TO FRANCES

Michael Stewart

KEYNES AND AFTER

Third Edition

PENGUIN BOOKS

PENGUIN BOOKS

Published by the Penguin Group
Penguin Books Ltd, 27 Wrights Lane, London W8 5TZ, England
Penguin Books USA Inc., 375 Hudson Street, New York, New York 10014, USA
Penguin Books Australia Ltd, Ringwood, Victoria, Australia
Penguin Books Canada Ltd, 10 Alcorn Avenue, Toronto, Ontario, Canada M4V 3B2
Penguin Books (NZ) Ltd, 182–190 Wairau Road, Auckland 10, New Zealand

Penguin Books Ltd, Registered Offices: Harmondsworth, Middlesex, England

First published in Pelican Books 1967
Reprinted with minor revisions 1969
Second edition 1972
Third edition 1986
Reprinted in Penguin Books 1991
3 5 7 9 10 8 6 4

Printed in England by Clays Ltd, St Ives plc
Filmset in Ehrhardt

CONTENTS

PREFACE

No one but the author is much interested in the differences between the successive editions of a book, and I shall not dwell on the matter here. Suffice it to say that the first edition of this book was written in the mid-1960s, when confidence in Keynes's analysis and prescriptions was at its strongest; and the second edition at the beginning of the 1970s, when monetarist views were only just starting to make themselves felt, and unease about accelerating inflation was not yet acute.

Written in 1985, this edition is very different from the second edition, as the second was from the first. In particular, Part Two is completely new. But what the present edition has in common with the two earlier ones is an attempt to explain what it was that Keynes said, and why it still seems of such immense importance. The experience of the first half of the 1980s makes his analysis, if anything, more convincing, and his policy recommendations, if anything, more urgent.

Michael Stewart
June 1985

... I believe myself to be writing a book on economic theory which will largely revolutionize – not, I suppose at once but in the course of the next ten years – the way the world thinks about economic problems.
Letter from John Maynard Keynes to
George Bernard Shaw, 1 January 1935.

INTRODUCTION

A couple of years after the end of the First World War Britain plunged into a depression which lasted for twenty years. Between 1921 and 1940 unemployment never fell below a rate of 10 per cent; in the early 1930s, when the whole world was experiencing the worst slump in history, unemployment in Britain was over 20 per cent.

This represented a total failure of the economic system. Desperate poverty lay cheek by jowl with idle men and unused resources. Governments were helpless. They did what the experience of the past, and their official advisers, told them, and things got worse. Capitalists shivered; Marxists rubbed their hands. In some countries democracy foundered. In Britain, as it happened, it survived. But could it survive for ever in the face of paralysingly heavy unemployment?

Mass unemployment was brought to an end by the Second World War. For more than thirty years – until the mid-1970s – Britain enjoyed full employment. Such a tremendous transformation might be expected to have many causes. But in fact the evidence points to one cause above all others: the publication in 1936 of a book called *The General Theory of Employment, Interest and Money* by John Maynard Keynes.

In Part One of the present book we discuss the historical background to Keynes's work, what it was that he said, and how it differed from prevailing views of how the economy worked and of what the role of the government should be; in short, why it was that Keynes's theory became, for a third of a century, the foundation of economic policy.

But in the course of the 1970s things started to go wrong. Unemployment rose, and inflation became an increasingly threatening problem. By the end of the decade a new doctrine, monetarism, had supplanted Keynesianism as the basis of economic policy-making. By the mid-1980s inflation had, at least for the time being, been brought under control; but unemployment had risen to levels not far short of those suffered in the 1930s.

What does monetarism say? Does it provide a long-term answer to inflation? Can full employment be restored by reverting to Keynesian policies? Are the new technologies a threat to jobs? What are the implications for employment of the increasing interdependence of the world economy? These are the questions discussed in Part Two.

Part One
KEYNES

———

Chapter One

KEYNES THE MAN

John Maynard Keynes has often been described as an economist of genius, ranking with such giants of the past as Adam Smith and Karl Marx. While this is true, it is not the whole truth. He certainly possessed superlative intellectual powers. Bertrand Russell wrote in his autobiography that

Keynes's intellect was the sharpest and clearest that I have ever known. When I argued with him, I felt that I took my life in my hands, and I seldom emerged without feeling something of a fool.

But Keynes was not just an intellectual; he was also a man of passionate emotions. During the first three or four decades of his life these emotions found their expression largely in the private domain: what was important to him was the pursuit of truth, the contemplation of beauty and, above all, the cultivation of friendships and the formation of romantic attachments, almost exclusively with members of the same sex. Later on, his passion assumed a much more public focus, and he used his formidable talents to denounce the follies of the world's policy-makers: the Versailles Peace Treaty of 1919, governments' acquiescence in the high unemployment of the 1920s and 1930s, and the unimaginative American approach to post-war reconstruction in 1944. Nevertheless, until the end of his life he remained a man of the widest possible cultural interests: he was captivated by philosophy and farming, old books and modern poetry, paintings and the ballet (two of the great loves of his life were the painter Duncan Grant and the ballerina Lydia Lopokova). But Keynes was a study in contrasts. He could entrance the people he liked with his wit and charm, and paralyse those he did not with his rudeness. He was the most civilized of men, who could dismay his more sensitive friends with his scatological coarseness. He revelled in gossip of the most intimate and trivial kind; and he wrote the *General Theory*. It is not surprising that those who never knew him feel the poorer for it, or that many worlds mourned him when he died.

Keynes was born in Cambridge in 1883 (the year Marx died), the son of a don who was himself a lecturer in economics and logic. Always a precocious child, from a local preparatory school he won a scholarship to Eton, where he soon blossomed out. He won prizes for classics, mathematics, history and English essays, wrote papers on contemporary problems, rowed, played the incomprehensible Wall Game, debated, acted, and still managed to read omnivorously and become something of an expert on medieval Latin poetry. His overall success at the school was attested by his election to 'Pop', Eton's ultimate social elite, traditionally composed more of athletes than of intellectuals; but it was his extreme cleverness which most made its mark on his contemporaries, and which won him an open scholarship to read mathematics at King's College, Cambridge.

At Cambridge, where the range of his activities widened even further, he came to live what could almost be seen as a double life. Publicly, he became President of the Union and President of the University Liberal Club, rowed, and did just enough mathematics to end up with a First. But his main interests were of a more private nature. He studied philosophy for his own pleasure, played bridge, looked at paintings, collected rare books, went to the theatre, and kept up a weighty correspondence with family and friends. Above all, he was soon elected to the Apostles, a secret and highly exclusive Cambridge society dedicated to intellectual discussion, the pursuit of truth and beauty, and the development of intimate personal relationships. Among its members in Keynes's day were Lytton Strachey and Leonard Woolf; its past members included A. N. Whitehead, Bertrand Russell, G. E. Moore and E. M. Forster. Election to this society had a marked effect on Keynes's life. Several of its members, and their relations and acquaintances, became his closest friends, not only in Cambridge but later on in London in the form of the Bloomsbury Group. The ideals of the Apostles, and particularly the philosophy of G. E. Moore, had a pronounced influence on him, emphasizing as they did the extreme importance of states of mind rather than of conventional morality or material success: what mattered above all was love between individuals, the pleasures of human intercourse, and the contemplation of beautiful works of art and literature. Although in one sense Keynes came to outgrow this aesthetic and unworldly milieu, with its hothouse atmosphere and homosexual dimension, it and its subsequent outposts in London and elsewhere always afforded him a physical and spiritual refuge after he had become immersed in public affairs and was a figure on the international stage.

A year after taking his Cambridge degree Keynes sat the Civil Service examination. He had spent much of the intervening period studying economics – devouring the existing literature, attending Marshall's lectures and being coached by Pigou; but this did not prevent him from getting a relatively low mark in the economics paper (as well as in mathematics, the other subject he really knew something about). With typical intellectual arrogance and, probably, accuracy, Keynes attributed this to the fact that he knew more economics than his examiners. Nevertheless, he passed second into the Civil Service and was assigned to the India Office. The work (or lack of it) he found irksome, and after two years of office hours spent mainly on a private project of his own (a dissertation on Probability) he resigned, claiming that his only official achievement had been to get ten pedigree bulls shipped to Bombay.

In 1908 he returned to Cambridge, first as a lecturer in economics and later as a fellow of King's, a post he retained for the rest of his life. He went on with his work on Probability and eventually, in 1921, and to considerable academic acclaim, published it as *A Treatise on Probability*. But although for some years his principal intellectual interest continued to be philosophy, his energies came increasingly to be directed towards economics – learning it, teaching it, and beginning to make original contributions to it. The economics he taught and embellished was, naturally enough, the orthodox, classical economics of the day. He was an enthusiastic expositor of the Quantity Theory of Money (discussed in Chapter 8 below), a strong believer in the virtues of free trade and international capital mobility and, in general, a subscriber to the notion that the capitalist system, if left to itself, will generate the best of all possible outcomes. It is not surprising that a quarter of a century later, in the Preface to the *General Theory*, he should write that the composition of this book has been for the author a long struggle of escape ... from habitual modes of thought and expression ... The difficulty lies, not in the new ideas, but in escaping from the old ones, which ramify, for those brought up as most of us have been, into every corner of our minds.

In 1911 Keynes became editor of the *Economic Journal*, at that time unquestionably the world's leading economic periodical. In 1913 he showed that his time at the India Office had not been completely wasted by publishing *Indian Currency and Finance*, an important book of which at least one chapter is still regarded as a classic. As a result of this he was appointed a member of a Royal Commission set up to examine the Indian currency question. In this capacity he made a marked impression both on the chairman (Austen Chamberlain, a former Chancellor of the Exchequer, later to be Chancellor again, and then Foreign Secretary) and on the other politicians and senior civil servants involved, not only with his mastery of complex technical detail, but also with his feel for the political and human problems involved. In fact, he started to establish a reputation as a top-flight economic theorist who understood how the world actually worked.

It was during the First World War that Keynes really came into his own. Early in 1915 he found himself in the Treasury, initially in a fairly junior capacity; but he rose rapidly and was soon in charge of one of the most vital aspects of the war economy, the problem of coordinating the foreign exchange expenditure of Britain and her allies on essential imports from abroad. He came to know and be relied on by Asquith, Lloyd George, McKenna and other war leaders, though even at this relatively early stage in his career he was no respecter of persons: on one famous occasion he told Lloyd George to his face that his views on French finance were 'rubbish'. But the war engendered a conflict within Keynes himself, a counterpart of the dichotomy between his public and private selves. On the one hand he wanted to (and did) throw all his energies into a successful pursuit of the war effort. On the other hand he felt, like most of his friends in Bloomsbury, that the war was madness, and the appalling slaughter it involved totally unjustifiable; hostilities should be brought to an end as soon as possible, if necessary by negotiating a 'peace without victory'. These two warring factions of his nature were uneasily reconciled by circumstances: when conscription was introduced in

January 1916, Keynes, like many of his friends, applied for exemption from military service as a conscientious objector; but he was exempted on the grounds that his work at the Treasury was of national importance.

Throughout the war Keynes was concerned not only with financial questions, such as how enough gold or foreign exchange could be accumulated to pay for American supplies, but also with questions of real resources and physical shortages: should scarce shipping capacity, for example, be used to transport troops, or munitions, or wheat? In this concentration on the use of real resources may have lain the seeds of the *General Theory*, which is ultimately concerned not with finance or money but with the volume of output and employment. However that may be, there is little doubt that the question of real resources coloured Keynes's approach to the issue of German reparations. Towards the end of the war, he was asked to consider how much the Germans should pay Britain and France by way of compensation for the damage they had suffered during the war. He saw clearly that reparations could not be based on the extent of the damage suffered by the Allies, but only on Germany's capacity to pay in the form of real resources: it was not a question of Germany simply signing a cheque, but of producing goods and shipping them abroad without payment (a process which, in so far as it could be achieved, in any case had the disadvantage of posing a threat to Britain's own export markets). Keynes formed the view that a reasonable figure for reparations would be £2 billion, to be paid over a period of years. Another estimate, arrived at largely under the influence of the Bank of England, was £24 billion. Keynes had always had a healthy disrespect for the economic wisdom of bankers; this incident did nothing to relieve it. In relation to the physical capacity of the post-war German economy £2 billion made reasonable sense; £24 billion made no sense whatever.

After a great deal of to-ing and fro-ing between the Allies (in the course of which Keynes proposed, unsuccessfully, that British and French demands for reparations from Germany should be substantially scaled down in return for a comparable remission of the debts owed by these two countries to the United States), the Versailles Peace Treaty was signed in June 1919. It contained no detailed figures, but the whole structure and tone of the Treaty made it clear that heavy reparation payments would be exacted from Germany. Keynes was convinced that the attempt to exact such payments would not only be unsuccessful, but would have disastrous political consequences. He resigned his post at the Treasury and set out his views in *The Economic Consequences of the Peace.* 'If we aim deliberately at the impoverishment of Central Europe,' he said, 'vengeance, I dare predict, will not limp.' There would before long be a war 'which will destroy, whoever is victor, the civilization and progress of our generation'.

To this day there are two views on whether Keynes was right. Some think that his intervention played a major part in preventing a permanent crushing of the power of Germany, and in encouraging the disastrous American withdrawal from Europe. Others think that the reparation demands were, as Keynes said, impossible (in the end the Germans paid far less even than Keynes's estimate of £2 billion) and that the attempt to exact them created a social revolution, and laid a foundation of bitterness, that were major factors behind the success of Hitler. The weight of the evidence is probably on Keynes's side.

Right or wrong, *The Economic Consequences of the Peace* soon became a best-seller. It caused considerable annoyance in the Westminster–Whitehall Establishment, but brought Keynes's name before a large – indeed international – audience as someone with well-informed and cogently argued views on some of the main economic and political problems of the day. The mantle of formidable and controversial public figure now descended on him, and his views on many aspects of economic policy became well known to readers of the *Manchester Guardian* and *The Nation* (later absorbed by the *New Statesman*; Keynes was Chairman of both). Throughout the rest of his life he remained a prolific author, as the twenty-nine volumes of his collected writings attest. Some of this work (such as *Essays in Biography* and *Essays in Persuasion*) is likely to be read for as long as anything else in the English language. But he continued to pursue many other interests: he lectured in Cambridge; talked in Bloomsbury; became Chairman of a life insurance company; made a great deal of money (both for himself and for King's, of which he became Bursar) by shrewd speculation in the foreign exchange and commodity markets; and married Lydia Lopokova, the leading ballerina from the Diaghilev Ballet.

In 1923 he published *A Tract on Monetary Reform*, in which he argued that Britain should not (as the government and everyone else obviously intended) go back to the pre-war gold standard system. This pamphlet constituted an attack on one of the main pillars of the British economic system, and Keynes found himself virtually alone. When it became apparent that the government was quite determined to go back to the gold standard, Keynes argued that at least it should not return at the pre-war parity; but here again he failed. In *The Economic Consequences of Mr Churchill* (the Chancellor who took the final decision to return) Keynes demolished the arguments behind the decision, insisting that the result would be an over-valued currency and a persistence of heavy unemployment. As so often, he was right. He called for large-scale government expenditure on public works to cope with unemployment, even though this would mean a large Budget deficit, but he could not provide a theoretical justification of this 'patently unsound' idea, and was largely ignored. However he had enough influence with Lloyd George to ensure that the Liberal party programme in the 1929 election consisted chiefly of promises of higher public expenditure to counter unemployment.

In 1930 Keynes published *A Treatise on Money*, a massive work which distilled all his accumulated knowledge of the subject and developed many of the concepts and relationships that were to be finally pulled into shape with such dramatic effect in the *General Theory*. He was appointed a member of the Macmillan Committee on Finance and Industry (set up by Snowden in 1929) and had a marked influence on its recommendations, though not succeeding in persuading it of the efficacy of public works.

In 1930 he was appointed by the Prime Minister as Chairman of a committee of economists to advise the government on what it should do about mounting unemployment. (Keynes's answer was again public works, and, a far cry from his earlier belief in free trade, protective duties on imports.) In 1935 he set on foot the building of the Arts Theatre in Cambridge. 1936 saw the publication of the *General Theory*. In 1937 he suffered a serious heart attack. He had always been dogged by ill health, and was now to be a semi-invalid for the rest of his days – though few of those who met him were allowed to realize it.

With the outbreak of the Second World War he was again brought into the Treasury, this time not as an administrator but as a free-ranging adviser of great reputation and influence. His *How to Pay for the War*, published in 1940, made radical new proposals on the problem of internal war finance; and he had more than a finger in many other famous pies – such as the Beveridge Report on social security and the 1944 White Paper on employment policy. He was given a peerage in 1942, and in the same year – as evidence that his versatility had not diminished – he was appointed Chairman of a new 'Council for the Encouragement of Music and the Arts', which a few years later became the Arts Council. But his main contribution during the Second World War was as negotiator – in effect, chief British negotiator – with the Americans, first over Lend-Lease, then in the discussions which led up to the establishment at Bretton Woods of the World Bank and the International Monetary Fund, and finally on the post-war US loan. All these negotiations were extremely complex and demanding, and in all of them Keynes was the acknowledged master of proceedings, displaying a quickness of grasp, a fertility of imagination, an understanding of large panorama and tiny detail, a wit and tact that brought him the unqualified admiration of all involved in them, and an outcome, some have said, considerably better than any other man could have achieved. But even Keynes could not always win. The US only granted the post-war loan (essential to Britain's survival once Lend-Lease had stopped) on terms which jeopardized Britain's economic recovery – a fact of which Keynes was bitterly aware. He strained every nerve in his efforts to get the Americans to understand the nature of the new economic problems the war had left, but he failed. Perhaps this failure literally broke his heart.

He died of another heart attack in April 1946, at the age of 62. His death removed from the scene a man whose wisdom might have been of immeasurable value to the battered and limping post-war British economy. But he left behind him an explanation of how the economic system works which transformed the world.

Chapter Two

ECONOMICS BEFORE KEYNES

There was one particularly alarming feature of the heavy unemployment between the wars. This was that although practical men tackled it in a common-sense sort of way, they not merely failed to cure it, but actually made it worse. Keynes had an explanation of this. 'The ideas of economists and political philosophers,' he wrote in the *General Theory*, 'are more powerful than is commonly understood. Indeed the world is ruled by little else. Practical men, who believe themselves to be quite exempt from any intellectual influences, are usually the slaves of some defunct economist.' It was precisely because the practical men of the 1920s and 1930s were the slaves of defunct economists – defunct in the sense that since their time the world had changed, invalidating as it did so some of the assumptions on which their theories were based – that things went so badly wrong. In order to understand the inter-war years, and the significance of Keynes's theory, we must begin by taking a look at what pre-Keynesian economists had said on the subject of employment.

SMITH, RICARDO AND MALTHUS

Economics goes back a long way – the ancients were by no means innocent of it – but for practical purposes one can take the founder of modern economics to be Adam Smith, who published *The Wealth of Nations* in 1776. Smith, possibly the original eccentric, absent-minded professor, dictated this book standing with his back to the fire, and perhaps in consequence it rambles over the whole field of human knowledge: in the vast index (not compiled by Smith) the As begin with *Abassides, during reigns of, Saracens opulent* and the Zs with *Zama, battle of, and armies engaged in.* Yet, despite its great

23

sweep, and its pre-eminent concern with what we would now call 'economic growth', the book contains no real discussion of why the level of employment is what it is. Clearly, this was not a question which interested the author; indeed it probably never occurred to him to ask it. In Smith's day agriculture was still by far the most important economic activity, and in an agricultural society the line between being employed and being unemployed tends to be blurred: the whole family works, but may be underemployed. Moreover wages were so low that the distinction between employed and unemployed, when it could be made, seemed much less significant than other divisions within society – for example those between landowners, businessmen and workers. In effect, Smith simply assumed that there was always full employment – i.e. that everybody who wanted a job either had one or could get one without much difficulty.

The next economist of major importance was David Ricardo, a wealthy stockbroker, and later an MP, who published the first edition of his *Principles of Political Economy and Taxation* in 1817. Like many nineteenth-century economists who came after him, his main interest lay in the factors which governed the distribution of a nation's income between the main social classes – landowners, capitalists and workers (in other words rent, profits and wages). We cannot get involved in Ricardo's main contributions to economics here; the relevant point for our purposes is that he regarded businessmen's investment in machinery and equipment as one of the most important activities in the economy. Businessmen must make large profits, he said, because they would invest them in new machinery; and this new machinery would enable more to be produced, and thus make the country richer.

In his view that investment in more and more machinery was a good thing, Ricardo found himself opposed by a clergyman and Cambridge don (Keynes called him 'the first of the Cambridge economists') called Thomas Robert Malthus. Malthus is best known today for his theory of population, according to which there is a tendency for the population to increase much faster than the supply of food – a tendency which results in periodic famines. With this part of Malthus's work Ricardo did not disagree. But there was another side to Malthus's work which proved far more controversial, and in the lengthy, friendly dialogue which developed between Ricardo and Malthus we come across – perhaps for the first time – an explicit discussion of what it is that determines the level of employment.

Perhaps because he identified himself with the landed classes (as opposed to Ricardo, the spokesman of the up-and-coming manufacturers) Malthus took a dim view of the process of accumulating capital and investing it in industrial machinery. There was a danger, he argued, that this investment would raise society's ability to produce at a faster rate than its ability to consume. The wages received by the workers, after all, represent only a part of the value of what they produce – so that only a part of all the goods produced can be bought by the workers. What is going to happen to the rest? Is there not a danger, as more machinery is installed in industry, and total production rises, that the country will find itself with a 'general glut of commodities' which cannot be sold? Will this not lead to unemployment? And is it not fortunate, he went on (overdoing it a bit, perhaps) that there is a large class of landowners who up till now, by producing nothing but consuming a lot, have managed to stave off the evil day when this general glut of commodities will appear?

Ricardo's reply was remarkable for both its plausibility and its durability: what Ricardo said in the 1820s was being solemnly repeated by orthodox economists in the 1920s (as Keynes said, 'Ricardo conquered England as completely as the Holy Inquisition conquered Spain'*). He agreed with Malthus that it was possible to have a glut of commodities – but only a temporary glut of a particular kind of commodity. Some sudden shock (a war, a change in fashion or taxation) could result in a fall in the demand for a particular commodity. There would, for a time, be a glut of this commodity on the market, and some of the machinery and men who produced it would find

---

* *General Theory*, page 32. It is impossible to resist quoting the next paragraph, a typically splendid piece of Keynesian irony:

'The completeness of the Ricardian victory is something of a curiosity and a mystery. It must have been due to a complex of suitabilities in the doctrine to the environment into which it was projected. That it reached conclusions quite different from what the ordinary uninstructed person would expect, added, I suppose, to its intellectual prestige. That its teaching, translated into practice, was austere and often unpalatable, lent it virtue. That it was adapted to carry a vast and consistent logical superstructure, gave it beauty. That it could explain much social injustice and apparent cruelty as an inevitable incident in the scheme of progress, and the attempt to change such things as likely on the whole to do more harm than good, commended it to authority. That it afforded a measure of justification to the free activities of the individual capitalist, attracted to it the support of the dominant social force behind authority.'

themselves idle. But meanwhile the demand for some other commodity would have risen, for if people spend less on one thing they will spend more on another, and there would be a shortage of this other commodity. High wages and profits could be earned by producing this new commodity, and so extra labour and capital would start moving into this industry; at the same time, of course, it would be moving out of the old industry whose products were no longer in demand. Before long, equilibrium would have been re-established with a new pattern of production. So the only kind of unemployment – of either men or machinery – that was possible was temporary unemployment, during the transitional phase of a shift in the pattern of demand.

As for Malthus's argument that there might be a *general* glut of commodities (and, by implication, widespread unemployment) because workers could only afford to buy a part of what they produced, this was absurd. Here Ricardo invoked the writings of a French economist called J. B. Say. What has come to be known as 'Say's Law' was first propounded in 1803, and has been a rich source of confusion ever since. It is usually summarized by saying, 'Supply creates its own demand.' This means that the very processes which result in a commodity being placed on the market also result in the creation of the income with which it can be bought. For the final price of a commodity is simply the cost of the materials and labour used to make it, plus the profit that accrues to the manufacturer. In other words the supplier of materials, the worker and the capitalist have between them made exactly enough money, by producing the article, to enable them to buy it. They do not, of course, buy the article they themselves have produced, but what is true of one firm is true of all firms taken together: exactly enough income is created to enable the population to buy everything that is produced. A glut of commodities – goods which get produced but for which no buyer can be found – is therefore an absurdity.

But what happens, Malthus wondered, if the capitalists do not *spend* their profits, but *save* them instead? Surely, in that case, one would get a glut of commodities? For some of the money which has to be spent, if the market is to be cleared, is not being spent; it is staying in the capitalist's pocket.

Again, Ricardo had an answer. The money that the capitalist saves, he explained, does *not* simply stay in his pocket; it is invested – that is to say, it is spent on machinery, equipment, buildings and so on. In other words, the fact that the capitalist does not spend all his profits on consumer goods does not mean that the profits do not get spent. On the contrary, they are spent on machinery and other capital goods, and it is for this reason that firms which manufacture machinery are able, like other firms, to sell everything they produce.

Malthus appears to have accepted the logic of this argument, and to have been diverted to less profitable areas of inquiry into why an economy might suffer from a shortage of what he called 'effective demand'. For what Ricardo said was more or less right, *at the time he said it*. During the early nineteenth century the only way most manufacturers could finance the new buildings and machinery needed to expand their business was out of their own profits. There was no organized Stock Exchange through which money could be raised, and bank lending was relatively undeveloped. There was rarely a problem of a manufacturer having more profits than he knew what to do with; on the contrary, after he had paid his household's living expenses, they were generally smaller than he could usefully employ. Indeed, the businessman who made himself and his family go short in order to plough every available penny back into the business was a favourite character of Victorian fiction.

Thus Keynes was perhaps reading too much into Malthus when he said, in his *Essay on Malthus*,

One cannot rise from a perusal of this correspondence [between Malthus and Ricardo] without a feeling that the almost total obliteration of Malthus's line of approach and the complete domination of Ricardo's for a period of a hundred years has been a disaster to the progress of economics.

Nevertheless, although Ricardo had the logic, Malthus had the intuition: there was, or in some circumstances could be, something wrong with Ricardo's argument that wages and profits would all get spent, and that general unemployment was therefore an impossibility. A number of other economists, such as J. A. Hobson, were later to worry over the same problem, but it was left to Keynes to put his finger on the truth.

MARX

After Ricardo and Malthus the main stream of economic thought turned away from macroeconomic problems – the questions of what determines the size of the national income, or its division between the main social classes, or the overall level of employment. For the best part of a century the fashion was for microeconomics – the question of what determines the output of an individual firm, or the price of a particular commodity or factor of production.* But to this general rule there were exceptions, and the most notable of them was Karl Marx.

As an economist Marx was very clearly in the debt of Adam Smith and Ricardo. He took over much of their framework of thought, and gave it a new twist. At the same time his work contained brilliantly original insights. He was the first major economist, for example, to notice that by the middle of the nineteenth century heavy unemployment was quite a frequent occurrence in the developing industrial countries of Western Europe – or at any rate the first to realize that the phenomenon required an explanation. He not only built the 'trade cycle'† into his analysis; he saw it as an expression of the inner contradictions of the capitalist system; he expected trade cycles to get progressively worse, and to lead eventually to the collapse of the system.

There is an eel-like quality about Marx's analysis of the economic development of the capitalist system: one no sooner thinks one has grasped it than it slithers out of one's hands. But one interpretation of the kernel of his argument would go as follows.

Competition forces capitalist firms to invest their profits in labour-saving machinery, for if they do not do this their efficiency will drop, and they will be forced out of business. But if labour-saving machinery is installed, there will be a fall in employment and hence a rise in the number of unemployed. As unemployment rises, wages (if not already at subsistence level) will tend to fall – for those who still have jobs will be forced by the capitalists to accept lower wages under threat of being replaced by some of the 'reserve army' of the un-

---

* A *factor of production* is something which contributes to the production of a commodity. In the simplest case three factors of production are distinguished – land, labour and capital.

† We discuss the trade cycle more fully a little later on (see page 35).

employed. But according to Marx, a fall in employment also meant a fall in profits, because the value of what is produced depends on the number of man-hours involved in producing it. This fall in profits leads before long to a crisis: profits fall so low that many businesses go bankrupt; investment in plant and machinery more or less ceases; more workers lose their jobs, and the reserve army of the unemployed grows. In fact, the economy is in the depths of a depression. Eventually the crisis comes to an end, as big firms swallow up small firms, buying their plant and equipment at knock-down prices, and thus getting back into a position where they can make profits. But in spite of these periodic recoveries, there is a long-term trend at work which makes each crisis worse than the previous one. The main factor in this is the growing monopolization of business – the result of bigger firms taking over smaller ones at times of crisis. As firms become bigger and the economy more monopolized, the competition which originally impelled firms to invest their profits in machinery weakens, and with it the incentive to continue this sort of investment. In the long run, therefore, firms will have little incentive to invest their profits (as Ricardo had assumed they would) and, since only a small part of the capitalists' profits can be spent on consumption, the general glut of commodities that Malthus had been afraid of will become a reality. As a result, unemployment will get heavier and heavier.

To many people in the 1930s Marx's work came as a blinding revelation. He had, it seemed, not merely predicted the slump and explained its underlying causes but even in a sense put forward a solution to it. (And since – contrary to Marx's own expectations – it happened to be in Russia that the revolution he had predicted and called for actually took place, it was therefore towards Soviet communism that many of the most intelligent and sensitive people in Western Europe were drawn in their search for a solution to the mass unemployment of the 1930s.)

But although there are great nuggets of truth in Marx's analysis, as an explanation of what happened in the 1920s and 1930s it will not really do. There were many similarities between what happened and what Marx said would happen, but the ineluctable fact remained that Marx's whole analysis depended on the standard of living of the average worker remaining in the long run at subsistence level, whereas experience had been quite different: in Britain real income per head in 1920 (and even in the worst year of the slump, 1932) was more than double what it had been in 1860.

Nevertheless, in spite of the fact that his theory of economic development cannot be swallowed whole, Marx did represent a very significant landmark in the evolution of economic theory. It was much more difficult, after he had written, to believe that the capitalist economy, if left to itself, would necessarily function satisfactorily. In particular, it was more difficult to accept Ricardo's view that profits were always invested in new machinery. For one of the points Marx was making was that society's capacity to produce *will* outstrip its capacity to consume: in the capitalist economy the workers cannot consume much because their wages are so low; the capitalists cannot consume much because there are so few of them; and there is no point in them putting their profits to their other possible use (investment), because there will not be enough demand for the goods that new machinery could turn out to make it worthwhile.

THE THEORY OF PRICE

Marx, as we have said, was an exception. Most economists during the century or so after about 1820 concerned themselves mainly with microeconomic problems. Much of this lies outside our field, but we must spotlight a few strands of this microeconomic theory because of their importance to an understanding of what economists thought in the 1920s.

The main concern of nineteenth-century economics was with what determined the *price* or *value* of an article, or a factor of production. (The price of something was not thought to be necessarily the same as its value – this distinction was itself the source of endless discussion.) Quite soon after the death of Ricardo the price of an article came to be explained less in terms of what it had cost to produce, and more in terms of what people were willing to pay for it. Adam Smith and Ricardo had said, in effect, that an article cost £10 because two hours' work, at a rate of pay of £5 an hour, had been needed to make it; the new 'theory of utility' said that it cost £10 because that was what someone was willing to pay for it. The new approach was summed up by an economist (later an Archbishop – the nineteenth century did not believe in too much specialization) called Whately who said, 'It is not that pearls fetch a high price *because* men have dived for them; but on the contrary, men dive for them because they fetch a high price.' As the century wore on more sophisticated theories came to be advanced, both of what determined how much it cost to produce an article, and of what determined how much people were willing to pay for it. The whole thing was summarized by the Cambridge economist Alfred Marshall, who said that supply and demand should be regarded as the two blades of a pair of scissors – both of them being necessary to explain the price of an article. For any article one could (if one had perfect knowledge) construct a 'demand curve', which would tell you how many of these articles would be demanded (i.e. bought) at different prices. In general, one would expect that the higher the price, the smaller the number of this particular article that would be bought. The exact number bought at any particular price would depend on such factors as people's income and tastes, the prices of other articles (particularly those which were close substitutes) and so on.

In the same way, said Marshall, one could, at any rate in theory, construct a 'supply curve', which would tell you how many of these articles would be supplied (i.e. produced) at different prices. In this case, there is a presumption that the higher the price, the greater the number that would be produced, but the exact number produced at any particular price would depend on the price the manufacturer had to pay for his labour, materials and equipment – and the profit he required for himself in order to keep him in business. The price actually established would of course be the price at which the number of articles demanded was exactly equal to the number supplied; in other words the price at which the number that customers wanted to buy was the same as the number that manufacturers wanted to produce.

Refinement and synthesis of supply and demand theory did not stop with Marshall. It continued to form the main preoccupation of economists until the 1930s – and indeed was given a new lease of life in the early 1930s by a revolutionary change in the theory's framework of reference – a change which resulted from new thinking (with which Keynes himself was to some extent associated) in Cambridge and at Harvard.*

* Nineteenth-century theory had assumed (reasonably enough, given the structure

31

DIMINISHING RETURNS
AND MARGINAL PRODUCTIVITY

Now the important point about this supply and demand analysis for our present purpose is that it was supposed to be of general application, explaining the price of anything which had a price. Thus it was supposed to explain not only the price of goods, but also the price of *money* (i.e. the rate of interest) and the price of *labour* (i.e. wages). It is convenient to hold over until later (page 37 and pages 101–102) a discussion of what nineteenth-century economists thought about interest rates; here we concentrate on what they thought about wages.

The average wage, they said, was simply the price of labour, and it was determined, like the price of anything else, by the interaction of supply and demand. In the short run the supply of labour was fixed – it was simply the total population, or at any rate those parts of it which were accustomed to work. (In the longer run, of course, the size of population changed, but we can ignore this for the purposes of the present analysis.) How, then, did elements on the demand side interact with this fixed supply of labour in order to determine its price – i.e. the average wage? In order to understand this we must take a brief look at two essentially simple bits of economic folklore, one rather confidently called the *Law of Diminishing Returns*, the other, more modestly, the *Theory of Marginal Productivity*.

The Law of Diminishing Returns was what Malthus had had in mind when predicting that world population would grow faster than world food supplies, leading to periodic famines. The Law said that beyond a certain point, the more of one factor of production you apply to a fixed amount of another factor of production, the smaller

---

of agriculture and industry at the time the theory was evolved) that firms in the same industry were in 'perfect' competition with each other – meaning that they were relatively small, and all produced exactly the same product. Consequently the individual firm had no control over the price of its goods – it had to accept the price established 'in the market' by supply and demand. For if it raised its price above the market price it would immediately lose all its business; while if it lowered its price below the market price it would make a smaller profit. The new theory, of 'imperfect' or 'monopolistic' competition, recognized that a modern firm's products are not in fact considered by its customers to be exactly the same as its rivals'. Consequently it does have some control over its price – it can raise its price without losing all its business, and in some cases make bigger profits by lowering prices because it can then expand its sales.

is the additional output. To take a concrete example, suppose that 10 men work on 1 acre of land and produce a total of 100 beetroot a year – 10 per man. Now assume an increase in the labour force (on the same 1 acre of land) to 11. Production of beetroot will rise, says the Law, but only to 109. The extra man only produces 9 beetroot, whereas each of the previous men produced, on average, 10. Add a twelfth man; production will rise again, but only to 117. The twelfth man has only produced 8 beetroot. Diminishing returns have set in. One result of this, of course, is that average production per man employed has dropped – from 10 beetroot per man when there were only 10 men to $9\frac{3}{4}$ when there were 12 men. (It was precisely this effect, on a much larger scale, that Malthus was afraid of.) But it is the fact that each additional man has the effect of raising production *less than the previous additional man* that is important in the present context.

Now let us look at the Theory of Marginal Productivity. This states that each factor of production will be paid the value of its marginal product. In other words the pay of labour (the average wage) will be equal to the value of what is produced by the marginal man – the man that the farmer or manufacturer thinks it is just worth his while to employ. Let us go back to the beetroot example in order to make the argument clear.

Suppose, for the sake of simplicity, that the demand for beetroot is such that each beetroot can be sold for £1, regardless of how many are produced. In our example, in which the Law of Diminishing Returns was operating, when the labour force increased from 10 to 11 the addition to output was 9 beetroot, which would be worth £9. If, therefore, the wages of this eleventh man were £8, it was obviously in the farmer's interest to take him on: his sales have risen by £9, his costs by only £8, and therefore his profits by £1. If, on the other hand, the eleventh man's wages had been £10 it would not have been worth taking him on – taking him on would have involved the farmer in a £1 loss. In fact, it will benefit the farmer to take the man on provided that his wage is £8·99 or less. Since it will also benefit other farmers to do the same, competition will ensure that the man *is* taken on at a wage of £8·99 (which let us call £9) – i.e. *at a wage equal to the value of what he produces*. But if this man is paid £9, then all other men (of similar skill etc.) will also be paid £9, for 'perfect' competition makes it impossible for different prices to be paid for identical articles or factors of production.

In our example, then, if the labour force consists of eleven men, the wage that each of them receives will be £9, since this is the value of the extra output that accrues as a result of taking the eleventh man on. But suppose, as in our previous example, that the labour force is increased to 12, and that the addition of this twelfth man to the same 1 acre of land only results in the production of 8 more beetroot, worth £8. In that case, of course, the wage of each of the 12 men will be only £8. In other words, *the larger the number of men employed, the lower the average wage.*

Nineteenth-century theory did not claim that this principle operated at all times and in all places. It was obviously not true that (as in our simplified example) an ever-growing labour force was being continuously added to a fixed amount of land. Land was not in practice a fixed factor of production – new land could be brought into cultivation in this or other countries (during the nineteenth century emigration from Britain to much more sparsely populated countries was, in fact, at its height). And the quantity of man-made capital (machinery and equipment) was of course being continuously increased. Moreover, even in the extreme case in which an increasing labour force was working with the same amount of land or capital, there might be a range over which there were *increasing* returns from each additional man.

Nevertheless it was broadly accepted that in most cases, and particularly in the short run (roughly defined as a period within which there would not be much change in the size of population or amount of land and capital) the Law of Diminishing Returns and the Theory of Marginal Productivity would both operate.

The implications of this are worth stressing. The Law of Diminishing Returns said that the more men were employed, the less would the last man produce. The Theory of Marginal Productivity said that the last man would be paid the value of what he produced. Therefore the more men were employed, the less would the last man be paid. But since competition will ensure that the last man is paid much the same as other men, this means that the more men are employed, the less will each man in the labour force be paid – in other words the less will be the average wage. This apparently inexorable connection between employment and wages lay deep in the subconscious minds of the practical men of the 1920s and 1930s, as we shall see.

THE TRADE CYCLE

As we have indicated, during the late eighteenth and early nineteenth centuries economists were not particularly interested in what determined the level of employment, or in the distinction between employment and unemployment. In a semi-agricultural society it is broadly true that everyone old enough to work does work, and widespread *underemployment* is a much more characteristic feature than a clear-cut division between those who have jobs and those who have not.

But as the nineteenth century wore on Britain became increasingly industrialized, and the distinction between being employed and being unemployed began to assume some substance. The phenomenon which drew attention to this distinction had probably been operating in a subdued way since some time in the eighteenth century, but it was only now that people really became aware of it. This was the 'trade cycle'.*

The trade cycle was, as the term implies, a pattern of events which was repeated in similar form at fairly regular intervals. From beginning to end it would last some eight or ten years. On the up-swing everything would expand: production, employment, wages, profits and prices would all rise, and unemployment would fall to a low level – perhaps 1 or 2 per cent of the labour force. This phase would last for perhaps four to five years. Then everything would level off and, sometimes immediately, sometimes after a year or two, would start to fall again. The down-swing would last, in a typical instance, for three or four years, with production, employment, incomes and prices all falling, and unemployment rising to a rate of 8 or 10 per cent. Then it would level off, and the stage would be set for another burst of expansion. The cycle was superimposed, however, on a rising trend: at each peak, production and employment tended to be higher than at the previous peak, and would not fall as low in each trough as in the

* The Victorians said 'trade' where we would tend to say 'production'. To avoid ambiguity the Americans use the term 'business cycle'.

previous trough. A graph of production or employment during the nineteenth century would look rather like a staircase tilted slightly forward.

As we have seen, Marx was one of the first people to give serious attention to the trade cycle. His account was soon to be followed by many others. One of the most engaging was provided in 1878 by W. S. Jevons, Professor of Political Economy in the University of Manchester. According to Jevons, the cycle was caused by sun-spots: sun-spot cycles caused weather cycles, which caused harvest cycles, which in turn resulted in trade cycles. In support of his theory Jevons argued that during the previous 150 years each trade cycle had lasted, on average, for some 10·44 years; the average length of the sun-spot cycle was 10·45 years. These figures were too close to each other to be a coincidence.

This pleasingly direct link between celestial and terrestrial events was soon abandoned. Later calculations suggested different figures for the average length of the trade cycle, and in any case those who supported the theory could never agree among themselves on the vital point of whether good harvests had good or bad effects on the rest of the economy. But the main reason for the abandonment of the kind of harvest theory originated by Jevons was simply that as the economy became more industrialized (and this applied to the United States and Germany as well as Britain) a theory of the trade cycle which relied so heavily on agricultural developments became less and less satisfactory. Instead, people began increasingly to look – as Marx had done – for sources of instability within the industrial system itself.

During the first twenty or thirty years of the twentieth century a great deal of thought was devoted to the trade cycle, not only in Britain, but in many of the other most advanced industrial countries as well – economists in the US, Germany, Sweden, Russia, France, Austria and several other countries contributed to the pool of ideas. At the same time a great deal of statistical information began to be collected and analysed, particularly in the United States, and it became easier to examine a theory in the light of the facts. By around 1930, when the first real impact of the Slump was being felt by the US and Western Europe, there was a fair amount of agreement about the main features of the cycle.

The most convenient place to start is at the lower turning-point of the cycle, when unemployment is at its heaviest. What starts off the recovery? There was pretty general agreement that the recovery begins with a rise in investment; in other words, with businessmen starting to build new factories, install new machinery and so on. Different economists emphasized different reasons for this rise in investment. One school of thought, for example, stressed the role of interest rates. During the down-swing, as more and more factories became idle, there became less and less reason for new investment – if existing machinery was unemployed what was the point of installing more? This meant that there was a fall in the demand for loans to finance the new investment. At the same time, it was argued, as the down-swing went on, and production fell and unemployment rose, the uncertain outlook caused people to cut their spending and save as much as they could; thus they accumulated more and more idle cash. This combination of a fall in the demand for what have been called *loanable funds*, and a rise in the supply of these funds, resulted in a fall in the rate of interest (for the same reason that a fall in the demand for, or a rise in the supply of, any other commodity tends to reduce its price). Well then, this school of thought argued, there comes a time when the rate of interest is pushed so low by the operation of these forces that it becomes profitable to borrow money, and invest it in new factories or equipment. The rate of return to be made on this new investment may not be very high, but money can be borrowed so cheaply that even a low rate of return makes the operation worthwhile.

Other economists thought it was not only the lower cost of borrowing money that stimulated new investment, but the lower cost of everything else as well. During the down-swing wages and prices always fell. This meant that at the bottom of the depression businessmen could buy or hire factors of production more cheaply than before: the price of raw materials and capital equipment would have fallen, and – more important still – wages would be a good deal lower than they had been a few years before. Other economists, again, took a more positive view about the reasons for the turn-up, arguing that new investment was stimulated not only by the lower costs of doing it, but also by the greater profitability of doing it. During the down-swing and the depression, they said, the existing stock of capital equipment gets older or more obsolete; new products and processes are invented; new markets appear; and sooner or later businessmen will start investing in order to exploit these new developments.

Whatever the differences in emphasis, there was wide agreement about the basic point: the thing that started off the recovery from a slump was a rise in investment, and one of the main factors behind the rise in investment was the fall in wages and interest rates that occurred during the down-swing.

There was also wide agreement about what happened after the recovery got under way, though again the emphasis varied. As some new investments started paying off, other businesses would be encouraged to start investing as well. These new investments would create more employment – some people would be needed to build the new factories and machinery, other people would be needed to operate them. As more people were brought into employment (i.e. as the demand for labour rose) wages and salaries would rise and so, in consequence, would the amount spent by wage- and salary-earners on consumer goods. This in turn would create an incentive to businessmen to increase their investment even more in order to meet the new demand. During the early and middle stages of the up-swing there would be no difficulty in financing this new investment. It would be financed out of the idle hoards of cash that people had accumulated during the down-swing and the slump; out of the profits being made by the newly erected factories; or (and some economists attached particular importance to this) out of credit advanced by the banks. For the banks make their living, after all, by lending money at a profitable rate of interest; little satisfactory business comes their way during a slump and they, like individuals, accumulate idle hoards. When the recovery brings a rise in the demand for loans, they are only too glad to make large amounts of credit available at relatively low rates of interest.

And so the up-swing gathers pace. As more money is spent on new investment, this creates more jobs and more incomes. This in turn results in more money being spent by consumers. In order to meet this higher demand for consumer goods, more raw materials are needed, more factories and equipment and components, more transport facilities, more warehouses and shops. And rising demand for labour and goods leads to rising wages and rising prices. Thus a cumulative process is set up. Sooner or later, however, this expansionary process comes to an end. The up-swing flattens out. Perhaps immediately, perhaps only after several years of stability, the economy starts to contract. Why?

The basic reason for the down-turn was thought to be that during the up-swing of the cycle the industries making *capital* goods expanded faster than the industries making *consumer* goods.* The result of this was that when full employment was reached the distribution of the nation's resources between capital goods production and consumer goods production was distorted: too much labour and capital was engaged in making steel and heavy machinery and cement, and too little in making cutlery and furniture and clothing. Production of capital goods fell, and men and machinery in these industries (unable to be quickly or easily transferred to the production of consumer goods) became idle. As men were thrown out of work, consumption fell, and as consumption fell, so did the incentive to invest. The down-turn had begun.

THE ACCELERATOR

There was a particular, and not immediately obvious, reason why the up-swing saw too big an expansion of the capital goods industries. This was called the *accelerator* principle. In essence, the principle states that a small change in the output of the kind of goods bought in the shops by consumers tends to result in a much bigger – or accelerated – change in the output of goods needed to make these consumer goods. The principle is easiest to grasp in the form of a simple example. Suppose that a firm produces 10,000 electric coffee grinders a year, selling them for £5 each. And suppose that to produce these 10,000 coffee grinders it needs machinery worth £200,000. And suppose, finally, that each year 10 per cent of its machinery wears out, so that it buys £20,000 worth of new machinery. This is an equilibrium situation which can go on for ever, with the firm selling £50,000 worth of coffee grinders each year, and buying £20,000 worth of equipment. Now suppose that for some reason there is a 5 per cent rise in the demand for coffee grinders, and the firm finds that it can

* Consumer goods, as the term implies, are the final goods bought in shops by consumers – everything from hi-fi sets to hairpins. Capital goods, on the other hand, consist of the machinery and equipment bought by firms, and used in the process of production.

sell 10,500 coffee grinders each year. Since it takes £20 worth of machinery to produce one coffee grinder, it will have to install another £10,000 worth of machinery in order to produce these 500 extra coffee grinders. Consequently this year it will buy not its usual £20,000 worth of machinery, but £30,000 worth. In other words, a 5 per cent rise in the demand for coffee grinders has led to a 50 per cent rise in the demand for the machinery needed to make coffee grinders. In order to raise its output by 50 per cent, the firm that makes the machinery may have to increase its own capacity by 50 per cent – and this might mean, according to the accelerator principle, that its own purchases of machinery and equipment were suddenly trebled or quadrupled. Obviously this is the extreme case – in practice the capital goods industries will have a lot of spare capacity at the beginning of the up-swing, and may in any case respond to a big rise in the demand for their products by lengthening their order books rather than increasing their capacity. Nevertheless one can see from the accelerator principle how fairly small and cautious decisions to expand output in the consumer goods industries can lead to a big expansion of the capital goods industries.

But the influence of the accelerator does not stop there. Precisely because it is responsible for the undue expansion of the capital goods industries, it is also a major factor in the down-turn. For after a while it goes into reverse: just as a small rise in the output of consumer goods may result in a much larger rise in the output of capital goods, so a small fall in the output of consumer goods may result in a much larger fall in the output of capital goods. This can be seen if we go back to our example. We saw that a 5 per cent increase in the output of coffee grinders (from 10,000 to 10,500) resulted in a 50 per cent rise in the output of coffee-grinder-making machinery. But if in the following year the output of the firm making coffee grinders falls by about 5 per cent (back to 10,000) its demand for machinery will fall from £30,000 to £10,000. For it will have £210,000 worth of machinery, but will only need £200,000 worth. Assuming that as usual £20,000 worth wears out, it will only need to buy £10,000 worth. So in this case a 5 per cent fall in the output of consumer goods has led to a fall of no less than two-thirds in the output of capital goods.

So far, for the sake of simplicity, we have been talking of the accelerated effect on the capital goods industries as being the result of an actual rise or fall in the output of consumer goods. But in fact nothing so dramatic is needed to bring the accelerator into play; it can be brought into play by a slight variation in the *rate of change* of output of consumer goods (e.g. a slight slowing down in the rate of increase). Without going through all the arithmetic, if in our example the output of coffee grinders in the second year had continued to rise, but only by 4 per cent instead of 5 per cent, then the firm's purchases of machinery (assuming it kept its capacity in line with its output) would still have been lower than in the first year. In other words a mere slowing-down in the rate of increase of consumer goods production can result in an actual fall in the output of capital goods. As the economy rapidly approaches the full employment ceiling during the up-swing of the trade cycle the rate of increase of consumer goods production is bound to be slowed down by an increasing shortage of labour, if by nothing else. The accelerator principle shows how this slowing-down will result in an actual fall in output and employment in the capital goods industries, and thus topple the economy over into a down-swing.

This, very briefly, is how economists in the 1920s and 1930s thought the trade cycle operated. Even today most economists would not dissent from many of the basic elements of the argument. But there are two intriguing aspects of the whole affair that need to be noted.

The first is that the various explanations, ingenious and plausible as they were, of why the economy toppled over from boom to slump, or recovered again from slump to boom, were propounded against the background of a theory according to which the trade cycle could not happen in the first place. In other words, at one level theory had had to come to grips with the phenomenon of the trade cycle, because it was so obviously there. But at a deeper level, full employment was still assumed to be the natural condition of the economy. 'Trade cycles cannot happen,' the economists seemed to be saying, 'but given that they do happen, this is why.'

The second interesting feature of the theory was the *inevitability* with which the cycle was assumed to operate. Given that during the up-swing the capital goods industries expanded too fast, it was taken for granted that before long the boom would come to an end and the economy would topple over into recession. It is true that some econ-

omists wanted to moderate the expansion of the capital goods industries at an early stage in the up-swing, by deliberately raising interest
rates and restricting bank credit, and thus making it more difficult
for businessmen to finance new investment projects. But there was a
tendency to regard this as a rather visionary approach; most people
took a curiously fatalistic view. Indeed one can almost detect a faint
Puritan satisfaction in the acceptance that a penalty must be paid for
the years of frenzied expansion – a penalty that could not be avoided
(though it might sometimes be postponed) by doing clever things
during the later stages of the boom. Some economists, in fact, appear
to have seen the economy as a somewhat dissipated member of the
human race, and to have thought of the trade cycle in terms of
getting drunk and suffering the after-effects – as is suggested by the
frequent use of words like 'excesses' and 'hangover'. The more
boisterously one drank, the more acute and prolonged would be the
eventual hangover. And human nature being what it is, there was
little hope of avoiding hangovers in the future by drinking more
slowly or stopping drinking sooner.

There was, however, a compensation for the inevitability of the
down-turn: the up-turn was inevitable too. During the down-swing
wages, prices and interest rates would fall, existing machinery would
wear out, and new inventions would be made and developed. Before
long investment would once again become profitable, and the stage
would be set for recovery. It was inconceivable that the economy
could get stuck at the bottom of the cycle as long as events were
allowed to take their natural course. If by any chance it did get stuck,
this could only be because some artificial restraint had been introduced which was impeding the smooth working of the system.

Or perhaps – one can say in the light of hindsight – it would be a
sign that the schizophrenia according to which the trade cycle could
not happen, but did, was no longer tolerable.

STATE OF THEORY IN THE 1920s

Let us now pull together the main threads we have been following in
this chapter, and summarize the theory of employment as it stood in
the 1920s and early 1930s.

First, and most basically, full employment was assumed to be part of the natural order of things. This assumption derived from Say's Law. Say's Law stated that supply created its own demand – that the process of creating an article also resulted in the creation of just enough purchasing power to buy that article. Therefore there could be no general surplus of articles, or of the labour employed in making the articles. This Law had been qualified as long ago as the early nineteenth century as far as surpluses in *particular industries* were concerned. Ricardo had argued that some shift in fashion could result in a sudden fall in the demand for the products of a particular industry, thus creating unemployment and spare capacity within that industry. But by definition the shift in fashion would have resulted in a rise in the demand for the products of some other industry. Capital and labour would move from the first industry to the second, so that the unemployment originally created would disappear.

The emergence during the nineteenth century of the trade cycle, and the attempts made to account for it, can be regarded as resulting in a further qualification to Say's Law. In addition to a process (perhaps fairly continuous) of unemployment appearing in one or two industries, and then being absorbed by the expansion of other industries, one now had the periodic and simultaneous appearance of unemployment in a large number of industries, particularly those making capital goods. So one had to agree not only (as Ricardo had done) that at any given time one or two industries might be suffering from unemployment; one also had to admit that every now and then the whole economy might suffer from it.

Nevertheless, Say's Law was still held to be valid. In principle, the economy would always absorb all the commodities it was capable of producing. The periodic unemployment associated with the trade cycle was an aberration, a consequence of the unbalanced structure of production caused by too rapid an expansion of the capital goods industries. Once this too-rapid expansion had occurred, a down-swing was inevitable. Many economists thought that all one could do was to stand back and let events take their course: as the existing (and excessive) stock of machinery and capital equipment which had been left over at the top of the boom wore out or rusted away; as falling employment led (as it always had done) to falling wages and prices; as the falling demand for loanable funds, and the rising supply of them, led to lower interest rates; and as time passed and new products and processes were invented – so, gradually, the conditions necessary for a recovery would come into being. Other economists were rather less passive than this – they felt that the down-swing phase of the cycle could be hurried up, for example by taking deliberate steps to reduce interest rates, instead of merely waiting for them to fall. But by and large there was agreement on the kind of things that had to happen before the up-swing could get under way again and full employment be restored.

Full employment, then, was accepted as the normal state of affairs. From time to time quite heavy unemployment would develop and, in so far as it could not be cured, must be endured. But such un-employment was a temporary phenomenon which always cured itself within a few years.

This was all very well. But what if, in fact, after the down-swing, the economy did not start to recover again; what if it simply got stuck at the bottom of the cycle, with heavy unemployment persisting year after year? How could this be accounted for?

To most economists in the 1920s and early 1930s the answer seemed obvious. Something must be happening to obstruct the adjustments which normally accompanied the down-swing of the trade cycle. These adjustments consisted, on the one side, of reductions in costs: wages, interest rates and the price of capital equipment were all supposed to fall, so that after a while it became cheaper (and therefore more profitable) to hire labour, borrow money and buy capital equipment. The other set of adjustments consisted of the emergence of new products or techniques of production which it was profitable to exploit. If, therefore, the economy refused to revive and heavy unemployment persisted, this must either be because one of the cost elements had not fallen as it should have done, or because no new products or processes were being developed which looked profitable enough to exploit. The problem was to identify the guilty factor, and then do something about it.

In the view of most economists and (though they might not have put it in quite these terms) of the overwhelming majority of the 'practical men' in business, the City and the Civil Service who took an interest in the matter, identification was made, with the devastating certainty of a fingerprint test, by the Law of Diminishing Returns and the Theory of Marginal Productivity. Together, these two bits of economic theory showed that the more of a factor of production that was employed, the less it would be paid. Therefore if the total available quantity of a factor of production is to be employed, each unit of the factor of production must be paid less than if only 90 per cent of it is to be employed. To be more specific, if there is to be full employment of the labour force, the average wage will have to be lower than if there is only 90 per cent employment (i.e. 10 per cent unemployment). Therefore if there is a persistent unemployment rate of 10 per cent, average wages must be too high. The only way to get back to full employment is to have some reduction in wages.

That was the theory. But did it provide a plausible explanation of the persistent unemployment of the 1920s and the refusal of the economy to budge from the bottom of the trade cycle? Had something happened to make wages too high in the first place? Or had something happened to prevent them falling in the way they had always fallen in previous down-swings?

The answer to both questions seemed clear. On the first point, the tremendous demand for labour during and immediately after the First World War had resulted in an enormous rise in wages: in the seven years between 1913 and 1920 wage rates nearly trebled. Past up-swings of the trade cycle had, of course, seen quite substantial increases in wages, but a rise on this scale was quite unprecedented.

On the second point, too, the evidence seemed conclusive. During the War there was a great increase in the size and power of the trade unions: the same seven years that saw a near-trebling of wage rates also saw a near-trebling of the number of trade unionists affiliated to the Trades Union Congress. By the early 1920s millions of workers who twenty or thirty years before would have had to bargain with their employers as individuals or small isolated groups were now spoken for by large and powerful unions.

To orthodox economic opinion in the 1920s the case was now made out. Wages were too high, and as a result part of the available labour force could not find employment. Full employment could only be restored if wages fell. During the nineteenth and early twentieth centuries this would have happened automatically during the down-swing of the trade cycle, and before long this would have enabled a revival to get under way. But now the unions were strong enough to resist wage reductions. Until they were persuaded, or forced, to see the error of their ways heavy unemployment would continue.

Economics is not an exact science: controlled experiments cannot be conducted on its subject matter, and there is plenty of room for disagreement among economists on how the economy works, or what cause will produce what effect. At any particular time, there are likely to be those who doubt or dissent from some aspects of the orthodox theory accepted and taught by the great majority of the profession. It would therefore be wrong to suggest that all British or Western economists in the 1920s and early 1930s necessarily adopted the theoretical approach outlined above, or favoured the policies which the theory seemed to call for. Several economists, in addition to Keynes himself, were uneasy about the state of the existing theory, and quite a number refused to advocate the policy measures – such as wage cuts – which the theory required.

Nevertheless, whatever the doubts and reservations of some economists, it was the theory outlined above which dominated economic thinking in the 1920s and early 1930s: this was the theory that was taught in the universities; this was the theory students got from their textbooks; this, above all, was the theory which underlay the basic approach to economic problems of all those in politics, the civil service, business and finance who were not themselves economists, but were daily making or influencing economic decisions. It was, in short, the conventional wisdom.

Let us now take a brief look at the 1920s and early 1930s in the light of this conventional wisdom.

Chapter Three

UNEMPLOYMENT BETWEEN
THE WARS

For the first couple of years after the end of the First World War the British economy boomed. There was pent-up demand for the consumer goods which had been unobtainable during the war; and heavy expenditure to replace buildings and capital equipment. Although the boom was more short-lived than most, it was in the classical trade cycle tradition, with a great burst of capital investment. But before the end of 1920 the usual down-swing started: production, employment, wages and prices all began to fall. As usual, after a couple of years or so the down-swing flattened out, and people began to look forward to the usual recovery.

But the recovery never came. Year after year went by, and every day more than a million men – often more than two million – were out of work. Not until nearly a generation later – in 1940, when the army had been pulled out of Dunkirk, and London was being pounded by the *Luftwaffe* – did unemployment fall convincingly below 10 per cent.

EXPORT PRICES

Looking at the problem in the early 1920s from a practical rather than theoretical standpoint, it was clear that much of the trouble lay in the export field: it was the traditional export industries – coal, cotton and shipbuilding – that were worst hit. During the war many of Britain's overseas markets had been lost to other countries, and attempts to recapture them after the war was over were hampered by the fact that our prices were now too high. During the war and immediate post-war period, wages and profits had nearly trebled, and

47

the general level of prices, including export prices, had risen at much the same rate. Wages and prices had risen in other countries as well, but not so much as in Britain, and our competitiveness had been substantially reduced. The result was that in the early 1920s the volume of British exports was only about two thirds of what it had been in 1913, with corresponding effects on production and employment.

Now if one's exports are too expensive, there are two things one can do. One can reduce wages, profits and other costs, so that, for example, a shirt which previously cost £10 to make now only costs £7·50 to make. Or one can lower the exchange rate between one's own currency and other countries' currencies, for example making £1 exchange for $1·50 instead of $2, so that a British shirt which cost £10 to make will now sell in America for $15 instead of $20. Either measure will have the effect of reducing the price of a British shirt in the American market by 25 per cent; but in other respects the effect of the two measures will be different. A good many of Britain's economic problems in the 1920s stemmed from the fact that successive governments preferred the first of these alternatives (a reduction in wages and prices) to the second (a reduction in the exchange rate).

One of the reasons for this preference we have already encountered, though in the context of general unemployment rather than unemployment created by lack of competitiveness in export markets. Experience of the trade cycle had convinced economists that wages and other costs must fall during the down-swing as one of the preconditions of eventual recovery. This conviction was reinforced, on a theoretical level, by the marginal productivity doctrine, which said that if there was unemployed labour it could only be re-employed at a lower level of average wages. So the moral pointed by both theory and experience was clear: if full employment was to be restored in Britain's export industries, wages must be reduced.

The other reason was more subtle than this, more elusive, and more difficult to pin down. To explain it, we must say a little about the gold standard, and the way the banking system works.

THE GOLD STANDARD

During the nineteenth century a country was said to be on the gold standard if the paper currency was backed by gold – in other words if a unit of its paper currency could be freely exchanged for a certain amount of gold. Britain was on the gold standard before the First World War because you could take a pound note along to the Bank of England and be given (in the form of a sovereign) a certain amount of gold in exchange. Obviously, any two countries that were on the gold standard must have a fixed rate of exchange between their currencies: in 1913 the same amount of gold that could be bought for £1 in London could be bought for $4.86 in New York, and therefore £1 had to exchange for about $4.86 if someone was not to make a fortune by shipping all the gold in one country across the Atlantic to the other.

Now if a country is on the gold standard it is supposed to preserve a pretty fixed relationship between the amount of gold in the Central Bank and the amount of money (in the form of bank notes and bank deposits) in the country. If there is too little gold in relation to the total amount of money there is a danger that the Bank will not be able to sell gold to all those who arrive flourishing £1 notes and asking for it. But if there is too much gold in relation to the total amount of money the Bank will be passing up a profitable opportunity – by simply sitting on the gold instead of using it as the basis of loans which bring in interest payments. Therefore the Central Bank will manipulate the total amount of money in the country in order to keep it in a fairly fixed relationship with the amount of gold it has in its vaults.

It does this by what are called 'open-market operations'. If there is too little gold in its vaults, in relation to the amount of money in the country, it will sell government securities in the open market – i.e. to anyone who wants to buy them. In return for these securities, the Central Bank will receive cheques, drawn on the purchasers' bank accounts, which it will present for payment to the commercial banks. The latter will then transfer an equivalent amount of cash to the Central Bank. The net result will be that the cash reserves of the commercial banks will fall by the amount of their customers' purchases of government securities. But the commercial banks have to maintain a minimum ratio of cash to deposits for much the same reason as the Central Bank – they would be in trouble if they could no longer cash their customers' cheques. If their cash reserves fall as a result of the Central Bank's open-market operations, they will have to reduce their customers' deposits to the point where the cash-to-deposit ratio is restored to the figure required by law or tradition. The commercial banks reduce their customers' deposits by reducing individuals' overdrafts, and the advances they have made to business firms – in fact all the measures which have now come to be known as a 'credit squeeze'. This is supposed to lead to a fall in consumption and investment, and hence in production and employment and hence (according to trade cycle theory) in wages and prices as well.

By acting in this way, therefore, the Central Bank reduces the amount of money in the country, hoping that the reduction will be just big enough to bring the total amount of money back into the desired relationship with its own stock of gold. In the opposite case – when the Central Bank has too much gold in relation to the amount of money in the economy – the reverse happens. The Central Bank buys government securities from the commercial banks or their customers in return for cash. This will lead to a rise in the banks' holdings of cash, which will impel them to increase their customers' deposits by lending more, and consumption and investment will start to rise. This leads in turn to rising production and employment, and rising wages and prices.

Now the crucial aspect of the gold standard system stemmed from the fact that countries settled their international debts in terms of gold. If Britain imported more from America than she exported to her, thus incurring a trade deficit, she would pay the difference in gold. This had a double effect. On one side of the Atlantic, the Bank of England would lose gold, and would therefore contract the amount of money in Britain. This would lead to a reduction in spending in Britain, and to some fall in wages and prices. This would lead in turn to a reduction in British imports and a rise in British exports – partly because the tighter British market would discourage foreigners from selling to Britain and encourage British manufacturers to sell abroad, and partly because these influences would be reinforced by the fact that British goods had now become cheaper in relation to foreign goods.

But meanwhile the same sequence of events would be happening, in reverse, on the other side of the Atlantic. The Federal Reserve Banks in America would gain gold, and therefore expand credit, with the eventual result that total expenditure in America would rise, as would wages and prices. American imports would accordingly rise, and American exports fall. Through the operation of this double effect, Britain's trade deficit with America would be eliminated.

This was the real trick about the gold standard. It provided, at any rate in theory, a beautiful, self-equilibrating mechanism which ensured that maladjustments in international trade would be automatically eliminated. In practice, according to recent historical research, the gold standard never worked quite like this. It is true that during the nineteenth century balance of payments maladjustments were fairly quickly and easily eliminated. But this was not in the main due to the workings of the gold standard – for on the whole Central Banks did not maintain the strict relationship between the amount of gold and the amount of money that the theory required, nor were prices so closely related to the amount of money as the theory implied. It was due rather to other factors – partly to the effect of interest rates on short-term capital movements, and partly to the fact that there really was some tendency for an imbalance in trade to cure itself: a rapid rise in exports may lead in the short run to a trade surplus, but it also creates incomes which will be partly spent on imports; in the same way the emergence of a trade deficit has effects on incomes which will tend to depress imports.

But these finer distinctions were not apparent to economists and politicians in the 1920s. As they saw it, in the nineteenth century the gold standard had been in operation, and the international payments mechanism had worked smoothly. If it was to work smoothly again, the gold standard must be restored. And this could only be done if Britain herself went back on to the gold standard.

RETURN TO PRE-WAR PARITY

Britain had formally abandoned the gold standard in 1919, but this was regarded as a strictly temporary measure designed to give the country time to get back to normal after the upheavals caused by the war. It was generally accepted that before long the country would return to the gold standard: without it there could be no order in international economic life, and no guarantee against limitless expansion of the currency and hence uncontrollable inflation (a point later driven forcibly home by the German hyper-inflation of 1922–3). Above all, perhaps, it was necessary to return to the gold standard in order to preserve sterling as the world's major trading currency, and to restore the City of London to the lucrative position it had held before 1914 as the capital of the world's financial system.

It was these last considerations which were probably decisive, not merely in causing Britain to go back on to the gold standard, but to go back *at the pre-war parity*. For to go back at a lower parity (i.e. with £1 being equal to a smaller amount of gold or dollars than before the war) would mean that foreigners who held sterling, or assets in Britain, would find the value of their holdings, in terms of gold or dollars, reduced. Everyone in the City, and indeed most economists and politicians, were convinced that this would constitute a default by Britain that would make it impossible to restore sterling and the City of London to their former status.*

Since 1919 the exchange rate between sterling and the dollar had been well below the pre-war level of $4.86. If the pre-war parity between gold and sterling (and therefore, since the US had remained on the gold standard, between the dollar and sterling) was to be restored, it was clear that wages and prices in Britain would have to come down sharply from their inflated post-war levels. The attempt to bring this about became one of the main features of economic policy in the first half of the 1920s. Eventually it resulted in the General Strike.

The severe recession which began late in 1920 was in fact accompanied, as both theory and experience suggested it would be, by big reductions in wages and prices: over the next three years they both fell by about a third. This augured well for a return to the gold standard at the pre-war parity, and the government finally took this step in April 1925. But it was clear that despite this big fall in wages and prices, British exports were still not fully competitive at the pre-war exchange rate, and that there would have to be some further cuts

---

* A typical comment came from Montagu Norman, Governor of the Bank of England, who said, 'I think that the disadvantages to the internal position [of going back at the pre-war parity] are relatively small compared with the advantage to the external position.' (Macmillan Committee, Minutes of Evidence, Question 3332.)

in wage rates. A small number of people thought that this would not happen automatically or easily. Keynes himself was the leading exponent of this view. He noted that the fall in wages had come to a halt in 1923, and believed that any further fall could only be brought about by a deliberate deflationary policy on the part of the government. With unemployment already at a rate of more than 10 per cent, he thought this was too high a price to pay for going back on the gold standard at the pre-war parity, and opposed the decision to do so. But in this he was pretty well a lone voice in the wilderness. Most economists, politicians and businessmen thought that the necessary wage cuts could be brought about fairly easily.

Not least among this group were the mine-owners. Faced with the additional difficulties in exporting created by the return to the pre-war, and less favourable, exchange rate, they decided that wages must be cut, and proposed reductions of 10–25 per cent. The miners refused, and in self-defence revived the Triple Alliance – originally a pre-war association between themselves, the railwaymen and the transport workers. For a while the clash was postponed by the government agreeing to give the industry a subsidy until 1 May 1926, so reducing the mine-owners' costs without reducing wages. At the same time it set up a Royal Commission to inquire into the industry. This Commission reported in March 1926, saying among other things that the subsidy must end on the appointed day and never be renewed. The government accepted this, and at the end of April many mine-owners announced reductions in wages. This led immediately to the General Strike.

The strike failed, in the sense that the miners eventually went back to work at substantially reduced wages. But it provided Britain with a taste of dissension and chaos that nobody much liked, and after it was over the unions and the Conservative government treated each other with considerable circumspection. Few attempts were made to force through wage cuts in other industries, and wage rates remained at about the 1925 level for the rest of the decade. As a result British exports remained uncompetitive and unemployment in the export industries (though not only in these industries) remained high. Indeed the export problem grew worse later in the 1920s when other countries, such as France, also returned to the gold standard, but at a much lower parity than pre-war, thus ensuring that their exports were considerably cheaper than ours.* And so our balance of *trade* remained highly unfavourable (in the sense that imports were much higher than exports). However our balance of payments as a whole was in reasonable equilibrium. The trade deficit was offset by the 'invisible' earnings which derived from the profits received from British investments overseas, and from the banking, insurance and shipping services provided through the City of London. Less satisfactorily, the long-term investments overseas that Britain continued to build up over this period were financed by short-term borrowing from abroad. This caused trouble later, as we shall see.

But although for these reasons the uncompetitiveness of exports did not have the drastic consequences for the *balance of payments* that it has had in more recent years, it was nevertheless an obvious source of *unemployment*. And, according to the economic theory of the day, which still relied heavily on the Law of Diminishing Returns and the Theory of Marginal Productivity, the same factor which caused exports to be uncompetitive – the excessive level of wages and prices – was itself responsible for unemployment quite apart from the effect on exports. So throughout the later 1920s orthodox politicians and economists continued to bewail the inflexibility of wages and prices, caused, as they saw it, by the strength of the trade unions on the one hand and restrictive business practices on the other, and to argue that only if this inflexibility could be overcome, and wages and prices made to fall, would full employment be restored.

THE WALL STREET CRASH

During the 1920s unemployment had been mainly a British problem. By and large, other countries prospered. But in 1929 came the Wall Street Crash and the beginning of the Great Slump. All over the world unemployment came to seem less the exception than the rule.

During the years 1922 to 1929 the US appeared not only to have recovered from such effects of the war as she had suffered, but to have found the secret of permanent economic expansion. Un-

* The French, as so often, were much more intelligent about this than we were. Their new parity was deliberately chosen as one which would make their exports competitive *without* requiring any reduction in wages.

employment was very low; employment, production, wages and profits all rose steadily year after year. On the other hand prices remained roughly stable, and this persuaded many economists and politicians that the economy was not just experiencing the usual up-swing of the trade cycle (for this should have been characterized by rising prices), but had found some more permanent stability. (In fact many prices did rise during this period, but this was masked by a steady fall in food prices caused by a steep rise in agricultural productivity.) The general optimistic, not to say euphoric, atmosphere engendered by the belief that employment, wages and profits (particularly profits) would not be hit by the usual down-swing, but would go on rising for ever, went to many people's heads. They decided that if profits were going to go on rising for ever they had better get their hands on some of the shares which entitled their holders to a portion of those profits. Even if the shares seemed unduly expensive, even if you had to borrow money in order to pay for them, or indeed merely promised to pay for them in the future, the only way to get rich was to buy as many as you could. As a result share prices shot up during the few years before October 1929 to ridiculous levels – levels which no conceivable future rise in profits could possibly justify. 'The present level of stock prices,' one observer commented in 1929, 'discounts not just the future but the hereafter.' Sooner or later, the market was bound to collapse.

The Crash actually came in October 1929, though there was no particular reason why it should have come in that month rather than in any other month. A wave of selling hit the New York Stock Exchange, and once a wave of selling gets under way in a situation where share prices are much too high, it tends to gather pace. Those who have bought shares on borrowed money decide they must sell before prices fall so far that the value of what they possess is less than the amount they owe. The more they sell, the more prices fall, and the more prices fall, the more they sell. Within a month of the beginning of the Crash industrial shares on the New York Stock Exchange had lost more than a third of their value. For more than two and a half years share prices continued to fall. By the middle of 1932 the average industrial share was worth less than a sixth of what it had been worth in October 1929.

THE GREAT SLUMP

The Wall Street Crash can be said to have ushered in the Slump and even, by its dramatic effects on business and consumer confidence, to have played a major role in aggravating it. But it was not the real cause. The factors which underlay the Stock Exchange boom and collapse were basically the same factors which had always caused the up-swing and down-swing of the trade cycle. There was a rapid rise in investment in the US during the later 1920s – not only in productive industry, but in the form of house-building as well. The output of capital goods rose by nearly a quarter between 1927 and 1929, and the great house-building boom which had begun in 1921 continued happily upwards. This investment boom broke in the middle of 1929 – several months before the Stock Exchange collapsed. Industrial production began to fall, and unemployment to rise. As usual, it was the capital goods industries which were worst hit. By 1932 the output of capital goods was only about a quarter of what it had been in 1929. The fall in the output of consumer goods, though much less sharp than this, was still fairly severe, and the net result was that in 1932 industrial production was no more than half what it had been three years before. Because of falling output in other sectors, the output of the economy as a whole, by 1932, was only two thirds what it had been in 1929. This fall in production was accompanied by a violent fall in employment. Unemployment rose from about $1\frac{1}{2}$ million in 1929 to more than 12 million in 1932.

This tremendous contraction of economic activity in the United States had repercussions all over the world. We shall be looking more closely at some of the reasons for this – the fall in American imports and the catastrophic decline in primary product prices – in Chapter 6. Here we concentrate on one particular reason – though an extremely important reason – for the devastating speed and intensity with which the Slump spread. This was the precarious structure of international debt which had grown up during the 1920s.

America had invested a great deal of money abroad during the 1920s, particularly in Germany. Much of this money was used to finance German industry, but a good deal of it was used to finance German reparation payments to France, Britain and a number of other countries. For although German reparation payments had been successively scaled down from the enormous figures fixed at the end of the war (and bitterly criticized by Keynes) she had proved unable to raise her exports or reduce her imports enough to finance even this reduced level of payments out of her own trade balance. What happened, in effect, was that money flowed from the United States to Germany; some of it went from Germany to France (and to a lesser extent to Britain); and some of the money that came to France went back again to America, in repayment for money that France had borrowed from America. In 1928 the American outflow of capital to Germany fell off, principally because Americans decided it was much more profitable to invest in their own booming Stock Exchange than in Germany. After the 1929 Crash, this fall became even more pronounced. As a result German industry found itself without adequate funds; investment fell, and the whole economy started to contract. Moreover Germany now found that she could no longer meet her reparation and other debt payments to France, Britain and other countries. This led to exactly the same kind of scramble for cash in the international field as the New York crash had led to within the United States. When people start defaulting on debt everyone who is owed money starts calling it in before those who owe it go bankrupt. This leads to more defaulting, and the spiral worsens. Countries started withdrawing from other countries the money they had lent to them. Since gold was the accepted medium for settling international debts, people in effect started arriving at the Central Banks of Britain, France and Germany waving IOUs and demanding gold in return.

Britain was particularly hard hit by this. Her gold reserves were relatively low, because her return to the gold standard in 1925 at the pre-war parity had made exports too expensive and imports too cheap. Consequently there were large deficits on the balance of trade, and although, as we have seen, invisible earnings from banking, insurance, shipping and similar services turned this into a surplus for current transactions as a whole, this surplus was too small to pay for the large outflow of capital into investments overseas. These investments were quite inappropriate to Britain's new and much weaker economic position, but nevertheless they continued to be made. Since they could not be financed by a current account surplus, they had to be financed by short-term borrowing from abroad, and this made Britain's position more vulnerable than ever. For of their very nature, Britain's long-term investments overseas, which represented factories in Australia or tea plantations in Ceylon, could not be quickly or easily liquidated; but the money Britain had borrowed to finance them, representing three-month Treasury Bills, or even ordinary deposit accounts in banks, could be called back virtually overnight. The situation was made worse by the fall in Britain's exports after 1929, the steep decline in invisible earnings which attended the falling-off of world trade, and the reduction in profits and dividends from investments overseas as production slumped in one country after another. Gold flowed out of Britain, and unemployment grew.

As if all this were not bad enough, this rise in unemployment in itself created a new crisis. For as unemployment rose, from 10 per cent in 1929 to 16 per cent in 1930 and 21 per cent in 1931, the unemployment benefits paid out by the National Insurance Fund rose, and the contributions paid into it fell. The result was that by 1931 the Fund was heavily in debt to the Exchequer. The Exchequer itself had already been running a small deficit for some years, and this development made things much worse.

THE BALANCED BUDGET

Ever since, in the nineteenth century, the government had become an important spending agency, it had been a cardinal principle of financial and economic orthodoxy – indeed of ordinary common sense – that the government must cover its expenditure out of its income. Exceptions were sometimes permitted in wartime; if the government could not raise enough money by taxation to cover the cost of fighting a war, it was accepted that it would have to borrow to make up the difference. But in normal peacetime conditions it was self-evident that the Budget must be balanced, with the government's income equalling or exceeding its expenditure. After all, it is important for any individual to keep his expenditure within his income; it was obviously infinitely more important for a government to balance its books – particularly the government of a country like Britain, in which large amounts of foreign money were invested, and in whose currency more than half the world's trade was conducted.

During the First World War government expenditure had, inevitably, risen enormously. Taxation had risen as well but not nearly enough to fill the gap, the rest of which was financed by borrowing. After the war government expenditure fell sharply but (even after allowing for the change in price levels) not nearly back to the pre-war figure. This was partly due to the effects of the war itself – the cost of paying pensions to disabled ex-servicemen and war widows, and the cost of paying interest on the money borrowed to finance the war (i.e. on the now much increased National Debt); and partly to the cost of implementing wartime and post-war pledges to build 'homes for heroes' and to pay increased scales of unemployment benefits.

This high level of public expenditure required high taxes to pay for it. Indeed, taxes had to be rather more than enough to pay for current government expenditure, for the government accepted the orthodox view that it was not enough merely to pay the *interest* on the sums it had borrowed during the war; it must start repaying the *principal* as well. In other words each year it must achieve a Budget surplus with which to pay off a little bit of the National Debt. During the first half of the 1920s this was in fact done. But the taxes needed to achieve this surplus were bitterly criticized, particularly by businessmen, who argued, predictably, that high taxation was throttling enterprise and was thus responsible for stagnation and unemployment. These arguments impressed the government, and taxes were reduced. With a fall in the yield of taxation, it was obvious to all that there must be a corresponding fall in government expenditure. But as countless politicians have discovered before and since, this was easier said than done. The government's expenditure was indeed cut, but not as much as its income. Consequently the small Budget surpluses achieved in the first half of the 1920s gave way to small deficits in the second half. These deficits were greeted with much lip-pursing and head-shaking, but it seemed impossible either to raise taxes or reduce expenditure, and nothing much was done.

But when it became apparent, in 1930, that the Exchequer deficit was rapidly increasing, considerable anxiety began to be expressed both in Britain and in other countries. A Treasury memorandum presented to the Royal Commission on Unemployment Insurance in January 1931 said that 'continued State borrowing on the present vast scale, without adequate provision for repayment by the [National Insurance] Fund, would quickly call in question the stability of the

British financial system'. In February the Labour government set up a Committee on National Expenditure, under Sir George May, to advise on what should be done; at the same time the Chancellor of the Exchequer (Mr Snowden) said that 'the national position is grave; drastic and disagreeable measures will have to be taken if the Budget equilibrium is to be maintained and industrial recovery is to be made'. (Note the assumed connection between a balanced Budget and industrial recovery.)

By the time the May Committee reported, at the end of July 1931, the international payments position had grown very much worse. The Credit Anstalt, the largest bank in Austria, had got into difficulties, and had partially suspended payments. Mistrust of European banks and financial institutions spread rapidly, and there was an intensification of the process by which countries called in their own money from abroad while doing their best to freeze their own liabilities to other countries. Inevitably Britain, unable to recall much of the money she had lent abroad, but committed by her adherence to the gold standard to selling gold to all those who wanted to remove their money from London, suffered particularly severely. By the second half of July gold was flowing out of the country at a rate of £12–15 million a week, and by the end of the month the gold reserves were down to £133 million.

BRITAIN GOES OFF THE GOLD STANDARD

The May Report forecast that at the end of the current financial year (1931–2) there would be a Budget deficit of £120 million, and recommended some increase in taxation and drastic cuts in expenditure, particularly on unemployment benefits, in order to close the gap. This report (which Keynes described as 'the most foolish document I have ever had the misfortune to read'), coupled with the obvious reluctance of the Labour government to cut unemployment pay and the wages of public servants, increased alarm at home and abroad. The outflow of gold accelerated, though the reserves were temporarily boosted by a £50 million loan from the French and American Central Banks at the beginning of August. Late in August the government fell, and was replaced by a National government (with Ramsay Macdonald still Prime Minister) pledged to preserve the value of the pound at any price. But although a further £80 million was borrowed from France and the US towards the end of August, and the new government announced increases in taxation and cuts in expenditure early in September, the situation was out of control. By 19 September the remaining gold reserves were rapidly disappearing. The government had no choice. On 21 September it suspended gold payments. After six years of struggle Britain had been finally forced off the gold standard.

The effects of this on the whole system of international trade and payments were far-reaching and long-lasting, but for present purposes the point to notice is the effect on employment in Britain. The immediate effect was favourable. The price of sterling was now free to fluctuate according to supply and demand, and since more people were trying to sell it than buy it, its price fell. By the middle of 1932 the price in relation to the dollar had fallen from the $4·86 implied by being on the gold standard to $3·58. This meant that Britain's exports were now cheaper and her imports more expensive, and there was some corresponding improvement in the trade balance. But the effects of this were small and short-lived. The countries which had not devalued in relation to gold took other steps to relieve their balance of payments and to protect their home markets from the foreign competition which threatened to further reduce their employment. Tariffs were raised, import quotas extended, and exchange controls imposed. Britain, and other countries which had left the gold standard, retaliated in the same way. By 1932 the value of world trade had fallen to a third of the 1929 level, and everywhere production continued to fall and unemployment to rise. In Britain, in 1932, unemployment was worse than ever before, at a rate of 22 per cent. In Germany and the US it was even higher.

SLAVES OF DEFUNCT ECONOMISTS

What should be done about this? Keynes himself was quite clear. Instead of attempting to cut wages, the government should reduce interest rates; should impose protective duties on imports; and above all – a policy he had been advocating since 1924 or so – should undertake large-scale public investment expenditures, financing them by borrowing from the banking system.

Keynes was by no means alone among professional economists in holding and advocating these views, though he was certainly one of the earliest and leading exponents of them. A considerable number of eminent economists joined him in calling for government expenditure on public works, for example, and in recognizing the practical difficulties of restoring full employment by cutting wages. In evidence to the Macmillan Committee on Finance and Industry in 1930; in the recommendations of the committee set up by the Prime Minister under the chairmanship of Keynes later in the same year; in letters to *The Times* in the early 1930s, and in other ways, several of the leading economists of the day, as well as Keynes himself, called for the sort of measures which would later be regarded as the right ones to adopt.

The government by no means set its face against all these measures. Protective duties were imposed – though the political pressures were such that it seems pretty certain they would have been imposed whatever the economists said. Interest rates were reduced – though this was an orthodox and time-honoured step. Widespread wage-cuts were not forced through – though the government did reduce pay in the public sector in 1931 and 1932. But in the most crucial area of all – expenditure on public works – the advice of Keynes and those who thought like him was totally rejected. Indeed not only was public expenditure not increased; the most strenuous, and successful, attempts were made to reduce it.

This refusal on the part of the government to respond to this most central and incessant of Keynes's exhortations can perhaps be traced to two principal factors. One was that on the question of public works – and on the even more politically-sensitive issue of wage-cuts – economists were far from unanimous. A letter to *The Times* from one group of economists advocating public works or opposing wage-cuts was liable to evoke a reply from another group of economists arguing the opposite. The second sort of view was more fully expounded in *The Great Depression*, a book by Professor Lionel (later Lord) Robbins published in 1935. Professor Robbins argued, for example, that ·

in general it is true to say that a greater flexibility of wage rates would considerably reduce unemployment ... If it had not been for the prevalence of the view that wage rates must at all costs be maintained in order to maintain the purchasing power of the consumer, the violence of the present depression and the magnitude of the unemployment that accompanied it would have been considerably less.

And his view on the unwisdom of incurring a Budget deficit in order to finance public works comes out in this passage (provoked by the fact that this was in effect what President Roosevelt – in sharp contrast to the British government – was doing in the US):

> It is yet too early to say whether the American emergency legislation will prevent the coming of some degree of recovery . . . The unbalancing of the Budget and the vast expenditure on public works have an inflationary tendency which may well override the various impediments to enterprise created in other directions and engender an inflationary boom – a boom which, if the analysis of earlier chapters is correct, would be likely to be followed by a deflationary collapse.*

But the problem was not only that a good many economists were strongly opposed to Keynes's line on public works and wage cuts; there was also the problem that staunch allies on one issue might vacillate or talk with a muted voice on the other. Professor Pigou, for example, one of the most distinguished economists of the day, did not advocate wage cuts, but he did not oppose them either; and – as Keynes justly observed – the conclusion of his *Theory of Unemployment*, published in 1933, was that unemployment is primarily due to a wage policy which fails to adjust itself sufficiently to changes in the real demand function for labour.

This, then, was one of the reasons why the policy-makers turned a deaf ear to Keynes's advice: the economists were divided among themselves in the advice they gave. The other reason was even more important, and Keynes put his finger on it in the immortal phrase in which he accused practical men of being the slaves of some defunct economist (see page 23). The practical men of the 1920s and early 1930s – the politicians and civil servants, the business executives and the men who were 'something in the City' – were the slaves of the economists of a century before. In particular, the politicians and civil servants who took the decisions about how much the Government should spend on public works were slaves of the view that full employment was the normal state of affairs. There was only a certain

---

* Note the assumption, which we have seen to be a constant theme of trade cycle theory, that once the boom had happened the slump had to happen too. It was better, the moral seemed to be, to have unemployment than to have employment which was created artificially.

amount of savings in the economy available for investment, they argued, and if more of these savings were devoted to public investment, less would be available for private investment. Therefore increased expenditure on public works could not help the economy. Indeed it was likely to harm it, and to delay the beginning of a proper and soundly-based recovery by diverting resources away from productive private investment, like factories which would soon employ men and produce goods, towards unproductive public investment, like houses and roads, which would not.

The official attitude to unemployment is well expressed in an extract from a speech made in the House of Commons in February 1935 by the Chancellor of the Exchequer, Mr Neville Chamberlain.

> There may be circumstances when it is right and sound to follow a policy of that kind [i.e. a large expenditure of public money, including expenditure on public works], but not for the purpose of providing employment, because the whole experience of the past shows that, for the purpose of providing employment, this policy of public works is always disappointing . . . The conclusion I draw . . . is that the quickest and most effective contribution which any government can make towards an increase of employment is to create conditions which will encourage and facilitate improvement in ordinary trade.*

Too much blame should not be attached to these practical men for arguing in this sort of way. The economic theory from which their opinions sprang might be a century old but it was still going strong; nobody had changed it. It was still the theory of the textbooks and the undergraduate lectures. Distinguished economists might be so bold as to issue policy advice which could not be derived from the theory they taught; practical men had to be more careful. Keynes might get away with it; the Chancellor of the Exchequer did not dare.

The picture is, perhaps, a little overdrawn. But the fact remains that the politicians and the civil servants were acting in perfect accord with the dictates of the traditional, received theory of how the economy worked. Until somebody came along with a new economic theory, which showed that the modern economy really worked quite differently, practical men, paradoxically, were going to be difficult to convince.

This is what Keynes did. Early 1936 saw the publication of the *General Theory*. At last he could provide a comprehensive theoretical

* *Hansard*, 14 February 1935, Cols. 2208–9.

justification for some of the views he had been expressing since the early 1920s.

It would be wrong to suggest that the *General Theory* appeared, totally unheralded and unexpected, from a clear blue sky. Many of Keynes's Cambridge colleagues knew how his mind was moving, and had indeed contributed, in their discussions and writings, to the evolution of his ideas. He paid tribute not only to them, but to the stimulus he had received from the works of several earlier economists such as Malthus, Hobson and the 'unduly neglected prophet' Silvio Gesell. And in hindsight it is possible to see Keynes's debt to a number of other economists, some long since dead at the time he was writing, some still alive today.

Nevertheless, the fact remains that the major intellectual discovery represented by the *General Theory* was made by Keynes. How he made it, we do not really know – whether it came in a flash or was pieced together bit by bit; whether he climbed a hill and suddenly saw the Pacific, or deduced its presence from the smell of the wind and the cries of the gulls. What we do know is that on 1 January 1935 he wrote in a letter to Bernard Shaw

... I believe myself to be writing a book on economic theory which will largely revolutionize – not, I suppose, at once but in the course of the next ten years – the way the world thinks about economic problems.

Never was such apparent arrogance so amply justified.

Chapter Four

THE GENERAL THEORY

The book is called *The General Theory of Employment, Interest and Money*, but it is not surprising that the title at the top of each page of the text has been abbreviated to *The General Theory of Employment*. For as Keynes himself put it, 'The ultimate object of our analysis is to discover what determines the volume of employment.'*

However, the volume of employment is significant not only on its own account, as a measure of whether or not people who want work can find it. It is also, because in the short run employment and output tend to move fairly closely in line with each other, a kind of shorthand way of describing the whole level of activity in the economy. Therefore although in this chapter we shall be discussing Keynes's theory mainly in terms of employment and unemployment – legitimately so, in view of the level of unemployment in the 1930s – we must remember that the subject matter might equally well be described as the level of output in the country, or the standard of living of its citizens. To this day, as we shall see in Part Two, there are those who refuse to accept that Keynes's analysis was right; but no one has ever questioned that the subject he was dealing with is at the heart of economic theory and policy.

Keynes was not interested in every kind of unemployment that had ever existed. He was not concerned, for example, with the question of why unemployment should sometimes appear in particular industries; this question had been satisfactorily answered by Ricardo, if not before. Nor was he primarily concerned with explaining the bouts of unemployment which would appear from time to time in a wide range of industries, grow worse for a year or two, level off and then

* *General Theory*, page 89.

66

disappear again. Although his theory did supply the key to understanding how the trade cycle could happen in the first place (the one aspect of the trade cycle which existing theory could not properly explain) this was essentially a by-product of his work.*

His main concern was with the factors which determine the overall level of employment in a modern industrial economy at any particular time. Inevitably, writing in Britain in the mid-1930s, his attention was focused on the reasons for the persistence of heavy unemployment year after year. How, he asked, could this happen? What was wrong with the prevailing theory, which assumed it could not happen? But although he was writing against the background of what seemed a permanent slump, Keynes's theory was essentially a short-term theory. He was not concerned with the factors which determine what the volume of employment will be in twenty or fifty years' time; in the long run, as he put it, we are all dead. He wanted to know what determines employment now and next year. In short, he was concerned with a sufficiently brief space of time for it to be reasonable to assume that such factors as the number of people of working age, consumer spending patterns, industrial techniques and so on do not change enough to have much effect on employment.

EFFECTIVE DEMAND

Keynes began † by rejecting the idea that one can rely on full employment being maintained (or, after the down-swing of the trade cycle, restored) by the operation of some self-adjusting mechanism. Wages, prices and interest rates do not, he said, move by themselves in such a way as to ensure full employment. And even if they *did* move in the way required by orthodox theory, this would not necessarily do the trick either. In fact, one must not simply assume that full employment is the normal state of affairs, kept in being by the flexibility of wages or interest rates in the same sort of way that the temperature of a room is kept at a constant level by the automatic

* There is a short chapter appended to the main text of the *General Theory* entitled 'Notes on the Trade Cycle'.

† This does not mean that he actually began the *General Theory* in this way. I have tried in this chapter to expound the essence of Keynes's argument rather than to follow at all closely the order or terminology of the *General Theory* itself.

operation of a thermostat. Instead one must regard the level of employment, like any other variable in economics (or life itself) as something determined by certain causal factors. One must think out what these factors are, and consider whether they might work in such a way as to result in a level of employment persistently lower than the numbers seeking work.

In the short run, he went on, the level of employment is determined by the level of output: if output is running at a high level, firms will employ more men than if it is running at a low level, and men will be engaged or laid off according to whether output is rising or falling. Output, in turn, depends on *effective demand*. Effective demand simply means demand backed by money – in other words actual expenditure. Total expenditure and total sales are the same thing from different viewpoints, and sales (apart from changes in stocks) are the same thing as output.* So one can see why output is determined by effective demand. The real question is, what determines effective demand?

To answer this question Keynes argued that one must break down effective demand into two components, consumption and investment, and study each in turn. The distinction between consumption and investment is conceptually fairly clear, though there are a number of technical snags involved which we must not spend too much time on. If an individual spends money on ice cream or a seat in a theatre, this is obviously expenditure on consumption. Equally obviously, if a firm spends money on a new factory and new plant and machinery to put in it, this is investment. Some other cases are much less clear-cut. Money spent on a car, for example, counts as consumption if it is spent by a private individual, but investment if spent by a firm. Houses are bought by individuals, but count as investment. But the best rough-and-ready distinction for the purposes of our analysis is that money spent by individuals on goods and services in order to satisfy their own wants is consumption; money spent by firms on

* Total output, total expenditure and total incomes are all equal: they are three different ways of measuring the same concept. Nowadays this is usually called the Gross Domestic Product, or GDP, a term we shall employ when discussing post-war developments in Part Two. At the time of the *General Theory*, however, this terminology had not been invented. Keynes himself mainly used the term 'income' or 'aggregate income', but the term 'National Income' soon came into common use, and it is this that we shall employ in this and the next two chapters.

buildings and machinery in order to produce goods and services in the future is investment.

Of the total annual income of a modern country, something like a fifth will be spent on investment, and the other four fifths on consumption. Or, to look at it from the side of output rather than income, a fifth of the annual output of the country will consist of what are called *investment* or *capital* goods such as buildings and machinery, and the other four fifths of consumer goods and services such as clothes and haircuts.* If, therefore, one wants to know what determines the total output of a country (and hence the level of employment) one must examine what determines the level of consumption and what determines the level of investment. Let us take consumption first.

CONSUMPTION

An individual's consumption is determined mainly by his income; and his consumption will normally be rather *less* than his income. There are of course cases in which the opposite is true, and a rich or optimistic individual manages to spend more on consumption than he receives in income, by borrowing or dipping into past savings. There are probably a good many cases where income and consumption are exactly equal, with each week's pay packet being spent down to the last penny. But the majority of individuals or households probably save a little bit of their income, even if the saving only takes the form of paying premiums on a life insurance policy, or contributions towards a pension. They therefore spend rather less on consumption than they earn (savings being defined simply as the difference between income and expenditure on consumption). The factors that impel people to save are various: some save to provide for their children, or their own old age; some as an insurance against future illness or unemployment; some to build up a small business of their own; some out of sheer miserliness; and some, no doubt, because they

* This breakdown of the National Income into only two categories – consumption and investment – is of course a simplification which takes no account of such real-world complications as government current expenditure and stock-building. But throughout this chapter we shall be drastically simplifying reality in order to make the gist of the argument as clear as possible. In particular, we shall be ignoring foreign trade and assuming – as Keynes himself did in the *General Theory* – that we are dealing with a 'closed economy'.

cannot think of anything interesting enough to spend their money on.

Whatever the relative strength of these various motives, it seems fairly safe to say that if you take all the individuals or households in an advanced industrial country together you will find that their total consumption is less than their total income – in other words that some proportion of their total income is saved. Just what this proportion will be – whether it will be a tenth or a fifth or a third – will depend on the way a whole host of factors affect a particular society at a particular time, such as the attitude to thrift, the generosity of state old age pensions, the extent to which the state provides free education or medical treatment, and so on. We must accept most of these factors as determined by historical or sociological processes outside our terms of reference, but two particular ones may be worth a brief mention.

First, the proportion of a country's income that is spent on consumption depends quite a lot on how the National Income is distributed. Not surprisingly, rich people save a larger proportion of their income than poor people. If income is distributed fairly equally no one may be rich enough to do much saving, and consumption may be relatively high. If on the other hand the distribution of income is very unequal, the rich will save a good deal, and the poor will not be able to offset this by dis-saving.* Another relevant point is the distribution of the National Income between wages (including salaries) on the one hand, and profits on the other. The proportion of profits that is saved is usually a good deal higher than the proportion of wages that is saved. Therefore the larger the share of wages in the National Income the higher will be the proportion of the National Income spent on consumption.

Secondly, the proportion of income spent on consumption may change as income changes. One might expect, for example, that in the long run, as a society grew richer and people's real incomes rose, the proportion of income saved would tend to rise as well. As it happens, there is very little evidence that this does in fact occur – perhaps, in some cases, because the effect of rising incomes is offset by the effect of a reduction in inequality (not to mention an increase in

---

* i.e. spending more on consumption than they earn. You have to have assets to be allowed to run up a decent overdraft. Since Keynes wrote the picture has, of course, been somewhat changed by hire purchase.

advertising). But that is in the long run. In the *short run* there is a good deal of evidence to suggest that the *proportion* of income spent on consumption does change as income changes – because the *amount* spent on consumption changes rather slowly. During the up-swing of the trade cycle, for example, when incomes are rising quite rapidly, it takes people a little time to adjust their expenditure patterns to their higher level of income, and while they are making up their minds how to spend the extra money, they save more. Consequently the proportion of their incomes that they spend temporarily falls, and the same goes for the proportion of the National Income that is spent on consumption. Conversely, during the down-swing of the trade cycle, as people are put on to short time or lose their jobs altogether, and the household's income contracts, people find it difficult to cut their expenditure immediately in line with their reduced income; the tendency is to keep on with previous consumption patterns as long as possible, usually by dipping into *past* savings. As a result many people are, for the time being, spending more on consumption than they are earning, and so the proportion of the National Income as a whole which is spent on consumption during the down-swing is generally quite high.

THE MARGINAL PROPENSITY TO CONSUME

Before we leave consumption it may be as well to say a word about a concept which we shall need later on, which Keynes christened the *marginal propensity to consume*. Despite the slightly technical language, this is a fairly straightforward concept. It is the proportion of any *increase* in income that is spent on consumption. Suppose that 90 per cent of income is spent on consumption. In this case one would say that the *average* propensity to consume was 90 per cent, or 0·9. Now suppose that income rises, and of this *extra* income only 80 per cent is spent on consumption. In that case the *marginal* propensity to consume will be 80 per cent, or 0·8. As we have seen, the marginal propensity to consume may be relatively low during the up-swing of the trade cycle. But the simplest case to have in mind is where the marginal propensity is *equal* to the average propensity – where, say, 90 per cent of existing income is spent on consumption, and 90 per cent of any increase in income would also be spent on consumption.

In that case both the average and the marginal propensity to consume would be 0·9. According to Keynes, the size of the marginal propensity to consume – whether it was 0·8 or 0·85 or 0·9 – was very important; but the really crucial thing about it was that it was almost certainly less than 1 – in other words that *some* part of any increase in income would be saved. As we shall see, this assumption – which is clearly a fairly safe one – played an important part in his analysis.

The main factor which determines a country's consumption, then, is its income, just as the main factor which determines a family's consumption is its income. The exact proportion of its income that a country will spend on consumption will depend on institutional arrangements, traditional attitudes to saving, the distribution of income, and so on. But we shall not go very far wrong, as far as getting to grips with Keynes's analysis is concerned, if we think of a country's expenditure on consumption as being a fairly high, and fairly stable, proportion of its income.

INVESTMENT

Now let us turn to the factors which, according to Keynes, determine the second element of effective demand, investment. Although at this point the story becomes a little more complicated (particularly in the way in which Keynes actually presented it), the essence of what he was saying is relatively simple.

The amount of money spent on investment, said Keynes, is determined by two things: on the one hand, by the amount the investment will yield, and on the other by the cost of borrowing the money needed to finance the investment. This seems fairly clear. Obviously, no one is going to borrow money in order to build a factory if the profits eventually made by the factory are smaller than the interest payments he has to make on the money he has borrowed. On the other hand, if the profits to be made out of a new factory are much larger than the interest payments, one would expect all sorts of businessmen to start borrowing money and building factories all over the place. The exact amount of new factory-building, or other kinds of investment, that takes place will therefore depend in some way on the relationship between the yield of investment on the one hand and the cost of borrowing money on the other.

But in saying this one has merely driven the crucial questions further back. One now wants to know what determines the yield of an investment? And what determines the rate of interest that a borrower has to pay? Let us take these two questions in turn.

THE YIELD OF INVESTMENT

In order to assess the yield of an investment, said Keynes, one must assess the probable returns from it over the whole of its life, and not just in the first year or two.* The future yield depends on the future volume of sales, and the price at which these sales will be effected. The businessman's assessment of this will in turn depend on the outlook for the economy as a whole, and in particular for the goods that the new investment is designed to produce. We have already seen, in our discussion of the trade cycle, the kind of factors which are relevant. Immediately after the trade cycle has gone into the down-swing phase, for example, the prospects for new investment will not look very exciting: with a large amount of fairly new capital equipment already standing idle there will not be much profit to be made by installing more. But a few years later, when some of this equipment has worn out, or rusted away, or been made out-of-date by the development of new products or techniques, it may again become profitable to build new factories and install modern machinery. This will apply particularly, of course, to the up-swing stage of the business cycle, when incomes have started rising and the demand for goods and services is beginning to expand again. During this stage the accelerator, which has a depressing effect on investment during the down-swing, acts as a stimulant.

It would probably not be too much of an over-simplification, therefore, to say that the main factors affecting the future yield of a new factory or piece of machinery are the *amount* of capital equipment already in existence, and the *extent* to which it is being used. If there

---

* Keynes actually employed a concept which he christened 'the marginal efficiency of capital'. He defined this 'as being equal to that rate of discount which would make the present value of the series of annuities given by the returns expected from the capital-asset during its life just equal to its supply price.' Those familiar with modern techniques of investment appraisal will observe that Keynes had precisely anticipated what is now known as the 'internal rate of return on a discounted cash flow basis' or, more briefly, 'DCF rate of return'. For simplicity, we talk in the text of the 'yield' or 'profitability' of an investment.

is a lot of equipment about (as at the end of the boom) the profitability of new investment will tend to be less than when there is a relatively smaller amount (as at the beginning of the boom). And if what equipment already exists is under-utilized, the incentive to invest will be smaller than if all existing equipment is being used to capacity. This is fairly easy to see, and was indeed an element in the theory of the trade cycle. Keynes accepted this analysis, but significantly strengthened it by the emphasis he placed on *expectations*. It was not simply the present state of the economy which affected investment decisions, he insisted, but the expectations different businessmen had about the way things would develop in the future. The prospect of large immediate profits would not necessarily tempt them to invest in new projects if they thought that these profits would disappear in a year or two's time with the onset of a recession.

So far we have been looking only at one side of the investment decision, namely the yield to be expected from the investment if the businessman decides to go ahead with it. But before he can make his decision he will also need to know about the other side of the ledger, namely how much it will cost to borrow the money needed to pay for the investment; in other words, what is the rate of interest he will have to pay.* Our second question, then, is what determines the rate of interest?

THE RATE OF INTEREST

Keynes's theory of what determines the rate of interest, though highly ingenious, is not always easy to follow, and indeed was never quite pulled together in the *General Theory*. But the gist of it is roughly as follows.

The rate of interest is essentially a price – the price of borrowing

* It is assumed, again for the sake of simplicity, that the businessman raises money by borrowing at a fixed rate of interest from his bank. In fact he might raise money by issuing shares, or he might already have the money himself. But in both these cases the rate of interest is still relevant to his calculations; in the first case it will affect the terms on which he can raise money by a share issue, and in the second it will determine the return he can get by lending his money to somebody else instead of investing it himself. So even in these slightly more complicated cases the rate of interest is still a determinant of investment decisions. In practice, of course, there are many different rates of interest; when one talks of *the* rate of interest one is inevitably simplifying reality.

money – and one would expect it to be determined, like any other price, by supply and demand. This, said Keynes, is correct. It is determined by the supply and demand for *money* – money, in this context, being cash, and bank deposits which can immediately be converted into cash. What, then, determines the supply of money, and the demand for money?

As far as the supply side is concerned the position is fairly straight-forward. The quantity of money in the economy is decided by the Central Bank (or the government); we have seen (page 49) how the Central Bank uses 'open-market operations' (i.e. buys or sells secur-ities) in order to affect the liquid reserves of the commercial banks, and hence the willingness of these banks to grant overdrafts or make advances, and hence the cash or bank deposits at the disposal of ordinary citizens. Thus the supply of money is determined, to all intents and purposes, by decisions of the government or Central Bank (subject only to whether or how far the gold standard rules are operating).*

The demand side is more complicated. Let us be clear about the question we are asking. We are not asking the somewhat naïve question 'Why do people want money?' We are asking 'Why do people want to hold their wealth in the form of *money* (i.e. cash or bank deposits, which yield no interest) rather than in the form of equity shares, government securities or other assets which yield some return?' In other words, what determines the amount of *money* that people want to hold, as compared with shares or other assets?

Keynes broke down the answer to this question into three parts, distinguishing three different reasons why people should want to hold some of their wealth in the form of money rather than interest-bearing assets. First, there is the *transactions* motive: people need ready cash for their everyday purchases. Secondly, there is the *precautionary* motive: they want money in their pocket, or at any rate immediately available in the form of a bank deposit, in case some unforeseen contingency arises – a sudden illness, a burglary, or a heavy fine for an alleged traffic offence. Finally, there is the

---

* The 'supply of money' or 'money supply' is not (as the phrase seems to imply) a *flow* over time, but the *stock* or quantity of money in the economy at any given time. How far the behaviour of the money supply can in practice be controlled by the Central Bank is a controversial matter, and is discussed in Chapter 9.

speculative motive: people (or some people) want to have money in hand to take advantage of any profitable situation that may suddenly arise – for example the expectation of a fall in the price of shares or government bonds; or, to put it the other way round, they do not want to be caught holding bonds if they expect the price to fall, and so they sell out and hold money instead.

According to Keynes, the transactions and precautionary motives for holding money, though quite closely related to the money level of the National Income, are not affected very much by the rate of interest; the amount of money people require for these purposes is much the same whether interest rates are high or low, though they will tend to economize a bit on these idle balances when interest rates are high. But the speculative motive is very closely affected by the existing, and expected, level of interest rates. If interest rates are already high, and people think that they are going to fall (which is another way of saying that the price of government bonds is going to rise)* then they will lend as much money at the present high level of interest rates (i.e. buy as much government stock at the present low level of prices) as they possibly can. In these circumstances the desire to make a speculative profit will prompt people to put their money into government securities, and they will hold very little cash; or, to use Keynes's own term, their *liquidity preference* will be very low. But in the opposite case, in which interest rates are low and there is a general belief that they will rise, the desire for cash to satisfy the speculative motive will be very high (i.e. liquidity preference will be very high). People will be anxious to have money immediately available to take advantage of the higher level of interest rates (lower level of government security prices) that they are expecting, and will not want to risk a capital loss by holding securities that are likely to fall in price.

What all this adds up to, then, is that the demand for money to satisfy the speculative motive will be high at low rates of interest, and

* A government bond (or security) normally pays a certain money dividend each year – say £10. If interest rates are 10 per cent, such a bond will be worth £100. If interest rates fall (say to 8 per cent), a bond which pays £10 a year will rise in value to £125, since only at this price will the bond yield 8 per cent. If interest rates rise to 12 per cent, on the other hand, the value of the bond will fall to £83.33, since only at this price will the £10 dividend represent a yield of 12 per cent. In other words, interest rates and government security prices move in opposite directions to each other.

low at high rates of interest. Taking into account the transactions and precautionary motives for holding money, which are related to the money level of the National Income but are not much affected by interest rates, it will still remain true that for any given level of the National Income the total demand for money will be higher the lower the rate of interest: as the rate of interest falls, the demand for money will rise. And the actual rate of interest that is established, said Keynes, will be that rate of interest at which the demand for money, as determined by these various motives, is equal to the supply of money, as determined by the Central Bank. In other words the rate of interest is determined by the amount of money created by the Central Bank on the one hand, and people's demand for money (or, as Keynes put it, their liquidity preference) on the other.

All this can perhaps be grasped more easily with the aid of a very simple diagram. The rate of interest is plotted on the vertical axis, the amount of money on the horizontal axis. The liquidity preference curve (LP) shows how the amount of money people want to hold varies with the rate of interest – the lower the rate of interest, the more of their assets they want to hold in the form of money. The rate

77

of interest actually established (r) will be the rate at which the amount of money people want to hold is equal to the amount of money (M) which the Central Bank has created.

Keynes did not in fact contend that this account was the full story of the rate of interest. As befitted a child of the Victorian era, he was very conscious of the influence on the 'real', long-term rate of interest of the twin deities known to nineteenth-century economists as Productivity and Thrift. How fast a sum of money can be made to grow by investing it in a project (Productivity) and how willing people are to save and lend money instead of spending it immediately (Thrift) he acknowledged to be powerful determinants of the rate of interest in the long run. But it was the short run he was interested in, and in the short run, he argued, these longer-term influences could be overborne by the relationship between the supply of money on the one hand, and liquidity preference on the other.

The full significance of Keynes's liquidity preference analysis will not become apparent until the next chapter, when we compare Keynes's views on interest rates with those of the 'classical' economists who inherited and developed the theories of Ricardo. But we do need at this point to take note of one particular feature of the liquidity preference curve to which Keynes attached great importance.

When interest rates are fairly normal, in the sense of being within the sort of range that people are used to, and expect to see in the future, the Central Bank has considerable power to vary them. It does this, of course, by using open-market operations. If it wants interest rates to rise, it will sell Government securities to the public by offering them at a lower price. The money supply (i.e. the cash and bank deposits owned by the public) will fall because some of this money will be used by the public to pay for the Government securities. The rate of interest, as represented by the relationship between the fixed annual payment on the security and the price of the security, will rise, and this will exert an upward influence on other interest rates in the economy. Just how far the rate of interest on Government securities will rise in response to a given reduction in the money supply will depend upon the strength of the public's liquidity preference – in other words on just how much of a reduction in the price of Government securities is needed to induce the public to accept the stipulated amount of them in return for ready cash.

The same considerations apply, in principle, in the reverse case, when the Central Bank wants to reduce interest rates. It buys Government securities in the open market by offering a higher price for them, thus reducing the interest rate represented by the fixed annual dividend payment on the stock. Again, just how far interest rates will fall in response to the purchase of a given quantity of securities will depend on how far the price of these securities has to be raised in order to induce the public to part with the necessary number of them. Or, to look at it the other way round, just how far the Central Bank will have to increase the quantity of money in order to reduce interest rates by some specified amount will depend on how far the price of the securities held by the public will need to be raised to persuade people to exchange them for money. Put crudely, if the price has to be raised a lot, interest rates will fall a lot. If the price hardly has to be raised at all, interest rates will hardly fall at all.

It was to this last aspect of the matter that Keynes attached importance. If interest rates are low, he argued, it may be difficult for the Central Bank to get them any lower. For if interest rates are low (in relation to what experience suggests is a normal level) this is another way of saying that the price of Government securities is high, compared with what is thought of as normal: in other words the price is expected to fall rather than to rise. In this situation it will take only an infinitesimal rise in the price of securities to persuade people to sell them in exchange for cash. So – to push the argument to its limits – the Central Bank is *unable* to raise the price of Government securities, and therefore *unable* to reduce the rate of interest. Liquidity-preference becomes near-absolute: however much money the Central Bank creates by open-market operations, people will not use it to buy securities, or to make loans of any other kind; they will hold their assets in the most liquid form possible – as money. In the last resort, interest rates cannot fall because no one expects them to fall. (This situation is illustrated in the diagram: an increase in the quantity of money from M_1 to M_2 has virtually no effect in reducing interest rates.)

Keynes himself did not push the argument quite so far. But it is quite clear from the *General Theory* that he regarded the inability of interest rates to fall far enough as a very important element in the continuation of the Slump. And a major reason for the inability of the monetary authorities to get interest rates down far enough (apart from the fact that they did not actually try very hard) was, in Keynes's view, that increases in the quantity of money were likely to be offset by increases in liquidity preference.

This has been something of a digression, though by no means a pointless one, as will become clear later on. Meanwhile let us return to our main theme, and briefly recapitulate the determinants of investment as Keynes saw them. The amount of investment undertaken in a country in any particular period, he said, depends on the yield businessmen expect to see from individual investment projects on the one hand, and the rate of interest on the other. We have looked at the factors which determine investment yields and interest rates, and have seen that they include, in the one case, such things as the amount of capital equipment already in existence, the extent to which it is utilized, the number of newly developed products or techniques and the general outlook for the economy; and in the other case the preferences people have for holding money rather than interest-bearing assets, and the quantity of money that the Central Bank decides to create. The amount of investment that is actually done will be determined by the interaction of all these forces. Obviously, if the outlook for the economy is good, if existing capital equipment is being used to capacity, and if the rate of interest is relatively low, a good deal of investment will be done. If, on the other hand, the outlook is gloomy and existing equipment is under-used, the amount of investment done will tend to be relatively small, particularly if at the same time interest rates are high.

THE LEVEL OF OUTPUT AND EMPLOYMENT

We have seen, then, the factors which, in Keynes's view, determine what the level of consumption will be in a particular country at a particular time, and the factors which determine what the level of investment will be. Since he began the exercise by breaking down the National Income into the two components consumption and investment, it is clear that if one knows what determines each of them, one knows what determines the National Income. For consumption plus investment equals National Income. Or, to use Keynes's own notation, in which consumption is C, investment is I and National Income is Y, $C + I = Y$. And since, as we have also seen, output (= National Income) and employment move closely together in the short run, it is clear that consumption and investment together determine the level of employment.

Now, at last, Keynes was ready to explode his bombshell. I have shown, he said, that a certain level of employment results from the amount of consumption and investment that takes place in a country. *Now why*, he asked, *should this level of employment be full employment?* What is there in the economic system which ensures that the amount spent by businessmen on investment, and the amount spent by households on consumption, should together call forth a level of output which can only be achieved by employing everyone who is seeking work? What prevents consumption and investment from imposing demands on the economy which it cannot meet even by drawing into employment every able-bodied person in the country? At the other extreme, what prevents consumption and investment from being so low that they call forth only a relatively small output of goods and services, which can be produced by only 80 or 90 per cent of the labour force? In short, what reason is there to suppose that the millions of individual decisions to consume or not to consume, to invest or not to invest, will just happen to add up to a level of effective demand which will imply full employment?

To these questions Keynes returned clear and uncompromising answers. The level of employment which results from the amount of consumption and investment a country undertakes will *not* necessarily be full employment. There is *nothing* in the economic system to ensure that consumption and investment will call forth just enough output to entail full employment. There is *nothing* to prevent consumption and investment from imposing too many demands on the economy (thus leading to inflation) or too few demands on the economy (thus leading to unemployment). In short, there is *no* reason to suppose that the sum total of millions of individual decisions to consume or invest will just happen to add up to a level of demand that will result in full employment.

These answers came as a terrific shock to orthodox opinion. As we have seen (Chapter 2) full employment had always been thought of as the normal and natural state of affairs: unemployment represented an exceptional and temporary departure from normality. Now here was Keynes rejecting the idea that there was something normal about full employment, and asserting that full employment was merely one possible level of employment out of a large number of possible levels. If one had full employment, he was in effect saying, this was not because it was inevitable; it was simply good luck.

This, then, was the dramatic and imperative part of what Keynes was saying: dramatic because it stood existing economic theory on its head, imperative because it implied the need for government action of a kind, and on a scale, never before contemplated. As Keynes himself put it, 'The central controls necessary to ensure full employment will, of course, involve a large extension of the traditional functions of government.'*

If the government wants full employment, the message ran, it cannot simply sit back and hope that full employment will just happen: it must take steps to see that there is enough investment or consumption to secure it. One implication of this may be, at some periods, a Budget deficit; so be it. The important thing is not that the government should balance its own accounts, but that it should attain and maintain full employment.

THE CONCEPT OF EQUILIBRIUM

But so far we have not penetrated to the heart of Keynes's theory. This becomes clear if one considers the incompleteness of the story so far. We said that the level of consumption is determined by the level, and distribution, of income. We then went on to say that the level of consumption, plus the level of investment, determines the total output of the country – which is the same thing as the total income of the couuntry. In other words one is saying *both* that income determines consumption *and* that consumption (with investment) determines income. Surely this is a circular argument?

Not exactly. It is, rather, an example of the fact that in the subject matter of economics, everything is determined by everything else. One is dealing here with a set of *mutually dependent* variables. This means that if one changes one variable, this will result in changes in other variables, and these changes in the other variables will eventually

* *General Theory*, page 379.

result in a further change in the first variable. In this case, we are saying that total income and total consumption are mutually dependent variables. Consumption is determined by income, and income is determined, at any rate in part, by consumption. If one changes income, consumption will change – as we have seen. But this change in consumption will itself lead to further changes in income – as we shall see a little later on.

Now when one is dealing with two mutually dependent variables like this one can only explain why each of them is at the level it is by bringing in the concept of *equilibrium*. A situation is an equilibrium one if there is no tendency for any of the variables to depart from their existing levels. It is not a sufficient explanation of the level of consumption to say 'consumption is £80 a year because income is £100', if in fact it is also true that income is only £100 because consumption is £80. Instead, one must explain the level of consumption by saying 'consumption is £80 because the mutual relationships between income and consumption are such that this is the only level of consumption compatible, over a period of time, with an income of £100'. In other words, given that income is £100, one will only have an equilibrium situation if consumption is £80. If consumption was *not* £80, but £70 or £90, then income would not have settled down at £100.

The *General Theory* is a theory of equilibrium. It analyses the process by which four inter-related variables – consumption, investment, saving and the National Income – are brought into equilibrium with each other; and shows that the equilibrium established may, or may not, result in full employment. Indeed the essence of the *General Theory* can be expressed even more simply than this, as an account of the way in which *saving* and *investment* are brought into equilibrium with each other. And it is this that we shall now examine.

INVESTMENT AND SAVING IN EQUILIBRIUM

Let us begin our examination by looking at a simple but immensely significant piece of arithmetic. We have seen that expenditure on consumption plus expenditure on investment is equal to the National Income. Therefore investment is equal to National Income *minus* consumption. But if one looks at the National Income from the other angle, as the sum total not of all *expenditure* but of all *incomes* one can see that the National Income *minus* consumption is also equal to saving, because saving is defined as the difference between income and consumption. Therefore investment and saving must be equal to each other.

All this can be expressed much less clumsily in Keynes's own notation. Writing S for total saving, we have

$$Y = C + I$$
$$\therefore I = Y - C$$
$$\text{But } S = Y - C$$
$$\therefore I = S$$

In other words, what one is saying is this: a nation's production is the same thing as its income; what it produces but does not consume is its investment; what it receives in income but does not spend on consumption is its saving. Therefore its investment must be equal to its saving.

The arithmetic is foolproof. But when one turns to apply it to the real world one cannot immediately see how it can be true. For, as we have seen, investment and saving are activities carried out by different groups of people for different reasons. Investment is decided on by businessmen in the light of the rate of interest and the return they expect from particular types of capital equipment. Saving, on the other hand, is decided on by millions of individual families, according to how much they think they should set aside out of current income for their own or their children's future. How is it possible, except by a fantastic fluke, for the total amount that tens of thousands of businessmen decide to invest to be exactly the same as the total amount that millions of families decide to save?*

This is where the concept of equilibrium comes in. The level of National Income that is finally established, said Keynes, will be a level at which saving and investment are in equilibrium with each other – i.e. at which the amount that households *want* to save is exactly equal to the amount that businessmen *want* to invest. Any level of National Income at which saving and investment are not in

* The distinction between 'businessmen' who invest and 'families' which save is a drastic simplification of reality used to aid the exposition. What actually happens is much more complicated, and is briefly discussed in the footnote on page 100.

equilibrium cannot persist; it will change until it reaches a level at which the amount that families want to save *is* equal to what businessmen want to invest. At this level the whole economic system will be in equilibrium – i.e. there will be no tendency for any further changes in any of the variables to occur. (But, to stress the main message again, this equilibrium level of National Income may involve substantial unemployment.)

Now before we go on to look at all this in more detail, we had better get absolutely clear a point that baffled even the experts when the *General Theory* appeared, and was responsible for some of the most eminent economists of the 1930s never really understanding what Keynes was getting at. This is the difference between saying that saving and investment are *equal* to each other, and saying that they are *in equilibrium* with each other.

We have seen that saving and investment are the same thing, looked at from different angles: in the case of a closed economy they are both the difference between the income or output of a country on the one hand, and the level of consumption on the other. That being so, they must always be equal to each other, however short a period of time one is considering. 2 is always equal to 2, however quickly one looks at it; not even for a millionth of a second is it equal to $1\frac{3}{4}$. Therefore what businessmen *actually* invest will always be equal to what families *actually* save.

But what businessmen *want* to invest, and what families *want* to save, is a quite different matter. These two quantities may be far from equal. But in that case, as a matter of logic, there will be a difference between what people want to do, and what they succeed in doing. If, for example, businessmen want to invest *more* than families want to save, then either the businessmen will find they cannot spend as much on investment as they want to (because, for example, the investment goods are simply not there to be bought); or families will find that they cannot consume as much as (i.e. are saving more than) they want to, perhaps because there is a diversion of output to investment goods, thus reducing the quantities of consumer goods available in the shops. Similarly, if businessmen want to invest *less* than families want to save either they will find they are investing more than they want to or, more probably, families will find they are saving less than they want to.

But although actual saving and investment will always be equal to each other, one will not have an equilibrium situation unless *desired* saving and investment are equal to each other, with the amount that businessmen want to invest being equal to the amount that families want to save. If one starts off in a situation in which businessmen want to invest more, or less, than families want to save, then, according to Keynes, the National Income will change, and go on changing, until it reaches a level at which what businessmen want to invest *is* equal to what families want to save.

THE MULTIPLIER

In order to see the process by which this happens, we must first of all look a little more closely at the marginal propensity to consume. We have already seen (page 71) that the marginal propensity to consume is that fraction of an increase in income that is spent on consumption. If, for example, a family (or a country) has an *increase* in income of £100, and spends £80 of this increase on consumption, then its marginal propensity to consume is $\frac{80}{100}$ or o.8. Since by definition it must save the £20 that it does not consume, its *marginal propensity to save* must be $\frac{20}{100}$ or o.2. (Just as any increase in income must be either spent on consumption or saved, so the marginal propensity to consume and the marginal propensity to save must together add up to 1·0, or unity.)

Now according to Keynes, the *size* of the marginal propensity to consume was the key to the size of the change in the National Income that would be needed to bring a disequilibrium situation, in which businessmen wanted to invest more or less than families wanted to save, into equilibrium. The higher the marginal propensity to consume, the bigger will be the change in National Income that results from a given change in investment, or saving. Let us look at a simple numerical example in order to make the argument clear.

Suppose that a country with a marginal propensity to consume of o·8 for some reason or other receives an increase in income of £100. Of this £100 it (or rather the actual individuals who receive it) will spend £80 on consumption. But the people who receive this £80 in the form of income (the retailers who sell the £80 worth of consumption goods, the manufacturers and workers who make them etc.), assuming they also have a marginal propensity to consume of 0.8, will themselves spend 80 per cent of this increased income of £80 (i.e. £64) on consumption goods. And the people who receive this extra £64 will spend 80 per cent of this (i.e. £51·20) on consumption – and so on. In other words the increase in the total income of the country (i.e. in the National Income) will not, at the end of the day, be £100; it will be £100 + £80 + £64 + £51·20 + ... If one works this series out one will find that it adds up to £500 – in other words one has to multiply the original increase in income by 5 in order to find out the eventual increase in total income. Or, as Keynes put it, the *Multiplier* is 5.* Numerically, the Multiplier is in fact the reciprocal of the marginal propensity to save: it is 5 in this case because the marginal propensity to save is 0·2, or $\frac{1}{5}$. If people had consumed only two thirds of their increased income, so that the marginal propensity to save was $\frac{1}{3}$, then the Multiplier would have been 3, and the final increase in total income only £300. Similarly, if they had consumed 90 per cent of their increased income, so that the marginal propensity to save was only $\frac{1}{10}$, the Multiplier would have been 10, and the final increase in total income therefore £1,000. This obviously accords with common sense. The smaller the fraction of any increase in income that people save, the larger will be their extra expenditure on consumption, and thus the larger their contribution to increasing the incomes of others, and thus the larger the eventual increase in the income of the community as a whole. In the limiting case, in which people consume *all* of any increase in their income, so that the marginal propensity to consume is 1·0 and the marginal propensity to save is 0, incomes will go on rising for ever, because the Multiplier will be infinity. In fact, Keynes argued, the marginal propensity to consume is less than 1, so that the Multiplier is of manageable size and the eventual rise in the income of the community not tremendously large.†

---

* The concept of the Multiplier had first been evolved by R. F. Kahn in 1931; Keynes modified it slightly and used it as one of the corner-stones of the *General Theory*.

†In practice, as Keynes made clear, the Multiplier in a country like Britain is unlikely to be greater than 2 or 3, even on the assumption that the marginal propensity to consume is 0·8 or 0·9. This is partly because the net increase in the income of those drawn into employment is smaller than the gross increase by the size of the unemployment benefits etc. received before; but chiefly because in present-day conditions

Now, armed with this concept of the Multiplier, let us return to the question of how saving and investment are brought into equilibrium with each other (in the sense that *desired* saving and *desired* investment are made equal to each other) by changes in the National Income. Let us start off by assuming an equilibrium situation, in which the level of the National Income is such that the amount that businessmen want to spend on investment is just equal to the amount that families want to save, so that saving and investment are not only equal to each other, but are also in equilibrium with each other. The situation is in equilibrium, in the sense that there is no tendency for either saving or investment to change.

Now suppose that for some reason, such as the development of a new product, or a fall in the cost of borrowing money, businessmen suddenly decide to increase their spending on investment. The equilibrium between investment and saving will be broken. Instead of wanting to invest exactly the same amount as households are saving, businessmen are now trying to invest more. What happens? According to Keynes, the rise in investment results in a rise in the National Income bigger than the initial rise in investment – just how much bigger depends on the size of the Multiplier. If the people whose incomes rise as a result of the businessmen's increased expenditure on investment – the men who build the new factories or make the new machinery to put in them – spend a large proportion of their increased incomes on consumption the Multiplier will be high, i.e. the National Income will have to rise by a large amount to yield the extra quantity of saving needed to finance the higher level of investment. If, on the other hand, people *save* a large proportion of their extra income – i.e. if the Multiplier is low – the National Income will not have to rise very much before it is yielding enough extra saving to finance the new level of investment. In short, as the National Income rises, so will the total incomes of families and so, correspondingly, will *both* total consumption *and* total saving. National Income will rise to the point at which the total saving that families want to make out

---

a quarter or a third of any increase in income will be swallowed up by direct and indirect taxation, and perhaps another quarter will go to increase imports, and thus the incomes of people outside Britain. So even if only £10 of a £100 increase in income is saved, the first-round increase in the incomes of those who make consumer goods in Britain may be not £90, but only £40 or £50.

of their higher incomes is large enough to equal the new, higher level of investment that businessmen are undertaking. The smaller the fraction of any increase in income people save (i.e. the larger the Multiplier) the bigger will be the rise in the National Income before desired saving is again equal to desired investment, and equilibrium is restored.

It may be easier to see exactly what happens if we take a simple numerical example. As before, we denote the National Income by Y, consumption by C, investment by I, and saving by S.*

Suppose that to start off with

$$\text{Actual } Y = £100$$
$$\text{Actual } C = £ 80$$
$$\text{Actual } I = £ 20$$
$$\text{Actual } S = £ 20$$

and that this is an equilibrium situation, in which businessmen *want* to invest exactly the £20 that they are investing, and families have an average propensity to consume of 0·8, and therefore *want* to save the £20 that they are saving. Now suppose that businessmen start taking a more optimistic view of things, and decide to raise their investment from £20 to £25. In the first stage, this extra £5 of expenditure will raise the incomes of those who manufacture investment goods by £5, so that Y will become £105. Assuming that the marginal propensity to consume (like the average propensity to consume) is 0·8, people will want to spend £4 of this extra £5 income on consumption, and save £1 of it. So one will have, as a picture of what people are *trying* or *wanting* to do,

$$\text{Actual } Y = £105$$
$$\text{Desired } C = £ 84$$

* We continue to keep the argument as simple as possible. As before, we assume only two kinds of expenditure (consumption and investment), thus taking no account of the complications introduced by government transactions and foreign trade, changes in both of which can in practice affect the level of demand and employment in exactly the same way as changes in consumption and investment. Similarly, we ignore as far as possible the problem of time-lags in the adjustment process, e.g. the fact that investment expenditures do not change immediately businessmen take decisions, but only after a series of time lags which differ for different types of investment. All these complications can be (and have been) built into systems of equations; and they must of course be taken explicit account of in the process of forecasting or attempting to influence economic developments (see Part Two of the present book). Here, however, they are better ignored.

$$\text{Desired (and} \\ \text{actual) I} = \text{\textsterling} 25 \\ \text{Desired S} = \text{\textsterling} 21$$

But some of these desires cannot be fulfilled. If actual investment is £25, then actual saving must, as a matter of arithmetic, be £25 too, and families will in practice be saving £25 and spending only £80 on consumption. What will have happened will be that the workers in the investment goods industries will, during this first stage of the adjustment process, have saved their extra income and not spent it – either because they have not yet made up their minds what to buy, or because there has not yet been time for the extra consumer goods to be manufactured or distributed to the shops. The actual position, in fact, will be this:

$$\text{Actual Y} = \text{\textsterling}105 \\ \text{Actual C} = \text{\textsterling} 80 \\ \text{Actual I} = \text{\textsterling} 25 \\ \text{Actual S} = \text{\textsterling} 25$$

As the gap between *desired* consumption and saving and *actual* consumption and saving indicates, this is not an equilibrium situation: there are further adjustments to come.

What happens in the second stage is that the workers in the investment goods industries succeed in spending the extra £4, because they have made up their minds what to spend their money on, or because the increased demand for consumer goods has resulted in an increase in the production of these goods. But by this time the Multiplier has come into operation: the very fact of an increase of £4 in consumers' expenditure has resulted in a rise of £4 in the income of those who manufacture the new consumer goods. So at this second stage the picture looks like this:

$$\text{Actual Y} = \text{\textsterling}109 \\ \text{Actual C} = \text{\textsterling} 84 \\ \text{Actual I} = \text{\textsterling} 25 \\ \text{Actual S} = \text{\textsterling} 25$$

But now that income has risen again, to £109, households are still spending less on consumption than they want to; they are actually spending £84, whereas out of a total income of £109 they *want* to spend (still assuming a propensity to consume of 0·8) £87·20. Similarly they *want* to save only £21·80, whereas they are actually saving £25. So the situation is still out of equilibrium (though less so than it was before) and the still unsatisfied demand for consumer goods will result in a further rise in their production, and hence a further rise in the incomes of those engaged in making them.

And so the process goes on, via successive increases in incomes and expenditure, until eventually households are once again actually consuming the same amount as they want to consume. The final picture will look like this:

$$\text{Actual } Y = £125$$
$$\text{Actual } C = £100$$
$$\text{Actual } I = £\ 25$$
$$\text{Actual } S = £\ 25$$

Out of the new level of income of £125 families are once again consuming the 80 per cent (£100) that they want to consume, and saving the 20 per cent (£25) that they want to save. Now that what they want to save is once again equal to what businessmen want to invest, saving and investment, and hence the whole economic system, are back in equilibrium. There is no tendency for any further changes to take place in any of the variables.

But why is the new equilibrium level of income £125, and not some other figure? Briefly, because we assumed a marginal propensity to consume of 0·8 (and therefore a marginal propensity to save of 0·2 or $\frac{1}{5}$). This means that the Multiplier was 5, and therefore that the eventual increase in total income would be 5 times the initial increase in investment expenditure, which was £5. Less technically, if businessmen want to invest £25 (and succeed in doing so) then equilibrium can only exist if families want to save £25 – and given a propensity to consume of 0·8, the only level of total incomes at which they will want to save £25 is £125.

So far we have been discussing what happens when the initial equilibrium is broken by an *increase* in investment, so that businessmen are investing *more* than households want to save. The same process operates in reverse when the equilibrium is broken by a *decrease* in investment, so that businessmen are investing *less* than households want to save. Suppose that in this case businessmen suddenly start taking a less optimistic view of the world, and reduce their expenditure on investment by £5. The first thing that happens is that those who build factories and make machinery find that their income has fallen by £5. The initial equilibrium situation, where

$$
\begin{aligned}
\text{Actual Y} &= \text{£100} \\
\text{Actual C} &= \text{£ 80} \\
\text{Actual I} &= \text{£ 20} \\
\text{Actual S} &= \text{£ 20}
\end{aligned}
$$

therefore becomes

$$
\begin{aligned}
\text{Actual Y} &= \text{£ 95} \\
\text{Actual C} &= \text{£ 80} \\
\text{Actual I} &= \text{£ 15} \\
\text{Actual S} &= \text{£ 15}
\end{aligned}
$$

whereas what individuals *want* to do in this situation can be represented as

$$
\begin{aligned}
\text{Actual Y} &= \text{£ 95} \\
\text{Desired C} &= \text{£ 76} \\
\text{Desired (and} & \\
\text{actual) I} &= \text{£ 15} \\
\text{Desired S} &= \text{£ 19}
\end{aligned}
$$

The actual situation, in fact, is now out of equilibrium, because households are actually spending £80 on consumption and saving only £15, whereas what they want to do out of a total income of £95 (still assuming a propensity to consume of 0·8) is spend £76 on consumption and save £19.

In the next stage consumption will fall to £76, because the workers in the investment goods industries, whose incomes have fallen by £5, will reduce their consumption by £4. But this £4 reduction in their consumption will lead to a £4 reduction in other people's incomes – and so the process will continue until a new equilibrium is established in which

$$
\begin{aligned}
\text{Actual Y} &= \text{£ 75} \\
\text{Actual C} &= \text{£ 60}
\end{aligned}
$$

$$\text{Actual I} = \pounds\ 15$$
$$\text{Actual S} = \pounds\ 15$$

Total income has now fallen to a level at which the amount that households want to save is equal to what businessmen want to invest. As before, the extent of the change in total income is determined by the size of the Multiplier and the size of the initial change in investment expenditure – only this time the changes are downwards.

Following Keynes, we have been assuming throughout this analysis that it is changes – either increases or decreases – in *investment* which cause an existing equilibrium to be disturbed. This is in line with experience, which suggests that saving and consumption do not change very much of their own accord, and that it is changes in investment which represent the most unstable element in the economy. But if it was a change in saving – or, looked at the other way, in consumption – rather than in investment which upset the equilibrium the analysis would proceed in exactly the same way.

EMPLOYMENT

It only remains now to relate the changes in National Income we have been discussing to changes in employment. In our two examples we have seen how an initial relatively small increase (or decrease) in investment eventually resulted in a 25 per cent increase (or decrease) in National Income. A 25 per cent change in National Income does not necessarily involve a 25 per cent change in employment. The number of manual workers in a factory may change in fairly direct proportion to the level of output, but the number of administrative, clerical and technical staff may not vary nearly so much – many of them have much the same amount of work to do whether the factory is running flat out or only at half-cock. Therefore total employment tends to vary rather less than total output. But these are complications which do not substantially affect the analysis. The point is that the level of employment is determined by the level of National Income, which is determined in turn by the levels of consumption and investment. One may start off with an equilibrium situation in which there is full employment – that is, in which consumption and investment are at such a level, and therefore National Income is at such a level, that everyone who wants to work is able to do so. But if there is then a fall in investment the National Income, and the volume of employment, will fall to a level at which saving is brought back into equilibrium with this lower level of investment. This may be an equilibrium at which there is a substantial amount of unemployment.*

Such an equilibrium, Keynes was saying, could persist for years – or indeed for ever. Unless investment (or consumption) rose and so, via the Multiplier, raised the National Income and the level of employment, heavy unemployment would just go on and on. Therefore if the government wanted full employment, it should either take steps to promote business investment, preferably by reducing the rate of interest, if that were feasible; or it should encourage an increase in consumption, preferably by taxation policies designed to improve the distribution of income; or – and here at last he justified his earlier advocacy of public works – it should itself undertake large-scale public investment expenditure. If it did, and judged the size of the Multiplier correctly, full employment would before long be restored. If it did not, unemployment would persist until investment or consumption eventually rose of their own accord – if they ever did.

In fact, if the government wanted full employment, it must itself accept responsibility for manipulating the level of demand in a way that would ensure it. The fact that this might involve Budget deficits was not particularly important.

SUMMARY

Although the basic message which emerges from the *General Theory* is clear, the underlying equilibrium analysis which forms the guts of the theory and the basis of the policy conclusions is not altogether easy to grasp, and it may be helpful to recapitulate briefly what this chapter has been saying.

* It is of course possible that one may start with a full-employment equilibrium and that investment may then *rise* rather than *fall*. In this case National Income will also rise (as in our example) but since there are no unemployed men to be drawn into employment the total amount of *output* cannot rise, and the rise in National Income will reflect a rise in prices – i.e. inflation. This was obviously not a situation with which Keynes was particularly concerned in the 1930s – though he did discuss it in the *General Theory* – but it was relevant to what happened during and after the Second World War, and we shall be dealing with it extensively in Part Two.

First of all, said Keynes, it is a mistake to imagine that full employment is part of the natural order of things, and that departures from it are abnormal and temporary aberrations. On the contrary, full employment is only one of a number of possible situations. It is, in fact, a special case.

The level of employment in a particular country at a particular time depends on the level of output in that country, and this in turn depends on *effective demand* – the amount of goods and services that individuals and institutions in that country purchase. All these purchases can be classified as either *consumption* (mainly done by individuals) or *investment* (mainly done by business firms). The level of employment, therefore, will depend on the level of consumption and the level of investment.

The level of consumption is the sum total of all the consumption expenditures of individuals or families, and families' consumption is determined mainly by their income. The level of investment is the sum total of all the investment expenditure of business firms, and this is determined by how profitable firms think investment would be – which is itself determined by their expectations of the return on a new investment on the one hand, and the cost of paying for it on the other. The level of output, then, and hence the level of employment, is determined by the total amount of money that families decide to spend on consumption, and firms decide to spend on investment. If it so happens that the sum total of families' consumption decisions and firms' investment decisions results in a level of output which it does not require the whole labour force to produce, then there will be unemployment. And until there is some change in either consumption or investment, this unemployment will continue.

This was the dramatic statement the book made – the peremptory message to the politicians and the public that if the unemployment problem was to be solved prevailing attitudes and policies must be radically changed. But Keynes had been issuing much the same advice for ten or fifteen years before the *General Theory* was published (so, particularly during the later part of the period, had a number of other economists) and no one had taken much notice. The real importance of the book lay in the fact that the policy implications to which it pointed were derived from a completely new and completely convincing theory of how the economy worked, and of how it was possible for there to be a permanent high level of unemployment.

This theory can best be understood by taking a close look at the statement that the total output of the economy is equal to consumption *plus* investment. This is true. But the total output of the economy is the same thing as the total income of the economy, and income *minus* consumption is saving. Therefore, by definition, saving must be equal to investment. But saving is determined by millions of individuals – it is the difference between their income and what they decide to consume. And investment is determined by tens of thousands of businessmen. Now why on earth should what millions of individuals decide to save just happen to be exactly equal to what tens of thousands of businessmen decide to invest?

The best way of answering this question is to assume that initially saving and investment are not merely *equal* (as by definition they always must be) but also *in equilibrium*, in the sense that the amount that businessmen *want* to invest is the same as the amount that families *want* to save. Now suppose that the equilibrium is broken – for example by businessmen deciding to reduce their investment below the current level. In this case, said Keynes, the fall in investment will cause a fall in incomes which will cause a fall in consumption; this fall in consumption will in turn cause a further fall in other people's incomes, and so on. The exact extent of the fall in incomes will depend on the marginal propensity to consume. The higher the marginal propensity to consume (i.e. the lower the marginal propensity to save) the greater will be the Multiplier, and the greater will be the fall in the National Income resulting from the initial reduction in investment. The new equilibrium level of National Income eventually established will be that at which *desired* saving (as well as actual saving) is equal to the (lower) level of investment. There is nothing accidental about this. The reason why the National Income will fall to just that point where what families want to save is equal to the new level of investment is that the size of the fall in the National Income is governed by the size of the marginal propensity to consume (or save). The lower the marginal propensity to save (i.e. the smaller the fall in saving resulting from a given fall in income) the further total incomes will have to fall in order to reduce the amount that people want to save until this is equal to the new, and lower, level of business investment.

This new equilibrium level of National Income may be attended by substantial unemployment. But there are no automatic forces, according to Keynes, which guarantee a return to full employment (at any rate in the short run), and heavy unemployment may last for years. The only way out of this situation is for the government to take action, perhaps by forcing down interest rates, or itself inaugurating public investment programmes, which will increase effective demand and thus, assisted by the upward drive of the Multiplier, raise the economy back to full employment.

Chapter Five

THE ISSUES BETWEEN KEYNES AND THE CLASSICS

Not everyone recognizes a revolution when they see one, not even its principal victims. Orthodox economists continued to propound classical remedies after the publication of the *General Theory* in much the same way as Louis XVI had continued to sign royal decrees after the fall of the Bastille. Professor Pigou, for example, perhaps the most distinguished and authoritative exponent of 'classical economics'* during the 1920s and 1930s, was not impressed by the book. 'Einstein actually did for Physics,' he observed blandly, 'what Mr Keynes believes himself to have done for Economics. He developed a far-reaching generalization, under which Newton's results can be subsumed as a special case.'† Clearly Pigou did not take very seriously the possibility that the theories he had been propounding and embel-

* Keynes made clear who he meant by 'the classical economists' in a footnote on the first page of the *General Theory*: ' "The classical economists" was a name invented by Marx to cover Ricardo and James Mill and their *predecessors*, that is to say for the founders of the theory which culminated in the Ricardian economics. I have become accustomed, perhaps perpetrating a solecism, to include in "the classical school" the *followers* of Ricardo, those, that is to say, who adopted and perfected the theory of the Ricardian economics, including (for example) J. S. Mill, Marshall, Edgeworth and Prof. Pigou.' If one were being pedantic, one would take pains to explain that not all economists think alike, that before the *General Theory* different economists taught the accepted theory with different degrees of fervour or scepticism; in short that Keynes's 'classical economist' was something of an over-simplification. But Keynes had no time for pedantry, and in this we shall try to follow him. There *was* a conventional wisdom in the 1920s and early 1930s, and although it was rarely set out in black and white – Pigou's *Theory of Unemployment* was the only satisfactory exposition Keynes could find – it did represent the way most economists, if pressed, would have said the economy worked. It is this that we shall mean by 'the classical theory' or 'the views of the classical economists'.

† *Economica*, May 1936.

lishing all his life might have met the same fate as Newton's. Nevertheless, this is more or less what had happened.

In this chapter we consider in some detail how Keynes's theory differed from the classical theory, and in exactly what way it represented a revolutionary change.

ARE SAVINGS AUTOMATICALLY INVESTED?

As we have seen, the classical economists, though they did not use the same language as Keynes, had nevertheless been perfectly aware of one important logical point – that if there is to be full employment, then the whole of the output that the economy is capable of producing, when running at full stretch, has to find a buyer. Looking at it from the income side, the whole of the income generated by a fully employed economy must be spent either on consumption or on investment; or, more precisely, all saving (i.e. that part of total income which is not spent on consumption) must be invested. But of course, said the classics: this is exactly what happens. And so indeed it did – in the early nineteenth century, when the classical theory was being developed. At that time saving consisted largely of the profits which farmers, merchants and manufacturers had left over after providing for themselves and their families. These profits were usually all ploughed back into the business in order to expand it – i.e. savings were automatically invested. Indeed saving and investment, being done by the same person, were hardly distinguished as two separate activities. This conviction that savings will automatically be invested is to be found most strongly in the work of Ricardo and his immediate successors, and there is no reason to doubt that what they were saying was substantially true, at the time they said it. And precisely because it was true that at full employment levels of output everything that was saved was automatically invested, full employment remained (apart from the occasional interruptions of the trade cycle) a permanent feature of the economy. The difference between Keynes and the classical economists was that while they thought of this as the normal, universal state of affairs, he saw it as a special case.

But although the earlier classical economists were content, on the whole, simply to assert that savings were automatically invested, their successors went beyond this and argued that there were certain forces at work in the economy which made it *inevitable* that at full employment levels of output all savings would be invested.* They had to do this because as the nineteenth century wore on a marked distinction began to develop between those who did the investing and those who did the saving. The small manufacturer or trader who could only expand his business out of the savings he made himself became less typical. Instead, there began to emerge bigger firms, owned not by those who managed them but by large numbers of shareholders who in practice had little or no say in the firm's decisions. The managers decided how much the firm should invest, and the increasingly prosperous middle- and even working-classes decided how much they were going to save. The close link of earlier days between saving and investment had been broken: no longer were they essentially the same activity carried out by the same person – they were now different activities, often carried out by different people for different reasons.†

There did not seem to be any obvious reason why the amount that thousands of managers decided to invest should happen to be the same as millions of people decided to save. But there was a reason, according to later classical economists, and they were quite clear what

* The occasional bouts of unemployment associated with the down-swing of the trade cycle were dismissed, in the words of John Stuart Mill, as a 'temporary derangement of markets', which did not alter the fact that there were certain forces at work which ensured that full employment was the normal state of affairs.

† This is very far from saying that all investment is nowadays done by business firms and all saving by families; the situation is much more complex than that. In practice, businesses save as well as invest and families can invest (in the sense in which the term is used in this book) as well as save. Moreover both saving and investment can and do take place in the public sector of the economy; and, in an open economy, the investment a country does at home can be less than its total saving if it invests abroad, or more than its total saving, if it borrows from abroad. Some businesses will be able to finance all their own investment out of undistributed profits, and maybe even have something left over with which to buy government securities or shares in other firms; others will have to finance all their investment by borrowing; many will fall somewhere between these two extremes.

But none of this affects the basic point, which is that there is no reason to suppose that nowadays (in contrast, on the whole, to the position in Ricardo's time) the sum total of all the decisions to invest which are made in the economy will happen to be the same as the sum total of all the decisions to save which are made in the economy. For simplicity of exposition in the text the complex pattern of investment and saving which actually exists is categorized as 'managers' or 'businesses' investing and 'people' or 'families' saving.

it was: saving and investment were brought into balance by changes in the rate of interest.

Their argument, if put rather crudely and explicitly, would go somewhat as follows. Suppose that one starts with an equilibrium situation, in which the economy is fully employed and people are content to save exactly the amount that businessmen are investing. Now suppose that for some reason people decide to save a larger proportion of their income, or that businessmen decide to reduce their investment. Will this not mean that some saving is unable to find an outlet in investment? And will this excess of saving over investment not lead to a fall in output and employment? No, said the classical econo-mists. If there is a tendency for savings to exceed investment – i.e. a tendency for the *supply* of 'loanable funds' to exceed the *demand* for loanable funds – then the rate of interest will fall. And it will fall until saving and investment are brought back into balance. For the rate of interest is the price of these loanable funds – the price that one pays to borrow them or receives if one lends them. If the supply of these funds is greater than the demand for them the same thing happens as in the case of shoes or ships or sealing-wax or anything else for which supply exceeds demand: the price, or rate of interest, falls.

This fall in the rate of interest has a double effect. The more powerful effect will be to stimulate investment, because some projects that were not profitable before will become so now that money can be borrowed more cheaply; but it will also tend to discourage saving, since the return on savings will now have fallen. Therefore any tendency for the saving of a fully employed economy to exceed investment will result in a fall in the rate of interest sufficient to bring saving and investment back into balance, either by reducing saving, or by increasing investment, or both. In fact, the rate of interest is a mechanism which will automatically ensure that whatever the level of saving generated by a fully employed economy, these savings will be invested.

The same point can be made in another way. Assume again an equilibrium position, in which the economy is fully employed and the saving being done by households is just equal to the investment being done by businessmen. What happens if people decide to reduce their consumption? Will this not result in a fall in output and employment? No, said the classics. A fall in consumption entails a rise in saving, and a rise in saving – i.e. an increase in the supply of loanable funds – will lead to a fall in interest rates and thus to a rise in investment. In fact any reduction in consumption will result in an equal increase in investment; and since it is consumption and investment, taken together, which constitute the National Income this, and hence the level of employment, will be unaffected.

In short, said the classics, full employment is the normal state of affairs. Full employment exists provided that all the savings generated by a fully employed economy are invested, and the rate of interest is a mechanism which ensures that this will happen. Just as a fall in the water level of a cistern will, by opening a valve, set in motion forces which will restore the water level, so any departure of the economy from full employment will, by its effects on the rate of interest, set in motion forces which will restore full employment.

KEYNES'S VIEW

This theory is simple, elegant and extremely plausible. Unfortunately, said Keynes, it is 'a nonsense theory'. The main reason why it is nonsense is that it fails to take account of the changes in *income* that result from any change in investment or saving; it fails to see that what people *want* to save, and what they actually *do* save, are in certain circumstances quite different things. Let us take another look at the example we have just given, of an equilibrium full employment situation, in which what families want to save (and are saving) is exactly the same as what businessmen want to invest (and are investing); and let us assume that people are saving (and businessmen are investing) 20 per cent of the National Income. Families then decide, for some reason, to increase their saving to 25 per cent of their incomes. The classical theory assumed that these extra savings would actually be forthcoming, and would force down the rate of interest, thus leading to a corresponding increase in investment. But, said Keynes, these extra savings would *not* be forthcoming. For in order to increase their saving people would have to reduce their consumption, and this would result in a fall in the incomes of those who made consumer goods. They in turn would reduce their expenditure, with further repercussions on other people's incomes – and so the process would go on, in accordance with the Multiplier analysis we discussed in Chapter 4. If people still stick to their new decision to save 25 per cent of their incomes, the National Income will fall (assuming that investment remains unchanged) to four fifths of its former level – for this will be the only level of income at which what families want to save is equal to what businessmen want to invest. To put this into numerical form, the situation was

$$\text{Actual } Y = \text{£}100$$
$$\text{Actual } C = \text{£}80$$
$$\text{Actual } I = \text{£}20$$
$$\text{Actual } S = \text{£}20$$

People were content with a situation in which they were saving 20 per cent of their incomes. They then decide to save 25 per cent of their incomes. But this leads to successive falls in consumption and income, until a new equilibrium is established in which

$$\text{Actual } Y = \text{£}80$$
$$\text{Actual } C = \text{£}60$$
$$\text{Actual } I = \text{£}20$$
$$\text{Actual } S = \text{£}20$$

It is true that people have achieved their ambition of saving 25 per cent of their income. But this has happened not because their saving has gone up, but because their income has gone down. The *amount* they save is the same as before; their income has fallen by 20 per cent. This 20 per cent fall in the National Income will have been accompanied by a severe fall in employment – so that a new equilibrium has been established in which there is substantial unemployment.

If anything, said Keynes, the final position will probably be even worse than this, for against a background of falling income it is unlikely that investment will be sustained at its former level. Supposing it falls by a quarter (and that individuals still persist in their new desire to save 25 per cent of their incomes) the final position will look like this:

$$\text{Actual } Y = \text{£}60$$
$$\text{Actual } C = \text{£}45$$
$$\text{Actual } I = \text{£}15$$
$$\text{Actual } S = \text{£}15$$

Once again people have succeeded in saving 25 per cent of their incomes, but in the meantime the National Income has fallen by a catastrophic 40 per cent, and unemployment has probably risen to 20 or 25 per cent of the labour force – and the economy will remain in this situation until either consumption or investment starts to rise again.

So, Keynes concluded, classical theory provided a wholly misleading picture of how the economy reacted to an attempt to increase saving, or to reduce investment. Such attempts did not set in motion changes in interest rates which automatically preserved full employment. On the contrary, they led to falling incomes and rising unemployment.

This, then, is a highly abbreviated account of the difference between the Keynesian and classical theories of how the economy reacts to changes in investment or saving. But if the full originality and force of Keynes's contribution is to be appreciated, one or two aspects of this difference need to be examined in rather more detail.

BEARS

It is a common belief that economists know better than others how to make money on the Stock Exchange. Usually this belief is, alas, erroneous, but in Keynes's case, as we have seen, there was something in it. But Keynes's feel for the way financial markets worked did not merely enable him to make money; it coloured his approach to the workings of the economy as a whole. Much of the *General Theory* is devoted to an analysis of the way the behaviour of the economy is affected by dealings in the financial markets; or, to paraphrase slightly, by the way that 'real' things (output and employment) are affected by 'money' things (in particular the prices of various kinds of assets). So far we have concentrated on the differences between the Keynesian and classical theories on the 'real' or 'physical' side – i.e. in terms of output and employment. Let us now take a look at the differences on the 'financial' or 'monetary' side.

Once again, suppose that the economy is initially in equilibrium at full employment, with families wanting to save what businesses want to invest; and that for some reason families then decide to increase their saving. On the *physical* side, the first effect of this decision is of course a reduction in consumers' expenditure; so that stocks of unsold goods pile up in shops and warehouses; and manufacturers find that their orders for new goods are falling, and accordingly cut back on output and employment. The counterpart of this decrease in the amount of money being spent on physical things is an increase in the amount of money being spent on *financial* things: the first effect will be that each week or each month a larger amount of money than before will be put into financial assets. These may be equity shares, industrial debentures, Treasury bills, government securities or any other kind of financial asset, including bank deposits or even pound notes under the mattress, that people favour as a safe or profitable haven for their savings.*

The effect of this larger amount of money being spent on an existing pool of financial assets will be to drive up the price of these assets; and in so far as much of the money will, in the Keynesian system, be channelled into government securities, this rise in price will entail, as we have seen, a fall in the rate of interest. So far, so good; this is in line with what classical theory said – an increase in the supply of loanable funds leads to a fall in the price paid for borrowing such funds – i.e. in the rate of interest.

It was at this point that Keynes dramatically unmasked the real villain of the piece – the *bear*.

A bear, in Stock Exchange parlance, is someone who expects the price of a stock or share to fall. He therefore sells the stock, in the expectation of being able to buy it back more cheaply later on. And the very fact that he sells, in the expectation that the price will go down, helps to make the price go down, or to prevent it from going up. Close to the heart of Keynes's theory is the supposition that bear selling will prevent the price of securities from rising very far or very fast in response to the bigger inflow of personal savings. Bears, he said, will supply securities out of their portfolios, and thus moderate the rise in security prices. This in turn will moderate the fall in interest rates, and prevent them falling far enough to encourage the additional investment that would be needed to

* In practice a large part of personal saving takes the form of contributing to pension schemes or paying the premium on various kinds of life insurance policies. In that case it is the pension funds or insurance companies that now have more money to channel into financial assets; but the essential picture is the same.

accommodate the larger amount that families now want to save.

But why do the bears behave in this way – denuding their portfolios of securities, and accumulating hoards of cash instead? Because, said Keynes, of their liquidity preference, and in particular because of the speculative motive for holding money rather than securities. As we have seen (pages 76–7), as interest rates fall (government security prices rise) speculatively-minded people become increasingly keen to hold money rather than securities – because experience tells them that the new (low) level of interest rates, or (high) price of government securities, will probably not last; and if one expects security prices to fall, one should not be holding securities; one should be holding cash.

In essence, Keynes's complaint against the bears was that in the course of pursuing their own speculative activities – activities designed solely to enrich themselves, which must be regarded as perfectly proper in a capitalist economy, and which had indeed received the blessing of Adam Smith – they messed up the process whereby interest rates might adjust themselves far enough and fast enough to keep the economy at a full employment equilibrium. And while they were messing it up, by preventing, or at any rate delaying, a large enough fall in interest rates, the Multiplier saw its chance, so to speak, and leapt into action. This was the really crucial point, which the classical economists had failed to see. The initial fall in consumers' spending led to a cutback in output and employment, and this in turn led to a further fall in consumers' spending, and deflation started to snowball. Any stimulus to a rise in investment expenditure which might have come from lower interest rates was swamped by the depressing effect of falling incomes and output, and rising un-employment of men and machinery.

Keynes himself provided another, less technical account of why it was that a decision on the part of individuals to save more was likely, in the absence of government intervention, to lead the economy to plunge downhill into depression. At the beginning of Chapter 16 of the *General Theory* he says:

An act of individual saving means – so to speak – a decision not to have dinner today. But it does *not* necessitate a decision to have dinner or to buy a pair of boots a week hence or a year hence or to consume any specified thing at any specified date. Thus it depresses the business of preparing today's dinner without stimulating the business of making ready for some future act of consumption. It is not a substitution of future consumption-demand for present consumption-demand – it is a net diminution of such demand.

To paraphrase: if a lot of people cut their expenditure on motor cars because they have individually decided to save up and buy a yacht, this would be all right if the manufacturers of motor cars knew what they were up to: the resources released from car production would be invested in preparation for future yacht production. But the car manufacturers do not know what consumers intend to switch their expenditure to (nor, in practice, may the consumers themselves). So employment falls in car production without rising anywhere else – and the Multiplier starts to operate.

The above discussion has been conducted in terms of a decision by families to increase their saving (i.e. reduce their consumption). But the argument would have been much the same if we had considered instead the effects of a decision by businessmen to reduce their investment. Such a decision would lead, like a decision to increase saving, to a rise in the price of financial assets, because the funds that business was previously investing in physical assets (building, machinery and equipment) will now be 'invested' in financial assets – i.e. used to buy existing government securities or other stocks and shares.* But because of the operations of the bears the price of government securities will not rise far enough (interest rates will not fall far enough) to restore the profitability of investment, and a cumulative deflation will get under way.

Keynes's main difference from the classics, then, might be briefly summed up as follows. The classics thought that a fall in investment or consumption would lead to a fall in interest rates sufficient to maintain, or at any rate rapidly restore, full employment. Keynes thought that interest rates were determined in a more complicated way than this, and that the activities of bear speculators would prevent interest rates from falling far enough to stimulate sufficient invest-ment to restore full employment. And the initial fall in investment or consumption would rapidly lead, by way of the Multiplier, to a decline

* If industry had been financing its capital investment out of borrowing, instead of from retained profits, the same result would be reached in a slightly different way: less household saving would now be needed by industry (e.g. new share issues would be fewer), and a larger volume of household saving could now be diverted to existing shares and securities, thus driving up their price.

in income and a further fall in investment or consumption. In short, the system was not an automatically self-stabilizing one: initial deviations from full employment were not *corrected* by movements in *interest rates*; on the contrary, they were *amplified* by movements in *incomes*. Keynes's policy conclusion was that the monetary authorities should intervene actively – much more actively than they were accustomed to do – in an attempt to drive down interest rates by open-market operations. But at relatively low interest rates such increases in the supply of money might be offset by increases in liquidity preference, and it might prove impossible to bring down interest rates far enough to stimulate investment. In this case the government should use other measures – such as public investment – to get the economy going again.

FALLING WAGES AND RISING EMPLOYMENT

The discussion in the last few pages has dealt with the really crucial difference between the Keynesian and classical theories. But for a full understanding of the way Keynes stood existing economic theory on its head it is necessary to examine not only how he differed from the classical economists on the determinants of the rate of interest, and on the other factors, in addition to the rate of interest, which determined saving and investment; it is also necessary to look at how he differed from them on the subject of wage flexibility, and on the effect of wage flexibility on the volume of employment. For according to the classical economists it was the flexibility of wage rates, even more than the flexibility of interest rates, which ensured that full employment was the normal condition of the economy.

The emphasis that classical theory put on the flexibility (particularly, of course, the downward flexibility) of wage rates reflected, it seems fair to say, a less sophisticated view of the workings of the economy than the view advanced by Keynes. To Keynes, heavy unemployment was essentially a symptom – though undoubtedly the most obtrusive and tragic symptom – of an economy in which the level of effective demand was too low, due to the operation of the forces discussed in the previous section. That is to say, the excess supply of labour represented by a large number of unemployed men did not necessarily mean that the price of labour was too high in relation to the price of other factors of production, or the price of finished goods. In Keynes's view wages, even at a time of heavy unemployment, might well be at the right level, in terms of the needs of full employment equilibrium; it was much more likely to be interest rates that were at the wrong level. The classical view was simpler. If there was an excess supply of labour, it was argued, then the price of labour must be too high. If the excess supply was to be eliminated, the price must be reduced. More bluntly, if unemployment was to be reduced, wage rates must fall.

We have already seen (pages 32–5) the theoretical foundation for this view. The Law of Diminishing Returns said that the more men were employed, given a fixed amount of capital equipment etc., the less would each additional man produce. The Theory of Marginal Productivity said that the wages of the last man employed, and therefore, given competition, of all other men, would be equal to the value of what he produced. Put these two bits of doctrine together, and there is no escaping the fact that if more men are to be employed, the average wage must be lower. It is easy to see why classical theory said, in effect: reduce wages, and employment will rise.

The interesting thing about this part of the story is that Keynes entirely accepted both of the classical premises. One is reminded of Houdini agreeing to be swathed in chains and locked in a leaky trunk under ten feet of water. For Keynes started off by agreeing that both the Law of Diminishing Returns and the Theory of Marginal Productivity operated in the circumstances he was concerned with. That is to say, he agreed that as output and employment increase in the short run, output will increase less than employment, so that each additional man will produce less than the previous man, and average output per man will therefore fall.* And he also agreed that it was, roughly speaking, true that the last man taken on would be paid only the value of the output he produced, and that since competition

* Nowadays one is more inclined to believe the opposite – that as output and employment increase in the short run (from an initial position in which unemployment is 10 or 15 per cent), output will increase *more* than employment, and average output per man (i.e. productivity) will rise. This is chiefly because in a complex and capital-intensive economy the proportion of overhead labour (administrative, clerical and technical workers) tends to be relatively high, and in the short run the amount of overhead labour needed is much the same whatever the level of output. Had Keynes accepted this in the *General Theory* (as he did a few years later in an article in the March 1939 *Economic Journal* entitled 'Relative Movements of Real Wages and Output') his task would have been easier, though his argument would have been fundamentally the same.

operates reasonably effectively, and one worker is much the same as another, this means that all workers would be paid about the same amount as the last worker taken on.

How then does one avoid the conclusion that in order to increase employment one must reduce wages? How does Houdini get out of the trunk? Basically, one turns the classical theory upside down. One does not reduce wages and as a result get an increase in employment. One does the opposite – one increases employment, and as a result gets a reduction in wages.

REAL AND MONEY WAGES*

The first stage in Keynes's argument was to establish the distinction between money wages and real wages. This is a familiar distinction nowadays; it was less familiar in the 1930s. *Real wages* represent the amount of goods a man can buy with his pay-packet. Whatever happens to the amount of money in his pay-packet, he will only have had an increase in real wages if he can buy *more* goods than before. In other words, an increase in *money* wages is only an increase in *real* wages if prices stay unchanged, so that the extra money really buys something. A 10 per cent rise in money wages is a 10 per cent rise in real wages if prices stay the same; but if prices rise by 4 per cent real wages only rise by 6 per cent; and if prices rise by 10 per cent real wages are unchanged. Similarly, a 10 per cent fall in money wages will only be a 10 per cent fall in real wages if prices do not change; if prices fall by 10 per cent as well, real wages will not have fallen at all. According to Keynes, one of the reasons the classics had got into trouble over this bit of theory was that they had failed to understand this distinction between money wages and real wages.

It is probably true, said Keynes, that if wage rates are cut in one firm or industry there will be a rise in employment of the workers concerned. Suppose that the money wages of shoemakers are cut by 20 per cent, for example, and that this leads to a 10 per cent reduction in the price of shoes. The incomes of everybody else in the economy will hardly be affected at all by the fall in the amount shoemakers can afford to spend on consumption, and now that shoes are 10 per cent

* Throughout this section (except where otherwise stated) we are talking about wage-rates, or hourly or weekly wages *per head*, not the sum total of wages paid out.

cheaper the country will buy more shoes; employment of shoemakers will rise. The corollary of this is that there will have been a fall in the *real* wages of shoemakers as well as in their *money* wages, for all prices (apart from shoes) will have stayed the same, while shoemakers' money wages have fallen by 20 per cent. So the rise in employment of shoemakers has been accompanied by a fall in their real wages – as both Keynes and the classics agreed was necessary.

But the classics tended to think that what was true of one group of workers, such as shoemakers, was true of all workers taken together; Keynes did not. What is true of the part, he said, is not necessarily true of the whole. If *everybody*'s money wages are cut by 20 per cent, it is not at all clear that there will be a rise in employment. To take the simplest case first, suppose that a 20 per cent cut in people's money wages leads to a 20 per cent reduction in the price of what they produce. If all wage rates are reduced by 20 per cent, all prices will be reduced by 20 per cent, and real wages will be unchanged. And if real wages are unchanged then, according to the laws of the classical economists' own theory, employment must be unchanged as well. Or, to look at it simply in terms of common sense, if real wages are unchanged there can be no reason to expect any change in the actual amount families spend on consumption, or businessmen spend on investment. In fact there will be no change in output and therefore no change in employment either.* There will not have been any real changes in the economy; all that will have happened is that everybody's income, in money terms, is 20 per cent less than it used to be, so that someone who used to earn £200 a week now earns £160; and all prices will be 20 per cent less than they used to be – so that £160 will buy exactly the same amount now as £200 used to.

This example is unrealistically simple, but it does at least throw a clear light on one important flaw in the classical theory: the assumption that labour as a whole *can* by its own actions reduce real wages, and thus move the economy back to full employment. Keynes was concerned to stress that a general reduction in money wages would lead to a general (though not necessarily proportionate) re-

* In an open economy there would be some rise in output and employment because one kind of demand would rise – demand for exports; for, assuming a fixed exchange rate, these would now be 20 per cent cheaper to foreign buyers. However for present purposes we can ignore this complication.

duction in prices. This meant that the reduction in real wages – which is what counted, in both his and the classical theory – would be smaller than the reduction in money wages, and possibly very much smaller. In short, while the classical theory might indicate that a general cut in real wages was needed to reduce unemployment, in practice there might be no way in which the workers could secure such a cut in real wages.

The likelihood that a cut in money wages will lead to no cut at all in real wages is, of course, remote. Wages account for only a part of the final selling price of an article, and there is no reason why a cut in wages should lead, at any rate immediately, to any reduction in the other elements going to make up the selling price, particularly the element representing profits. Thus a more likely set of figures would be those given in our shoemaker example: a general reduction of 20 per cent in money wages might lead, at any rate at first, to only a 10 per cent reduction in prices; real wages would therefore fall, but only by 10 per cent.

But the effect of this cut in real wages, said Keynes, would not be to increase employment; it would be to reduce it. For people's consumption depends on their incomes, and if their incomes have fallen, in real terms, their consumption will fall as well. And as we have seen, a fall in consumption will lead, via the Multiplier, to a fall in output and incomes, and a further rise in unemployment.

Keynes recognized that not everyone's real income would have fallen: in money terms there would be no immediate fall in profits, and therefore in dividend incomes, or in incomes received in the form of rents, interest on government securities and so on. These same money incomes would now represent higher real incomes, because of the fall in the prices of commodities. But Keynes thought that any tendency towards higher consumption out of these higher real incomes would be insufficient to offset the lower consumption of wage-earners, and that the net effect of the original cut in money wages would still be to depress output and employment. The same point can be put in a slightly different way: it is likely that the total of non-wage incomes will fall less than the total of wages, so that there will be a redistribution of the National Income away from wage-earners and in favour of those who receive incomes from dividends, interest and rent. But this latter group of people is wealthier than the average wage-earner, and has a lower propensity to consume. This shift in the distribution of the National Income will therefore result in a fall in total consumption.

Keynes did make one concession in the *General Theory* to the view that cuts in money wages could have a favourable influence on employment.* As money wages and prices fall, he said, and hence the money value of the National Income falls, people will need less money to satisfy the 'transactions motive' – i.e. to cover their day-to-day needs. Assuming that the quantity of money remains unchanged, this will mean that they have more money than they need in liquid form, and they will therefore increase their purchase of government securities and other financial assets. This will drive up the price of such assets, and thus result in a fall in the rate of interest. And this fall in the rate of interest will lead to some rise in investment.

Keynes did not think that this particular repercussion of a cut in money wage rates was likely to be very important. And in any case, as he pointed out, the same result that one obtained from a fall in money wage rates and an unchanged quantity of money could be obtained from unchanged money wage rates and a rise in the quantity of money – the effect on interest rates would be the same. In other words, the only favourable effect on employment Keynes could see resulting from a policy of wage cuts would follow just as much (or just as little, in the face of bear speculation) from a policy of increasing the supply of money. To try to force through wage cuts, with all the political and social disruption such a policy was likely to entail, rather than to increase the money supply, was a policy that to Keynes made no sense. As he said,

Having regard to human nature and our institutions, it can only be a foolish person who would prefer a flexible wage policy to a flexible money policy, unless he can point to advantages from the former which are not obtainable from the latter. Moreover, other things being equal, a method which it is comparatively easy to apply should be deemed preferable to a method which is probably so difficult as to be impracticable.†

But all this assumes that increases in the quantity of money can lead to a reduction in interest rates. As we have seen Keynes was

* This particular channel by which wage cuts might affect employment came to be known in the literature as the 'Keynes effect'.

† *General Theory*, page 268.

convinced that in certain circumstances an increase in liquidity preference, particularly on the part of bear speculators, might prevent
interest rates from being driven down very much, even if the monetary
authority does take steps to increase the supply of money. So, said
Keynes,

> It follows that wage reductions, as a method of securing full employment,
> are also subject to the same limitations as the method of increasing the
> quantity of money. The same reasons as those mentioned above, which limit
> the efficacy of increases in the quantity of money as a means of increasing
> investment to the optimum figure, apply *mutatis mutandis* to wage reduc-
> tions.*

To summarize: the main effect of a cut in money wage rates,
according to Keynes, was to depress effective demand and hence
employment. The only feature of this policy which might exercise a
stimulating influence on demand and employment was a feature
which could be matched, at far less social cost, by monetary policy.
But, like monetary policy, it might turn out to be least effective just
when it was most needed.

One final puzzle remains, perhaps, to be resolved. As we have seen,
Keynes agreed with the classics (unnecessarily, one would now tend
to say) that if the economy is to move from 15 per cent unemployment
to full employment, there must be a reduction in average real wages,
i.e. in the amount the average worker can buy with his wages. Yet
here he is questioning how far workers as a whole can in fact reduce
their real wages by agreeing to reductions in money wages, and saying
that in any case such reductions in real wages as they do secure will
lead not to a rise but to a fall in employment. How can this apparent
inconsistency be explained?

The answer is that Keynes was demanding from his fellow-
economists much the same sort of mental somersault that Copernicus
had demanded from his fellow-scientists. The evidence, said
Copernicus to his contemporaries, is consistent with your theory that
the sun goes round the earth, and from this theory you have made
many deductions. But the same evidence is also consistent with another theory – that the earth goes round the sun. This theory is
correct, and your deductions are wrong. Similarly, according to
Keynes, the agreed evidence of an association between rising em-

* *General Theory*, page 266.

ployment and falling real wage rates was consistent with the classical theory that it was real wages which determined the level of employment – and from this theory they deduced that one must first reduce real wages, and that this would result in a rise in employment. But the same evidence, said Keynes, is also consistent with the theory that it is the level of employment which determines real wages. This theory is correct, and therefore the classical economists' deduction is wrong; the right deduction is that one should first increase the level of employment, and that this will result in a fall in real wages.

We have seen how Keynes proposed that the level of employment should be increased: an attempt should be made to force down interest rates by an active monetary policy, so that private investment would be stimulated; tax measures should be introduced to reduce the inequality of income distribution, and thus raise the propensity to consume; and the government should engage in large-scale public expenditure. If the Law of Diminishing Returns and the Theory of Marginal Productivity were both true and both in operation (as Keynes agreed with the classics they were) then this increase in employment would result in a fall in real wages, for as employment increased, output would increase less than proportionately and costs per unit of output would therefore rise. Rising costs would lead to rising prices and therefore, since money wages would not rise proportionately, to falling real wages.* One will therefore end up with full employment and lower real wages, which is what the classics were trying to achieve. But one has only ended up here because one raised employment first; lower real wages followed. If one took the classical economists' advice one would probably succeed in reducing real wages (though not as much as they expected, because of the fall in prices) but one would also reduce effective demand, and what would follow would be lower employment and not higher employment.

THE PIGOU EFFECT

The differences between Keynes's theory and the 'classical' theory which it effectively replaced have now been discussed at some length.

* Of course the fall in real wages (i.e. real wages per head of those in employment) is outweighed by the rise in the number of wage-earners in employment, which is why total consumption rises.

But if the classical theory had been mortally wounded by Keynes's onslaught, it was nevertheless quite a long time a-dying. It seems appropriate to end this chapter by taking a brief look at the resistance it put up in the years immediately after 1936. (We discuss later on – in Part Two – its resurrection, disguised as Monetarism, in the 1970s.)

The resistance to Keynes's theory centred mainly on the importance attributed to what became known as the 'Pigou effect'. So christened because it represented the core of the argument immediately advanced against the *General Theory* by Pigou, it was subsequently developed, under the title of the 'real balance' effect or 'wealth effect', by other economists (sometimes known as the 'neo-classical' school, precisely because of their unshakeable faith in the essential rightness of the old classical economics).

The purpose of this *deus ex machina* was to demonstrate that Keynes was wrong, and that in a properly functioning economy the system did automatically return to full employment after an initial disturbance. The argument, in its simplest possible form, went as follows. As the economy goes into a recession, wages and prices fall, and as wages and prices fall, the value or purchasing power of a given sum of money increases: if prices fall by 50 per cent, for example, £1,000 will buy twice as much as it did before. Those people who hold money, therefore, will find that they can buy more than they could before, and so they actually will buy more than they did before. This increase in demand will lead to a rise in output, and will bring the economy back to full employment.

Clearly, there is something in this argument; the question is how much. The pros and cons of it were still being debated many years after the publication of the *General Theory*. Curiously, some of Keynes's own followers appear to have conceded more to the Pigou effect than they need have done. 'It is true,' some of them in effect said, 'that *if* wages and prices were flexible downwards then the real balance effect might lead to full employment being restored without government intervention; but in practice, nowadays, wages and prices are not flexible downwards – i.e. there is great resistance to a fall in wages or prices even when the economy is going downhill into a recession. This being so, the real balance effect has no chance to operate, and Keynes was therefore right to say that the economy could settle into a long-term equilibrium in which there was substantial unemployment.'

This kind of argument does less than justice to Keynes and indeed, if accepted, would imply that the *General Theory* was much less important as a contribution to economic theory than most people had originally supposed. For it would imply that Keynes had merely been saying, 'Classical theory is correct so long as wages and prices are flexible downwards; but since they are not in practice flexible downwards, classical theory is wrong.' In other words, his theory would not have been a *general* theory at all, but simply a special case of the classical theory – relevant only in the special (though in the real world important) case in which wages and prices were not flexible downwards.

In fact, as we tried to show earlier in the chapter, Keynes's quarrel with the classical economists was much more fundamental than this. He was not merely saying that wages and prices were not in practice flexible downwards; he was saying that in no sophisticated economic system in which money was used as a medium of exchange was it possible for wages, prices and interest rates to fall far enough and fast enough to maintain full employment, or at all rapidly restore it, once some major change – such as a fall in investment or an increase in saving – had occurred. Ignorance, inertia, bear speculation, human nature itself would prevent the kind of instantaneous adjustment of wages, prices and interest rates that classical theory had assumed; and this inevitable, fatal, delay in adjustment would permit the Multiplier to come into play, amplifying the original fall in consumption or investment, and driving the economy into a cumulative decline.

Keynes's own position, then, was not that the Pigou effect would not occur because in practice wages and prices were not flexible downwards; it was, rather, that it would simply not be of much importance by comparison with all the other changes that occurred when the economy went into recession. Keynes discussed in some detail in the *General Theory* ways in which changes in the prices of goods or financial assets affect the volume of expenditure on consumption or investment. He devoted a good deal of attention to the way in which an individual's consumption could be influenced by changes in his wealth resulting from changes in the price of any government securities he possessed; and as we have seen (page 113) what is known as the 'Keynes effect' is a real-balance effect of the

Pigou kind, though it primarily affects investment, not consumption.

Thus the fact that Keynes devoted little or no attention to what subsequently came to be called the 'Pigou effect' can hardly have been due to a failure to appreciate the kind of mechanism involved. His view seems rather to have been that because the amount of 'outside money' (i.e. the amount of money not itself reduced by the process of deflation and falling prices) was limited in extent, it was not possible for the expansionary effect of its greater purchasing power to be more than a minor offset to the contractionary effect of falling incomes, consumption and investment, particularly when account was taken of the Multiplier. In so far as this was Keynes's position, it is difficult to argue that it was wrong, and even more difficult to believe that the validity of the *General Theory* has been much diminished by the line of attack represented by the various versions of the Pigou effect.

The Pigou effect has been dealt with at some length not because, in perspective, it seems to have much importance, but because for many years it was at the centre of the arguments of those economists who claimed that the *General Theory* did not represent a radically new way of looking at how the economic system worked, but merely a theoretically trivial (albeit perhaps practically important) gloss on orthodox classical theory. The neo-classical counter-attack was a bold move to wrong-foot the Keynesians into agreement that Keynes's theory was a special case of the classical theory, applicable only when wages and prices were inflexible downwards. In fact, Keynes's own claim still seems the more valid one: it was the classical theory that was the special case, applicable only when all saving was automatically invested at full employment; and the general theory was the one propounded by Keynes.

Chapter Six

THE TWENTIES AND THIRTIES IN THE LIGHT OF KEYNES

In Chapter 3 we traced some of the history of the 1920s and 1930s, noting the contemporary comments of one or two economists and politicians. It seems appropriate to round off the first half of this book by looking again at some aspects of the twenties and thirties in the light of Keynes's analysis. This will serve both to give a more precise indication of what went wrong during the inter-war years, and to provide an introduction to the kind of approach that successive governments have adopted towards the economy since the Second World War.

The most obvious question about the inter-war period was simply why there was so much more unemployment than there had ever been before. Why was the present so different from the past? During the century before 1914 unemployment in Britain probably averaged no more than 3 or 4 per cent; between 1919 and 1939 it averaged 13 per cent. The world economy as a whole had progressed quite happily throughout the nineteenth and early twentieth centuries – lurching about a bit from time to time, yet clearly on an upward trend; but at the end of the 1920s it plunged into a slump incomparably worse than any that had occurred before, and one which looked like going on for ever. What was the cause of this heavy and seemingly endless unemployment? According to Keynes, unemployment was a symptom of too low a level of effective demand. But this merely pushes the question one stage further back. Why should there have been too little effective demand in the 1920s and 1930s when presumably there had always been enough before?

To answer this question properly we need to break effective demand down into a few more categories than we have done up till now. In our analysis so far we have broken down total demand (or total expenditure) into only two components, consumption and invest-ment, since these were all that were necessary to demonstrate the essence of Keynes's argument. But we now need to take specific account of two other categories of demand – exports, and government expenditure.* These are both components of effective demand in exactly the same way as consumption or investment. Exports represent a purchase by someone (in this case a foreigner) of goods or services produced in Britain; so a fall in exports has exactly the same adverse effect on incomes, output and employment as a fall in consumption or investment. The same is true of government expenditure.

PRODUCTIVE POTENTIAL

But before we look in detail at the demand side, let us spend a moment on the supply side. The amount that a country can produce when its labour force is fully employed – let us call it the country's *productive potential* – depends on two factors. The first is the size of the working population – i.e. the number of people either in em-ployment or looking for employment. The second is the average level of productivity, or output per head of working population – something which will be related to the state of technology in the country, and to the amount of capital equipment per head. The bigger the working population and the higher the level of productivity the larger will be the economy's productive potential. Now in spite of the vast numbers killed and disabled during the war, Britain's working population was bigger in 1920 than it had been in 1914, chiefly because of a big wartime rise in the employment of women and older men. There was also some rise in productivity during the war years – output per man was perhaps 5–10 per cent higher during the early 1920s than it had been 10 years before. Taking these two factors – the rise in working population and the rise in productivity – together, one would estimate that in the early post-war period Britain's productive potential may

* Technically, government (central and local) current expenditure on goods and services. Government expenditure on transfer payments (such as pensions or un-employment benefits) is not included here, since it is already allowed for under con-sumption; and capital expenditure by the government or other public bodies is included in investment.

have been some 10–15 per cent higher than it had been before the war, so that with full employment the economy would be producing 10–15 per cent more than before the war. The corollary of this was that if unemployment in the post-war period were to be as low as it had been in the years immediately before the war (when it averaged about 3 per cent) output, and hence effective demand, would have to be 10–15 per cent higher.

INADEQUATE DEMAND

Unfortunately, so far from being 10–15 per cent higher, demand was lower. The main villain was exports. As we saw in Chapter 3, Britain lost export markets during the First World War to other countries less involved in the fighting. Many of these markets were never recaptured, even when the economy moved off a war footing and industrial capacity again became available to meet export orders, because the rapid rise in British incomes and prices during the war had left many of our exports uncompetitive. As a result, exports of goods in the early 1920s were running at only about two thirds of the pre-war level; and since before the war exports had accounted for a fifth of the National Income the effect on employment was serious. Lack of competitiveness also affected employment, though to a much smaller extent, through the other side of the trade account, since manufactured imports were now higher than they would otherwise have been, thus displacing some domestic production.

A more favourable factor was government expenditure. As one would expect, this had risen very sharply indeed during the war, and although it fell away again afterwards it remained at a higher level than before the war. Unfortunately, however, the beneficial effects on employment of this rise in government expenditure were swamped by government policy on the other side of the balance sheet, which was one of the factors responsible for keeping consumption in the early 1920s down to the pre-war level. As we saw in Chapter 3, in order to pay for war expenditure the government had increased taxation very sharply, but this did not nearly fill the gap, and there was also a big rise in government borrowing. After the war the government's expenditure fell off rapidly and so, correspondingly, did the need for taxation to pay for it. But orthodox financial practice required that each year there should be a Budget surplus so that some part of the money the government had borrowed during the war could be paid back. Therefore, it was argued, taxation must not be reduced by as much as government expenditure, because a high level of taxation was still needed to finance these repayments. As a result the standard rate of income tax, which had stood at 1s. 2d. (5·8 p) in the £ at the outbreak of war in 1914, remained at the peak wartime figure of 6s. (30 p) until 1922, and only came down to 4s. (20 p) in 1925.

The effects of a high rate of income tax on effective demand, and in particular on consumption, depend in large part on what the government does with the tax revenue it collects. If it uses it to raise old age pensions or employ more nurses or primary school teachers consumption will probably rise, because the propensity to consume of these people is almost certainly higher than the propensity to consume of the people (roughly speaking the richer half of the community) who pay the great bulk of income tax. But to the extent that the government uses the proceeds of a high rate of income tax to redeem the National Debt, as it did in the early 1920s, the effect on consumption is almost certain to be adverse. Those who benefit from repayments of government debt are merely receiving one kind of asset (cash) in exchange for another (government securities); though economists might differ on whether or not this would increase their consumption most of them would probably agree that any such effect would not be very marked. Those from whom the money has come, on the other hand – the income-tax payers – although the richer half of the community, will nevertheless in most cases have a considerably lower level of consumption than they would have had if they had not been required to pay the tax. There is no doubt that the government's policy of keeping taxes up in order to pay off some of the National Debt had a depressing effect on consumption in the early 1920s.

But probably the most important factor behind the stagnation of consumption in the early 1920s was not that because of higher taxes (or, perhaps, greater inequality in the distribution of income) people were spending less of a given income on consumption. It was simply that the level of incomes was relatively low – and incomes were relatively low because of too little demand, including demand for consumer goods. To make the point clear: the lower level of exports obviously reduced the level of employment and incomes in the export industries. Workers attached to these industries spent less on consumption, and this meant in turn (as we saw when discussing the Multiplier) that the incomes of those making certain consumption goods were depressed, and that they in turn had less to spend on consumer goods. But the chain did not end there. The fact that in the early 1920s consumption, for whatever mixture of reasons, was low in relation to the economy's productive potential had implications for investment: if existing capacity is under-utilized there is little point in installing more. Not surprisingly, investment during the early 1920s, like consumption, was no higher than it had been a decade before.

However we must not let ourselves get too tangled up in the cobweb of economic inter-relationships. The simple fact was that because of an increase in productivity, and in the size of the working population, the British economy was capable in the early 1920s of producing 10–15 per cent more than it had before the war. But consumption and investment were no higher than they had been before the war and exports were substantially lower, so that effective demand in total was 5–10 per cent lower than it had been. With actual demand and production therefore some 15–25 per cent lower than what the economy was capable of producing, heavy unemployment was inevitable. And whatever weight one assigns to different factors it is clear that two of the basic causes of this heavy unemployment were the high price of exports, and the high rate of taxation.

GOVERNMENT POLICY

The unemployment consequences of excessive export prices were perfectly apparent in the 1920s – no Keynesian spectacles were needed to see them. Moreover although the mechanism by which high rates of taxation can result in unemployment was not properly understood, no community ever lacks those who ascribe the worst contemporary ills to high taxation; certainly there were plenty of influential businessmen in the 1920s who said that unemployment would never be reduced until taxes were reduced. One might have expected, therefore, that the government would aim to cope with the unemployment problem by trying to reduce export prices, or tax rates, or both. And so it did. But it did so in a way that certainly made things no better, and if anything made them worse.

As we have seen, in order to achieve the objective of lower export prices the government did not adopt the obvious course of lowering the exchange rate – for its avowed objective, eventually achieved in 1925, was to *raise* the exchange rate back to the pre-war level. Instead it tried to reduce wages and prices enough to ensure that even though the exchange rate went up the price of British exports to foreigners would go down. In the event, resistance to wage cuts, culminating in the General Strike, prevented the reduction in wages and prices being carried far enough to restore competitiveness, and there was little change in the volume of exports for the rest of the decade, and hence little boost to employment.

But wage cuts were a more positive failure than that: although they did not go far enough to solve the export problem, they probably did go far enough to have an adverse effect on consumption. We have seen that the classical economists thought that general wage cuts would directly increase employment, and this was undoubtedly part of the rationale behind government policy; Keynes, on the other hand, thought the effects on employment would at best be neutral and at worst adverse. In this case consumption and employment almost certainly suffered from the effects of wage cuts: during the early 1920s prices fell less than wage rates so that there must have been a decline in real wages, and therefore in consumption and employment. One is therefore led to conclude that the government's policy was exactly the opposite of what was needed; had it supported *increases* in wages the effect on employment would probably have been better, at any rate as far as domestic demand was concerned. In practice, of course, the best way for a government to increase consumption is not to encourage an increase in money wages, since much or all of this will before long be offset by a rise in prices, but to reduce taxation or increase pensions and other social security payments.

This brings us back to the second thing the government did, but did in such a way that the effect was almost certainly to reduce employment rather than increase it. It reduced taxation. But each time it reduced taxation it tried to follow the golden rule that in peacetime a government must avoid a Budget deficit as it would avoid the plague, and reduced its expenditure as well. The good effects on employment of higher consumption out of higher post-tax incomes were probably more than offset by the bad effects of lower public authority expenditure.

The story was not very different during the second half of the 1920s. It is true that effective demand rose quite strongly, mainly because of increases in consumption and investment. But this rise in effective demand was no greater than the rise in the economy's productive potential engendered by the growth of productivity and the working population. Consequently there was no narrowing of the gap between full employment output and actual output, and unemployment continued, year after year, at a high level of 10–12 per cent. None of the steps which Keynesian hindsight now suggests should have been taken, were taken. Government current expenditure was not significantly increased, for this would have meant an even larger Budget deficit than the one the government was already unwillingly running – and Budget deficits were simply assumed to be undesirable and indeed potentially disastrous. For the same reason, there was (after 1925) no cut in taxation which might have stimulated consumption. Nothing was done to cheapen the price of exports: the government was stuck as a matter of dogma with the pre-war, and therefore too high, exchange rate; and following the traumatic experience of the General Strike it was stuck as a matter of political reality with an inability to enforce wage reductions. It was unthinkable for a government to interfere with private enterprise by trying to persuade businessmen to increase their investment, except perhaps by reducing interest rates, and during the 1920s Britain was so dependent on short-term borrowing from abroad that interest rates could not safely be reduced very far. On the other hand public investment could not be increased (as Keynes and some others were advocating in the later 1920s) because this would use up precious savings that might otherwise find their way into more profitable and productive private investment.

In short, nothing could be done. There was heavy unemployment in Britain throughout the 1920s because the economy had settled down into an equilibrium situation in which there was too little effective demand, and because the prevailing political and economic orthodoxy made it impossible for people to recognize that a shortage of demand was the root of the trouble, let alone to take steps to deal with it.

THE SLUMP: UNITED STATES

Throughout the 1920s Britain had been virtually alone in suffering from prolonged unemployment, but with the onset of the Slump she was soon to be joined by practically every other country on earth. The origins of the Slump lay in the down-turn in American investment which occurred at the end of the 1920s. This down-turn in investment was not in itself at all surprising – in the United States, as in Britain, the trade cycle had been a familiar phenomenon for over a century. What was surprising, and what past experience provided no precedent for, was the depth of the depression which followed this down-turn in investment; the severity with which many other countries were affected; and the refusal of the US economy to recover. Some of this ground was covered in Chapter 3, and here we only glance at some of the more salient points in the light of Keynesian theory.

The severity of the down-swing in the United States (the fact that within a few years from the top of the boom, unemployment had risen to 25 per cent instead of the 6–10 per cent customary at the bottom of the trade cycle) can perhaps be attributed to two main factors (besides the confidence effects of the Wall Street Crash). Both of these factors had their ultimate origins in the First World War.

One was the sheer strength of the investment boom which developed during the 1920s. Between 1919 and 1927 American investment nearly doubled, rising so much faster than other kinds of expenditure that it increased from 16 per cent of the National Income in 1919 to 22 per cent in 1927. Such a rapid increase in investment meant that the country's stock of capital – the number of houses and factories, the amount of plant and machinery – was being added to at an unusually rapid rate. Sooner or later it would become clear that the capital stock was big enough – perhaps more than big enough – to meet current needs: factories would be easily able to meet all the orders they received, and builders would find new houses increasingly difficult to sell. When this happened, businessmen would stop adding to their existing productive capacity, and house-building would drop;

in fact the 'accelerator' would go into reverse with a vengeance (see page 40), and there would be a sharp fall in investment – much sharper than it would have been had the rise in the stock of capital been slower, and more in line with the rise in demand.

This is precisely what happened. Investment flattened out in 1928, and turned down in 1929. As Keynes's analysis would lead one to expect, this fall in investment led, via the Multiplier, to a substantially bigger fall in the National Income. With a lower National Income there was less reason than ever to add to existing productive capacity, so that there was a further fall in investment; and this in turn led to a further fall in the National Income. One reason why the fall in the American National Income between 1929 and 1932 was so large was that the fall in investment was so large: National Income fell by about a third, investment by three quarters.

The other main reason why the American down-turn was so severe lay in the agricultural sector. The productivity of American farms had risen enormously under the stimulus of world-wide food shortages brought on by the war; and it continued to do so during the 1920s after pre-war sources of food and agricultural raw materials (such as Europe) had been restored. As a result world surpluses of many primary products began to emerge during the 1920s, and prices started to drop. This led to a vicious spiral, in which farm prices and farm incomes chased each other downward. Unlike an industrialist, a farmer who is faced by a lower price for his product tends to *increase* his output, for only by selling more can he offset lower prices and maintain his income; there was in fact a slight *increase* in American farm output between 1929 and 1933. But the consequence of millions of farmers trying to increase their output is a further fall in prices and farm incomes. When the over-supply which already existed in the late 1920s was accentuated by the fall in demand for food and raw materials that followed the downturn in investment in 1928–9 the situation became desperate. The prices of farm products fell by more than half in the three years after 1929, and American farm incomes suffered accordingly; and of course this fall in farm incomes itself brought the Multiplier into play, and led to a further decline in consumption and hence, as a result of the operation of the accelerator, in investment as well.

THE SLUMP: REST OF THE WORLD

International trade and payments were fairly peripheral to the operation of the US economy, and the cause of the severity of the American Slump must be sought internally in the kind of factors we have just been examining. But the same is not true in reverse; the American balance of payments was a major factor in the affairs of the rest of the world, and the origins of the world Slump lay in America. ('When America sneezes,' as someone once put it, 'the rest of the world catches pneumonia.') One factor we have already examined in Chapter 3: the repatriation of American money from abroad, and the immense contraction in international lending to which this gave rise.

Another factor was the fall in American imports which accompanied the fall in the National Income. Foreign trade may have been unimportant to the American economy, but the US was nevertheless, next to Britain, the world's biggest importer, and the 70 per cent fall in her imports between 1929 and 1933 brought bankruptcy and unemployment to export industries all over the world. Worse even than the direct effect on the exports of manufacturing countries such as Britain was the indirect effect on the value of primary producing countries' exports. Just as falling demand for primary products led (because of inelastic supply) to a big fall in their price within America, so a fall in the demand for these products on the part of Britain, Germany and other manufacturing countries led to tumbling primary product prices all over the world. The less developed countries whose exports consist very largely of primary products saw their export earnings fall catastrophically, and having little in the way of reserves were quickly forced to clamp down hard on their own imports of manufactured goods from the industrial countries. In the international sphere, just as within individual countries, falling incomes led to falling expenditure, and falling expenditure led to further falls in other people's incomes.

There was, however, one difference: in the international sphere the fall in incomes and expenditure was not entirely automatic. No doubt there were cases in which a country's imports (and therefore other countries' exports) fell solely because National Income fell. But in many cases industrial countries took deliberate steps, by raising tariffs or imposing quotas or foreign exchange restrictions, to reduce imports, with the idea of diverting expenditure from foreign goods to home-produced goods, and thus giving a boost to employment. Such measures came to be known, not surprisingly, as 'beggar-my-neighbour' policies: countries were trying to solve their unemployment problem by passing it on to some other country. With nearly everyone forced to pursue these policies (for a country which failed to do so would soon find itself with few exports, huge imports and vast unemployment) no one benefited very much; indeed in a sense everyone suffered, for many of the benefits of greater specialization, which are the underlying reason for international trade, were inevitably lost. Yet import restrictions, however self-defeating, seemed to many desperate governments the only quick and practical step that might alleviate a little the unemployment that threatened to swamp them.

In Keynesian terms, then, the Great Slump was a reflection of too little effective demand on a world-wide scale. Expenditure was too low; therefore incomes were too low; therefore expenditure was too low. The initial cause of this was a big decline in investment in the United States, which was not offset by a rise in consumption or any other category of expenditure, and therefore led to a progressive slide in output and employment. Partly as a result of special factors owing their origins to the war the great American contraction convulsed countries all over the world. Banks failed, businesses went bankrupt, incomes plummeted and tens of millions of men were thrown out of work. By 1933 there were probably 30 million unemployed in the industrialized countries alone.

NO RECOVERY

This down-swing in world economic activity was not only much more severe than any previous down-swing; it was not succeeded by an up-swing. In the US unemployment rose from 3 per cent in 1929 to 25 per cent in 1933, but then fell very little, to 22 per cent in 1934 and 20 per cent in 1935. The US economy – and with it the world economy – had got stuck at the bottom of the down-swing. What was supposed to happen in this situation, according to all the trade cycle literature, was a recovery in investment, induced by the emergence of profitable opportunities on the one hand, and lower costs, including lower interest rates, on the other. Keynes broadly agreed with this. But, as we saw in Chapter 4, he believed that the yield of new investment was largely determined by the amount of existing capital equipment in the economy and the extent to which it was being used. In the US in 1933 there was a very large amount of capital equipment and a great deal of it was not being used. The yield to be obtained by installing yet more capital equipment seemed likely to be pretty low. But what about the other determinant of investment, the rate of interest? This, said Keynes, was determined by liquidity preference and the quantity of money, and it seemed that when interest rates got down to a certain level (perhaps $2-2\frac{1}{2}$ per cent) it proved impossible to force them down any further, because any increase in the quantity of money (which should have the effect of reducing interest rates) was offset by an equal increase in liquidity preference. It could therefore happen, said Keynes, that the yield of new investment was lower than the rate of interest: a man might be unable to borrow for less than 2 per cent, yet be unable to find an investment project that yielded more than $1\frac{1}{2}$ per cent. When this happens no sane businessman will invest. According to Keynes, this is precisely what happened in the United States, and to a lesser extent in Britain, in the 1930s.

If investment is very low then saving will have to be equally low, and given a fairly normal propensity to consume among the population this will only happen if the National Income is low. An equilibrium gets established in which the National Income is much lower than the economy's productive potential, and unemployment is high. Until either consumption or investment or exports or government expenditure rises this low-level equilibrium will persist. It is virtually impossible for consumption to rise of its own accord, for incomes and saving are now so low that even if people cut their propensity to save in order to increase their consumption it would not make very much difference. And as long as consumption stays so low there is no particular reason why businessmen should chance their arm by increasing investment. And exports are unlikely to rise as long as there is heavy unemployment in other countries. If anything is to be done, therefore, it must be done by the government, which can stimulate consumption by cutting taxation, or (the remedy Keynes preferred) can create employment by itself spending large sums on public works.

THE NEW DEAL

Curiously enough, it was not in Britain, the country most exposed to Keynes's views, and one which had a supposedly left-wing government for the first two years of the Slump, that an attempt was made to alleviate unemployment by public works, but in the United States, supposedly the last bastion of capitalism. The 'New Deal' which Roosevelt introduced in 1933 got off to rather a shaky start, by trying simultaneously to raise wages, in order to increase consumption, and to raise prices, in order to provide businessmen with an inducement to invest; obviously one or other of these measures might have had some effect, but the two together were self-defeating. But after a year or two the public works programmes which are now thought of as the essence of the New Deal got under way. The Administration started to spend large sums of money *over and above what it received in tax revenue* on roads, dams, harbours, irrigation and land reclamation works, public buildings, housing estates and projects of many other kinds. Thus the Administration directly provided a large amount of employment, and indirectly a lot more; for the men it paid to build the roads and dams spent the money on goods and services and thus provided employment for others. The increase in government expenditure put the Multiplier into operation in exactly the same way as a rise in investment or consumption would have done.

The counterpart of this policy, under which the Administration spent more than its income, was of course a Budget deficit of the kind so dreaded by orthodox economists and politicians. In 1929–30 the federal Budget had been in modest surplus, as was considered correct and necessary to help pay off the National Debt: expenditure was $3·4 billion and tax revenue $4·2 billion. By 1935–6 expenditure had risen to over $8·5 billion, though tax revenue was only $4·1 billion; as a result there was a deficit of nearly $4·5 billion. Every year throughout the rest of the 1930s there was a Budget deficit (indeed the next time there was a surplus was 1946–7) and by the time the US again found itself at war the National Debt, which had stood at some $20 billion when Roosevelt became President, was over $50 billion. In fact the National Debt, which in the eyes of the faithful is only supposed to increase in wartime, and then only if really necessary, had more than doubled in eight peacetime years. This fact was – and indeed still is – held bitterly against Roosevelt by many people in the United States. Yet looking back today any economist or politician who has assimilated Keynes must feel that the only trouble with the US Administration's deficit spending in the 1930s was that it did not go nearly far enough. Under the stimulus of large government expenditures there was a substantial rise in employment, but the total labour force was also rising, and unemployment only fell to 14 per cent (in 1937) and actually rose again (to 19 per cent) in 1938. A large part of the trouble was that despite the rise in consumption resulting from government spending, private investment still refused to revive properly; even in the later 1930s, though there was some recovery from the very low levels in the depth of the depression, investment was still much lower than it had been immediately before 1929. Those hostile to Roosevelt claimed at the time that this was because his policy of deficit spending had destroyed confidence among the business community; other critics advanced the old theory with which Keynes had been confronted in the 1920s by the British Treasury, that expenditure on public works uses up savings that would otherwise have been used to finance private investment. In fact a much more compelling explanation seems to have been the excessive amount of idle productive capacity referred to earlier. Until demand was high enough to call existing capital equipment into use there seemed no point in installing more. Only an even greater increase in government expenditure could have led at all quickly to this. As it was, it was only with the massive re-armament programme on which the United States embarked at the end of the 1930s that any real impact was made on unemployment; and so vast were the numbers out of work that it was not until 1941 – the year of Pearl Harbor – that unemployment fell below 10 per cent.

GERMANY

Another country whose heavy unemployment was tackled by large-scale public expenditure was Germany. When the Nazis came to power in early 1933 they started a vigorous spending campaign: roads and railways were built and rebuilt, large-scale land improvement schemes were embarked on and, in the private sector, businessmen were given subsidies to encourage them to invest. These measures effected a drastic reduction in unemployment, which was carried further when re-armament got under way in 1935. By 1936 or soon after, while Britain and America were still struggling with unemployment rates of 15 per cent or more, the problem had virtually disappeared in Germany. Within three or four years Hitler's policies had resulted in a big enough rise in effective demand to re-employ most of the six million men who had been out of a job when he came to power. No wonder he enjoyed a certain popularity. Of course he also incurred very large Budget deficits, but what is an unbalanced Budget or two to set against the building of an Empire that will last for a thousand years?

BRITISH POLICY IN THE 1930s

Britain, of course, had long since left the Empire-building business; it might have suffered less in the 1930s if it had not. Throughout most of the decade the principal aim of the British government was not world domination but prudent housekeeping. From about the middle of the 1920s, as we saw in Chapter 3, the Exchequer had suffered from a small but growing deficit. After the onset of the world Slump in 1929 this deficit leaped alarmingly. The government reacted like any worried housewife. On one side of the account steps were taken to cut back expenditure – steps that faltered a little at first but became much firmer after the formation of the National Government in August 1931: public expenditure was reduced in 1932 and continued to fall for several years. On the other side of the account steps were taken to increase the government's revenue: the standard rate of income tax was raised, and so were various indirect taxes, notably the duties on tobacco, beer and petrol. These tax increases did not, in fact, succeed in raising government revenue very much: higher rates of income tax were offset by lower incomes, and higher taxes on expenditure by falling expenditure. Nevertheless the combination of cuts in public expenditure and increases in taxation did put the Exchequer back on the road to the black: the Budget deficit started to fall and by 1934 there was again a small surplus. The government's satisfaction with this state of affairs was summed up in 1935 by the Chancellor of the Exchequer, Neville Chamberlain.

Speaking with the air of a man recalling some arduous but in the end victorious military campaign he said, 'By cuts, by economy and by severe taxation the Budget was balanced.' He failed to add that in the meantime unemployment had doubled. Yet in the light of Keynes's analysis one can see that this was bound to be the result: cuts in public expenditure, and increases in taxation which force individuals to reduce their consumption, both lead to falling incomes and further reductions in expenditure. In Britain, even more than in the United States, where at least government policy was aimed in the right direction, it was only the onset of re-armament and finally of the Second World War itself that really solved the unemployment problem.

THE INTER-WAR YEARS IN RETROSPECT

We have seen that during practically the whole of the inter-war period Britain suffered from too low a level of effective demand; during much of the second half of the period the disease afflicted the rest of the world as well. Some of the immediate causes of this deficiency of demand we have traced – for example, the weakness of exports in the case of Britain, and the slump in investment in the case of the United States. Yet unemployment as severe and long-lasting as this was an entirely new phenomenon, and prompts the question of whether there was some more fundamental force at work which had permanently upset the balance of supply and demand; or, to put it in the simplest Keynesian terms, which made people want to save more at full employment levels of income than businessmen wanted to invest.

As is clear both from the *General Theory* and from one or two other writings, Keynes himself took fairly seriously the notion that the industrial countries of the West, and particularly Britain and America, were reaching a stage of economic maturity in which there was a danger of a chronic tendency for effective demand to fall short of productive potential. He pin-pointed likely weaknesses in both consumption and investment. A principal element in the latter was the ever-increasing quantity of capital equipment in such advanced industrial countries and – as he saw it – a corresponding long-run decline in the marginal efficiency of capital. If investment were to be large enough to make a substantial contribution towards maintaining full employment in this situation, interest rates must be kept very low (indeed he thought the rate of return on capital to be expected in a capital–plentiful economy would be so low as to lead before long to the 'euthanasia of the rentier' – i.e. the disappearance of incomes derived solely from the ownership of capital). But not even these very low interest rates would ensure the right amount of investment, and Keynes came to a fairly radical conclusion about the main measure the situation would require; in his own words, 'I conceive, therefore, that a somewhat comprehensive socialization of investment will prove the only means of securing an approximation to full employment.'*

On the consumption side, too, the requirements of the kind of mature industrial economy Keynes thought he was contemplating seemed to call for a significant change in traditional attitudes and arrangements. From the beginning of recorded time (or at any rate from the time of Aesop, which is much the same thing) it has been an axiom of organized society that sensible people will put aside a bit of their current income in the form of saving. And if it is sensible for an individual to save, it must also be sensible for a nation to save; as Adam Smith put it, 'What is prudence in the conduct of every private family can scarce be folly in that of a great Kingdom.'

But only in an economy which is fully employed is saving a virtue; in an economy with a chronic tendency to under-employment, it becomes a vice: attempts to save lead, paradoxically, to incomes and saving being lower than they would otherwise have been.† For in an

---

* *General Theory*, page 378.

† See the numerical example on page 103. The heresy that saving is a vice rather than a virtue has a long history, and Keynes briefly traced it in one of the Notes appended to the *General Theory*. He referred in particular to a work by Bernard Mandeville, entitled *The Fable of the Bees* (and significantly sub-titled *Private Vices, Publick Benefits*). The heart of this work (which was convicted as a 'nuisance' by the Grand Jury of Middlesex in 1723) is an allegorical poem called *The Grumbling Hive: or, Knaves Turn'd Honest*, which describes the dreadful fate of a prosperous community in which the citizens suddenly decide to abandon their extravagant way of life and start to save in the sort of way that conventional morality would prescribe. Before this misguided decision,

> 'The Root of evil Avarice,
> That damn'd ill-natur'd baneful Vice,
> Was Slave to Prodigality,
> That Noble Sin; whilst Luxury

economy in which investment is unlikely to be very great because the rate of return on capital is unlikely to be very great, saving must be kept relatively low. Or, to put it the other way round, consumption must be kept at a high level. This was unlikely, according to Keynes, to happen by itself in an advanced capitalist economy like Britain in which there were very great disparities in the distribution of income and wealth; tax policies designed to distribute income more equally would be required if the propensity to consume were to be kept at a high enough level.

Keynes himself, then, made some play with the notion that there was something rather new about the unprecedentedly heavy unemployment of the 1930s. He was inclined to take it as a reflection of a deep-seated problem increasingly afflicting advanced industrial economies as the stock of capital grew and the rate of return on it declined, and as the propensity to consume – given a very unequal distribution of income – remained too low to absorb the output the economy was capable of producing. But Keynes – unlike contemporary Marxists – believed that this problem could probably be solved within the framework of a liberal capitalist society: it might not be easy, it might require a very considerable degree of government intervention in the economy, but it probably could be done. A number of other economists who accepted Keynes's analysis took a much gloomier view of the possibility of coping with the problem, arguing that the British and American economies were settling into a state of

---

> Employed a Million of the Poor,
> And odious Pride a Million more.'

And afterwards.
> 'But, Oh ye Gods! What Consternation,
> How vast and sudden was th'Alteration!
> In half an Hour, the Nation round,
> Meat fell a Penny in the Pound.'

And later,
> 'As Pride and Luxury decrease,
> So by degrees they leave the Seas,
> Not Merchants now; but Companies
> Remove whole Manufacturies.
> All Arts and Crafts neglected lie;
> Content, the Bane of Industry,
> Makes 'em admire their homely Store,
> And neither seek, nor covet more.'

permanent stagnation, and that government action of the kind re-commended by Keynes would never be able to increase demand sufficiently to employ the country's resources to the full.

Today, in spite of the high rates of unemployment which have scarred the 1980s – the reasons for which will be discussed in Part Two – this latter appraisal is difficult to comprehend. Even Keynes's own views, with their implication that in such countries as Britain and America it would for evermore be a hard and unremitting struggle to maintain full employment, seem absurdly gloomy. But they serve, perhaps, as a salutary reminder of how hopeless the unemployment problem appeared in the 1930s, and of how difficult even Keynes must have found it to envisage an economy in which too many calls on resources, rather than too few, would be the constant pre-occupation of economists and politicians. For, looking back over the last forty or fifty years, one can see no real signs of a long-term decline in the rate of return on capital, or of any disposition on the part of the population as a whole to save more of their full-employment incomes than can be absorbed in investment. The story might have been different in the absence of some of the most character-istic features of the period since the Second World War – the near-frenzied development of new products and processes, and the explosive growth of advertising. But these are the offshoots – desirable or not – of the very capitalist economy that Keynes was analysing. They hardly suggest that the heavy unemployment of the 1930s was a reflection of a new situation in the advanced industrial countries of the West, in which society could now produce more than it would ever again want to consume. They are consistent, rather, with the basic idea expounded in the *General Theory*, that in such economies an equilibrium can be established a long way below full employment, in which both busi-nessmen and families lack either the incentive or the means to increase their expenditure; and that it is only the government, if necessary by deficit financing, which can break into the circle, increase effective demand, and set the economy on the path back to full employment.

This is not to say that the Great Slump had nothing to do with some of the changes which had taken place in the economies of Western countries over the previous fifty or a hundred years. The emergence, for example, of a situation in which savings were not automatically invested (partly because to an important extent saving and investment were now different activities carried out by different groups of people) was, as we have seen, a crucial factor in the mechanism of prolonged unemployment. But the search for some great cosmic factor which decreed that although great slumps had not been a problem in the past they would, unless one was very cunning in countering them, be a continual problem in the future – such a search, even though Keynes himself showed some disposition to join in it, seems to have been a wild goose chase. The more prosaic kind of investigation we have been engaging in, of examining the specific factors which influence particular components of demand at particular times, seems a better guide to the truth. Or so post-war experience would suggest.

It is to some aspects of post-war experience that we now turn.

Part Two
AFTER

Chapter Seven

UNEMPLOYMENT AND INFLATION SINCE THE WAR

SUCCESS OF KEYNESIAN POLICIES

With stunning suddenness, the Second World War transformed Britain from a great power to a minor one, from the ruler of an Empire to a member of a Commonwealth. But the war had other, more parochial effects as well. It acted on the nation's values and attitudes like a microwave oven on a piece of steak. Changes that would normally have taken decades were compressed into a few years. It would have seemed inconceivable in 1939 that within five years the government would have passed the 1944 Education Act which ensured that all children should receive a secondary education, or would have started to construct the welfare state foreshadowed in Sir William Beveridge's report on *Social and Allied Services*. It would have seemed equally unlikely that in 1944 the government would publish a White Paper on *Employment Policy* in which it pledged itself to maintain full employment after the war by regulating effective demand. 1939, after all, was the nineteenth consecutive year in which unemployment had averaged 10 per cent or more. Was it possible that only five years later the government could have found both the will and the weapons to maintain full employment?

As far as the will was concerned there was no doubt. The national mood demanded that everyone who wanted to work should have a job. There were plenty of jobs in wartime; there had better be plenty of jobs in peacetime too, and woe betide the government that failed to provide them. By 1944 the weapons were there as well. For by this time the economists and civil servants, and even some of the politicians and businessmen and trade union leaders, had absorbed what Keynes had been saying. It was accepted that the government could and should regulate expenditure so as to maintain a level of effective demand sufficient to preserve full employment. In the words of the White Paper,*

The government accept as one of their primary aims and responsibilities the maintenance of a high and stable level of employment after the war ... Total expenditure on goods and services must be prevented from falling to a level where general unemployment appears.

It is true that not everyone believed in the government's willingness to preserve full employment, as was perhaps demonstrated by the massive defeat in the 1945 General Election of Winston Churchill and the Conservative party, the senior partner in the Coalition government. It is also true that some economists were still doubtful about the government's ability to control demand in such a way as to maintain full employment; some of them predicted that the Second World War, just like the First, would be followed by a temporary boom which gave way to a prolonged depression. But such worriers and sceptics were proved totally wrong – at any rate for a quarter of a century. Between 1945 and 1970 unemployment averaged 1·8 per cent. This was a good performance even by the apparently optimistic standards laid down during the war by Beveridge, who said that if unemployment could be kept down to 3 per cent the country would be doing very well. By the standards of the inter-war period, when unemployment averaged 13 per cent, the achievement was monumental. Moreover the achievement was not confined to Britain. In the two countries hardest hit by the slump in the 1930s – the United States and Germany – there was also, by pre-war standards, permanent full employment. In the US, unemployment was somewhat higher than in Britain, but in Germany it was even lower. In none of the other advanced industrial countries was there anything remotely like a recurrence of the unemployment of the 1930s.

But how far, it might legitimately be asked, was this the legacy of Keynes? How can we be sure that there would not have been full employment anyway? In the nature of things, no categorical answers can be given to these questions; nevertheless, a few observations can be ventured.

* *Employment Policy*, Cmd. 6527, May 1944.

The case of Germany is of some interest. It seems clear that Germany was a country which – after post-war reconstruction had been completed – enjoyed full employment and rapid economic growth throughout the 1950s and 1960s without needing much in the way of Keynesian demand management. The main reason for this seems to have been that Germany benefited from 'export-led growth' during this period. The exchange rate established between the Deutschemark and the dollar in 1949, under the Bretton Woods fixed exchange rate system, made Germany's exports distinctly competitive, and this competitiveness increased over time as Germany's inflation rate remained even lower than that of most other countries. Rapidly rising exports encouraged increased investment in export-oriented industries, and this led to the development of new and improved products which in turn further enhanced the country's export competitiveness. Thus rising exports and rising private investment caused effective demand to rise rapidly enough to maintain full employment without Keynesian policies being needed. However, one crucial point needs to be noted: Germany could hardly have pursued this route to full employment if there had not been full employment and rapid growth in the rest of the world as well. Had there been a severe world recession in the 1950s or 1960s German exports would have been hit hard, and Germany would have had to choose between active Keynesian policies and unemployment.

An example of a rather different kind is provided by the United States. There were signs that by the end of the 1940s the American economy was beginning to slide into recession, and that full employment was maintained in the early 1950s only because of the high level of defence expenditure required by the Korean War. After the end of that war in 1953 recessionary forces reasserted themselves, and for the rest of the decade – precisely because President Eisenhower did *not* pursue Keynesian policies, but concentrated on the pre-Keynesian objective of trying to balance the federal Budget – unemployment rose. By 1960 it had reached 7 per cent, and although this was a far cry from the levels experienced in the early 1930s, it was certainly not considered at the time to constitute full employment. Things began to change under President Kennedy, whose election in 1960 undoubtedly owed something to discontent over unemployment. Kennedy surrounded himself with Keynesian advisers and, after a certain amount of hesitation, started taking their advice. He took a series of steps to encourage private investment and increase government expenditure, but relied mainly on tax cuts to get the country moving again. In fact, he found it impossible to get Congressional agreement to tax cuts: a majority of the Congress was still locked in a pre-Keynesian cast of thought. A cut in taxation, it was believed, would mean a Budget deficit, and a Budget deficit was coincident at best with inflation and at worst with nameless evils waiting in the wings to destroy the American way of life. It took the shock of Kennedy's assassination in 1963 and the long-practised manipulative skills of his successor, Lyndon Johnson, to get the tax cuts through Congress. But once they were enacted (income tax was cut in 1964 and indirect taxes in 1965) they had exactly the kind of multiplier-accelerator effect that Keynes had stressed thirty years before: lower taxes led to higher consumption, which in turn stimulated investment; and higher investment raised incomes and led to further increases in consumption. Output rose rapidly, and unemployment came tumbling down. The moral would seem fairly clear: in America – in contrast to Germany – Keynesian remedies were needed in both the 1950s and the 1960s. In the 1950s they were not applied, and unemployment rose. In the 1960s they were applied, and unemployment fell.

Britain's experience in the 1950s and 1960s was more akin to that of the US than of Germany, in that the country did not enjoy the continuing stimulus to demand that resulted from Germany's export-led growth, and in consequence had more need for effective demand to be consciously maintained by the government. It is true that this was not the situation in the early post-war years. The pent-up demand of consumers and businesses who had been unable to spend much of their incomes during the war because of rationing and other controls, combined with the physical destruction and dislocation caused by the war itself, meant that for several years after 1945 the problem was one of too much demand, not too little. The government responded to this not only by continuing with rationing but – in line with Keynes's recommendations in such a situation – by running budget surpluses designed to reduce effective demand and thus damp down inflationary pressures. After the adjustment to a peacetime economy had been completed, however, the situation changed. On a number of occasions during the ensuing twenty years – in the early 1950s and again in the late 1950s, in the early 1960s and again at the beginning of the 1970s – the growth of demand fell below the growth of the economy's productive potential, as determined by increases in productivity and in the labour force. Consequently, spare capacity appeared and unemployment started to rise. On all these occasions the government of the day responded by using a combination of fiscal policies (increases in government expenditure and reductions in taxation) and monetary policies (reductions in interest rates, relaxation of controls on bank advances, hire purchase agreements, etc.) in order to increase effective demand. In an ideal world, of course, these mini-recessions would never have happened in the first place: the forecasts regularly made by the government's economists would have given due warning that effective demand was going to fall away, and action would have been taken in time to prevent this from happening. But, although forecasting techniques became more sophisticated as time wore on, the world remained an unpredictable place, and the forecasts sometimes got it wrong. Moreover, it was not really known precisely what effects particular changes in fiscal or monetary policy would have on effective demand, nor how long it would take for the effects to be felt. Thus it was not possible for governments to prevent some fluctuations in the growth of effective demand and some fluctuations in unemployment. But such fluctuations that did occur were relatively minor, as indicated by the fact already mentioned, that the average rate of unemployment, until the beginning of the 1970s, was kept below 2 per cent.

None of this, of course, constitutes irrefutable proof that unemployment stayed as low as this *because* successive British governments pursued Keynesian full employment policies. It could be claimed that even in Britain such 'autonomous' items of expenditure as exports and private investment were buoyant enough to keep the economy growing at a more or less full employment level of output, and that the mini-recessions which occurred would still have been as shallow and short-lived as they were even if the government had concentrated simply on balancing the budget. But such a claim would not be very credible. In particular, it is implausible to suppose that private investment would have been the same as it was if successive governments had not made clear their commitment to honour the full employment pledge laid down in the 1944 White Paper. The belief that governments would take whatever action was necessary to maintain full employment gave businessmen the confidence to invest, since they knew that their newly installed plant and equipment would not be rendered idle by a general recession. In the absence of the full employment pledge, business investment would probably have been a much less buoyant element in effective demand than it actually was.

The question of what would have happened to the post-war British – and world – economy had Keynes not existed can hold the same fascination for economists that the question of what would have happened to the world had Cleopatra's nose been half an inch longer is supposed to have held for generations of teachers of Roman history.* A particularly satisfactory feature of the game is that no one can ever be proved wrong. But the commonsense conclusion is that Britain and other Western countries had full employment for a quarter of a century after the war because their governments were committed to full employment, and knew how to secure it; and they knew how to secure it because Keynes had told them how.

GROWTH AND INFLATION

So successful did Keynesian policies prove in Britain that less than a decade after the end of the war full employment had come to be taken for granted, and attention had shifted to another objective – faster growth. The total output of the economy (gross domestic product, or GDP, at constant prices) was growing at an average rate of about 3 per cent a year, and although this compared favourably with the rates of growth Britain had achieved in the past, it was distinctly lower than the rates being achieved in other European countries. In 1954 the Chancellor of the Exchequer, Mr Butler, talked in terms of doubling the standard of living in twenty-five years, which implied an annual growth of GDP of about $3\frac{1}{4}$ per cent. Later on, this target (though it had not in the meantime been attained) came to seem too modest, and by the early 1960s it was fashionable to talk in terms of a

---

* The question is not entirely fanciful. Lord Kitchener, the Secretary of State for War, was on his way to Russia in 1916 when his ship hit a mine, and he and most of those on board were drowned. Keynes (and Lloyd George) had been due to go on this voyage, and only withdrew at the last moment.

4 per cent growth rate. Indeed one of the main issues in the 1964 General Election was which political party would be more likely to achieve this faster rate of growth.

However, although the secret of maintaining full employment seemed to have been found, so that policy could now focus on how to raise productivity so as to increase the output of a fully employed labour force, the fact was that full employment had only been achieved at a cost. The cost was inflation.

Inflation consists of a rise – not just a once-for-all rise, but a fairly continuous rise – in the cost of a basket of goods and services. The most comprehensive basket of goods and services is the total output of the economy, or GDP. If the actual volume of output, or GDP in real terms, stayed unchanged but the GDP in money terms rose by 5 per cent, one would say that the inflation rate was 5 per cent. The inflation rate would also be 5 per cent (approximately) if the GDP rose by 8 per cent in money terms ('at current prices') but only by 3 per cent in real terms ('at constant prices'). In fact the most widely used index of inflation in Britain is not this so-called 'GDP deflator', but the retail price index, which measures the cost of the whole basket of goods and services bought in an average month by an average household. For present purposes, however, the difference between these two indices is of no significance, and we shall use the word 'inflation' in a loose way to refer to either or both of them.

Inflation has now been going on for half a century: the retail price index has risen in every year since 1935. Thus only a diminishing minority of the population can remember what it was like to live in a non-inflationary era. Yet by historical standards this continuous inflation is unusual, if not unique. There have of course been periods of rising prices in the past, but they were nearly always succeeded by periods of falling prices, so that over quite long stretches of time the inflation rate was almost imperceptible. In the first decade of the eighteenth century, for example, prices in Britain were only about 25 per cent higher than they had been a hundred years before. At the time of the outbreak of the First World War in 1914, prices were if anything lower than they had been at the time of the Battle of Waterloo in 1815. The unusual nature of what has happened since 1935 can be put in another way: in the 650 years before 1935 prices rose about

14-fold. In the fifty years or so since, they have risen 28-fold.*

One must be careful about concluding that the continuous inflation of the last fifty years has necessarily been a bad thing. What really matters is not what is happening to prices as such, but what is happening to prices in relation to money incomes. To put it another way: it is the growth of *real* GDP that counts, not the growth of money GDP. It does not make any difference to the rise in people's living standards whether money GDP rises by 3 per cent a year and prices are stable or whether money GDP rises by 8 per cent a year and prices rise by 5 per cent a year. In both cases real GDP, and thus real incomes, rise by 3 per cent a year. The 28-fold increase in prices between 1935 and 1985 was accompanied by a 75-fold increase in the money GDP, so that real GDP rose more than $2\frac{1}{2}$ times. Even after allowing for the fact that the population grew by about 20 per cent over the same period, it is clear that living standards, or real GDP per head, more than doubled. It is by no means self-evident that this rise in living standards would have been faster if inflation had been slower.

None of this is to say that inflation does not matter. In view of the immense lengths to which most Western governments have gone to reduce inflation, particularly since about the mid-1970s, this would indeed be a surprising conclusion. But it is important to be clear as to exactly why inflation matters and what its adverse consequences can be.

A useful starting-point in this inquiry is British experience during the quarter century that followed the war – the same quarter century that saw unemployment average 1·8 per cent, and also saw living standards, as measured by real GDP per head, rise by well over 50 per cent. Between 1945 and 1970 inflation in Britain averaged about 4 per cent a year, being a bit more in some years and a bit less in others, but showing little sign of either accelerating or decelerating.

There were two principal reasons why this rate of inflation, modest and stable though it was, was thought to matter, and why successive governments made a series of attempts to reduce it. First of all, it hit those whose money incomes did not adjust fully to inflation. Powerfully organized groups of workers might be able to secure

* These figures are taken from the Appendix to Douglas Jay, *Sterling* (Sidgwick & Jackson, London, 1985), which draws on the work of E. H. Phelps Brown and S. Hopkins. Immense difficulties attend the calculation of price indices over long periods of time because of changes in the nature and quality of commodities, in social habits and tastes etc., but these figures are probably as good as it is possible to provide.

annual wage and salary increases that kept them well ahead of inflation, but not everyone was in this position. Recipients of state benefits, such as old age pensions and unemployment or sickness benefits, did all right in practice since governments found it politically necessary to uprate these benefits regularly in line with the rise in prices, or even with the (usually bigger) rise in earnings. Those who really suffered were people partly or wholly dependent on fixed incomes, notably those living on private pensions which were fixed in money terms and where there was no provision for upward adjustment. Some of these people were well off, but many were relatively poor, and inflation made them progressively poorer and increasingly critical of the government.

The second cause of concern about Britain's 4 per cent inflation rate was that it was faster than the inflation rate of many other countries. Under the fixed exchange rate regime established at Bretton Woods in 1944, this meant that Britain's goods gradually lost competitiveness in export markets, and foreign goods gradually became more competitive in the British market. Throughout the 1950s and 1960s this process contributed to a series of balance of payments crises, which successive governments responded to with deflationary packages that had damaging effects on business confidence and investment, and hence on the country's rate of growth. If inflation in Britain could be slowed down or stopped, it was argued, these damaging consequences could be avoided.

Some people would take the view that the adverse effects of a 4 per cent inflation rate are not very great. As people come to accept the fact that there is likely to be inflation in the future as there has been in the past, it could be argued that it is up to them to adjust their behaviour and the disposition of their assets to take account of it; and in any case there are many worse aspects of the distribution of income in Britain than the inequity caused by inflation to those on fixed incomes. Similarly, the adverse effects on international competitiveness of an inflation rate faster than that of other countries can be taken care of – as they were in 1949 and again, belatedly, in 1967 – by devaluation of the currency. Alternatively, the currency can be floated, as was in fact done in 1972, so that – in theory at any rate – Britain's above-average inflation rate can be offset by a gradual decline in the exchange rate, leaving competitiveness unchanged.

Nevertheless, although there was some sympathy for these arguments in the 1950s and 1960s, the reluctance to devalue or float the currency, and the electoral dangers of appearing to condone inflation, by and large proved stronger. At one time or another all the governments in office between 1945 and 1970 adopted policies designed to reduce inflation. It stands to reason, however, that policies to reduce inflation are unlikely to be successful unless the causes of inflation have been correctly identified; and this has not proved quite as straightforward a process as might have been expected.

DEMAND-PULL AND COST-PUSH

It is a fairly natural presumption that inflation is in some sense the mirror-image of unemployment. Keynes had demonstrated in the *General Theory* that if there is too little effective demand in the economy, the result will be unemployment. It seems a reasonable inference that if there is too much effective demand in the economy, the result will be rising prices. By definition, a fully employed economy cannot produce any more, at least in the short run. If demand increases in a fully employed economy, the extra spending cannot call forth more output, and will therefore merely lead to a rise in prices (although in an open economy there is also likely to be a rise in imports). If one wants to prevent inflation, therefore, one must avoid too high a level of effective demand, just as one must avoid too low a level of demand if one wants to prevent unemployment. Keynes himself had made this point in *How To Pay for the War*, published in 1940: during the war civilian spending would have to be kept down by high taxation, compulsory saving schemes, etc., if there was not to be excess demand and hence rampant inflation.

After the war this simple idea continued to hold sway. It received a boost in the late 1950s from the work of A. W. Phillips, who discovered that during the past hundred years there had been an inverse relationship in Britain between the level of unemployment and the rate of increase of money wages. When unemployment was high, wages increased slowly; when unemployment was low, wages increased a good deal faster. Since wage increases and price increases are fairly closely correlated (the difference being mainly the growth of productivity) one can infer that there is an inverse relationship between unemployment and inflation, of a kind that can be illustrated by what came to be called a 'Phillips curve'.

The idea underlying the Phillips curve is intuitively plausible. If unemployment is high, workers will be in a weak position to press for big wage increases, and employers, faced by a depressed economy, will be very reluctant to concede them. Wages and prices will not increase very much, and there will be little or no inflation. If unemployment is low, on the other hand, workers' bargaining position will be strong, employers may bid against each other to secure skilled labour needed to meet profitable orders in a booming economy, and wages and prices are likely to rise relatively rapidly: the inflation rate will be high.

It would appear to follow from the Phillips curve analysis that if one wants to reduce the inflation rate all one need do is to reduce the level of effective demand in the economy, and permit some rise in unemployment. This is certainly how a number of economists in Britain saw it in the late 1950s and early 1960s. It was argued, for example, on the basis of the Phillips curve, that the reason why

Britain had an inflation rate of around 4 per cent was that an un-employment rate averaging around 1·8 per cent represented some excess demand in the economy. If demand had been kept a little lower, and unemployment had averaged about 2·5 per cent, inflation would have been zero. A good deal of the debate – taking the validity of this argument for granted – revolved around the political or moral question of whether it was acceptable to endure this extra un-employment in order to eliminate inflation.

But the argument was faulty, as some economists pointed out at the time. The fact that excess demand will lead to inflation does not necessarily mean that an absence of excess demand will lead to an absence of inflation. Avoiding excess demand may be a necessary condition of avoiding inflation, but it may not be a sufficient condi-tion. In other words, inflation may be caused by other factors, as well as by an excessive level of demand.

Experience in Britain in the 1940s and 1950s strongly suggested what had already been foreshadowed in the 1944 White Paper – that there was indeed another such factor which caused inflation. This cause of inflation came to be referred to as 'cost-push', by contrast with the 'demand-pull' cause identified by the Phillips-curve analysis. Instead of prices being pulled up by excessive demand, they were pushed up by rising costs, notably rising wage costs. For, so the argument went, in a situation in which the government was committed to maintaining full employment, unions could demand large wage increases without much risk of becoming unemployed, or, in the phrase much used in the 1980s, of 'pricing themselves out of jobs'. And employers had no great incentive to resist these large wage demands, since the fact that their competitors were facing the same wage demands, combined with the government's guarantee of full employment, meant that they could pass higher wages on in higher prices without much risk of losing business. It would be much more risky, in many cases, to resist these wage demands and face the prospect of a prolonged strike which might lead to bank-ruptcy.

If this explanation of inflation, which laid crucial emphasis on the new situation created by the government's pledge to maintain full employment, was correct, then the stage was set for an endless upward spiral, in which big wage increases would lead to price increases, which would in turn become the justification of further wage increases. This new kind of cost-push inflation was by no means incompatible with the traditional demand-pull inflation: indeed it might well be that a period of excess demand could, by pulling up certain key prices and wages, set off the rising spiral of cost-push inflation in the first place. But the crucial point was this: once cost-push inflation had got under way, it could continue even when demand had ceased to be in any sense excessive. Thus cost-push inflation could not be eliminated simply by reducing demand – or at any rate by reducing demand on a modest enough scale to avoid jeopardizing full employment. It had to be tackled by breaking into the spiral directly, by taking action to slow down the growth of wages, or prices, or both. In other words it had to be tackled by what came to be called a prices and incomes policy.

It is a remarkable fact that sooner or later every single post-war British government came to recognize this, until the election of Mrs Thatcher's Conservative government in 1979. The first incomes policy was operated by Mr Attlee's Labour government in the late 1940s. Thirty years later – from 1975 to 1979 – an incomes policy was in operation under the Wilson–Callaghan Labour government. In between, the 1951–64 Conservative government, the 1964–70 Labour government, and the 1970–74 Conservative government had all, if sometimes belatedly, come to the conclusion that, if full employment were to be maintained, inflation could not be dealt with simply by managing the level of effective demand; an incomes policy was needed as well.

The subject of incomes policies will come up again in Chapter 9. Meanwhile, let us try to summarize the state of informed economic opinion in Britain in the late 1960s – a quarter of a century after the publication of the 1944 White Paper. There would probably have been widespread support for something like the following statement.

'Experience has demonstrated that governments can, by influencing effective demand, maintain full employment: Keynes was right. Unfortunately full employment seems to have an undesirable companion: inflation. Although the inflation rate is relatively low and fairly stable, it is a nuisance, both because it hits those on fixed incomes and because it reduces our competitiveness in world markets.

Although these drawbacks can to some extent be overcome by suitable domestic policies or by changing the exchange rate, it would be better to eliminate inflation, or at least reduce it to the level experienced by other countries, and in order to do this it is necessary to have a workable incomes policy. Nevertheless, now that full employment has been achieved, the main objective of economic policy should not be the elimination of inflation, which would not in itself do much to increase people's living standards; it should be the achievement of a faster rate of economic growth. For this is the only way, in a fully employed economy, that living standards can be progressively raised; and the raising of living standards is the ultimate objective of economic policy.'

ACCELERATING INFLATION

However, life is full of surprises. The kind of statement just made would soon have come to look premature and over-complacent. For around 1970, things started to go wrong. In particular, the inflation rate started to accelerate. The retail price index, which had been rising at a little over 4 per cent in the later 1960s, rose by $6\frac{1}{2}$ per cent in 1970 and $9\frac{1}{2}$ per cent in 1971. There was a brief lull, and then the rate accelerated again, to 16 per cent in 1974 and 26 per cent by the middle of 1975. This was frightening. A stable inflation rate of 4 per cent or so is one thing; an accelerating inflation rate is quite another. For many people, as inflation accelerates, pay increases lag well behind price increases and living standards drop. Many others face the prospect of their lifetime savings becoming nearly worthless within a few years. Alarm spreads, and newspapers remind their readers of the hyper-inflation in Germany in the early 1920s, which destroyed the German middle class and paved the way for the rise of Hitler.

Things would not have looked so bad if this rise in the inflation rate could have been explained in terms of the Phillips curve. If unemployment had been falling to an extremely low level, so that the economy had been moving up the left-hand segment of the curve, the cause of rising inflation would have been clear, and so would the solution: reduce effective demand from an obviously excessive level, allow unemployment to rise to a more normal figure, and the inflation rate would fall back again towards the customary 4 per cent. But this was not the state of affairs at all. On the contrary, unemployment was actually *rising* over most of this period. It had been 1½ per cent in 1966, 2–2½ per cent from 1967 to 1970, 3½ per cent in 1971, and nearly 4 per cent in 1972. It fell back briefly in 1973 and 1974, in response to major Keynesian expansionary measures undertaken by Mr Heath's Conservative government, but then rose again, and by the end of 1975 was around 5 per cent. What was happening during this period, in fact, was not that the economy was moving along the Phillips curve; what was happening was that the Phillips curve itself was moving smartly upwards in a north-easterly direction. Unemployment and inflation were no longer inversely related. Unemployment and inflation were both rising at the same time.

It must be said that to those Keynesian economists who had never accepted the validity of the Phillips-curve analysis, there was nothing very surprising about this disappearance of the curve off the top right-hand corner of the page. To them, as was indicated earlier, unemployment was determined by effective demand, and the inflation rate – though by no means impervious to the level of demand – was to a large extent determined by the strength of the cost-push process. There was no reason why various factors should not intensify the wage–price spiral even at a time when demand was weakening and unemployment rising. And it was in fact possible to identify half a dozen factors in the late 1960s and early 1970s that boosted inflation in Britain, even though demand in Britain was in no sense excessive. Some of these factors might reflect excessive demand in other countries (the way in which excess demand can trigger off a cost-push inflation has already been mentioned); but the strength of these forces could not have been significantly curbed by anything done to reduce demand in Britain.

One of these factors was the combination of America's deepening involvement in the Vietnam war and President Johnson's 'Great Society' programme – an attempt to have both guns and butter which promoted inflation in the US itself and, through the agency of the Bretton Woods fixed exchange rate system, passed a good deal of it on to the rest of the world. Another was the devaluation of sterling in November 1967, which raised Britain's import prices by about 15 per cent. A third was the explosion of student violence in Paris in May

1968 and the revolutionary atmosphere which developed when large numbers of industrial workers joined the students on the barricades. The French government bought off the industrial workers by conceding very large wage increases, and a number of other European countries, also touched by student and worker unrest, did the same. A fourth factor was the rapid rise in world commodity prices in the early 1970s, the consequence of a simultaneous boom in most of the industrial countries, together with bad harvests in 1972 in both North America and the Soviet Union: wheat prices doubled between 1972 and 1973; world commodity prices as a whole rose by about 50 per cent. A fifth factor – itself a reflection of the excessive wage and price increases already taking place in Britain, but in turn augmenting these increases further – was a 15 per cent depreciation of sterling between June 1972, when it was floated, and the early autumn of 1973. And on top of all this came OPEC's quadrupling of the oil price between September 1973 and January 1974.

Thus it was quite possible for Keynesians to explain why the inflation rate in Britain rose markedly between the late 1960s and the mid-1970s, even though demand, so far from being excessive, was increasing more slowly than productive potential over much of the period, with the consequence that unemployment was on a rising trend. But to many people the explanation sounded a little hollow. Somehow, rather suddenly, the Keynesian image had become tarnished. Keynes's analysis had, above all else, provided an answer to the question of how to maintain full employment. But if full employment meant an accelerating inflation rate – i.e. if the Phillips curve were moving north-eastwards – then the answer was not very helpful, because accelerating inflation must end in catastrophe. If, to look at the rising Phillips curve the other way, a stable inflation rate meant an ever-increasing unemployment rate, then the Keynesian answer was no answer at all.

Into this scene of uncertainty and confusion stepped a new breed of critics – the monetarists. It is to their analysis that we now turn.

Chapter Eight

THE MONETARIST COUNTER-REVOLUTION

Monetarism is a school of economic thought associated particularly with the names of Milton Friedman (a Nobel Prize-winner) and the University of Chicago. Developing slowly from around the mid-1950s, by the late 1960s it had gained a large number of adherents in the United States and had begun to make a significant impact on economic thought in Britain. By the early 1970s many British economists, politicians and civil servants, not to mention a probable majority of those in the City of London, were looking at things through monetarist spectacles, and by the end of the decade, with the election of Mrs Thatcher in Britain and Mr Reagan in America, the capture of government by the monetarists was complete.

There seem to be a number of reasons why, between the late 1960s and the late 1970s, monetarism displaced Keynesianism as the guiding light of economic policy in Britain. One reason, perhaps, was simply that it was (or appeared to be) new, and in an era beguiled by novelty the appeal of a new way of looking at the world – particularly to the increasing tribe of economic journalists who had to write daily or weekly articles about the economy – should not be underestimated. Another reason for the appeal of monetarism lay in its essential simplicity: the fundamental prescription which emerged from it could be grasped by the dimmest banker or stockbroker. Thirdly, it was a message in tune with the instincts of the more right-wing elements in the Conservative party, which held sway in 1970–72 (before Mr Heath did his famous U-turn) and again, more pronouncedly, after 1979. But the most important reason of all for the emergence of monetarism as the predominant economic doctrine of the 1970s and 1980s was the simplest of all: monetarism promised a cure for inflation.

There are many versions of monetarism, just as there is a variety of interpretations of Keynes. In this chapter we try to set out, as clearly and objectively as possible, the essence of the monetarist argument.

THE SELF-STABILIZING ECONOMY

One of the most fundamental tenets of monetarism is that a modern industrial economy, if left to itself, is self-stabilizing at full employment (though what is meant by full employment is not entirely straightforward, and is discussed in the next section). This is because there are powerful forces at work, including particularly the flexibility of real wages, which ensure that the normal condition of the economy is one in which available resources are fully utilized. If some external shock impinges on the economy, throwing things out of kilter and causing unemployment to rise, these powerful forces will see to it that full employment equilibrium is soon restored. Looked at from another angle, one could say that monetarism postulates that *agents optimize* and *markets clear*. Agents (businessmen, workers, households) optimize in the sense that they take rational decisions about the course of action that is best for them, and then follow these decisions through in a consistent way. Markets clear in the sense that all prices – including the price of labour – adjust in such a way as to equate supply and demand. It is therefore not possible for there to be excess demand for, or excess supply of, any commodity or factor of production. In particular, it is not possible for labour to be in excess supply – except perhaps temporarily, in the wake of some unexpected disturbance; in other words it is not possible for there to be workers who want a job but are unable to find one. It can be seen that the parallel between monetarism and the nineteenth-century classical economics discussed in Chapters 2 and 5 is a striking one, and it is not surprising that in its most sophisticated, 'rational expectations' form (see page 166 below) monetarism is often referred to as the 'New Classical Economics'.

The most important implication of the presumption that the economy is self-stabilizing is that the government's role should be a neutral one: the government should keep its hands off the economy. For if the economy is basically stable, the effect of government intervention at the macroeconomic level is likely to be to destabilize it. So far as fiscal policy is concerned, the government should balance its budget or, at the very least, maintain a stable relationship between the budget balance and the GDP. And monetary policy should be neutral as well. It is this insistence on the need for a neutral monetary policy that is close to the heart of monetarist doctrine, and in order to understand its nature and rationale we need to take a look at a fairly ancient piece of economic theory – *the quantity theory of money*.

The quantity theory of money, developed in the early years of the twentieth century, is based on a very simple equation. The equation is nowadays generally written as

$$MV = PQ$$

where M is the quantity of money (or 'the money supply'), V the average velocity at which this money circulates, Q the quantity of output produced by the economy, in real terms, in the course of a year, and P the price of this output. Thus PQ is the same thing as the GDP at current prices; and this must equal the money supply, multiplied by its velocity of circulation.

The quantity equation is simply an identity or tautology; there is so far no indication of which terms in the equation cause change, and which accept it. What the quantity *theory* does is to assert a particular causal relationship. Put crudely, it says that V does not change very much (or changes in a steady and predictable way), and therefore there is a close correlation between M and PQ; and that it is changes in M that cause changes in PQ, and not the other way round. Thus changes in the money supply cause changes in the GDP at current prices. This is what the monetarists say (the fact that they are sometimes called 'neo-quantity theorists' is a valid reminder of their intellectual ancestry). We now need to examine the mechanism whereby, according to the monetarists, changes in the money supply generate changes in the GDP at current prices, or money GDP.

The key bit of this mechanism is what is termed the 'stable money demand function' – a piece of doctrine based on historical observation which says that people's demand for money is a stable function of their money income.* In other words, the amount of money people

---

* Milton Friedman stressed that it is people's *permanent* income (i.e. what they think of as being their normal or expected level of income), rather than the actual income they happen to receive in a particular period, that is important; but for present purposes this makes no significant difference to the analysis.

want to hold, in cash or bank deposits, is related in a fairly fixed way to their income (and hardly at all, as in the Keynesian liquidity preference theory (see page 76) to the rate of interest). If the Central Bank increases the money supply by open-market operations, people who have sold securities in return for money, or who find it easier (because of the increase in the commercial banks' monetary base) to get overdrafts or bank advances, will find that their holdings of money have risen in relation to their income. To restore their preferred ratio, they will spend the excess money: some of it, no doubt, on financial assets, but much of it on goods and services. And this expenditure on goods and services, while reducing their money balances, will at the same time increase the money GDP or PQ. Thus according to the monetarists there is a direct causal connection between changes in the money supply and changes in the GDP. This is because all other assets – not just other financial assets – are seen as a good substitute for money. Therefore an increase in the money supply, which leads to a fall in the rate of interest, or the yield on holdings of financial assets, causes people to shift into a whole range of other assets – houses, durable goods and any other consumer goods which yield up their services over a period of time. It is precisely because the yield on these non-financial assets – which is not normally expressed in money terms but is a valid concept all the same – has *not* fallen that people, in order to maximize the yield they receive on all their assets taken as a whole, will increase their expenditure on these non-financial assets and thus cause a rise in the GDP. This is in marked contrast to the traditional Keynesian view, discussed on pages 74 to 80, according to which it is only other *financial* assets that are a good substitute for money, so that an increase in the money supply only affects the level of expenditure, and hence the GDP, *indirectly* – by reducing interest rates, which may in turn influence the level of investment and, possibly, of consumption.

But the fact that increases in M generate increases in PQ is not the end of the matter: the question now arises of how far the increase in PQ takes the form of an increase in P, and how far of Q. In other words, how far does an increase in the money supply lead to a rise in output, and how far does it simply lead to a rise in prices? At its very simplest, the monetarist theory says that it cannot lead to a rise in output because the normal condition of the economy is one of full utilization of resources and hence maximum output; therefore it simply leads to a rise in prices. But since maximum output (the productive potential of the economy) does rise over time because of improvements in productivity and increases in the labour force, there is some scope for the money supply to rise over time without causing a rise in prices. In Britain, taking the conventional figure of a 3 per cent annual rise in productive potential, there is therefore scope for the money supply to rise by about 3 per cent a year without causing inflation. This, then, is what the monetarists would regard as a neutral, and therefore appropriate, monetary policy in the British context: the money supply should be increased by 3 per cent a year.

But what if the economy is clearly not at the level of full employment and maximum output? Surely in that case it would be legitimate to increase the money supply by more than the usual 3 per cent a year, since there would be scope for PQ to rise by more than 3 per cent without there being any increase in P. In this way the economy could be brought back to full employment, by allowing output to rise by more than 3 per cent a year, without there being any rise in prices. In other words one could increase the money supply by, say, 5 per cent a year for a couple of years, thus increasing the real GDP by 5 per cent a year for these two years, restoring full employment but not raising the price level.

Absolutely not, the monetarists would reply. Although there is a causal relationship between the money supply and money GDP, the timing of this relationship is a bit unpredictable: to quote Milton Friedman, there are 'long and variable time-lags' in the system. Thus one could not be sure that the extra rise in M would come through soon enough to raise Q; by the time it had its effect, Q might – as a result of the self-stabilizing forces mentioned earlier – be back at its maximum, full employment level, so that the effect would all be felt by P. In other words the extra rise in the money supply would simply lead to a rise in prices. The only safe thing to do is to rely on the long-run relationship between M and PQ and increase M steadily, in line with the long-run scope for the rise in Q.

For this argument to carry conviction, however, one needs to penetrate more deeply into the question of why the monetarists presume that the economy is basically self-stabilizing at full employment. And this brings us to the concept of the natural rate of unemployment.

THE NATURAL RATE OF UNEMPLOYMENT

To the monetarists, the labour market works like any other market: supply and demand are brought into balance by the price mechanism. The demand curve relates employers' demand for labour to the real wage rate they have to pay: the lower the real wage rate, the greater their demand for labour. The supply curve relates the working population's offers of work to the real wage it receives: the higher the real wage rate, the more people will offer themselves for employment. The intersection of demand and supply curves will simultaneously determine the real wage rate actually paid and the level of employment. This is full employment, in the sense that everyone who wants a job at the real wage rate established in the market has a job. Thus the economy and the labour market are in equilibrium at what Milton Friedman has called 'the natural rate of unemployment'. The natural rate of unemployment will never be zero, for the same reason that Keynesian full employment was never defined as zero unemployment: in any economy there will always be some degree of frictional and structural unemployment. And because attitudes and institutions vary over time and in different countries, the natural rate of unemployment will vary at different times and in different countries – a point to which we shall return in the last section of the chapter. For present purposes, however, we can say that according to the monetarists the economy, left to itself, will establish equilibrium at the natural rate of unemployment, and that this will represent full employment of the labour force.

There are two features of the natural rate of unemployment, as conceived by the monetarists, which are of key importance to their argument. The first feature has already been mentioned, but deserves to be emphasized. It is that at the natural rate of unemployment everyone who wants to be employed at the real wage rate established by the forces of supply and demand in the labour market, is employed. Thus there is no such thing as 'involuntary' unemployment: unemployment is voluntary. Anyone who is unemployed is unemployed because he has decided that it is not worth his while to work for the real wage which market forces have established. Obviously, the higher the real wage rate, the more likely he is to decide to work. Conversely – a point much stressed by politicians of a monetarist bent – the higher the level of unemployment benefit provided by the state, the more likely he is to decide not to work. But if he is unemployed, and wants a job, all he has to do is to offer himself at the going real wage rate, or a fraction below it, and he will find someone who is willing to employ him. Because the demand curve slopes downwards, a substantial increase in employment will be forthcoming only at a reduced level of real wages, so that if 10 per cent of the labour force is unemployed but wants to work, they will have to accept a lower real wage rate than the one currently prevailing. But they *can* find employment *if* they are willing to accept a lower real wage. It is in this sense that unemployment is assumed by the monetarists to be voluntary.

The second feature of the natural rate of unemployment is at the crux of the monetarist argument. At the natural rate of unemployment – and *only* at that rate – the inflation rate will be stable. If the inflation rate is zero – i.e. the overall price level is stable – it will stay at zero. If the inflation rate is 4 per cent a year, it will stay at 4 per cent a year. Whatever the initial inflation rate, in fact, it will show no tendency to accelerate or decelerate. If, on the other hand, unemployment is below the natural rate – because of the kind of government intervention advocated by Keynesians and seen by the monetarists as misguided – inflation will accelerate. If it is above it, inflation will decelerate. But if unemployment is at the natural rate, the inflation rate will be stable.

The reason for the stability of the inflation rate at the natural rate of unemployment lies in the role of *expectations*, a feature of economic life to which the monetarists attach great importance, as Keynes himself had done. According to Friedman, at the natural rate of unemployment, with the economy and the labour market in a state of equilibrium, the *actual* inflation rate is equal to the *expected* inflation rate. Not to put too fine a point on it, if the inflation rate is, say, zero, then everyone will expect it to continue to be zero; and if they expect it to continue to be zero, it will continue to be zero. It is only when something happens to confound these expectations, and the actual inflation rate rises above the expected inflation rate, that trouble begins. And it is this that we shall now examine.

THE KEYNESIAN MISTAKE

The mistake the Keynesians had made, according to the monetarists, was to think that one could select any particular rate of unemployment and then manage effective demand in such a way as to achieve this unemployment rate while maintaining a stable rate of inflation. In other words, the Phillips curve – an essentially Keynesian construct, despite the scepticism felt about it by some Keynesians – is a chimera. It is not possible to choose any given combination of unemployment and inflation, unless by a fluke the unemployment rate chosen happens to be the natural rate of unemployment. If, in response to political pressures, the unemployment rate selected as a target is below the natural rate, there will be accelerating inflation. And if for any reason – such as structural changes in the economy, improved social security benefits or increasing trade union power – the natural rate of unemployment is itself rising over time, then it is perfectly possible to have *both* rising unemployment *and* accelerating inflation – precisely the phenomenon that appeared at the beginning of the 1970s.

Let us consider this monetarist version of events in terms of a very simple example. Suppose that the economy initially has an unemployment rate of 5 per cent; that this is, as it happens, the natural rate of unemployment, so that the inflation rate is stable; and that the stable inflation rate is a zero rate. (In terms of the diagram on page 151, the economy will therefore be at the point where the Phillips curve intersects the horizontal axis.) Now suppose that the Keynesian managers of the economy decide that 5 per cent unemployment is too high, and that it should be brought down to 3 per cent. They will take steps to increase effective demand: cutting taxes, increasing public expenditure, or expanding the money supply and bringing down interest rates. The demand for goods and services will increase, and so will employers' demand for labour: the demand curve for labour will shift upwards. This increased demand for labour will lead to a rise in money wage rates. This rise in money wage rates is interpreted by unemployed workers as a rise in *real* wage rates – which is perfectly reasonable, since they have been accustomed to a zero inflation rate and understandably expect this zero inflation rate to continue. Accordingly, they will now offer themselves for work, which they were unwilling to do at the previous, lower, wage rate; and so unemployment will fall.

However, as unemployment falls, inflation will rise: the economy will move up the Phillips curve. Inflation will rise because wage rates have risen; this is particularly true, in the monetarist version of events, because the monetarists believe in diminishing returns to scale (as did Keynes in the *General Theory*, though not later – see page 109), so that as output rises, unit costs rise, and prices have to rise as well if profit margins are to be maintained. As unemployment falls from 5 per cent to 3 per cent, the inflation rate rises from zero to, say, 2 per cent.

This rise in the inflation rate – the story goes on – comes as a nasty shock to the workers who have allowed themselves to be drawn into employment by the rise in money wage rates. For it has now become apparent that the rise in money wages has been offset by a rise in prices, so that their real wage is no higher than the previous real wage, which was not high enough to make it worth their while to work. Accordingly, disillusioned, they quit their new jobs and rejoin the ranks of the unemployed. Thus the supply curve of labour shifts upwards, negating the effect on employment of the previous upward shift of the demand curve, and unemployment moves back up to the natural rate of 5 per cent.

But though unemployment goes back to where it was, inflation does not. People have now experienced a 2 per cent annual inflation rate, and they are inclined to believe that it will continue at 2 per cent – just as previously the zero inflation rate led them to expect the continuation of a zero inflation rate. And because they expect inflation to be 2 per cent, it will be 2 per cent. So the economy will not move back down the Phillips curve to where it was before; it will move laterally to the right, to a new point of equilibrium at which unemployment is at the natural rate of 5 per cent and inflation is at 2 per cent. In short, one can say that the Phillips curve has moved upwards, in a north-easterly direction. And it has moved upwards in order to take account of the higher expected inflation rate. (Thus economists came to talk in the 1970s of the 'expectations-augmented' Phillips curve as a better guide to reality than the original, static,

Phillips curve.) The upward movement of the Phillips curve will of course continue if further attempts are made to reduce unemployment below the natural rate by administering further doses of fiscal or monetary expansion to the economy. By the same process outlined above, the inflation rate, whose starting point is now 2 per cent a year instead of zero, will rise further as unemployment is reduced and the economy moves up the new, higher, Phillips curve. People will adjust their expectations to this higher inflation rate, and so it will persist even after unemployment has returned to its natural rate. Only if unemployment moves *above* the natural rate, and stays there for some time, is there likely to be a reduction in the inflation rate.

This, then, is the story according to the monetarists. And the particular conclusion which emerges from it is that it is only in the short run that the Phillips curve is sloped as it is in the diagram on page 151. In the long run the Phillips curve is vertical. In the long run the economy can only be at the natural rate of unemployment. But the inflation rate associated with the natural rate of unemployment, though stable, will be at a level determined by past policy, and particularly by past increases in the money supply. If the money supply has been increased only in line with the growth of the economy's productive potential, the inflation rate will be zero. It is only if misguided attempts have been made to reduce unemployment below the natural rate that the stable inflation rate will be a positive and perhaps a high one.

THE ROLE OF GOVERNMENT

In the view of the monetarists, then, the government is able to influence *real* variables, such as output, employment and unemployment, only in the short run. (Indeed, there is one group of monetarists, known as the rational expectations theorists, who claim that the government cannot influence real variables even in the short run.) Attempts by Keynesian-inspired governments to maintain 'full employment', if this means trying to keep unemployment below the natural rate, will only result in accelerating inflation. In the long run the Phillips curve is vertical – meaning that the government can affect the rate of inflation by macroeconomic policy, but not the level of unemployment. And the rate of inflation will depend upon the rate of growth of the money supply. Thus as far as macroeconomic policy is concerned, the government should confine itself to balancing its own budget and ensuring that the country's money supply grows at a stable rate over time. If it does this, the economy will settle down at the natural rate of unemployment; growth will occur at whatever rate is permitted by increases in productivity and the labour force; and the inflation rate will be stable. If this stable inflation rate is itself regarded as too high, because of past mistakes, then the growth rate of the money supply should be progressively reduced so as to bring the inflation rate down to an acceptable level, perhaps even to zero, even if this means that for a while unemployment rises above the natural rate.

But what if following this monetarist prescription leaves unemployment unacceptably high? Can nothing be done about this? Certainly it can, say the monetarists. But the answer is not to try to reduce unemployment below the natural rate. The answer is to reduce the natural rate itself. And this calls not for macroeconomic policies, but for microeconomic policies – or what are sometimes called 'supply-side' measures. The supply-side measures that are needed are essentially measures to increase the flexibility of the labour market. Many monetarists consider that there was a marked reduction in the flexibility of the labour market in Britain between the early 1960s and the early 1970s, which explains why inflation accelerated after the late 1960s despite high and, indeed, rising rates of unemployment. In other words, there must have been a very substantial increase in the natural rate of unemployment. The reasons for this increase in the natural rate, they would argue, included a rise in tax rates; the introduction of redundancy payments and earnings-related unemployment benefits which cushioned the effect of unemployment; and, more generally, an increase in the power of the trade unions.

Measures to increase the flexibility of the labour market are likely to be controversial, in some cases highly so, since they not only encroach on some powerful vested interests, but are seen by many as an unforgivable attack on the Welfare State constructed during the war and early post-war years. This was particularly true of the steps taken by the Conservative government led by Mrs Thatcher, elected in 1979 and re-elected in 1983. Mr Heath had flirted with some monetarist ideas in 1970–72, and there was a fair dose of monetarism in the policies pursued in its later years by the 1974–9 Labour government. But Mrs Thatcher's government was the first to embrace monetarism wholeheartedly and pursue it consistently. Thus in addition to the macroeconomic measures designed to move the budget deficit down towards zero and to reduce the rate of growth of the money supply (which are discussed in the next chapter), the Thatcher government adopted a series of microeconomic or supply-side measures designed to increase the flexibility of the labour market and thus reduce the natural rate of unemployment. Much emphasis was put on reductions in taxation (which, particularly since the budget deficit was to be progressively reduced, required cuts in the level of public expenditure) so as to increase the proportion of a person's gross income left in his pocket and thus, it was supposed, his incentive to work. Correspondingly, a series of steps were taken to reduce the value of unemployment and supplementary benefits in relation to wages: earnings-related unemployment benefits were abolished, unemployment benefit itself became taxable, supplementary benefits were increased only in line with prices and not with earnings, and so on. The aim was to make unemployment more unpleasant, and thus to increase the incentive to find a job. On a different front, steps were taken to phase out the subsidies enjoyed by existing council-house tenants so as to eliminate the advantages to sitting tenants of staying put in a particular council house or flat, and thus increase the incentive for those in depressed areas to look for work in more prosperous parts of the country. (No corresponding steps were taken, as cynics observed, to phase out the housing subsidies which accrued mainly to the middle class in the form of tax relief on their mortgage interest payments.)

But the main target of the monetarists, and of Mrs Thatcher's government, was the so-called 'monopoly power' of the trade unions. The unions, the argument goes, insist on being paid real wages which are above the 'market-clearing' real wage, and on enforcing this insistence by such measures as the closed shop, which prevents the employment of non-union members who might be prepared to work for less; and, more generally, by the threat of strike action. The consequence is a high natural rate of unemployment. This is all right for the union members in employment, drawing an excessive real wage, but bad luck on those who are unemployed and unwilling – or not allowed by union closed-shop provisions – to work for the lower real wage which would make an employer willing to employ them. This problem can only be overcome by weakening the power of the trade unions, for example by outlawing the closed shop, reducing picketing, making secret strike ballots compulsory, and so on. In this way, real wages can fall and more people can be employed; in other words there will be a reduction in the natural rate of unemployment. Of course, not all the unemployed may wish to work for this lower real wage, even if the alternative is only a very modest level of state social security provision. But that is their problem; their unemployment is voluntary, and it is certainly not the job of the state to increase effective demand in order to provide them with jobs.

That, at any rate, is the monetarist view.

Chapter Nine

THE NEO-KEYNESIAN
RESPONSE

Just as there are many different versions of monetarism and a variety
of interpretations of what Keynes really meant, so also has there been
a wide range of responses by economists and policy-makers to the
monetarist case, as summarized in the last chapter. Some economists
became instant and permanent converts, as did many politicians of
conservative bent whose instincts seemed validated, and whose interests were often promoted, by the monetarist message. At the other
end of the spectrum were those who regarded monetarism as complete
nonsense, seeing nothing in it to make them relinquish an inch of the
ground that the Keynesian revolution had won. Forming a more
numerous group, perhaps, were those who initially embraced the new
doctrine with some enthusiasm but whose ardour waned as the pursuit
of monetarist policies in Britain and other countries led to the kind of
high and persistent unemployment that they had thought Keynesian
economics had banished for ever. Finally, there were those
who conceded that the monetarists were making one or two useful
points, and that Keynesian theory and policy-making should be
modified accordingly; but who considered that the basic thrust of
monetarism was thoroughly misconceived, and should be resolutely
resisted.

It is this last point of view that is reflected in the present chapter.
Two particular monetarist insights which seem illuminating are discussed; and it is acknowledged that mistakes were sometimes made in
the way that Keynesian policies were applied in Britain, notably in
the early 1970s. Nevertheless, the main burden of the argument is
that the monetarist theory of how the economy works is simply wrong;
that the policies derived from this theory are consequently misguided;
and that essentially Keynesian policies, though suitably amended to

take account of what we have learnt over the past twenty years and thus reasonably described as 'neo-Keynesian', are the right ones for a government to pursue.

FINE TUNING

One of the basic tenets of monetarism is that changes in the money supply have a predominant influence in determining changes in the money GDP (and not, as will be argued later in this chapter, the other way round); but that although, as Milton Friedman has put it, this is true 'over any considerable period of years', one cannot predict the relationship at all accurately 'month to month, quarter to quarter, or even year to year'.* The inference the monetarists draw from this, as we saw in the last chapter, is that the money supply should not be adjusted in a short-term way in an attempt to offset any fluctuations that might occur in the economy, since this is as likely to destabilize the economy as to stabilize it; it should, instead, be made to grow at a steady pace in line with the long-term growth of the economy's productive potential. Now, one may reject monetarism as a whole, but still accept that it is an important notion that there are unpredictable time-lags between a change in monetary policy (or for that matter fiscal or exchange-rate policy) and the effect of this on the relevant economic targets. The unease that this unpredictability aroused was particularly apposite in the case of the refinement of Keynesian macroeconomic policy that came to be known as 'fine tuning'.

Since the acceptance of Keynesian economics during the war, macroeconomic policy in Britain had consisted of forecasting the growth in the economy's productive potential over the next year or two; forecasting the likely change in effective demand over the same period; and using policy instruments to bring the second into line with the first. It was the forecasting of effective demand that was difficult (the growth in productive potential, in the short run at least, was fairly predictable), with such items as exports and private investment being particularly tricky. However, as time went on the fore-

* Evidence submitted to Congress in May 1959, and republished as 'Monetary Theory and Policy' in Ball and Doyle (eds.), *Inflation*, Penguin Books, London, 1969, pages 136 to 145.

casting process became more elaborate, and knowledge of how different policy instruments might affect different economic variables became more sophisticated. Confidence grew that the government had a pretty good idea of how to manage the economy.

But in due course confidence became over-confidence. The belief that the government could manage the economy in a rough-and-ready sort of way gave way to the belief that it could influence its development in a rather precise way. Some economists and civil servants came to believe that one could monitor the performance of the economy quarter by quarter and even month by month, and make minor adjustments in the settings of the instruments of policy in order to keep the economy on the desired course. As new figures became available on unemployment or production or retail sales, for example, small changes could be made in taxes, public expenditure, interest rates or hire-purchase regulations in order to keep the economy as a whole growing at the desired rate and, indeed, particular sectors of the economy behaving in the desired way. One does not want to overstress the point; nevertheless it is clear that during the 1960s and early 1970s the idea was fairly prevalent that the right approach to macroeconomic management was to make frequent adjustments to policy in order to keep the economy on course; in short, that the government could fine tune the economy in rather the way that a musician fine tunes his piano or violin.

For a number of reasons the analogy was false. One reason is the monetarist point mentioned above – that time-lags in the system are difficult to predict, and can be long. But there are other compelling reasons for questioning the validity of fine tuning as well. One is that it takes time to collect and process economic data. Some figures, such as the unemployment figures, become available within a week or two of the date to which they relate. Others, such as consumers' expenditure or private investment, become available only several months after the end of the period to which they refer. Worse still, many figures are subsequently revised, sometimes significantly, since there is a conflict between speed and accuracy, and if statistics were to be published only when accurate, the delays in publication would be even longer. Thus at any given moment, the government has only an imperfect idea of where the economy is or how it has recently been moving (as government forecasters put it, it is almost as difficult to forecast the past as to forecast the future). This uncertainty about what has been happening and where one is now must at least raise doubts about the wisdom of making frequent adjustments in policy instruments in order to keep the economy on course. The motoring and yachting metaphors much beloved of politicians and journalists in the 1960s ('a slight pressure on the brake', 'a touch on the tiller') were, in short, inappropriate.

There is another kind of uncertainty as well: the magnitude of the effect of a change in a policy instrument, as well as its timing, is often in question. Suppose, to take a simple example, that a government that believes in fine tuning is told by its forecasters that over the next year consumers' expenditure looks like growing by 1 per cent less than the government thinks desirable, and that simulations on the Treasury's economic model show that consumers' expenditure can be raised by 1 per cent by cutting value added tax by 2 percentage points (e.g. from 15 per cent to 13 per cent). Quite apart from the awkward possibility that the forecast itself may be wrong, the difficulty about the government making this small adjustment in taxation lies in the fact that the prediction that it will lead to a 1 per cent increase in consumption is simply the central point of a probability distribution, based on what has happened in the past. The actual increase in consumers' expenditure induced by a 2 percentage point cut in VAT could be considerably more than 1 per cent, or considerably less. An important influence on what actually happens (as monetarists would emphasize, in a way that Keynes himself would probably have approved) is people's expectations. If, for example, consumers for any reason expect the tax cut to be only temporary, they may increase their expenditure a lot. If, on the other hand, they interpret it as the government's response to a threatened recession they may react very cautiously, saving a bit more against a rainy day; their expenditure may not increase, and may even fall.

It should perhaps be mentioned in passing that the importance of people's expectations to what actually happens in the economy has been developed by one school of monetarists – the 'rational expecta-tions' theorists – to the point of absurdity represented by the so-called 'policy ineffectiveness proposition'. This states that no act of government policy can have any effect on any real economic variable because it will always have been fully anticipated by the actions of agents in the private sector of the economy who are all blessed with the possession of rational expectations. We shall not follow this school of thought any further into this fairy-tale other than to observe that it is hard to see how anyone could believe anything so far removed from the reality of the world we actually live in.

For present purposes the basic point is this. At any given time the government lacks precise knowledge both of where the economy is and where it is going, and of the size and timing of the effects of minor adjustments in the instruments of economic policy. In these circumstances it is unwise to tinker endlessly with the economy in an endeavour to keep it moving smoothly along some preordained path, since it may turn out that the government has been nudging it in the wrong direction.

The dangers of this kind of fine tuning are not just theoretical; they were graphically illustrated by British experience in the early 1970s. Faced in March 1971 by a sluggish economy and rising unemployment, the Conservative Chancellor of the Exchequer, Mr Barber, introduced a mildly expansionary Budget. Only four months later, further expansionary measures were taken on the grounds that unemployment was still rising, and that it was now estimated that real GDP in the first half of the year had been 1 per cent lower than had been assumed at the time of the Budget: in particular, purchase tax (the predecessor of VAT) was reduced by approximately 20 per cent, and all hire-purchase controls were abolished. But unemployment continued to rise, the forecasts suggesting that by the beginning of 1972 it would be close to 4 per cent, or what was regarded at the time as the politically suicidal figure of one million (which, indeed, turned out to be the case). And so, throughout the rest of 1971 and early 1972, further steps were taken to stimulate the economy: interest rates were reduced, bank lending to the private sector was encouraged, major increases in public expenditure were announced and, in the March 1972 Budget, there was a substantial cut in income tax.

The extent of the consensus on the desirability of fine tuning that existed at the time is illustrated by the fact that, with the exception of some monetarists, there was no criticism of these successive expansionary measures either from the Labour Opposition, or the economic establishment, or the serious press. If anything, Mr Barber was judged to have done too little, too late. Yet with hindsight the outcome does not seem very surprising. The effects of the earlier expansionary measures had not shown up at the time the later expansionary measures were decided upon; but they were in the pipeline. Before long, they all came crashing through, one on top of the other. The result was a very rapid rise in effective demand during 1972 and the early part of 1973, more rapid than British industry could cope with: between 1971 and 1973 total final expenditure, in real terms, rose by 12 per cent, but total output rose by only 8 per cent. In consequence, inflationary pressures increased sharply, imports rose much faster than exports, and by the early autumn of 1973 – before the first oil shock – the balance of payments had deteriorated to an alarming degree.

The episode which came to be known as 'the Barber boom' served to discredit the fine tuning approach to economic policy, and legitimately so. Unfortunately, it also strengthened the hand of those – mainly the monetarists – who argued that there should be *no* discretionary government intervention in the economy. This conclusion was not legitimate. We shall return to this issue later on. But before that something needs to be said about the second monetarist insight which has led to an important modification of the original Keynesian position.

'CONSTANT PRICES'

Keynes's *General Theory* and the macroeconomic policies which it inspired were essentially concerned with what is sometimes called the 'real' economy – the level of output and employment. Keynes's analysis said that if demand was deficient, actual output would be lower than potential output and unemployment would get stuck at an unnecessarily high level. Keynesian policy was thus a matter of maintaining enough demand in the economy to ensure that actual output was equal to potential output and that there was full employment. It was therefore natural for Keynesian policies to be conceived of 'in real terms'. If the growth in productivity and in the population of working age meant that the volume of output could rise by 3 per cent a year, then the object of policy was to ensure that effective demand, in real terms, rose by 3 per cent a year, so as to achieve maximum output and maintain full employment.

Provided that there is no inflation, i.e. that the overall price level is stable, this is perfectly straightforward: total expenditure, in money terms, must be kept rising at 3 per cent a year. But, as was noted in Chapter 7, there has not been a condition of zero inflation in Britain for half a century: retail prices have risen every year since 1935. With inflation, the situation becomes slightly more complicated. In money terms (and it is, after all, *money* that the government and businesses and families receive and spend), effective demand has to rise by 3 per cent *plus* the inflation rate if demand is to rise by 3 per cent in real terms. So, in managing the economy, the government needs to make a forecast of the inflation rate. If it reckons that the inflation rate during the coming year is going to be 4 per cent, for example, then it must ensure that, in money terms, effective demand rises by 7 per cent. In this way demand and output in real terms, or 'at constant prices', will rise by 3 per cent.

This is all right as long as the government forecasts the inflation rate correctly. But what happens if it gets it wrong? The interesting case (and, in the real world, the characteristic one) is where the inflation rate turns out to be higher than the government had allowed for. If the government is focusing exclusively on the growth of demand in *real* terms, it will react to a higher than expected inflation rate by increasing demand faster in money terms. Thus if inflation turns out to be, say, 6 per cent rather than 4 per cent, because of a rise in import prices or an unexpectedly big round of wage increases, or for some other reason, a government determined to keep demand in real terms rising at an annual rate of 3 per cent so as to maintain full employment will have to ensure that in money terms demand rises by 9 per cent. The trouble is that this will validate the higher inflation rate, and correspondingly raise inflationary expectations – as the monetarists pointed out. The process will be particularly striking in the public sector – which is very important, since in Britain and other Western European countries it typically accounts for 40 to 45 per cent of the GDP. Government departments and other public sector agencies will initially be provided with funds by the Treasury on the assumption of a 4 per cent inflation rate. If, however, the inflation rate is faster than this, and the pay of civil servants or nurses or teachers rises by more than was expected, the Treasury will have to provide extra funds if the real level of the output or services provided by the public sector is to grow in the way originally intended. One of the unfortunate consequences of this way of doing things, as Britain discovered to its cost in the mid-1970s, is that public sector bodies will have little or no incentive to resist large wage demands or exorbitant increases in the prices of inputs generally. Given that their output (and in many parts of the public sector, because of the difficulty of increasing productivity, this often means their input as well) is supposed to be rising by, say, 3 per cent, the Treasury will simply have to make available whatever extra funds are required to finance this higher level of wages or input prices. A more effective recipe for encouraging inflation would be difficult to imagine.

This, then, is the second useful insight which can be attributed to the monetarists: conducting macroeconomic policy in terms of constant prices – or what has been called 'funny money' – can only too easily encourage inflation and raise inflationary expectations. The need for neo-Keynesian policies to come to terms with this insight is taken up in the penultimate section of this chapter.

MONETARISM'S UNREAL ASSUMPTIONS

In the last two sections we have discussed two specific monetarist criticisms of the sort of Keynesian demand management that was practised in the 1960s and early 1970s, and indicated that these are valid criticisms and need to be taken on board by those who still believe in the Keynesian approach to macroeconomic policy. But, it is argued here, that is about as far as one should go in accepting the monetarist case. Some unreconstructed Keynesians would argue that even this position is too charitable to the monetarists, since the problems involved in fine tuning the economy, and thinking and acting in terms of constant prices rather than current prices, are not specifically monetarist concerns but have long been apparent to many Keynesians. This seems ungenerous, however, particularly as far as the second point is concerned. By concentrating, as they did, on the behaviour of economic variables in real terms or at constant prices, Keynesians failed to build into their models the consequences of expectations that there would be a *change* in the inflation rate. Monetarist models grasped this nettle of inflationary expectations, and accordingly provided a more illuminating account of an important part of the story.

But none of this alters the basic fact that monetarism is fatally flawed. The ultimate reason for this is that it starts from unreal assumptions about how the economy works. The most unreal assumption of all is the same assumption that underlay the classical economics of the nineteenth and early twentieth centuries, to which monetarism is in many respects a throwback. This is the assumption that the economy is self-stabilizing at full employment. Shocks of one sort or another may cause temporary fluctuations; but there are powerful forces at work within the economy which will, before long and of their own accord, lead to the restoration of full employment equilibrium. Thus no intervention by the government is called for; indeed such intervention is almost bound to destabilize the economy rather than stabilize it. That is the monetarist message.

It is one thing to construct an econometric model in which prices, wages and interest rates are all fully flexible, so that markets continually clear and full employment equilibrium is maintained or at any rate, after some external shock, rapidly restored. It is quite another thing to argue that such a model bears any resemblance to the real world. By and large, agents do not optimize and the crucial markets do not clear. A strong case could be made for saying that given the conflicting drives and emotions that characterize any individual, given the imperfect knowledge that attends most decision-making, given uncertainty about the future, and given the time it takes individuals and businesses to adapt to new developments, it is inconceivable that any human society could behave in the way postulated by monetarist theories. However, whether or not this is so is somewhat academic; the fact is that the world we actually inhabit is not like the world of monetarist models. The point was put succinctly by Keynes himself on the first page of the *General Theory* (he was talking of classical theory, but the point applies equally to its resurrected version, monetarism):

The characteristics of the special case assumed by the classical theory happen not to be those of the economic society in which we actually live, with the result that its teaching is misleading and disastrous if we attempt to apply it to the facts of experience.

Now it is of course conceivable that some creature newly arrived from outer space, knowing nothing of this planet or the ways of its inhabitants, might be unconvinced that the description of the economic system contained on the monetarists' computers was a thoroughly inaccurate one. For all he knows, the world does work like this. How to persuade him that this is not the case? A good starting-point would be to draw his attention to what has actually happened since monetarist policies were adopted.

Although there was a monetarist element in the economic policies of the 1974-9 Labour government, at least after 1975, it was only the election of Mrs Thatcher's Conservative government in 1979 that unleashed full-blooded monetarist policies on Britain. Keynesian demand management was completely abandoned. Instead, the budget deficit was to be brought steadily down to zero, or close to it, over a period of three or four years. This was seen as the main way of reducing the rate of growth of the money supply over the same three or four year period, until it was roughly in line with the economy's real rate of growth, thus ensuring – according to monetarist doctrine – the elimination of inflation. At the same time income tax was to be cut in order to increase incentives. In consequence – if the budget was to be balanced – there had to be big reductions in what was seen as the grossly excessive level of public expenditure. (Some of these public expenditure cuts would reduce the support available to the unemployed, and to strikers and their families; this would – following the argument set out in Chapter 8 – provide additional incentives to people to go to work, thus reducing the natural rate of unemployment.)

According to the monetarists, this set of policies would soon bring inflation down to a low rate but, given that the economy was basically self-stabilizing at full employment, would have no more than a temporary effect on the level of unemployment. This point of view was expressed very clearly by Milton Friedman himself. In a memorandum submitted to the House of Commons Treasury and Civil Service Committee in June 1980 he said, in support of the policies the Thatcher government was pursuing,

I conclude that (a) only a modest reduction in output and employment will be a side effect of reducing inflation to single figures by 1982, and (b) the effect on investment and the potential for future growth will be highly favourable.

It would be difficult to find an economic prediction that proved more comprehensively inaccurate. Inflation was indeed brought down to single figures by 1982 (though, as will be argued in a later section, this was not for the reasons adduced by the monetarists). But total output fell by $2\frac{1}{2}$ per cent in 1980, and another $1\frac{1}{2}$ per cent in 1981. Although there was then some recovery, in 1984 it was still only $3\frac{1}{2}$ per cent higher than it had been in 1979. Moreover, much of this recovery was accounted for by the rather special factor of rapidly rising North Sea oil production. Manufacturing output in 1984 was still 10 per cent *lower* than it had been in 1979. Much the same applies to investment. Total gross fixed investment fell in 1980 and 1981, and by 1984 had recovered to a level only 3 per cent higher than in 1979. For manufacturing investment – closely related, one might think, to the future growth Friedman referred to – the effect of monetarist policies was catastrophic. In 1984 manufacturing investment was 30 per cent lower than in 1979. Indeed, this was the third or fourth successive year in which *net* manufacturing investment was negative: in other words, gross investment was insufficient to make good depreciation, so that the size of the capital stock in manufacturing was shrinking.

As if all this were not bad enough, unemployment, which had been around 1·3 million or 5 per cent of the labour force in 1979 (the lowest it had been since 1975), rose and went on rising. Six years later it was still rising: in the middle of 1985 it was around 3·2 million, or 13 per cent of the labour force (and would have been even higher but for a change in the method of measuring unemployment in 1983). So much – the visitor from another planet could reasonably be told – for the monetarist assumption of an economy which stabilizes itself at full employment.

But – our visitor might, if well informed, riposte – how does this denunciation of monetarism square with the experience of the United States over the same period? The American central bank (the independent Federal Reserve Board) adopted fairly hardline monetarist policies in October 1979, and this was followed a year later by the election of the most conservative and monetarist-inclined president for fifty years. Yet total American output, though it fell by 2 per cent in 1982, rose by more than 10 per cent between 1982 and 1984. Unemployment in the US, though it rose sharply from mid-1981 onwards, peaked at around 10 per cent of the labour force at the end of 1982 and then started to fall. By the middle of 1985 it had come down to about 7 per cent, or half the British level. At the same time, the inflation rate was brought down from around 12 per cent in 1980 to around 4 to 5 per cent five years later. Is this not a vindication of monetarist policies?

Ironically enough, it is nothing of the kind; it is a vindication of *Keynesian* policies. For, whatever he said he was doing (or, indeed, thought he was doing), President Reagan, inheriting the recession promoted by the second, 1979–80 oil shock, adopted thorough-going Keynesian policies. Taxes were reduced by a very substantial amount, particularly those on the better-off; and a large acceleration of military expenditures was embarked upon. Although other kinds of public expenditure were cut back, the net effect was a large fiscal stimulus, which raised the budget deficit between 1980 and 1985 from around $60 billion, or 2 per cent of the GDP, to around $200 billion, or 5 per cent of the GDP. This Keynesian expansion had a massive effect in increasing employment and reducing unemployment. The fact that it was accompanied by a significant fall in the inflation rate was partly a tribute to the flexibility of the American labour market (something that Conservative governments in Britain and other European countries look at wistfully, without knowing quite how to emulate), but was also a consequence of the combination of a loose fiscal policy and a tight monetary policy. This led to very high real rates of interest, which in turn led to a large inflow of capital into the US from abroad. This capital inflow both financed the budget deficit and had the effect of inducing an enormous rise in the value of the dollar. The rise in the dollar in turn reduced American import prices and thus helped to bring down the inflation rate.

This section might be summarized as follows. Monetarist assumptions bear little relation to reality. To assume in 1986 that the economy is self-stabilizing at full employment is as absurd as it was in 1936. To argue that any unemployment that exists must therefore be voluntary is equally nonsensical. Monetarist policies can create a high level of involuntary unemployment; in Britain, between 1979 and 1985, they did so. Keynesian policies can create rising output and falling unemployment; in the United States, between 1982 and 1985, they did so.

THE NATURAL RATE AND THE NAIRU

If, on both theoretical and empirical grounds, one rejects the notion that the economy is self-stabilizing at full employment, one is bound to reject also the monetarist concept of the natural rate of unemployment. For the natural rate of unemployment is the rate that emerges when the economy has settled at its equilibrium point, at which the supply of labour is equal to the demand for labour at the existing real wage rate and the actual rate of inflation is equal to the expected rate of inflation. At this point of equilibrium, as was explained in Chapter 8, there is full employment in the sense that everyone who wants a job at the real wage rate established in the market will have a job; or, to put it the other way round, there will be no 'involuntary' unemployment. If, however, one takes the Keynesian view that there are no good theoretical reasons for supposing the economy to be self-stabilizing at full employment in this way, and that the whole idea is in any case abundantly contradicted by experience, then the concept of a unique natural rate of unemployment ceases to have any meaning. The plain fact is that the economy can settle for long periods of time at any one of a wide range of unemployment rates, depending on the level of effective demand.

There is, however, one feature of the natural rate of unemployment concept which has commended itself to some Keynesians. This is the idea that there is some rate of unemployment at which the inflation rate is stable. In any given economy at any given time, it is postulated, there is a unique non-accelerating inflation rate of unemployment or, to use its ugly acronym, NAIRU. If unemployment is below the NAIRU, the inflation rate will rise; if unemployment is above it, the inflation rate will fall. If one seeks a stable inflation rate, one must ensure that unemployment is equal to the NAIRU. But – and this is the crucial difference between these Keynesians and the monetarists – the government must do this by influencing the level of effective demand, since there are no powerful self-equilibrating forces in the economy that will automatically bring unemployment into line with the NAIRU.

Other neo-Keynesians do not find the NAIRU a particularly helpful concept. Estimates of what the NAIRU actually is, in numerical terms, vary so much over time and between different studies that it is of little practical use. While conceding that inflation is more likely to accelerate if unemployment is low than if it is high, these Keynesians see no reason to suppose that there is some unique unemployment rate at which inflation will be stable. The inflation rate during any given period is determined by many factors, of which the unemployment rate (or, perhaps more usefully, the *change* in the unemployment rate) is only one. Others include changes in import prices, the outcome of particular industrial disputes, shifts in government priorities and political developments generally. The NAIRU, they believe, is as much of a chimera as the original Phillips curve.

However, the operational significance of this difference of view is not very great. Most neo-Keynesians would agree that if an economy is to achieve a low level of unemployment and a stable rate of inflation, demand management, though essential, is not by itself enough. 'Supply-side' policies, such as more training and re-training of the labour force, are needed as well; and so, almost certainly, is some kind of incomes policy (an issue discussed in the final section of this chapter). Whether, like some neo-Keynesians, one thinks of such measures as being ways of reducing the NAIRU or whether, like others, one simply sees them as necessary in their own right, is a somewhat academic point.

REDUCING THE REAL WAGE

We saw in Chapter 8 that an important strand in monetarist thinking is that unemployment is the consequence of workers refusing to work for the real wage rate established in the market. If workers reduced their supply price – i.e. offered to work for lower real wages – they would find employment. For a fall in the price of labour will increase the demand for labour just as a fall in the price of apples will increase the demand for apples. In short, for unemployment to fall, all that is needed is for workers to accept a cut in the real wage. So the argument runs.

Although the argument may have a certain intuitive plausibility, the truth is not so straightforward. The issue of the relationship between real wages and unemployment is surrounded by controversy. One reason for this is that the matter arouses strong passions. The price of labour is not quite the same thing as the price of apples; it represents, viewed from another angle, the money on which a worker and his family have to live. Since it is the lower-paid workers who suffer most from unemployment – those who lack skills, or who possess skills no longer in demand – talking of reducing real wages in order to bring down unemployment is to talk of reducing even further the living standards of people in the poorest 10 or 20 per cent of the population. Moreover, the devices which monetarist-inclined governments may adopt in order to persuade people to work for lower real wages can also be highly contentious. Reducing income tax or employees' social security contributions, so that employers can pay lower wages to unskilled workers without these workers' take-home pay being affected, is one thing. It is quite another thing to adopt a series of measures, as the Thatcher government did, to reduce the real value of the social security benefits received by the unemployed. To monetarists who think that the unemployed are making a cool calculation about the advantages of being out of work rather than in work, this may seem reasonable. But to those who do not believe that most unemployment is voluntary, it represents an inexcusable attack on the living standards of people who are already poor through no fault of their own.

Whatever the emotions aroused by this issue, it is at an intellectual level that it must be resolved. And it is clear that the idea that unemployment is caused by excessive real wages, and that real wages must be reduced if unemployment is to fall, is open to challenge along a number of different lines. It is a measure of the extent to which monetarism represents a resurrection of the fallacies of classical economics that some of these lines of argument amount to little more than a restatement of some of the points made by Keynes in the *General Theory*, and discussed in Part One. But there are other arguments as well.

First of all, as was pointed out above, wages, although a cost to the employer, represent income to the employee. A cut in real wages is therefore likely to reduce workers' consumption and, via the Multiplier mechanism discussed in Part One, the incomes and consumption of other workers. Thus there will be a fall in the output of the economy and a rise, not a fall, in unemployment. (To put it slightly more technically, the downward shift in the supply curve of labour represented by the cut in real wages may be offset, or more than offset, by a downward shift in the demand curve for labour, leaving the level of employment unchanged, or even lower than it was before.) With Keynesian techniques of demand management this adverse effect on incomes and employment could of course be counteracted by tax cuts or increases in public expenditure. But, as we have seen, monetarists reject the need for demand management, and argue that wage cuts will *in themselves* lead to a rise in employment. The reason why this should be so is very difficult to discern.

There is, it should be noted in passing, one case where it can be said that real wages are too high, and that if they are reduced there will be a rise in employment. This is where there is an open economy with an overvalued exchange rate. At this exchange rate, exports are uncompetitive and imports are only too competitive with home-made goods. The country is asking too much for its products, and the result is unemployment in export industries, and in the industries that compete with imports. One answer to this is for the country to reduce, or try to reduce, its prices and money wages. A more intelligent approach is to change the exchange rate by devaluing the currency, as Keynes pointed out at the time of the gold standard controversy in the mid 1920s. This will have the effect of reducing real wages, restoring the country's competitiveness both in export markets and in the home market, and will thus lead to an increase in output and employment.

However this is not the case the monetarists have in mind. Very little of the increase in employment which their models predict will follow a reduction in real wages comes via this route; or, to put it another way, they believe the effect will work nearly as powerfully in a closed economy as in an open one. And the reasons for this remain obscure.

Secondly – a point that Keynes was particularly at pains to establish in the *General Theory* (see pages 110–113 above) – even if one were to accept on trust the classical or monetarist view that a cut in the real wage would lead to a fall in unemployment, it would remain unclear how workers are supposed to achieve this real wage cut or, to put it in the phrase fashionable in the mid-1980s, 'price themselves into jobs'. Real wages are determined only in part by money wages; the other determinant is prices, and workers have no control over prices. If all workers voluntarily accepted a 10 per cent cut in *money* wages, there is no guarantee that *real* wages would fall by 10 per cent, or indeed at all. There is much evidence to suggest that many prices are based on a standard percentage mark-up on some normal level of unit costs, of which labour costs are usually the most important component. So a 10 per cent reduction in money wages could in principle lead to a 10 per cent cut in prices, leaving real wages unchanged. Moreover, even if one conceded that a 10 per cent reduction in money wages would in practice lead to some reduction in real wages, there is the commonsense question of how such a cut in money wages might be achieved. Are workers who have jobs to demand of their employers on a Monday morning that their wages be reduced by 10 per cent so that some of those without jobs can be taken on to the payroll? No doubt it is not impossible; but it is not a scenario that stuns one with its realism.

Thirdly, there is the troublesome fact that in many industries there are increasing, not decreasing, returns to scale: in other words, as output and employment increase, labour productivity rises and unit costs fall. This fact has some awkward implications for much conventional economic theory; in particular it means that as the economy expands and unemployment falls from, say, 10 per cent to 5 per cent, real wages must rise, not fall. (As we noted in Chapter 5, Keynes did not incorporate this insight into the *General Theory*, but highlighted it in an article in the *Economic Journal* in 1939.) If it is true that real wages will rise as unemployment falls, to postulate, as the monetarists do, that it is necessary to reduce real wages in order to reduce unemployment would seem to be startlingly perverse.

Finally, there is some evidence about what actually happened when unemployment in Britain started its big rise early in 1980, and in particular what happened to different groups of workers. Between 1979 and 1983 the real earnings of adult male manual workers rose by 10 per cent, while the employment of these manual workers fell by 8 per cent. The real earnings of non-manual workers, on the other hand, rose by 19 per cent – but employment of these workers *rose* by 12 per cent. Even more striking is what happened at the top and bottom of the earnings scale. The real hourly earnings of the top 10 per cent of adult male earners (among whom unemployment is very low) rose by 19 per cent between 1979 and 1984. The real hourly earnings of the bottom 10 per cent, which suffered heavily from the rise in unemployment during these five years, actually fell slightly over the period. Thus it is very hard to believe that what happens to real wages determines what happens to employment. The correct inference is surely that the demand for labour determines employment *and* real wages. Over the four or five years after 1979, groups of workers whose services were in demand suffered little unemployment, and enjoyed rising real wages. Groups of workers whose services were not in demand suffered heavy unemployment, and found it difficult to maintain, let alone increase, their real wage.

The moral of these figures, then, is that if unemployment is to be reduced among low-paid manual workers, the demand for their labour must be increased. One way of doing this (a crucially important 'supply-side' measure) is to train or re-train them in skills that are in demand. Another, more controversial, measure is to reduce or eliminate employers' social security contributions for the low paid, thus making them more attractive to employ without reducing the take-home pay of the workers themselves. But the basic answer is the Keynesian one: to increase effective demand. This will raise employment and reduce unemployment. It may or may not lead to a fall in real wages, depending on the shape of the average cost curve. But any such fall in the real wage will be the effect, not the cause, of the rise in employment. As Keynes himself put it,

> The propensity to consume and the rate of new investment determine between them the volume of employment, and the volume of employment is uniquely related to a given level of real wages – not the other way round.*

THE MONEY SUPPLY AND INFLATION

As we saw in Chapter 8, monetarists believe that changes in the money supply determine changes in money GDP. In terms of the Quantity Equation, where $MV = PQ$, it is the left-hand side of the equation that determines the right-hand side; and because the velocity of circulation of money is fairly stable, and the trend rate of growth of output or real GDP pretty slow and predictable, the important point is that the rate of growth of the money supply determines what happens to prices. In Britain, where the underlying growth of real

* *General Theory*, page 30.

total output may be about 3 per cent a year, keeping the money supply growing by 3 per cent a year will ensure a zero inflation rate.

Keynesians regard this account of the causes and cure of inflation as highly questionable, if not downright incorrect. In the long run, there may well be a broad correlation between movements in the money supply and movements in the price level. In the short and medium run, however, this relationship is not nearly so clear, due in particular to the fact that the velocity of circulation can in practice be distinctly volatile. Much more important is the question of how far it is changes in the money supply that determine changes in the price level, and how far it is the other way round. There probably are times when changes in the money supply cause changes in the price level. In the course of the sixteenth century, for example, the price level in Britain quintupled – a much faster rate of growth than experienced over any other sustained period of time until after the Second World War, and more specifically after 1970. It seems highly likely, at a time when money consisted of gold and silver coinage, that this reflected the large influx of gold and silver into Western Europe that followed Columbus's discovery of the New World in 1492, so that in a real and direct sense a rise in the money supply caused rising prices. But even here there is some room for doubt. Some historians argue that a more important factor behind rising prices in the sixteenth century was that the population was growing more rapidly than the food supply.

Whatever may have happened in the sixteenth century, monetarists have found it very difficult to demonstrate convincingly that it is changes in the money supply that cause changes in prices – or, more generally, the money GDP – and not the other way round. Arguably the most important single event behind the growth of monetarist ideas from around the mid-1960s onward was the publication in 1963 of a vast tome by Milton Friedman and Anna Schwartz which was supposed to show the crucial importance of the behaviour of the money supply in explaining what had happened in the United States over the previous century.* Yet what appears to be the concluding summary of the book (on page 695) reads as follows:

Changes in the money stock are therefore a consequence as well as an

* Milton Friedman and Anna Schwartz, *A Monetary History of the United States, 1867–1960*, Princeton University Press, 1963.

independent source of change in money income and prices. Mutual inter-action, but with money rather clearly the senior partner in longer-run move-ments and in major cyclical movements, and more nearly an equal partner with money income and prices in shorter-run and milder movements – this is the generalization suggested by our evidence.

More nearly an equal partner? Generalization suggested by the evidence? It is little short of extraordinary that such a qualified and tentative finding should have become the basis of the widespread assertion that changes in the money supply determine money incomes and prices, rather than the other way round. And some Keynesians would argue that the detailed statistical tables in the book do not in fact bear out even such a qualified and tentative finding as this.

The plain fact is that in a modern economy money does not consist – to more than a very limited extent – of notes and coins (let alone gold or silver coins) that are printed or minted by the government or central bank. Money consists mainly of bank deposits, and these deposits are the consequence of credit creation by the commercial banks, which are profit-making institutions. If a bank grants a firm a loan, or provides an individual with an overdraft, it does so in order to make a profit; and by doing so, it creates money. Of course it must not over-extend itself, and it will take care (or be required by law) to keep its deposits to a figure no greater than, say, five times its reserves, as represented by its holdings of cash and its deposits with the central bank. Nevertheless, the basic point is that banks create money in order to satisfy their customers' demand for it. In other words, the supply of money is determined by the demand for money or – to put it technically – the money supply is endogenous, not exogenous. Viewed from this angle, it can be seen that it is not changes in the money supply that *cause* changes in money GDP or prices. It is changes in money GDP or prices that *cause* changes in the money supply. A big rise in prices or money wages, for example, will increase the demand for money, and this increased demand will lead to increased supply. In terms of the Quantity Equation, P rises, and this causes a rise in M.

Although this, Keynesians believe, is the essence of the matter, the argument should not be taken to extremes. It would certainly not be true to suggest that the central bank has no control over the money supply. As we have noted, the commercial banks are constrained in their deposit-creating activities by the need to maintain a certain ratio of reserves to deposits, and these reserves, consisting of cash and deposits with the central bank (and also known as 'the monetary base'), are ultimately controlled by the central bank. But controlling the money supply by controlling the monetary base is not as simple as it sounds. It could lead to (and in the United States, during the period after October 1979 when the technique was rigorously used, did lead to) very big fluctuations in interest rates. Taken to extremes, moreover, monetary base control would require the central bank to refuse to supply liquidity to the banking system – in other words to refuse to act as lender of last resort; and this would undermine the foundations on which the entire financial system rests. In practice, therefore, governments and central banks control the money supply indirectly, by influencing the demand for money. At any given level of the money GDP, the demand for money will be determined by the level and structure of interest rates, and it is in the skilful manipulation of interest rates that the heart of monetary policy is to be found. To a much greater extent than even Keynes conceded in the *General Theory* (despite his great practical knowledge of the workings of financial markets) the money supply is not under the control of the government or central bank. It is essentially endogenous, not exogenous.

The moral of all this is that one cannot slow down or stop inflation by controlling the money supply. One has to operate on the inflation rate directly. How this is to be done is discussed in the next section. But before going on to consider this question, it may be useful to give some brief consideration to British experience after 1979. For it might reasonably be objected to the argument set out above that Mrs Thatcher's Conservative government did pursue monetarist policies after its election in 1979, and the inflation rate did fall dramatically. Was the one factor not the cause of the other?

It is necessary, first of all, to get the facts straight. The inflation rate (as measured by the percentage increase in the retail price index over the previous twelve months) had reached 26 per cent in June 1975, as a result of the first oil shock and of very large wage increases in 1974. The Labour government of the day, taking fright at the prospect of inflation accelerating out of control, introduced a tough incomes policy which, together with fairly tight fiscal and monetary policies, had brought the inflation rate down to 8 per cent in May

1979, when Mrs Thatcher assumed office. By the summer of 1980, however, the inflation rate had risen to 22 per cent – not far short of the mid-1975 figure. The factors behind this steep rise were similar to those on the previous occasion: the second, 1979–80, oil shock and big wage increases in 1979, though some 4 per cent of the 22 per cent rise was a direct result of the new Conservative government's decision to double the rate of Value Added Tax. Thus the fact that under the Thatcher government the inflation rate had come down to about 5 per cent by 1984 should be kept in perspective: it was not very different from what had happened under the Labour government between 1975 and 1979.

The basic point, however, is that the fall in the inflation rate in Britain in the early 1980s owed little to the success of monetarist policies. For one thing, the government found it much more difficult to control the growth of the money supply than it had expected, for the reasons discussed above. During 1980 and 1981, for example, the money supply, as represented by the government's favourite measure, 'sterling M3', rose at an annual rate of about 17 per cent – far above what had been intended. But even more interesting is the fact that these comparatively large increases in the money supply had a quite different effect on prices from that predicted by monetarist theory. Despite their talk of 'long and variable time-lags', many monetarists have a rough and ready rule of thumb, deriving originally from Friedman himself, according to which increases in the money supply affect prices after a two-year time-lag. Allowing for an underlying growth rate of the British economy of about 3 per cent, this should have meant an annual inflation rate in 1982 and 1983 of around 15 per cent. In fact, the inflation rate during these two years averaged barely 5 per cent.

There were two reasons for the steep decline in the inflation rate from the peak reached in 1980. One was the rapid and sustained rise in unemployment that began early in 1980 and was still continuing five years later. As we saw earlier, this rise in unemployment, from about 5 per cent of the labour force to over 13 per cent, had not been foreshadowed by the monetarists, and was certainly not anticipated by the government. But it undoubtedly had a major effect in restraining wage increases. At a time of rising unemployment and growing numbers of bankruptcies, workers are cautious about demanding big wage increases, and employers very reluctant to concede them.

The second reason for the fall in the inflation rate was the effect on international commodity prices of the world recession which followed the 1979–80 oil shock. Between 1980 and 1982 world commodity prices fell by 20 to 30 per cent, to their lowest level, in real terms, for more than thirty years. This led to a sharp fall in Britain's import prices, measured in sterling terms, and was thus a significant factor in reducing the domestic inflation rate.

Of their very nature, however, neither rising unemployment nor falling commodity prices can go on for ever. It was apparent that when unemployment stopped rising and started to fall, and when commodity prices stopped falling and started to rise, these two favourable effects on inflation would go into reverse, and the factors making for accelerating inflation – even at an unemployment rate of 10 per cent or more – would become increasingly powerful. In these circumstances, attempts to keep the inflation rate down simply by controlling the money supply would prove futile.

THE NEO-KEYNESIAN WAY AHEAD

The most fundamental argument in this chapter is that the economy is not, as monetarists believe, self-stabilizing at full employment. In a modern economy there are, to be sure, the so-called 'built-in stabilizers': a progressive income tax structure dampens the effects on demand when the economy expands rapidly, and unemployment benefits cushion the impact of a recession. But this is not enough. The government needs to engage in discretionary intervention in the economy if these fluctuations in demand are to be minimized, and if, in particular, effective demand is not to get stuck at too low a level, leading to a high rate of unemployment which may persist for many years.

It was conceded earlier in this chapter that the kind of fine tuning in which governments engaged in the 1960s and early 1970s was over-ambitious, given the limitations on our knowledge of where the economy is heading at any given moment, and how the instruments of economic policy affect the target variables. But it would be quite wrong, in rejecting fine tuning, to go to the opposite extreme and embrace the monetarist view that all a government ought to do is to balance the Budget and maintain a steady growth of the money supply. The economy does need to be managed: effective demand needs to be monitored and influenced by the government in order to ensure that it is neither deficient nor excessive. The frequency with which adjustments should be made is ultimately a matter of judgement. The main stock-taking exercise in the British economy is conducted once a year, at the time of the Budget in March or April. At that time the Chancellor of the Exchequer announces changes in taxation for the coming financial year (changes in public expenditure are often, somewhat illogically, announced a month or two earlier). Once a year is probably about right, as a general rule, for significant changes in the instruments of economic policy, though this should not preclude more frequent adjustments when it becomes clear that the assumptions underlying the last Budget were wrong, or when major unexpected developments such as an oil shock occur. It would be foolish, in such circumstances, for the government to wait woodenly until the next Budget before reacting. At the same time, the converse of this point needs to be stressed: a government should make clear (as the 1964–70 Labour government did in its – admittedly ill-fated – National Plan, published in 1965, and as Mrs Thatcher's government did – however perversely – in its Medium-Term Financial Strategy, published in 1980) what its key economic objectives are for the next three or four years. Changes made in the Budget, or between Budgets, should be designed to keep the economy moving along this planned course, or should represent a reasoned response to unexpected developments; they should not be seen as arbitrary changes with little rhyme or reason to them. The desirability of firms and individuals having a fairly clear idea of the government's economic priorities is, perhaps, the one practical point to emerge from the literature on rational expectations. But the essential fact remains: the economy cannot be relied on to follow the right course by itself – it needs to be managed by intelligent Keynesian policies.

Such policies need to take account also of the second monetarist criticism which was acknowledged earlier in this chapter to be a useful one. This was that by focusing very largely on what was happening to the real GDP, or GDP at constant prices, the Keynesian policies of the 1960s and early 1970s tended to validate inflation and increase inflationary expectations. Clearly, this fault must be corrected. But, as in the case of fine tuning, recognition that mistakes were made in the past does not mean that in the future one should go to the opposite extreme. To conduct economic policy solely in terms of money or nominal GDP (GDP at current prices) would be as bad, or worse. It would beg the whole question of what was happening to the real GDP, and hence to output, employment, unemployment and living standards. Of course, if the inflation rate stayed at a low and stable rate, focusing solely on nominal GDP would be perfectly all right. But in these circumstances it would also be perfectly all right to focus solely on real GDP.

The point can be illustrated by what happened to public expenditure (which accounts for some 40 per cent of the GDP) after the Conservatives took office in 1979. To remedy the disastrous effects of planning public expenditure in terms of constant prices in the way described earlier in the chapter, the 1974–9 Labour government had introduced a system of 'cash limits', which made it much more difficult for government departments and other public sector bodies to claim extra cash from the Treasury if the inflation rate turned out higher than expected. The new Conservative government not only tightened up this system, but before long was planning and controlling public expenditure purely in cash terms. This was all very well if the inflation rate was correctly predicted, but if it was underestimated – as was usually the case – the effect was inevitably that the volume of public expenditure, or expenditure in real terms, was less than had been intended or desired. Because public authorities' current expenditure is difficult to cut in real terms, at any rate in the short run, most of the brunt was borne by capital expenditure. Capital expenditure was in consequence cut back in a wholly unplanned and irrational way. By the mid-1980s, the damaging effects on the country's basic infrastructure – the housing stock, the schools and hospitals, the roads and sewers – were increasingly in evidence.

What was needed, then, was a middle way: a method of managing the economy which avoided equally the pitfalls of looking at the economy only in real terms and the dangers of looking at it only in money terms. And by the mid-1980s what might be called a neo-Keynesian consensus on this issue was beginning to emerge. The essence of this consensus can be simply stated. It was that the government should use all the conventional instruments of economic policy (fiscal policy, monetary policy and, perhaps, exchange rate policy) to achieve a chosen rate of growth of *nominal* GDP, while using other weapons to ensure that as much as possible of the annual rise in nominal GDP took the form of a rise in output, and as little as possible took the form of a rise in prices.

Suppose, for example, that the inflation rate is 5 per cent, that un-employment is at a satisfactory level, and that the productive potential of the economy is reckoned to be growing by 3 per cent a year. The aim of policy would then be to keep nominal GDP growing at a rate of 8 per cent a year. As long as the inflation rate remains at 5 per cent, all is well: total output, or real GDP, grows by 3 per cent a year, and unemployment neither rises nor falls. Now suppose that, for whatever reason, the inflation rate rises to 7 per cent. As we saw earlier, Keynesian governments in the 1960s and early 1970s would have responded to this by raising the growth of total money demand, or nominal GDP, to 10 per cent a year, so as to ensure that real GDP still grew by 3 per cent and unemployment remained unchanged. But this would have validated the rise in the inflation rate, and encouraged it to rise further. The neo-Keynesian response would be different: the rise in nominal GDP would remain at 8 per cent. In consequence, the rise in output would be cut back to an annual rate of only 1 per cent, and unemployment would rise; but by the same token no en-couragement would be given to inflation.

One can envisage more sophisticated examples of the neo-Keynesian approach. If, for instance, as in the mid-1980s, there is a high level of unemployment and a good deal of unused capacity in the economy, it should be possible to expand output by 4 or 5 per cent a year for a number of years, even if the underlying growth rate is only 3 per cent. In this case, again assuming an initial inflation rate of 5 per cent, nominal GDP would be expanded by 9 or 10 per cent for a number of years, and only after that brought down to 8 per cent. A rather trickier situation arises when it is the inflation rate, rather than the unemployment rate, that is too high. If inflation is running at 10 per cent, and the aim is to bring it down to 5 per cent over two or three years, then the annual growth of nominal GDP must be brought down from 13 per cent to 8 per cent over two or three years. Trickiest of all, of course, is a situation in which initially both unemployment and inflation are too high. The arithmetic is simple enough: the growth of nominal GDP would start off high, but would have to be brought down fast to a figure of 8 per cent over a period of a few years. In real life the difficulties would be formidable: better not to get into a situation of simultaneous high unemployment and high inflation in the first place.

Let us, however, focus on the simple case discussed above, where unemployment is satisfactory, inflation stable at 5 per cent, and the government keeps nominal GDP rising at 8 per cent a year. The main advantage of this way of managing the economy, compared with the conventional Keynesian way, is clear: it would be a powerful factor preventing inflation from accelerating. With nominal GDP as the target, if the inflation rate rises the growth of output will automatically slow down and unemployment will increase; and to some extent this will discourage inflationary forces. Even more important, perhaps, is that a ceiling will be put on inflation. If the rate of growth of output falls to zero, inflation will still be only 8 per cent. Even if output falls by 2 per cent a year, inflation will not go above 10 per cent as long as the growth of nominal GDP is not allowed to rise above 8 per cent; and it is hard to envisage total output being allowed to fall by 2 per cent a year for very long.

This, however, brings us to the nub of the matter. If inflationary forces are so strong that the 8 per cent growth of nominal GDP can only be stuck to at the cost of a large and sustained fall in output, and consequently high and rising unemployment, then the whole policy may collapse. The growth of nominal GDP will accelerate, and so will inflation. If this is to be avoided, a requirement of the neo-Keynesian approach is that some other factor be invoked to discourage inflationary wage and price increases. The rational expectations school of monetarists would deny the necessity for this, arguing that if people were convinced that the government was going to stick to an 8 per cent annual growth in nominal GDP, then this is what would happen: a 3 per cent growth in real GDP would be combined with a 5 per cent inflation rate, since this is the most rational outcome on offer. Unfortunately, the world does not work like that. The Conservatives came into office in 1979 with a closely related point of view: that since everyone believed in the government's policy of steadily reducing the rate of the growth of the money supply, their wage claims and price-setting behaviour would be consistent with a decline in the inflation rate, over the four-year period of the Medium-Term Financial Strategy, to approximately zero. That would be the rational thing to happen, and so it would happen. This notion was trebly misconceived. First, most people neither knew nor cared what was happening to the money supply. Secondly, even if they had both known and cared, many would probably not have believed (and, as we have seen, with good reason) that the government would achieve its targets. Thirdly, even if they had known, cared and believed, there is no reason to suppose that this would have affected individual behaviour. Even if it is in the interests of society as a whole for average pay increases to be no greater than average productivity increases, so that the inflation rate is zero, it remains in the interests of the individual or group to secure the biggest pay increase possible. And what all this boils down to is that keeping nominal GDP growing by 8 per cent a year is not, by itself, going to be enough. An essential requirement of the neo-Keynesian approach to economic policy is an incomes policy.

Keynesians have long attached importance to incomes policies. The 1944 White Paper on Employment Policy, written under Keynes's influence, had stressed the difficulty of trying to combine full employment, stable prices and free collective bargaining; and a year earlier Joan Robinson, one of Keynes's closest colleagues, had written that if such free wage bargaining was continued in conditions of full employment 'the vicious spiral of wages and prices might become chronic'.* With the exception of the Thatcher government elected in 1979, every single British government since the war has sooner or later, however reluctantly, recognized the logic of the dilemma and introduced an incomes policy. Even the Thatcher government is less an exception than it may appear: not only did it impose the most stringent restrictions on pay increases in the public sector, but it soon abandoned its initial idea that it did not matter what happened to pay increases in the private sector provided that the money supply was controlled, and before long was calling for wage restraint in the private sector just like all its predecessors.

* Article in *The Times*, 23 January 1943.

The degree of success achieved by all these post-war incomes policies is controversial. Some observers regard the Labour government's 1975–9 incomes policy, for example, as a major success: as we saw earlier, it brought the inflation rate down from 26 per cent to 8 per cent without significantly increasing the level of unemployment. Others cite the way the policy broke down in the 'winter of discontent' of 1978–9 as an inevitable consequence of the strains that had developed within the policy, rather than simply the result of bad luck or clumsy handling. Much the same points are made in arguments about earlier incomes policies. Without entering into this controversy, three considerations should perhaps be stressed.

First, past incomes policies have nearly always been introduced as a crisis response to acute balance of payments or inflationary difficulties. They have thus been perceived as a short-term measure, which people are prepared to put up with for the time being, but not for long. As time goes on, people become increasingly fed up and increasingly ready to kick over the traces. What is envisaged as part of a neo-Keynesian economic strategy, on the other hand, is a long-term policy that would become a permanent feature of economic life.

Secondly, until 1979 it was possible to criticize incomes policies for the distortions and rigidities they introduced into the workings of a mixed economy, without appreciating that the welfare losses occasioned by these distortions might be small compared with the welfare losses involved in not having an incomes policy. Since 1979 this argument has been much more difficult to sustain. The costs (in terms of lost output and high unemployment) of keeping inflation at a low and stable rate without an incomes policy have been apparent for all to see. The result may be a greater willingness to cooperate in an incomes policy in the future than was the case in the 1960s and 1970s.

Thirdly, an incomes policy is not, as so many people in Britain still seem to imagine, some sort of socialist or collectivist arrangement that has a chance of working only in a Soviet or East European type of command economy. Some of the West's most successful economies have for many years operated some form of incomes policy, in substance if not in name. This is true not only of the more familiar cases of Sweden and Austria, but also of Germany and Japan. Both these countries have a mixture of formal and informal understandings between government, employers and workers which ensure that by and large wages and salaries do not increase at a rate which jeopardizes the nation's economic progress. These arrangements are not perfect, and from time to time there is a hiccup; but they work well enough. If Britain had done as well as Germany and Japan over the last twenty years in restraining inflationary wage increases, it seems likely that growth would have been significantly faster and contemporary living standards substantially higher.

Precisely because of the unacceptable costs in terms of unemployment (not to mention the dubious long-term effectiveness) of Mrs Thatcher's way of bringing down inflation, a vigorous debate about future incomes policies got under way in Britain in the early 1980s. There is general agreement that any future policy should be as decentralized as possible, avoiding the over-centralized and bureaucratic nature of past policies and the inhibiting effects they sometimes had on productivity increases and the movement of labour from declining to expanding sectors of the economy. One specific idea is for what James Meade (like Milton Friedman, a Nobel prize-winner) has called 'not-quite-compulsory arbitration'. Where employers and unions failed to agree on a wage settlement, the two parties would go to arbitration, and abide by the result. Either party which refused to do this would be penalized, for example by fines or (in the case of the union) loss of legal immunities. An extension of this idea is that the arbitration should be 'pendular': the arbitrator would be obliged to opt for either the union's last demand or the employer's last offer – perhaps whichever was most likely to maximize employment – and not simply split the difference. The effect of this, it is hoped, would be to make both the union's demands and the employer's offers more realistic. It is true that arrangements of this kind would only work if the unions agreed to them. In the low unemployment climate of the late 1960s and early 1970s this would have been unlikely. In the later 1980s, at a time of high unemployment, with the unions weakened by declining membership and the restrictions imposed on them by the Thatcher government's legislation, it might be a different story. Another idea is for a tax-based incomes policy: employers would be deterred from conceding inflationary wage increases and passing them on in higher prices by having the excessive part of the wage increase treated as profits, not costs, for tax purposes. And there are various other ideas around. Whatever the merits and demerits of different forms of incomes policy, it is difficult to deny the logic of the insight achieved by some Keynesians more than forty years ago. If, in the longer term, full employment is to be combined with a stable inflation rate, some form of permanent incomes policy is unavoidable.

A FINAL WORD

This chapter has been concerned with the demand side, rather than the supply side, of the economy. This in no way detracts from the importance of supply-side measures. If Britain is to compete successfully in the modern world, it needs to educate more scientists, engineers and technologists, and to train and re-train more people in the skills demanded by the new technologies. More investment is needed, too, particularly in manufacturing industry and in the country's decaying physical infrastructure. There may, moreover, be some changes to be made in the structure of taxation and social security benefits in order to reduce disincentives to work, though it could readily be argued that the Thatcher government went far enough in this direction – indeed, too far. All these measures can play a part in raising the productivity of the economy, and in increasing the speed and efficiency with which it adapts to the new opportunities and challenges provided by a rapidly changing world.

Nevertheless, it is the management of demand that is the critical factor in achieving the basic objectives of economic policy – full employment, a reasonable rate of growth, and a low and stable rate of inflation. It has been argued in this chapter that the economy is not self-stabilizing, as monetarists assume, and that simple rules of thumb like balancing the budget and controlling the money supply are not enough either to reach and maintain full employment or to achieve a low and stable rate of inflation. Nor are attempts to reduce real wages of much help. Instead, the government must engage in a process of monitoring and influencing the level of effective demand. Macro-economic policy must, to be sure, eschew the excessive ambitions which characterized attempts to fine tune the economy, and must be conscious of the imperative need to prevent inflation from accelerating out of control. This requires some adaptation of traditional techniques of Keynesian demand management, but the animal is essentially the same. Finally, it has got to be recognized that if full employment and a stable inflation rate are to be achieved and maintained, some form of incomes policy will be a crucial element in the strategy.

Chapter Ten

TECHNOLOGY AND THE FUTURE
OF EMPLOYMENT

The conclusion that emerged from the last chapter was that the economy does not tend to settle itself at a full employment equilibrium, as the monetarists claim; that Keynesian demand management is therefore essential to the maintenance of full employment; but that these Keynesian macroeconomic policies need to be supplemented by incomes policies and appropriate microeconomic or supply-side policies if full employment is to be compatible with a low and stable rate of inflation. On this interpretation, the heavy unemployment experienced by Britain and, indeed, the rest of Western Europe throughout most of the 1980s was in large part the consequence of pursuing the wrong economic policies – monetarist policies rather than Keynesian ones. Some people, however, take the view that the Keynesian-monetarist debate is not the only issue relevant to unemployment and that the rapid pace of technological change in the 1970s and 1980s has a bearing on it as well. On this reading, it is the microelectronic revolution, as well as the monetarist counter-revolution, that is part of the problem. In this chapter we examine this view.

THE EFFECTS OF THE CHIP

Technological progress has been going on down the ages, since before somebody invented the wheel and somebody else the sail. It is, of course, the foundation of the increases in productivity that create economic growth and rising living standards, which is what economic policy is all about. Technological progress is therefore thoroughly desirable. But it does have adverse effects on those whose skills are displaced by the new products or the new techniques. In the 1830s the hand-loom weavers of Lancashire were put out of business by the new power looms. In the same way, in the 1980s, semi-skilled car workers are being put out of business by robots. For the displaced workers, the only answer has been to find other jobs, perhaps in other places and perhaps as a result of acquiring new skills. By and large, though not without much hardship, this has happened, sometimes purely through the operation of market forces, sometimes with government assistance. There has been a huge increase in employment in Britain over the past 150 years, as the population has grown from seventeen million to fifty-five million; and there has been no long-term upward trend in the rate of unemployment.

But the chip is different, the worriers say. Although its development is very recent – the microprocessor, or central processing unit of a computer contained on a chip, appeared only in 1971 – the new microelectronic technology has already created new products and led to new techniques of production on a very significant scale. Because the scope for the displacement of labour by the chip is so vast, and the pace of change so great, it is difficult to see what kind of jobs large numbers of semi-skilled and unskilled workers are going to be needed to do. To take a simple example: electronic typewriters, or word processors, are much cheaper to produce than electro-mechanical typewriters because they contain fewer components to manufacture and assemble; they significantly increase the productivity of secretaries and typists; and, having few moving parts, need less repair and maintenance. In consequence, the demand for three different kinds of labour has, at least in principle, been reduced by their introduction. Where are these displaced members of the labour force going to find jobs? More generally, what is going to happen to those whose work is taken over by robots and computers? Is there not a danger of an increasingly polarized society, in which there is plenty of work for the highly qualified people who design or manufacture or service robots and computers, but less and less work for the semi-skilled and unskilled – those with few qualifications, or none at all?

In its crudest form, this kind of worry is misguided. Only when all wants are satisfied will there be no work for people to do, and the world is still a long way from that situation. One must avoid what has been called the 'lump of labour fallacy', which posits that there is only a certain amount of work to be done, and deduces that the more of it that is done by some people, the less is left over to be done by others. Put like that, the view does not make sense. Nevertheless, it is too facile to dismiss the kind of worries expressed above – as some economists do – as simply an example of the lump of labour fallacy, not worth further discussion. No one knows what the implications for employment of the microelectronic revolution are going to be, nor for that matter what consequences will stem from technological advances in other fields, such as biotechnology and new man-made materials. There are, as always, optimists and pessimists. But one does not have to be too much of a pessimist to see that there are going to be problems.

A major problem will arise – indeed has already arisen – in manufacturing industry. Employment in manufacturing has been on a downward trend in most Western countries for many years. In Britain, for example, it fell by around three million, or 30 per cent, between the early 1960s and the early 1980s. This is quite a natural process: as an economy becomes more developed, labour typically moves first from the primary sector (agriculture and mining) to the secondary sector (manufacturing); and then into the tertiary sector (services). This process has been enhanced over the past twenty years or so by a shift of comparative advantage to the newly industrialized countries, first in the older and technologically less sophisticated industries such as textiles and clothing, steel and shipbuilding, and more recently in such industries as car assembly and some kinds of consumer electronics. The microelectronic revolution is likely to prove yet another factor reducing manufacturing employment in countries like Britain; indeed one could say that Britain's only hope of becoming or remaining competitive in fields like consumer electronics is to offset its high unit labour costs (compared with those of the newly industrializing countries) by the high productivity made possible by the increasing use of computers and robots. Thus one has something of a paradox: the more successful Britain is in retaining a vigorous and competitive manufacturing sector (of increasing importance to the balance of payments as North Sea oil production falls away) the less employment in manufacturing industry there is likely to be.

Less employment in manufacturing will mean more employment in services, if there is to be full employment. And because some parts of the service sector are themselves very much affected by the labour-saving consequences of the microelectronic revolution, other parts will have to increase employment that much faster. Some observers see no great difficulty about this, and point to the example of the United States, where total employment rose by thirty-five million, or 53 per cent, between 1961 and 1983. All of this increase in employment occurred in the service sector, the great bulk of it in wholesale and retail trading; finance, insurance and real estate; and professional, scientific and miscellaneous services. Thus there are some grounds for optimism.

However, there are also some reasons for concern. One is that much of the rise in employment in the service sector, in the United States and elsewhere, has taken the form of increased employment of married women, often on a part-time basis. In itself, this is all to the good; in particular, as is suggested in the next section, the greater availability of part-time work has much to recommend it. But the corollary is that increased employment in the service sector does not necessarily provide a solution to the problem of finding full-time jobs for adult men.

A second cause of concern (though again one on which opinions differ) might be put like this: is there enough entrepreneurship available to create employment in the service sector on the necessary scale? Entrepreneurship is the ambition to make money, combined with the talent for spotting a gap in the market and the opportunity to make a profit by filling it, backed up by the ability to organize capital and labour in the way required to get the project off the drawing board and into the form of goods or services which are actually produced and sold. Not everyone possesses these characteristics. In the late nineteenth and early twentieth centuries the most dynamic entrepreneurs built up great manufacturing industries which employed huge numbers of men. In the microelectronic age, such entrepreneurship is more likely to be engaged in the knowledge-intensive field of high technology, where the work force is characterized more by its advanced qualifications than its size. Thus it is probable that much of the increase in employment in the service sector will have to be provided by small businesses. American experience in this respect is encouraging: there has been a remarkable growth in employment in the small business sector in the US over the past decade. Whether this record can be sustained, however, remains to be seen: the death rate of small firms, as well as the birth rate, is high. It also remains to be seen whether small firms can create new jobs on a comparable scale in Britain, with its less individualistic and striving social tradition, less aggressive business environment, and less ruthless attitude towards those who fail to make good. Many people certainly want to start their own small businesses, and some of those who already have small businesses want to expand them. There is no reason why such people should not be taught some of the managerial and technical skills required to run a small firm; nor why the state should not simplify or eliminate some of the baffling array of regulations and disincentives which small businesses often feel they face. But whether, at the end of the day, there are going to be enough entrepreneurs to create enough small firms to provide as much employment and self-employment as is going to be needed, must remain an open question.

There is another factor which raises doubts about whether enough employment is going to be generated in the service sector. It can be argued that many of these extra jobs ought to be created in the *public* service sector. But will this actually happen?

One reason, it can be argued, why new jobs should be created in the public sector lies in the fact that as a society becomes better off it increasingly demands what are called 'public goods', such as cleaner air, safer water, better roads or improved parks and open spaces which cannot be charged for, or can only be charged for at prohibitive expense, and thus have to be provided by central or local government, which will pay for the extra manpower needed to increase or improve these services out of general taxation. Moreover in Britain and many other European countries there is a quantitatively much more significant example of this phenomenon: it has for many years been widely accepted that education and health services should be provided free or at subsidized prices through the public sector to all those who want them.

More education is needed in an increasingly technologically sophisticated society, and so accordingly are more teachers in the public sector. More health care is demanded as a society grows wealthier, and more is required in a society, like Britain in the closing years of the twentieth century, in which an increasing proportion of the population is over seventy and in need of specialized medical or institutional care. Thus more doctors and nurses are needed, and more home helps and community care workers. In Britain, at least, the facts of life suggest that if there is to be increased provision of educational, medical and other services, a great many of them will be provided through the public sector.

A second reason why there should be increases in employment in the public sector is that there is limited scope for improving the productivity of many public-service workers. This is true of teachers and nurses, and also of policemen and firemen, social workers and playground supervisors, road sweepers and dustmen. Although there are exceptions, by and large the microchip is not going to raise the productivity of workers like these very much. If there is to be an improvement in the services they provide – which would seem a reasonable objective in a society in which per capita income is growing – then there will simply have to be more of them.

It follows from all this that if many of the unsatisfied wants referred to earlier in this chapter are to be met, they will have to be met by increased employment in the public sector. And this raises a problem. For this requirement is plainly inconsistent with the hostility to public-sector employment which developed around the mid-1970s, partly in sympathy with the growing influence of monetarist ideas, and was given further impetus by the election of Conservative governments dedicated to cutting back the public sector, in Britain in 1979 and the US in 1980. Of course governments can change their views, or be replaced by governments with other views. But the climate in the mid-1980s was not propitious. At that time neither President Reagan nor Mrs Thatcher was showing any sign of soft-pedalling their attack on the size of the public sector – despite, in Britain's case, a very high and still-rising level of unemployment. Thus, in the medium term at least, this is another reason for wondering whether the service sector will in practice create enough new jobs to offset the effects of the microelectronic revolution. Of course, it may be all right in the long run; but in the long run, as Keynes observed, we are all dead.

A SHORTER WORKING LIFETIME?

It seems possible, therefore, that over the next decade or two, as the effects of the microelectronic revolution continue to spread throughout the economy, there may be a persistent problem of unemployment, particularly among adult men. This would not be Keynesian unemployment, in the sense that it could be eliminated by increasing effective demand: an increase in effective demand would raise the output of the goods and services produced by robots and computers, but might have no great impact on the demand for this kind of labour. Nor is it useful to see it as the kind of 'natural' unemployment posited by the monetarists. The monetarists would, to be sure, deny this, claiming that such unemployment simply reflected the unwillingness of the workers in question to accept a real wage equal to the (very low) value of their output. But this is an unrealistic way of looking at the issue. In a civilized and democratic society there is a limit to how far unemployment benefits can be reduced, and this in turn sets a floor to real wages. The problem is that at this level of real wages, and taking account of all the time and trouble involved in hiring (and later, perhaps, firing) additional labour, there may not be enough entrepreneurs around who find it profitable to employ these unemployed workers.

The prospect of this kind of 'technological' unemployment has prompted a number of people in recent years to propose some form of work sharing, the basic idea being that if there is a cut in the hours worked by people who are employed, then, for a given output, more people will be employed. Employers are usually strongly critical of these proposals, seeing them as being (as indeed they sometimes are) an attempt by unions to secure a cut in working hours without any cut in pay. This would of course add to unit costs, and lead to either lower profits or faster inflation. But this is a bit of a red herring: the serious proposals on this issue fully recognize that pay would have to be cut in line with hours of work. The obvious example is where an employer, instead of employing one full-time worker at, say, £200 a week, employs two part-time workers at £100 a week each. His unit costs will not have risen, but unemployment will have fallen.

This is clearly an extreme example, and is open to the obvious criticism that the full-time worker may not wish to – and should certainly not be compelled to – lose half his income, even though he would now only have to do half as much work as before. But the basic issue should be looked at in a broader context. There is nothing sacrosanct about the forty-hour week, forty-eight-week year, forty to forty-five year working lifetime which is the contemporary norm. Over the last couple of hundred years the fruits of rising productivity have been enjoyed in two different forms – higher incomes on the one hand, and more leisure on the other. People nowadays consume far more goods and services than they did a century ago. But they also, by and large, work fewer hours per day, fewer days per week, fewer weeks per year and fewer years per lifetime. No doubt this will continue in the future. What is at issue here is how far the process should be allowed to take its own course, and how far it should be given a bit of an extra shove if this would help to reduce unemployment. Longer periods of education and training; shorter daily or weekly hours of work; longer annual holidays; occasional 'sabbaticals' in the course of a working lifetime to learn new skills or develop new interests; an earlier age of retirement: these are all ways in which lifetime hours of work might be reduced. Provided it was clearly understood that for the individual this greater leisure was an alternative to higher income and not an addition to it, this process would not raise unit costs and not be inflationary; and, for any given level of the GDP, more people would be employed.

Some participants in the debate dismiss this kind of idea as foolish and unworkable, arguing that people demonstrably want more income to spend on goods and services, rather than more leisure. Others are not so sure. They point out that people's choices between income and leisure are not God-given, but influenced in particular by the structure of the tax and social security system and, more generally, by the prevailing ethos of the society in question. There might be a significant shift to part-time work if tax changes made it more attractive to both employers and employees. There might be a considerable move towards earlier retirement if the government rejigged the regulations and allowances relating to private pension schemes. More generally (and perhaps over-optimistically), anything which reduced the incentives directed towards individuals in a market economy to prefer more income to more leisure – such as an increased emphasis on education for leisure, or less generous tax treatment of business advertising expenditures – would work in the same direction.

Two points must, however, be stressed. First, measures designed to encourage people to reduce the number of hours they work during their lifetime would have the effect of reducing unemployment only if they also had the effect of encouraging employers to take more people on to the payroll than they otherwise would. In some degree this would almost certainly happen, since – provided the overall level of demand were kept the same – there is no reason why any employer should reduce the size of his workforce in these circumstances, while many would wish to take on more employees in order to maintain the total number of hours worked, and thus the level of output, at what it would otherwise have been. Nevertheless, the extent of the reduction in unemployment that would ensue is something that opinions will differ about.

The second point that needs to be emphasized is that work sharing is unlikely to be more than a fairly small part of any rational strategy for maintaining full employment. The chief determinant of the level of unemployment will remain, as was argued in Chapter 9, the total level of demand in the economy, combined with the degree of flexibility in the labour market: the extent to which labour is trained or re-trained to do the jobs that are available. Moreover, the work-sharing approach, designed to encourage private employers to take on more labour, is only one of several possible ways to deal with technological unemployment. A simpler way might be for the state to pay subsidies to employers who take on certain categories of unemployed workers, or indeed to act as employer of last resort itself, guaranteeing a job at a low but viable real wage to everybody.

However, these speculations are beginning to take us too far afield. The basic point made in this chapter is that the microelectronic revolution holds out the prospect of significant increases in productivity and living standards. Some of this will be taken in the form of higher consumption, and some in the form of greater leisure. It is very important that the increased leisure should, so to speak, be spread equitably across the entire population, and not accrue to only 10 or 15 per cent of the population in the form of enforced idleness. And work sharing, properly handled, may well have a role to play in achieving this objective.

Chapter Eleven

THE INTERNATIONAL DIMENSION

The *General Theory* was about a closed economy: Keynes was concerned to analyse the workings of a modern industrial economy without complicating the picture by bringing in its relations with other economies. But no book about Keynes's contribution to economic theory and economic policy-making would be complete without some reference to this international dimension. There are two reasons for this. First, throughout his life Keynes was concerned with international economic issues. As we saw in Chapter 1, his first major book, *The Economic Consequences of the Peace*, published in 1919, attacked as potentially disastrous the attempt to extract reparations from Germany. A quarter of a century later, towards the end of his life, he was one of the principal architects of the post-war international economic order.

The second reason is that the world of the late 1980s is characterized by a much greater degree of economic interdependence than the world of thirty or forty years ago. In the 1950s, for example, the international dimension of economic policy-making in Britain consisted of little more than casting an occasional eye across the Atlantic to check whether or not the American economy was moving into recession. Things are very different today, when policy-making has to be responsive to a host of developments and decisions in other countries over which Britain has no control.

These two aspects of the international dimension are discussed in turn.

THE IMF AND THE WORLD ECONOMY

An important reason for the severity of the slump in the 1930s was that many countries tried to increase employment by imposing import restrictions and devaluing their currencies. The main effect of these beggar-my-neighbour policies was to export unemployment to other countries, which led to further retaliation and further increases in unemployment. A principal objective of those who created the post-war international financial institutions was to ensure that this kind of thing did not happen again. One outcome of their endeavours was the General Agreement on Tariffs and Trade (GATT), which led to a series of multilateral negotiations that have reduced barriers, particularly tariff barriers, to international trade. Most germane for present purposes, however, is the International Monetary Fund (IMF) which, together with its sister organization the World Bank, was set up following a conference held at Bretton Woods, New Hampshire, in 1944. One task with which the Fund was charged was to supervise the operation of a new system of fixed exchange rates that was to replace what was regarded as the unstable floating exchange rate regime of the 1930s. Under the new arrangements, competitive devaluations were to be outlawed: a country could only devalue its currency if its balance of payments was in 'fundamental disequilibrium' – and the Fund had to be satisfied that this was the case. This fixed exchange rate system worked well for more than twenty years. By the late 1960s, however, it was beginning to crumble, mainly because by that time different countries were experiencing very different rates of inflation. By 1973 the world had reverted to a regime under which the major currencies were floating fairly freely against each other, and this state of affairs, subject to some modifications such as the creation of the European Monetary System (EMS) in 1979, was still in existence in the mid-1980s. By that time the International Monetary Fund's role in relation to exchange rates had become little more than one of trying to nudge countries into adopting fiscal and monetary policies that would avoid serious currency misalignments, such as the overvaluation of the American dollar, which had reached massive proportions by the beginning of 1985.

Our main concern here, however, is with the IMF's second principal function, which related to the creation of what was sometimes called 'international liquidity'. To Keynes, Britain's chief negotiator at Bretton Woods, it seemed essential that in the post-war era countries should not be forced by temporary balance of payments difficulties to deflate their economies in an effort to reduce their import bill: this would create unnecessary unemployment both at home and abroad. They should instead possess or be able to borrow enough foreign exchange to tide them over, without reducing imports, until things improved. To this end he proposed the setting-up of what he called an International Clearing Union, which would create credit in a world context in much the same way that a central bank creates credit in a national context. Individual countries would in effect have overdraft facilities at the Clearing Union, and a large part of these facilities would be available without conditions; it would be for the individual country to decide that it wished to avail itself of them. Moreover the scheme was conceived on an ambitious scale: total overdraft facilities would amount to around $26 billion, equivalent to half the value of world imports in 1948.

The Americans did not like Keynes's plan. They saw its scale as wholly excessive, and the lack of conditions on which much of the credit would be made available as a standing invitation to profligate behaviour and chronic balance of payments deficits. (One cannot help wondering what these stern-minded moralists would have made of the colossal balance of payments deficits the US was running in the mid-1980s.) They had some justification for their attitude. America would clearly emerge from the war as far and away the world's strongest economic power, and accordingly it would be America which would foot most of the bill: the goods on which other countries would spend the money they borrowed from the Clearing Union would be made in America and shipped, unrequited, overseas. (In fact this happened later anyway, under the Marshall Plan.) So the Americans insisted on establishing not Keynes's International Clearing Union, but the International Monetary Fund. The Fund did not create credit, as the Clearing Union would have done; instead it received subscriptions from its members in proportion to their economic size, and allocated them quotas equivalent to their subscriptions –the advantage of the arrangement being that 75 per cent of the subscription was paid in national currency, whereas the quota could be drawn on in terms of dollars. But the quotas could only be drawn on subject to certain conditions. And the total size of the quotas was only $9 billion, barely a third of the figure Keynes had thought necessary.

It can certainly be argued that the resources available to the IMF were inadequate to start with, and have become more inadequate with the passage of time. The $9 billion figure was raised over the next forty years by a series of quota increases: the eighth quota increase brought it to around $90 billion in the mid-1980s. But world trade grew faster. IMF quotas were equivalent to 16 per cent of world imports in 1948, for example; in 1983 to only 4 per cent. However, from the point of view of ensuring adequate international liquidity so that countries do not have to deflate in the face of temporary balance of payments problems, the size of countries' quotas with the Fund cannot sensibly be separated from the conditions under which these quotas can be drawn on. And this issue of 'IMF conditionality' has become an exceedingly controversial one.

Of its very nature, the IMF is in the business of making short-term loans to countries to help them cope with temporary balance of payments problems. (It is the job of the World Bank to make long-term loans to assist with economic development.) In the typical case, an IMF loan has to be repaid within three to five years. Moreover, the Fund's relative lack of resources makes the timeliness of these repayments important: it cannot always lend to a new borrower until an old one has repaid. But the Fund can only be sure that countries to which it lends money are going to be able to repay it within three to five years if these countries follow policies which will rapidly restore their balance of payments to surplus, thus making available the foreign exchange needed for the repayment. And to make sure that the appropriate policies are followed, the Fund establishes certain performance criteria which the country must meet. These criteria will vary in detail from country to country, but in broad outline are usually much the same: they involve reductions in the budget deficit, cuts in public expenditure (and particularly in subsidies), a slowing down of the growth of the money supply, and often devaluation and removal of import restrictions as well. Only if the country follows policies of this kind, the Fund will argue, will the balance of payments come right. And to make sure that the country does follow these policies, it is only allowed to draw down the IMF loan in successive tranches. If the performance criteria are not being met, the next tranche of the loan will be withheld.

The issue of IMF conditionality is too complex and too contentious to discuss in any detail here. But two points can be made. First, it is not difficult to infer from the kind of medicine the Fund prescribes that its economic philosophy is essentially a monetarist one. Cut public expenditure, balance the budget, control the money supply, let market forces rip: the voice may be that of the multi-accented Fund staff, but the philosophy is that of Milton Friedman. The perversity of this philosophy has been argued earlier in this book in the case of Britain and, by implication, other developed countries. In the case of developing countries (the Fund's main clients, now that developed countries rely mainly on the private international capital markets) the perversity is often even greater. Inequalities are more glaring in these countries; monetarist remedies tend to increase them. Many people are on the margin of subsistence; cuts in subsidies can push them over the edge.

Secondly, the IMF's approach seems to be based on the idea that if a country has an unsustainable balance of payments deficit on current account (i.e. a deficit that cannot be financed by an inflow of long-term capital) then that is the country's own fault. Consequently, it is right to impose tough conditions on the country to force it to get its balance of payments back into surplus. But if one country has a current account deficit, some other country must have a current account surplus: for the world as a whole, surpluses and deficits must necessarily sum to zero. And it is by no means clear that imbalances are always the fault of the countries running deficits; they may be the fault of countries running surpluses. Keynes himself was acutely conscious of this point, and throughout the Bretton Woods negotiations he stressed the need to ensure that creditor countries, as well as debtor countries, should shoulder their obligations. To this end a 'Scarce Currency Clause' was inserted in the Articles of Agreement of the IMF, under which countries whose currencies became scarce, because they were in chronic balance of payments surplus, could be discriminated against. But the clause was never invoked, and the Fund has generally shown itself unwilling to distinguish between deficits which are a country's own fault – the result, for example, of massive arms purchases from abroad – and deficits which are not.

The classic example of deficits of the latter kind were those which followed the first oil shock in 1973–4. Within a few months, non oil-producing developing countries found that the cost of their oil imports had quadrupled; and other essential imports based on oil, such as fertilizers and pesticides, increased sharply in price as well. This plunged most of these countries into deficits which could in no sense be described as their fault. There was some recognition of this on the part of the Fund, but not enough. It was clear that tough conditions would apply to most borrowings from the Fund, and even if the developing countries were to accept these conditions, the inadequacy of the Fund's resources referred to earlier meant that what they got would in many cases be insufficient for their needs. The upshot was that many of these developing countries, particularly those in Latin America, turned to the private international banks to finance their deficits. These banks were awash with cash in the form of the OPEC countries' surpluses, which were largely deposited with them. Consequently they were only too eager to lend money to all but the poorest developing countries, without any conditions, without any coordination between themselves, and without thinking very hard about how they were going to be repaid. For a few years all was sunshine and roses. But by the early 1980s there had been a second oil shock and repayments had started to fall due; it was apparent that most of these debtor countries could not repay the principal, and some could not even afford to keep up the interest payments. Massive and continuous debt-rescheduling negotiations got under way between the developing countries and the private international banks, with the participation of the IMF, and the problem was just about contained. But the situation remains critical. The external debt of the non-oil developing countries, which had been $130 billion in 1973, had risen to over $700 billion by 1985, and was still rising. How this problem is ultimately going to be resolved is unclear; but it is certainly not going to go away.

The increase in the oil price from about $2 a barrel in 1972 to $34 a barrel ten years later (though there has subsequently been some decline) was inevitably an extremely disruptive factor. Oil-importing countries had to cope with it as best they could in the short run, and restructure their economies in response to higher energy prices in the longer run. What Keynes would probably have been extremely critical of is the highly imperfect way in which these necessary adjustments were made, and are still being made. The resources and conditionality of the IMF were inadequate to the task, and although the World Bank made some effort to bridge the gap, it was not enough. One consequence, as we have seen, was the debt crisis. Another – particularly since 1980, when borrowing new money has been much harder – was one that Keynes had been especially concerned to avoid: developing countries, and some others, have had to cut back hard on their imports because they have simply not had the cash to pay for them. The result has not only been severe domestic hardship in many of these countries, but an adverse effect on the exports of both developed and other developing countries. This has slowed down world growth, and in turn made it even harder for debtor countries to export enough to pay for essential imports. The whole vicious circle is a sad example of the kind of situation that Keynes, in the closing years of his life, had hoped the post-war international arrangements would make it possible for the world to avoid.

INTERDEPENDENCE

In the previous section a number of criticisms were levelled at the philosophy and operating procedures of the International Monetary Fund. Some of these criticisms lie at the door of certain strong personalities who have shaped the development of the Fund over the past forty years. In the last resort, however, even the conditions on which the Fund lends money, and unquestionably the amount of resources at its disposal, are determined by its members. In practice this means the major Western powers, and particularly the United States. If the governments of these countries are of conservative and monetarist bent, as was the case during the first half of the 1980s in the US, Britain, Japan and (during the later part of the period) Germany, it is not surprising that the Fund's role in the world economy should be a less helpful one than many Keynesians would like. But there is another and more direct way in which conservative governments, and the interests they represent, can be seen as exercising a dampening influence on employment and growth in the world as a whole.*

In economic terms, the world is much more interdependent than it was two or three decades ago. One measure of this is that for most advanced industrial countries exports and imports represent a much

* I have argued this at length in *Controlling the Economic Future*, Wheatsheaf Books Ltd., Brighton, 1983.

larger proportion of the GDP. Another is the build-up of large sums of money – $1,500 billion or more in the Eurocurrency markets alone – which, given the virtual elimination of exchange controls in most Western countries, can be moved from one country or currency to another with a single telephone call. These changes have had major implications for the conduct of macroeconomic policy. The increased importance of international trade means that the level of output and employment in a country is much more dependent than it used to be on what happens in other countries. By the same token, a much larger proportion of the effect of policy measures a country adopts will leak abroad: an expansionary budget, for example, will have more of an effect than it used to on imports, and less of an effect than it used to on production and employment at home. On the capital side, too, the changes are very significant. If observers abroad (or, for that matter, at home) believe that an expansionary macroeconomic policy is going to re-ignite inflation and lead to a depreciation of the currency, they will move their money elsewhere. This will itself lead to a fall in the exchange rate, which may already be under pressure, because if the country is alone in adopting expansionary measures its imports will probably be rising faster than its exports and its balance of payments will be deteriorating. The consequence may well be a forced abandonment of its expansionary programme. There is nothing imaginary about this scenario: it is exactly what happened to the Mitterrand administration which took office in France in 1981 pledged (alone among major Western countries at that time) to adopt expansionary economic policies, but which had to abandon them in 1982.

It need not happen quite like that, as was demonstrated a little later by the experience of the United States. The strong Keynesian expansion which got under way in the US at the end of 1982 was accompanied by a tight monetary policy which led to very high real interest rates at a time when the inflation rate stayed low. The result was a large inflow of capital, which for quite a long time more than offset the deteriorating current account position, and caused a very big rise in the value of the dollar. But two points must be made about this American experience. First, it highlighted the interdependence of the world economy, in that high interest rates in the US led to high interest rates around the world, discouraging productive investment in other countries and increasing the debt burden of developing countries. Secondly, the American boom contained within it the seeds of its own destruction. The soaring dollar meant that effective demand in the US was increasingly being met by imports, and the huge and ever-rising current account deficit to which this led transformed the US within a few years from the world's biggest creditor to the world's biggest debtor. Sooner or later the dollar would come crashing down, and the effects on the world economy would probably be severe.

Thus the recent experience of the United States does not provide an encouraging exception to what seems the general rule: that in individual economies as open as most are today, expansionary measures of a Keynesian type aimed at reducing unemployment (even if accompanied by an incomes policy designed to prevent inflation from accelerating) can lead to trouble, and may before long have to be abandoned.

There are two ways in which this difficulty might be tackled. One would be a policy of opting out, at least partially, from the inter-dependence of the world economy – reducing the openness of the country's economy by imposing import restrictions and exchange controls. Such a policy cannot be rejected out of hand, but it seems likely, particularly if it led to retaliation, that the costs would outweigh the benefits, at any rate for a transitional period that would be too long for politicians to contemplate.

The other way is to coordinate the economic policies of the main Western countries, so that a general expansion at a time of high unemployment gives some assurance that an individual country's exports will rise as much as its imports, and severe balance of payments and exchange rate problems will thereby be avoided. This was done, with some success, as a result of the Bonn Summit of the heads of government of the seven major Western countries in July 1978. But of course this approach will only work if the leaders of the most important countries believe in an economic policy which incorporates the view that effective demand should be managed in order to in-fluence the level of output and employment. In Bonn, in 1978, President Carter, President Giscard d'Estaing, Chancellor Schmidt and Mr Callaghan did believe this, on the whole. At the next summit whose turn it was to be held in Bonn, in 1985, President Reagan, Chancellor Kohl and Mrs Thatcher manifestly did not, and even

President Mitterrand seemed to have modified his views following his experiences in 1981–2.

The conclusion, then, is that the growth of interdependence has made it more difficult for a single country to use Keynesian policies to bring down a high rate of unemployment if other major countries are not doing the same. But too sombre a picture should not be painted. Keynesianism in one country may be more difficult than it was; it is not impossible. If the financial markets believe that a Keynesian expansion designed to reduce unemployment is going to be accompanied by an effective incomes policy which will prevent inflation from accelerating, and if necessary by a monetary policy designed to discourage any excessive fall in the exchange rate, things should work out all right. And once a country has achieved full employment and a stable rate of inflation, all the instruments of economic policy should be used along neo-Keynesian lines to ensure that this happy state of affairs continues.

Chapter Twelve
CONCLUSION

In the social sciences, as in the natural sciences, revolutions in thought occur when the prevailing theory can no longer be reconciled with the observable facts. But another ingredient is needed as well – a genius: a Copernicus, a Newton or an Einstein; an Adam Smith, a Marx or a Keynes.

The heavy unemployment which was suffered in Britain through-out the 1920s, and the even heavier unemployment which afflicted the whole world in the 1930s, could not be explained by the orthodox economic theory of the day. According to this theory, unemployment was a transient phenomenon: full employment was the condition to which the economy naturally tended. What Keynes did was demonstrate that, whatever may have been the state of affairs a century earlier, the economy did not behave in this way: there were no strong automatic forces at work which could be relied on to bring it back to full employment. It was the job of the government, he concluded, to achieve and maintain full employment, by ensuring that there was enough effective demand in the economy.

In something under ten years, as Keynes had predicted in his letter to Shaw, the world had largely come to accept Keynes's revolutionary new theory; and for another thirty years after that Britain and other Western countries enjoyed full employment. But the very success of Keynesian full-employment policies carried within it the seeds of another intractable problem: inflation. Around the beginning of the 1970s the inflation rate, until then fairly stable, started to accelerate. This brought into question the long-term success of the Keynesian revolution itself, for accelerating inflation is an unsustainable con-dition, and if the price of full employment is accelerating inflation, then full employment cannot be maintained.

Monetarism was the economic doctrine advanced in the 1970s as the answer to inflation. But monetarism is no answer. It rests on assumptions about the self-stabilizing nature of the economy which, like the assumptions which underlay the classical economics of the 1920s and 1930s, are manifestly false. When introduced in a hardline form by Britain's new Conservative government in 1979, it simply did not work. The unemployment rate trebled to a level not far short of the average suffered throughout the 1930s, and six years later it showed no sign of any significant fall. The inflation rate fell, but this owed much more to the rise in unemployment and the effect of the world recession on international commodity prices than to the government's control of the money supply; and there was little assurance that inflation had been brought down to the 4 or 5 per cent level for good. By the mid 1980s it was beginning to be widely recognized that the abandonment of Keynesian demand-management policies in 1979 had been an appalling mistake.

However, no informed observer would now argue that traditional Keynesian policies, by themselves, are still enough. Quite apart from Britain's desperate need for appropriate supply-side policies – notably training and re-training in the skills required by the new technologies – some means must be found of controlling the growth of money incomes (this has been done, with considerable success, in high employment and fast-growing economies such as Germany and Japan). The problem of reconciling full employment with a low and stable inflation rate will not be solved without clear economic thinking and resolute political action. But it seems likely that if such thinking and such action are to be successful, they will have to take as their starting-point the explanation that Keynes provided of how a modern economy works. Too much may have changed since 1936 to make it appropriate to describe the right macroeconomic policies for the late 1980s and 1990s simply as Keynesian. But it will surely be correct to describe them as neo-Keynesian.

BIBLIOGRAPHICAL NOTE

The literature on the subject-matter of this book is already vast, and expanding (or so it sometimes seems) at an exponential rate. Anyone who wishes to learn more about Keynesian economics or monetarism will find these matters treated in literally scores of textbooks, most of them containing copious references, and can take it from there. Here I simply list, rather arbitrarily and in roughly relevant sequence, a dozen works which seem to me to deal in an interesting and illuminating way with many of the issues discussed in this book.

Robert Skidelsky, *John Maynard Keynes, Volume One: Hopes Betrayed 1883-1920* (Macmillan, London, 1983). The fascinating new biography of Keynes; a second volume is due to appear in 1986.

Robert Heilbroner, *The Worldly Philosophers* (Penguin edition, 1983). A very entertaining historical account of various economists and economic ideas.

John Kenneth Galbraith, *The Great Crash 1929* (Penguin edition, 1961). A witty analysis of the Wall Street Crash.

Milton Friedman, *Free to Choose* (Penguin Books, 1980). Some controversial thoughts from the great guru himself.

Samuel Brittan, *The Role and Limits of Government* (Temple Smith, London, 1983). Wide-ranging economic and political essays by a thoughtful and sceptical monetarist.

William Keegan, *Mrs Thatcher's Economic Experiment* (Penguin Books, 1984). A powerful critique from an economic journalist with strong anti-monetarist views.

Ian Gilmour, *Britain Can Work* (Martin Robertson, Oxford, 1983). A sophisticated and well-argued onslaught on Mrs Thatcher's economic policies by a leading Conservative MP who survived in her cabinet for only two years.

W. W. Rostow, *The Barbaric Counter-Revolution* (Macmillan, London, 1984). A short but pithy attack on monetarism from an American perspective.

J. E. Meade and others, *Stagflation* (two volumes, George Allen & Unwin, London, 1982 and 1983). The first volume deals with incomes policies; the second, which is more technical, with neo-Keynesian ideas about demand management.

Stephen Marris, *Managing the World Economy: will we ever learn?* (Princeton Essays in International Finance No. 155, Princeton University, October 1984). A succinct overview of the shifting attitudes to national and international economic policy-making since the 1940s.

David Worswick and James Trevithick (eds), *Keynes and the Modern World* (Cambridge University Press, 1983). The proceedings of a conference held at King's College, Cambridge, to celebrate the centenary of Keynes's birth. Not really for beginners, but gives a good idea of how leading contemporary economists assess the significance of Keynes's contribution.

John Maynard Keynes, *Collected Writings*, twenty-nine volumes, including Bibliography and Index (Macmillan for the Royal Economic Society). If you have the time and the money, probably the best value of all.

INDEX

Discover more about our forthcoming books through Penguin's FREE newspaper...

Penguin
Quarterly

It's packed with:

- exciting features
- author interviews
- previews & reviews
- books from your favourite films & TV series
- exclusive competitions & much, much more...

Write off for your free copy today to:
Dept JC
Penguin Books Ltd
FREEPOST
West Drayton
Middlesex
UB7 0BR
NO STAMP REQUIRED

READ MORE IN PENGUIN

In every corner of the world, on every subject under the sun, Penguin represents quality and variety – the very best in publishing today.

For complete information about books available from Penguin – including Puffins, Penguin Classics and Arkana – and how to order them, write to us at the appropriate address below. Please note that for copyright reasons the selection of books varies from country to country.

In the United Kingdom: Please write to *Dept. JC, Penguin Books Ltd, FREEPOST, West Drayton, Middlesex UB7 OBR*

If you have any difficulty in obtaining a title, please send your order with the correct money, plus ten per cent for postage and packaging, to *PO Box No. 11, West Drayton, Middlesex UB7 OBR*

In the United States: Please write to *Penguin USA Inc., 375 Hudson Street, New York, NY 10014*

In Canada: Please write to *Penguin Books Canada Ltd, 10 Alcorn Avenue, Suite 300, Toronto, Ontario M4V 3B2*

In Australia: Please write to *Penguin Books Australia Ltd, 487 Maroondah Highway, Ringwood, Victoria 3134*

In New Zealand: Please write to *Penguin Books (NZ) Ltd, 182–190 Wairau Road, Private Bag, Takapuna, Auckland 9*

In India: Please write to *Penguin Books India Pvt Ltd, 706 Eros Apartments, 56 Nehru Place, New Delhi 110 019*

In the Netherlands: Please write to *Penguin Books Netherlands B.V., Keizersgracht 231 NL–1016 DV Amsterdam*

In Germany: Please write to *Penguin Books Deutschland GmbH, Friedrichstrasse 10–12, W–6000 Frankfurt/Main 1*

In Spain: Please write to *Penguin Books S. A., C. San Bernardo 117–6° E–28015 Madrid*

In Italy: Please write to *Penguin Italia s.r.l., Via Felice Casati 20, I–20124 Milano*

In France: Please write to *Penguin France S. A., 17 rue Lejeune, F–31000 Toulouse*

In Japan: Please write to *Penguin Books Japan, Ishikiribashi Building, 2–5–4, Suido, Tokyo 112*

In Greece: Please write to *Penguin Hellas Ltd, Dimocritou 3, GR–106 71 Athens*

In South Africa: Please write to *Longman Penguin Southern Africa (Pty) Ltd, Private Bag X08, Bertsham 2013*

READ MORE IN PENGUIN

POLITICS AND SOCIAL SCIENCES

National Identity Anthony D. Smith

In this stimulating new book, Anthony D. Smith asks why the first modern nation states developed in the West. He considers how ethnic origins, religion, language and shared symbols can provide a sense of nation and illuminates his argument with a wealth of detailed examples.

The Feminine Mystique Betty Friedan

'A brilliantly researched, passionately argued book – a time-bomb flung into the Mom-and-Apple-Pie image … Out of the debris of that shattered ideal, the Women's Liberation Movement was born' – Ann Leslie

Peacemaking Among Primates Frans de Waal

'A vitally fresh analysis of the biology of aggression which deserves the serious attention of all those concerned with the nature of conflict, whether in humans or non-human animals … De Waal delivers forcibly and clearly his interpretation of the significance of his findings … Lucidly written' – *The Times Higher Educational Supplement*

Political Ideas David Thomson (ed.)

From Machiavelli to Marx – a stimulating and informative introduction to the last 500 years of European political thinkers and political thought.

The Raw and the Cooked Claude Lévi-Strauss

Deliberately, brilliantly and inimitably challenging, Lévi-Strauss's seminal work of structural anthropology cuts wide and deep into the mind of mankind, as he finds in the myths of the South American Indians a comprehensible psychological pattern.

The Social Construction of Reality
Peter Berger and Thomas Luckmann

The Social Construction of Reality is concerned with the sociology of 'everything that passes for knowledge in society', and particularly with that 'common-sense knowledge' that constitutes the reality of everyday life for the ordinary member of society.

THE SAME AUTHOR

es in the 1990s

in's most recent recession has been the worst experienced by any
r country in the past 25 years. How did it happen? What went
g? What can be done to bring about changes?

roviding answers to these crucial questions, Michael Stewart,
or of *Keynes and After*, advocates a return to Keynesian
omics. He starts with an evaluation of monetarism and its cen-
doctrine of low inflation. From the mid 1970s onwards monetar-
began to have a major impact on Europe, particularly in Britain,
re it was readily taken up by Margaret Thatcher. He shows how
etarist policy has manifestly failed, with low inflation having
n achieved only intermittently, and at great cost. At the start of
3 the number of unemployed in Britain was 3 million more than
per cent of the labour force. In contrast to the monetarist belief in
ply balancing the budget and controlling the money supply,
ynesian policies emphasize the need to create jobs by ensuring
ugh spending in the economy.

READ MORE IN PENGUIN

POLITICS AND SOCIAL SCIENCES

Conservatism Ted Honderich

'It offers a powerful critique of the major beliefs of modern con-
servatism, and shows how much a rigorous philosopher can contribute to
understanding the fashionable but deeply ruinous absurdities of his times'
– *New Statesman & Society*

Karl Marx: Selected Writings in Sociology and Social Philosophy
Bottomore and Rubel (eds.)

'It makes available, in coherent form and lucid English, some of Marx's
most important ideas. As an introduction to Marx's thought, it has very
few rivals indeed' – *British Journal of Sociology*

Post-War Britain A Political History Alan Sked and Chris Cook

Major political figures from Attlee to Thatcher, the aims and achievements
of governments and the changing fortunes of Britain in the period since
1945 are thoroughly scrutinized in this stimulating history.

Inside the Third World Paul Harrison

This comprehensive book brings home a wealth of facts and analysis on
the often tragic realities of life for the poor people and communities of
Asia, Africa and Latin America.

Medicine, Patients and the Law Margaret Brazier

'An absorbing book which, in addition to being accessible to the general
reader, should prove illuminating for practitioners – both medical and
legal – and an ideal accompaniment to student courses on law and
medicine' – *New Law Journal*

Bread and Circuses Paul Veyne

'Warming oneself at the fire of M. Veyne's intelligence is such a joy that
any irritation at one's prejudice and ignorance being revealed and exposed
vanishes with his winning ways ... *Bread and Circuses* is M. Veyne's way
of explaining the philosophy of the Roman Empire, which was the most
successful form of government known to mankind' – *Literary Review*

READ MORE IN PENGUIN

BUSINESS AND ECONOMICS

From Boom to Bust David Smith

When Margaret Thatcher took office for the third time in 1987 her monetarist experiment had been replaced by more pragmatic policies, inflation and unemployment were both low, and there was even talk of an 'economic miracle'. By 1991 this short-lived boom was just a distant memory.

Atlas of Management Thinking Edward de Bono

This fascinating book provides a vital repertoire of non-verbal images that will help activate the right side of any manager's brain.

Almost Everyone's Guide to Economics
J. K. Galbraith and Nicole Salinger

This instructive and entertaining dialogue provides a step-by-step explanation of 'the state of economics in general and the reasons for its present failure in particular, in simple, accurate language that everyone could understand and that a perverse few might conceivably enjoy'.

The Economist Economics Rupert Pennant-Rea and Clive Crook

Based on a series of 'briefs' published in *The Economist* , this is a clear and accessible guide to the key issues of today's economics for the general reader.

The Rise and Fall of Monetarism David Smith

Now that even Conservatives have consigned monetarism to the scrap heap of history, David Smith draws out the unhappy lessons of a fundamentally flawed economic experiment, driven by a doctrine that for years had been regarded as outmoded and irrelevant.

Understanding Organizations Charles B. Handy

Of practical as well as theoretical interest, this book shows how general concepts can help solve specific organizational problems.

READ MORE IN PEN

BUSINESS AND ECONOMICS

The Affluent Society John Kenneth Galbrai

Classical economics was born in a harsh world
left us with a set of preoccupations hard to adap
richer age. Our unfamiliar problems need
reception given to this famous book has shown
ideas.

Understanding the British Economy
Peter Donaldson and John Farquhar

A comprehensive and well-signposted tour of the
a sound introduction to elements of economic
account of recent policies are provided by this bes

A Question of Economics Peter Donaldson

Twenty key issues – the City, trade unions, 'free ma
others – are presented clearly and fully in this ma
television series.

The Economics of the Common Market Dennis S

From the CAP to the EMS, this is an internationally
the Common Market – now substantially revised.

The Money Machine: How the City Works Philip

How are the big deals made? Which are the institutions
What causes the pound to rise or interest rates to fall? T
clear and concise answers to these and many othe
questions.

Parkinson's Law C. Northcote Parkinson

'Work expands so as to fill the time available for its comp
underlies this 'extraordinarily funny and witty book' (Steph
Sunday Times) which also makes some painfully seriou
those in business or the Civil Service.

Contents

DYNAMIC
POSITIONING
BRIDGE

PIPE
TRANSFER
CRANE

PIPE
TRANSFER
BOOM

MOON
POOL
COVER

HELIPAD

STERN
THRUSTERS

AFT GATE (OPEN)

TUBULAR
STORAGE

MOON

PROPULSION MOTORS
(GENERATORS ABOVE)

PIPE
STRING

AFT
DOCKING
LEG

BREAKOUT
LEGS (4)

CAPTURE DAVITS

THE TAKING OF K–129

The Most Daring Covert Operation in History

JOSH DEAN

AMBERLEY

For my dad,
who needs to stick around
for a few more books

First published by Dutton 2017
This edition first published 2018

Amberley Publishing
The Hill, Stroud
Gloucestershire, GL5 4EP

www.amberley-books.com

British Library Cataloguing in Publication Data.
A catalogue record for this book is available from the British Library.

ISBN 978 1 4456 8384 3 (paperback)
ISBN 978 1 4456 7475 9 (ebook)

Hughes Glomar Explorer illustration on pages viii–ix courtesy of Antonio Raspa
with minor modifications by Dutton.

Book design by Amy Hill.

Printed in the UK.

HUGHES GLOMAR EXPLORER

DERRICK

GIMBAL PLATFORM

"A" FRAME

NAVIGATION BRIDGE

HYDRAULIC PUMPS

POOL

FORWARD GATE (OPEN)

FORWARD PUMP ROOM AND STABILIZER TANKS

BOW THRUSTERS

BRIDLE & YOKE

FORWARD DOCKING LEG

CAPTURE VEHICLE

STRONG BACK

by Antonio Raspa

The ability to get to the verge without getting into the war is the necessary art.

—*John Foster Dulles*

The only way of discovering the limits of the possible is to venture a little way past them into the impossible.

—*Arthur C. Clarke*

In wartime, truth is so precious that she should always be attended by a bodyguard of lies.

—*Winston Churchill*

If ever legends and stories of American technological genius were deserved and not yet realized, they would be about the scientists and engineers—the wizards—of [the] CIA.

—*Robert M. Gates*

PROLOGUE
Unexpected Visitors

NOVEMBER 1969

As he often did in the morning, Curtis Crooke was reviewing projects with members of his engineering staff when his intercom chimed. A resolute rail of a man with buzzed hair and metal-rimmed Wayfarer-style glasses, Crooke, then just forty-one, was one of the most influential minds in the emerging field of deep-ocean drilling, directing all engineering for his employer, Global Marine, from a large office on the second floor of its headquarters in downtown Los Angeles. The building was an area landmark, an ornate art deco tower with a soaring three-story lobby, known as the Fine Arts Building, and informally as the Havenstrite Building, for the eccentric oil wildcatter Russell E. Havenstrite, who once occupied its posh full-floor penthouse.

Global Marine was only nineteen years old but already an industry leader, with "the most versatile offshore drilling fleet in the world," according to its 1968 sales brochure. In just two and a half years, from 1965 to the middle of 1967, Global Marine had designed and built five "heavy, ocean-going, self-propelled drilling ships"—including two four-hundred-foot, eleven-thousand-ton vessels that were the largest of their kind ever built—and every one of them came to be under the direction of Curtis Crooke, who had been with Global Marine since its founding.

Crooke grew up in New York City as the youngest of four kids. His father, a GMAC executive, was wounded in World War I and eventually died

1

of complications from those injuries when Curtis was only seven, but he left the family well-off, and Curtis had a happy, uneventful childhood and adolescence in Forest Hills, Queens, home of the US Open at the West Side Tennis Club, until going west for college, to learn everything he could about boats and the ocean at UCLA and then UC Berkeley.

Dozens of talented men worked under the handsome, charming, disarmingly easygoing Crooke, who favored loosely knotted ties and off-the-rack button-downs at a time when executives wore suits. He drove a red Ferrari 250 California, typically very fast, and was known for being the calm, reasonable person in any room. Crooke was the only man on the executive floor who never closed his office door, which endeared him to his engineers, who loved him and the work. They came to Global Maine for the opportunity to build ships and plunder the deep ocean, a realm that, in 1969, was as much of a mystery to humankind as outer space. Crooke was a development engineer himself, with experience in fluid mechanics, hydrodynamics, and oceanography, but his real talent was in management and business development. He was a born leader so comfortable in his position and skin that he often took afternoon naps upright in his chair with his feet on the desk and the door wide open.

"I've got a man on the phone who says he needs to see you," Crooke's secretary said, interrupting the meeting.

"Who is he?" Crooke replied.

"He won't tell me, but he says it's extremely important."

"Tell him I'm in the middle of something and please take a message."

Crooke resumed the conversation with his engineers, but moments later, the intercom sounded again. This time, his secretary reported that the man was very persistent and wasn't taking the hint. He wanted Crooke to know that he was a potential customer with a large piece of business requiring immediate attention. He absolutely could not wait.

This was certainly unusual. Crooke was annoyed but also curious about the man and the message he so desperately wanted to share. Still, he was in a meeting. Crooke asked his secretary to tell the man that, as he'd already stated, he was busy, but he'd be willing to see him later that morning, when the schedule cleared, if she could set something up.

Five minutes later, the intercom buzzed again.

"I'm sorry, Mr. Crooke, but now the man is *here*, with two other men, and he says he needs to see you immediately."

The engineers sitting around Crooke looked at their boss, wondering how he might react. And he was chewing on that notion himself when his door opened and three men, all in suits, strutted through. The one who appeared to be in charge was about forty and of average height but thick in the shoulders and middle. He had black hair, parted on the left and slicked back, and as soon as he and his colleagues were through the office door, he closed it behind them—a brash display even more jarring to Crooke because he rarely ever shut that door himself.

The entry was so sudden, so surprising, so brazen, that Crooke just stared up at the intruders through the tinted lenses of his glasses. He apologized to his engineers and asked if they could resume the meeting later.

As soon as they left, the man with the slicked hair spoke.

"Mr. Crooke, I'm John Parangosky," he said. "This is Alex Holzer and Paul Evans, and we all work for the Central Intelligence Agency. I assume you know what that is. Now," he said, approaching the round table where Crooke had been sitting, "do you mind if we sit down?"

Parangosky took the chair across from Crooke, while the two other men both pulled up chairs on the same side, to his left.

"Am I supposed to just accept that this is true?" Crooke said. He wasn't sure what to think. Global Marine was not a government contractor and he'd never met an officer from the CIA, let alone done business with one. It felt like a prank. "Do you have an ID?"

"We don't carry those," Parangosky replied, explaining that in his field it wasn't good for a man to ever really be himself in public. He had plenty of business cards in various cases and desk drawers, but none of them identified his actual job. Or his real name.

"So you're saying you rarely tell the truth about who you are?" Crooke said and cracked a smile. "With that name you gave me you could be Russian." By this point, he was more intrigued than annoyed. The whole episode was so bizarre and unlike anything he'd experienced before that he was curious to see what happened next. "Anyway, you've ruined my meeting and got my attention. What can I do for you?"

Parangosky explained that he had been reading up on ocean drilling and

3

was convinced that Global Marine was the only company in the country—really, on the planet—that could complete a job that interested the Agency; a job important enough that he, his chief scientist (Holzer), and his chief of security (Evans) had flown from Washington, DC, to Los Angeles with no advance warning to ask a single question in person. The larger context was classified, Parangosky said, so he wasn't going to be able to go into detail or answer any questions—at least not at this point. Those things would come later, if they decided to work together.

Crooke nodded and told the man to continue.

"Is it feasible, using your current technology, or technology that's within the realm of possibility, to lift something weighing several thousand tons from the bottom of the ocean, at a depth of fifteen thousand to twenty thousand feet?"

The question surprised Crooke, but he wasn't shocked by it. Global Marine was in the business of extraordinary engineering—innovation, especially in the deep ocean, was the company hallmark. But it also wasn't something he could answer offhand.

"Honestly," Crooke replied, "I don't know. I'm going to have to think about it."

"That's fine," Parangosky said. "Please do that. We'll be in touch."

And that was it. He shook Crooke's hand, and all three men rose and left, closing the door behind them—Holzer and Evans without having uttered a single word.

Crooke was young by any measure. He studied at UC Berkeley's acclaimed marine program under some of the giants of ocean science, and he was in charge of Global Marine's engineering for the same reason twenty-five-year-olds run technology companies today—because this was a new industry. Established oil companies had no experience working offshore and didn't have research arms set up to explore it. This left a market hole for innovative start-ups, and Global Marine was basically that, an ambitious engineering shop spun out of a collaboration between the Continental, Union, Shell, and Superior Oil companies that had, very quickly, become a global leader in developing technology to access natural resources under the ocean.

For a few minutes after his visitors left, Crooke sat and thought about what this strange man with the slicked hair had just asked him. What weighs several thousand tons and would be important enough that the CIA would want to pull it off the bottom of the ocean? His first thought was a submarine.

This wasn't a total guess. Global Marine had recently consulted with the Navy following the loss of the nuclear sub the USS *Scorpion,* which had sunk in the Atlantic on May 22 of the previous year, resulting in the loss of ninety-nine American lives. The Navy had come in search of ideas for recovering or even scuttling the wreck so that its reactor could be neutralized, and Crooke had given them several proposals based on a concept Global Marine favored and had become very proficient with—using a long strand of interconnected steel pipe known as a drill string to deploy equipment such as drill bits to the seafloor. The simplest idea, he thought, was to pump the hull full of concrete, eliminating the risk of a reactor leak. He didn't get the job.

Crooke walked over to a large bookcase on his office wall and scanned the titles until he saw the spine of *Jane's Fighting Ships,* a tall, thin volume wrapped in a laminated blue cover. He flipped through until he found Soviet submarines, and the numbers matched up, more or less.

Later, he scratched some calculations with a pencil on graph paper and consulted a copy of the Spang Tubular Products catalog in search of industrial pipe cased in HY-100 high-strength military-spec steel—the highest-grade steel possible, and the primary type used in submarine and ship construction. What Crooke wanted to figure out was whether it was technically possible to deploy and control a tapered string of HY-100–cased pipe three to four miles long in the open ocean—and not just that, but also whether or not some kind of device on the end of the string could grab and lift a massive object back to the surface.

The answer was inconclusive. This wasn't the kind of problem even a brilliant marine engineer could solve quickly on a scratch pad, but Crooke decided that it was compelling enough to investigate further. The job might not be possible, ultimately, but according to some very rough math—and the knowledge accumulated over a decade of drillship work—it didn't seem to be impossible, either.

A day later, Parangosky returned, again without warning. This time, Crooke told his secretary to send the men right in.

"Did you think about it?" Parangosky asked.

"I did," Crooke replied. "I think it's possible."

"Good," Parangosky said. "I'll get the papers drawn up and have a work order sent over."

Once those were signed, he said, he'd be at liberty to tell the entire story.

1

K–129 Down

FEBRUARY 1968

The Soviet nuclear ballistic missile submarine K-129 left Petropavlovsk, on Russia's remote, frigid Kamchatka peninsula, with a crew of ninety-eight after dark on February 24, 1968, for a routine but unexpected patrol. No external markings signified the sub's name, and even its hull number was painted over so that the vessel would be unrecognizable to any ship that happened to notice it when it surfaced to gulp air and run the diesel motors that recharged its onboard batteries.

The Golf-class sub, which the Soviets called by its side number, PL-574, was under the command of an ascendant thirty-eight-year-old Ukrainian captain first rank named Vladimir Kobzar, who was leading his final mission aboard the boat he'd commanded for four years. When the submarine returned to its home base, Kobzar would move to Soviet fleet headquarters to assume a more senior position commanding multiple subs from a desk.

Kobzar was one of the most experienced captains in the fleet, a rigorous, demanding man so highly regarded that many in the submarine service thought he might one day command the entire fleet. He had been given the Order of the Red Star for service and was being rewarded for his four years at sea with a promotion that was certain not to be his last. Kobzar was loved by his crew and respected by his superiors, who noted how he personally helped train watch officers, oversaw survival training, and could capably handle any job on the sub. He had a question he liked to repeat to men under his command: "Who is the most dangerous man on a submarine? The one who doesn't know what he's doing!"

Upon return to port, Kobzar's second-in-command, Captain Third Rank Alexander Zhuravin, would take over the K-129. The two officers knew each other well, having served more than a year at sea together, and were comfortable working in unison.

Zhuravin was sharp, polished, ambitious, and, at thirty-four, one of the youngest senior officers in the fleet. He was tall for a submariner, at six foot two, and good-natured, fond of practical jokes and of occasionally fishing from atop the sub with the enlisted men when it wasn't on war patrol. Alex was introduced to his wife, Irina, by her brother, while the two were cadets at the Leningrad Naval Academy. She was in high school at the time, back in Moscow, so their relationship began as a series of letters that Irina would sometimes read aloud in class, to impress her friends with the romantic notion that she was being wooed from afar by this handsome naval cadet. This went on for seven years, with Alex traveling to Moscow to continue his pursuit in person whenever his schedule allowed.

When Irina graduated from college, she finally agreed to marry him, making a commitment that came with an unfortunate asterisk: Alex was to join the Pacific Fleet, forty-two hundred miles away, on Kamchatka. Worse, he was to serve on submarines, leaving Russia for several months at a time, during which she would be home alone, unable to communicate with her husband for days and sometimes weeks. And yet, the marriage came with an upside, too. Being a Soviet naval officer was a prestigious job and Irina enjoyed the residual luster and of course the benefits—especially a nice house and a salary that was high for a young family in the Soviet Union. When Alex left port, his wife missed him, but she never feared he wouldn't come back.

None of the sub's officers expected to be at sea in February. The boat had completed a normal two-month combat patrol in the northeast Pacific on November 30, 1967, and upon return the crew was split into two for the duration in port, as was the custom. Half of the personnel went on vacation, while the other half were assigned to routine maintenance—cleaning, painting, repairs. Halfway through the break, they swapped roles.

8

What little rest the crew got during the break wasn't just welcome; it was necessary. Autumn storms had rocked the boat almost incessantly for the entire time K-129 was at sea, making the previous mission a rough one, physically. And the men assumed, fairly, that they'd have several months to recover. Subs of this type typically did two combat patrols a year, but when two different sister ships experienced mechanical problems early in February and were deemed unfit for combat patrols, the Soviet Navy decided to send the K-129 back to sea so as to not disrupt the fleet's scheduled activities.

Telegrams from Central Command went out, ordering the crew to report to base between February 5 and February 8. When Division Commander Admiral V. A. Dygalo heard the news, he complained that the decision was cruel and potentially reckless. He filed a report stating his concerns to Rear Admiral Krivoruchko, commander of the Fifteenth Squadron, but Krivoruchko handed it right back, with a very clear message.

"You can take your report to the latrine," he said. "Direct your energy to getting the sub ready for service."

Dygalo was irritated enough that he didn't heed the warning. Instead, he went up the chain of command, sending his report to the fleet commander, who had the same response.

"Comrade Dygalo, this order comes from the Supreme Commander," he replied. "And nobody, not I, nor the Commander of the Navy will be asking him to postpone the mission by two weeks in hopes that [another] sub might be able to work through all its problems and report to active duty."

Sufficiently chastened, Dygalo focused instead on trying to get his submarine ready for duty. Submarine K-129 wasn't new; in fact, it had been in service since 1960, but it was outfitted to be as advanced as any of the forty subs stationed at the Soviet Navy's Petropavlovsk-Kamchatka base. It was the first sub in the division to be given an award of excellence, and it sailed with the newest, most advanced navigation system in the Pacific Fleet.

Like all subs operating during the height of the Cold War, K-129 went to sea in full battle rattle. She was 328 feet long from nose to tail, propelled by three two-thousand-horsepower diesel engines when at the surface or in recharge mode, and three electric propulsion motors when cruising underwater, when the silence provided by electric motors is essential to mission success.

The sub carried three R-21 ballistic nuclear missiles—also known as SS-N-5 Serbs. Each R-21 had a white nose cone stuffed with a nuclear warhead and was loaded into one of the three vertical launch tubes that stood behind the sub's conning tower. A single R-21 warhead carried one megaton of punch—more than sixty-five times the explosive power of Fat Man, the bomb that leveled Nagasaki—and had a range of 755 miles. It was also a historic weapon, the first Soviet missile that could be fired from a submerged submarine, giving the K-129 the ability to launch a preemptive nuclear strike from an undetectable position far from the American coastline if war were to break out.

Missile subs are relatively slow and vulnerable to attack. So to defend herself, K-129 carried two nuclear-tipped torpedoes loaded into the forward launch tubes, each one capable of sinking a US aircraft carrier, as well as a second set of conventional self-guided torpedoes in the stern bays to defend against attack from other submarines.

Boats like the K-129 were particularly critical to the Soviet Navy's mission. The Pacific Fleet was still young, and these diesel-powered ballistic missile subs of the Twenty-ninth Division provided the most direct threat to America's major West Coast cities—a threat that the Americans couldn't easily track. The sub's role was to patrol the Pacific quietly and stand ready to act in the event of nuclear war.

The end result of the schedule change was that Kobzar and his men were yanked out of shore leave they had earned, tearing them away from neglected hobbies, upcoming anniversaries, and family birthdays they missed all too often in the course of serving the motherland. Zhuravin, his wife, and their two children had joined several other officers and their families at a spa resort, where the pristine air of the Kamchatka peninsula helped clear up the respiratory irritation he had developed on the previous mission. But the arrival of a telegram announcing orders to return to port could not be ignored, and though the young captain had reservations about returning to sea so soon, with the sub in need of repairs, he knew better than to express that sentiment aloud.

A Soviet submarine's precise directives were never known to its captain upon departure, but Kobzar and his crew knew the broader plan: to follow a prescribed course to K-129's station, a relatively small block of ocean well to the northwest of Hawaii, and more or less sit there—in a remote section of the Pacific, infamous for heaving seas and flotillas of flotsam and for being largely barren of nautical activity except for the silent passage of American hunter-killer subs that stalked Soviet ballistic missile subs. The K-129's mission was to stay out of sight of these subs, or any other hostile American vessels, until returning to base on May 5 at no later than 1200 hours.

The sub slipped out of her bay, docked briefly alongside a floating barracks ship, then cruised on to the fleet weapons depot to pick up the ballistic missiles and nuclear-tipped torpedoes. Once loaded, the K-129 moved farther into the bay and anchored, to await the arrival of a large antisubmarine ship that escorted her as far as the booms, a standard procedure meant to signal loud and clear to any Americans watching that the sub leaving port was on a combat mission, carrying live nukes.

At twelve fifteen A.M. on February 25, the submarine passed the booms and headed into the open ocean. At one A.M., a monitoring station picked up a signal that the K-129 had submerged, and then it went quiet. After leaving Russian waters, the sub headed south until it reached 40 degrees latitude, then turned toward Japan, under orders to spend at least 90 percent of her time submerged, mostly at a depth of around one hundred feet, running on underwater diesel power (UDP). This was a hybrid stealth mode mandated by fleet command to keep Soviet subs hidden yet still within range of radio signals from shore. It was a far more risky (and noisy) position than cruising under battery power at a deeper and safer depth, but Soviet sub captains were under orders to operate according to UDP protocols as much as possible—and a mission's success was in part judged by the percentage of time spent in this mode.

The K-129 cruised more or less in a straight line, with periodic zigs and zags to seek out and shake any American subs that might be trailing. Submarine warfare during the Cold War was a game of hide-and-seek. All captains of slower ballistic subs considered their vessels prey for attack subs and were trained to move evasively, making unpredictable course changes regularly. A sub might ascend or descend suddenly and would occasionally shut down all engines so the crew could just sit silently and listen for any external sounds that would indicate American hunter-killers lurking nearby.

At 180 degrees longitude, the K-129 was to turn again, toward the US coast. To prevent detection, especially considering the rising geopolitical tensions in the region, the K-129 traveled for two weeks in silent mode, running on battery power. As far as anyone back at command was concerned, she was proceeding as directed.

Vulnerable at snorkel depth, diesel-powered boats routinely and unavoidably traveled there. Golfs were the last generation of Soviet subs to have diesel power (all later generations had nuclear power, which eliminated the necessity to surface), and those noisy engines cranked up when a sub surfaced to charge the electric batteries that made cruising silently underwater possible. Ascend, charge, submerge. The pattern repeats over and over.

Inside, there was no fresh air. The caustic, bitter smell of diesel fuel permeated every inch of the submarine, seeping into clothes, mattresses, and sheets. And there was precious little freshwater. Each crewman was allowed a single liter per day, and that had to cover drinking, bathing, and—very occasionally—laundry. The entire crew shared three toilets and slept in bunks stacked so tightly that there was barely room for a man to lift his head.

When a sub is on or near the surface, all personnel stand at the ready, with key officers manning the boat's two periscopes: the sky-search scope, which points straight up to spot sub-hunter planes; and the attack scope, which scans the ocean surface in search of foreign vessels. At prearranged times, the K-129 would also use these opportunities to send word back to Kamchatka, in the form of encoded burst communications that told superiors back at base that the mission was continuing as planned and that no problems had arisen en route.

A submarine's most important attribute is stealth, and what made subs so important during the Cold War was that they enabled both sides to move nuclear missiles from land—where their fixed positions were easily located and, in theory, destroyed if a war were to break out—to sea, where on these

12

silent, mobile launch platforms they would remain capable of striking and prolonging a war even if the homeland's nuclear arsenal had been eliminated. Locating Soviet subs, then, was a huge priority for the US Navy, which had an almost unlimited budget for intelligence and antisubmarine warfare tactics—a line item so important that it required no congressional oversight.

The Soviets were aware that any radio transmissions sent between the subs and the mainland were intercepted by a network of land-based installations. What frustrated US Naval Intelligence was that analysts could not unlock these communications—typically short bursts of code sent at prearranged times and from specific locations—so while they could hear when and from where a particular burst originated, analysts had no idea what specific information was being transmitted.

Like any Soviet captain, Kobzar did not learn his official orders until the sub was in the open ocean. They were contained in a packet handed to him by his commander just before departure. The envelope was marked with clear directions: "To be opened on the third day after leaving base." Kobzar bore a heavy burden—he was in a position to start a war if necessary, and should that happen, he would be asked to target and destroy three of the most critical US military installations in the Pacific: Pearl Harbor, Hickam Air Force Base, and US Pacific Command Headquarters, in Oahu.

Nothing about this was new, and there was nothing new about the mission, either. It was a routine combat patrol, hopefully doing very little. Only in the event of combat was Kobzar allowed to think freely and react, and even then, very specific instructions for handling himself and the precious ballistic load on board had been drilled into his head.

Pacific Fleet command expected to hear from all deployed subs at prearranged times, but the K-129 was to travel in silent mode for the first two weeks at sea, so until March 8, there was no reason for anyone back in Kamchatka to worry. On the eighth, however, a watch officer at Soviet Navy Central Command noticed that the sub failed to transmit a radio message as scheduled, and he brought the matter to his superiors. An alert was declared.

Rear Admiral Dygalo was at the home of one of his captains that night when the phone rang at ten o'clock. The squadron commander wanted to see Dygalo immediately. A quarter of an hour later, he arrived at headquarters to find Krivoruchko pacing frantically while smoking a cigarette as if he were in a race to finish it. His previous cigarette was still smoking in an ashtray.

There has been no communication from the K-129, Krivoruchko said. The fleet commander was already on a plane from Moscow and would be at headquarters in the morning expecting a full report with explanations for the apparent disappearance of a submarine carrying ninety-eight men and three ballistic nuclear missiles.

"When ready, report to me on the possible reasons for Kobzar's silence, and on the forces necessary for the search operation," Krivoruchko told Dygalo.

A failure to communicate didn't necessarily indicate disaster. Radio transmitters are not infallible, and Soviet submarines were notorious for equipment failure. Weather can also be an issue. And if a sub's commander felt his boat was under threat of discovery or attack by American vessels, he might also choose to remain silent. Thus, Soviet admirals didn't automatically assume the worst when a sub failed to communicate. But it was rare for one to go completely dark for more than a full day, and when the K-129 missed a scheduled communication for the second consecutive day, fleet command began to panic.

Although the Soviet Union had never lost a submarine with nuclear missiles on board, the idea of it happening was a nightmare for command. The crew of officers that Dygalo assembled offered a number of possibilities for the silence—damage to the ship's antennas, a collision with another vessel, a sudden loss of buoyancy caused by a leak or massive water intake through the snorkel while under diesel power, or a catastrophic fire caused by a leak of rocket fuel or oxidizer from the ballistic missiles. In some rare cases, they noted, freakish ocean conditions—a zone of higher-temperature or low-salinity ocean water, or a run-in with subsurface waves—can even push a sub suddenly toward its depth limit, the point at which its hull collapses.

Dygalo recalled one such rare case. In March 1965, the sub K-163 was on patrol in the North Pacific when, in less than two minutes, it plummeted from forty meters nearly to its crush depth—the point at which the integrity of its steel hull is compromised—and was saved only because the watch officer noticed the change immediately and ordered the engine room to go full power toward the surface. This slowed but did not stop the sub's plunge, and it kept descending right up to the precipice of its crush depth again, when the sub, its steel hull groaning violently from the ever-growing water pressure, finally stabilized and began to rise.

There were plans for rescuing vessels in distress, and the Soviet Navy put them into effect on March 9, dispatching a flotilla of ships, from various ports, out to sea. A damaged submarine will always surface, if possible, so the fleet's reflex is to commence a rapid search for a crippled sub somewhere inside a predetermined area, in this case one measuring about 854,000 square miles. Searchers were to look for a submarine bobbing on the surface, probably without power or communication. Provided the sub's structural integrity hadn't been compromised, it would be safe there. Every sub in the fleet carried enough provisions on board to keep a crew alive for three months.

The US Navy maintained a constant presence off the Kamchatka Coast, and the USS *Barb* was sitting quietly in radio silence near Vladivostok when the Soviet Navy's mobilization began. The *Barb*'s captain, Bernard "Bud" Kauderer, was initially confused by the frantic reaction. It was unlike anything he'd ever seen—an entire sub group racing out of port, with active sonar going full bore, and no apparent worry about detection. Kauderer ordered the *Barb* to follow the group from a safe distance, observing as these Soviet subs dove, resurfaced, then dove again, talking openly over the radio channels to fleet command and calling out, again and again, for a boat that never called back. "Red Star, come in. Red Star, come in. Red Star."

Kauderer reported back to US Fleet Command and asked for orders.

"Stay on station," he was told.

The search intensified. Two destroyers, three frigates, three minesweepers, two mother ships, and ten support vessels—in addition to the four submarines—participated in a methodical search led by planes that circled overhead. In total, thirty-six flagged vessels participated in the hunt for

K-129, working day and night, using echo and sonar sounders and dragging photographic equipment that scanned the depths far below the surface. All the while, surveillance planes flew ahead—at least fifty-three took part—tracking the sub's intended path, looking for any wreckage on the surface that could help narrow the search area. Over the next seventy-three days, Soviet planes would make a total of 286 flights over the zone.

Weather made matters worse. Winters can be brutal in the North Pacific, and the Soviet fleet ran smack into violent storms, with heavy snow, gale-force winds, and waves cresting as high as forty-five feet. During the early days of the search, the ocean was as wicked as it could be, with conditions registering at or near a 9 on the Douglas Sea Scale—a scale designed to express the sea's roughness for navigation that goes only as high as 9. At that level, waves can reach fifty feet and the sea is described, bleakly, as "phenomenal."

Dygalo joined the search personally, aboard a nuclear sub, and at snorkel depth, his watch officer wore a full diving suit over a fur coat and pants and was strapped using a harness and chain to an iron brace on the bridge. There, Dygalo recalled, "he bobbed up and down like a cork in waters foaming about his chin whenever the sub plowed into an oncoming wave." On the downside of waves, the sub would nearly roll onto its side. "To make anything out in those seething waters, in those conditions, was highly improbable," Dygalo later said.

All the while, American Orion-class antisubmarine planes circled overhead, constantly audible to the Soviet watchmen but visible through sky scopes only on the rare occasion when the weather broke and the clouds parted.

The biggest problem was that the Soviets didn't actually know where to look; they knew only where the K-129 had been last—on March 7—and where it was headed—to the Hawaii station—so they focused the search along that line, looking for oil slicks, debris, or anything else on the surface that could indicate a disaster. The initial search zone was vast, more than eight hundred thousand square miles, and got bigger as the search failed to locate any signs of the sub, growing to 1 million square miles, an almost impossibly large area, especially considering another factor: the ocean's depth. In that area of the Pacific, the bottom was nearly four miles below, and because all signs pointed to a catastrophic loss, the K-129 wasn't likely to be found on the surface. In all likelihood, it lay shattered on the bottom, more than three miles below.

The K-129's return to port had been scheduled for May 5, and when that date came and went, the wives and parents back in Petropavlovsk, who'd been told almost nothing by the fleet leadership, began to accept that their husbands and sons weren't coming home. They gathered in a square next to a monument erected for another lost sub, wearing black. Irina Zhuravina, wife of the submarine's second-in-command, had been clinging to faint hope. "He loved life so much that he simply couldn't die," she told herself, and the friends from the fleet who fished with her husband and made caviar in their home kept coming by. "Sasha can't die," they told her. "He'll come up. He'll figure out a way." For weeks, her eight-year-old son, Misha, kept asking the same question: "Where is Daddy? He's never gone this long." "Daddy's at sea," she told the boy.

Officially, the families were told very little. It wasn't until September 12, six months after the K-129's disappearance, that the supreme commander of the Soviet Navy issued an order stating that the sub had been lost while on duty in the Pacific and that all the men on board were "presumed dead." That description wasn't just insulting; it was financially cruel, because instead of the full salary and pension awarded to military men lost in the line of duty, it meant the families were awarded only a single lump-sum payment of fifteen hundred rubles plus a partial pension—the same pitiful amount they'd have been given if the men had died accidentally by slipping and falling.

Many within the fleet, including Admiral Dygalo, were ashamed of the Soviet response. Dygalo suffered a heart attack while writing personal letters to each of the families and was hospitalized for a month. "By the order of the Minister of Defense, K-129 was removed from the register of naval vessels, as though it never existed," he later wrote. "Moscow decided that it was the end of the story."

2

Is This What You Were Looking For?

APRIL 1968

Back in Washington, deep inside the Pentagon's inner ring, Jim Bradley had an idea. Bradley, a captain, was officially the assistant for undersea warfare in the Office of Naval Intelligence, but his real job was as the Navy's chief underwater spy. A former submariner himself, Bradley oversaw the Navy's growing clandestine efforts in undersea intelligence, where advanced technology was beginning to give the United States an advantage that it desperately needed to make up for a distinct gap in on-the-ground human espionage, which the intelligence community refers to as HUMINT.

Bradley, forty-seven, was an enigma even to most people in his own branch. If you looked him up in the Pentagon's official record, you'd see his assignment as "Naval Operations, Navy Department," a designation about as specific as referring to a professor of chemistry as "Faculty, University." In reality, Bradley oversaw highly compartmentalized black programs from an unmarked bunker on the fifth floor of the Pentagon, hidden behind three sets of locked doors. There, Bradley considered ways to use some of the Navy's most sophisticated and secret tools to unlock mysteries of the Soviet arsenal, in particular its submarine, encoded communications, and ballistic missile programs.

It was obvious to Bradley and anyone else who had been told about the Soviets' vast and fruitless search of the North Pacific that they'd lost a sub—a sub the Navy suspected with some confidence to be the K-129. This presented a tantalizing thought: If the US Navy could locate the sub's precise location, it might be able to access the wreck and mine it for a host of valuable intelligence—including communication codes, code-breaking machinery, and most compelling of all, the nuclear warheads atop the ballistic missiles. Any combination of these things would provide the greatest intelligence haul of the Cold War to date.

Both the United States and the Soviet Union knew basically what the other side was packing, but when it came to the specifics of those atomic missiles and warheads, the two adversaries were guessing. Getting their hands on an actual Soviet missile, intact, would allow US nuclear analysts to unlock any number of secrets about the enemy's arsenal, in particular the makeup of the warheads and the design of the guidance system, which could enable the United States to build better antimissile defenses specially calibrated to the Soviet design.

While the idea of finding a missing submarine in the Pacific Ocean, even when they had a general idea of where to search, proved so daunting to the Soviets that they'd ultimately given up looking, Bradley was fairly optimistic. He had a better way of locating it.

Starting in the early 1950s, the US Navy began installing a system of underwater hydrophones, anchored to the seafloor, designed to listen for the telltale sounds of enemy submarines. By the 1960s, it was increasingly clear that the balance of power in the Cold War was likely to be tipped under the oceans. Locating Soviet subs and maintaining an awareness of their positions at all times became tantamount for Naval Intelligence. It was the single most important part of the job.

The Navy recognized that every submarine—owing to the unique manufacture and wear of its moving parts, such as its propeller, cooling system, and diesel-electric engine—had a unique sound signature. It was basically a sonic fingerprint that analysts could listen for and locate. And putting large, fixed hydrophones at the bottom of the ocean provided a network of ears that were always listening.

The first hydrophone arrays were designed in secret by Western Electric, a division of the American Telephone and Telegraph Company (today's AT&T), in a program code-named Project Jezebel. It came together rather quickly, since most of the key components were already in use for other purposes. For instance, the "LOFAR actuator," a low-frequency signal analyzer that recorded submarine sounds onto paper, was based on a technology built at AT&T's famed Bell Labs to study human voice patterns in the hope of improving customer service.

The Navy's prototype array was forty hydrophones on a one-thousand-foot-long line installed at a depth of 1,440 feet off of the Bahamian island of Eleuthera in 1952. Once turned on, the system successfully detected a US submarine, and the program was rapidly expanded to cover the entire East Coast, stretching in an arc pattern from the Caribbean to Nova Scotia.

Two years later, the network was installed off the coast of California, and then Hawaii. Collectively the passive acoustic listening network was known as SOSUS, for Sound Surveillance System, and by the time it was finally operational on both coasts, in 1958, the US Navy had spent an estimated 16 billion dollars on the program. That was money well spent.

The ocean turns out to be a useful and efficient conveyor of some sound frequencies. Sound energy is absorbed by seawater at a very low rate, so it travels a great distance without losing much intensity. What's more, the deep ocean has a horizontal layer known as the Sound Fixing and Ranging channel (SOFAR), which serves as a wave guide for sound, allowing the waves to travel extreme distances in a horizontal direction without much dissipation. The specific depth of that layer varies around the world and is dependent on the effects of temperature and water pressure, but awareness of this depth is very important in submarine warfare. Commanders are careful to avoid spending much time inside this layer because they know to do so means sending out the equivalent of a radio broadcast that says, "Hey, y'all! I'm here!"

Being a SOSUS operator was a highly specialized and often boring job. There were long stretches, days upon days, of no activity, but occasionally something exciting happened. The analysts, all trained at a secret school on Key West, began to identify particular submarines, and even to pick up spooky unexplained sounds, such as the deep, eerie howl of the so-called Jezebel monster, which was later identified as the never-before-heard ultra-low-frequency vocalizations of blue whales.

Bradley knew that the network of hydrophone arrays in the Pacific was especially vast and that SOSUS was likely to pick up any abnormally loud sounds that occurred in the ocean. Analysts were trained to distinguish signal from noise, and the sudden and violent sounds of a submarine in trouble—one that had either exploded on the surface because of an accident, or sunk and imploded at crush depth—would be picked up by SOSUS. So he asked Captain Joseph P. Kelly, who oversaw SOSUS, to pull the acoustic data from the area of the Soviet search during the period of March 1 to 15 and have his analysts look it over closely for anomalous events.

Kelly's analysts found nothing suspicious. But there was another way.

As the arms race ramped up rapidly following World War II, President Dwight Eisenhower directed the US Air Force to find a means to eavesdrop on Soviet missile tests. He wanted the United States to have the ability to know when the enemy was detonating bombs and, to the best of its ability, where.

Working above a cigar shop in downtown Troy, New York, a young engineer named Carl Romney and a small team began a highly classified project funded by a secret group known as the Air Force Office of Atomic Energy. Romney's team built a system that used seismography to sense abnormal signals in the earth that could indicate explosions—and by 1951 it was ready for installation.

When a particular site picked up a suspicious signal, that data was rushed to Troy by encrypted message for analysis so that Romney and the few other men trained to interpret the signals could try to determine the origin of the explosion.

This became the Atomic Energy Detection System (or AEDS), a top secret global network of seismic sensors that greatly enhanced the Air Force's awareness of Soviet nuclear testing. But the increase of underwater testing in the late 1950s presented a new problem that would be addressed by a new agency, the Air Force Technical Applications Center (AFTAC). The land-based sensors easily picked up most underwater explosions, but if those explosions were to occur in an area with high natural seismic activity—and much of the Soviet east coast was exactly that—it was extremely difficult to distinguish between a nuclear test and an earthquake. Romney needed to put sensors under the water.

He knew that there were other secret acoustic intelligence-gathering systems at other departments, and SOSUS, with its wide coverage of the Pacific, was particularly attractive. Romney asked Kelly if he could piggyback on the Navy's array and was given the okay, so long as the Air Force agreed to maintain the same level of secrecy. That wasn't a problem.

Romney's group designed a custom system of recording and installed their own hydrophones, tuned to listen to different signals. Whereas the Navy was looking for long, continuous, narrow-band signals—the kind of sounds put off by machinery that's working—the Air Force was in search of short, broadband impulses that indicated short, violent episodes: explosions.

These sensors were also tuned for a second, even more secret purpose. The CIA wanted AFTAC to listen for the impact of Soviet intercontinental ballistic missiles (ICBMs) that were tested over the Pacific. The Soviets routinely launched dummy ICBMs into orbit and out over Kamchatka, where they'd splash down harmlessly in the Pacific. There was no reason for the Soviets to worry that those missiles, or their secret guidance systems, could be recovered, but the Agency recognized an opportunity. If it could precisely locate the splashdowns using AFTAC, then perhaps a new kind of secret spy sub, already in development, could pick them up.

Romney had long since realized it was inefficient to sit in Troy and wait for data to reach him and had built up a network of listening stations where analysts studied data twenty-four hours a day. He himself had moved to Fairfax County, Virginia, where AFTAC centralized its operations. He was in his office there on May 14, 1968, when Commander Jacob from the Office of Naval Intelligence (ONI) paid him a visit.

Jacob told Romney that a curious episode had been observed in the Pacific in mid-March: The Soviet Navy mobilized an abnormally large fleet off Kamchatka, a ragtag armada of submarines, cruisers, and fishing trawlers. This fleet formed a tight line in an east-west direction and moved slowly to the south until it reached 40 degrees north, east of Japan's Honshu Island. Here, the line turned and swept east, moving along the fortieth parallel, and searched all the way past the International Date Line, at 180 degrees east/west, before finally abandoning the mission.

Other intelligence suggested that a Soviet Golf-class submarine had been on patrol in that area in the weeks prior to the search but had not been heard from since. The ONI—and others in naval intelligence—suspected this was the target of the search.

Romney didn't have to be a submariner to know that a sub that sinks is going to explode one way or the other—either on the surface, as a result of some catastrophic event (a battery explosion, a missile failure, a collision with another ship, enemy fire), or when it, an airtight vessel, reaches crush depth.

"Would your boys have heard such a thing?" Jacob asked.

Probably, Romney replied. A sub explosion or implosion would be far less powerful than a nuclear test, so analysts most likely wouldn't have reported it. But it wouldn't be hard to go back and look at that data and find such an event, he said.

And sure enough, there it was. A number of AFTAC hydrophones in the North Pacific showed a strong, short pulse on March 11. The signal was strongest at a single hydrophone attached to the SOSUS array off Alaska's Aleutian Islands. Analysts were able to measure the time of the signal as it arrived at each station, and then—because they knew the speed at which sound travels through that area of the ocean—they could triangulate the signal and pinpoint its origin, with some precision.

The explosive event occurred at almost exactly 40 degrees north, 180 degrees west—the International Date Line—thirty seconds after midnight, local time. Romney knew immediately that this was a human event, because there was virtually no way that some natural occurrence—an earthquake, volcanic activity, or an especially loud whale—would be heard at the intersection of two important coordinates at almost exactly midnight. Nature is reactive and unpredictable; only people plan activities around precise times and locations.

Six minutes later, a second, similar signal appeared in the data, and both were located well within the area where the Soviet fleet had been searching.

This had to be the missing sub, and since the Soviets had called off the search and gone home, it was still there, lying almost seventeen thousand feet under the Pacific—1,560 miles northeast of Oahu, Hawaii—just waiting for the Americans to come and find it.

3

Finders Keepers

The idea of recovering key components of a Soviet ballistic missile submarine with a full arsenal of nuclear warheads was quite a carrot to dangle in front of the US intelligence leadership, but actually pulling it off was an absurdly complicated matter. Without understanding what caused the sub to sink suddenly, before it had a chance to call out in distress, there was no way for any US analyst to know what kind of shape the K-129 was in, and that was critically important.

A catastrophic explosion aboard the sub on or near the ocean's surface would have likely incinerated anything of value inside, while a violent implosion of the pressure hull at crush depth followed by a collision with the ocean floor would probably have left it in a pile of twisted pieces, no single one of them of much use as anything but an unnatural habitat for blindfish and other bottom dwellers. And the problem was that all of these questions could be answered only by actually getting close enough to analyze a wreck that lay more than three miles under the ocean, far beyond the capabilities of anything in the Navy's chest of toys.

Or so it seemed.

Reaching the unexplored realms of the ocean bottom had been a focus of the US Navy since the mid-1950s, when a group from the Office of Naval Research contacted the sixty-nine-year-old Swiss inventor Auguste Piccard and his son, Jacques, after observing their quixotic experiments in deep-sea exploration from afar.

Piccard the elder was a physicist who'd made his name assisting Albert Einstein, but he matured into a genius inventor with eccentric ideas who very much looked the part, with oft-bent wire-rimmed glasses and long gray hair that was infrequently attended to. He dabbled in all kinds of projects, including a high-altitude balloon, which he flew to a height of nine miles in 1931, breathing oxygen from a bottle—and doubling the record for highest manned ascent—but it was an obsession with the work of William Beebe, a bird curator turned ocean explorer at the New York Zoological Society, that turned Piccard's attention to the sea.

Beebe was confounded by the limitations of underwater exploration, so in the 1930s he built the bathysphere, a perfectly round steel sphere with thick windows that could hold two men and be lowered a half mile into the ocean on a steel tether. Beebe made his first manned dive in June 1930, and he went on to explore the murky dark of the deep ocean from inside his metal ball for much of the subsequent decade, making numerous discoveries despite his inability to move the craft once he was on the seafloor, therefore limited to observing only what happened to swim through the cloudy yellow tunnel of his spotlight.

Piccard met Beebe at the 1933 Chicago World's Fair, and he couldn't get the notion of these indestructible steel spheres out of his head. They became his new obsession. For years, he tinkered with similar submersible concepts, and by 1948, he was ready to test his own prototype.

Piccard's bathyscaphe was improved in many ways, most notably in its lack of a tether. It also had thicker walls and more interior space than Beebe's sphere and used a huge tank filled with gasoline to provide buoyancy (since gasoline is lighter than seawater). To descend, Beebe would flood an upper tank with water, creating negative buoyancy, and when he was finished down below, iron ballast was dumped overboard, which restored positive buoyancy and caused the sphere to bloop-bloop its way back to the surface.

The French Navy bought his first version of the contraption, and Piccard—with Jacques at his side—began work on its successor, the *Trieste,* named for the Italian city that helped fund the project as part of a public relations effort to become known as a hub of innovation. The *Trieste* was larger—twice as long—and safer than the bathyscaphe. In 1953, Auguste and Jacques hopped inside, closed the hatch, and plummeted nearly two miles into the Mediterranean, where they were disappointed to observe mostly just darkness and mud. Funding was difficult to come by, so a despondent Piccard was on the verge of abandoning his life's work, when the US Navy appeared on his doorstep.

In 1957, the Office of Naval Research contracted with the Piccards for fifteen dives in the Mediterranean, so that summer Jacques essentially operated a deep-water taxi for Pentagon scientists who asked puzzling questions and scribbled illegible notes. Eight of those dives, it was later revealed, were for the study of sound propagation through the sea—studies that were critical to the development of the SOSUS hydrophone network. In the end, the Navy was so pleased with the vessel that it bought *Trieste* from Piccard, hauled it back to San Diego, and hired him to train additional pilots as well as serve as a consultant.

Two years later, an improved *Trieste* was ready, and on January 23, 1960, Piccard and Navy Lieutenant Don Walsh traveled seven miles down toward the deepest known point in the Pacific, into a section of the Mariana Trench known as Challenger Deep. They spent only twenty minutes on the floor, staring agog at all manner of never-before-seen creatures, then began the long ascent back to the surface. The entire trip took nine hours and only one human (the film director James Cameron) has been that deep since.

To the Pentagon hierarchy, these experiments seemed like follies. All the momentum at the Navy's highest levels was toward preparations for warfare. Vice Admiral Hyman G. Rickover, the so-called father of the nuclear Navy, was probably the most influential man in the branch and maybe in the entire military establishment at that time. In Rickover's view, anything that didn't improve the war-fighting capability of American submarines was a waste, and because subs didn't ever descend beyond two thousand feet (and were rarely even that deep), exploring realms past twenty-five hundred feet under the surface was a waste of money.

On April 10, 1963, a single devastating accident changed everything. The USS *Thresher,* powered by a nuclear reactor and named for a type of long-tail shark, was the fastest and quietest attack sub ever built. It was to be the first of a new wave of twenty-four nuclear attack subs, which would ultimately be designated Thresher-class, armed with passive and active sonar and a new type of antisubmarine missile. *Thresher'*s main job would be to protect the growing fleet of subs that carried Polaris missiles, the new solid-fueled ballistic missiles that could be fired without surfacing.

Commissioned in August 1961, the *Thresher* underwent extensive tests up and down the Eastern Seaboard and impressed every submariner in the fleet. At eight A.M. on April 9, 1963, it left Portsmouth on a shakedown cruise in preparation for active duty. The submarine rescue ship *Skylark* accompanied *Thresher* during dive trials as a precaution and carried a Mc-Cann submarine rescue chamber, which could be lowered, with the assistance of divers, to evacuate and rescue personnel at depths up to 850 feet. It was the only sub rescue system in existence.

During one of these tests, just as the sub approached thirteen hundred feet, the commander of the *Skylark,* Lieutenant Commander Stanley Hecker, received a series of garbled messages from *Thresher'*s bridge. "Experiencing minor difficulty . . . Have positive angle . . . Attempting to blow . . . Will keep you informed." And then communications were lost.

The most advanced submarine in the American fleet sank more than eight thousand feet to the bottom of the Atlantic, with 129 men aboard. A frantic search involving fifteen ships began immediately, but everyone in the fleet knew rescue was futile. Subs lost in the open ocean are not going to be saved. Two days later, on April 12, President John F. Kennedy ordered all flags to fly at half-staff for four days to honor the men lost in the worst submarine disaster in naval history.

John Piña Craven, the Navy's chief scientist, was the only civilian at a meeting of the Navy's top submarine officers at the Pentagon on April 10, when word reached the group about the *Thresher'*s loss. The admiral in charge of Submarine Forces Atlantic had been leading the meeting, a celebratory technology review, when he was called away and returned to the room with a sunken expression that every man immediately recognized. Craven was sitting next to Captain Harry Jackson, one of the Navy's best naval architects and the engineering duty officer for the *Thresher*. Jackson had overseen all stages of *Thresher*'s development and was aboard every test until he declared the sub fit for duty.

The news devastated the room, and no one took it harder than Jackson, who just kept repeating the same phrase, over and over: "I should be there, I should be there."

"What could you do, Captain?" asked Craven. "What could anyone do?"

The loss of the most sophisticated submarine in the Navy's fleet created a cascading effect of short-term damage to the nuclear program. Fleet command was battered, the program's engineers stunned, and volunteers to serve in the silent service plummeted. Worst of all, the Navy had no idea what caused *Thresher*'s loss, and without that knowledge it was impossible to prevent the problem from recurring, let alone assure the public and potential future submariners that it would be fixed. Among the many realities exposed by *Thresher*'s death was the futility of a submarine rescue system that reached a depth of only 850 feet; it was essentially useless once a boat had traveled even a short distance from shore.

A year later, a committee chaired by the Navy's chief oceanographer recommended the creation of a new program that would provide the Navy with a way to reach the seafloor, perform rescues, and salvage lost materiel— and it would be run by the Special Projects Office, the Navy's experimental R and D shop, which carried a deliberately generic name.

Admiral Arleigh Burke, who ran the office, felt that his team was already too busy with development of a new ballistic missile and next-generation submarines to take on another project that carried such importance, so he created yet another new group, the Deep Submergence Systems Project (DSSP), and put John Craven, the Navy's chief scientist, in charge.

A forty-year-old Brooklyn native, Craven had previously worked on nuclear submarine hull designs and helped lead the development of the Polaris ballistic missile system. Placing a civilian in charge of a major initiative ruffled feathers up and down the chain of command, but Craven's appointment stood; to help assure the bureaucracy that order would not be upset, he was given the full legal status of a commanding officer.

Craven reveled in being an outsider and flaunted his iconoclastic nature, talking proudly of his direct lineage to both Moorish pirates (on his mother's side) and the Union ship *Tecumseh* (through his father). Rejected by the Naval Academy, Craven had joined the reserves and then became a maritime engineer with big dreams, which ultimately got him into the Navy's upper echelon anyway.

Craven's team of engineers and deep-sea experts at the DSSP focused first on the creation of the Deep Submergence Rescue Vehicle, also known as the DSRV. Everyone associated with the program understood the unspoken truth that saving a lost submarine that sank in deep water was an impossibility—once a sub reaches crush depth, no one on board could possibly survive, and on the West Coast, a sub leaving port was at that depth in twenty minutes; on the East Coast, it took about two hours. Craven knew that a strong, maneuverable DSRV would help expedite shallow rescue and also could provide the Navy with access to whole new areas of the ocean, for whatever reason.

Craven contracted with Lockheed Corporation's Ocean Systems Division and with MIT's Draper Laboratory, the only place in the country capable of designing the complex control and display system Craven had in mind. Draper, founded by the man who changed the face of naval warfare in World War II by inventing a more accurate gunsight, had built the computer and landing displays for the Apollo moon lander. The systems it created for the DSRV turned out to be even more complicated, because it's actually much harder to control a hovering craft in a fluid medium than it is in the low gravity of outer space.

But Craven wasn't just looking at sub rescue and recovery. In 1965, he was called to the Pentagon to meet with a mysterious intelligence officer who gave him strict orders to tell no one on his staff where he was going. There, he was told of Sand Dollar, a top secret program created by the Defense Intelligence Agency (DIA) to use whatever tools possible to retrieve Soviet war materiel—mostly the dummy warheads from test launches—from the seafloor. Sand Dollar was compartmentalized even from other cleared naval intelligence officers, meaning that information about the program could be stored only in very specific secured areas and could not be removed except in the company of an armed guard.

These so-called black programs had personnel and offices that couldn't very well be hidden from other military and political figures, as well as funding that was accountable to the Congress that provided it. Thus, every black program needed a plausible explanation for its existence—an accompanying white cover. One tenet of all successful white programs is that many of the participants have no idea they're participating in a cover. And the DIA saw in Craven's DSSP a perfect home for programs like this.

It was widely known that the Pentagon demanded the creation of the DSRV to help save American lives and to investigate future disasters. But it also happened to be the perfect vehicle for doing underwater espionage.

This is how John Craven came to know Jim Bradley, the captain in the secret Pentagon office who recognized that the United States was in a better position to find submarine K-129 than the Soviets were. Sand Dollar was devised to find and recover warheads off the seafloor so that engineers could pick apart their guidance systems and construction.

The program was a new realm militarily and also legally. Hardware on both sides of the Cold War lost in international waters was essentially abandoned. It had no value to the original owner and was considered useless to adversaries because the floor of the ocean was such a distant and formidable place. If the Navy could hone its tools to get down there, and actually be operational, there was a wealth of knowledge to be stolen.

To really do this job, Craven decided, he needed nuclear submarines, which can travel long distances without surfacing. This is critical when the task is going deep inside Soviet waters, or when you don't want to be observed searching for pieces of missing or abandoned equipment, often right under your enemy's nose.

Among Bradley's numerous responsibilities was oversight of the clandestine Office of Undersea Warfare, which conducted deep-ocean intelligence, and that gave him the authority to requisition certain very expensive machines—for instance, older nuclear subs that were no longer of much use to Rickover's fleet.

One of those, the *Halibut,* suited his purposes exactly. The *Halibut* was an ungainly thing, a hulk of a sub with a bulging nose that looked as if it was inspired by the silhouette of a blue whale. That lump housed the Regulus cruise missile, and on March 25, 1960, it became the first nuclear sub to launch a cruise missile.

The Regulus was quickly obsolete, replaced by the Polaris, making the *Halibut* a slow and cumbersome mobile launch platform that had virtually no use to the nuclear Navy. But one of her primary elements—the twenty-foot-diameter hatch from which the Regulus was launched—caught Craven's eye. To do the kind of intelligence gathering the DIA was looking for, he and Bradley would need a sub that could covertly deploy a new kind of submersible, and the *Halibut* and her gaping maw, with a few tweaks to the design, were uniquely suited to what Craven had in mind.

In February 1965, the *Halibut* was sent to Pearl Harbor to begin a 70-million-dollar renovation that was, as far as the world knew, to transform the sub into an oceanographic research vessel. In reality, the *Halibut* was kitted out with everything John Craven needed to deploy and operate a fleet of submersibles and other towed vehicles that could gather intelligence from the deep sea—cameras, electronics, sonar gear, sound recorders. After Pearl Harbor, the *Halibut* was tested, but Craven wasn't quite satisfied. The boat was sent to Mare Island, an inland Navy base east of San Francisco, for a second round of improvements. There, her sail was raised to make space for National Security Agency (NSA) antennas that could intercept communications, and a system was installed that would allow the *Halibut* to hover in water, so that her crew of NSA and CIA analysts could study a specific site and even deploy saturation divers to take a closer look.

The biggest changes were in the *Halibut*'s telltale hump, a space that Craven renamed the "Bat Cave" and which became the sub's hub of special operations. He remade the cavernous space into a three-level command center for special intelligence operations, with a darkroom, a data analysis center, and the largest computer ever installed on a submarine, the Univac 1124. The sub was given a two-ton aluminum "fish"—a twelve-foot-long robot outfitted with radar, sonar, cameras, and strobe lights that could be deployed from the hatch and towed under the sub on several miles of steel cable, providing Craven with a way to photograph the ocean depths.

Bradley's first test for the group's new toy was a mission to locate the nose cone of a Soviet ICBM in the South Pacific. Most of the crew wasn't even told what the *Halibut*'s goal was, and when they began to deposit transponders on the seafloor through the torpedo tubes, the majority of the crewmen thought the sub was laying mines.

Then the problems began. The computer crashed, mechanical systems malfunctioned, and Craven's precious fish—one of three in existence—was nearly lost when the threaded, seven-mile-long cable that tethered the 5-million-dollar gadget to the sub snapped on the spool and jammed the entire mechanism. After another follow-up mission during which the fish again malfunctioned, the *Halibut* headed back to Pearl Harbor, unsuccessful in its search for the nose cone.

The *Halibut* was in port at Pearl Harbor when word of the K-129 plan reached Craven. He'd been privy to conversations about the missing sub from the beginning and had attended the secret meetings in which the SO-SUS and AFTAC data was discussed, including a key gathering at the Naval Observatory in Washington on May 20, 1968.

Between the sinking of the USS *Scorpion* and the K-129's disappearance, Craven's deep-sea tools were suddenly in great demand. Each disaster showed up differently on the acoustic data. The *Scorpion* had very clearly suffered some kind of catastrophic accident while submerged. The K-129, on the other hand, appeared to have exploded while on the surface, and though the blip on the data was smaller for the Soviet sub than for the *Scorpion*, this difference seemed to be a compelling clue: The sound of a surface explosion wouldn't be conveyed very well through the water, so the fact that a "good-sized bang," in the words of SOSUS inventor Joseph Kelly, showed up on the hydrophone readings meant that whatever happened up top was a significant event. Craven saw something else in those results. There was no second large blip in the data, which some expected to see when the crippled sub passed through its crush depth. Most likely K-129 had sunk with its hatches open and the sub had been flooded with water that equalized the pressure and prevented an implosion. In theory, this meant the wreck would be more intact, and would have gone basically straight down from the coordinates where it was last identified. Craven wanted to test that idea.

He requisitioned a World War II–era sub and sank it with the hatches open out at sea, in a place where the hydrophones would be listening. There was no implosion.

It seemed very likely, Craven thought, that the K-129 was lying on the floor in one piece.

4

Enter the *Halibut*

O n July 15, four months after the K-129 was lost, the *Halibut* slipped from her berth in Pearl Harbor and cruised out of Oahu, navigating past an armada of sailboats and fishing vessels anchored around the harbor. Up in the cockpit, atop the sail, Captain Edward Moore scanned the surface and ordered the engine room to increase power as the sub reached clear, calm water, with only ocean ahead for thousands of miles. Down in the engine room, the turbines began to whir, and Moore watched his boat's white wake grow outward in a V shape behind the sub's stern.

"Let's take her down," Moore said as he stepped through a hatch into the sail and climbed down to assume his normal station in the main control room.

Once the *Halibut*'s CO departed the sail, two lookouts lowered the American flag and followed the captain inside, leaving only the officer of the deck alone outside the hull. He inhaled a final gulp of fresh air, clamped the hatch shut, and climbed inside as the USS *Halibut* dropped under the surface of the Pacific, where she'd spend at least the next two months conducting one of the most ambitious and secret intelligence operations of the Cold War.

The *Halibut,* her sail number painted over and hull now covered in a pattern of gray and dark gray camouflage, went to sea with a full house aboard—fifteen officers, 123 enlisted men, and six "technical specialists," from government agencies that were not named—and the vast majority of the crew were not given specific details on where they were going, or for what. Among the Navy crew, only Moore and his executive officer knew of the sub's true mission. To the submariners who served under them, it was known simply as the Special Project.

Submarine duty is challenging for anyone, but the crew of the *Halibut* was asked for even more sacrifice, since her missions were secret and of open-ended duration. For months, those 144 men would be sharing a space with no windows, no TV, and no telephone. Personal space was virtually nonexistent, and no man on any submarine is ever completely comfortable with the knowledge that only a thick layer of steel separates him from an environment that will kill any human instantly. As if to remind himself of the fragility of the boat that protected so many men, Captain Moore had hung a wooden sign in his stateroom. It read: O GOD, THY SEA IS SO GREAT AND MY BOAT IS SO SMALL.

Under the sea, there is no night or day, and men set schedules according to shifts, sleeping when they're told. Showers, when possible, were extremely cold and extremely brief, because freshwater is a precious commodity that cannot be wasted on vanity. So long as everyone on board stinks more or less equally, any individual's nose adapts, at least to the human odors. The waste matter is something else. Sub toilets can't flush to the sea outside the hull, because the water pressure there is too extreme. Instead, toilets flush into a tank that is emptied periodically, when conditions allow. A man sits on a cold steel horseshoe over a bowl, finishes his business, then works a series of valves to open the pipe that leads to the tank, as well as the one that brings in seawater to do the flushing, and each time a man does this, hideous waste gases escape through the pipe opening from below. No one gets used to this smell.

Days at sea can be tedious, and inevitably they blur together. A submariner on duty has little time to think, consumed with whatever critical operation he's doing to keep the machine that keeps them all alive afloat. The Navy does what it can to bring comforts to the crew, stocking high-quality food that doesn't spoil easily—subs famously have the best food in the Navy—and providing a library of entertainment. The *Halibut* went to sea with seventy-five reel-to-reel movies, many of them first-run Hollywood films.

After about a week, the *Halibut* crossed the International Date Line. The crew wasn't given specific details about their location, but everyone deduced from the cold water outside the hull that they'd been heading north and west and that by this point they were almost certainly inside waters where Soviet subs lurked. That suspicion was validated when the order came down from Captain Moore to the engine room: Do not cavitate.

When a submarine propeller spins rapidly in water, it creates low-pressure areas that form bubbles. These, in turn, collapse against the propeller and make a crackling noise that is easily heard by any nearby craft. When a captain orders his engine crew not to cavitate, it means that he either knows or suspects that an adversary is nearby. Additional orders instructed everyone to be wary of excessive noise. Until further notice, silence was to be the norm, which meant that while the crew could talk and work and conduct normal activities, they should all take special care not to do anything that resulted in loud noises that might be audible from the outside—such as slamming doors or dropping tools on the deck. Before any garbage was jettisoned, it was to be searched for anything that could implode in the sea, especially lightbulbs, which popped like little depth charges the moment they were ejected into the water. The *Halibut*'s crew was accustomed to dangerous work, and they knew the boat's missions were secret because they were conducted in places other submarines couldn't reach. The increased vigilance about silence only intensified the realization that somewhere out there—possibly quite close—were ships and subs actively hunting for incursions just like this.

Once the technicians up in the Bat Cave were certain they'd reached the correct five-mile zone, they went to work. First, a search grid was laid out. Acoustic transponders were launched through the sub's bow torpedo tubes at specific intervals. Once a transponder came to rest on the ocean floor, its location was noted using inertial guidance and added to a chart. Over the next thirty-six hours, the *Halibut* ejected and plotted the location of the entire array of transponders to establish a navigational grid that would be used to build a detailed map of the search area so that when the fish and its cameras passed over any particular point, it could signal the transponder and get its location within about five hundred yards—a remarkable accuracy considering the water was nearly three miles deep at that point.

Technicians prepped and launched the fish through the hatch in the bottom of the *Halibut,* then began lowering it for thousands of feet. The process was slow and tedious. It took hours and was conducted with extreme care, considering the fish's troubled history and the critical nature of the job it was about to undertake. The two-ton device hung from its wire tether a few tens of feet above the ocean floor—close enough to get a decent picture of what was down there but not so close that it might collide with underwater hills, thermal vents, or seabed lava flows.

Then the hunt for K-129 began.

For weeks, Captain Moore ordered the sub to sweep methodically over the target area, maintaining a constant depth to protect the fish, and varying the search patterns to ensure that no areas were missed, especially when the sub was changing course—all of this requiring meticulous cooperation between the bridge, the reactor crew, the ballast control operator, the helmsman, and the planesman. In the Bat Cave, analysts squinted and stared at the fuzzy side-scan sonar images, in search of large objects that warranted closer inspection with cameras.

And as the days ticked away, frustration rose. Moore and the civilian technicians conferred and made adjustments, varying the search pattern and the depth at which the fish was deployed, hoping for a break. The crew did what they could to stay occupied, knowing that their sub—which was moving at a crawl with its precious surveillance tool trailing on eighteen thousand feet of cable—was about as vulnerable as a boat could be.

Periodically, operators would reel the fish in so that the camera's film could be retrieved, and the crew's photo technician, Billie Joe Price, would then vanish into the adjacent darkroom to develop the photos. What Price was seeing wasn't valuable intelligence, but it was the first and best look any human had ever had of this remote realm of deep sea. Hundreds and thousands of black-and-white eight-by-tens came out of the darkroom, and because these weren't sensitive documents, the photo tech was free to share them with the crew, who excitedly passed around shots of giant sea slugs, fish with huge eyes and bat wings, and all kinds of animals that looked like creations from a sci-fi film.

At the mission's one-month mark, morale began to sag. The operation seemed futile and doomed to fail. But all indications from above were that it would continue. It had to continue. Tempers simmered. Boredom settled in. Everyone on board had seen every film, and the best of the food had long since been eaten. Exhausted from seven weeks of searching, Captain Moore ordered the fish reeled in, and the *Halibut* limped home to Pearl Harbor.

By the time the *Halibut* got back to base for servicing, there was enough uranium—the reactor's lifeblood—for only one more deployment, so after a short break, Moore gathered his crew and the spooks and set out again toward the search area.

Everything about this final mission was more hurried and less well planned. The galley ran out of milk two days into the trip and the lettuce disappeared two days after that. By the time they reached the search area, there was nothing fresh to eat—only canned, frozen, and pickled foods remained.

It hardly mattered. The *Halibut*'s final mission was all about purpose, about expedience. To return to Pearl Harbor this time without success would mean that months of work and stress and discomfort would have been a waste, and though the crew still had no idea what they were looking for, it was obvious that it was of incredible importance to the Navy, and the nation.

Four and a half weeks into the second search, Price was given new film canisters and disappeared back into his darkroom just off the Bat Cave's port side. As usual, the shy, soft-spoken crewman saw mostly similar frames of milky gray sea. At this point, even the freakish sea creatures weren't interesting to him. He simply added those shots to the stacks on his light table, which had begun to resemble a small mountain chain. Even Price hadn't been fully cleared for the mission. The young photo tech wasn't sure exactly what he was looking for. He'd been told only to keep an eye out for anything unusual and that he'd probably know what that meant when he saw it.

Then he did see it: the conning tower of a submarine. Price's pulse quickened. The fish's strobe was bright and allowed for remarkably clear pictures, even at twenty thousand feet. And there was no doubt as to what he was seeing:

the intact steel section of an unfamiliar sub, with four periscopes extended. He flipped through and saw more photos of sub parts, in clear contrast to the darker mud of the seafloor. There was a rudder. And there, the diving bell.

When the photos were assembled into a montage, it was clear that the sub had broken in two main parts, and the larger section was lying on its side, with holes and tears. Some hull sections appeared to have fully buckled. What the tech was seeing was so strange, so shocking, so unreal after thousands of useless photos over dozens of endless days, that he froze there for a minute. He reached for the phone to dial the captain's stateroom, and as he did, Price came upon the most shocking photo yet: A partial human skeleton, wearing a storm raglan, quilted pants, and boots, lying in the mud next to the wreck.

"Captain Moore?" Price said, as his CO picked up the phone on the other end.

"Yes, go ahead," Moore replied.

"Captain, it's the photo hangar. We've found what we are looking for."

It took three weeks for the *Halibut* to reach Pearl Harbor, and despite the fact that only the captain, his executive officer, the photo tech, and a handful of intelligence analysts inside the Bat Cave knew exactly what the boat had just accomplished, every man on board knew that they had finally completed their critical mission. The sense of triumph on the sub was palpable, and all those months of bad food, bad hygiene, crushing boredom, and near paralyzing frustration had been forgotten by the time the sub pulled into its berth.

As the men greeted their families, several of them noted three naval officers wearing dress uniforms bedecked in medals climb from a black limousine, accompanied by two armed guards. They walked toward the *Halibut* and waited for Captain Moore and his XO, the last two men on board the sub, to disembark. The XO carried a black briefcase that was locked to his left wrist with handcuffs that the guards clicked open, so that he could hand the case over to the officers. Each of them shook his hand, turned around, and got back into the limo, which drove them off to the base airfield, where the briefcase began its trip back to Washington, DC, carrying a stack of photos that were about to change history.

5

Okay, Now What?

Captain Jim Bradley was briefed about the photos long before they actually reached his secret office at the Pentagon, but he still wasn't prepared for what he saw when they were actually fanned out on his desk: Here was a largely intact Soviet nuclear submarine captured in such clarity that the photos could have been taken in shallow water. The detail was incredible. Bradley could see that one of the sub's ballistic missile tubes was empty and that there was substantial damage to the steel hull around it, but two of the R-21s were clearly still there, standing in their silos, and presenting an incredible opportunity for the United States to get its hands on something that seemed almost unfathomable: a Soviet ICBM with an intact nuclear warhead.

Bradley took the photos straight to his new boss, Frederick "Fritz" Harlfinger II, who hadn't even been in his job as the director of naval intelligence for a month.

Prior to taking over Naval Intelligence, Harlfinger had been the Defense Intelligence Agency's assistant director of collection, a job that required him to find ways to steal foreign military equipment for analysis. Under Harlfinger's direction, the DIA obtained a Soviet MiG fighter in Syria, a Soviet surface-to-air missile from Vietnam, another Soviet missile from Indonesia, and the engine of a Soviet plane that crashed in Germany.

These photos offered him a chance for the greatest theft yet—possibly the greatest theft in the history of military intelligence.

The legality of this wasn't an immediate concern, especially not in the wake of what had transpired off the North Korean coast earlier in the year. On the evening of January 22, 1968, the USS *Pueblo,* a spy ship flagged as an environmental research vessel, was collecting electronic intelligence just outside North Korea's boundary waters, when a North Korean sub chaser and three torpedo boats appeared on its periphery. The Korean ships harassed the *Pueblo,* which was only lightly armed, and ultimately opened fire. Korean guns strafed the flying bridge with fifty-seven-millimeter explosive rounds, wounding the captain and two other crewmen. The captain ordered the crew to begin destroying sensitive materials and attempted to buy time by obeying an order from the North Korean ship to follow it toward port. While the *Pueblo* cruised slowly toward the hostile coast, intelligence officers worked furiously to smash machines with hammers, burn the most sensitive classified files in the onboard incinerator, and throw others overboard.

When the *Pueblo* stopped just outside North Korean waters, the sub chaser opened fire again, this time fatally wounding an American sailor named Duane Hodges. Seeing no choice, the captain finally relented and surrendered his ship. The North Koreans boarded, bound, and blindfolded the crew, and then docked at Wonsan, where they paraded the captive crew past a crowd of cheering, jeering civilians.

Months later, the United States was still stung by the loss of the *Pueblo.* The ship was held and plundered by the North Koreans, and anything of value had no doubt been shared with their Soviet proxies. It was later revealed that the raid was almost certainly ordered by the Soviets to obtain a Vinson KY-58 radio encryption unit, in order to decrypt and read the old cards that the American traitor John Anthony Walker had been handing over to the Soviets.

Fury over the *Pueblo* incident only sweetened the opportunity to snatch the K-129 for anyone who worked intel at the Pentagon. Bradley selected the best of the photos into a collection that he code-named Velvet Fist.

He and Harlfinger approached the rear admiral in charge of submarine warfare, and he couldn't believe what he was seeing, either. This was something they had to try.

There was little argument over whether the submarine was worth targeting. Everyone invited into the conversation agreed that the opportunity was unprecedented.

There were two primary motivations. The first was the tantalizing possibility of obtaining actual Soviet nuclear warheads. Everything understood about the enemy's foremost weapon to date was gleaned from telemetry captured during missile tests. The telemetry provided analysts with information about overall performance of the missiles, but it didn't tell them how the Soviets achieved that performance, or what was inside a live warhead. To actually possess, deconstruct, and reverse engineer a Soviet nuclear weapon could inform American warhead design, guidance, and missile defense systems. US analysts had no idea how accurate Soviet missiles really were. They also had no idea of the true power of submarine-launched warheads, nor how many of those warheads were on board a given attack sub. It was widely theorized that the Soviet subs (and land bases) carried two types of ballistic missiles—those with live warheads, and dummies. Why would a sub carry dummies? Because a nuclear warhead is expensive to produce and a dummy is nearly as effective a weapon considering that American radar and missile defense can't tell the difference and aren't about to start guessing as missiles approach the US mainland.

For the Navy, though, there was another, arguably even more valuable prize—the cryptography. To recover a submarine's communication systems for enciphering and deciphering code was the kind of thing that could upset the balance of power for years. Sure, the Soviets changed their codes and keying materials regularly, but the machines themselves could be studied to see how the codes were made and read. Capturing a Soviet cryptological machine would, in theory, enable naval intelligence analysts to decipher all of the classified chatter that NSA satellites were already intercepting. With the machines and the cards, analysts could go also back and read all the messages received in the recent past, to study movements and commands.

A few months before the K-129 sank, a top-ranking admiral told Congress that the single most dangerous threat to the United States was the rise of the Soviet Union's "huge underseas fleet of 250 attack submarines and 100 missile-firing submarines, the largest force of submarines ever created." A comprehensive 1969 survey by the Naval War College warned that not only were the Soviet subs a formidable opposition—they were part of a force growing at an unprecedented rate. "It has been estimated that the Russians can build 20 to 30 nuclear submarines a year in covered shipyards protected from satellite reconnaissance," the survey stated. The United States, in contrast, could build only "10 to 12 a year in shipyards open to public view."

Harlfinger's next stop was the White House, where he showed the photos to Lyndon Johnson. The president, he later said, was blown away by the photographs, but Johnson was also in the final months of his presidency and had little motivation to put something in motion that might not survive under his successor, the Republican Richard Nixon.

The submarine, of course, was going nowhere. And the Soviets had long since given up searching for it, so the matter was tabled until Nixon was sworn in on January 20, 1969. Not long after America's thirty-seventh president took office, according to an interview Harlfinger later gave to reporter Christopher Drew, he called Jim Bradley. "Get your ass over to the White House and take Velvet Fist with you," Harlfinger said.

It wasn't Nixon himself who'd asked for them. It was Alexander Haig, deputy to the country's new national security adviser, Henry Kissinger. Haig wanted the photos, and he wanted to hold on to them, so that he could show Nixon personally. This request shocked Bradley and horrified Harlfinger. It was a gross violation of protocol to transfer documents that serious outside of Naval Intelligence custody, but it was also clear that Haig was really going to get them in front of the president, so they made an exception. Haig could keep the photos, for twenty-four hours.

Kissinger, then just forty-five, was chosen to be the key foreign policy adviser on the president-elect's transition team, and he worked quickly to consolidate power, taking over the responsibility of receiving the important President's Daily Brief from the CIA, which he had presented every morning in a basement room at 450 Park Avenue in Manhattan, the home of Nixon's presidential campaign.

Haig passed the photos to Kissinger, who took them to Nixon. During his campaign, Nixon had argued that the US military had diminished under Johnson's presidency. One of the examples Nixon cited most often to prove this was the capture of the USS *Pueblo*. Here, then, was a thrilling opportunity for revenge.

John Craven assumed that the job of looting K-129 would be his. All of the Navy's deep-water innovation to that point had come out of his office, including the *Halibut,* and it seemed only natural that he'd be the one they asked to get the sub. Craven had already been thinking about how he'd go about such a thing, from the moment *Halibut*'s fish had found it, and the simplest concept in his mind—the only one that made sense to him—was to use robots. Craven was confident that he could outfit existing gear to deploy from the *Halibut* that could breach the hull and retrieve specific equipment from the inside.

But that was also a huge step beyond anything he'd done so far. And the targets were very delicate. It seemed very unlikely to others at the Pentagon that any robot could be remotely operated seventeen thousand feet under the ocean with enough care and accuracy to get inside of a wrecked submarine and pick up a code book, or, for that matter, a nuclear warhead.

The chief of naval operations agreed. Craven was pushed out.

CIA director Richard Helms wanted very badly for the Agency to take over the project. Whereas the notion of trusting an intelligence outfit with complicated engineering might once have been an insane idea, the Agency had proven over the preceding decade an ability to succeed in aerospace, another complicated area where it previously had no experience.

As soon as Nixon's White House let on that a submarine theft might be in play, Helms began to build a case for having the CIA run the operation. And his lobbying worked. On April 1, 1969, Deputy Defense Secretary David Packard, the tall, barrel-chested electrical engineer who cofounded Hewlett-Packard, drafted a memo to Helms asking the CIA to prepare a study of how the Agency's technical group might get the submarine, or at least its most sought-after components.

Helms knew exactly whom to hand that job to—Carl Duckett, deputy director of the Agency's burgeoning hub of innovation, recently renamed the Directorate of Science and Technology.

6

America's Top Secret Hub of Innovation

spionage is as old as warfare, and America's first president was among its first spymasters, but there was no national department for intelligence gathering empowered by the executive branch of the US government until July 26, 1947, when President Harry Truman established the Central Intelligence Agency, as well as the National Security Council and the Department of Defense, as part of the National Security Act. The act took more than a year of debate and compromise on Capitol Hill but established the CIA as an independent organization outside the control of the military that could spy and conduct clandestine operations but which would have no law enforcement powers. "I believe that this act will permit us to make real progress toward building a balanced and effective national defense," Truman said.

A year later, John Parangosky joined America's nascent spy agency at the age of twenty-nine. He was born on December 4, 1919, in Shenandoah, Pennsylvania, the oldest of three children from an American mother and a father who'd immigrated from Lithuania. John stayed close to home for college, getting his bachelor's in economics at Washington & Jefferson College and, because he loved to play violin, a minor in music. When World War II broke out, Parangosky joined the Army Air Forces as a first lieutenant and excelled in covert ops. After the war, he enrolled at Columbia Law School before leaving to join the brand-new CIA, which was then headquartered in a brick building with white columns on E Street that formerly housed its World War II predecessor, the Office of Strategic Services (OSS).

Parangosky was shipped back overseas, to Trieste, Italy, which at that time was an active post for running agents inside the Communist Eastern Bloc of Europe, and when he returned to the United States a few years later, Parangosky moved into the Directorate of Plans—the branch of the Agency responsible for clandestine operations—as a specialist in program management.

In 1956, he was assigned into Detachment B of a new top secret spy plane program and sent to Turkey to serve as the administrative officer at Adana Air Base, which later became known as Incirlik. This was a very different role for Parangosky. He was the senior CIA officer within the detachment, charged with managing security, logistics, general housekeeping, and personnel matters—in particular, Parangosky had to navigate the complicated and often tense relationship between the Air Force, which provided the pilots (or "drivers," as the program called them), and the CIA, for whom they were actually working while in Turkey. The pilots had to blend in as civilians. They were asked to grow their hair out and wear street clothes, to look more like "tech reps" working on an experimental weather plane program that was openly discussed in order to provide cover. The job was Parangosky's first exposure to compartmentalized black programs, as well as to an increasingly important but lesser-known core of employees within the Agency: scientists and engineers. Helping brilliant men execute increasingly audacious projects would become the focus of Parangosky's career, as he developed into one of the most wide-ranging and effective intelligence officers in US history.

The CIA's original science and technology group consisted of a small team of scientists and engineers plucked from various defense contractors, or from within the military branches, and housed in a cluster of Quonset huts on the National Mall originally built for personnel that poured into the nation's capital during World War II. The wooden structures were so rickety that the heavy safes necessary to protect classified documents occasionally broke through the floors, like a scene out of a Bugs Bunny cartoon. It wasn't unusual to see PhDs chasing away the rats that lived behind the radiators.

Inside, men—and only men; the few women hired were exclusively in secretarial jobs—crammed around makeshift desks, working with hand-cranked calculators and slide rules, wiring together prototypes for early guidance systems, and then, at lunch and after work, strolled directly out onto the mall, a short walk from the Tidal Basin, the Lincoln Memorial, and the Potomac River, which in those days was actually still clean enough to swim in.

The original name of that group was the Office of Scientific Intelligence (OSI), which oversaw a wide slate of projects that used technology as a method of gathering intelligence.

President Eisenhower had spurred the creation of such a group after recognizing that lapses in postwar spy practices had caused the US intelligence apparatus to develop enormous blind spots. When the first Soviet nuclear test was carried out in 1949, for instance, the United States was shocked because its own experts had predicted that the Russians were at least three years away.

In July 1954, Eisenhower approached MIT president Dr. James R. Killian, Jr., with a critical task. Killian had overseen the vast Radiation Lab (RadLab) during World War II and became president of MIT when he was just forty-five. RadLab had been the largest scientific operation in America, larger even than the Manhattan Project. At its peak, it employed more than 20 percent of the country's physicists and was the birthplace of various radar systems (including those small enough to mount on planes as well as direct-fire systems) and the first long-range navigation system.

Killian wasn't a scientist himself. He was a science administrator, but he revered science and technology, had an easy grasp of complicated subjects, and was convinced that small groups of smart people could solve any problem on earth. He'd seen it again and again during World War II, and the Manhattan Project in particular solidified his philosophy—that the United States, he later wrote, "was capable of almost any engineering accomplishment that it considered necessary to national survival. It possessed in its manpower and industrial base the power to achieve almost any single goal it set, provided only that it was willing to concentrate its energies and resources on that goal."

Eisenhower summoned Killian because he was worried. He and his closest advisers were increasingly aware that America was vulnerable to surprise attack from the Soviet Union. Several 1950 intelligence estimates had actually recommended that the United States prepare for a global war in 1954, which one report called the "year of maximum danger."

The president asked Killian to commence a study "of the country's technological capabilities to meet some of its current problems"—and the highest priority of the study should be a rapid and accurate counting of Soviet nuclear capability, especially the number and dispersion of its new Bison long-range bombers, which a US military attaché spotted for the first time in 1953. The result was the Technological Capabilities Panel (TCP)—which gathered forty-two of the nation's brightest scientists, with Killian in charge.

The TCP created three separate projects—offensive capabilities, continental defense, and intelligence—and Killian hand-selected the members, putting Polaroid founder Edwin "Din" Land in charge of the intelligence project. Land was another of America's great scientific minds, the forty-five-year-old inventor of the polarizing filter and instant camera who was at that time on leave from Polaroid and living in Hollywood, helping Alfred Hitchcock figure out a way to make three-dimensional movies. When Killian came calling, Land chose national security over entertainment and selected just five men to serve on his panel, employing one of his favorite management tenets—that any effective committee should fit inside a taxi.

Beginning on September 13, 1954, the members met 307 different times and were given access to every major unit of the US defense and intelligence community. The panel's assessment completely changed the way in which the United States went about intelligence gathering over the next two decades. Covert operations inside Russia were failing, the report stated. And the way to make up for that gap was to use science and technology.

The rapid reinvention that Land wanted required an entirely new "laboratory facility where broad fundamental research in intelligence can be concluded." This should serve as the beginning of an entirely new unit within the CIA—a group that would "pioneer in scientific techniques for collecting intelligence," Land wrote to CIA director Allen Dulles—a group that would eventually become the Directorate of Science and Technology.

All along, Eisenhower fretted about leaks, and some of the TCP's ideas were too sensitive even for distribution among the entire national security leadership. In October 1954, Killian and Land met privately with the president to discuss two ideas so highly classified that they didn't want to put them in print. One was the development of a submarine that could fire ballistic missiles—this would soon be the Polaris class of subs that changed the nuclear battlefield and started a new undersea arms race with the Soviet Union. The other was a project proposed by Kelly Johnson, the maverick aeronautical engineer who ran Lockheed Corporation's Skunk Works in Burbank: a high-altitude photo reconnaissance plane that could soar undetected, seventy thousand feet above the Soviet Union, in search of bombers, fighters, radar installations, and ground-to-air missile defenses.

Johnson's real name was Clarence, but he'd gone by Kelly since grade school, after some classmates took to calling him Clara. He joined Lockheed, one of America's primary military aircraft contractors, in 1933 and was the company's chief research engineer by 1938. In 1952, he was put in charge of Lockheed's Burbank plant, and a few years later assumed control of research and development, turning that plant into a quasi-secret laboratory for advanced technology projects that was nicknamed the Skunk Works because of the overpowering stench that wafted over from a nearby plastic plant.

Although the Air Force initially dismissed Johnson's idea as "too optimistic," he was certain that he could build the plane, and quickly. For approximately 22 million dollars, Johnson said, he would build twenty high-altitude spy planes and he'd "have the first one flying in eight months."

To Killian and Land, this was exactly what America needed to get an accurate handle on the Soviets' war-fighting capability. If your concern is finding those Bison bombers, Land told Eisenhower, this is the way we do that. Eisenhower agreed. He told them on the spot that he wanted to build this plane—but rather than go through the slow bureaucracy of the Defense Department, he wanted the CIA to do it.

CIA director Allen Dulles was also in the meeting and was worried that the Agency wasn't set up to run such a project. It didn't build missiles or airplanes. That's just not our business, he said.

You're in that business now, Eisenhower replied.

On December 9, 1954, the CIA and Lockheed signed a contract and work officially began at the Skunk Works on the most secret project in the Agency's short history. It was code-named Aquatone. Dulles handed the program to Dick Bissell, a Yale-trained economist who was working as his office coordinator. Unable to serve in World War II for medical reasons, Bissell helped run logistics for war purchasing, and afterward he imagined and then directed the Marshall Plan, helping to rebuild Europe from 1948 to 1951. Bissell was intimidatingly smart, a dapper man with a mind so sharp that one former colleague described him as "a human computer." He could memorize anything, and he often did. His parents recalled him memorizing the timetables for the Connecticut railroad line between New York City and Boston in a single day, for no apparent reason.

Bissell was surprised by the assignment. He found out a day after Eisenhower's decision, when Dulles summoned him to the director's office and told him, he later recalled, "with absolutely no prior warning or knowledge that The President approved a project involving the development of an extremely high-altitude aircraft to be used for surveillance and intelligence collection over 'denied areas'" in Europe and Russia. Bissell was to go directly to the Pentagon and work with Trevor Gardner and two of the Air Force's top generals to figure out how the project would be organized and run.

"Okay, Richard," Dulles said, upon briefing him. "It's yours."

Dulles told Bissell that Kelly Johnson would build the plane, and then he patched Johnson in over the phone. In the subsequent conversation, Dulles and Johnson agreed on a schedule, Bissell thought, "that was almost impossible to meet."

Granted, Bissell knew very little about airplanes, and he wasn't an engineer, but he was an autodidact with a photographic memory. He arranged an overnight flight to Los Angeles to visit the Skunk Works and meet Johnson; instead of sleeping he read a book on aeronautical engineering en route, learning enough to become conversant in technical details, which made Johnson like and trust his new CIA supervisor from the outset.

The organization that emerged under Bissell's direction was tiny and extremely secret. For Aquatone's initial stage, only fourteen CIA officers were assigned to the project, including Bissell. Each was detailed from his home office position and remained on the home office payroll. As far as the record would show, they were all doing their regular jobs, and even their closest associates wouldn't know their true assignment.

At the Skunk Works in downtown Burbank, the program was just as tightly controlled. Johnson handpicked twenty-five engineers and told the team that they were all now working for the CIA and must operate as such. No one, not even spouses, could know what they were doing. "This project is so secret that you may have a six-month to one-year hole in your résumé that can never be explained," he told Ben Rich, one of his top engineers. "You'll tell no one about what we do—not your wife, your mother, your brother, your girlfriend, your priest, or your CPA."

Even the other engineers at the Skunk Works—known officially as Lockheed Advanced Development Programs—had no idea what was happening inside the windowless two-story concrete warehouse that housed the spy plane program, a building filled with cigarette smoke that was always dirty because the CIA was too skittish to clear any secretaries or janitors for work there.

The CIA plucked pilots in secret from the Air Force and had Lockheed put them on its payroll. As far as the public, and everyone at Lockheed and the Air Force who hadn't been cleared into the program, knew, these pilots had been selected to participate in a government-contracted "high-altitude weather and performance study," and their salaries were paid from a special account filled with untraceable government funds.

As an economist, Bissell understood risk. When the payoff is big enough, significant risk is acceptable. And Eisenhower agreed. Bissell was given basically a blank check to deliver the plane, and fast, but without anyone knowing about it. To maintain absolute secrecy, Bissell set up an independent organization within the CIA that he called the Development Projects Staff. The DPS existed outside of the regular Agency operations, with its own security and communications system.

Aquatone was, in Agency parlance, compartmentalized—a project that only a few people outside of the director were to be told about—and its creation gave rise to many methods that still make up the basic blueprint for how a black project is designed and run today. That includes careful handling of files, which would be labeled "top secret/special handling," and the use of code names. When Bissell made frequent visits to the Skunk Works, he came alone (or nearly alone) and walked in the shadows, known, if he was referred to at all, as Mr. B.

Along with secrecy, speed was the primary directive. To prevent delays and allow his staff the ability to learn on the fly, Bissell opened channels to the most important minds in America. Even the least-experienced and lowest-ranking workers on Bissell's special project staff were introduced and also given access to Land and Killian, as well as other living legends of science and technology. Because the program couldn't just run rogue—even a black program used money that had to be trackable and explainable to Congress—Bissell built out the back office, clearing security men to vet the contractors, lawyers to draw up contracts, and even a few IRS officials to ensure that all the arrangements met US tax codes.

The money trail called for creative accounting; to allow Kelly Johnson to begin work before the official financial arrangements were in place, the Agency used a portion of its black funds, funneled through subsidiary accounts attached to front companies, to pay Lockheed using personal checks. More than a million dollars arrived that way, by regular mail at Johnson's Encino home, and he deposited the checks into a phony corporation he called C&J Engineering. This process, Johnson's deputy, Ben Rich, remarked, "has to be the wildest government payout in history."

Eight months later, the plane was ready. Lockheed needed somewhere to test it in total secrecy, so the CIA selected a small patch of Nevada desert directly abutting an Atomic Energy Commission territory used for nuclear tests. The area was remote and completely off-limits to air traffic.

Bissell arranged for a presidential action to add Groom Lake, as the test area was called, into the AEC territory, so that on maps it would just look like more land partitioned off for nuclear tests. The new CIA base—later nicknamed Area 51—was built for a total of eight hundred thousand dollars. "I'll bet this is one of the best deals the government will ever get," Johnson observed.

On July 24, 1955, the first Aquatone plane—now known as the U-2—was disassembled in Burbank and delivered to the secret test facility inside the belly of a C-124 cargo plane.

The U-2 looked bizarre, like no plane on earth. It had a fifty-foot-long fuselage built of "wafer-thin aluminum" and wings that extended eighty feet. This enormous wingspan gave the U-2 tremendous lift—so much lift that the plane went airborne on its first taxi and throttle test and was thirty-five feet off the ground before its test pilot even noticed.

Within a month, CIA pilots had broken the existing altitude record, reaching 74,500 feet, and flew up to five thousand miles over ten hours on a single tank of gas, causing one early pilot to crack, "I ran out of ass before I ran out of gas."

It was a grueling job: "A pilot was jammed inside a cockpit smaller than the front seat of a VW Beetle, laced into a bulky partial-pressure suit, his head encased in a heavy helmet, hooked up to an oxygen breathing tube, a urine tube, and fighting off muscle cramps, hunger, sleepiness, and fatigue," explained Ben Rich. "If the cabin pressure and oxygen supply cut off, a pilot's blood would boil off in seconds at more than 13 miles above sea level." The skill and focus required were also extreme. A U-2 pilot had to maintain speed within a very small and specific range. If he dropped below 98 knots, the plane would stall and fall out of the sky; if he went over 102 knots, it was in danger of breaking apart. So, Ben Rich wrote, "the slowest it could safely go was right next to the fastest it could go."

Thanks to Walt Lloyd, the young CIA officer Bissell had placed in charge of Aquatone's security apparatus, the public believed Lockheed's bizarre new plane was part of a weather research program conducted by the National Advisory Committee for Aeronautics (NACA)—the precursor to NASA. Lloyd, a rising star within the Agency's security wing, cleared only two people—NACA Director Hugh Dryden and his public relations man, Walt Bonney—and the cover story was so plausible that everyone else at NACA really believed this was an experimental plane.

Six weeks later, the U-2 was operational. It flew its first official mission over Germany and Poland on June 20 under the guise of weather reconnaissance, assigned to a fictional Air Force detachment known as the First Weather Reconnaissance Squadron Provisional.

On July 4, the first U-2 overflew the Soviet Union, photographing naval bases where submarines were built, as well as several airfields. A day later, another pilot took the plane over the plant where Soviet Bison bombers were being built, a bomber test facility, and important missile and rocket plants.

The Agency was surprised to see that the flights weren't as stealthy as they'd hoped; the Russians picked the planes up on radar and scrambled fighters to intercept them; fortunately, neither those fighters, nor the ground-based antiaircraft defenses, could reach a U-2 cruising at seventy thousand feet. Still, it gave Eisenhower pause, and the Air Force urged him to stop the flights, which he did only temporarily, until the CIA told him what had been accomplished in only a few weeks. "For the first time we are really able to say that we have an understanding of much that was going on in the Soviet Union. . . . Five operational missions have already proven that many of our guesses on important subjects can be seriously wrong."

One of the big ones: The US military was using bad maps. Photo interpreters noticed that the geodetic data used to make the Air Force's nuclear target maps were wrong. The U-2 showed the earth to be slightly oblong and not a perfect sphere, meaning that the targets assigned to all of the US ICBMs were each about twenty miles off. Had war broken out, every missile would have missed.

Eisenhower had told CIA director Allen Dulles that locating and counting the Soviet Bison bomber fleet was the single most important item on his national security agenda. And four days after the first U-2 flight, the film was delivered to CIA headquarters, where Dulles and Bissell saw it for the first time together. "From 70,000 feet you could not only count the airplanes lined up at ramps, but tell what they were without a magnifying glass," Bissell later said. "We had finally pried open the oyster shell of Russian secrecy and discovered a giant pearl. . . . The accumulated weight of evidence from these flights caused the President to . . . relax a bit. I was able to assure him that the so-called bomber gap seemed to be nonexistent."

The Soviets, meanwhile, tried everything possible to disrupt the flights. They scrambled fifty-seven fighter jets against a single U-2, but not one of them could get close enough to fire. When the Soviets accepted that no plane was going to reach a U-2, they adopted a new tactic. Entire squadrons of jets flew in tight formation fifteen thousand feet under the spy planes to try to obscure their view of the ground—a tactic the CIA jokingly called "aluminum clouds."

The Soviets worked frantically to raise the target altitude on their SA-2 missile systems and began training MiG fighter pilots to make very brief flights straight up into the upper altitudes in order to get in firing range. According to one early pilot, the Soviets even tried to ram the plane with MiG-21s stripped down to become, in essence, piloted missiles. "They flew straight up at top speed, arcing up to 68,000 feet before flaming out and falling back to Earth," he recalled. "It was crazy, but it showed how angry and desperate they were becoming."

On May 1, 1960—May Day in the USSR—thirty-four-year-old pilot Francis Gary Powers was flying at about seventy thousand feet over Sverdlovsk in Russia when ground-to-air positions fired multiple newly redesigned SA-2 missiles at the plane. None of them were direct hits, but one exploded in close proximity, behind and below Powers' plane, and the resulting shock wave tilted the U-2's nose upward, upsetting the delicate balance that kept the plane aloft. Powers fought to regain control, but he couldn't. The plane stalled and began to maple leaf out of the sky—falling and spinning at once.

All U-2 pilots had orders to destroy a disabled plane before ejecting. The planes had a built-in lever out on the wing that would blow up the aircraft, the camera, and the film, and once it was pulled, the pilot had a short time to eject away from the explosion. In Powers' case, the centrifugal force of the spinning prevented him from reaching the lever and he could only save himself. He pushed away from the plane and free fell until a preset change in barometric pressure opened his parachute. As he drifted slowly down to earth and his imminent capture, Powers looked around at a rare sight in the Russian spring—a clear, sunny day that, he thought, would be just perfect for taking pictures.

Kelly Johnson learned of Powers' fate late at night from Bissell and trudged into the Skunk Works the next morning to share the grim news: "We got nailed over Sverdlovsk," Johnson told his team. "That's that. We're dead."

Which didn't mean the program was a failure—far from it. The U-2 program made thirty flights over four years, gathering 1.2 million feet of film that covered more than a million square miles of Soviet territory. The planes photographed bomber fleets, atomic energy facilities, weapons-testing sites, air defense systems, submarine fleets, and missile bases.

As CIA director Richard Helms later wrote, "For the first time, American policymakers had accurate, credible information on the Soviet strategic assets. . . . Those overflights eliminated almost entirely the ability of the Kremlin ever to launch a surprise preemptive strike against the West. . . . It was the greatest bargain and the greatest triumph of the Cold War."

The Powers incident forced Eisenhower to shut down overflights of Russia, and while the U-2 continued to conduct missions elsewhere for decades after its creation, a new program was already under way to design a successor plane that could evade Soviet radar.

Kelly Johnson didn't want an incremental improvement on the U-2. That, he told his team, would buy only "a couple years before the Russians would be able to nail us again. I want us to come up with an airplane that can rule the skies for a decade or more."

He told his engineers that he wanted to fly at ninety thousand feet in a plane that could reach Mach 3 with a range of four thousand miles. It was, to say the least, a ridiculous goal.

When Johnson brought his sleek, futuristic design to the CIA, he claimed that he could build it in twenty months, although the world's first Mach 2 airplane at the time, the F-104 Starfighter (also a Lockheed design), could reach that speed only on takeoffs or for short periods in what was called "dash mode." As Ben Rich later observed, Johnson was asking for a plane that could *cruise* at "twice the fastest fighter's dash speed." The U-2 "was to the A-12 [its successor] as a covered wagon was to an Indy 500 race car," Rich wrote. But to Johnson, he said, "the word 'impossible' was a gross insult."

7

Faster and More Furious

I n January of 1960, Dick Bissell handed the task of developing the most technologically advanced aircraft in history—in total secrecy—to his favorite program manager, John Parangosky.

Parangosky, then forty, had been one of Bissell's key officers on Aquatone. In Turkey, he was known as "Big John," for his sizable, sometimes volatile personality and for the fact that he was, physically, a large man. Not tall, so much; Parangosky was five foot ten at best, but he had broad shoulders and amply filled out his shirts, with a rounded midsection that revealed his love of fine dining, especially French food.

He lived alone in a small, tidy apartment not far from the original CIA headquarters on E Street in downtown Washington and took cabs to and from work. When the office moved to Langley in 1961, Parangosky kept taking cabs, but security protocols at the new headquarters prohibited taxis from passing beyond the compound's outer gate, so he had to walk a half mile from the taxi drop to his office every morning, and then make the same walk in reverse at day's end. This was uncomfortable for a heavy guy in any weather, and downright insufferable in the heat and humidity, which in Washington starts in May and lasts well into September.

Parangosky's aversion to driving was a common topic of conversation around the office. Various friends offered to help him find a car, but Parangosky, who'd never even been to a car dealer, refused all assistance and went himself one night after work to a Renault dealer he'd heard about. He bought the cheapest car on the lot, writing a check on the spot for the

precise amount on the sticker, and then drove off in a tiny car that was terribly uncomfortable for a man his size. There was barely even room for a
passenger.

So he took the car back and tried again. This time, Parangosky bought a
Ford Mustang—a huge, loud, green eight-cylinder version with two doors.
And he loved it so much that he drove that car for the next fifteen years,
even after it started breaking down regularly and spent much of its time at
a gas station near the apartment he eventually bought in Fairfax.

Parangosky was meticulous in many ways, finding comfort in routine.
He had a uniform: dark suit, typically black but sometimes navy, solid tie,
black socks, pointy black patent leather shoes, and white shirt—which he
washed and ironed himself. His only jewelry was a simple watch with a
leather band. He didn't take vacations. On a day off, he'd go to the library
and read, or maybe, occasionally, see an opera across the Potomac in Washington. He was an aficionado of fine dining and liked to cook, but he rarely
did so because he loved eating out in restaurants so much. He especially
liked French cuisine, and that, along with a notable lack of physical activity,
helped explain his shape.

His days had a consistent rhythm, when possible, to make up for the wild
unpredictability of life in the field. He liked a simple breakfast at home, then
lunch out with one or more of his senior officers, where, at a table in the
darkest, quietest corner of one of several continental cuisine restaurants
near Langley, Parangosky would conduct informal debrief sessions, typically with a single black martini close at hand. The designated company was
never given much warning; rather, the boss would stop by late in the morning and say, "Let's go to lunch." Saying no was never a good idea.

Parangosky used these lunches to get more intimate exposure to key officers who might have things to say that they wouldn't otherwise bring up in
the group. And the restaurant was always selected that day, from a rotation
of about five, so that he was never seen to be developing a pattern that could be
predicted. This was basic tradecraft—as spies call the methods and practices
of espionage—and Parangosky was obsessive about the pursuit of secrecy, to
the point that it seemed almost silly at times to members of his staff.

He wasn't a scientist or an engineer. As one of his favorite engineers often said, "John P wouldn't know a motorcycle from a megacycle." He was, at

heart, a manager, but also a keen observer and voracious consumer of information. He knew how to identify and empower talented individuals while also keeping them under close watch. His MO was trust but validate. Parangosky could approach a complicated subject and do a quick study to become conversant enough to help actual engineers see the strengths and weaknesses of the matter at hand. If he didn't understand something technical that came up in a meeting—a regular occurrence in this line of work—he'd ask his people what he needed to read about the subject, and by the next meeting he'd be versed enough to ask tough questions.

Men loved to work for Parangosky, too. He listened well and remembered everything, supplementing his impressive memory with three-by-five-inch note cards that he carried in his jacket pocket and wrote on in tiny, careful script during meetings. He could be funny but was usually extremely polite, which often came off as formal, especially to those who didn't know him well. You were free to argue with him so long as you recognized the point at which he was done hearing your side. If you missed that point, he would certainly let you know. Parangosky could be volatile when pushed, and he wielded that temper strategically, to keep order and maintain respect within the hierarchy. The best way to set him off was to challenge his authority in front of a group, and nearly everyone inside the CIA's technical branch had some story of a naive junior officer questioning an idea and getting fired on the spot. Often, Parangosky would rescind that firing later, particularly if it turned out he'd been wrong, and to see a man who loathed apologies swallow his pride and forgive an underling was as powerful as watching him lose his temper in the first place.

He could be, at times, parsimonious with his words. Parangosky knew what he wanted and how to get it, and he preferred to avoid conflict unless it was absolutely necessary. When he entrusted a subordinate to handle a matter, that trust was absolute and he didn't want to get options in return.

Tact was a specialty, but he moderated its use depending on the audience. In the presence of women, younger employees, or anyone with a fragile ego, Parangosky operated gently, but he was ready and willing to stand up and face down bigger, blunter personalities, too. He could smooth out the rough edges of a meeting within fifteen minutes of sitting down.

People didn't want to disappoint the boss or miss a deadline, and much was accomplished based solely on fear of John Parangosky.

He was a master of the butchered metaphor, often telling his security guys, when something required better oversight, that "I want a fly on the wall with his feet planted firmly on the floor in that meeting so I can know what's really going on." And the answer was never to correct him. You just said, "Okay, John."

Playing a key role in a second compartmentalized CIA Science and Technology program, code-named Oxcart, this time in a much more direct and intimate capacity, deeply influenced Parangosky's management style within the Agency. It changed him from a promising project leader to one of the most effective managers at the CIA.

Parangosky admired what Kelly Johnson was doing at the Skunk Works, where he was simultaneously reinventing management and designing some of the most impressive machines ever created. The Skunk Works was its own airplane company inside of the larger Lockheed Corporation, and it had its own rules, written by Johnson.

The Oxcart team was even smaller than the one that designed the U-2, and to hasten progress Johnson and Ben Rich removed the door that separated the aerodynamics group from the structures team. That worked so well that they decided to remove all the doors, mashing the whole bunch together, so that solving a problem became as easy as yelling across the room.

After eleven rejected but incrementally better airplane designs, the twelfth was approved. Johnson called it the A-12 and returned from a one-on-one meeting with Bissell with clear and simple orders: The CIA would buy five planes at a cost of 96.6 million dollars. They would allow Johnson's shop to do work exactly as it had on the U-2, with one change: even more secrecy.

Actually building the A-12 required a complete rethinking of every single piece on the plane, starting with the metal used for its frame and skin.

Johnson settled on titanium, which has the highest strength-to-density ratio of any metal on earth, but which no one had ever used on a plane before. Titanium worked—while causing all sorts of problems. For instance, it was so strong that all of the Skunk Works' existing tools and bolts were rendered useless, forcing Johnson to reinvent those, too. What was more, there wasn't enough titanium available in the United States, so the CIA had to use subcontractors and dummy companies to covertly buy the rare alloy from, of all places, the Soviet Union.

Virtually every piece of the A-12 had to be designed to withstand the extreme stresses the plane would be under. The hydraulic lines were stainless steel, the plumbing lines gold plated. Some parts required alloys that sounded like they'd been made up—Hastelloy X for the ejector flaps, for instance, or Elgiloy, more typically used for watch springs, on the control cables. In total, the Skunk Works would manufacture 13 million different parts by the time the A-12 project was completed.

Johnson underestimated the complexity of the project, and by the end of 1960 he swallowed his pride and told Parangosky that Lockheed wasn't going to hit the original deadline. He needed another year.

The engine, in particular, was a struggle, and Parangosky's patience was under constant assault as delays and costs increased by the day. The A-12 required the most powerful engine ever made, which would allow it to fly continuously on its afterburners. To build an engine this complicated, Pratt & Whitney had to build a new factory at its Florida complex, and the CIA, after much hand-wringing by Bissell and Parangosky, swallowed the 600-million-dollar tab. Parangosky called it the "Macy's engine" after he told a colleague, at the height of his frustration, that "if we gave as much money to R. H. Macy's they could build that engine in time for Christmas."

Parangosky reached his limit. He and Bissell agreed that Johnson needed a babysitter, and in mid-1960 he flew to Burbank and told Kelly that if he wouldn't allow a CIA engineer to work inside the Skunk Works, he couldn't guarantee the project's survival.

Johnson hated that idea, of course. "I'm not gonna have one of your spies poking into my business!" he yelled. "Bissell promised me you guys would keep hands off and let me do the thing my way."

"Be reasonable, Kelly," Parangosky replied. "We won't get in your way. We just want someone here you can trust and we can, too."

Seeing no choice, Johnson acceded. Parangosky made it easier for him by offering up an engineer he knew Johnson liked and trusted—Norm Nelson, an old acquaintance from World War II.

"I'll let Norm in, but not another goddamn person," Johnson snapped. "You tell Nelson he can have a desk and a phone, but no chair. I expect him in the shop, not sitting on his fat duff."

Nelson was a sharp engineer and a better office politician, so despite being the first government employee ever to work inside the Skunk Works, he turned out to be both welcome and useful. Nelson was unafraid to challenge Johnson and proved his worth numerous times, such as when the CIA gave the Skunk Works 20 million dollars to build special wing tanks to extend the plane's range. Nelson looked at the design, scratched out some calculations, and told the engineers that they were extending the range by only eighty miles. In Nelson's estimation, that didn't justify the time and engineering required to build the tanks. Johnson agreed and sent the 20 million dollars right back to Langley.

When the CIA's new director, Richard Helms, witnessed his first A-12 flight, in January 1962, the experience was so visceral that he could hardly process what he was seeing. "I was so shaken," he told Ben Rich, "that I invented my own name for [the plane]. I called it the Hammers of Hell." The A-12's more popular nickname was the Blackbird, named for the black body paint chosen because it lowered the temperature of the titanium by thirty-five degrees.

Every test flight was an event. The pilots covered huge distances in small amounts of time, often moving so fast that they'd witness three or four sunrises on a single three-hour flight. Pilots flew from New York City to London in an hour and fifty-five minutes, London to Los Angeles in three hours and forty-seven minutes, and Los Angeles to Washington in sixty-four minutes, breaking records on a daily basis.

To fly the long distances required to reach the Soviet Union, the plane would require multiple in-air refuelings, and every one of them was hair-raising. In order to mate, the hulking KC-135 tankers had to fly at their absolute maximum speed while the Blackbird pilot would throttle his plane back as much as possible, so that he was on the verge of stalling out. When the supersonic planes returned to base, pilots and mechanics puzzled over the tiny black dots that pitted the windshields. Test samples came back as organic material. The source: insects that had been sucked up into the stratosphere during Russian and Chinese nuclear tests and were just winging around the earth in the jet stream, seventy-five thousand feet up.

Once operational, the Blackbird proved its worth again and again. The primary detachment of CIA pilots and crew was based on Okinawa, outside of the town of Kadena. The location was ostensibly secret, but the Blackbird was so loud and peculiar-looking that the locals took notice almost immediately. Within days, they began gathering on a hill that overlooked the base in hopes of watching this incredible plane take flight. They nicknamed it Habu, for a highly poisonous jet-black pit viper indigenous to the island.

Word of the location spread quickly. Soviet spy ships disguised as fishing trawlers would cruise off the coast, observing takeoffs and relaying the departure times back to North Vietnam, the primary target of overflights in the late 1960s. It didn't matter. The planes were too fast for antiair defenses, so the CIA paid no attention to the spying. They chose flight times based on when the light was best, and every twelve-thousand-mile round trip resulted in reams of intelligence. A single Blackbird could photograph one hundred thousand square miles per hour, with the ability to zoom in up to twenty times, providing enough resolution from eighty-five thousand feet to look down into the hatches of container ships unloading materiel in Haiphong harbor.

When the North Koreans boarded and commandeered the USS *Pueblo* in January 1968, it was a Blackbird that helped prevent war. President Johnson was furious at the North Koreans' brazen act and was seriously considering attacking Pyongyang from the air to force the Koreans to release the ship, but CIA director Richard Helms convinced Johnson to wait until a Blackbird—which could photograph the entire country in under ten minutes, and would be there and gone by the time the North Koreans even knew they'd been filmed—provided better intelligence.

Johnson agreed. On January 26, a Blackbird flown by CIA pilot Jack Weeks took off from Okinawa and a few hours later had made three passes, photographing the *Pueblo* in Wonsan harbor. The photos proved the Koreans had the ship, as well as the crew, and made it clear that bombing the area would likely result in American casualties. The president opted to stand down and negotiate. Less than six months later, in June, Weeks was killed when his A-12 malfunctioned during a test flight off the coast of the Philippines. He was one of two CIA pilots killed in crashes during the A-12 program; both are honored by stars on the Memorial Wall in the lobby of CIA Headquarters, in Langley.

8

Same Man, Different Mission

John Parangosky oversaw the Blackbird's first test flight on April 30, 1962, its operational certification in 1965, and its eventual deployment overseas under the code name Black Shield. "The main objective—to create a reconnaissance aircraft of unprecedented speed, range, and altitude capability—was triumphantly achieved," Parangosky later said. "It may well be, however, that the most important aspects of the effort lay in its by-products—the notable advances in aerodynamic design, engine performance, cameras, electronic countermeasures, pilot life-support systems, antiair devices, and above all in milling, machining, and shaping titanium."

The CIA's regard for Parangosky was obvious in his appointments. Seemingly every time a major science and technological project arose, the round man with the slicked hair was asked to make sure it worked out, as quickly as possible. The Agency formalized that regard in January 1963, when Herbert Scoville, the deputy director for research, promoted Parangosky to so-called super grade—naming him deputy director for special activities. Even in the internal commendation letter, Scoville was vague about Parangosky's clandestine work, noting his "great deal of developmental responsibility" with "special projects of the highest national priority." In particular, Scoville pointed out his "exceptional ability to work with our varied contractors so as to obtain maximum results in a diversity of scientific fields."

Between the U-2 and the A-12, Parangosky had been assigned to a very different task devised with the same goal in mind: to capture high-quality photographic intelligence of the Soviet military complex without being detected. The loss of the U-2 in 1960 caused Eisenhower to push for something that could replace it: What he wanted was a spy satellite.

The Air Force was already working on a photographic reconnaissance satellite, but the progress had been slow, and Eisenhower's trusted technology advisers, Killian and Land, recommended that the president take the satellite project from the Air Force and hand it to the CIA, which had proven its ability to develop and implement important technology quickly and in secret with the U-2. Ike agreed, and the CIA satellite project was codenamed Corona.

The operation was assigned to Bissell's Development Projects Staff, and Parangosky, who began the project as its deputy, quickly rose to chief. Once again, Parangosky showed a unique ability to assemble and manage a team that included both government workers and five different private contractors—Itek, Fairchild Camera and Instrument, General Electric, Eastman Kodak, and Lockheed—leading a joint effort that designed and deployed the world's first photo reconnaissance satellite.

Launching satellites into space is difficult to do in secret. Corona, then, required a plausible cover story to explain why the United States was sending so many rockets into space and then scrambling to recover things that were dropped back down from the heavens. The answer: Discoverer, a white science program that was allegedly doing biomedical research for future space travel. The story, as far as the public (and the Soviets) knew, was that the Air Force was blasting small animals into space and then recovering them as part of its ongoing research on human space travel.

There were twelve failed Corona launches between February 28, 1959, and August 10, 1960, when Navy SEALs finally retrieved a "recovery package" from *Discoverer 13* after it completed seventeen orbits around the earth. The package fell into the Pacific Ocean, 330 miles northeast of the Hawaiian Islands. It was the first time in history that humanity had launched something into the earth's orbit and then retrieved it—but the Soviets weren't far behind. Ten days later, *Sputnik 5* blasted off, orbited, and fell back to earth with its two brave pioneers, the space dogs Belka and Strelka—as well as a rabbit, two rats, and forty-two mice—alive and well.

The *Discoverer 13* basket contained no film. Engineers weren't about to waste an expensive, hand-built camera on a satellite that had yet to work, but once they proved that a satellite could reach orbit, then drop a payload for retrieval, it was time for Corona to go live.

On August 18, the fourteenth spy satellite blasted off, this time with a KH-1 Keyhole panoramic camera—built by Itek—on board. It reached orbit and began circling the earth. One day, seventeen orbits, and seven passes over the Soviet Union later, the satellite ejected its film-return capsule, which was snatched out of the air over Hawaii during its descent by a C-119 recovery plane.

The satellite wasn't just a replacement for the U-2; it was an evolutionary leap in overhead intelligence gathering. That single day of surveillance produced more photo coverage than all of the U-2 flights combined—more than 1 million square miles, albeit with lower resolution.

The CIA's science and technology group had solved a tremendous problem, but they weren't done tinkering. For the next two years, successive versions of the Corona went up and circled Earth, with progressively better cameras. Over that period the Agency methodically honed in on one of the biggest mysteries of the Cold War: Just how large and advanced was the Soviet's intercontinental ballistic missile program?

Estimates varied widely, but the prevailing theory among analysts was that the Soviets were dangerously far ahead when it came to ICBMs.

Those assessments had been wrong. The Corona flights showed that there was little if any missile gap. The United States was in excellent position and might even have had an advantage. Technology prevailed, again.

For the CIA to continue the evolution of this growing branch, which by 1962 had three separate billion-dollar projects under way—in the U-2, Corona, and Oxcart—it needed a distinct home for activities of this kind. In 1963, Killian and Land gave then CIA director John McCone a proposal for "the creation of an organization for research and development which will couple research done outside the intelligence community, both overt and covert, with development and engineering conducted within intelligence agencies, particularly the CIA."

They wanted completely new thinking, wherein researchers across the country would share ideas with CIA engineers who could implement them. On August 5, 1963, Albert "Bud" Wheelon, former director of the Office of Scientific Intelligence, assumed leadership of the all-new Directorate of Science and Technology, and over the next few years he helped build arguably the most powerful development and engineering establishment in American history, a government-funded Skunk Works for outlandish projects—like figuring out how to retrieve a submarine wrecked seventeen thousand feet below the ocean's surface.

A year before the K-129 sank, John Parangosky was given the Distinguished Intelligence Medal, one of the CIA's highest awards. When it came time to pick a man to lead the submarine recovery, the choice wasn't difficult. And the fact that John Parangosky, in early 1969, happened to be between jobs made it even easier.

A top secret CIA task force assigned to the submarine recovery was formed on July 1, 1969, with Parangosky in charge. Within the Agency, only Carl Duckett knew of the task force's existence. It was listed in official records only as "Special Projects Staff, DDS&T."

9
Need to Know

Starting with the U-2, the CIA's Special Projects Office built and perfected a model for clandestine operations on a massive scale—projects that involved hundreds if not thousands of people, many of them employees of the private sector—and John Parangosky and Walt Lloyd, who helped devise the original security structure for the U-2, played a critical role in all of them.

Black contracts were always complicated. Many companies, small and large, had no interest in making their work with the CIA public. And the Agency was sensitive to this concern. To facilitate one skittish optical company recruited to work on the Blackbird, the CIA arranged for a major university to hire the company instead, and used a third-party attorney to write checks and pay for the work on that university's behalf.

This was a new kind of security support. Each contractor had its own individual needs and concerns, and the scope of these new, highly compartmentalized programs was unprecedented. Thousands of personnel had to be vetted and then taught how to work within the strict security protocols, which often required entirely new methods of communication and secrecy.

To handle the growing portfolio of black work, a new security clearance desk code-named Project Rock was established within the Special Projects Office once the U-2 was up and flying. No one within the larger CIA knew which operations Project Rock handled, only that they were top secret and that its officers were all over America doing full background investigations on contractor employees. Project Rock security officers were looking for obvious things (criminal records, drug problems) and also potential weaknesses (affairs, unconventional sexual proclivities) that could make a person susceptible to threats, coercion, or blackmail.

Having skeletons in the closet wasn't an automatic disqualifier. Project Rock staff made it a point not to sit in judgment. What mattered was not that a man had done something that might embarrass him. What mattered was that he was willing to cop to this incident, because a guy who's willingly owned up to his own demons has undermined his inquisitor's leverage.

It wasn't unusual for security staff to clear more than a thousand people for a black program, but even within a program, how much information a particular person received was directly correlated to his or her need to know. There were three primary levels of clearance. Category 1 was for the administrative staff—people who handled paperwork, especially, and either knew the client was the CIA or were likely to find out at some point. Category 2 was for people who knew they were working on a project for the CIA but didn't know what the end result of that work was. They might, for instance, be working on tooling for experimental airplane parts, but they didn't know that the airplane was a high-altitude supersonic spy plane. Category 3 was for people whose job required full knowledge of the operation.

It was hardly a science. Project Rock staff were authorized to make judgment calls, and the sensitivity of who should be given full disclosure was often a point of conflict between CIA security staff and their military counterparts. When Walt Lloyd was setting up security protocols for the U-2, he butted heads with the Air Force about clearing technicians who worked on certain key components, such as the camera systems. The military's opinion was that these people didn't need to know the geographic targets of their equipment. But Lloyd felt very strongly that handing a man that kind of information fixed him with responsibility. It elevated his connection to the work, making it more personal because he now carried the burden, too.

That belief was vindicated one night in an English pub during early test flights when an extremely sober young tech introduced himself and said, "I just want to tell you that you almost gave me nightmares." How did I do that? Lloyd replied. "You had them brief me on what we're doing and I don't want to go to town or to a bar and have a drink for fear I'll reveal it."

To emphasize the importance of what these men were signing, Lloyd asked for a new kind of secrecy agreement. Traditionally, agreements were fairly simple and nondescript—legalese on white paper. Lloyd asked for "something that really snaps"—bonded paper "with a blue eagle someplace, or a symbol buried in the paper." That way, he said, "When the guy signs this, he feels like he's signing his goddamn death away." It made sense. The CIA's Document Department produced a new, extremely official-looking secrecy agreement that—despite having basically the same verbiage as the old one—carried far more visual weight.

To isolate these programs, they were given code names so that anyone who saw a code name, or heard it, wouldn't have any idea what it meant. A code name relates in no way to the actual nature of the program; that's the point. Oxcart, in Walt Lloyd's words, "is just a great big lumbering goddamn cart"—the complete opposite of a sleek, supersonic spy plane. Corona came about when Lloyd was sitting in an office with the satellite program's contracting officer, George Kucera, puzzling over what to call the program. Kucera, looking at the typewriter on his desk, noticed the label: Smith Corona. "How about Corona?" he said.

And the submarine job, known internally as "the boat project," became Azorian. Code words are intentionally meaningless. The CIA maintains a register in a room at Langley that program security officers visit with proposed names. These names are checked against the existing registry to make sure they have never been used before. Provided a name is clear, it's added to the registry, along with the security officer who filed it, but with no additional information. Somewhere, then, is a card with the code name Azorian and the name Paul Evans, but Azorian's security lead is dead and no one connected to the program knows or can recall exactly why a word referring to the Azores island chain was chosen—other than it was available and meaningless in regard to stealing a submarine.

If there's any deeper significance, it's a part of the story that's been lost to time.

10

So, How Do We Steal a Submarine, Anyway?

JULY 1969

A mong the reasonable arguments raised for not going after K-129 was that it might be illegal. A submarine is considered a man-of-war, and international maritime law states that salvaging another country's military equipment is forbidden. But there seemed to be a loophole. A nation retains ownership of a sunken vessel only until it has been abandoned. And the CIA pointed out that the Soviets had mounted a massive search for the submarine after it vanished but then gave up that search and never resumed. In that sense, the K-129 was abandoned.

There was also historical precedent. The Russians had stolen a sub themselves. In 1929, the Russian government raised the British submarine HMS L55, which had been sunk in 1919 by the Bolsheviks when European forces attempted to meddle in the Russian Civil War. The Russians returned the remains of the British sailors who'd been on board, then repaired the sub and reengineered it, using it as the basis for the Soviet L-class submarine.

The legal argument, then, seemed moot. And the potential intelligence value of the haul was so significant, so potentially balance-of-power shifting, that those few in the know—extending to the highest levels of government—decided to green-light the project before the technical feasibility studies had even been completed.

Carl Duckett, the dapper autodidact from rural North Carolina running the Directorate of Science and Technology, was ecstatic. This was exactly how he envisioned his division: as the government's own Skunk Works for high-risk, high-reward operations. But when he took the news that the CIA was being considered for the sub snatch to DCI Richard Helms, the Agency's director wasn't nearly as excited. "He almost threw me out the window," Duckett later said.

One man who didn't think the idea was crazy was John Parangosky. Though neither he nor the Agency had ever worked on underwater projects, Parangosky didn't see why they couldn't. When anyone asked him what aerospace engineers knew about underwater work, he liked to say that most of them weren't aerospace guys, either—until they started making airplanes.

On July 1, 1969, the Project Azorian task force was formed and given office space in a secret satellite location in Tysons Corner, known only as the "think tank." Officially, and in all internal records, Parangosky's group was designated as Special Projects Staff, and anyone within the directorate knew better than to ask what that really meant.

Duckett turned Parangosky loose to begin initial planning for the sub recovery, giving him the freedom to consider all possible concepts. Parangosky first recruited his chief scientist, Alex Holzer, along with Dave Sharp, an electronics engineer who'd worked on both U-2 and Oxcart.

Sharp, who later wrote a memoir about his experience, recalled Parangosky phoning him at the University of Virginia, where he was in graduate school while on leave from the Agency.

The two men had a long history of working together, and it had mostly been positive. Parangosky was a fair boss, occasionally even friendly, but no one was immune from his temper. Sharp discovered this firsthand in 1964 while the two were working on the Oxcart program.

Sharp worked on radar cross sections of the A-12 at Area 51. The plane was ostensibly invisible, but it was brought to his attention that the Air Force had been tracking Blackbird flights on its air defense radar systems. Sharp did what seemed obvious: He told his boss. But Parangosky was under tremendous pressure to get the plane into service as soon as possible, and he completely lost it. He told Sharp that this was "impossible" and that he "didn't want to hear it." When the young engineer replied that it was the truth, whether or not he wanted it to be, Parangosky snapped and fired him on the spot. "Pack your bags and go home!" he barked.

A day later, Norm Nelson intervened. Parangosky trusted Nelson, the man he'd picked to embed within Kelly Johnson's Skunk Works, as much as anyone. And Nelson talked the boss off his ledge. Sharp was allowed to keep working. Shortly thereafter, the CIA's own study of the stealth capabilities of the "Ox," as they called it, proved what Sharp had reported. The improved capabilities of Soviet long-range radar, as a memo to the Agency leadership stated, meant that the Russians—like the United States' own Air Force—would be able to see the plane. "Therefore," the memo stated, "it is impossible to fly the Ox over the Soviet Union without detection."

Sharp was happy to rejoin the program, and he didn't carry a grudge. Dealing with sudden storms was part of working for one of the Agency's most talented program managers.

"Dave, I've found a new job for you that you're going to love," Parangosky said when he reached Sharp in Charlottesville six years later, and then noted that he was unable to share any specifics of that job at that time.

"Do I have a choice, John?" Sharp replied.

"No," he said. "Be here next week!"

At the beginning of July, Dave Sharp and the rest of the task force began a series of all-day meetings at the think tank to discuss concepts for plucking a Soviet sub from the bottom of the ocean.

His first job was to help Holzer and Parangosky identify the directorate's sharpest minds, or at least those that would be most useful for this particular challenge. They selected five men: Erwin Runge, an oceanographer who'd already been studying ways to collect intelligence from under the ocean as part of the S&T's Office of Research and Development; Dr. Jack Stephenson, a chemical engineer better known by code name Redjack; a mechanical engineer from the aerospace world; a Soviet submarine expert; and Parangosky's longtime associate Doug Cummings, who eventually became Azorian's deputy program manager.

Here was a group of men, only two of whom had any experience working in the oceans, tasked with solving perhaps the single largest engineering challenge in intelligence and maritime history: How to retrieve a

3-million-pound submarine from 16,700 feet under the Pacific Ocean—a feat that was exponentially more complicated than any deep-sea recovery ever attempted. And to do it in total secret, without arousing Soviet suspicion. Discovery of any attempted sub theft—before, during, or after the operation—would, in the most optimistic scenario imaginable, greatly damage improving relations at a time when the public badly wanted a thaw; in the worst case, it could start a nuclear war.

Given two months to prepare a proposal of concepts for the recovery, Parangosky told his task force that it was their job to solve a problem that even the Agency's director considered impossible. Because there was no time for his small security staff to clear new contractors, Parangosky recruited technical assistance from a little-known California aerospace engineering company called Mechanics Research Inc., a small shop staffed by engineers who already had top secret clearance from previous CIA projects, and from a naval architect in Seattle named Larry Glosten. His old friend Kelly Johnson also chipped in some eggheads.

Then the debate began. No idea was too outrageous, and considering that most of the men in the room had absolutely no experience with naval architecture, oceanography, or undersea warfare, radical and sometimes ridiculous concepts were proposed. One early proposal typified the learning curve necessary for a group that had built its reputation on aerospace: What if deep-sea submersibles were used to attach rocket boosters to the wreck? The boosters could launch the sub up through the ocean and to the surface, at which point—well, that's where that idea fell apart, since no one knew how to catch the rocket-boosted wreck once it hit the surface and before it began to climb into orbit.

A suggestion that they could use enormous bags filled with gas to float the sub up to the surface was also rejected, though it was slightly less outrageous. It was theoretically possible to make gas on the seafloor—using electrolysis of seawater, for example—but the team's lone submarine expert raised an important point. Submarines all carry compressed air in bottles for buoyancy, and without knowing how many of those were still on board the K-129, or how they'd react as the sub rose—they would expand and quite possibly explode or leak—it was very likely that the sub would become uncontrollably buoyant, rising through the sea at a tremendous rate and perhaps crashing into and sinking whatever was sitting on the surface above it.

Both ideas had another major problem in common: How do you hide a wrecked Soviet submarine once you've blasted or floated it to the surface?

The group pressed on. In mid-July, the deputy secretary of defense, David Packard, was briefed and came away impressed enough that he gave Parangosky approval to continue with the task force.

One of the most challenging realities was that engineers were trying to envision a complex system to achieve something never before attempted—a system that would have to work the first time it ran. Because of the time and financial constraints, any kind of full-scale systems test just wasn't possible. As the Agency's own internal assessment stated, "Azorian would be a single-shot, go-for-broke effort."

More and more, the debate focused on two concepts: a so-called keyhole barge with a large hole in its bottom that would be lowered on cables and placed over the sub, essentially swallowing it, and some method of brute lift. Both would require an engineering solution that seemed to the men of the think tank every bit as daunting as the moon landing. Calculations showed that the amount of pentane gas required to float that much weight would be equal to two years' worth of the entire planet's supply. And the deep-sea lifting record in 1968 was held by an all-aluminum research vessel named the *Alcoa Seaprobe,* which had raised fifty tons from eighteen thousand feet. The submarine weighed fifteen hundred tons, a thirty-fold increase.

"You can't pick up the goddamn submarine or it will fall apart," the Navy's chief undersea spy Jim Bradley told Duckett when he delivered the CIA's preferred concept. "That's a pipe dream." Others at the Navy were more receptive. In particular, Thomas H. Moorer, chief of naval operations, found the CIA's plan to grab the entire submarine compelling and relayed his support up the chain of command to Defense Secretary Melvin Laird, who had his doubts but assigned the heavy-lift project to the CIA anyway. If nothing else, Laird thought, building a system like the Agency was proposing could help the United States retrieve its own distressed or abandoned subs in the future.

11

Epiphany

The solution to this vexing, almost impossible-seeming engineering problem originated from an unlikely source: the National Science Foundation. In the spring of 1957, a review panel of scientific heavyweights for the NSF had gathered to consider sixty-five research projects proposed for government funding and rejected them all, disappointed that not a single one would result in a major advance in earth sciences.

Unsatisfied, Princeton geologist Harry Hess and geophysicist Walter Munk from the Scripps Institution of Oceanography met in the aftermath to discuss what project would substantially advance current thought, given no restraints on cost or difficulty. The answer, they decided, was to obtain a sample of whatever lay below the Moho.

The Moho, short for Mohorovicic discontinuity, is the name given to the boundary between the earth's crust and its mantle, named for the Croatian seismologist who discovered it in 1909. The mantle makes up 85 percent of the volume of the earth, but no geologist in 1957 had any idea what it was actually made of. That's because the Moho was, using any existing technology, completely out of reach—an average of twenty-two miles below the earth's surface, and up to sixty miles deep in certain places, meaning that even in the best of circumstances it was far beyond the capabilities of any drilling equipment.

The only way you might reach the Moho, scientists argued, was under the ocean, where the depth below the seabed was more like three to six miles. And at a 1958 meeting of geophysicists at the NSF, an engineer from

Union Oil named A. J. Field showed a movie of a ship called the *CUSS I*—named for the four companies that owned it: Continental, Union, Shell, and Superior—drilling in two hundred feet of water off the California coast. Moving to the deep sea was a much more difficult proposition, but the *CUSS I*, a World War II barge converted into a drillship by a new company called Global Marine, proved at least that a full-size drill rig on a ship could work on the open ocean. The NSF was impressed enough to fund a feasibility study on drilling for the Moho in the ocean, and the engineer, adventurer, and bon vivant Willard Bascom gave it a name that stuck: the Mohole.

In 1959, Bascom wrote a story about the Mohole for *Scientific American,* laying out the project's various goals, sparking a frenzy of press attention, and freaking out certain members of the public, including one crackpot who began sending daily telegraphs to the secretary of the Navy that said "Stop the Mohole!" and stated his fear that drilling a hole in the ocean floor would cause all the water to drain out.

When the NSF formally announced the Mohole Project, Bascom was named technical director. The plan called for refitting the *CUSS I* to drill in the deep Pacific, and Bascom quickly identified and began working on the single greatest problem: keeping the ship stationary atop an ocean that churns and surges. In a 1959 report, he coined the term "dynamic positioning" for the concept of using four thrusters—essentially giant outboard motors, one at each corner of the ship—to constantly adjust the ship's location in response to signals from radar buoys positioned around the drill site. An operator monitored radar signals and used a joystick to maneuver the ship back into the center point of the buoy circle whenever the radar told him the ship had shifted out of position.

The actual boring would be done with an industrial drill with a diamond bit at the end of a tapered steel pipe string, but that worked only if the ship could stay relatively still; more than a little motion and the string would snap.

In February 1960, the *CUSS I* went to sea off San Diego. Two weeks later, a drill bit touched the seafloor in 3,100 feet of water and drilled to 115 feet. "We believe that today's experiment at a water depth which is nearly an order of magnitude greater than the previous record clearly establishes the feasibility of deep sea drilling," Bascom wrote in a cable to the National Research Council.

A year later, following modifications to the ship and rig, the *CUSS I* headed for the deep ocean, off Mexico's Guadalupe Island. There, on April Fools' Day 1961, in heavy weather and heaving seas, the *CUSS I* drilled 560 feet under the seafloor, at which point the drill bit slowed suddenly, indicating that a new layer had been reached. Bascom and the crew nervously waited as the core sample came up with the pipe string and proved to be exactly what everyone thought it would be: basalt. None other than John Steinbeck, Bascom's friend, was there to report, as the project historian, that "everyone wants a fragment as a memento . . . of the second layer which no one has ever seen before. I asked for a piece and got a scowling refusal so I stole a small piece. And then the damned chief scientist gave me a piece secretly. Made me feel terrible. I had to sneak in and replace the piece I had stolen."

More holes were drilled, more samples taken, and accolades from the earth sciences community rained down upon the Mohole. "CUSS I's drilling has about the same emphasis as Columbus' first feeble voyage of discovery: on this first touching of a new world the way to discovery lies open," Steinbeck wrote in *Life* magazine. Even the president took notice. "I have been following with deep interest the experimental drilling in connection with the first phase of Project Mohole," Kennedy wrote to the president of the NSF. "The success . . . constitutes a remarkable achievement and a historic landmark in our scientific and engineering progress."

The deep-sea drilling work aboard the *CUSS I* turned out to be a revelation for Parangosky's task force, which learned about the Mohole through Bascom's book *A Hole in the Bottom of the Sea*. In particular, the team was taken with the ship's ability to maintain position over a specific location within a six-hundred-foot radius, which was accurate enough to avoid any serious damage to the pipe string.

Further investigation revealed that the field of deep-sea drilling had continued after the Mohole. Union Oil funded the spin-off of Global Marine, which had been set up to engineer experimental drillships starting with the *CUSS I,* and the company took off from there. The *Glomar II,* built in 1962, was the world's first drillship built specifically for that purpose from scratch. And by 1968, the year the K-129 sank, Global Marine had refined the drill-ship concept through various evolutions leading up to the *Glomar*

Challenger, their most impressive ship to date. The *Challenger* was commissioned by the NSF for the Deep Sea Drilling Project and went to sea in 1969. Over the next year, it drilled 1,092 holes at 624 sites, working at depths up to 20,146 feet, in every ocean except the Arctic, and—making penetrations into the seafloor more than three thousand feet deep—recovered ninety-six thousand meters of core.

What really got the Azorian team's attention was the *Challenger*'s new, automated dynamic positioning system that enabled the four-hundred-foot ship to maintain station over a specific point within a radius of one hundred feet or less. It was the largest commercial vessel ever outfitted with dynamic positioning, an incredible leap in technology that allowed the ship to basically stand still over a target area, no matter how bad the weather or waves might be. It was also the first commercial ship with satellite navigation. Finally, Global Marine had devised a way to retract the drill string, then lower it back down and continue drilling in the same hole, at depths up to ten thousand feet. To do this, the ship had maintained its position within a circle with a radius of approximately fifteen feet. The *Glomar Challenger* was a monumental achievement in ocean engineering, a ship that could stand still and take drill samples sixteen thousand feet under the surface of the sea. Earth scientists from all over the world begged to get aboard one of its cruises, and the ship was highly visible, having been featured in numerous science journals and magazines.

As Curtis Crooke later explained it, Global Marine had, by the time of John Parangosky's surprise visit to his office, "proven our ability to design and operate highly sophisticated vessels, lift and handle heavy work in deep water under adverse conditions in virtually every part of the world."

This wasn't just the best company on earth for achieving the CIA's extremely particular task; it was the only company.

12

The Secret Office of
Underwater Spies

ene Poteat was at his desk in Langley one day that fall when his phone rang and he picked it up to hear a familiar baritone on the other end. It was John Parangosky. The big guy wanted to talk.

Poteat had joined the Agency in 1959 from Bell Labs, where he worked on missile guidance for ICBMs, and he distinguished himself within the Directorate of Science and Technology as a specialist in electronic intelligence, or ELINT as the spies call it. Poteat helped the Agency devise a method for intercepting Soviet missile telemetry, figured out how to locate and test Soviet radar installations using the reflection of their signals off the moon, and created a method for fooling those same radars by flying ghost planes—electronic signals that appeared to radar operators to be actual American jets and were so convincing that the Cuban Air Force scrambled fighters to intercept one such ghost during the 1962 missile crisis.

Poteat's expertise with radar was why Parangosky recruited him for Oxcart, and the two became good friends over their many months in the Nevada desert. Poteat wasn't cleared into Azorian, but he'd heard enough chatter to know that something was up. Fifteen minutes later, Parangosky barreled into his office before a secretary could announce him and sat down in a chair opposite Poteat's desk.

"It looks like we're going to have to create an office similar to the NRO," he said, referring to the National Reconnaissance Office, a joint Air Force–CIA organization set up inside the Pentagon to coordinate activities for overhead surveillance after the U-2 and Corona programs created a sudden boom in photo intelligence. Poteat had helped design the agency and was the first man assigned to the NRO after it was officially formed.

The "boat project," as Parangosky called it, was necessitating a similar partnership between the Agency and the Navy. "So tell me how in the hell that thing was organized."

Poteat laughed. "You mean the fighting and struggles?"

"Well, yeah," Parangosky said. "It's not a lot different now. Only instead of with an Air Force, it's with a Navy."

Once David Packard decided that the submarine recovery project should go to the CIA, a process was initiated to build an extremely small but powerful and well-provisioned support structure to facilitate the Agency on the project, while also keeping the Navy involved with major decisions. Parangosky was handed the job of figuring out what that might look like.

Poteat gave his old friend an organizational diagram for how the NRO was formed, and Parangosky used it as a model for setting up the Navy–CIA office that would oversee Azorian. That office would be known to the very few who were even aware of it as the National Underwater Reconnaissance Office, or NURO—a group so secret that its existence wasn't officially acknowledged for decades.

On August 8, 1969, Carl Duckett outlined the framework for NURO to the Executive Committee of the National Security Council, better known as ExCom, a small, shadowy advisory group formed by Kennedy in response to the Cuban Missile Crisis, which met whenever a major foreign policy decision was at hand.

The organization the Agency was proposing, Duckett explained, would be based on the model of the NRO, which had been successful in its mission of overseeing and distributing intelligence gathered by aerial surveillance. The submarine recovery would be NURO's first program, but the idea was that other underwater espionage operations would surely follow, particularly if this was successful, and NURO could shepherd those, too.

ExCom approved the establishment of the new organization, as well as the allocation of resources and personnel, and agreed that the president should be told. Kissinger shared the plan with Nixon, who approved, and on August 19, 1969, NURO's creation was formalized, with the dictate that its operations should include the best talent available from the Navy and the CIA.

The Agency had learned many things from its early experiences with planes and satellites, especially that tension with the military is inevitable. Top brass at the Air Force were angry from the onset that the CIA was put in charge of the U-2, Oxcart, and Corona programs—all of them high-tech flying objects—and the Agency helped lessen that friction by putting an Air Force man in charge of the NRO, with a CIA employee as his deputy. It was an org-chart decision as much as a hierarchical one, since in reality the chief and deputy worked side by side, as near equals, but rank means everything to the military, and the move was a persuasive symbol.

So that's what they did with NURO, too. Robert Frosch, the Navy's assistant secretary for research and development, was named founding staff director, with Ernest "Zeke" Zellmer, a World War II submariner who'd been working in management for the S&T, as his deputy.

The new program was based on the fifth floor of the Pentagon and was not included in official Defense Department records or organization charts. Anyone who walked by the office entrance would have no idea what lay behind its unmarked doors.

Primarily, NURO's job was to appropriate and manage the money for underwater projects—in particular, those involving the "special project subs" like *Halibut*—but having senior Navy staff alongside S&T managers was also meant to facilitate coordination, so that if Parangosky's team needed some specific naval expertise or the use of a ship, there was a system in place to make that happen.

Frosch was a theoretical physicist from the Bronx who climbed the Navy ranks through the Office of Naval Research, where he helped develop active sonar. He moved into nuclear test detection at the Advanced Research Projects Agency (ARPA) before rejoining the Navy in 1966 to oversee all research. He was a bright man, well-liked by his underlings, and he really embraced his role at NURO, as the head of a secret office that existed basically off the books, nearly always arriving late to meetings, after everyone was seated, with a lit cigar in his mouth.

Zeke Zellmer was an excellent counterbalance to his more flamboyant boss. He'd gone to war in the Pacific as a communications officer aboard the submarine USS *Cavalla*, commissioned on February 29, 1944, making her a rare leap-year sub, which the boat's CO considered to be a lucky omen.

After the war, Zellmer spent three years in his hometown of St. Louis, working for Washington University, and then was recruited by the Agency to study Soviet submarines and other naval vessels. Eventually—after numerous assignments, and a four-year stint at the National Security Agency—Zellmer came back to Langley to join the staff of Bud Wheelon's brand-new DDS&T, where he was given directorship of the weapons and equipment division. It was in this capacity that he first met John Parangosky.

Zellmer's cover at the Pentagon was as special assistant to Frosch, and that's how you'd find him in the building's phone book. He had a staff to keep activities coordinated and, most important, to keep the money coming. And they were going to need lots of money.

As a former Navy man who had established himself at the CIA, Zellmer was an ideal fit at NURO, possessing an ease and comfort in working with either organization. No quality was more important, though, than his ability to work with Parangosky.

Zellmer liked Parangosky but was never confident in his ability to read the man. Even in a realm filled with workaholics, Zellmer marveled at Parangosky's singular obsession with work. He appeared to have no life outside of the Agency and wasn't at all upset about that fact.

From the outset, Azorian was given the highest possible security protocols. Even within the DDS&T and Naval Intelligence branches, only those who absolutely needed to know about it would be cleared and given details. Parangosky and his security chief, Paul Evans, built a new security system, code-named Jennifer, which set very specific parameters for the handling of information. The name Jennifer appeared on the cover of every file exchanged and became so common that it was soon almost synonymous with the operation.

Jennifer was also designed to protect the methods from the intelligence gathered—the "take," as it was known. The Agency established a security protocol during the U-2 program specifically to deal with the matter of intelligence distribution. The program itself needed to remain highly classified, but the products of those flights—the pictures, and the results of analysis by photo interpreters—were of value to many people and departments. It was logistically impossible for CIA security officers to be responsible for deciding who could be trusted with the intel, so to remove that overwhelming responsibility the group created a system to separate the data from its origins. That system would have a code name. Certain valuable pieces of intelligence might show up at Air Force, or State, or the NSA, and they would be stamped with that code word but would include no other information about its origins. You didn't ask where the photo or telemetry data came from. You just worried about what you could do with it.

If the Azorian's mission were successful, there might be code books to distribute, as well as ballistic missile guidance information, or maybe valuable insights into Soviet construction.

The moniker for Azorian's intel haul has a sad origin story. It was chosen as a tribute to Paul Evans' young daughter, who, according to Dave Sharp, "had recently and tragically died." The so-called Jennifer control system for classified documents was named in her honor.

13

Global Marine to the Rescue

NOVEMBER 1969

Within a week of ambushing Curtis Crooke in his office, Big John Parangosky hired Global Marine to do some preliminary engineering on the boat project. To disguise the contract and expedite the work, he used an intermediary company named Mechanics Research Inc. (MRI), the same one he'd selected to provide technical assistance for his task force. MRI was an aerospace contractor that had been doing work for the CIA for years and had in place an infrastructure for secure communications as well as a cleared office space in the Tishman Building on Century Boulevard, near Los Angeles International Airport. MRI also had an existing contract with the CIA that included a team of cleared workers who were free to subcontract to others, when it seemed fortuitous to keep a level of separation in place. MRI's location was strategic, as well. The Agency's Los Angeles base for the Services and Support Group of the DDS&T—known as the Western Industrial Liaison Detachment, or WILD—was located in the basement of the Tishman Building.

For this early work on a proof of concept, Crooke was asked to keep a low profile. He pulled in just two men, both engineers from the oil industry: Jimmy Dean, hired away from Mobil Oil following work on the *CUSS I,* and Jack Reed, a structural and petroleum engineer who'd previously worked at Humble Oil. Not even Global Marine's CEO, Bob Bauer, was told what they were doing. Bauer trusted Crooke, who ran a division of experimental projects, and didn't need to know all of the details of a prospective job, especially if Crooke told him that he wasn't yet at liberty to discuss them. In due time, if things worked out, all would be revealed.

The three men were given a windowless room accessed by double doors secured by cipher locks inside MRI's cluster of offices. This was new territory for Global Marine, and the message was very clear: What happened inside that room stayed inside the room, unless the Agency said otherwise.

Parangosky gave Crooke what he called "the green book," a collection of about a dozen concepts proposed by CIA engineers for how one might raise a submarine off the ocean floor. The book contained all of the task force's ideas, outlandish or otherwise, as well as Craven and Bradley's original Navy plan, which suggested using robots to access the sub's interior.

It took very little time for Crooke, Dean, and Reed to shoot down nearly all of the ideas in the green book. The only way the Agency was going to get that sub up from the bottom—if such a thing were even possible—was by using the "brute-strength" or "dead lift" method. They would have to pull it up on the end of a string of pipe, the longest and heaviest ever built.

MRI was as secure as any contractor facility could be, but Crooke and his men had no experience with secure communications, and Parangosky didn't want to take any risks, especially in the tenuous early days of an operation that didn't yet have official approval from the White House. Phone calls were brief and very general. No specific names or details were to be discussed. When it was time to go over design specifics, Parangosky wanted Crooke to deliver his findings in person to his engineers on the East Coast, in surroundings they controlled.

A few weeks into the project, Crooke and Dean ran out for lunch across Sepulveda, one of the major north-south thoroughfares near LAX, and on the way back Dean misjudged the traffic and was struck by a US Postal Service truck. He was only bruised, fortunately, and when Paul Evans heard the story he explained how fortunate they all were that Dean hadn't been injured enough to require surgery. No one knew yet how trustworthy Dean was, and it's not uncommon for people under anesthesia to blab uncontrollably, so a recently cleared contractor with an unproven track record going under for surgery is a security man's nightmare. Who knew what Dean might have said under the influence of gas?

Ultimately, the CIA briefed and cleared Global's lawyer, Taylor Hancock, Bob Bauer, and A. J. Field, all of whom endorsed the project, as devoted patriots as well as businessmen who realized that this was going to be a large and lucrative job for GMI.

To move forward with the design, though, Crooke needed additional brainpower, so he asked Parangosky to clear more Global Marine engineers. He knew that the kind of pipe string the operation was going to require could be deployed only from a massive ship, the kind of floating island Global had begun building for its deep-sea drilling, and it wasn't just as easy as designing a giant ship.

That ship would have to be unlike anything ever built, and on top of that, it had to make narrative sense to the world—especially to the Soviets, who would be paying attention to any unusual activity in the Pacific. One of the first Global men cleared to join the effort was Russ Thornburg, vice president of Oceanics, or what Crooke liked to call OTO—for "other than oil."

Thornburg and Crooke set upon the challenge of explaining why a giant ship would be operating at a standstill in a remote area of the Pacific. What reason could a ship plausibly have for being parked out there? Pretending the ship is crippled buys only a few days, maybe a week. And it wasn't like other ships wouldn't come to help. Considering weather delays, rough seas, and technical problems, a mission to lift the sub could take weeks or even months. To Thornburg, the answer was obvious: Global Marine was going into the mining business.

14
Ocean Mining 101

Pretending to mine the ocean floor wasn't some crazy idea that came out of nowhere. By the late 1960s, deep-ocean mining was widely discussed in the marine industry press, and some of Global Marine's competitors were also exploring how harvesting minerals from the seafloor might be done. The technological hurdles were extreme, but the potential payoff was enormous: billions of tons of variously sized manganese nodules, which, depending on their location around the planet, contained a mix of valuable rare earth elements, including copper, nickel, and cobalt.

Nodules were first identified by John Young Buchanan, the staff chemist on the scientific voyage of the HMS *Challenger,* a British vessel that sailed the oceans from 1872 to 1876, covering seventy thousand nautical miles in the hopes of opening up the mysteries of what lay under the sea. Buchanan discovered many things in the buckets attached to hemp rope that the ship used for dredging, including life on a seabed that was thought to be frozen, as well as lumpy gray nodules he recognized to be an almost pure oxide of manganese. The nodules, his expedition leader noted, ranged in size from mustard seed to cricket ball and were formed like pearls inside of oysters— minerals precipitating out of the sea and solidifying around a solid nucleus that could be almost anything. Often, the *Challenger* observed, it was "a bit of volcanic glass, a shark's tooth, or the ear bone of a whale for a nucleus," but it could even be a grain of sand. The average nodule was about three centimeters in diameter, but because the objects grow in perpetuity, they can reach giant size. One manganese boulder found "entangled in a telephone cable" that was being salvaged near the Philippines weighed eighteen hundred pounds.

These dull, lumpy objects were found in all of the world's oceans, but the largest and best concentration was in the Pacific, especially in a large area south and west of Hawaii, where studies found an average of eleven kilograms of nodules per square meter of seafloor. Nodules have an "exceedingly slow rate of accumulation," growing in size by just one millimeter every thousand years, but their spread is so vast—there is a mind-blowingly large amount of seafloor on earth—that the total growth in volume over a year is 6 million metric tons, which makes them, essentially, an infinitely renewable resource. The best estimate on the total tonnage in the Pacific alone, as of 1969, was 1.66×10^{12} metric tons.

In 1963, the oceanographer John Mero turned his PhD thesis into the book *The Mineral Resources of the Sea,* and most experts cite it as the birth of the notion that the seabed was a location that could be mined commercially. Manganese nodules in particular were singled out. "From an economic standpoint," Mero writes, "they are the most important sediment of the deep-sea floor."

Mero's book inspired groups to organize research voyages into the world's oceans to begin sampling nodules. And Global Marine, in 1968, listed ocean mining as one of several areas of future growth for the company in its annual report, written before Crooke ever met Parangosky. The company's Engineering and Construction Division, it noted, had already developed "specialized equipment" to investigate occurrences of valuable minerals, including manganese and phosphorite, on the seafloor.

Initial studies estimated the start-up cost of a deep-sea-mining operation, plus processing facilities, at between 30 million and 300 million dollars. Even then, according to a 1969 report by the US Army School of Naval Warfare, "a manganese mining operation in the deep ocean is possible and could be economically feasible."

There was, if not immediately then at least in the long term, both an economic and a national security rationale for pursuing ocean-mining technology. Copper and manganese were both fairly plentiful in 1969, but the United States had only minimal deposits of either—95 percent of manganese and 92 percent of copper used in the United States came from foreign sources—and to find its own domestic supplies of these and other import-dependent resources was always in America's best interests. Mero predicted that within two decades "the entire free-world copper supply will come from the sea, radically changing the balance of world trade."

The challenges in harvesting these minerals, however, were significant. Designing and building a system to do the physical mining—locating and retrieving the nodules in enough volume to justify the cost of the machines being used—was a massive task. And only half of the problem. The nodules are a conglomerate consisting of multiple elements smashed together with other materials that have no value. To get at whatever you actually want— nickel, cobalt, or copper—you have to process them, and as of 1969, no one had yet devised a way to do that.

People were thinking about it, though. In November 1968, the oil and natural gas company Tenneco formed Deepsea Ventures. The company built a 152-foot research vessel and announced a plan to invest from 100 million to 150 million dollars in an ocean-mining program, including a "prototype noncommercial mining operation" in shallow water off the coast of Florida, as well as a mini pilot plant to demonstrate how the company would process the nodules. When the first test was conducted successfully in the summer of 1970, wire reports carried the story across the country. They quoted Deepsea's marketing director, James Victory, as saying the deposits held enough copper "to rewire the whole damn country."

Americans weren't alone in wondering how humanity might tap the seafloor. The Germans and Japanese had projects to explore ocean mining, and while the Russians had yet to launch any kind of mining experiment, they were actively studying the distribution of nodules around the central Pacific, including locations in the general area of the K-129 wreck.

Concerns about exploiting areas of the globe that belonged to no country became an inflection point at the UN, where landlocked nations began to agitate for a treaty that would ensure that all countries benefited equally from whatever was harvested from the seafloor.

On May 3, 1970, Richard Nixon stepped into the conversation. "The nations of the world are now facing decisions of momentous importance to man's use of the oceans for decades ahead," he said in a formal statement about the United States' National Ocean Policy. "The stark fact is that the law of the sea is inadequate to meet the needs of modern technology and the concerns of the international community."

It was time, Nixon said, for all nations of the world to establish some basic standards about shared use of the oceans, and he called upon the United States to move this effort forward.

Tension on the subject had been building for years at that point. In September 1967, the Maltese ambassador to the UN delivered a three-hour speech to the General Assembly in reaction to fears that the United States and Soviet Union might soon place nuclear weapons on the bottom of the sea. The deep ocean and its vast mineral wealth, he said, should be "the common heritage of mankind." And three years later, in 1970, the UN formally adopted that idea.

15

Every Great Ship Has a Great Naval Architect

O nce the CIA and Global Marine had a plausible story, they needed a ship. And the man to conceive of such a vessel was obviously John Graham. Graham, then fifty-five, was Global's chief naval architect, a brilliant, confident redhead who had designed all of the company's break-through ships, including the *Glomar Challenger,* which had so impressed Parangosky's task force.

Graham joined Global Marine in 1958 after relocating to California from Houston with his wife, Nell, and three children. He hadn't moved west for ca-reer reasons. Graham was running from his demons. He was an MIT graduate from a proud family. His father had been an engineer, too, until he was named chief justice for the Court of Customs and Patent Appeals by presidential ap-pointment. Graham's father was also an amateur archaeologist who would take his son digging along the Potomac River, where they'd find arrowheads, as well as pieces of old ships that had wrecked in the rapids outside Washington. Father and son studied up on these wrecks and then built models to re-create them, and Graham went off to college with the idea that he would like to build ships, for real, as a job. At MIT, he married the secretary of the school president and specialized in naval architecture and marine engineering. He didn't actually like sailing, or even being in the water. He just liked building boats.

94

After college, John and Nell Graham moved to Long Island, where he worked and thrived at one of the largest shipyards in the area, establishing a reputation as a clever engineer who knew how to do big jobs on time, within a budget. The Grahams raised their children on a dead-end street where twenty-eight kids lived on a single block. His career took him to New Jersey, and then to Houston, with each destination bringing a better job and a bigger house. In Houston, Graham went into business with a friend, founding a naval architecture firm called Graham and Christensen. He was a serious man, rarely easygoing, and as his workload intensified, the only way Graham seemed to know how to relax was by drinking, a longtime habit that escalated and then finally spun out of control in Texas.

There were cocktails at lunch, cocktails after work, and then, at home, Graham would drink beer from cans that piled up around his chair until he fell asleep. It began to affect his work, and Graham's partner ultimately kicked him out of the business, an event that he failed to mention to his family until his young daughter Jenny came home after school and found her dad passed out in bed in the middle of the afternoon.

That was enough for Nell. Her father had just died, suddenly, of a heart attack in California, and she told John that she and the kids were moving west to help her mother.

Graham absorbed the news that his family was leaving him and asked Nell for one more chance. She gave it to him, with the caveat that she was still moving to California. If he wanted to save the family and make it work, he'd have to come along.

"I will sober up and we'll start again," he said.

Nell and the kids piled into the family car with the dog and cat and a trunk full of luggage and headed for Newport Beach. John Graham caught a flight to Long Beach and checked himself into rehab. A month later, his soul and spirit revived, he was discharged and went immediately to his first Alcoholics Anonymous meeting. He never drank again.

John Graham became a fervent member of the Southern California AA community. He attended two meetings a day and devoted much of his free time to helping other alcoholics in trouble. The men of AA became his best friends. He took up golf, rediscovered the saxophone, and took a job as a draftsman, a job far beneath his abilities, but which reconnected him to his love of shipbuilding. Quickly, his talents stood out, and he began consulting, in particular to the famous Todd Shipyards, in San Pedro. Then, one day in 1960, he saw an ad for a position overseeing all naval architecture for a company called Global Marine.

The interview was at Global's headquarters in downtown LA, and Graham's credentials—an MIT grad with extensive experience building ships—made him an attractive candidate. At the interview, Global Marine's three top executives, President Bob Bauer, VP A. J. Field, and Curtis Crooke, were impressed by the man. Graham made it clear that this was his dream job, that he'd basically been born, reared, and trained to build the kinds of ships Global needed, but he wanted the men to know the whole story before they considered his candidacy.

"There's one thing you need to know about me," Graham told the men. "I'm a drunk. And I've been a drunk for a long time. If I can keep sober I will give you the best years of my life."

He got the job. And Global Marine took off.

Crooke knew that Project Azorian couldn't succeed without Graham. Global Marine was acclaimed for innovation, and that innovation almost always began in the brain of the company's chief architect. The drinking, however, created a quandary. The idea of putting a reformed alcoholic in charge of engineering on the largest operation in CIA history gave John Parangosky and his security staff serious concerns. It was basically a nonstarter.

The most important factor in clearing an individual for a covert operation—especially one as sensitive as Azorian—was the likelihood that the person could compromise the project. And an alcohol or drug problem, even a former problem, was among the behaviors most feared by CIA security personnel. Dark secrets can be exploited. And drinkers often relapse. On the other hand, Crooke made it very clear that Global couldn't pull this off without John Graham, and he staked his word on the company's best engineer. He asked Parangosky to do whatever was necessary to get Graham cleared. While not impossible, Parangosky explained, it was going to take time. And work on Azorian couldn't just freeze.

While he waited for the CIA to figure out a way to get Graham cleared,

Crooke brought the project to his chief architect under its white cover, telling Graham that the company had an anonymous client who was exploring the possibility of deep-ocean mining. This wasn't an outrageous story to tell. Global had now proven it could build huge ships equipped with station keeping that could operate on the ocean floor, and the subject of ocean mining was bubbling up all over the industry. If there was money to be made there, why wouldn't Global Marine at least pursue concepts? So what, Crooke asked his head naval architect, would a mining ship even look like?

Graham's first reaction was that Crooke was nuts. Sure, he could design a ship that would sit in place and deploy a long pipe that sucked up rocks from the bottom of the ocean, but such a ship would be prohibitively expensive. You'd have to operate it for years just to break even. And the point of Global Marine was to make profits, so that would be stupid. Crooke told Graham not to worry, that he already had potential partners willing to share in the cost. Global's risk was small. He just needed a ship.

To work at Global Marine in 1970 was to be employed at a company that could do no wrong, where resources and intellectual energy seemed almost limitless and the drive to innovate and explore in an industry that didn't even exist before 1961 created an atmosphere of relentless optimism. Led by Crooke and Graham, Global Marine's engineers just kept thinking bigger and bigger, and though they knew eventually they'd run afoul of the laws of physics, they fully intended to push the boundaries of what was possible in the deep ocean until they reached that point.

Graham was an intuitive engineer who worked from his gut and Crooke knew how to set him free to create, by not drilling down on detail. Graham's concepts were almost always right, and Crooke surrounded him with technical engineers to refine the detail. But on this job, with its epic scale and frantic schedule, there was little time for noodling over detail anyway. They weren't designing a prototype for future mining ships. Every system on Azorian's ship could and should be purpose-built only for this mission.

When Crooke brought him the mining concept, Graham called in a few of his closest engineers and began to sketch out a ship. His loyal secretary, Laura Crouchet, protected his schedule and office, keeping him provisioned with cigarettes—which he smoked often and enthusiastically—and coffee, which he consumed by the gallon. Crooke told Graham to keep the early design work quiet, at least from upper management. If he needed to call in a little help, that was okay, but it would be best to keep it all low-key. One of Graham's first recruits was his least-experienced naval architect, a recent University of Michigan graduate named Charlie Canby, whom he liked for his youthful enthusiasm and unpredictable nature.

Graham asked Canby, who'd yet to design anything of note, to "draw some lines of a Glomar Grand Isle–class ship." This was Global Marine's largest class—more than four hundred feet in length and weighing at least eleven thousand tons—the same size and type of ship as the *Challenger*. Like all of Global's new drillships, it also needed to have automated pipe handling and a hydrophone-enabled station-keeping system.

Graham was asking for something even bigger, though. He wanted thirty-five thousand tons of displacement and a cavernous opening inside the ship—a feature known as a moon pool—that was 125 feet long by 50 feet wide.

Canby loved to visit Graham's office. The boss was often tough but always encouraging. He'd accept the latest drawings, slap them on his desk, and then take the old dime-store slide rule, the kind, Canby says, "they give you in sixth grade," out of his shirt pocket. Most naval architects had a favorite slide rule, a showpiece, maybe made of bamboo and accented with ivory, but Graham's was cheap and plastic. He'd slide it back and forth across whatever print was on his desk, whipping from line to line like an architect in a film that was being fast-forwarded, pausing periodically to tap along to the beat of whatever big-band classic was playing on his office stereo. Almost inevitably, if he took some prints home to study, they'd come back splattered with red pencil marks and coffee rings.

Graham liked what Canby was doing, but he couldn't make up his mind, either. He kept increasing the size of the moon pool as the specs passed on by Crooke—who was getting them from Parangosky back in Virginia—changed. The ship's gaping center cavity went from 125 by 50 feet to 175 by 65 feet to 199 by 75 feet, on a ship with a displacement of sixty-five thousand tons—a set of specs unlike any Canby had ever seen and very odd dimensions for a mining ship, which he might have noticed had he not been twenty-one and thrilled simply to be designing ships alongside John Graham.

Graham was always the smartest person in the meeting, a man who didn't equivocate and who inspired awe in his employees. One of his best qualities as an employee and a collaborator was that he rarely said no, at least not right away. He never reflexively said an idea wasn't possible, even if he believed that was the case. In his office, all ideas were entertained, and the architect never dismissed one until he'd done some scribbling on a napkin to test it out first.

Gradually, the team assigned to what had become known as the "Deep Ocean Mining Ship" expanded. Graham pulled in the best of what he called, endearingly, his "grunt engineers," including Sherman Wetmore, a prodigy who had worked for Global Marine since 1961, when he graduated from college. Wetmore was involved as design engineer on all of the important drillships, including *Glomar II, III, IV,* and *V* and the *Challenger.* Graham also drafted the mechanical engineers Jim McNary, Abe Person, and Charlie Johnson to work on ship and "mining" support systems.

In fairly short order, the group had designed a mining ship that, they thought, could do the work to fulfill the bizarre and increasingly onerous specs that Crooke was feeding them. In addition to being enormous—more than six hundred feet—with a moon pool the size of a college gymnasium, it would have dynamic positioning, a semiautomated pipe-handling system, and a set of sliding doors in the bottom of the hull through which seventeen thousand feet of steel pipe could be lowered and raised by the largest and most powerful heavy-lift system ever built—deployed from a rig floor atop a gimbaled A-frame derrick that could stay perfectly still even as the ship itself pitched in rough seas. The only thing missing was a mining machine—whatever was going to be on the end of the pipe to locate and suck in nodules. But that wasn't John Graham's responsibility. Lockheed Corporation had been hired to handle that part.

Eventually, Graham got his clearance—Parangosky had worked around the drinking issues—and when Crooke briefed him on the ship's true purpose, Graham stared a hole through him. "I knew there was something screwy about this whole thing," he said.

The design was constantly evolving, but as soon as Graham and Crooke felt that it was far enough along to share with the Agency's engineering group, Paul Evans' security team arranged a trip to Washington and booked the two nautical wonks into a hotel in Fairfax County as senior executives from Graham Pharmaceuticals.

When they arrived at the hotel and checked in, Graham as CEO and Crooke as vice president, the two men were asked to fill out a card with their work details and contact information. The clerk laid two cards out and then stepped away as Graham and Crooke began to fill them out and then stopped at the same point. They looked at each other, whispered, and then couldn't contain their amusement, doubling over in a convulsion of laughter at the same realization: Neither of them knew how to spell "pharmaceuticals."

It didn't take long, at most a few meetings, for Crooke to recognize that Parangosky and Graham were best kept apart. Graham was at heart a friendly guy, even loose around those he trusted, but the engineer stiffened reflexively when he felt uncomfortable. He was a tall guy who stood erect, and he entered every meeting with an aura of the man in charge. If you didn't know Graham, he could come off as curt or standoffish, and Parangosky wasn't the warmest individual in the workplace, either. He was, in every sense of the word, professional, with little time for politics or negotiating around prickly personalities. Fortunately, there wasn't much reason for them to interact. Graham attended briefings, but it was Crooke who ran them.

Once the decision was made to pursue the "grunt lift" concept, with Global Marine as chief contractor, concern among the CIA's engineers focused mostly on the pipe. What would happen if the pipe broke while the string was under maximum stress, turning a relatively static 17-million-pound load into a dynamic one? The answer, according to a nuclear physicist who sat in on one of the advisory meetings, was that the broken pipe would become a runaway spring, with "the energy equivalent of setting off a nuclear explosive of 8 kilotons."

This and other horrifying potential outcomes were not enough to deter Parangosky, NURO director Bob Frosch, or David Packard. Parangosky trusted that his task force, when given access to real-world experts who built ships and pipes, could solve these problems. He also knew there just wasn't time to fret. There were perishable aspects to Azorian, both tangible and otherwise. Certain things on the seafloor—paper documents, such as the battle orders, and the cryptographic machines, likely made of weaker metals—would decay, in time. And the bigger risk was secrecy. To pull this off would require a massive operation, involving hundreds or more likely thousands of people, and keeping a program of that scale hidden from the Soviets would be hard. Especially if it dragged on for years. And then there was the matter of the location. The area where the sub went down was notoriously rough, and there was only a brief two-month window during the summer when a ship might be able to sit on station in relative calm. If Parangosky's team missed that date, they'd have to wait a year, so that a delay of even two months somewhere late in the design would likely result in the loss of twelve months in real time. That would pile up more costs and allow more time for a leak.

The only way to do this was to do it. So in October 1970, Parangosky was given the okay to begin design and construction of the major hardware components simultaneously despite the fact that his task force had identified eleven "major unknowns or technical risk areas." These included such "basic items as the exact dimension and condition of the target, the ship design, the working machinery to provide the lift capability, and the pipe string." Allowing four to eight months for study and analysis of each component—as a real-world engineering environment might require— would add three or four years to a program that needed to start as soon as possible to have even a slight chance of success. Everyone understood that the designs would need to be flexible enough to accommodate changes that might be necessary during the construction.

If this sounds like a ridiculous set of parameters, that's because it was.

16
Big Bertha

The plan would require four primary pieces: First, an enormous ship built around a moon pool large enough to hold the wrecked sub, with sliding gates in the hull's bottom that could open and close to lower the string, retrieve the sub, and then pull the sub inside without anyone on the surface knowing that it had been done. Second, a mechanical grabber or claw at the end of the drill string to grab and hold the sub while it was raised. Third, the pipe-string system, which would be the largest and toughest ever built. And finally, a submersible barge/dry dock that would serve two purposes. It would need to be large enough that the claw could be built inside, out of view. Once the claw was completed inside the barge, the barge itself, with the claw inside, would be put into the water and sailed out to sea to mate with the ship.

No one company could possibly handle all of the major systems, nor would Parangosky's ambitious schedule allow such a thing, so the work was divided up, with Global Marine building the ship, Lockheed Missiles and Space handling the claw and the barge, and Summa/Hughes Tool Company making the pipe string. Global Marine would also be the primary contractor, coordinating the program office and the various subcontractors.

And there were many. Aside from the three primary contractors, Parangosky's task force selected numerous others to contribute specific components, including Western Gear to build the heavy-lift system and Honeywell to handle data processing, which included the automatic station keeping that would enable the ship to hold its position over a fixed location.

The project was a race from the outset. Work needed to begin as quickly as possible, even in some cases before there was official approval in Washington. Once bases had been established on both coasts, the CIA would install ciphered phones so that officers on the two coasts could communicate by voice without fear of being overheard. But that would take time, and the CIA task force needed to be in regular contact with Global Marine, MRI, and the other West Coast contractors. There was no reason to suspect leaks at this point, but Parangosky still insisted on the strictest precautions. Until encrypted phone lines were installed, anyone in Washington who wanted to call Curtis Crooke or John Graham had to go outside and use one of dozens of phone booths around Fairfax County that the Agency had identified as safe for use. Known officers were also forbidden from meeting publicly with any of the contractors or even entering their headquarters unless they'd been scrubbed by security officers and given disguises. If an engineer did need to travel—say, to Seattle to visit Honeywell—it had to be under a false name and with a nonrelatable, nonproject explanation for his presence.

John Graham determined a rough blueprint for a ship that he thought could handle the load and then assigned architects to focus on specific functions. A young architect named Chuck Cannon was assigned to design the hull, which included the sliding moon-pool gates in the bottom that would open and close to allow the capture vehicle—and, hopefully, the submarine—to come in and out of the ship without detection.

Something that troubled Graham from the moment the ship's lines were drawn was how having such a large hole in the middle—and the extremely long, relatively narrow wing walls on either side of that hole—would affect the ship's structure and stability at sea. Even after Global Marine began to submit its drawings to the American Bureau of Shipping for approval, Graham asked Cannon to perform manual calculations to predict how the ship would react structurally in a seaway. It took Cannon three weeks, but he determined that the ship would undergo stresses at acceptable levels even in fairly heavy wave conditions. But not everything was predictable; certain factors would be unknowns even after the ship was finished.

Cannon was thrilled by the responsibility, but also intimidated, which typified his experience under Graham. Shortly after he was hired, at age twenty-three, Cannon was ordered to fly to New York and read a paper (that Graham had written but was too busy to deliver himself) to the national Society of Naval Architects and Marine Engineers (SNAME). The paper was a critique of a SNAME technical paper titled "Vehicles for Ocean Engineering," and it was withering. These meetings were known to be polite and complimentary, but after a trembling Cannon finished the paper, he looked out at a "stunned" room that, he later recalled, "was pin-drop quiet."

He was still a little shaken when he returned to LA and reported back to Graham, who patted him on the shoulder, smiled, and fired up a cigarette.

The mining ship that began to emerge on Graham's drafting table was like none ever built, a massive vessel sturdy enough to pick up 3.92 million pounds—the equivalent of a World War II destroyer—from the bottom of the ocean, lift it more than three miles, and then carry it home in the ship's belly, without anyone seeing it. This required a very clever design, and Graham was free to try basically anything without worrying about revealing the ship's true purpose, since no one had ever built a mining ship before. A mining ship could look like whatever Graham wanted.

There were certain necessities, of course. The ship would need berthing for more than one hundred men, many of whom weren't experienced seamen and who, being away from home for a month or more, would need some legitimate comforts in order not to lose their minds. And it would have to withstand some of the most punishing weather and ocean conditions imaginable. While under way, that could be storms with one-hundred-foot waves, winds reaching one hundred knots or more, and temperatures that ranged wildly, from 40 to 105 degrees Fahrenheit. The Agency task force had compiled a list of these ridiculous requirements, which Graham tacked on a wall over his desk and often fixated on while chain-smoking his way through a problem.

To meet the program's rigid deadlines, materials had to be ordered before designs were finalized. Long lead procurement began in March 1971, starting with the biggest pieces of steel, such as the ones required for the hull, the ship's center well, the A-frame derrick, the gimbal platforms, the gimbal bearings, and the enormous five-foot-diameter by twenty-foot-long heave-compensation and heavy-lift system cylinders, which would take fifteen to eighteen months to manufacture.

Curtis Crooke left Graham mostly alone to do his work, but he also knew his chief architect better than anyone. The two had been working together for twelve years, on one massive project after another. Crooke recognized Graham as a genius, but not a perfectionist, and considering the pace at which Azorian had to come together, he needed to be sure time wasn't wasted on ideas that weren't going to work. So Crooke assigned a human safeguard, a quiet, sharply dressed, obsessively detail-oriented engineer named Dayton Knorr, to watch over his chief architect's shoulder and check his math. Graham was the kind of engineer who solved problems on the fly, who "did his work on the back of matchboxes," as Crooke liked to say. Knorr's job was to be Graham's shadow, to stay quiet and make sure the technology required to build whatever he was proposing actually existed, or would soon.

17

Paging Howard Hughes

he mining cover struck everyone as perfect, but it had one flaw. Global Marine wasn't big enough to plausibly go into such an expensive and speculative business on its own. No one would believe it. And because Global was a public corporation, Curtis Crooke needed a way to explain to investors why this drilling company would embark on such an experimental concept, not to mention how it was going to finance the hiring of the contractors required to help bring it to fruition. The money had to come from somewhere—ideally from a "client" who could hire Global Marine to do the work.

Nearly all of the companies large enough to plausibly pay for such a venture were publicly traded, and the CIA wasn't about to drag in a public corporation, which would then have to explain to its shareholders why it was paying hundreds of millions of dollars to hire Global Marine to start a new industry that was speculative at best. That presented too much risk.

There was, however, one company that made sense: Howard Hughes's Hughes Tool Company. The true origin of the idea remains a mystery. CIA engineers, including Dave Sharp, recall that it came from inside Parangosky's task force and was fairly obvious when they made a list of companies that fit the extremely narrow criteria of (a) being large enough to actually launch a mining venture, and (b) already operating in a business space where embarking on such a venture would make sense to the public, the media, and the Soviets. Curtis Crooke is sure that it was his idea. In either case, the only real option turned out to be the perfect choice.

Hughes Tool was a private corporation that didn't have to explain its activities to investors. Even better, it was a private company owned by a reclusive billionaire industrialist who was famous for investing in risky ventures and had no apparent concern for his public image. Hughes was sixty-four years old and a virtual ghost at this point in his life. The once brash pilot, film producer, airplane maker, and real estate investor was now profoundly paranoid, addicted to prescription opiates, and germophobic. He almost never spoke to the media or saw daylight and was, as far as anyone knew, holed up in a hotel suite with the shades pulled on the top floor of his own Desert Inn Hotel in Las Vegas. He was still wealthy and powerful, however, with a sprawling empire of businesses, including some that had done work—occasionally clandestine work—for the US government.

On top of that, Hughes Tool was a sensible partner. The Hughes fortune was built on the invention of a new type of rotary drill bit that opened up new areas for oil exploration by Howard Sr., and the company's experience in mining by 1969 was widespread. No one would doubt a mining venture backed by Hughes Tool, and the company had a history with Global Marine, which had been using Hughes drill bits for years. Howard Hughes's own interests in mining had mostly drifted away and been replaced by things like aviation and Hollywood, but he was still accumulating mining claims in Nevada and was rumored to be developing revolutionary mining methods using computers. "We just kept coming back to crazy old Howard," Crooke later said.

Several weeks after the CIA had agreed to recruit Hughes, Parangosky came back to Crooke with a problem. He couldn't find a route to the man that didn't go through Robert Maheu, the longtime boss of Hughes's Las Vegas operations who had become radioactive to the Agency for numerous reasons, including his involvement with alleged attempted bribes of former presidents and a failed CIA plot to have the mafia assassinate Fidel Castro. Hughes had a long history with the government through his many-tentacled operations, and in fact numerous functions within the Agency had worked with his companies at one point or another, but none of these paths were clean enough for Parangosky to consider them viable.

Crooke had a solution. Wendell Williams, one of Global's main sales-men in Houston, was close personal friends with James Lesch, a Hughes Tool vice president. Parangosky quickly cleared Williams into the program, and he went to see Lesch, who agreed to take the idea to Raymond Holliday, the president of Hughes Tool and one of the few people who could get a mes-sage directly to the reclusive billionaire.

Whether or not Hughes himself actually heard the proposal wasn't clear to anyone. It was a mystery of the program that lived on to the end—that lives on to this day, in fact. At no point did any of the principals ever see Hughes himself. Crooke suspects he was nearby once, on the other side of a wall on the penthouse floor of LA's Century Plaza Hotel, when the key indi-viduals from the Agency, Global Marine, and Hughes Tool were meeting to finalize details. In certain critical moments, a phone in the room would ring and Chester Davis, Hughes's lawyer, would answer it, listen, then leave the room, returning a few minutes later with a question that could only have come from Hughes. He was either listening through the wall or via a device that piped audio to a nearby room where someone was relaying messages to him. Whatever the method, no one in that room ever saw the mogul's face or heard his voice.

Howard's trio of lieutenants—Chester Davis, Raymond Holliday, and Bill Gay, often referred to as the mogul's Mormon Mafia—claimed to speak for their boss and reported back that he was happy to provide Azorian's critical cover. Hughes was honored to do this service for his country, and so were they.

The arrangement was to be very simple. The CIA and Hughes Tool would sign a classified black contract signifying that Hughes would serve as the Agency's secret proxy for the operation. Once the contract was signed, Hughes Tool would hire contractors chosen by the CIA using white con-tracts stating that they were doing work for hire on a deep-sea-mining operation. The first and most important of those contracts would be with Global Marine.

Parangosky sent a memo to Henry Kissinger summarizing the proposed structure for Azorian. "From the outset it has been recognized that there could be no overt U.S. Government involvement in AZORIAN without at-tracting close Soviet scrutiny, and possible realization of the actual purpose for the program," he wrote. "The alternative was to structure the program as a commercial venture." Deep-ocean mining, specifically, had been chosen, he reported. The industry was "in its infancy," commercially viable, and so new that no one knew what an ocean-mining machine even looked like, giving them plenty of room to engineer freely. Furthermore, Parangosky noted, the Hughes Tool Company's (later Summa Corporation's) "participation as the sponsor and sole source of funding" could not be more perfect. "Mr. Howard Hughes is the only stockholder; he is recognized as a pioneering entrepreneur with a wide variety of business interests; he has the necessary financial resources; he habitually operates in secrecy; and, his personal eccentricities are such that news media reporting and speculation about his activities frequently range from the truth to utter fiction."

Parangosky got his first go-ahead. On December 13, 1970, Global CEO A. J. Field, Hughes Tool's Raymond Holliday, and Parangosky's contracting officer, George Kucera, signed and executed classified Government Contract No. S-HU-0900, which legally established the parameters for Project Azorian's cover structure. The three key parties were Global Marine Inc., referred to as the "Contractor"; Hughes Tool Company, the "Agent"; and the US government, called the "Sponsor." The specific agency of the government was not named, but the contract stated that Hughes was uniquely positioned to be the agent, to be a believable front for the project's true purpose. "WHEREAS due to necessity for cover purposes to operate the mission under the guise of an overt commercial deep sea mining project the Sponsor desires to enter into a contract with the Agent who shall represent and act in the stead of the Sponsor who shall at all times remain an unidentified principal."

This was the so-called black contract, which laid out each party's responsibility in the operation: "Whereas the Agent"—Hughes Tool—"acting on the behalf of the Sponsor"—the CIA—"shall enter into an overt commercial contract with the Contractor"—Global Marine—"for the design, fabrication, delivery and subsequent operation of the aforesaid overt deep sea mining Project. The Hughes Tool Company shall act as the undisclosed Agent for the Sponsor. The Agent shall represent itself to be the owner and operator of the Deep Sea Mining Project and as directed by the Sponsor enter into an overt commercial contract with Global Marine Inc." This would be the white contract, the one that would be shown to Global's investors, the media, and the Securities and Exchange Commission, should they wish to see it.

The black contract laid out very clear terms. Global Marine was "responsible for technical direction of design, fabrication and delivery" of the actual "mining" system, while the Agency was responsible for security and funding. Because other contractors were going to be necessary, Global Marine would hire and pay them and serve as the primary engineering contractor, overseeing design and handling systems integration.

Most important, there could be no direct link between the US government and Global Marine, so in addition to providing cover, Hughes Tool would be the pipeline for moving money from the CIA to Global Marine to pay for its own work and for hiring the contractors. Not even Global Marine's accountants knew the true nature of the relationship. Like everyone else, they thought the work was really going to be done for Hughes.

18

Building a Bulletproof Lie

very con needs an artist. And Parangosky had the perfect man: his old friend Walt Lloyd. Lloyd had run security on the S&T's three most important programs to date: the U-2, the A-12, and the Corona satellite. In that capacity, he had all but created the model for compartmentalized security programs and protocols. A sharp, good-natured sort, Lloyd was specialized in solving unusual problems in creative ways. And this was going to be one hell of a problem.

Lloyd grew up poor, the oldest of five sons whose father worked in a General Motors factory for twenty-five years and died of leukemia at sixty-five. All five boys joined the military. Walt chose the Coast Guard, enlisting at the tail end of World War II only to be told he had a red-green color deficiency. Upon discharge, he washed cars for a while in Detroit, then in 1948 enrolled in a basic college program at Michigan State to pursue criminal justice. In 1951, CIA recruiters visited the program in search of investigators and hired eight of the twelve criminal justice graduates in his class, Lloyd included, to do background investigations on Agency hires, a job formerly done by the FBI, until J. Edgar Hoover decided that his men were too busy.

Lloyd was initially based out of those old Navy barracks on the National Mall, in a Quonset hut filled with mice, and after a period of doing general investigations, he was put on the special operations desk, which was for cases that had extra sensitivity—such as the investigation of safe houses, covert locations, or other potential security department hires. The Agency wasn't looking for spotless records, because nobody is truly pure. Lloyd's father had given him some advice when he was a teenager. "You don't have to be absolutely perfect," he said. "But be prepared to not do anything you would be embarrassed to tell me about." And that became Walt's basic standard at the Agency, too. He could forgive many things as long as the person was honest, but lies were unforgivable—and nearly always caught.

When Parangosky first reached out about the "boat project," Lloyd had just returned from a stint in Taiwan, where he'd been in command of one of the CIA's most closely guarded secrets: Detachment H. This was a squadron of U-2s sold to the Chinese nationalists on Taiwan, nicknamed the Black Cats, and used for overflights of mainland China. Taiwanese pilots flew the U-2 missions, but the CIA ran the base and its operations, while Lockheed provided the ground crew.

Upon his return, Lloyd was assigned to the S&T's Special Projects Staff, the incubator for black programs. Specifically, he was told to report to Parangosky, who was very quietly building up a mysterious new program at an unremarkable office park in Tysons Corner.

As he'd done with Oxcart and Corona before, Parangosky built out an autonomous division that had all the essential components of the larger CIA. The Azorian program office had its engineering section, obviously, as well as a security staff, a communications department, a finance officer, and a small but efficient administrative group. As the project began to transition from a theoretical operation to one that would actually hire contractors and build things, however, Parangosky needed someone very clever to run the so-called Commercial Operations Division—which maintained the cover story—and he wanted Walt Lloyd to be that man.

Lloyd arrived for his meeting with Parangosky in the afternoon. He looked at the address given to him by his assigning officer, which matched the numbers on the building that he had just parked in front of. Lloyd went inside and up the stairs, where he entered a door with no sign. The receptionist recognized this visitor's name and took Lloyd past a warren of desks—many occupied by men he knew, who smiled and greeted their old security boss—and into Parangosky's office.

"Good to see you, Walt," he said. He shook Lloyd's hand, nodded at a chair, and asked his assistant to get them some coffee.

For the first half hour, the two men talked and laughed and reminisced about "the U-bird" years until finally Parangosky asked his old friend why he'd come back to headquarters.

"I think I'm bored," Lloyd answered.

"Well, I don't think you're going to be bored here," Parangosky replied. "I'm going to put you in a position as a director in my office. Let me tell you what the program is."

And he did, starting with the fate of the Soviet submarine, and running through the chronology of events that led to him sitting there, ready to offer Lloyd one of the most unusual jobs in Agency history. Lloyd sat there, expressionless, as only a man who'd helped launch two experimental planes and the world's first spy satellite could be under the circumstances.

"What do you want me to do?" he asked, when Parangosky finished.

"I want you to explain it publicly."

The "germ" of the plan was already in place, Parangosky explained. Howard Hughes—under the umbrella of the Hughes Tool Company—had agreed to provide the cover. What he needed Lloyd to do was to make the world believe that story, from now until the moment the Soviet submarine was in an American hangar being picked apart. Your job, he said, "is to develop a socially acceptable public explanation."

Azorian's success required two giant and complex operations to succeed perfectly. First, engineers had to build and integrate all the novel components into a machine that could actually reach and retrieve the submarine. And Walt Lloyd had to convince the world that all the parts, and the mission, were just Howard Hughes's latest outlandish lark.

Work had been under way for nearly a year at this point, and Lloyd tried to get up to speed as quickly as he could. He studied the engineering plans, met with key contractors, and went deep diving into the minutiae of ocean mining.

There were already a few Navy men attached to the program office as consultants, and Lloyd sat in on a meeting with the ranking officer, a captain who was going over John Graham's ship design with some of his operational guys, including a few divers.

"Walt, you're just the guy I'm looking for," the captain said.

"What can I do for you?" Lloyd replied.

The captain gestured at a set of drawings on the table, pointing specifically at the ship's cavernous moon pool. He had concerns about its size and possible effect on stability.

"Well now, Captain, that's not for me to decide," Lloyd replied. "Let the engineers decide what the hell the goddamn thing looks like and I'll figure out a way to explain it. I don't give a shit whether it floats or not. I'll explain it."

Lloyd wasn't being flip. He knew that his job, as creator of the Big Lie, had to be subordinate to the job of the engineers, and he wanted them all to know it. There was no way the designers could possibly build a tool as outlandish as the one needed for Azorian—an enormous ship that deploys an enormous claw at the end of an enormous string of pipe to steal a submarine from three miles under the ocean, ten times deeper than any previous salvage operation in history—if they had to stop and ask themselves how to explain this thing to the public. He also knew that the Navy captain wasn't enthusiastic about the operation in the first place, and wasn't going to make it easy on the engineers.

Besides, Lloyd said, the explanations were obvious. The mining machine was huge and novel and the ship was configured in a specific way to accommodate it. Any specific questions were deflected by one simple answer: Because that's the way it needs be done.

As Curtis Crooke would explain, years later in a deposition, offshore mining was the perfect cover. "Because there was no expert on what an offshore mining rig looks like, I daresay I can take anybody and convince them either way, because there's no background. Nothing's been established."

Lloyd was given a staff of four and for weeks they met, day after day, to look at every piece of the mission's equipment and timeline and figure out how to explain it publicly.

He liked to imagine himself watching the operation from above, observing it from a distance in an effort to anticipate and work around potential flaws in the cover. But he knew he couldn't possibly see everything, especially not from the inside. The Agency had long drawn from a loose network of academics and experts who could be consulted when necessary, unofficially. Lloyd went to see one of them, a professor of ocean science at a university he has never named. When Lloyd arrived, the man seemed relieved. He'd been worried, he said, when a mysterious man showed up and was clearly checking up on him. "You're the son of a bitch who started that," he said.

Lloyd apologized for the security precautions. "I don't want you to be involved," he said. "I just want you to watch us from a distance. If we're goofing somewhere, tell me."

A fundamental tenet, from the outset, was that Paul Reeve should be the public face of the project. The tall, polite, soft-spoken Texan had been hand-selected from the Hughes organization to be the ostensible head of Hughes's ocean-mining project, and once the project was publicly announced, Lloyd wanted Reeve to be the only person who addressed the media or represented the operation whenever public appearances were required—especially at industry conferences and confabs. Reeve was a mining engineer already, and though he wasn't an expert in manganese at the outset, he quickly became one.

Lloyd assigned a single man from his group to Reeve—known to history only as Tom—to be his point of contact should he require research or expertise, and asked everyone else to avoid contact wherever possible. Parangosky, obviously, could speak with him, and so could Global Marine and all the Agency engineers embedded inside the Program Office, but Reeve's job was to go out and look like a man thrilled to his soul to be launching the world's first ocean-mining ship, funded by Howard Hughes.

And then there was Lloyd's logistics man, John. John's job was to plot the cover story, to fit the various lies over the top of the actual things that were happening in the wild, so that every step of the operation made sense in the context of the con. Lloyd understood that the engineering work must not be interrupted. It was not his job to tell the engineers working for Parangosky, or at any of the contractors, what to do. Instead, if something they were doing looked fishy, he was supposed to find a way to cover for it. John became his milestone tracker, the guy assigned to talk to Lloyd's various sources who told him what should be happening when—for instance, this is when you should announce the involvement of a certain subcontractor, or this is a conference you should not miss, in which case Tom would call Paul Reeve and tell him to register.

A big part of Lloyd's job was to worry. And the increasingly loud chatter over what the United Nations was calling the Law of the Sea—in particular, laws related to mining the ocean—worried him a lot. He wanted to get as close as possible to the conversation inside the UN without actually putting someone there. So he identified an analyst inside the Directorate of Intelligence who was already assigned to watching the UN, and went to see him at his office in Langley. This analyst wasn't cleared into Azorian, and there was no reason he should be.

Lloyd explained to him, in the vaguest terms possible, what he wanted to know. The science and technology group, he said, was very active in the ocean, and "that Law of the Sea could kick us in the ass." For the next three years, that analyst was Lloyd's eyes and ears in the UN, without ever knowing why he was actually reporting information.

19
The Big Con

Eva Krutein had just walked in from running errands when the phone began to ring. She was only stopping quickly at home to pick up sheet music for her harpsichord class and had wanted to let the answering machine pick up, only it didn't. One of her two kids must have unplugged the machine or maybe Eva forgot to turn it on, so after eight or nine rings the feisty German émigré stomped over to the phone and snatched the receiver from its cradle.

"This is Jack Reed from Global Marine," a man's voice said. "May I talk to Manfred Krutein?"

Eva apologized and said that her husband was on the other side of the country, at a conference in Washington, DC. Could she take a message?

"Please tell him that the Los Angeles office of Global Marine wants him for a big ocean-mining project," Reed answered. "Do you think he would be interested?"

Eva didn't need to ask. Her husband was employed by General Dynamics, his latest job in a long and circuitous path through the world of naval engineering. A German U-boat engineer during the war in Europe, Krutein fled Germany after the Soviet tanks rolled in, settled in Poland, married, and became a naval architect who founded his own shipyard, which thrived. When the Soviets seized Poland, Krutein sold the shipyard and attempted to emigrate to the United States but was unable to get a visa. In 1951, he went to Chile instead and worked as an engineer at a copper mine until 1959, when the Soviets launched *Sputnik* and the United States was suddenly very

117

receptive to foreign scientists. Krutein flew to New York in May 1960, caught a Greyhound to California, and within a day got a job as a design engineer with Utah Construction and Mining in Palo Alto.

Because of his experience, Krutein took an extreme, almost obsessive, interest in a new field that was just starting to bubble up: ocean mining. He saw in this emerging field a great opportunity for developing new ships and equipment.

General Dynamics saw potential, too. The company hired Krutein in 1966 to move to San Diego and work on submersibles, with an eye on utilizing them to do research for deep-sea mining.

Then, with the president's 1970 UN announcement, the Nixon administration ceased all funding for oceanography. Among the projects this affected was General Dynamics' research into ocean mining, Krutein's passion. He was crushed. Jack Reed's call, then, was an answered prayer.

When Krutein returned to California, he drove up to Los Angeles for a meeting near LAX with Reed, who introduced himself as Global's personnel manager, Curtis Crooke, and John Graham. After some discussion about Krutein's background in ship design and submersible research, the men probed him about the feasibility of ocean mining, and though he was thrilled to discuss this subject, Krutein couldn't help but feel like there was some part of the story they weren't telling him.

Reed left the room and returned with a sheet of paper that referred to an important government project "whose data and actions were the property of Global Marine and had to be kept secret." Krutein scanned the document, took the pen that Reed offered him, and signed it. At which point Curtis Crooke smiled and unspooled the most incredible story Krutein had ever heard. "I was shocked to my bones," he wrote in a journal that he kept secret for years and later published as part of a memoir cowritten with his wife.

He sat there a moment, stunned, and then told the men that what they were proposing would require a massive ship of a kind never before built. Graham, exhaling a cloud of blue smoke, chuckled. That ship was already being designed.

Krutein was told to gather the research he'd been accumulating on ocean mining and present it to the CIA, to assure the Agency that this cover would plausibly allow for the actual operation. Then he was to join the project and help to create a story that would explain the ship, its equipment, and the area in which it would be working.

What Krutein had already learned in his limited exposure to companies pursuing ocean mining was that they disclosed almost no details about their technical plans. And the area where the Soviet sub lay, by some miracle of luck, would support the story, so long as no one else studied it too closely. It wasn't the ideal zone for mining manganese—the nodule quality wasn't great there—but it wasn't an unbelievable story, either.

"Manfred, you've got a hell of a job!" he recalls Crooke telling him. "Everything depends on the efficiency of the cover. If it breaks, we can close shop."

For the last decade of his life, Krutein had been collecting articles, papers, and studies about ocean mining, and shortly after that meeting, he gathered the best of them into a briefcase and flew to Dulles, outside Washington, where he checked into a hotel and, as directed, never let the briefcase out of his sight. (He even slept with it under his comforter.)

The next day, Krutein caught a taxi to a prearranged address and—as he tells it in his very colorful diary—was met by two men in suits who showed him into an elevator that went down from the ground level, at least three stories. There, he was ushered past a security guard and into a small electric vehicle that drove him through a long tunnel to another elevator that took him back up into another building, where he was shown into a room filled with men.

"Well, here he is—our U-boat captain," he recalls the leader of them saying.

"I was only a Third Watch Officer in the Atlantic," Krutein replied. Then, over the next three days, he presented his ocean-mining expertise, answered questions, and helped John Parangosky's team begin to construct the cover operation. "On this trip I entered the Great Game of Intelligence," he wrote. "What an adventure!"

Back in the program office, Krutein attended all design meetings so that no question about the ship or its equipment would stump him. He would also travel with Crooke, Graham, and security personnel whenever they needed to visit a potential customer, serving as "Manager, Ocean Mining

Technology." Mainly, though, his job was to attend conferences as a representative of a mysterious mining operation with major ambitions and an expedited timeline, and say very little. Until instructed, he wasn't even supposed to disclose the name of Global Marine's "customer," who, he was to tell people, preferred to stay silent for now.

Even Krutein's family had no idea what he was doing, and on his frequent travels, he had to cover his tracks with lies. Occasionally this created awkward situations of his own doing, like when he ran into a neighbor after returning from a visit to San Diego. Unprepared for the encounter, he panicked and said he'd been in New York, where the weather had been "beautiful."

"That's strange," the neighbor replied. "I talked to my sister there today and she said it's been pouring for days."

Flustered, Krutein explained that he'd been stuck in his hotel the entire trip and had rarely seen the outdoors.

Krutein decided that he needed help. A legitimate mining effort of this size would have a larger staff of scientific experts, so he asked Global Marine to find him a geologist.

The company already had one: Dave Pasho, who was working on offshore mineral deposits such as tin and phosphorites in GMI's exploration group. Pasho was hired by GMI in the fall of 1969 to bridge the period between completion of Army Reserve basic training and the start of grad school at the University of Southern California in the spring.

In early 1970, Curtis Crooke offered him a full-time job working on seabed mining and assigned him to work under a gregarious German named Manfred. Pasho quit his grad program with a master's in offshore phosphorites and went into the business of seabed exploration.

Krutein told his young geologist to look at ten offshore sites and to analyze marine resources like gold, phosphorites, and manganese in these locations to determine if there was commercial potential in harvesting them. He said that Global Marine was especially interested in manganese, and he wanted Pasho to absorb all of the scientific literature on the subject and learn everything he could about nodules—especially where they were found in greatest concentrations, and what the company would need to know in order to potentially mine them.

Every time Pasho reported back to Krutein, however, he was met with peculiar questions. His boss was insistent that he focus on the viability of the North Pacific as a mining site.

Yes, there are manganese nodules there, Pasho would tell him, but they were particularly deep, much more so than in other locations he'd been studying, and of a lower quality than deposits in other areas. What's more, that area of the Pacific Ocean was notoriously difficult to operate in, known for bad weather and violent seas. But it was the sampling device designed for a ship the engineers were working on that really didn't make sense to Pasho. The ship was the *Glomar II* and it was supposedly being prepared for a prototype mining trip out in the Pacific. Pasho had seen the sketches and models of the so-called sampling device, and he knew that no sane engineer would sign off on a design like that if the real purpose of the mission was to reap sample nodules from the floor.

He grew more and more suspicious. The concept—essentially a big clamshell to grab things off the seabed—just didn't seem right. Pasho wanted to know and have a better understanding of what he was doing, so he typed out a memo explaining his confusion about the project and delivered it to Krutein's desk.

A day later, Pasho was summoned to the office of Global's VP, John Evans. The moment he walked through the door, he knew he'd stumbled into something. Three men in suits, one wearing sunglasses, stood around the office, looking almost stuffed. Evans handed Pasho a piece of paper.

"Maybe you want to take a look at this and sign it," he said.

Pasho signed Walt Lloyd's secrecy form, embossed with a bald eagle, and got the story. The next day, fully cleared, he moved out of Global Marine's downtown headquarters and into a new location known as "the program office."

20
The Program Office

The hub of Azorian's operations became the West Coast program office, a two-floor complex just five minutes by car from the Tishman Building, where Curtis Crooke and his small team had done the initial assessment studies with MRI. The choice of location was fairly simple: Howard Hughes had a building abutting the airport to house some of his smaller operations, with only a few outside tenants, one of which was the US government. The building, at the corner of West Century Boulevard and Sepulveda, was a local landmark. People who flew into LAX knew it for the large HUGHES logo up near the roof that was lit up in blue after dark.

Visitors who came to the program office via its ostensibly public but rarely visited cover headquarters took the elevator to the fifth floor, walked down a long hall, turned right, and stopped at the door marked with a brass plaque that read SUMMA CORPORATION—GLOBAL MARINE (Summa Corporation being the new name of the various Hughes businesses that remained after Hughes Tool was sold off earlier in 1970). Through the door was a large office with low-pile industrial carpet, a drop ceiling, and pegboard walls.

Visitors encountered a cheerful secretary and walls festooned with engineering drawings and schematics for the exciting new industry that was being created across the lobby, in the offices beyond a single closed door. In reality, that door led to a secured warren of spaces where Global employees, representatives from each of the subcontractors, Agency personnel, and consultants all worked together designing a system to steal a Soviet submarine without anyone on earth knowing that they'd done it.

All of those people who worked in the open arrived and departed by this fifth-floor entry, and did so with no pretense of cautiousness. They were supposed to be showing up at their jobs—building the world's first deep-sea-mining company.

Government agents, however, were to avoid the fifth floor. They came and went according to schedules that seemed erratic but were actually highly planned, and went instead to the sixth floor, where a single door marked DEFENSE CONTRACT AUDIT AGENCY, or DCAA, led into a typical government office, sparsely decorated and filled with dated furniture and disinterested bureaucrats.

The DCAA was a legitimate office that did indeed audit defense contracts, making it a useful cover for federal employees who happened to be CIA officers, but the operations were mostly remote. The bulk of the work here required no interaction with the public.

Like the Deep Ocean Mining Project (DOMP) office downstairs, the DCAA also had a lobby leading to a second entry, which held more bureaucrats and also a second, less-visible area. The most secure section was a small communications vault, which connected the program office to Parangosky's base back east in Washington, and to the various cleared contractor offices, via secure telex, secure cable (an electronic transmission with NSA-enabled encryption), and the so-called bubble phone, nicknamed the Donald Duck phone because even the most dignified voice sounded like a cartoon duck when run through the scrambler. "It was hard just trying to tell yes from no," as Curtis Crooke recalled it, only half joking.

Messages between the coasts were encrypted and sent by high-frequency radio link. A radio operator would receive the message, then use a key to decipher it. CIA policy required accountability and a record of all communications, so, using the Jennifer code system, every message began with an indicator of its destination—the program office was "Jot"; the Washington office was "Jungle"—followed by the message itself. It was signed using the sender's designated code name—Mr. Lion for Parangosky, the king of the Jungle, for instance—and then stored away.

The sixth floor contained all of the necessary Agency security—a document safe, cipher locks, guards, and of course a hidden staircase. The link between the two floors was in the rear of the DCAA space, in an area that visitors would rarely, if ever, enter. There, two metal storage cabinets could be slid aside to reveal a secret door that opened to a stairway.

Every morning, the security staff opened this secret door, and they left it open for the duration of the day. And every night, they closed it up, so that the cleaning crew—which was CIA approved but had only limited clearance—was never aware of its presence. Rumor had it they even buffed the floor around the cabinets to remove any signs that they had been moved.

The staircase was nicknamed Harvey, for the six-foot-tall invisible rabbit that costarred in the 1950 Jimmy Stewart movie of the same name, and the secret door that led to it was known as Harvey Wallbanger, after the popular cocktail that employees ordered late at night at the Oar House in Venice Beach, once it became too difficult to enunciate the bar's specialty, the JC Fudpuckers.

At the end of every workday, all documents, notes, plans, and photographs were locked away in special safes approved for use in the Jennifer security system. Nothing even remotely sensitive was to be left on desks, and the most secret documents were stored in a special vault up on the sixth floor, secured with cipher locks and accessible only by the security staff. If someone needed a document from that vault, it had to be requested and signed out so that there was always a clear chain of custody.

As far as the outside world was concerned, the DOMP was a Summa/Hughes project with a tall Texas gentleman named Paul Reeve in charge. In reality, Curtis Crooke ran the project engineering, and John Parangosky was the man behind the curtain, in an unmarked office building three thousand miles away.

To the majority of the contractors in the program office, Parangosky was a ghost. Virtually no one knew his actual name, and those who ranked high enough to have occasional interactions with the operation's chief knew him only as "John P.," "Mr. P.," or "JP."

Parangosky was fanatical about security and along with his other top lieutenants—Agency lifers—considered himself "sight sensitive," meaning that he assumed his true identity was known by foreign intelligence services and so under no circumstances could he be seen anywhere near the open parts of the DOMP operation—the shipyard where construction would take place, Lockheed's Redwood City base, or the program office.

Every so often, Parangosky would fly to LA for program review meetings, requiring that he be "scrubbed" by the security team en route. Upon landing, he would proceed to one of several designated safe houses in Marina del Rey, pick up new identification, and be given a disguise—typically, new clothes, a wig, and sometimes a set of lifts to alter his height.

Once at the office, sight sensitive visitors would stay in the building, away from the windows, until it was time to leave. There was no going out for lunch; security guys would bring food in, and in the case of some of the longer design reviews, which could stretch over most of a day, attendees might sit in the office's windowless conference room through both lunch and dinner. And when a meeting wrapped, there was no happy hour with the Summa and Global engineers, either. The East Coast staff would head back through Harvey up to the sixth floor, then slip quietly out through the garage, where cars took them directly onto the runway to the plane.

These arrivals and departures were some of the most carefully orchestrated activities of the program. Newbies—for instance, technical specialists who might be coming for a onetime visit—arrived by plane and were taken to a car with flashing blue lights on the tarmac and driven straight across to an unmarked garage on the airport's south side, where a security guard checked them in at an unremarkable entrance and arranged a transfer to the program office.

One tentpole of CIA protocol was that no agency operative should travel on his own name. They all had official cover, often multiple covers, and which one was used at a particular moment depended on the program. When Parangosky worked on the U-2 and the A-12, he traveled under Air Force cover, as a civilian employee. He'd carry Air Force credentials, which included a phone number that appeared to be at the Pentagon but actually rang through to Langley, to a special cover office. There, a dedicated security officer answered the phone and vouched for whoever the caller was asking about. "Oh, yes," he'd say. "Mr. McIninch"—Thomas McIninch being one of Parangosky's cover names—"works here, but he's not in the office at the moment."

Mr. P never relaxed, and in an operation this complicated, with so many people and points of entry, he was always looking for ways to minimize risk. He considered the frequent and predictable travel of his Agency engineers from the East Coast to the West Coast a potential weak spot. A trained foreign intelligence officer who had even slight suspicions about activity from either office might begin studying passenger manifests in search of names that repeated often and flew regular routes and times. These people could then be followed or even approached. Parangosky asked Paul Evans to create a way to cover their tracks.

The solution became a project legend that Dave Sharp later revealed in his memoir about the operation. An Azorian security staffer asked one of the program's contractors to negotiate a series of unusual agreements with a major car rental company and a national hotel chain with locations in all the major project cities—Los Angeles, San Francisco, Seattle, and Philadelphia. Anyone who checked into that car company or hotel chain using the name "Bob James" would be given a car or room without being asked for identification or any further information. This worked well, so long as the men were traveling alone, but also resulted in some Abbott and Costello–style scenarios such as the time, according to Sharp, when five different program officers were traveling together and checked in for cars at a busy airport rental desk at the same time.

The first Bob James got a car without question, and the second one got his with some raised eyebrows, but when the third man in a suit with the same name arrived at the counter, the bemused clerk looked out at the line and asked, "Are there any more Bob Jameses in the line?"

Two men raised their hands.

"How can you all be Bob James?" she asked.

"We're an acrobatic team," one replied. "The Flying James Boys."

Crooke and his staff had to learn similar practices. Anytime Global's boss went east, he flew under a fake name, and even mundane paperwork was done using a system of code.

The largest CIA contingent in the program office was made up of security officers working under Paul Evans. Evans himself rarely came west—he, too, was sight sensitive—so he put a young officer named Steve Clark in charge of the program office security with a cover as office manager. Paul

Ito, a security officer hired in from TRW, was installed as the program's head of human resources, "hired" by Global Marine. And the rest of the security staff was made up of new hires. The most notable of these was Brent Savage, a retired California police detective who favored aviator sunglasses and garishly printed Hawaiian shirts. Savage took the work of maintaining program security extremely seriously, but he also relished his role as an antagonist, annoying workers who had little experience in project cover.

In a few cases, CIA engineers were asked to embed directly in key positions within the office. Parangosky's most important plant at the program office was Norm Nelson, a fifty-three-year-old former Air Force captain with white hair who wore tailored suits and large black-framed Wayfarer glasses. Nelson moved from the aviation industry into the CIA in 1961 and was the man Parangosky handpicked to babysit Kelly Johnson during Oxcart. Parangosky relied greatly on Nelson's ability to converse with contractors and especially military personnel, who often resented the Agency's role in defense projects. At the program office, Nelson was Parangosky's spy—his eyes and ears—and the two had daily debriefs by phone.

Nelson was less popular with the men who worked under him. He was, as one said, "about 200% politician," excellent at ingratiating himself to Parangosky and also to the people who mattered—especially contractors who might one day employ him. Said one: "He was a sneaky, lying, son of a bitch. But he was smooth."

Contractors who'd worked with Parangosky on other programs recognized that he had a very unusual and effective management technique that one former electrical engineer called "management by uncomfortableness." Parangosky was always focused on progress and on the schedule, and he understood that if you give technical people too much time to contemplate a problem, they'll always take it. Those same people are capable of working much more quickly, and often you don't need a perfect solution. You can always iterate. So what he did, according to a former employee, was keep a "cadre of four or five really dumb engineers in his office." It's unlikely that these engineers were actually dumb, but they may well have been less sharp than the ones who worked for the various contractors. On occasions when a problem arose and no immediate solution was suggested, Parangosky would dispatch two of these engineers to "help." And the mere threat of this, according to a former program worker, was remarkably effective. "There was a huge incentive to get it fixed before they got there."

There were very few Navy men officially detailed to Azorian, but certain officers would appear regularly for consultations and meetings, and Brent Savage had a grand old time pointing out how badly they filled in. The CIA was formal, as any federal agency has to be, but it was nothing in comparison to the Navy, which considers order and respect sacrosanct. But in a CIA operation, even the Navy officers have to follow the Agency rules, and no rule was more important than maintaining cover. Savage gleefully scolded Navy officers for their poor civilian outfits and never missed a chance to speak his mind in meetings, either. For years afterward, engineers traded Savage stories, one favorite being the time a captain, working in the office as a civilian, pulled him aside to point out what he considered a lack of respect. "Perhaps you don't know this, son, but I'm a naval officer," the man said, and Savage nodded glumly. "I know that," he replied. "I noticed the Navy ring when you were picking your nose."

The program office was the nerve center for the operation, keeping watch and control over the multiple distinct and extremely complicated engineering projects, each one moving at a frantic pace, and based elsewhere with subcontractors who were trusted but also closely watched. The primary function of the office during the design phase was to monitor each piece of the puzzle—the ship, the barge, the claw, the pipe, the electronics, and the many smaller contributions by contractors scattered around America—and to make sure they all worked and could be assembled together in the end into a working tool—a sub-snatching supership.

Crooke placed Sherman Wetmore in a critical role, as the systems engineer in charge of integration. Wetmore was talented, affable, and a bit of a savant. John Graham could have used him on the ship design, but Crooke wanted him in the program office instead.

Wetmore was a babe, relatively. He joined Global Marine in 1961, straight out of college, and bounced around various departments, learning more about maritime engineering in a few years than he could have in a decade of grad school. While in college, he'd worked as a draftsman for John Graham at his Houston naval architecture firm, and Graham hired him upon graduation.

Wetmore first heard about a secret mining project when Crooke and Graham called him into some early meetings, where they were just figuring out how such a thing might be possible. It was an ocean engineer's dream job—to contribute to the creation of a completely new industry—and he was thrilled to join the project. Once Wetmore was cleared and heard the true story, he was even more excited. He was by that time no longer green at all. The company was in a period of almost unbelievable productivity and innovation, and Wetmore had contributed significantly to *Glomar II, III, IV,* and *V* and *Challenger,* which was christened in 1968.

This was new work for Wetmore. As a systems engineer, he would not be contributing to the design of any particular component of the ship. Instead, he met daily with the embedded reps from every major contractor and made frequent trips to San Diego, Seattle, Philadelphia, and Redwood City (as well as Rochester, New York; Houston; and Detroit) for progress checks at the various facilities where construction was under way. He was easy to work with, he was clever, and he possessed an ability to see solutions where others were missing them. The contractors trusted Wetmore, and so did the CIA.

Even as work began in earnest at locations across America, the feeling in Washington was that Azorian was a long shot at best. When the program was formally approved, the Agency's internal analysis stated that the chance of success was only about 10 percent, but as the engineering work progressed, that number began to steadily tick upward.

21

Back to the Wreck Site

I n September of 1970, the engineering staffs in Los Angeles and Tysons Corner realized that they needed more data before finalizing design of the Lockheed machine that would grab the sub off the ocean floor, which was typically referred to as the "capture vehicle" or just the CV. The engineers wanted a new round of photographs of the wreck, looking in particular at the precise orientation of the sub on the seafloor, and needed more information about the site itself. Specifically, they wanted to know the slope of the land where the sub lay, as well as the composition of the seabed sediment there—how soft or sticky it was—which would impact how much force was required to pull the wreck out of the mud.

The work could be done with almost any drillship capable of lowering equipment to the bottom of the ocean. Curtis Crooke offered up the *Glomar II,* a 268-foot drilling barge that had been working summers in Alaska since 1964, and assigned the mechanical engineer Jim McNary to lead a rapid overhaul that would enable the ship to deploy a robot kitted out with cameras and strobes at the end of a pipe string to move around the site and take newer, better pictures.

McNary worked quickly and very quietly, as was his style, which earned him his office nickname, Silent Jim. He outfitted the ship with dynamic positioning to keep it on station and a heavy-lift system that was a smaller, lighter version of the one that would ultimately go on the Azorian mission ship. Steel pipes would be assembled into a string and hung from the derrick, then lowered 16,500 feet down into the ocean. There, a suite of machinery on the pipe string's end could gather more detailed information.

The ship's most important job was to obtain better photos than the ones *Halibut* provided, but it wasn't as if Graham's engineers could just snatch some parts off the shelf and throw together a contraption to capture the kind of detail required, remotely, at three miles under the sea. There was no such camera. So John Parangosky went out and found a company that could build him one.

Joe Houston was barely awake at his desk inside the Lexington, Massachusetts, headquarters of Itek Corporation when John Wolfe, the company's vice president for special projects, called to invite him to a lunch meeting. Houston was Itek's chief optical engineer for underwater projects, and he had just finished testing a new submarine periscope the day before. He'd arrived home late the previous night, having driven straight from New London, where he'd departed the sub upon return to its base. Houston assumed he'd have some time to ease back into work before moving on to a new project. Wolfe had other ideas.

It wasn't often that Houston was called into the executive offices, and he'd never been summoned to see Wolfe, a burly bear of a man with wide shoulders and a thick mass of hair, whose primary responsibility was overseeing Itek's secret government contracts.

"I've got this problem," Wolfe told the young engineer. "I know you know about periscopes and underwater optics and I have a job for you. We need to find some manganese nodules." Houston had no idea what a manganese nodule was, but he sat attentively as Wolfe laid out the challenge—a US government client had asked him to develop a high-resolution camera system that could take precise, detailed photos in a "very hostile environment."

This hostile environment was the bottom of the ocean nearly 17,000 feet down. And the client needed to obtain photographs accurate to the millimeter so that it could build a model of the machine that would ultimately mine these nodules, which were rich in rare earth minerals.

"You're talking about three miles down," Houston replied. The pressure alone would destroy most cameras, and even if one were put inside a housing sturdy enough that it wouldn't be crushed, there was sure to be distortion in the images. And then there was the issue of lighting. If the goal was truly to obtain metric data three miles under the ocean, well, that couldn't be done based on current technology.

"That's why I called you," Wolfe replied.

Houston was an engineer, and an ambitious one. A favorite saying of his, tossed around among engineers at the top levels of government contracting, was "The difficult we do tomorrow; the impossible might take a little longer." He probed Wolfe for specifics, and the area he described had an oddly familiar shape—it was long and thin, rectangular but oblong, with rounded ends. "I just got off something that size," he said. "You're talking about something the size of a submarine."

Wolfe laughed and deflected the conversation back to the problem he wanted Houston to help him solve. On top of the project's complexity, he said, the clients were in a huge rush, so Houston would need to begin immediately. He'd have six days to prepare a proposal that he would present personally, explaining how he'd pull this off.

Houston wasn't sure how to process it all. He was both excited and overwhelmed to try to solve what was objectively a preposterous problem. As he rose to leave, Wolfe handed over an official document from the client that he needed to sign. The form was embossed with the unmistakable logo of the Central Intelligence Agency and stated that the work he was signing on for was highly classified, and that he wasn't to discuss it with anyone. Ever.

One week later, Houston walked into a dark, windowless conference room on the second floor of Itek's lavish headquarters. There, at the table, were Wolfe; Itek's president, Frank Lindsay, a former OSS officer; and the client's representatives, one of whom was a stocky man in a suit with slick-backed hair who was introduced only as John P.

Standing in front of a whiteboard with a marker in his hand, Houston launched into his presentation, telling the men that the principal challenge of this task was the lighting: He needed to create a system of lights that would fully illuminate an area much larger than the beams, because as light is diminished outward from the center of a beam, objects on the periphery get distorted. Shadows also create distortion. And if this project required absolutely perfect images with zero distortion over an area as large as the one that was described to him, he had to illuminate it all equally, in flat, broad light.

The solution was multiple lights and multiple cameras. It would be expensive, and he'd need to buy the lights from a very specific source.

John P listened carefully and then approved the concept without hesitation. He also said that he needed the final product in six months, so that it could go to sea in the fall.

Houston still wasn't totally sure his concept would work. The slightest failure, even a microfracture, would cause a catastrophic implosion of the equipment. But he had the full financial and engineering support of the CIA. Mr. P assigned his chief scientist, Alex Holzer, and a second engineer, Floyd Alvarez, to provide Houston with whatever technical or logistical assistance he needed. And Houston was energized by the importance of his task—designing an entirely new optical system that would help open up a new frontier of natural resources, to the benefit of his country and the planet.

Once a month, John P, Holzer, and Alvarez would arrive for review meetings with Houston and his bosses, and whenever someone questioned the engineer's judgment, Parangosky found a way to reassure him. He recognized that the young man's approach was ultraconservative, but utterly necessary to finish the job.

Unlike his corporate work, Houston had no strict oversight on this project, and he didn't have to keep detailed records—in fact, he was told not to. Similarly, when he needed a part, it just appeared, with no discussion of cost or process. When it came time to order the lamps, from a source in California, Houston wrote out a simple one-page request to purchase with the caveat that he needed the lamps as soon as possible. Someone, he wasn't sure who, picked them up and caught a plane to Boston. They were in his office by the next day, with no sign of a bill.

Houston needed a way to test his concept. Behind his home in Sudbury, Massachusetts, was a small, shallow cranberry bog with a large tree limb arching over its center. He waded out to the center and placed seven two-by-two-foot square white panels mounted at forty-five degrees on stakes and pushed the stakes into the muddy bottom. The panels were set one foot apart, facing an extremely bright strobe-light source placed underwater at the edge of the bog. Houston then climbed the tree with his thirty-five-millimeter Pentax camera and, while sprawling precariously on the large limb, asked his fifteen-year-old son, Brant, to press a trigger to flash the strobe-light source. Using several different time exposures, he obtained plenty of sample images.

A few days later, the CIA team returned to the dark room on the second floor and Houston laid the images out in front of John P, who picked up a magnifying glass and studied them intently. "Very nice," he said. "But where did all these catfish come from?"

Thereafter, it became known as the catfish solution.

Once he handed his design off, Houston heard nothing more about it or how it was used. But he and Holzer stayed in contact and the CIA scientist encouraged him to write a technical paper on his innovative new optical system for deep-sea mining that he could present at the Marine Technology Society meeting held in Washington, DC. In March 1971, he met Holzer in Honolulu, where the two attended a seminar on underwater photo-optical applications. They hiked Diamond Head, ate out like old friends, toured the exhibits, and attended technical sessions on the development of underwater equipment and new techniques in underwater imaging. Houston had no idea at the time that he had designed a critical piece of the Azorian salvage project, and bolstered the cover story in the process.

22

A Minor Complication

I n October, Manfred Krutein was sent to Hawaii to begin preparations for a mission aboard the *Glomar II,* a drillship that, as far as anyone knew, would be doing tests of some prototype-scale mining equipment as part of a new but mysterious commercial mining project.

The *Glomar II* was already en route from Long Beach, and Krutein was instructed to rent an apartment in downtown Honolulu close to the office of RCA Communications, where telegrams from the ship would be sent. He was to wear a beeper at all times when away from the apartment, so that RCA could notify him of a message's arrival, and was to never leave that beeper's range. If the telegram was addressed to "Manfred Krutein, ocean mining engineer," it was a fully open message and required no decoding. But if it was addressed to "M. Krutein, ocean mining engineer," the telegram contained a hidden message and required decoding. In either case, Krutein was to call his local Agency contact, a mathematician from Parangosky's team named Bob Schied—whom Krutein knew only as "Jim"—and suggest the two meet for a beer or to play cards, always at a new location.

Krutein loved the cloak-and-dagger work especially, but when he'd told his wife about the assignment, Eva made a very reasonable demand: She and the two kids wanted to join him for this short-term assignment in paradise. The Agency was less enthusiastic about the idea. Ultimately, Parangosky decided that having a family around made Krutein even less suspicious, and as long as he could agree to certain very specific constraints, it was fine for him to take them along. The ground rules: The family could never meet any CIA representatives, they could never answer the telephone, and if it was deemed necessary to hold a meeting at the apartment, he'd have to get them all out, no matter what time of day or night.

A week after his arrival, Krutein picked the family up at Honolulu Airport in a rented Toyota sedan and drove them back to their penthouse one-bedroom, two blocks from Waikiki Beach. He showed them around the nice but sparsely decorated apartment, which had a heavy-duty file cabinet with padlocks on every drawer, and explained that "the customer" paying for the mining project was very odd, and demanding. Krutein said that he would be on call twenty-four hours a day, could never travel outside the range of his beeper, and might have to clear the apartment on short notice. In addition, neither Eva nor the kids could answer the telephone. "Our customer does not want to be identified at this point," he said.

Hawaii was beautiful, so Eva and the kids were happy to spend their days exploring the island instead of sitting around the spartan environs of the apartment. Often, "Jim," a security man with a dour expression and oversize ears, would arrive for meetings, held in the kitchen, next to the humming refrigerator. Krutein knew to prep for his arrival by closing windows, pulling shades, and turning up the radio to create background noise.

In late October, the *Glomar II* made a public stop in Honolulu to resupply before heading to the Pacific to pretend to take mining samples at various locations, including the wreck site. The night before it left, the ship's captain hosted a dinner for the crew and invited Krutein to Pier 8, where the harbor was abuzz with activity because of Aloha Week, the annual celebration of Hawaiian heritage. The tops of palm trees were spotlit for the occasion, and locals carried colorful Japanese lanterns, but the sight that got the most attention was the inky black *Glomar II.* Its hulking silhouette, especially the derrick that jutted up from the center of the hull, stood out among the harbor's fleet of fishing boats, freighters, and catamarans.

Once the *Glomar II* had arrived in port, Jim told Krutein to prepare for a meeting of the ship's mission team—the *Glomar II*'s captain, plus key scientists, technicians, and Agency personnel, including Dr. Jack Stephenson, the chemist better known as Redjack, who would be leading the mission. The next day, eleven men arrived at sporadic intervals, either alone or in pairs, and took seats around his living room, half of them on the floor.

Jim handed out an agenda, typed on sheets of white paper, and ran through the mission plan. Since the ship's crew would include only a few Agency men, and minimal security, he wanted to be clear about threats and contingencies. The Soviets had thousands of spies embedded in American society, Jim warned. Certainly, they were here in Honolulu, too. Every man needed to watch his own back and to follow the security protocols precisely.

Jim said that Soviets might send a ship to lurk and spy on the *Glomar II* and could even use false pretenses to come on board. "They know all kinds of tricks," he said. "They could try to ask for medical help for a sick crew member as they have done on two previous occasions in order to come aboard American ships." He recalled a time when a Soviet ship tried to entangle a rope around a ship's propellers to keep it in place.

Jim explained that Krutein was to serve three key roles during the Hawaii operation. He was first and foremost the project's ocean-mining expert. His job was to talk openly about the industry, as he'd already been doing at conferences around the world. During the time that the *Glomar II* was at sea, he was also to be the communications link between the ship and the mainland. Because he could travel freely without suspicion, he would receive the messages from RCA and make arrangements to pass them to Jim. And he was to be the local coordinator, a glorified admin assistant who booked hotel rooms, rented cars, arranged for meeting spaces, and ferried around "special guests of the customer" who came to town.

A government man whom Krutein didn't recognize pressed him about his time in Hawaii so far. Had anyone questioned him about his reasons for being there? Did he notice the same people in unusual locations? "If you see the same person twice, start getting concerned," Jim said. "If you see him three times, you know you're onto something."

It would take at least a week for the *Glomar II* to reach the target area, eighteen hundred miles north and west of Hawaii, because the ship couldn't just sail a straight line there. It had to appear to be working at various sites, and the crew scheduled three or four potential stops en route where the ship would pause to pretend to deploy its equipment and retrieve nodule samples.

Back in Honolulu, Krutein assumed he'd have a week of quiet, and he was looking forward to a break from the stress of meetings with paranoid spies who had him convinced that he was always a tiny mistake away from foiling the largest covert operation in US history. But the ship hadn't even been out of port a day when Jim called, requesting an urgent meeting. Ten minutes later, he arrived, clearly tense. His brow was sweaty, and he pulled two chairs next to the refrigerator.

Jim had made a huge mistake. He'd forgotten to give Redjack the underwater navigation charts that showed the precise location of the Soviet wreck. Without them, the crew had only geographic coordinates, which were imprecise enough that they could lead to days of fruitless searching for an object they could hone in on immediately using the charts. He'd sent urgent word to the *Glomar II* to stop, and now they needed to figure out a way to get the charts out to the ship as quickly as possible.

Krutein unlocked the heavy cabinet and pulled out a set of nautical charts to check the ship's position. It was just about two hundred miles north of Hawaii. That was close enough to reach in a high-speed Navy vessel, but to do that would blow the *Glomar*'s cover. The other option was to fly over the ship in a plane and drop the package by parachute, but that seemed too risky, considering the rough seas and the very real possibility that the package would miss the ship and fall into the ocean. And poor weather was coming, which ruled out a return to port.

What about a helicopter? Krutein pulled his phone book out of another drawer and found the listings for commercial helicopter services. He started with the first.

"Do you have a pilot who could fly at least two hundred uninterrupted miles in a row and back?" he asked. The answer was an unequivocal no, and he got the same reply from the next few listings, until one operator who couldn't do it thought he knew someone who would.

When Krutein arrived at the office of Eric Hatcher—"a tall, blond, Scandinavian-type man in his thirties," he later wrote—the pilot was already studying the flight plan on a set of large charts that lay butterflied on his desk. Hatcher was retired Navy and said that his chopper—"my good pal Jenny"—had a total range of two hundred miles.

The ship is two hundred miles away, Krutein replied. The helicopter's range was basically half of what they needed.

Hatcher didn't scoff at that number. There was a way, he said. It was risky, but he was fairly certain that he could pull it off, provided the weather was decent. He could fly the helicopter with a single passenger to carry the package, plus an extra fuel drum in the jump seat. Once at the ship, they'd land, refuel, and leave the empty drum behind. "But the ship can't go any farther," he said. "It has to wait for us."

Being a CIA officer, Jim couldn't go. Krutein would have to take the plans. And his anxiety about that prospect wasn't helped by Hatcher's casual warning that if the ship were to move beyond two hundred miles, even a little, they'd run out of gas and have to "get out and swim."

Back in Tysons Corner, Parangosky was furious. He blamed Schied. On an operation this sensitive, that single mistake could ruin everything. He decided that Schied would be fired from the program after finishing up in Hawaii, then transferred back to headquarters for reassignment.

And given no better option, he approved the helicopter mission.

As the guy in charge of the cover story, Walt Lloyd was angry, too. Delivering the plans introduced a number of bad scenarios, any one of which could spoil his elaborate ruse. He'd learned on the U-2 mission that the best way to handle very sensitive information, even in perilous environments, was to be as low-key as possible. He used to send unarmed CIA couriers to pick up the film after U-2 flights and fly it back via commercial jet to the United States for analysis. "I want you to walk through the forest and not disturb any of the leaves," he told the men.

Of course, the situation in Hawaii was entirely different. The urgent hire of an uncleared private pilot to deliver top secret plans via helicopter across the Pacific was the exact opposite of "disturbing no leaves." It was pouring kerosene on the leaves and setting them on fire. But what choice did any of them have? The flight would go forward, and Parangosky, Lloyd, and the entire Azorian leadership would sit back east, sweating every moment.

The next morning, Krutein left home at five A.M., telling his wife he was flying out to visit the mining ship and would be back sometime after dark. Jim had already arranged with the Navy to ensure that the flight would be tracked by radar and that a rescue team would be standing by off the coast to pick Hatcher and Krutein up if they should happen to run out of fuel and be forced to bail out. He met Krutein in the parking lot outside the apartment and gave him three things to deliver to the *Glomar II*: a hard-case tube with the charts inside, a bag of mail for the ship's crew, and a collapsible red rubber raft painted with a material that reflected radar, making it easy to locate in a search.

The sun had yet to rise when Krutein reached the airport and found Hatcher doing final safety checks. They reviewed the evacuation plan, which wasn't complicated: "Open the door, throw the raft into the water, jump out, and swim for it," Hatcher said. "Don't drown. Avoid sharks. Wait for help."

Space in the two-seat cockpit was tight, as both Hatcher and Krutein had to make room for the metal tank, which stunk of Jet A, the pungent aviation gas. Hatcher lifted off and flew over the seventy-two-mile-wide Kaieie Channel to Kauai, where they touched down in a field for long enough that a grizzled, middle-aged Hawaiian with a limp could top off the fuel. From there, they went northeast, over the towering green cliffs of the Napali Coast, which rise to three thousand feet, and then out over the sea, straight north for two hundred miles—heading, Krutein thought, "for a tiny ship in the immensity of the Pacific Ocean."

For minutes that dragged like hours, they flew a few hundred feet over the slate-colored water, Krutein fighting the urge to fixate on the fuel-gauge needle, which ticked slowly downward.

"Watch out for the ship!" Hatcher yelled. "Look east. I'll look west."

It was unsettling to fly along seeing nothing but water in every direction. Krutein stared ahead, where he knew the ship should be, where he desperately wanted it to appear—and then it did, a small dark spot that grew to "a ship the size of a toy," and then finally to an enormous metal island, populated by men in hard hats who waved emphatically as the chopper circled, dipped, and landed on the giant yellow "H" of the helipad.

The mission leaders greeted the men with champagne, and Krutein handed the mail bag and the tube—once he'd signed the receipt certifying the transfer of secret documents—to the captain, who invited them inside for a lunch of filet mignon, green beans, potatoes, and chocolate ice cream.

After lunch, Hatcher and Krutein climbed back into the chopper. It felt twice as spacious without the stinking metal tank between them, and Krutein, who was physically and emotionally drained by the tension of the experience, fell asleep and didn't wake up until they were just off the coast of Kauai, where thick gray clouds cloaked the coasts, enveloping the three-thousand-foot cliffs. Because he couldn't see the mountains between them and safety, Hatcher would have to fly high enough to clear them, and that extra stress on the chopper was going to push the fuel near exhaustion, again.

Ten extremely hairy minutes later, he pointed to an opening in the cloud cover. "I can see Lihue!" he said. "Ain't we lucky?"

When Krutein returned the raft and the receipt to Jim back at Honolulu Airport, the officer admitted that the whole thing had been terrifying from afar, especially on the return, when the helicopter vanished from radar just off the coast of Kauai.

A week later, Krutein was at lunch with his wife and a Buddhist who had been mentoring her when his beeper went off. He excused himself and went to RCA, where he was handed a cable addressed to "M. Krutein, ocean mining engineer." He called Jim and arranged to meet him at a café, where following prearranged protocol the two pretended to be old friends who'd just happened to run into each other. They sat at a table and, when the waitress brought two oversize menus, used them as shields so that Krutein could pass the cable, folded like a letter, to Jim, who slipped it inside his long sleeve and said he wasn't really hungry after all.

This process repeated itself every few days while the ship was on station, with Krutein stealing off suddenly, often while out or eating with his wife, whose patience was beginning to fray. On November 2, an unusually large group of CIA men—five of the thirty who'd decamped to Hawaii for the *Glomar II*'s operations—gathered at the apartment to discuss a concern of the security team that, while remote, could not be dismissed. According to the latest cable, several Soviet trawlers had shadowed the *Glomar II* as it cruised north, and one in particular had gotten very close and was obviously photographing its activities.

It could well be just industrial espionage, the spies explained. The Soviets weren't just interested in military secrets, and they'd surely have taken an interest in ocean mining, if they had any sense there was money to be made in it. But if they had been tipped off that the mining story was just a cover, and were suspicious of the *Glomar*'s motives, they'd have men on land waiting for it to return with whatever data had been gathered out there.

Jim proposed an elaborate trap. When they arranged to meet for the photographs and data from the *Glomar II,* as scheduled, they could do it in a way that would reveal or possibly even smoke out Soviet spies who might be watching. He instructed Krutein to rent a box truck with two doors in the rear, as well as two station wagons with tinted windows. Krutein would meet the ship in port, receive the boxes to be shipped back to the mainland, and carry them away in the truck. He should leave the port in a convoy with the two wagons, one in front, one in the rear, each filled with armed security officers. In total, twenty-four men would be watching and protecting him and the documents.

Krutein's face went white at that figure. Why would he need twenty-four armed guards?

Jim explained that a KGB team had recently intercepted documents on a box truck back east, by staging an accident in an intersection, crashing into the truck's rear hard enough to force the doors open. When the driver got out to summon help, KGB agents rushed in and stole the boxes as the truck's driver watched helplessly.

If they were after the documents on the *Glomar,* Jim said, they might be lured into trying something similar. "Manfred," he said with some gravity. "That's the moment to find out if we continue or stop the raising of the sub."

Shortly after sunrise on November 17, Krutein drove his Toyota to the pier and parked just behind the truck and wagons, which he'd parked there the day before. He crossed the gangway and boarded the ship, where Jim and twenty-two men sat in the galley drinking coffee.

Jim pointed to four cardboard boxes in the corner. In six minutes, those boxes would be carried out and loaded onto the truck. Krutein should take his time walking out behind them, looking as casual and unconcerned as possible, then get into the truck, and at 10:02, fire up the engine and leave. Five minutes later, at 10:07, he would pull into a restaurant called Koa.

And that's what he did. At 10:07, Krutein turned the truck into the lot, which was completely filled with cars. Just as he arrived, a tiny Opel hatchback pulled out, opening a space. Krutein parked the truck, locked it, and went inside. Like the lot, the place was filled when he entered, with every table taken, and just like in the lot, a table opened precisely when he needed it. Jim and two other officers arrived and joined him, and for thirty minutes the four men talked and laughed as security teams outside watched the truck for any signs that the Soviets were watching. At 10:40, they paid and left.

Krutein was instructed to drive the truck slowly back down Ala Moana Boulevard, while officers standing off with cameras filmed any possible pursuit, then make his way to the Ilikai Hotel. There, as ordered, he parked in a space on the third level of the garage that opened up upon his arrival and got into the elevator. Inside, as promised, he found an officer named Hank with "thick black eyebrows" along with three other CIA officers. Krutein handed over the keys, got off on the tenth floor, and felt a wave of relief.

There had been no interference, no sign of Soviet surveillance. Reassured that the cover was intact, the local security team delivered the boxes to an unmarked jet waiting at the airport to carry the new data back to Washington so that ship construction could begin.

Before Krutein could return to Los Angeles and resume his work promoting the cause of deep-ocean mining, the Agency had one last job for him. Parangosky and Lloyd had decided it was time to reveal "the customer" to the public. On December 7, 1970, Krutein's apartment phone rang early in the morning. On the other end was Jack Reed, the man who'd hired him into the program, whom Eva had called "the harbinger of good news." Global Marine and "the customer"—which in this case meant the Agency—were ready to reveal the name of the Deep Ocean Mining Project's mysterious sponsor.

Krutein was to prepare a party for thirty people at the Ilikai Hotel the next day, in the penthouse, if it wasn't already booked. He should reserve twelve rooms for three nights for top officials from all the publicly participating companies, plus ten rooms for managers from the customer. Those officials were all already en route and would be arriving throughout the day, so he'd also need to arrange for sixteen cars at Hertz, all of them reserved under Global Marine.

Invite the media, Reed said. Make sure the hotel provides an elevated stage, lectern, and microphone. Arrange some catering and drinks—and don't forget the champagne. And tell everyone the party starts promptly at eleven A.M.

The next morning, Manfred greeted Reed, who arrived first with Curtis Crooke, both of them looking surprised at how well the room had been staged in less than twenty-four hours. Crooke patted Krutein on the back. "I wondered, 'How will Manfred manage all this in a short time?'" he said, laughing. "But then I told myself, 'Why do we have a former U-boat captain in Hawaii?' He can do anything."

By eleven A.M., the seats were filled with executives, several reporters, and a number of men in suits whom Krutein didn't recognize. Crooke approached the stage, stepped behind the podium, and said, "Aloha, gentlemen!" He welcomed everyone to Hawaii and apologized for the secrecy of the mining project to that point. "Until now, there's been a reluctance to tell the world who the customer is for this private venture. But now, our customer has decided to lift the curtain and indicate who is behind our secret project. Mr. Holliday, please come up here and lift the veil of secrecy."

Raymond Holliday, a handsome man with a helmet of thick gray hair, replaced Crooke at the podium and thanked him. Then he delivered the lines that quieted the room: "It was a pleasure for me and my colleagues from the Howard Hughes Tool Company in Houston to work with you and all the other directors of the companies. Our boss, Mr. Howard Hughes, has decided to show the world that he personally provided the finances for the unique task of mining manganese nodules from the seabed."

Krutein took the podium as soon as Holliday finished, announced that the buffet was open, and watched as the reporters all scrambled to get quotes from representatives of the major contractors. He smiled and stifled a laugh, realizing in the frantic reaction of this small group that the cover story he helped to perpetrate was even more powerful than he'd anticipated.

Here was Howard Hughes—"a courageous pilot, flying planes at record speeds, who built the *Spruce Goose* out of plywood, put film stars on ice for future films which were never realized, bought all the silver mines of this country to get control over the silver market," he wrote in his memoir—now giving birth to an entirely new industry. The newspapers would soon be full of stories about him, Krutein thought. "The hoax will go on."

23
We Need a Bigger Boat

The *Glomar II* mission had mixed results. It was a success in that Joe Houston's catfish solution did its job precisely as intended, and the ship's rig captured incredibly detailed photos of the wreck site. But it was also a failure, because the sampling device that was supposed to penetrate and grab a chunk of the seafloor snapped off the end of the pipe string when it struck the bottom. That meant there was no soil sample, and the capture vehicle design would have to continue with no clear knowledge of what material the wreck was lying in. It was yet another unknown to toss atop the growing pile.

Nonetheless, the mission had an impact on John Graham's design. The new photos showed that the ship he'd drawn up wasn't big enough for the job. Graham's original design called for a hull 105 feet 8.5 inches wide—a size that was stable enough to support the various bulky systems and that allowed for a sixty-four-foot-wide moon pool, wide enough to fit the recovered submarine and capture vehicle, while still being narrow enough to fit through the Panama Canal, which provides the shortest path to the West Coast.

But the new photo survey revealed that the K-129 was leaning over more than previously thought, so that it would be coming up with the sail tilted sideways, rather than straight up. Because of this, a portion would protrude out, creating a wider profile. A sixty-four-foot-wide moon pool wasn't going to be wide enough.

Fortunately, this was something that John Graham was already coming to terms with, for other reasons that had arisen at almost the same time that the information from the *Glomar II* came back to Parangosky's group. Graham had asked his young architect Chuck Cannon to maintain a vessel weight and center-of-gravity estimate, and to recalculate this estimate every month based on the latest information from Global Marine's engineers and the contractors. What worried Graham the most was how this center of gravity would change when the moon pool was open and flooded, with the pipe string fully deployed and loaded with the capture vehicle and submarine. His concern was that if the ship were to list too far to the side during the recovery, the fully loaded pipe string could come into contact with the edge of the moon pool. And this would be very bad.

One of the ship's cleverest designs was the gimbaled platform, which used bearings and shock absorbers to keep the derrick and pipe steady, even when the ship was rolling in an active seaway. But the ship could roll only so much before its hull would hit the pipe, and the design needed to allow for plenty of leeway. The loaded pipe would be close to its maximum stress limit during the recovery, and if it were to contact the hull, it would almost certainly break, "with disastrous consequences to the ship, crew, and mission," according to Cannon.

Just about the time the CIA team back east was realizing that the moon pool wasn't wide enough, Cannon noticed a problem. Based on his latest numbers, the hull wasn't nearly wide enough to keep the ship stable and safe during pipe-string operations. And Cannon panicked. Being relatively junior, he took the results first to his immediate superior, who said he would take them to Graham and then didn't. After a week of silence, Cannon mustered his courage and took the result to Graham himself. Graham exploded. "Get your calculations together, we are going to Langley in the morning!" he barked.

Global Marine's chief architect knew that his ship was going to have to get wider and that a change of this magnitude so late in the process was unprecedented. The ship's drawings and calculations had already been submitted to the American Bureau of Shipping and the Coast Guard for regulatory approvals, and preliminary construction was under way outside Philadelphia. Steel for the hull plating had been ordered and the 20-foot 11.75-inch-wide wing walls were already being built at the shipyard.

Curtis Crooke ordered a temporary stop on work and he, Graham, and Cannon flew east to tell Parangosky they were going to have to increase the ship's beam by ten feet. That would set construction back, sure, and also create a logistical problem. The redesigned ship was going to be too wide for the Panama Canal; it would have to sail around the southern tip of South America instead.

This would be Cannon's first and only trip to the East Coast program office. The Global group caught a direct flight to Washington Dulles the next day and went first to see an old colleague of Graham's at the David Taylor Model Basin to discuss the problem and get his opinion on the results. A day later, Cannon found himself in a large conference room at a remote CIA site in northern Virginia next to his two bosses and looking out at more than twenty unfamiliar faces. Graham introduced Cannon and explained what he'd found.

No one was less happy than Parangosky to hear that the ship's construction would need to pause while they widened the hull, costing the program time and money, neither of which was abundant or easy to come by, but he recognized that this was necessary—and would simultaneously solve the problem indicated by the new round of photos from the *Glomar II*. Sure, divers could go into the water with torches and cut away the K-129's conning tower's top and periscopes, but a wider moon pool would make that unnecessary. This ship had to get bigger.

24

The Mother of All Barges

The first major Azorian component finished was the submersible dry dock, known as the *Hughes Mining Barge 1,* or the *HMB-1.* Necessity dictated this, because work on Lockheed's capture vehicle couldn't begin until the barge had been moved to Redwood City, fifteen minutes south of San Francisco International Airport, to become the enclosure in which the claw—or the mining machine, as the press and public understood it—could be constructed in secret.

Work on the barge began on May 11, 1971, at National Steel and Shipbuilding Company, in San Diego, the only new-construction shipyard on the West Coast, and one that specialized in building ships for the Navy, meaning it was accustomed to large and complicated jobs.

Lockheed hired Larry Glosten, one of the country's most innovative naval architects, to handle the barge, and gave him fifteen months to deliver it. Glosten served in the Pacific during World War II and later worked in the Navy's Bureau of Ships before opening his own shop in Seattle. Glosten asked Tom Bringloe, a young graduate of the University of Michigan's Department of Naval Architecture and Marine Engineering, to be the primary architect, and by the spring of 1971, he'd finished the project, on schedule and on budget.

Bringloe got his first hint that the barge wasn't really going to be used for mining when a neighbor stopped him to say that a private investigator had come by asking questions about his background and character, ostensibly as part of the evaluation process for a large insurance policy. He hadn't applied for any insurance policy, but he suspected that wasn't the true story, anyway—a hunch confirmed when Glosten summoned him to a meeting where two men in suits explained that his services were required for the national security of the United States and that he should never speak about the work he was about to do, even to family.

Glosten and Bringloe didn't have a lot to go on. Their primary Lockheed contact gave them only the barest of details—the principal dimensions of the barge and its structural requirements, written, literally, on a single sheet of eight-and-a-half-by-eleven-inch copy paper. What Bringloe created was a barge so immense that it could host basketball tournaments or rock concerts. But the *HMB-1* was clever, too. It had to be submersible to a depth at which John Graham's ship could moor over it and extract the claw, using the ocean as a cover so that the transfer could be made covertly. Bringloe put hard and soft tanks on the bow and stern that would be flooded to sink the barge and then pumped dry to bring it back to the surface. This process could be started from a small control room aboard the *HMB-1* and completed remotely from a tug.

Construction of the barge progressed from stern to bow and keel to roof in stages. The work wasn't secret, and there wasn't anything terribly unusual about a giant dry dock, but it wasn't openly promoted, either, and Parangosky wanted it that way. He was very surprised, then, when word arrived on January 3 that President Nixon would be appearing at the shipyard the following day to make an official announcement. Parangosky cringed at the idea of a huge public spectacle, but there wasn't anything he could do about it.

On January 4, Nixon stood at a podium in front of two thousand union men in hard hats and announced a 54.6-million-dollar contract to National Steel to build three new tankers for the US Merchant Marine fleet. The president arrived by helicopter from his mansion in San Clemente and toured the yard, then told the assembled crowd that other maritime nations were outbuilding the United States, putting this proud naval power in "a second class position around the world." It was critical for America to amend this emerging crisis, he said, to return to its rightful place as "number one." To Parangosky's great relief, the speech was widely covered, but the stories made no mention of the barge or the mining operation.

Construction of the *HMB-1* was fast and furious, taking only nine months. On April 14, the hull was launched and moved to the outfitting dock, where the roof was added and the wiring completed. By April 20, the world's largest submersible barge was ready for progressive sea tests. The first was a partial submergence, held off of Coronado Island, in San Diego Bay, and it went smoothly. Anchors were set and the tanks filled. By evening, the *HMB-1* was sitting on the seafloor in fifty-five feet of water. There were no complications, and by morning it had surfaced again.

From there, a tug towed the barge north, to Isthmus Cove, off Catalina Island, where a series of four tests in progressively deeper water would be held until the barge had proven it worked up to 182 feet, the depth required for mating with the ship. On the first dive, conducted April 24, a pocket of air got trapped inside, just under the roof, so that as quickly as the *HMB-1* descended under the water, it popped right back up to the surface. That air slowly escaped through holes in the roof, however, and once it was all gone the barge sank again.

This wasn't a difficult fix. Operators merely blew the ballast tanks prior to the next dive to make the barge negatively buoyant, and the next two dives— to 125 and 165 feet—were uneventful. But on the fourth and final dive, to maximum depth, a valve failed during submersion, causing the surface crew to lose control of the actuators that regulated buoyancy. As a result, the *HMB-1* sat parked on the bottom, helpless, until divers were sent down and into the flooded control room to reopen the valves by hand. Engineers under Tom Bringloe's direction quickly solved this problem, too, and on May 10, a tug pulled the *HMB-1* out of the test site and headed north, up the coast, under the Golden Gate Bridge, and through the bay to Redwood City, where construction of the last and most sensitive piece of submarine salvage equipment could finally begin.

"Somehow I sense with the launching of this vessel, we are witnessing the birth of a new industry," Howard Hughes's Ocean Mining Project chief Paul Reeve told reporters.

25

Oh My Darling, Clementine

I t was fine to build the ship and barge in public. John Parangosky and Walt Lloyd wanted the media to observe the enigmatic processes of Howard Hughes, the one man just crazy enough to mine the ocean. That was the whole con. But there was one component of the system that had to remain secret: the capture vehicle. This was the thing that would actually grab and lift the sub from the ocean floor, and it was the only piece of machinery that couldn't be explained in public.

Lockheed's Ocean Systems Division leased a plot of land along some undeveloped marshy waterfront in Redwood City, fifteen minutes south of San Francisco International Airport, erected two corrugated tin hangars— one large and one small—and encircled the lot in an eight-foot chain-link fence topped with razor wire. Light towers went up at the corners, and a single guard shack was manned twenty-four hours a day just inside the gate.

The smaller building was storage, and the larger one was divided into two sections, one for the machine and welding shop, the other for the small army of engineers who worked in tight rows at drafting boards and desks.

Lockheed's involvement wasn't a secret, nor was the fact that the company was building a mystery machine inside the giant barge that had been docked at Redwood City, and certain activities were staged in service of the cover. Close watch was kept on the schedule of Russia's spy satellites, which passed overhead at the same time every day. Eight-foot steel squares were built as prototype storage containers for the manganese nodules that would be sucked up off the ocean floor and placed outside on the docks at strategic times, so that they'd be seen and photographed by the passing satellites. Then they'd be moved inside, so that the next time the satellites passed over they would see the containers had been relocated, most likely onto the mining barge.

The CIA picked Lockheed because of the long-standing cooperation between the two entities on black programs. Parangosky had worked only on aerospace jobs with Kelly Johnson and the Skunk Works, but he knew the Navy had hired Ocean Systems for several secret deep-sea submersible projects, and he'd called upon Jim Wenzel, the division's head, in the early days of the task force to serve as an additional set of technical eyes when the CIA was considering concepts. Later, when the group had decided on the gruntlift method, Parangosky went back to Wenzel with a project. He wanted a proposal for what a theoretical capture vehicle might look like.

Wenzel had a problem. No one in his group was cleared into Azorian, and Parangosky wasn't willing to grant any more clearances at that early stage. As a result, Wenzel couldn't even use his secretary to type his proposal; he wrote it by hand on a legal pad and carried it himself to Virginia, where the task force liked the concept enough to give Lockheed the job.

The first design submitted by Wenzel, according to CIA electrical engineer Dave Sharp, was "a disaster . . . a concept that embodied the type of structure that one might expect from a high-tech missiles and space company." It was overly complicated, heavy, and "resembled a large birdcage." On top of that, the projected costs were well above what the CIA had budgeted. Fearing lost months, Parangosky called in Kelly Johnson to troubleshoot, and Johnson dispatched his star engineer, Henry Combs, to Ocean Systems.

Combs was "an irascible genius" who led the structures team on the A-12 Oxcart and was the man responsible for making it the world's first titanium airplane. Combs and Johnson, who sat in on the design reviews himself, helped steer Wenzel's ocean guys toward a far simpler design, based on a huge spine—or strongback—made of HY-100 steel. The strongback would be the largest single weldment structure ever made, and it would support the grabber arms of the capture vehicle.

The final concept had giant arms consisting of davits (think forearms) and beams (upper arms) that looked like an enormous set of metal claws.

That's how it got its nickname "the claw," a descriptor so accurate that Parangosky forbade anyone on the program from uttering it. Should anyone see the claw, it would blow the whole cover, because a device of that design was clearly not a miner; it could logically do only one job—pick up a huge object in the ocean.

The CV wasn't symmetrical. It had five davits on one side, which would grab the port side of the sub, and three on the other side, which would handle the starboard side. This was the direction in which the sub was listing, and the direction engineers feared the missiles might slip out during lift, so that side of the CV also had a set of beams that held a steel mesh net that would, everyone hoped, catch any missiles that slipped out.

Considering that they weren't allowed to call it the claw, Lockheed's engineers gave the CV a nickname—Clementine, for the old Western song about the daughter of "a miner, forty-niner." This name didn't have to be secret, and because it referred to mining, it actually worked in service of the cover story. Walt Lloyd wanted people in the Bay Area, and in the industry, to know that there was a secret mining machine under construction behind the razor wire in Redwood City, because no one—no one—was to see Howard Hughes's latest, greatest toy until it was ready to plumb the deeps.

A second Lockheed base, thirty minutes away, worked on electronic systems. Many of these control systems were subcontracted to Honeywell, in Seattle, but Lockheed handled certain components itself, in particular the critical digital data link (DDL), which would provide commands to, and telemetry from, Clementine on the seafloor and the controls up on the ship. The primary engineer for the DDL design was Ray Feldman, a veteran of the Corona satellite program who had seen the mysterious John P at several key design reviews but was never important enough to actually be acknowledged.

Lockheed's small Corona office was hidden in a building leased from Hiller Helicopters, in Menlo Park, and it was basically like a smaller version of the Skunk Works. The sign outside said ADVANCED DEVELOPMENT, HILLER HELICOPTERS, and its true nature was known by very few people.

The Hiller shop was classic Parangosky: small, quiet, and nimble. Rather than create a bureaucracy of secret keeping, Mr. P's security team instructed contractors to use their own methods. In Menlo Park, the engineers were given no official DOD or CIA classification system; they simply went to the local stationery shop and bought a stamp that said SPECIAL HANDLING to mark sensitive materials in a way that wouldn't be obvious to anyone flipping through their files. There were no secure lines, either. Engineers spoke on open phones, using a dictionary of code given to them by Walt Lloyd's Corona security—the word "film," for instance, was never used; it was only "payload"—and Lockheed workers in Sunnyvale weren't even aware that the facility in Menlo Park existed.

Ray Feldman had spent years working on the Corona project in secret. So when Ocean Systems' VP Ott Schick called to offer him work on a new mining project, he was excited to move out of the black world and into commercial operations that he could actually talk about. He went for an interview at Redwood City, saw the barge, and found himself right back at Hiller, this time working on the data link for a project even wilder than Corona.

Clementine needed two redundant electromechanical umbilical cables. Each one was three inches in diameter and had to be capable of sending and receiving data and controls for electrical, acoustic, command, telemetry, and hydraulic systems. It was a fantastically complex system, made up of integrated circuits, because microprocessors didn't yet exist, and once the cables were designed, they had to be moved out to Redwood City and integrated into both the capture vehicle and the controls, which were being built inside a van that would later be slipped into the *Explorer*.

After surveying the country for the best company to make the umbilicals, the program office electrical engineer in charge of underwater electronics selected a small outfit in Sugar Land, Texas, that was a subsidiary of the oil services goliath Schlumberger. The engineer put on his fake beard and some glasses and flew to Houston with another Agency plant from Lockheed. They walked into the office of the company's president looking like two hippie academics and got what one later described as "the Houston howdy." The man had never been so poorly treated by a contractor in his career and reported back to Curtis Crooke, who called the head of

Schlumberger, who called the executive who'd been so rude, to make it clear that those two fellas really needed the cables they'd asked about and he should probably be nice to them. When the two men went back, one recalled, "they did everything but slobber on us."

The same engineer was charged with finding Clementine's cameras, and for those he hired the electronics division of Cohu, in San Diego. These were incredible cameras, developed for use on American helicopters in Vietnam, and sensitive down to 10^{-5} lumens, meaning that they could capture recognizable pictures in even incredibly low light. The military was buying as many of these cameras as possible, so what was available for Azorian were technically "rejects," but actually they worked just fine.

The complexity of Clementine's task was difficult to imagine, even for a company that had consistently pushed the boundaries of aerospace design. The CV had to be remotely controlled from a ship three miles above, by men who needed to have a live, well-lit picture of the target and its surroundings. It had to be strong enough to endure the crushing pressure of that depth—almost eight thousand pounds per square inch—as well as the impact with the seafloor; dexterous enough to navigate forward, backward, and from side to side using a set of eight thrusters mounted to the hull; and delicate enough to grab and hold the object without damaging or dropping it. This was as challenging a task as any Lockheed or CIA engineers had ever faced, even on the A-12.

Later, the CIA would try to capture the enormity by comparison in a review. "Analogies to help grasp the complexity of the task are not completely satisfactory," an engineer wrote. "But imagine standing on the top of the Empire State Building with a 4-by-8-foot grappling device attached to one end of a one-inch-diameter steel rope. The task is to lower the rope and grapple to the street below, snag a compact-sized car full of gold (for weight simulation, not value) and pull the car back up to the top of the building. And the job has to be done without anyone taking note of it. Mission Impossible? One might think so."

The *Glomar II*'s failure to take an accurate survey of the ocean floor in 1970 meant that the engineers had no way to know what kind of muck the sub was resting in. It could be a soupy, porous material or a thicker, gummier mud. Designers would now need to provide enough lifting power so that the CV could deal with any situation. They solved it by giving the CV four massive legs—each one twelve feet in diameter with fifteen-by-sixteen-foot pads, or feet—that would rest on the ocean floor. Once controllers on the ship had positioned the claw around the sub and closed its fingers, cylinders inside each leg would begin to push against the floor. These cylinders were capable of extending up to thirty-five feet using hydraulic pressure provided by 1,240 gallons of seawater pumped down from the surface in the pipe string every minute.

The four legs together were capable of 5.74 million pounds of lifting force, and once the sub was free of the muck, a controller up on the ship would activate a release that pulled pins—again, hydraulically—leaving the legs behind, on the floor, where they would remain in perpetuity, or until they rusted away to fragments and dust.

From that point, it would be up to Clementine.

What Clementine had to do required technical precision of a kind that would be difficult to accomplish on the surface, considering the size of the machines in question, but to do it under the ocean—three miles away from the men who'd be operating the device—would require the most advanced technologies on the planet, including some that would have to be invented for the operation.

The capture vehicle was outfitted with a suite of sensors, including long-range sonar, high-resolution sonar, and altitude/attitude sonar, plus eleven television cameras lit with twenty-two lights to provide the eyes for the men on the controls up on the surface. Really, Clementine needed only the acoustic or the optical system, but because the Azorian team would get only one shot at this mission, every facet of the vehicle's operation had a redundant system to provide a backup if the primary system failed.

To locate and place itself over the wreck, Clementine carried an array of beacon transponders that were to be dropped around the target. Hydrophones on the CV would listen to these beacons, and onboard software used that data to position the CV over the target with an accuracy of one foot.

All of the audio and video data was transmitted back and forth to the ship by the two fully redundant, 18,500-foot electromechanical cables that would run along the pipe. These were two-way cables, providing up-down telemetry, video data, and acoustic sensor data, so that Clementine's operators could receive data from the bottom and then give direction in return. The system could handle at least ninety-six hundred bits of data per second and the electrical network that ran it all was also fail-safe—the failure of any one circuit or component would not foil the mission. Every facet of this system was pushing up against the limits of existing technology.

Assembly of Clementine finished near the end of June 1972, and on the final day of the month, the last dry test of the capture vehicle was completed inside the barge. The engineers who built Clementine would also operate her, not only to conserve time, but also because the men on the controls would truly, intimately understand what they were operating.

26
Across the Airport

U p to this point, John Graham had been overseeing the ship's design from Global Marine's headquarters downtown. Graham believed in keeping his projects lean, and though he had pulled in engineers to handle the detail work on all of the ship's major systems, the design team was still small, not even fifteen men. Even that, he'd often grumble, was too many people.

Graham liked to say that managing people was like growing roses, a hobby that had become a passion since he'd quit drinking. He was a gifted manager who made good (often impulsive) hires and then trusted his engineers to do what was asked of them. Every night, he'd take an armful of plans with him when he got into his convertible to drive home to Newport Beach, and the next morning, without fail, they'd all have been checked and marked up by the time he arrived, always within a few minutes of eight A.M. Mostly what Graham asked for was loyalty and hard work, and he often announced himself by barking, "I only want to see assholes and elbows," as he strode through the engineering sections.

Being inside Global Marine did pose some challenges for Graham in terms of maintaining secrecy, but he had so far succeeded in explaining the rash of closed-door meetings by saying that the "customer" for the mining ship was very concerned about maintaining silence to prevent competition. Still, it wasn't easy.

Once the board voted to split Global Marine Development off into a separate company, Crooke told Graham that his group would be moving

159

from downtown to the Tishman Building, near LAX, and Graham was happy to hear it. He'd have more freedom to operate without stress, in a larger space where he'd have full autonomy, a short drive from the program office.

While the program office had both white and black sections, the new headquarters of Global Marine Development Inc., at 5959 West Century Boulevard, was fully in the open. Here, in a fourteen-story midrise identifiable from great distances thanks to the enormous TISHMAN letters just below the roofline, was the new base of John Graham's engineering group.

Crooke rented a high floor, just about level with the 747s that would lumber past on their descents into LAX, barely a mile west. Graham had filled his team with young engineers like Chuck Cannon, who'd been hired directly out of the University of Michigan, after he read about Global Marine in a magazine and wrote the company a letter.

Cannon thought he was working on the hull of a mining ship, even after the group moved to Tishman, but shortly after the group relocated, Graham's secretary told Cannon that "something's come up" and that he should proceed to a phone booth on Sepulveda at a specific time and wait for instructions. When the phone rang, he followed a series of bizarre and precise steps that led him to the program office, where he sat across from Paul Ito—the security officer who'd been planted at Global Marine as the head of HR—and got the entire story. By the end of the conversation, Cannon had finished several cups of coffee and had seen numerous unbelievably detailed photos of a wrecked Soviet submarine. In subsequent days, and always without warning, Ito would appear at the Tishman office at the end of a workday to make sure no one was leaving plans out on desks overnight.

Any engineer cleared into the program got the same cloak-and-dagger entry into the secrets, but not everyone was granted knowledge of the true story. In some cases—such as those on the small administrative staff—there was simply no need to know. In others, there was some security exception, such as in the case of one of the chief electrical engineers, who was unable (or unwilling) to account for a few years of his life in China after World War

II, at least in a way that satisfied Mr. P. So that engineer never knew the truth, and he wasn't alone.

Steve Kemp, one of Chuck Cannon's closest friends, was hired into GMDI to work on an exciting prototype mining ship and then handed the immense job of calculating weights and centers—which involved looking at every single drawing of the ship, from every angle, and determining the weight of all the steel plates, beams, and pillars, and where that weight was in relation to the ship's geographic center. The calculations took months, and were done by hand, on desktop calculators.

Kemp was never cleared, perhaps because he was unabashedly anti-Nixon, and he saw every drawing of every piece of the ship except for one. Whenever he requested a drawing or details for the "mining machine," Graham made an excuse for why that wasn't possible. Instead, Kemp got weights and measures for the miner, nothing more, and those would have to do.

Arguably the two most complicated and critical components of the ship itself were the heavy-lift and heave-compensation systems. Heavy lift would deploy and hold the enormous weight of the steel pipe string, the capture vehicle, and the submarine—if the pickup was successful. The heave compensators would keep the string from being stretched and stressed as the ship moved up and down in the water; they were, in essence, gigantic shock absorbers. Graham handed those designs to a pair of mechanical engineers named Abe Person and Vance Bolding.

Both systems depended on another key feature—the gimbaled platform. For the heavy-lift concept to work, the pipe would need to remain as still as possible. Were the string to buck and whip like the ship, according to the motion of the ocean, it would snap. That meant that the enormous A-frame derrick that held the pipe string up over the moon pool needed to be self-stabilizing, so that it would sit still no matter how much the ship was rolling around. This required the entire platform to float on giant steel bearings. Graham's engineering deputy, Bill Skipton, gave Silent Jim McNary the job of figuring out how to design and make these bearings, and when McNary sent the specs out to various manufacturers, only one on earth had the ability to produce them—FAG Bearings, of West Germany. Graham found FAG's solution elegant. He wanted to give them the contract, if "the customer" would allow the job to go to a foreign company.

Graham sent McNary off to share the proposal with Mr. P and one of his engineers. Prior to leaving, McNary was given a ticket by Howard Imamura, the security officer who handled travel for the program on the West Coast, and told to follow specific instructions upon arriving in Washington. He was to rent a car and check into an Arlington hotel, where a "customer representative" would be waiting. When McNary entered the room, all of the blinds had been pulled and the TV was turned up nearly to full volume. A security officer followed him inside and then swept the room for bugs. He found none, but when he discovered a hatpin under a couch cushion, the officer pinched it between his fingers, held it up to his face, then smashed it in dramatic fashion.

The CIA approved the concept and FAG got the contract to manufacture a set of ninety-seven-inch-diameter triple-ring bearings that, at thirty-five thousand pounds each, were the heaviest bearings ever manufactured. Each one had a static load rating of 10 million pounds, and the rollers inside were the size of basketballs. McNary used one to prop open his office door.

The *Explorer*'s design was novel in many ways, with some of its features highly concerning to John Graham, who looked at every unique system as one more way to sink his ship. The fact that the moon pool left a vast hole in the middle, with only two narrow sidewalls holding the bow to the stern, was of particular worry. In fact, it gave him nightmares.

This required further study, and Graham had the nation at his fingertips. Carl Duckett had built the DDS&T with the idea that the architects and engineers who were asked to help win the Cold War through innovation should be given any resource possible.

For several months, one of Graham's old MIT classmates, a hydrodynamicist named Jacques Hadler, flew back and forth from the David Taylor Model Basin at the Naval Surface Warfare Center, outside Washington, to meet with specialists who'd been given the sole job of assuring John Graham that the moon pool wouldn't destroy his ship. They were to study what would happen when the moon pool had been flooded and was full of millions of gallons of water sloshing back and forth.

Hadler, then fifty-four, was a specialist in propeller design and had contributed to the design of many of the propellers that served US ships and submarines throughout the Cold War. He needed to establish two things for Graham: the effects of that water sloshing around the pool, and the limits of the ship—the maximum seas in which it could operate.

The model basin was accustomed to testing ship models in what they called "regular waves"—waves of a common length and height. But Hadler knew the ship wouldn't be working just in regular, predictable seas. He was able to increase the intensity and unpredictability of the waves in the model basin to more specifically mimic the conditions of the Pacific in the summer, when the ocean was calmest but when so-called rogue waves were also a threat.

The work was so sensitive that Hadler had to carry his calculations and drawings personally to the West Coast to deliver the results. At the model basin, only technical director Alan Powell knew of his work. And Powell also wanted regular briefings, which required that the CIA build and bug a special room for the sole purpose of holding their meetings. What was most awkward for Hadler was that his own supervisor, the manager between himself and Powell, wasn't cleared, but he knew enough to recognize that there was a reason for this. He never asked questions when one of his top engineers flew off every other week for six months to a mystery destination. Or, upon his return, met their department head in a room he wasn't allowed to enter.

When Hadler's work was completed—when the CIA and John Graham were satisfied that they'd studied the potential for wave damage in the moon pool to the extent that was possible—he was thanked for his service and asked to pack all notes and files, as well as the models he'd made, into boxes that a special moving company would pick up and take to secure storage.

And then he never heard from the program office, or the CIA, again.

About a month after the Tishman office opened, on a rare day in which John Graham and his senior engineers were all in Los Angeles and not flying around to contractors, a "representative" of Summa Corporation stopped by and announced that the company was going to host a media reception that night in the office and that everyone was invited to stay.

Caterers rolled in steam trays and set up a bar. Reporters poured in and chatted freely with Paul Reeve and Manfred Krutein while nibbling at enormous shrimp plucked from sprawling beds of ice. Reeve played host and interrupted the cocktail hum to give a brief speech. He held up a small plastic box with a dull gray lump inside and told the media that this was a manganese nodule picked up on a recent test by the *Glomar II*.

That trip was an important one, Reeve told the crowd. It proved that a miniature mining prototype designed by some of the men in this room could pick up nodules. More important, testing of those nodules, from a location in the central Pacific where they were found to be in great abundance, showed that they contained enough manganese, nickel, and cobalt to justify going forward.

I'm here to tell you, Paul Reeve said, that Howard Hughes is ready to go mining, hopefully by the summer of 1974.

27

Accountability Matters

F rom its earliest stages, Azorian was under fire for its costs. A frequent and easily understood misconception about black programs is that they are free of oversight, and likely if not certain to go wildly off the rails. But even covert programs must justify their costs. The first level of responsibility is internal, with the CIA's own budget office. Program managers go to this finance group to ask for funding and must be able to explain and justify the amounts they're requesting. Within the larger US government, people are cleared as needed in the process of requisitioning funds.

Azorian's security staff didn't just clear contractors. They had to open channels around Washington so that conversations about funding could actually be conducted. A small team was cleared at the General Accounting Office to follow the money, filling a critical oversight role—to make sure that whatever funds went into the project were spent as intended, and that the trail could be retraced if necessary, in case any of it was called into question later.

At the direction of the Agency, Hughes Tool adopted a strategic posture through the contracting process. It said little but hid nothing. On January 15, 1972, the same month the *HMB-1* was completed, Hughes Tool issued a brief press release officially announcing its key partners for the mining project. "The Hughes Tool Company, Oil Tool Division, Houston, Texas, has announced that it is utilizing the Lockheed Missiles & Space Company, Inc., in the development of hardware for its Deep Ocean Mining Operation," the release stated, and then also mentioned that Global Marine was building the "surface ship" and "will operate the mining system for Hughes Tool upon its completion and is coordinating the overall construction activities."

Western Gear, in Washington State, was assigned to build the giant gimbaled platform. Honeywell, in Seattle, was picked to develop a number of the key system components, including the station keeping and sonar, as well as data-processing systems for Clementine. The idea was to put controls for the ship and the capture vehicle all in the same room, on the same console, and it was all based on the very cutting edge of computing power at that time. Specifically, Honeywell would use six computers, each with thirty-two kilobytes of core memory, and a suite of peripherals, including magnetic tapes, alphanumeric CRT displays, card readers, line printers, and plotters. The system's primary responsibilities were station keeping for the ship, operation of the capture vehicle, and data handling. Nothing like the *Explorer*'s station keeping—which communicated with the ship's main propeller and bow and stern thrusters to automatically keep the ship in position over the target—had ever been deployed.

Honeywell's Dick Abbey signed three separate contracts with Lockheed—for acoustic sensors, dynamic positioning, and the control and software systems for Clementine. He put his old college friend Hank Van Calcar, who had black program experience from his work on missiles with TRW, on dynamic position, and when Van Calcar went for his initial meeting with the security staff, he was briefed, but not fully. They described the target only in terms of dimensions, calling it "cylindrical." Van Calcar knew better than to ask questions, but once he did some math, the shape looked more and more strange. So he went to Abbey. "What the heck is it we're going after?" he said. Abbey laughed. "You mean they didn't tell you?"

The five diesel-electric drives would be made by General Electric, an obvious choice, considering the company had been making Global Marine's switchboards, motors, and hydraulics for years, on all of the big ships. The smaller hydraulic drives, for the pipe-handling system, came from Vickers via a dealer in LA named Paul Monroe. These pumps, though, drove Graham nuts. Flex in the system kept tearing the motors apart, and finally Crooke convinced his architect to switch to a different pump, but not before smoothing over a potential complication, when Monroe couldn't understand why this one job was exhausting so much of his supply, causing him to put other clients on a waiting list for pumps. Monroe was annoyed, and to appease a dealer he'd worked with for years, Graham asked Parangosky to clear Monroe. After that, the problem went away. The pumps kept coming.

No single component of the system gave engineers and managers more worry, over a prolonged period, than the pipe string. Mechanically, the string wasn't complex—it was just tapered steel pipe—but the stresses it would be under, the loads it would be asked to carry, made this the most difficult piece of the entire operation. Hughes Tool Company was selected to make the pipe, in part because it would make no narrative sense for an ocean-mining company owned by Howard Hughes to buy its pipe from someone else. But Hughes Tool was also the best source. The Hughes family made its fortune in mining, by manufacturing drill bits, and understood both drill pipes and metallurgy.

The original CIA task force had concluded in 1970 that it was impossible, given current technology and metallurgy, to manufacture a pipe string strong enough to carry a maximum fail-safe load of 17,126,000 pounds, but when Global Marine took over the engineering study, Curtis Crooke's engineers convinced the Agency that, while the job was daunting, it wasn't impossible.

The closest anyone could come to the kind of pipe required to handle that load was the one used for the sixteen-inch gun barrels on World War II battleships, which hadn't been made in decades, meaning that there weren't any sixteen-inch-gun makers still around to help. There was, however, a metallurgist who specialized in gun barrel technology at the Watervliet Arsenal—home of the Army's artillery development. The Agency asked the Army to bring the man to Washington with virtually no advance warning, and without telling him or his superiors why he was so urgently needed at the Pentagon. All he knew was that it was a matter of great importance to national security.

Two of Paul Evans' officers picked the man up at the Pentagon and, following the tradecraft for covert meetings—using unusual routes, with frequent backtracks—they delivered him to a secret location to meet with some of the team's engineers. The metallurgist was exactly who they needed. He helped the team determine the material, manufacturing process, testing, and contractors who might be able to produce the components—without ever learning what the pipe was for.

Three different steel companies combined to pour, forge, and trepan 590 rough-machined forgings, each one thirty feet long and made of a standard alloy of steel and vanadium, which increased the strength, toughness, and ductility. These segments all had a five-inch-diameter bore, but they came in six different body diameters, all of them tapered, and with a unique thread pattern that allowed the pipe to reach maximum torque with just one and a half turns of a special wrench on the ship's rig floor.

The pipe was tested first at one-eighth scale, using a custom-designed, computer-controlled stress-testing machine, and when that showed the string would hold up to the conditions of the actual operation, it was sent to Hughes Tool's facility in Houston for final machining and coating. There, the sections were also color-coded based on size.

This scale testing, though, didn't provide enough assurance to the engineers back in LA. Those who worried about the string's tensile strength weren't comfortable doing the first full-scale proof test in the open ocean, with a stolen Soviet submarine on the end, so Crooke convinced Parangosky that they needed a full-scale test. There was no proof-test machine in existence large enough to do the job, so Mr. P had no choice but to approve the design and manufacture of a custom system capable of subjecting the string to a maximum load of 21,460,000 pounds.

The job of building the largest tensile test machine in history fell to the Battelle Memorial Institute in Columbus, Ohio, and on January 30, 1972, a design engineer "with much trepidation," according to a CIA report, "initiated the first full-load test of the pipe and machine." He was nervous for many reasons, especially because there were no existing standards to set measurements at the required stress levels and the machine had to be designed to (hopefully) absorb the impact of whatever happened if the pipe failed under tension. It was a success. And when the machine was moved to Houston and installed at the Hughes factory, it worked again. Every single one of the 584 pipe sections passed the test. Subsequently, they were combined into doubles and, in October of 1973, loaded onto trains and shipped to the port in Long Beach.

28
We Need More Proof

SPRING 1972

Walt Lloyd's job wasn't just to develop the cover story. Once the edifice had been constructed, he had to protect it, keeping an eye out for potential holes in the story while anticipating problems that could later arise and put the whole program in jeopardy. And a part of that was keeping an eye on his contractors.

He had been through this process three times before. The U-2, Oxcart, and Corona programs all worked because the players conducted their roles in the cover story as if what they were doing was real. The best contractors were the ones who didn't actually know they were playacting, of course, but operational security depended on keeping those who did know in line, every step of the way.

The CIA ran covert operations, but the Agency was subject to governmental oversight and Lloyd took that responsibility very seriously. He kept a very close watch on legal issues, and when concerns were raised about potential tax complications resulting from confusion over the ship's true ownership—it was, ultimately, a CIA ship, even though everyone needed to believe Howard Hughes owned it—Lloyd set out to head those problems off at the pass.

The man in charge of Hughes's legal affairs was Chester Davis, a sturdy, intimidating man who protected his boss's interests with fervor. Davis, according to Hughes's longtime PR man, was "an action figure, a volcano bubbling under the surface, a legal mind with a Machiavellian bent.... Victory was his goal. To him, failure was intolerable."

Davis wasn't just the defender of Howard Hughes's businesses; he was his personal counsel and a director of Summa Corporation, the company that held all of the mogul's remaining corporate assets after he sold off the Hughes Tool drill-bit business for 300 million dollars in 1972.

Along with Bill Gay and Raymond Holliday, Davis was essentially running Howard Hughes's affairs. Although Davis kept an office in Washington, he worked primarily out of the lavish Lower Manhattan offices of his firm, Davis & Cox, which he'd opened with the huge fees garnered by his work with Hughes.

That was where Lloyd went to see him, to discuss the matter of the Azorian vessel's ownership.

Like his boss, John Parangosky, Lloyd didn't arrange his appointments in advance. That only gives a person a chance to dodge you, or plan some subterfuge, so as he always did, Lloyd simply showed up in the ornate lobby of Davis & Cox, near Wall Street, and told the receptionist that he needed to see Chester Davis.

He was, like the best security officers, calm, clearheaded, and seemingly unflappable, the kind of person who can keep a straight face no matter the circumstances. Lloyd projected a quiet importance and wasn't a man you brushed off easily. Davis' secretary sensed that right away. She sent Lloyd through to see Davis, who presided over Hughes's interests from a spectacular corner office with floor-to-ceiling windows revealing the entire southern tip of Manhattan, the Statue of Liberty, Ellis Island, and the waterfronts of Bayonne and Jersey City. Davis was an immigrant himself, the son of an Italian mother and Algerian father who'd died when he was young. He arrived in the United States with his mother as a twelve-year-old named Caesar Simon, on a boat that sailed right past Lady Liberty, and he often looked out at the statue and remembered how far he'd come.

"Who are you?" Davis said, as this strange man with an unfamiliar name strode in.

Lloyd explained that he was a representative of the Agency affiliated with a certain mining operation that Davis was obviously familiar with. When

Davis asked for credentials, Lloyd replied that, for security reasons, he carried only cover identification.

"Well, how do I know you're who you say you are, then?" Davis asked.

"Because I'm telling you who I am."

Davis stared at the man a moment. "Okay. Tell me this: Who's the senior partner in your law firm?"

This was a clever question. The answer would be obvious to anyone who actually worked at the CIA, but an impersonator would likely not know the name of the Agency's general counsel.

Lloyd smiled. "It's Larry Houston."

At that, Davis warmed up. He fished a little further, checking Lloyd's knowledge of the Summa Corporation, but he was increasingly certain that the visitor was who he claimed to be. He recommended they go for a walk outside to discuss the ship's ownership, then returned to his office to wrap the meeting up with a glass of sherry, served in crystal rocks glasses.

"One more thing," Davis asked before Lloyd left. "Are you collecting any nodules?"

Lloyd replied that yes, they'd collected some nodules.

"Good," Davis replied. "The only problem I saw in this whole operation is that if you pretended to be doing something, and you didn't do it, it could be considered fraud."

Lloyd lingered a moment. This was a smart man, a pure cover officer. And when he got back to the program office in Virginia, he went straight to Parangosky's office.

"JP," he said, "you have got to show nodules."

"What do you mean?" Parangosky replied.

"Well, I don't know how many nodules you collected, but I want some."

"You can't have them," Parangosky said.

"Goddamn it, JP—this is what I want. I want them in glass cases and I want every one of the men admitted to this program to have one on his desk. I want some of the security guys out there in Redwood City to get one, and go to the bar and show some other guys a nodule in front of the goddamn bartender. And then let the bartender play with it."

And of course Parangosky got it. He knew that Lloyd was right, just as Lloyd knew that Davis was right. You have to do what you say you're doing.

Up to this point, specific positions on the ocean were still identified the way they had been for centuries—by using a sextant. The *Sea Scope* was one of the first vessels ever equipped with satellite navigation, which at that time was the size of a refrigerator and built by Magnavox.

Parangosky's one directive for the mining tests was that they be done quickly. There was little need—or time—to perfect any of the systems, and he told Graham that he needed only to get a fake ship seaworthy, with credible-enough-looking tools on board to make it look legitimate and withstand any scrutiny from other companies that would be watching closely.

The quality or abundance of the nodules in this case was of no importance. The ship merely had to find some samples and suck them up, and that's what the *Sea Scope* would do.

The job of outfitting the old World War II minesweeper was handed to John Parsons, a young engineer who served in Vietnam with the Marines. After Vietnam, Parsons went to Berkeley to study engineering with a focus on ocean mining, and that's where he met and befriended Jack Graham, John's son, then married his daughter, Jennifer, before joining the old man in the engineering department at Global Marine.

Parsons worked various projects under Graham and was in the Philippines when Crooke summoned him home to do the thing he wanted to do more than anything—design an ocean-mining system. He was thrilled to get the chance and then, after arriving at the program office and receiving a brief from Paul Ito, deeply disappointed that it wasn't going to happen.

Crooke promised Parsons there would be some actual mining, at least enough to convince doubters, and assigned him to work under Manfred Krutein and his geologist, Dave Pasho, in a windowless room that was probably better suited for storing brooms.

Parsons had two projects. One was to design what they'd nicknamed the "mini-miner," a prototype mining vehicle that could be loaded onto the ship once it reached California and then taken out and deployed on sea tests, in order to check the various systems while also doing a little pretend mining. Really, it was to be a feature player in an expensive piece of theater.

But after Lloyd's trip to New York, Parsons' focus was shifted to the *Sea*

Scope. He spent a few weeks modifying the ship's enormous fantail to hold a winch with thousands of feet of cable atop an A-frame. Using that winch, they would raise and lower a drag bucket to pick up nodules from the sea-floor off the coast of Mexico.

Dave Pasho had been chief scientist on several cruises for his graduate work, so he was familiar with life on the ocean when he joined the *Sea Scope*'s small crew. But the conditions on this cruise were punishing from the outset. Almost as soon as they departed Long Beach harbor and pointed a course north, the weather turned nasty. Pasho did his best to ignore the misery and even found a way to enjoy the rough water. He and some of the other young crewmen would go up to the top of the bridge, on the deck outside, and wait for the ship to rise and crest a giant wave. Just as the ship reached the lip and was about to drop over the back side of the wave, he would jump as high as he could into the wind and hang there, as the ship plunged over the side, so that by the time his feet touched back down on the deck it would be ten feet lower than it had been when he jumped.

That was the ship's pattern for hours and days—up the slope of a big wave, and then over the cliff and into the gap on the back: *Boom!* The relentless pounding made it hard to sleep or even relax, and Pasho actually began to worry after a while. He sought out James Drahos, the ship's first mate, and asked, with a clearly concerned expression, "Are we okay out here?"

Drahos—whose company nickname was Drainhose—nodded blankly.

Another worry was the Soviets. The crew had been briefed before the trip that while there was no reason to fear any specific actions, the Soviets considered a large rectangle of the Pacific to be a sensitive zone, and there was always a chance that unfamiliar vessels entering that vast area could be harassed. Walt Lloyd and Parangosky had asked the ship's captain to get somewhat close to the target area, at least in the same general vicinity, to establish even more precedent that this Howard Hughes mining operation was known to operate out there.

The *Sea Scope* sailed first to an area off the Mexican coast, to retrieve nodules of high quality, and then headed north, toward the target site, pausing periodically for additional tests that, everyone hoped, the Soviets would be watching. In the North Pacific, it conducted a few additional tests. One attempted to take a soil sample in an area not far from the target site employing a commonly used method of core sampling. An open-ended metal tube on a string was released and allowed to free fall from fifty or so feet above the seafloor in the hopes that it would penetrate the soil and snatch some material, like a straw in Jell-O. It works, however, only if the floor is soft, and in this case the sampler bounced and its nose crumpled.

As the ship sucked in nodules—nearly forty thousand pounds in total, valued at twenty to thirty dollars a ton—Pasho analyzed them in the ship's onboard wet chemistry lab. He had to measure and document the size of every nodule harvested, then use a hacked-together still built out of flasks and glassware from the galley to perform analytical chemistry—and also make moonshine. Every scoop brought in a hodgepodge of sea life, much of it bizarre, and Pasho logged that, too. He made notes about octopi, sea cucumbers, and lots of tunicates that came up along with the nodules, preserving a sample of each species in formaldehyde and then carefully recording the sample, the location of its discovery, and other pertinent data into a record that was taken back to headquarters and then filed away.

Arguably the most important thing the *Sea Scope* did was establish a pattern of activity. It sailed a course that would later be followed by the real mining ship, made a port call in Hawaii, and broadcasted radio chatter with the intention that it would be monitored by competitors and the Soviets.

When the ship returned to California, the nodules were boxed up and sent off to various locations, one of them a company that Walt Lloyd hired to clean, prep, and mount individual black rocks inside of small, clear cases that would be marked with the logo of Summa's Deep Ocean Mining Project for distribution to anyone who might want a souvenir.

29
A Ship Rises in Philadelphia

lobal Marine designed vessels; it didn't build them. To construct Azorian's ship, Crooke and Graham strongly recommended to Parangosky that the Agency select Sun Shipbuilding and Drydock Company
in Chester, Pennsylvania, just south of Philadelphia.

Sun Ship belonged to the Pew family, owners of Sun Oil, better known
as Sunoco. The site had been in operation since the late 1800s, but the Pews,
one of America's wealthiest families, bought it in 1916 and built the yard
into a booming operation that was, by World War II, the world's preeminent
site for the manufacture of oil tankers. Sun Ship also had a reputation for
taking on unusual projects. So when a contract came in to build the world's
first ocean-mining vessel, an enormous modified drillship designed to suck
nodules off of the floor of the Pacific, it didn't strike anyone in the engineering department as all that strange, particularly considering that Howard Hughes was involved.

Only Bob Dunlap, the chairman of Sun Oil, was fully briefed on the true
nature of the project. Even Paul Atkinson, the president, was uncleared
when the job arrived, in part to prevent him from driving up the price,
which he might have done if he knew that the US government was writing
the checks.

Jon Matthews was a rising design engineer in the yard, a cocky twenty-
seven-year-old eager to prove how skilled he was in a department loaded
with experienced shipbuilders. He began the Global Marine project as one
of many engineers, but by the time Azorian's ship was ready to leave Chester,

175

more than a year later, Matthews had become the youngest man ever to run the yard's engineering shop and had nearly 250 men working under him.

Press reports about the ship's owner inevitably questioned the commercial viability of deep-ocean mining, but the only thing that concerned Matthews was how his staff could actually build the extremely complicated ship that arrived in his office as a set of plans drawn up by John Graham.

The actual construction of a large vessel is an interplay between its naval architect and the engineers who have to figure out how to convert those drawings into pieces of steel that are assembled into a ship. But this was John Graham's baby, and although his office was technically back in California, he became a bicoastal commuter for the duration of the ship's construction, spending six of seven days every week in Philadelphia and the seventh in LA, visiting his engineering staff, as well as Nell and the kids.

When he was in Pennsylvania, Graham essentially lived out of the Sun Ship engineering shop, leaving only briefly to sleep a few hours at a Holiday Inn just south of Chester. He began each morning with a meeting of the various section chiefs to discuss what would be done that day, and ended his shift after dark with a debrief that covered progress, problems that had come up, and what could be done the next day.

Over and over, Matthews studied Graham's ideas and challenged the yard's teams to figure out how to bring them to life. Without computers to run the modeling, there was only faith, and pencils. Matthews did his best to design in a way that predicted problems that might occur, but he estimated that as much as 50 percent of what his crew did was guesswork.

More than anything, what challenged Sun Ship's capabilities was the heavy-lift system, which would be the most powerful ever constructed. This was the largest and most complex drillship ever conceived, with the unique ability to store and move twenty thousand feet of threaded gun-barrel steel pipe, built in thirty-foot sections of six tapered diameters ranging from fifteen and a half to twelve and three-quarters inches. These sections were stored in six bays in sixty-foot "doubles" that, when it came time to deploy the string, would all assemble into a robust umbilical for a mining machine that could be lowered and raised from the bottom of the ocean.

To deal with this pipe, the ship had a semiautomatic handling system that would retrieve the doubles from the storage bays and convey them to a vertical position in the derrick for sequential assembly into the pipe string. The system was designed to retrieve and deliver to the derrick one forty-thousand-pound double every ten minutes, using a system of cranes, conveyor belts, and elevators, even in rough seas.

Before they attempted to build the real thing, Sun's engineers constructed a one-tenth-scale model in an empty room next to the engineering office. There, Jon Matthews would have weekly meetings with his production superintendents, who had never built anything so intricate. Each section of pipe put tremendous load on the yard's cranes. When it came time to actually lift items such as the gimbaled platform, derrick, and heavy-lift system components from the docks onto the ship, a custom crane barge was built specifically for the job. It was, naturally, the largest on the East Coast.

The mining ship was a dream job for everyone in the yard. At first, Sun's estimators were wary of taking their price projections for certain parts and systems to Global Marine, expecting to be chased out of the office over what seemed like outrageous costs, but every time, they were told, "That's fine. Whatever it takes." It was, as Matthews liked to say, a pure muscle project. When in doubt, throw talent and money at a problem, and soon enough a solution appears. If the staff couldn't do it, they'd call in a contractor. If he failed, they'd try another one. From the onset, the total cost was going to top 50 million dollars (and could be as high as 100 million dollars), at a time when the average ship built in the yard cost 12 million dollars.

Sun's management was frequently reminded that the customer was a very secretive man who greatly valued privacy and intellectual property, and that whenever possible, the work should be concealed from view. Meetings were held to discuss how to disguise the ship's inner workings from airplane flyovers.

Periodically, new faces would appear—guys in suits, guys in mufti, guys who just looked official—and the Sun crew knew better than to interact or ask any questions. When in doubt, any mysterious person or matter could be explained in two words: Howard Hughes.

The final product was absolutely John Graham's ship—it was the concept he designed, at unprecedented scale—but to bring it to life required constant iteration, and the reengineering of nearly everything on a detailed level in order to actually make it work. In that way, Sun Ship's engineers played as large a role as anyone in Graham's California shop.

Unlike any other ship built in Chester, the Hughes ship was a fluid vessel, designed by necessity on the fly, and this made it impractical for Global Marine and Sun Ship to draw up a single, definitive contract for the job. Instead, the two companies worked according to a very basic agreement that was expanded and amended as needed. Anytime Graham came up with a new idea, necessitating an unexpected piece of work, lawyers for both sides would write up a change order and execute a price. In practice, this was exhausting work, especially for the project's in-house counsel, an ex-Navy man named Dave Toy, who had worked with Global Marine on drilling contracts since the early 1960s. He was based in LA but spent much of 1972 on planes crossing America.

Toy was essentially on call in California, waiting to hear from Graham or the shipyard lawyers, who would call and say, "We've got a problem. Can you come out and help us fix it?" One week, Toy made three separate round trips between Sunday and Friday—each one on a different airline, and at a slightly different time, on orders from the hypercautious security staff—and by the week's end, he was so visibly exhausted that a kind stewardess moved him from his coach seat to first class, gave him the whole row, and told him he didn't even need to sit up to eat. She just put a pillow on his chest, laid the tray on the pillow, and helped Toy eat. By the time the project was finished, he had drawn up 150 different change orders, and similar patterns were also in play at Lockheed, Western Gear, and all the other contractors.

This was how big contracts worked, particularly ones that were on an accelerated pace. As a CIA officer planted in the program office's purchasing department liked to explain it, the way to get audacious projects through Congress was to low-ball the cost and complexity, and then—once work was under way—there was little choice but to approve the budget changes. More pointedly, he said: "We give 'em the tree and fuck 'em on the lights."

Ship construction is controlled chaos under the best of circumstances, but on a project as urgent as the Hughes mining ship, the chaos was magnified, and keeping the ship on schedule while accommodating the inevitable complications was one of the biggest day-to-day challenges for Sun's staff.

Materials run low, parts arrive late, and mistakes in the plans appear, but Sun Ship was running three shifts a day—seven A.M. to four P.M., four P.M. to eleven P.M., and eleven P.M. to seven A.M.—with no time built into the schedule for delays, so when the delivery of a thirty-five-foot generator scheduled to go in on a Tuesday turned out to be delayed for two weeks, Jon Matthews had to re-orchestrate construction so that work could continue while still allowing a way to get the generator installed once it finally arrived.

The first shift did the biggest and most complicated jobs, the second shift focused on detail work, such as production welding and painting, and the third shift served more or less as grunts—doing rough welds and moving materials from storage to the ship so that the skilled laborers would arrive at their stations in the morning with everything they needed already in place. Matthews worked twelve hours a day, six days a week, arriving by seven A.M. and getting home most nights after eight, which gave him only a few hours, plus Sundays, to spend with his wife and three children.

It was a thriving miniature city in the yard, with 250 engineers, twenty purchasers, and more than three thousand men working on physical production. Hourly workers loved the job; there was as much overtime available as any single man could handle. All the while, John Graham stalked the pier with a cigarette dangling from his lips.

The worksite and the ship were epic in scale. Once the derrick and docking legs were installed, the ship towered over the yard, the town, and the surrounding area. You could see the gigantic mining ship from all of Philadelphia's bridges and from most any open point on the city's east side. From up close, it was like working on a skyscraper—it took riggers fifteen minutes of perilous climbing, using ropes and stairways, with only two-foot-by-twelve-foot planks in some places between their boots and the deck two hundred feet below, to reach the top. The perch there was so high that some supervisors refused to climb it, and that made the derrick the ideal spot for young men to hide out and smoke a joint. The view up there, for those who did brave the climb, was glorious; you could see across New Jersey nearly to the sea.

John Parangosky couldn't visit Chester. It was too risky. The senior program officer he sent as his proxy was a retired Navy commander, and his primary job was to keep an eye on Graham and the engineers. Graham, though, hated the oversight—hated any oversight. He began and ended every day with an engineering meeting, and Parangosky wanted to be sure the commander attended every one. Graham, though, took some pleasure in taunting Parangosky's on-site spy. He would vary the time and location of those meetings so that the commander would often arrive late and miss key portions. When he confronted Graham angrily, snarling, "You treat me like a spy!" the architect laughed and replied, "Well, you are, aren't you?"

He wasn't the only spy prowling the yard. The Navy sent three of its own active-duty officers to monitor the *Explorer*'s construction—two captains and another commander. Everything about the construction was supposed to look like a legitimate commercial venture, and the presence of these rigid military men gave the CIA security team fits.

All three showed up the first day in matching civilian disguises—dark blue pants, dark blue shirts, and dark blue duck-billed caps. The officers also couldn't help but act in the formal manner that had been imprinted into their personalities, carrying themselves with unnecessary rigor and following ridiculous rules of propriety. When the CIA's senior security officer on the site witnessed the commander walking in front of the two captains and holding a door open as they walked through, he snapped and pulled the men aside, telling them that, with all due respect, if he saw them do that again he would "deck them."

Officially, the Navy men were in Philadelphia as advisers, but their actual purpose was to monitor construction for skeptics in the hierarchy, to be sure that the CIA was really doing what it claimed to be doing—and to prove what they already suspected: that this audacious plan cooked up by spies was never going to work.

Shortly after the keel was laid, doubts about the *Explorer*'s engineering within the Navy ranks forced a stoppage in construction. Since the funds originated from Navy budgets, the branch had a right to vet the plans again to be sure that money wasn't being wasted. The Navy sent Rear Admiral Nathan "Sonny" Sonenshein, along with a staff, to inspect the operation and make sure the money wasn't going to some CIA boondoggle. Sonenshein was a respected, open-minded officer who'd taken command of the Bureau of Ships in 1970, making him the Navy's top shipbuilder.

Down in Virginia, Parangosky fretted. Fully aware that a bad report from Sonenshein could slow if not cancel the project, Parangosky instructed Crooke and Graham to cooperate with the admiral while sharing as little information as possible. They were to allow him to tour the ship and speak with workers, but all questions were to be answered with the fewest words possible. "Just say, 'Yes, sir; No, sir; or I don't know, sir,'" Parangosky instructed.

For an entire week, construction paused while Sonny toured the ship, attended briefings, and probed Graham and his engineers. Then he returned to the Pentagon and reported to a frustrated command that not only was the ship well designed and on schedule, but that if the Navy were attempting to do the same thing, they'd be at least three years behind. "He went back and told them he thought it was slick," Curtis Crooke later said. Not long after, Sonny resigned his commission and joined Global Marine.

The project's pace was the clearest evidence possible of why the job was given to the CIA and not the Navy. Graham's mining vessel was arguably the most complicated ship ever built, and its keel was laid less than a year after he started sketching the design. And a little more than a year after construction began, the ship was finished.

30

Come One, Come All!

n late October 1972, contractors, yard workers, and select members of the media and their families received flyers from Sun Shipbuilding inviting them to "Family Day, featuring the launching of the Hughes Glomar Explorer, constructed for Global Marine." The event's ceremonial host was Mrs. Zelma Lesch, wife of James Lesch, the Summa Corp. CEO who'd first agreed to link Howard Hughes to Global Marine and the Azorian project. The invitation included a short description of the enormous ship rising in the yard—designated Sun Hull #661—as well as a brief list of specs.

The event was to be held on November 4, from eleven A.M. to one thirty P.M., and would include an open-house tour of the US Navy destroyer USS *Lowry,* anchored nearby; an employee arts and crafts exhibit; and the official launching of John Graham's ship, the *Hughes Glomar Explorer* (*HGE*), at high noon. Refreshments would be provided, as well as "balloons for children."

The launching of a ship is often a misnomer, and that was certainly the case with the *Explorer.* The version of Graham's ship that was slid down the ramp and into the murky Delaware River was only tack welded, meaning it was only barely able to float without sinking. At that point, the ship was just a hull, with the inner bottom, wing walls, main engines, generators, tunnel thrusters, shafts, motors, and a partial amount of bilge and ballast piping.

It had at best 50 percent of the wiring installed, a portion of the fire-main system, and some but not all of the sewage tanks.

Still, it had taken Graham and his team, as well as the full might of the Sun Ship engineering shop, working full bore six days a week since the previous December, just to get to this point. Pressure had been intensifying throughout construction, with "early 1973" set as the delivery target to the client, and every time some change or complication added a day to the schedule, John Parangosky's patience frayed a little more. To help reassure himself, and the nags at the Pentagon, he added a new layer of oversight. On the recommendation of a CIA naval architecture adviser, Parangosky called Larry Glosten, the designer of the *Hughes Mining Barge 1* (which was now hiding Clementine's construction out in Redwood City), in to help.

Every few weeks, Glosten would fly from Seattle to Philadelphia and carry out a system of numerical progress reporting that drove John Graham nuts—but which accurately predicted the completion and cost of every major step along the way, including the launch.

All of the key contractors, as well as the media and several undercover CIA officers, attended the launch, held on one of the few days when work on the *Explorer* actually paused. Paul Reeve spoke first, on behalf of Summa Corporation, standing under a gray sky on a raised dais in front of the ten-story ship, painted black except for the enormous white letters that spelled out HUGHES GLOMAR EXPLORER. Reeve turned over the microphone to Curtis Crooke, who cited the work of John Graham and his engineers, as well as Sun Ship, and then apologized that Howard Hughes himself wasn't in attendance. "He's always in seclusion," Crooke joked. "But who knows? Maybe he's watching us from around the corner."

Finally, it was time to christen the ship, a job that fell to Mrs. Lesch, who ascended a ladder in a wildly patterned overcoat, her stiff arch of skunk-striped hair standing firm in the breeze. In her hand was a bottle of bubbly, for the ritual champagne bath—a ceremonial act that could have gone better. "Mrs. Lesch was a bit late with her swing as the ship had begun to pull away before she splattered the bottle," *The Philadelphia Inquirer* reported. Mrs. Lesch missed twice and looked unsure of what to do until someone rushed up with a third bottle and hurled it at the ship's side, where it exploded with a pop that caused the crowd to erupt.

That night there was a dinner at the Radley Run Country Club, in West Chester, and as a parting gift, everyone in attendance was given a small plastic box that contained a single manganese nodule about the size of a red potato—each one sucked up from the floor of the Pacific in the wire-and-bucket contraption that John Parsons had designed for *Sea Scope*. Some attendees also got a sterling silver medal embossed with the ship's silhouette, commissioned by Global Marine and paid for by the Agency at Walt Lloyd's direction.

31
Surprise, Surprise

urtis Crooke was himself an engineer, and a very good one. But he'd thrived at Global Marine as much for being a popular manager who excelled at selling the innovative products his company was turning out—both to funders of these projects and to the commercial market. As Global grew, so did Crooke's reputation and salary, and as the Azorian program came together, it did not escape him that the company was turning out some truly remarkable technology on the federal government's dime. This was technology that could and probably would revolutionize offshore drilling and would certainly have value after the program was completed. This was something he needed to think more about, but he just didn't have time.

Toward the end of 1972, Crooke called John Hollett, a young naval architect and classmate of Chuck Cannon's who'd worked for Graham on some previous projects but left in 1969 to join a shipyard back east. Crooke had always liked Hollett, who was colorful and a little brash and, unlike so many of the more taciturn engineers, enjoyed wandering the building and talking to whoever might be around. He especially liked visiting Crooke.

Crooke recalled hearing from Chuck Cannon that his old friend Hollett had left ship design to pursue his MBA, and that combination of business and technical expertise, Crooke thought, made him the perfect candidate to come out and help him market the technology from the mining program. "We're working on a project for Howard Hughes," Crooke told Hollett. "We don't have anyone working on what we can do with this stuff we're developing when it's over. So come on out here and head up our new business group."

Hollett moved back to LA and into a cubicle at the Tishman Building, where he was impressed with Crooke's beautiful new office, which had a teak desk, a teak conference table, and sweeping views of both LAX runways. Hollett could tell that the mining operation was all-consuming for Crooke, and the two rarely communicated for the first few months. Hollett had what seemed to be full autonomy, and once he'd devoured all of the engineering and technical specs of the *Hughes Glomar Explorer* and its many impressive and innovative features—dynamic positioning, a gimbaled platform, a semiautomatic pipe-handling system—he began to consider what clients might be able to afford such machinery, and, well, he couldn't think of many.

Very few companies would have a need for a ship this elaborate and specific, at the cost required to operate it, especially when he ruled out Global's competitors in the offshore drilling market, whom Crooke and Graham would never want to share their proprietary technology with. In Hollett's mind, there was only one good answer: Uncle Sam.

Hollett asked the office administrative assistant to book him a trip to Washington, and he made the rounds of all the major agencies and departments that he thought might have interest in this remarkable ship—primarily military groups that worked in deep water, such as the Supervisor of Salvage and the Defense Logistics Agency. The meetings went well; several groups showed interest over the course of his four-day tour, and Hollett flew home on a Friday feeling pretty darn good about himself.

First thing Monday, Crooke called and asked to see Hollett immediately. He sounded angry.

Hollett wandered over to his boss's office suite and found only his secretary. He asked where Crooke was.

He's at the program office, the secretary said.

"What the hell is that?" Hollett answered. He'd never heard of "the program office."

It's in the Hughes Aircraft building, she replied, and gave him directions over to the Summa tower on Sepulveda. Hollett drove over, got into the elevator, and exited on the fifth floor. This place was—different. Much less luxurious than Tishman. It felt almost industrial, and the program office itself had peculiar security—thick double-glass doors and a secretary behind glass who buzzed him in and through a second set of doors into a hall lined with small, spartan offices, each one with minimal decoration, an uncomfortable chair, and a small metal trash can sitting next to a steel-case desk. These looked like workspaces for entry-level clerks, and Hollett nearly fell over when he saw Crooke, the cocky boss he adored, sitting in one of them.

"This is your office?" he asked.

Crooke gestured for Hollett to come in and asked him to close the door. He was not happy. "You fucked this whole thing up by wandering around Washington going to see the Supervisor of Salvage at the Navy," he said. "As soon as you left he called me and said, 'What the hell is this guy doing here trying to sell us our own technology?'" Crooke said, dumbfounded. "You keep stumbling around and you're going to screw this up. I need to show you something."

Crooke led a very confused Hollett down the hall into a conference room that was completely dark except for a set of spotlights pointing straight down at the table. The lights illuminated a large collage of grainy photos that, together, contained the unmistakable outline of a wrecked submarine.

"Goddamnit, this is what we're going after," Crooke said. "Not manganese. The CIA is our customer, not Howard Hughes. Now we need to get you briefed up so you can do your job without ruining everything."

32

Ongoing Resistance

AUGUST 1972

A s far as the contractors were concerned, Azorian was a go, but back in Washington the program's status remained under constant threat. By the summer of 1972, ExCom had a new chairman, Kenneth Rush, who had succeeded David Packard as deputy secretary of defense. An unheralded part of Parangosky's job was to shelter those working on Azorian from the noise and political interference in the capitol, and over July and August of 1972, he, CIA director Richard Helms, and the NURO leaders were regularly called upon to defend and justify their work. Ongoing worries about the program's escalating costs were bolstered on August 4, when Rush handed Helms copies of three separate memos—from Chief of Naval Operations Admiral Elmo Zumwalt, Assistant Secretary of Defense Albert Hall, and Defense Intelligence Agency director Vice Admiral Vincent de Poix—stating that the actual value of the potential intel gain from the K-129 was less than originally argued and that all three had begun to think that the program should not go forward. Admiral Thomas Moorer of the Joint Chiefs of Staff joined the chorus of dissent, telling Kissinger and the powerful 40 Committee—which monitored covert activities for the White House—that he, too, felt that Azorian should probably be canceled.

Rush and Helms went back and forth—the former pointing out reasons not to go forward, with the latter countering, almost always with the same underlying message: The target was just as valuable as it had been the day the whole thing was initiated, when all of the defense and intelligence hierarchy agreed. Helms also warned that to cancel the operation at this juncture, after so much of the work had been completed, would be viewed by contractors as capricious and might jeopardize relationships with these companies like Lockheed and Honeywell, which had already contributed enormously to intelligence gathering and national security. The subtext, essentially, was: Do you really want to infuriate Kelly Johnson?

Rush listened and decided to place the program's fate in the hands of a review committee that would take the fall to study cost data, projected savings if the program were canceled, and technical risks that might still arise if it went forward.

On December 11, the panel reported back and was surprisingly positive about the work that had been done to date. In particular, the panel was in awe of the engineering work, including "developments on the boundary of state-of-the-art"—such as some of the largest forgings ever made and entirely new pipe metallurgy—but raised a warning at the same time. The members were wary of a reliance on such unproven technology, including a heavy-lift system that could not be tested until the actual mission was under way, and were concerned about the costs. The overall budget had grown 66 percent since the first estimates in October 1970 and was likely to continue climbing.

The message was mostly positive but also mixed. Parangosky had no idea what to think.

At last, after six furious months of debate and what seemed to be increasing certainty that Azorian would be killed, Henry Kissinger delivered a memo to the 40 Committee stating that President Nixon "was impressed by the project's creative and innovative approach to a complicated task" and wanted to praise the cooperation among various elements of the intelligence and defense communities in the cause of national security.

In other words: Nixon had given the program a green light.

Nearly four years after the first meetings about the lost Soviet sub—and two months after the keel was laid in Chester—Project Azorian had the president's official support.

33

Graham's Masterpiece

B y the time 1973 rolled around, John Graham's masterpiece had taken shape in Chester. The *Glomar Explorer*'s diesel-electric-powered engines were installed and running, and it was no longer necessary for the ship to be connected to shore power.

Every step of the assembly had been chewed over and preplanned, but it was all more difficult than anyone anticipated, and nearly every one of those steps had some kind of complication. The shipyard had run out of ways to add men and shave time. Ultimately, Parangosky was forced to clear a second Sun Ship vice president, the yard's production manager, to convince workers to stay on the job.

It worked. Over the next two months, the plumbing, wiring, and lift-system control equipment were all installed, and the massive docking legs were lowered into their tilting cradles over the deck. The moon-pool gates were installed on rails below the ship's bottom and their hydraulic drive motors hooked up and tested. Everything was lining up, with just one minor delay. The main radio wasn't working.

The maximum power allowable for a radio transmitter on a commercial ship in 1972 was one thousand kilowatts, but the *Explorer* was going to require far more power to handle the CIA's needs, so engineers had quietly installed a ten-thousand-kilowatt transmitter, purchased from the Collins Radio Company, under the cover of darkness. When it failed, Crooke was forced to call in a Collins engineer to do the service, and when the man saw the unusually powerful transmitter, he looked stunned. "If I didn't know any better, I'd say this is a CIA operation," he joked.

With the end in sight, John Graham set a target date of April 12 for the initial builder's sea trials, which would test the ship's basic systems—to make sure it all actually worked.

T he *Hughes Glomar Explorer* left the Sun shipyard for the first time on exactly the date that John Graham had circled: April 12, 1973. The ship sailed down the Delaware River, under the Delaware Memorial Bridge, and through Delaware Bay into the Atlantic Ocean for the builder's trials. Things went well. The tests were smooth. And an assessment stated that "overall seaworthiness, mobility and response is excellent."

Next, the *Explorer* would have sea trials, conducted in deep water just a few hours' sail from the mouth of the Chesapeake Bay. Late in the construction, Sun's engineering office did some calculations and determined that the giant ship rising on the pier was going to be too tall to actually get to sea. The derrick—almost certainly the largest ever built—was about thirty feet too high to get under the lowest point on the Delaware River, where a high-voltage power line runs across the water. The solution, Jon Matthews determined, was to leave the top section of the derrick unattached. The *Explorer* would depart Chester with that portion lying horizontally on the deck, and then, once the ship was past the wire and under the Delaware Memorial Bridge, it would be picked up by Sun's enormous floating crane and re-attached at sea.

The *Explorer* had an unusually large number of personnel on board for these trials: 203 in total, including 58 from Global Marine, and a small group of CIA representatives working undercover as consulting engineers.

To the contingent from Sun Ship—which included supervisors, engineers, electricians, pipe fitters, and operating crew—the number of men who went out for trials was unnecessary. Typically, you'd send a handful of men, plus a few representatives from the American Bureau of Shipping, which assessed a ship's seaworthiness before issuing the official certification.

Old-timers from the yard who had started out building Liberty ships during World War II—at the yard's peak during the war, Sun launched one ship a day—and who usually jumped at the chance to go on sea trials stayed home in this case. Many were uncomfortable with the *Explorer,* which they called "the Ghost Ship" because when they went into the hull, there was nothing there—just the vast moon pool, and even that had a bottom that opened up. To men who had grown up building large ships, something about the monster of a vessel just didn't seem right.

Once at sea, the crew ran every important system—propulsion, water purification, sewage treatment, air-conditioning, electrical and galley, and heave compensation. They ran the engines at full speed, then threw them into reverse to determine the distance the ship would travel before coming to a "crash stop," ran the fire system, and stress-tested various pumps.

To test the ship's ability to maintain position in open water, the crew laid a series of transponders on the bottom past the thousandth fathom line and then fired up the station-keeping system—three bow thrusters, two stern thrusters, and a twin-screw propulsion system that, together, could hold the ship still within six feet of a fixed point for twenty-four straight hours. That worked, too.

The final test, of the heavy-lift system, would be limited. There was no capture vehicle to attach, and no time to deploy the entire pipe string, but Graham's crew needed to know how well the gimbaled platform actually worked. Could the platform be held still even as the ship bucked and rocked? The captain sought out rough water and, yes, the platform didn't budge. It was so steady, in fact, that Matthews sent some of the engineers who weren't used to being at sea, and who were suffering for it, to sit up there and stare at the horizon to stave off nausea until the ship reached calmer water.

The tests were scheduled to run for seven days but finished a day early. They weren't perfect. They never are. But while normal shipbuilding protocol is to take the discrepancy list from the tests, return to port, and fix any problems, that wasn't an option in this case. The *Explorer* was needed on the West Coast as soon as possible, so at Crooke's order, all fixes would be made during the voyage around South America, toward Long Beach, California.

34

Bon Voyage

O n July 24, only seventeen days behind schedule, the *Hughes Glomar Explorer* left the yard in Chester for the final time. The giant ship repeated its previous voyage down the Delaware, this time as a nearly final version of itself, and once again dropped anchor after passing under the Delaware Memorial Bridge, so that Sun Ship's floating crane could pull up alongside and attach the upper portion of the derrick permanently.

To mark the occasion of the ship's sailing, Sun's PR man John Jordan faxed a press release to the media announcing the departure of the *Hughes Glomar Explorer*, "a 36,000-ton experimental mining ship," noting that "Sun's delivery of the vessel brought to a close a new ship construction program that was heavily engineering oriented." The release ran through the ship's most impressive features and innovations and informed readers that once on the West Coast, "it will be outfitted with mining equipment fabricated by Lockheed . . . and the ship will then engage in a program of experimental deep ocean mining and testing of various mining systems in the Pacific."

The departure kicked off a new round of press, including a bizarre report in *The London Observer* that linked the ship's intended path, down the coast of Latin America, with a rumor that Howard Hughes's secret partner in the mining venture was Nicaraguan president Anastasio Somoza, who was said

193

to be offering the "reclusive multimillionaire" a secret tax-free base for his mining operations.

The first leg of the journey, from Philadelphia to Hamilton, Bermuda, served as the second sea trial, and Curtis Crooke flew in to serve as mission director. Crooke had begun the operation with a buzz cut and vowed not to cut his hair until the ship left the East Coast. By the time the ship was ready, his hair had grown so long that he was constantly having to tuck the bangs behind his ears. One of the last things he did before leaving California was cut it all off again.

For the next week, first in shallow water, and then in deep ocean, the crew performed forty-seven different tests of the *Explorer*'s systems. When the ship was within eighty miles of Bermuda, three essential tests were done: the automatic station-keeping system got its first trial in deep water, six hundred feet of pipe string was deployed through the moon pool, and the gimbal platform was given its first operational test. All three systems performed ably. Nothing indicated significant issues with any of them, and the mood on board was so loose that when the moon pool was flooded for the first time, several crewmen dove into the saltwater pool and swam around, proclaiming the water "delightful."

All in all, the ship impressed Parangosky's engineers. The major systems all seemed to work, and though there were many, many deficiencies to address, there was no indication from anything experienced in the sea trials that the *Explorer* or its critical components were not up to the task of raising the submarine.

Most of the crew hired to sail the *Hughes Glomar Explorer* around South America to the future home in Long Beach, California, was uncleared. These men were hired in the open, to operate and deliver an unfinished mining ship from its place of construction to the port where work would be completed. But they'd gone into the offshore oil and mining business, in many cases, for the adventure and the good pay. They expected to be treated well, and Global Marine didn't disappoint.

As a celebratory gift in honor of the *Glomar Explorer*'s departure from Philadelphia, a major accomplishment on the road to the actual mission, the

CIA allowed Global Marine to charter an airline jet to fly the A crew, which would sail aboard the *Explorer* from LA, where they'd been training, to New York, where they'd refuel and continue to Bermuda, to meet the ship and begin the voyage around South America.

The plane was stocked with steaks and alcohol and flew the rowdy bunch of roughnecks across the country on what one participant later called "a booze-filled orgy." The party got wild and, according to one report, even involved the pilots, who were said to have flown the whole trip with the cockpit door wide open.

By the time the jet landed on the East Coast, the plane was trashed, numerous men had puked, and when a head count was taken before the crew transferred on to Bermuda, one person was missing. It didn't take long to find him. A search of the plane found the man, a twenty-eight-year-old bedroom steward—a BR, in shipping parlance—dead in the bathroom; he'd choked on either a piece of steak or his own vomit or both.

His parents, who knew only that their son had gone off to work on a mining ship built for Howard Hughes, filed suit, and the case—had it gotten into the courts—could have blown the whole cover. But the CIA, using intermediaries, settled. The terms and other details of the case remain a mystery, and almost certainly always will be.

35

On to Long Beach

On August 11, with a new crew of ninety-six men on board, the *Explorer* left Bermuda to begin the 12,700-mile journey to Long Beach with Captain Louis Kingma in command of the marine crew, a CIA operative carrying Global Marine credentials overseeing the mission, and Chuck Cannon serving as the chief naval architect. It was a thrilling assignment for Cannon, made all the more exciting by the return of his old pal Charlie Canby, who'd joined the crew as an ordinary seaman and welder. This was a lowly crew job, but Canby was happy to have it and be back with Global Marine after quitting earlier in the year to work for a competitor. Canby hated that job and begged to come back when the *Explorer* went to sea, in any role the company would give him.

The ship had been rushed out of the yard to meet Parangosky's ambitious deadlines, set by a calendar that was disappearing in front of his eyes, and Crooke and Graham were okay with the decision because they realized they could take advantage of the lengthy trip to make basic repairs and improvements. Graham assigned Cannon to make engineering sketches and help Leon Blurton oversee the work of thirty men with a list of eighty jobs to do, including the installation of numerous small components, improvement of some of the ship's temporary welds, and testing various smaller systems. It was, in a sense, an extended sea trial, and Cannon worked much of the time with a Scotsman from the contractor hired to install and calibrate the ship's anti-roll stabilizing seawater tanks.

The *Explorer* was still operating as a white vessel on this trip and had only a very small Agency contingent, with Brent Savage, the former cop, handling security. Savage could fade into any crowd, especially in the baseball cap he often wore, making him ideal as an embed on a ship that was supposed to be an open ocean miner. Savage wasn't the friendliest guy, and he had little to do on the voyage, a combination that made him something of a nuisance for the crew. He chastised three embedded program officers who weren't blending in well enough with the roughnecks, busted some of the engineers for swimming in the moon pool, which had partly filled with water due to leaks in the sea-gate seals, and confiscated Chuck Cannon's film, after he was caught taking pictures of seabirds.

The trip was expected to take fifty days, at an average speed of ten and a half knots, and would take the *Glomar Explorer* all the way down South America's east coast, and up the other side to California. This was a long and difficult course that included passage through one of the narrowest and most dangerous shipping channels on earth: the Strait of Magellan.

The weather was good—pleasant, warm, and with calm seas—save for a single storm that livened things up for a few days, bringing sixty-knot winds and twenty-foot seas. The crew settled into a routine, working in two shifts. Most men focused on repairs and tests and during downtime enjoyed first-run films and filet mignon from the *HGE*'s well-equipped galley, staffed by three cooks and two bakers.

A grunt crew of mostly college kids—one of whom was Curtis Crooke's eighteen-year-old son, Steve—had been hired to do basic maintenance as well as other menial jobs, like painting and cleaning. But not every job was so simple. The ship had numerous giant, one-thousand-horsepower air compressors, installed in Philadelphia and then lubricated before the voyage with PCBs, which immediately began to curdle the paint on the inside of the compressors. Some of the grunts spent nearly the entire voyage picking off those paint chips with dental picks.

The Agency's security team had debated the risk of including kids who, being in college in the early 1970s, were probably at least occasional pot smokers, and after a series of interviews decided that they were too risky to clear even for the ship's white mission. When Crooke heard that decision, he was furious. He pushed back, urging Parangosky to stop being so conservative. And Mr. P relented, on the condition that Crooke give the kids a stern lecture about marijuana while in Bermuda. So he did. The kids sailed.

The *Explorer* would make just a single stop on the voyage, in Valparaíso, Chile, and what awaited the ship there was increasingly unclear. In the month since the *Explorer* left Chester, Chile had been unraveling. Socialist leader Salvador Allende's regime was wobbling, and public unrest was growing by the day. Allende had ridden a wave of antibusiness, anti–foreign investment populism to power, overcoming covert American efforts to foil his election, and causing great concern within the US military and intelligence communities because the unrest brought Cold War worries over the growth of communism that much closer to home. Nixon ordered a series of economic sanctions against Chile, and various US groups and proxies worked behind the scenes to weaken Allende and encourage his generals to turn on him.

A coup attempt in June 1973 failed, but bad economic policies and a loss of support from both the Chilean supreme court and congress had left Allende on extremely weak ground, so rumors of another coup, this one with the full support of the military and—according to rumor—backed by the CIA, began to swell. Demonstrations and protests broke out and continued throughout the summer, and as the *Glomar Explorer* moved down the South American coast, rumblings of a massive labor strike that would further inflame tensions on the ground caused the Agency to begin making contingency plans.

If the ship was unable to enter the strait, Parangosky was given three options, none of them good: Hold position off the coast until the situation improved; change course and make a far more dangerous passage around Cape Horn; or reverse course entirely, heading east around South Africa's Cape of Good Hope, through the Indian Ocean, and finally across the Pacific—a trip that would add at least a month to the schedule.

Fortunately, Parangosky never had to make that call, as the situation had stabilized enough by the time the *Explorer* reached Possession Bay, on the Atlantic side of the strait, on September 5. Global Marine's representatives in

South America had prearranged for two Chilean pilots to join the ship there and guide it through the 320-mile channel to the Pacific. Provided that all went well, the pilots would disembark in Valparaíso, Chile's largest port, and the only one big enough to accommodate a ship the size of the *Explorer.*

The strait itself wasn't bad. Two pilots are required by Chilean law because a captain who doesn't know the geography would certainly run into trouble, especially in the fog and rain that constantly hang over the channel. But with pilots who'd grown up sailing this tricky nautical passage that divides the Chilean mainland from Tierra del Fuego, the voyage is simple, and for the *Explorer,* those twenty-four hours were quiet and uneventful.

Exiting the strait was much less pleasant. As soon as the *Explorer* sailed out of the mouth, on the afternoon of September 6, the weather worsened and a storm set in. Gale-force winds buffeted the ship and it heaved in seas up to twenty-five feet, forcing the captain to slow the *Explorer*'s progress from ten knots to just over one knot, the maximum speed at which the *Explorer* could safely move in those conditions.

More concerning to Brent Savage and the ship's small security team was that the situation in Chile had deteriorated and was worsening by the hour. On the morning of September 11, General Augusto Pinochet led a military coup that quickly overwhelmed the weakened Allende government. The president remained defiant until the end, making a final radio broadcast from inside the palace at 9:10 A.M., urging his supporters to stand up and resist by yelling, "Long live Chile! Long live the people! Long live the workers!" He then joined his detachment of bodyguards—known as the Group of Personal Friends—in defending the palace against a full-frontal assault by the military, including bombers, helicopters, and tanks, until it was clear the effort was futile. His options exhausted, Allende told his men to surrender and killed himself before he could be arrested.

The *Explorer* entered Valparaíso's outer harbor on the night of September 12, one day after the coup. It was late, and the harbor was quiet, having been seized and then shut down by the Chilean Navy in the early moments of the upheaval. The plan was to stop only long enough to drop off the pilots and receive a resupply of provisions and parts that had been shipped to Chile in advance, but as the ship approached, the situation was very much in question.

A half day's sail down the coast, the *Explorer*'s crew had observed a small cargo ship flying a Cuban flag heading south and then, three hours later, a Chilean submarine in pursuit. As the *Explorer* entered Valparaíso's harbor, a destroyer and a submarine cruised slowly past but left the ship alone. The bridge radioed to shore requesting a pilot to come guide the ship in, and when the *Explorer* dropped anchor, a small Chilean naval launch arrived instead. Two young men in uniform, barely out of their teens, climbed up the *Explorer*'s pilot ladder with machine guns strapped to their backs and asked to meet in private with Captain Kingma, who brought along a CIA rep, in the guise of a Global Marine engineer who was overseeing the mining work on board. After a short discussion, the ship was formally permitted to "take entry" into the port, and the Chileans skittered off on the launch with the two borrowed pilots.

The other reason for stopping in Valparaíso was to rendezvous with a contingent of Global Marine personnel who'd flown to Chile with twenty-eight boxes of supplies and a bag of personal mail on September 7. Once in-country, the men cleared the supplies through customs and waited for six additional technicians from Honeywell and Western Gear who were flying in to join the crew. The whole lot of them had traveled to Valparaíso on September 10 and checked into the Hotel O'Higgins to wait for the *Explorer*'s arrival. They were at the hotel when all hell broke loose.

At six A.M. on September 11, the Americans woke up to chaos outside the hotel. Smoke filled the air and the streets were packed with military personnel, armored cars, and tanks, all mobilized to overwhelm any remnants of Allende's regime. The hotel was surrounded and the phone lines disconnected, so that no guests could communicate with the outside, nor was anyone allowed to leave. For two days, the Americans were trapped inside the O'Higgins, subsisting on snacks, as Tom Williams, Global Marine's personnel representative, negotiated with his local contacts to try to arrange some solution in the middle of a revolution. Somehow, despite a curfew, limited communications, and chaos in the streets, Williams arranged safe passage for the group and its supplies to the *Explorer*. Whether he had any back-channel assistance from the State Department or Langley was never revealed, though a week before the ship arrived in Chile, Parangosky called Crooke and told him not to worry about any news he might hear coming from Santiago. He wasn't more specific than that, other than to say that the ship and its crew would be fine, no matter what happened. The joke among the crew, who'd taken to climbing the rig platform to watch the fighting on plains high above the city, was that someone on board called Howard Hughes, who called down to the Chileans to order them to let the ship go or he'd tell the Peruvians to invade.

However it happened, the problem was resolved, and at three P.M. on September 13, the *Hughes Glomar Explorer* pulled anchor and set a course for Long Beach as revolution raged in the streets of Valparaíso.

36

Paint It Black

The *Hughes Glomar Explorer* arrived in Long Beach at five P.M. on September 30—fifty days, seven hours, and thirty minutes after leaving Bermuda. At an average speed of 10.8 knots, the ship had burned through 20,643 barrels of fuel, at an average of sixty-eight gallons per mile. As directed, the captain pulled alongside Pier E, just north of the gigantic hangar where Howard Hughes's famous wooden plane, the *Spruce Goose,* had been parked for two decades.

The ship's journey from East to West Coast was the operation's pivot point. Up to the arrival in Long Beach, everything (or most everything) had been carried out in the open, as parts of a commercial mining venture. The ship left Philadelphia as an overt (white) mining ship, but it would transition in California into a covert (black) vessel purpose-built to steal a submarine, and that also meant a shift in leadership. Parangosky told the engineering team, led by Curtis Crooke, to stand down and handed the program lead to his operations crew.

A few days before the *Explorer* arrived, a convoy of trucks rolled up to Pier E and workers unloaded modular vans stamped with HUGHES on the side. The vans weren't suspicious themselves; they were the standard-size metal containers you see on cargo ships or freight trains, but no one on the outside could get close to them anyway. The pier was off-limits to the public.

Parangosky's plan called for the ship's conversion to take fifty-one days, an ambitious schedule for sure, but a realistic one provided there were no major complications. It wasn't like the operations crew had been sitting around waiting for the ship to reach California to begin the conversion. The *Explorer* was designed to be modular, with the empty spaces that puzzled the yard workers in Chester, but which made perfect sense once the work began in Long Beach. Within hours of the ship's arrival, a dockside crane was lifting the vans over the *Explorer*'s deck and sliding them into slots, at which point electricians would step in and connect them to the ship's power.

These vans had been prefabricated to a standard size (eight by eight by twenty feet) and delivered to contractors a year before so that they could design, engineer, and install the various components necessary for recovery and exploitation of whatever was found in the sub. Honeywell, Western Gear, and Lockheed had all outfitted vans with electronics and controls for their systems, the vans for handling nuclear material came from Lawrence Livermore National Laboratory, an hour's drive east of Oakland, and the CIA's own engineers built out vans containing all the spooky stuff.

The ship's nerve center would be a set of two control vans installed in an empty compartment on the upper deck of the deckhouse, while vans that had been prepared specifically to deal with recovery of intelligence from the sub were put in a row just forward of the moon pool on the main deck. There was a darkroom for processing photos and film, a van for careful drying of material, a van for ultrasonic cleaning and preservation of items recovered, multiple vans for decontamination of objects, including nuclear materials, a van for the delicate work of handling and preserving manuals and documents, a van for waste handling, a refrigerated van that would serve as a morgue for any bodies or human remains recovered, several vans for wrapping and crating any items of special value that would be shipped to exploitation facilities on the mainland, and a suite of rooms set up by Livermore Lab so that men on the exploitation crew could suit up for work around radioactive materials and then properly dispose of clothing and clean themselves after a shift.

Pier E was secured for the conversion work. A towering chain-link fence topped by snarls of barbed wire had been installed around the pier, and any vehicle or personnel had to pass through a second entry manned by guards who appeared to be hired security but were really Agency employees.

Off the pier, people were curious. The *Explorer*'s arrival had made news, and its association with Howard Hughes, attempting yet another bold, questionably viable venture, was bait for the media and the public. Yachts sailed into the harbor and cruised by the pier, sometimes with the rich and famous on board. Barry Goldwater, head of the Senate Intelligence Committee, had a boat moored nearby. So did Curtis LeMay, the famous Air Force general who ran for vice president as George Wallace's running mate in 1968. It was not uncommon to see John Wayne, chilling in shorts on the deck of his own boat, and the oil workers hollered when Peter Fonda cruised past on a yacht loaded with beautiful women in bikinis and offered the *Explorer* men beer, which they had to politely decline because alcohol was officially banned from the ship.

The crew that made the trip from Bermuda had done its best to patch and repair the ship's many operating systems, but the *Explorer* was also sent to sea with the knowledge that it was a work in progress. And the ship's arrival meant that Wayne Pendleton, who'd been twiddling his thumbs for months in the program office, was suddenly very busy.

Pendleton was an electrical engineer and a veteran of the Oxcart program, where he worked on radar cross sections on the A-12 for EG&G, a defense contractor born at MIT that had been a major contributor to America's nuclear weapons program since the Manhattan Project. Pendleton's boss on the A-12 was Don White, and once Azorian's program office was up and running, Parangosky ordered Crooke to hire White, which he did, putting the CIA veteran on Global Marine's payroll as VP in charge of electronics. White, in turn, immediately called in his old friend Wayne Pendleton to help.

As an engineer with high security clearance and a long history of working with the CIA, Pendleton was the ideal go-between for the mission's most classified components (communications gear, for instance) and the ship's engineers. When the *Explorer* arrived at Pier E, he would walk from job to job, assembling a wish list of parts and repairs, and then report back to the program office for design assistance and money. It was a never-ending process. With so many complex systems, most of them purpose-built from scratch and never tested, something was always failing.

Messages pinged back and forth between Pier E and the program office, by telephone, teletype, or—for the most sensitive communications—via memos hand-delivered by the many staff members who traveled back and forth. Every day, a security officer was assigned to courier a package of documents, including daily reports, to the East Coast on a chartered plane, because Parangosky had begun to worry about the threat of hijacking, which almost overnight had become a popular activity for revolutionaries, roustabouts, and seemingly any young person with a grievance to air in spectacular fashion.

One of the biggest tasks in the *Explorer*'s conversion was wiring the ship up to its many systems and vans. The vessel contained a rat's nest of wires that needed to be located, cataloged, and connected. And Pendleton knew right away that he needed more labor to get it done. Solving that problem wasn't as easy as calling the local union and hiring some electricians. A Navy captain assigned by the Pentagon to observe the progress had recently stirred up trouble by complaining back to Washington that too many civilians were being cleared—each one, he feared, a potential security risk.

If Pendleton was going to add workers, they'd have to be spies. A call went out, and more than twenty Agency "consultants" with high security clearances were pulled from various locations around the country and put on planes to LA, where security officers scooped them up at the airport and took them to nearby hotel suites rented specifically for the purpose of scrubbing personnel. Each man turned over his wallet and was issued false identification and credit cards in a new name, as well as new clothes and, if sight sensitivity was a concern, also a few changes to his appearance—a wig, some hair dye, occasionally a fake mustache.

When the makeover was complete, they were dropped off on the pier and put straight to work. Pendleton tried to be accommodating and to lighten the mood, as these highly educated men—many of them engineers or scientists who were unlucky enough to have had clearance and been available—were handed grueling grunt jobs, connecting wires or adding filters in the ship's bowels, often working for entire days inside of tiny passages filled with stuffy, stifling air.

But that wasn't the end of the indignity. Because they were undercover, the men weren't allowed to leave the site. They had to live on the boat, sleeping in bunks or, when space ran out—because there were other crews at work on other projects at the same time—on the deck.

Pendleton tried to keep a straight face when he found one such man up on deck, cursing and scratching his scalp like a flea-bitten dog.

"Goddamn, this wig is so itchy I wish I could throw it overboard," the man said. "But the security guys would kill me."

Inside the control van, Honeywell engineer Hank Van Calcar installed what was, at least in the interim, the most important piece of new equipment on the ship. Van Calcar had been hired to lead development of the ship's automatic station-keeping system back in Seattle, but once that was finished, he turned to a new project—a simulator that would allow Clementine's operators to practice for the mission.

Van Calcar had built simulators for missiles and airplanes and even for ship-stabilization systems, and he told the group that there was no reason he couldn't do that for Lockheed's claw.

Eighteen months and a seemingly infinite number of flights and meetings later, Van Calcar delivered the simulator to Long Beach. It used a beautiful scale model of the wreck, cast in gold by a sculptor hired by the Agency, and a "motion manipulator" that was a movable array of miniature lights and cameras meant to work like a scaled-down Clementine, all inside a large box. That was all linked up to software that simulated motion, forces, and movement and loaded into the CPUs in the same console where actual capture-vehicle operations would be carried out.

Van Calcar rigged it all up and commenced training sessions for the Lockheed engineers who designed the claw and would now drive it. He would let them get a feel for the controls, which were awkward and touchy, then add complications and contingencies so that the operators learned to expect the unexpected and would be prepared to act accordingly and find a workaround.

Watching hour upon hour of this made an impression on Dave Sharp, the CIA engineer whom Parangosky had named director of recovery for the mission. Sharp fired his original deputy of recovery and handed the job to Van Calcar, who with three young kids wasn't even supposed to go out on the operation. Van Calcar didn't hesitate. As he later explained it, "If you had the opportunity to be on that kind of a mission, and be part of something as exciting as that, there's no doubt in your mind that you would say, 'Yes!'"

37
Strike!

Some problems arise unexpectedly. Others you bring upon yourself. And when the *Explorer* arrived in Long Beach, Crooke made a strategic mistake that put the entire operation in jeopardy. He fired the working crew. Global Marine wasn't a union shop and the company wouldn't be using union labor on the *Explorer*, either, even for the most basic ship operations. Crooke assumed that when he dismissed the crew from the overt ship voyage—none of whom had been cleared—the men would grumble a little, take their pay, and then head off to other jobs.

The plan had always been to minimize exposure on the white voyage by operating it under the program's cover. For the purposes of that twelve-thousand-mile trip, the *HGE* was just an experimental mining ship being moved to California for final conversion.

But the local chapter of the Marine Engineers' Beneficial Association (MEBA) was already upset with Global Marine and Hughes for not hiring union men to work on the upcoming sea voyage, and when the dismissed crew took their grievances public—saying not only that they'd been fired without notice, but also that there had been no overtime pay and they'd been given shared staterooms, a violation of standard practice on the high seas—a labor action began.

At first, members of MEBA merely set up a picket line in an attempt to keep workers off the pier and create a boycott that would force Global Marine to the negotiating table. But on November 12, the situation escalated.

The small group of mostly peaceful men waving signs grew to a mob of more than one hundred angry protesters who didn't just get in the way of workers arriving at the site; they physically prevented them from crossing the line. The protesters harassed crew and managers, including Agency personnel, and began to stop delivery trucks, as well. They scattered nails on the road approaching the pier and even, in a few cases, slashed tires of work trucks parked at the site.

For days, work slowed and nearly stopped, causing an irate Parangosky to push the sea trials scheduled for mid-December back into January. Parangosky was furious with the protesters but also sensitive to the possibility that the situation could get much worse, so he and Paul Evans met to discuss options. They considered setting up a back channel to the union's leaders, who could be cleared into the program and asked to help quell the rebellion in the interests of national security, but both men felt that there were already far too many people aware of Azorian, and there was no guarantee that the union even had the ability to kill the strike without exposing the story.

The only solution was for Crooke and GMDI management to open legitimate negotiations with the union at the National Labor Relations Board, as Evans and his security team revised protocols for arrival at the site. All workers who weren't living on the ship were instructed to meet at several parking lots away from the waterfront, where they were loaded into vans driven by security officers and taken to the site in convoys. Word was passed to the picket lines that these vans would not stop and the convoys would speed across the dock—everyone holding his breath that no agitator had laid out spikes or nails to pop the tires—and through the gates, which were opened only long enough for the vans to get through, and then locked immediately behind them.

Azorian's West Coast security officers were already on high alert, busier than they'd been at any point of the program so far. They had to manage site security, the constant churn of workers who came and went, and now a strike, while maintaining constant watch for Soviet spies or slips in procedure that could potentially expose the program. Brent Savage took obvious pleasure in prowling the docks in mufti in search of anything that might raise eyebrows.

Everyone on the staff was under constant scrutiny, and the security team was prepared to act swiftly to eliminate any possible leaks, even before they developed. One secretary was fired after two staff members spotted a nude photo of her in the window of a novelty shop. Another was removed after she was linked to the Symbionese Liberation Army. And then there was a local prostitute with a long history of servicing Long Beach seamen recruited to lure anyone she could befriend from the *Explorer* back to her apartment, where instead of sex they'd get a sales pitch from a union rep. This worked once, but when the two men who accepted her offer saw the union rep, they left immediately and reported the breach to a security officer, who asked many detailed questions, including the location of this apartment. No one ever saw her again.

As if there weren't enough stresses accumulating, Soviet merchant ships had begun to make regular port calls in Long Beach, docking for two or three days at Berth 10, four hundred yards across the channel, off the *Explorer*'s starboard side.

Then there were the Navy guys. Parangosky accepted that the Navy was going to spy and meddle. Officers in obvious mufti had been regular visitors to the *Explorer* since construction began in Chester, and that didn't change in Long Beach.

To Parangosky's chagrin, NURO's first choice as mission director was a diminutive Navy captain named Chuck Richelieu, and Savage noticed him the moment he arrived in Long Beach with his deputy, a commander at least a foot taller, in tow. Each day, the two would appear in identical disguises bought the night before off the rack at a local department store: brown shoes, brown pants, brown belts, and starched shirts tucked in—the shirt seam, belt buckle, and trouser fly seam arranged in a perfect gig line. On their heads, they wore baseball caps, with brims as flat as pancakes.

What irked Savage most was that the two career officers were incapable of acting normal. The big guy was constantly opening hatches for his boss, and when either of them spotted a cigarette butt or candy wrapper on the ship's deck, he couldn't help but pick it up and throw it overboard. Such was the overwhelming force of order in Navy men.

Savage couldn't take it. As politely as possible, he asked the two to join him in a small conference room near the ship's bow, past the galley. There, out of sight of any nosy crew members, he leveled with these two esteemed officers.

"You're so blatantly Navy that you're going to blow our cover," Savage said. "You can't do that." He explained that as a security officer, he was trained to help people blend in. "Pull your shirt out of your pants. Screw up your gig line. Talk about beers and"—to the commander—"don't walk around opening doors for him all the time!"

38

Graham Gets Sick

FALL 1973

S trikes and delays weren't the only problems hanging over Pier E. John Graham's health, never excellent, was deteriorating rapidly. Azorian's chief architect had learned to live with emphysema. It was, for him, an uncomfortable but tolerable trade-off for the incomparable pleasures of nicotine. But the relentless pressure of three years of nearly nonstop work had elevated his already impressive smoking habit to a level that defied possibility. Throughout the ship's design, construction, and testing, Graham basically lit each new cigarette with the burning end of the last one, and his office and car were stacked with extra cartons of smokes.

Just before Labor Day, Graham began to exhibit signs that something else was wrong. His wife, Nell, noticed it first. Her seemingly tireless husband had begun to take vitamins, and also naps. He brushed her concerns aside, saying it was probably just pneumonia, and at first Graham's doctor agreed, prescribing only antibiotics and rest.

Graham was fundamentally incapable of resting, a condition exacerbated by the realities of a project that was, to him, the culmination of his already impressive life's work. To no one's surprise, Graham tried to power through his problems. He showed up to the pier just as early, and stayed as late as necessary, but his declining health was obvious to anyone who worked with him.

As his lungs failed him, Graham's energy sagged, too. It became too much for him to walk up the gangway to the ship, and he asked Steve Kemp, the young architect who'd been ably calculating the *Explorer*'s weight and centers with no knowledge of the ship's true purpose, to serve as his gopher in Long Beach. He also asked his secretary, Laura Crouchet, to locate and book a nearby motel room for an indefinite period, so that there was a place nearby to take an afternoon siesta when his energy flagged.

Kemp, a nonsmoker, moved into Trailer No. 1 along the pier, which housed Graham and Crouchet. He sat at a round table in the middle between their two desks, underneath a thick cloud of smoke, and did whatever Graham needed him to do.

Questions arrived at the trailer and Graham would dispatch Kemp with his answers, or on a mission to wander the ship, asking the various departments to think of anything that they might need from the architects. Kemp spent much of his time in the engine room, with the chief engineer, Gene Coke. They installed a set of overhead rails with trolleys and high-capacity chain falls so that if (and when) any of the five massive diesel engines blew a piston or cylinder, they'd have a way to pull it out and get a new one installed.

When a request came down to move thousands of gallons of highly toxic hydraulic fluid, Kemp went to go look for a pump. Graham stopped him first. "Tell me what you know about pumps," he said.

"I don't know a lot," Kemp replied sheepishly.

"Come here," Graham said, and gestured at the chair next to his desk, where he often taught the young architect things he hadn't learned in school. For ten minutes, Graham offered an impromptu lecture on pumps, and then said, "You need an explosion-proof submersible electric pump for that job."

Graham knew that Kemp wasn't cleared, and he managed to conduct the final ship preparations, with Kemp as his envoy, without tipping any secrets. Kemp, however, was suspicious. He still had never been shown plans or pictures of the mining machine. And there were many men in plaid pants and sunglasses who weren't the kind you typically see around ships. He was told they worked for Howard Hughes.

Kemp was in the engine room when a call came down that the air-conditioning wasn't working up on the superstructure deck, a restricted area that he'd never visited. The chief engineer told Kemp to come along, and when they got to that level, where a series of vans had been parked, he was surprised to see an array of electronics and TV screens.

"Who are you?" a man asked, surprising them.

Coke explained that he was the engineer and Kemp was a naval architect working for John Graham.

"Well, he doesn't have a red badge," the man said. "He can't be in here."

Eventually, Graham's breathing became so labored that Nell insisted he go back to the hospital, and doctors admitted him. This came at an inopportune moment. The accumulation of systems and equipment, tons upon tons of gear, was shifting the ship's center of gravity, and the issue was stressing Graham out. The *Explorer*'s stability had been his greatest worry from the beginning, and he knew there was little margin for error.

Graham barked orders at Kemp from his hospital bed. He wanted the ship's center of gravity tested again using what's called an "inclining experiment," and if the result was unsatisfactory, it would be Kemp's job to fix it. The result was unsatisfactory. The *Explorer*'s center of gravity had shifted up. In fact, Kemp calculated, when the moon-pool gates were open, and the derrick was loaded with pipe, the center would be so high that the ship could become unstable and roll beyond the seven-degree limit.

Kemp was twenty-six and in a job he adored, a job he was in no way qualified for, but he wasn't going to blow it, either, not if he could help it. He walked around the ship and looked at drawings and consulted with other engineers in search of a solution, until he finally had an idea.

The ship's massive docking legs—which would reach below the ship's bottom through the open moon-pool gates and grab the CV once it was within one hundred feet of the ship's bottom—had "rat holes" (or empty gaps toward the bottom) that were filled with freshwater. Kemp calculated that if he could replace that water with drilling mud, which is three times as dense as water, he could add 180 tons to each leg. Then, when the gates were open, the heavy legs, with extra density at their ends, could be manuevered into position and thus dropped into the ocean to lower the ship's center of gravity during the point at which it was most top-heavy. The math worked out. Problem solved.

Graham was thrilled.

The declining health of Azorian's key architect cast a pall over everyone in the program, especially at the Tishman Building and on the pier. But it probably hit John Parsons hardest. Parsons was both disciple and son-in-law, and he was watching his wife's father fall apart in a way that she couldn't, since as soon as he got out of the hospital, Graham went right back to work and was too busy finishing preparations on the ship to get away and see his family.

Really, though, not even Graham was aware of the severity of his condition. He acknowledged that he felt weak, but it came as a terrible surprise when he went to see physicians at a hospital in Newport Beach and was diagnosed with oat-cell carcinoma in his lungs—a particularly fast-growing cancer that, because it had already spread out of the lungs, was most likely incurable. His wife and kids were in the room as the oncologist delivered the news, and when his son Jack, a doctor in his final days of residency, heard the words he slid down the wall and onto the floor in shock.

"This is it for Dad," he told his sister Jenny. "He's going to die."

Ever a pragmatist, Graham took the news and went home, vowing to beat the disease. Nell drove him to the cancer center for chemo every week, and he loved the place, which was filled with friendly people, including many beautiful nurses who tolerated his flirting and paid him lots of attention in return. And his strength did improve. Graham even did something no one thought possible: He quit smoking. It was one of the hardest things he did in his life, but he went cold turkey, and it actually stuck—for a while.

For a man with terminal cancer, Graham struck everyone as surprisingly upbeat. Had the *Explorer*'s architect been healthy, he might even have been talked into going out on the mission, but it became increasingly clear in the months before departure that he would be in no shape to do so.

In fact, Graham decided, the most important thing he could do was focus what energy he still had on his health. His most critical work on the ship was finished anyway, and he had dozens of capable men under him, so when Graham told Crooke about the cancer, he said he was going to step away from the program.

From a bed at Hoag Hospital in Newport Beach, Graham dictated a letter by phone to Laura that was delivered to all of his engineers and the Azorian hierarchy. "My dear friends and associates," it began. "It is kind of a shock for me to have to write this letter, but, I would rather you know all the facts, and, you can count me in or out of future planning for Global Marine. Last Sunday, I was admitted to Hoag Memorial Hospital in Newport Beach, where my illness was quickly diagnosed as milignant [*sic*] lung cancer. In the next 8 days, we have been trying to find the exact extent and type of this cancer, and, thus far have seen nothing to positively state that it is incurable."

He went on to say that when the specialists at Hoag had finished studying his charts, a second team from UCLA would be consulted. "Obviously, I will be totally concerned with this No. 1 problem for some time. The most optimistic time would be 3 months for recovery and conjecture as to the worst is anybody's guess. I called Curtis Crooke and told him that I was totally, completely, and irrevocably finished with the Deep Sea Mining Project. Under no circumstances will I return to this program, except as a consultant with no responsibility or official capacity."

If he was "fortunate enough to recover from this problem," Graham continued, he would be happy to take on new projects in the future. But in the meantime, he wanted to make sure "the massive amount of technical files" he had accumulated in his sixteen years at Global Marine were collected and sorted. Even in this, his letter of resignation from Azorian, Graham couldn't pass up a chance to point out inferior work. "I have never been impressed with the central filing system Global Marine has had in the past and I would like to think that we could do better." He asked that Laura be able to spend "all her time on this effort for a period of at least 6 months, or until the job is finished."

For a time, the treatments worked. Graham's energy returned. He got stronger and would even work in the garden, tending to his roses. Then, in the spring, he felt pain in his back. The cancer had returned and was on the move. It had spread into his bones and was more than likely heading toward his brain, too. Graham was strong enough to attend his daughter Callie's wedding in Palm Springs in March, but he was in considerable pain. By April, he was smoking again.

39

We Need a Crew

Secret agents, undercover Navy captains, and mechanical engineers would comprise just part of the *Glomar Explorer*'s population. They were actually the minority. The majority of the men on the crew would be manual laborers who made the ship and its mechanical systems work. These were blue-collar men, mostly from the South and lower Midwest, where the American oil industry was based—roughnecks and good ol' boys who worked months at a time on drill rigs or at remote oil fields and began to show up at the Tishman Building in the spring of 1974 to apply for exotic, high-paying work on a mysterious mining ship that was the worst-kept secret in the industry.

GMDI's primary recruiter for the crew was Wayne Collier, better known as Cotton. A former undercover narcotics officer for the Justice Department in the Deep South, Cotton had also worked as an oil field roughneck and a steelworker. He arrived in LA in early 1974 and spent the first month absorbing what he could about the mining project while often wondering why so many of the engineers acted as if they were protecting a state secret—as well as why the office's cabinets were all secured with heavy-duty locks and meetings were often held behind closed doors.

Six weeks into his new job, Cotton was called to the Hughes building, where he was led into the office of Paul Ito.

Cotton knew Ito only by voice, as the man who approved all personnel decisions for the mining project. He was a stylish, stone-faced Japanese American with a pressed suit and hair the color of fresh tarmac. Ito didn't smile as he shook Cotton's hand and pointed him to a chair opposite his desk. He then sat down himself and beckoned his secretary on the intercom.

"Bring me six cups of coffee, please, and hold all calls," he said. Ito told Cotton he was about to receive a detailed briefing on the secretive Hughes operation and asked him to save his questions until he was finished. "All will be answered," Ito said.

Ito talked for hours, or that's how it felt, pausing only to swig coffee. He laid out the history of the Hughes company's interests in mining, as well as the structure and detailed roll-out plans for this experimental and speculative venture, which would establish an entirely new industry. He explained why Global Marine, the world's leader in deep-water drilling, had been chosen to build the mining ship, and showed Collier samples of the manganese nodules that would be suctioned from the seafloor and processed to access the rare valuable metals inside. Samples of these oblong black rocks, the size of fingerling potatoes, sat on his desk. He handed one to Cotton, who passed it from one hand to the other. It looked and felt like volcanic basalt, only lighter.

Cotton's eyes were about to cross from the deluge of detail when Ito stopped and fixed his gaze on the man who would recruit the men who would run the mining machines.

"Have you been paying attention?" he asked.

Cotton nodded.

"What you've heard about our plans is a complete lie," he said. "Mining is not our business. We are going to recover a sunken Russian submarine, and you are actually working for the Central Intelligence Agency."

There were actual Hughes employees at the program office. The cover story depended on that. But Ito wasn't one of them. He was a security officer hired to represent the CIA, inside the program, and charged with making sure every man hired was honest and trustworthy. Cotton, then, would be one of his most critical employees. As the guy who would hire the rugged men required to operate the ship and its equipment, he needed to find talented, experienced people who he was also certain would never reveal a word about the ship's true purpose. Ito told him that the CIA actually preferred men from the American South, who were considered to be more loyal, patriotic, and easy to clear.

Cotton placed ads in industry publications, and red-blooded roughnecks, many with southern accents as thick as sausage gravy, poured into LA. Aspiring pipe fitters, ironworkers, and crane operators were told they'd play a part in starting a new industry and would be working on the most advanced drillship ever built. Cotton handed applicants samples of the nodules pulled up by the *Glomar II,* allowing them to feel what they'd be seeking out. If a particular candidate seemed good enough to undergo further scrutiny, Cotton would offer twenty-five dollars in good-faith holding money to keep the man from taking another job while the CIA security team ran background checks, which he explained were personally ordered by Howard Hughes.

He hired nearly 150 men—75 each for the A and B crews—and each time a new hire was cleared, Cotton escorted him over to the DOMP office to receive an abbreviated version of Ito's famous briefing, sometimes delivered by one of the other security officers who worked in "human resources," often Howard Imamura. Then they were taken to the LA Airport Medical Center, across the street from Tishman, for a mandatory physical.

These, Cotton later wrote, were "men of true grit," recruited for their reliability, expertise, and patriotism. They had nicknames like Curley, Cowboy, Bimbo, and Big John and came from places like Bridge City, Texas; Brookhaven, Mississippi; Shreveport, Louisiana; Millry, Alabama; and Little Rock, Arkansas. The ideal man was, according to Cotton, "patriotic, loyal, flag-saluting, apple-pie-eatin', mother-lovin', tobacco-chewing and he swallowed the juice."

Clearing so many men was onerous work for the security group. An arrest or two, especially for minor crimes, was forgivable, but a surprising number of applicants had been jailed eight, nine, ten times, often for drunk and disorderly, a pattern of being reckless in public that the CIA obviously couldn't tolerate.

A background check wasn't entirely science. To some degree, a CIA security clearance was up to an officer's gut feeling. Often the best way to build loyalty was to put the responsibility directly into that person's hands in terms as blunt as possible. As Walt Lloyd explained it, "You tell them, 'You're carrying the goddamn subject that will get us into war. How are you going to treat it?'" The CIA called it "the team spirit approach."

The trickiest part of Cotton's job was hiring divers. The mission required sixteen highly experienced divers, far more than a typical drillship would need, meaning that the number itself was potentially a security risk and had to be kept secret. To cover his tracks, Cotton was instructed to hide the divers in other jobs and to cover the paper trail, so they weren't hired directly by Summa. A subsidiary called Oceanus was set up exclusively for this purpose.

Applications for the diving jobs came to Cotton's desk in batches and were often fishy. Some names were clearly faked, and he began to notice identical information—education, references, work history—repeated over and over. When Collier told Ito this concerned him, that it was an obvious red flag if anyone should decide to audit the files, he was told not to worry about it and to keep those personnel files locked away separately. Almost certainly, he later decided, this was because they were all Navy SEALs.

40
So, Who's Going?

The debate over crew size had been ongoing for months by the time the ship reached Long Beach. With so many specialized systems, each one requiring backup personnel trained to operate them, plus the need to include experts who were prepared to handle all of the intelligence recovered from the wreck, the crew list could easily have topped two hundred. But in the end the operations team settled on a total of 178 men—the final number determined by the maximum capacity of the *Explorer*'s lifeboats. There were eight key positions in the ship's hierarchy: mission director; deputy mission director; deputy for recovery; deputy for handling; deputy for exploitation; deputy for operations; deputy, technical staff; and ship's captain.

On most any ship, the captain is in command, but because of the nature of this operation, and the fact that this was a US government vessel, the captain would not be truly in charge. The mission director would run the operation. That job went to Dale Nielsen, a civilian physicist from Lawrence Livermore National Laboratory, the Bay Area nerve center of America's nuclear weapons program.

Nielsen was hardly just any physicist. He was a World War II and Korean War veteran who joined Livermore and was named founding director of that facility's secret Z Division, also known as the Special Projects Group. The Z Division was created in 1965 out of Livermore's Nonproliferation, Homeland Security, and International Security Directorate, as part of an agreement with the CIA to study the Soviet nuclear arsenal.

Z Division's primary responsibility was to learn as much as possible about Soviet nuclear weapons, so much of the group's emphasis was put on detecting nuclear tests and sampling particles from those tests to analyze the specific types and power of the warheads.

For the purposes of the mission, Nielsen was hired as a CIA contract employee and, like all Agency men, he was given a cover name. As far as anyone on the *Glomar Explorer* knew, the mission's director was a CIA man of mysterious origins named Dale Nagle. That he happened to know an inordinate amount about nukes struck no one as odd.

His selection meant that Curtis Crooke would be staying home, despite his deep experience on drillships and intimate knowledge of the *Explorer*'s complex systems. This was a gut punch to the individual who'd had as much to do with the Azorian program's success to date as anyone, but Crooke was a proud man who didn't easily cede command.

Parangosky didn't need to deliver this news personally, but he did it anyway, and he got exactly the response he expected from Crooke. The program office chief was either going to run the operation, or not go at all.

"I have no interest in going out there to be number two," Crooke said.

Privately, he thought that the CIA was making a mistake. In his opinion, the Agency was putting too much of the control in the hands of its own people, underestimating the difficulty of the physical ship work and the extent to which it was mostly a drilling and salvage job—the kind of thing best handled by grunts and roughnecks, who should have one of their own in charge.

Too many eggheads are great for imagination and not so great for operations. The engineers had worked almost literal miracles to design and build the ship, and certainly they'd be needed at sea to operate and fix complex systems, but having too many of them around—particularly with authority—was seen as extraneous, and possibly even detrimental, when it came to operations. An engineer's tendency is to analyze and discuss and make solid decisions based on data, but in the case of crisis—when a system has gone haywire and the entire ship could sink if a decision isn't made in minutes—they're not always the best people to have around.

CIA operatives were placed in many key jobs, including all of the director slots, as well as other strategic positions, such as the purser—the guy whose job is to be aware of exactly who comes on or off the boat. That, obviously, was an ideal place for a security officer.

Sherman Wetmore was offered a position as the senior Global man on the mission. And Wetmore, who considered himself almost as much a seaman as he was an engineer, didn't even need to consider the matter. He would go, without question. His job on the ship was to oversee all of Global Marine's engineers—but not the operating crew in the engine room or the marine crew run by the ship's captain. Another Global Marine employee put in a key role was Leon Blurton, a confident, friendly crew favorite who was named superintendent of drilling, which meant that he was in charge of the pipe-handling and heavy-lift systems, overseeing the army of roughnecks.

Ray Feldman, the Lockheed engineer who'd designed the telemetry cables, would also go. He was, he said later, "too young to know better." Jim McNary would help run the heavy lift, along with "Electric" John Owen, a Global Marine engineer who was excited but also worried about the prospect of Soviet interference—a real risk made obvious by a life insurance policy that every crewman had to sign. It stated that under certain circumstances the mission could be considered an act of war, and if anyone on the crew were to lose his life under those conditions, Summa would pay an award to whoever was named as the policy's beneficiary. Rumor had it that Owen learned just enough Russian in secret to say, should he be detained, "I'm just an engineer hired to work on the positioning system. I don't know what's going on."

To his own surprise, Charlie Canby was also going to sea. When the ship got to Long Beach, John Graham finally prevailed upon Paul Evans to clear Canby, vouching for him personally. So Canby, like so many before him, was summoned to the office of Paul Ito. Canby, who'd been involved in some capacity for more than a year, and had sailed the ship through the Strait of Magellan, had zero doubts about the mining story. Then Paul Ito blew his mind. "It was like learning the facts of life when you're eleven," he said many years later. "When your mom and dad tell you the truth for the first time."

That wasn't the only surprise in store for Canby. Graham had originally chosen Chuck Cannon to be the naval architect on the mission, but Cannon's wife, Harriet, objected. He'd been gone for long stints during ship construction in Chester, for ship trials, and on the West Coast delivery, causing him to miss a third of his eighteen-month-old son's life. Graham's next choice was Steve Kemp—his gopher at the port—but the Agency again refused to clear him. That left Canby, who'd been working happily as a ship's plebe. By process of elimination, he was the last architect standing and found himself offered the job he was actually educated for. He was, Cannon later admitted, the best choice anyway, being a certified welder, mechanic, and naval architect who'd sailed in the engine department during the West Coast delivery.

Canby loved the *Explorer* even when he was working as a grunt, but as the designated naval architect, he returned to Long Beach with swagger, his eyes now open to all of the spies he'd somehow failed to notice before. He immediately liked a cryptospecialist who worked in one of the vans that was off-limits to most of the crew, and when the man introduced himself, Canby asked if that was really his name. "No," he said, pulling out a license. "This isn't me."

The man explained that when any government employee—whether he was an Agency officer, a Navy man, or someone contracted to the Agency for the purpose of Azorian—arrived in LAX, he was met by a security officer and driven straight to a big apartment on Ocean Boulevard in Long Beach, where he would enter as himself and leave as someone else.

One afternoon, Canby was called upon to consult with Jack Poirier, who'd been selected to be the security chief for the mission. His nickname among the crew was Grayjack, for the color of his hair and beard. Poirier was a devout Catholic and Korean War vet who loved poetry and had a calming influence on everyone in his presence. He spoke in a thick New England accent and told Canby that he and his officers had been working out a procedure for classified material that would accumulate during the trip—charts, photos, cables from headquarters, and so on. These things were too risky to store, since they'd give away everything if the Soviets were to board the ship. The policy, then, would be to dump most of the paper overboard every day, by stuffing it into weighted wire baskets designed specifically to sink.

But officers couldn't throw away everything. Poirier asked Canby to help design a place to store a few key documents—including instructions for how to restart certain systems, and the cryptography keys. He wanted a large and impenetrable safe that could be padlocked. Canby listened patiently to the instructions and then told Poirier that this was a terrible idea.

"It's going to be like a cowboy movie when the guy robs a stagecoach," he said. "You know that's where the supersecret stuff is! So the guy takes out his .44 and shoots the lock off."

Instead, Canby said, he'd build them a secret tube, a fourteen-inch "magic pipe" that would come up from the CO_2 room below, on the main deck, and would appear to just connect into the other pipes. They could drop in the documents, which would slide down into a false section, accessed if necessary by a small steel door. No one else would know it existed.

Canby also took a liking to two Navy captains who were to serve important roles on the mission but who had little to do while the ship was anchored at Pier E. One was Harry Jackson, a kind, jovial man with a tremendous résumé. Jackson had worked at the Bureau of Ships, was one of the first officers in the Navy's nuclear power program, and was a key contributor to the design of the Navy's Thresher- and Polaris-class submarines. The year before Azorian began, Jackson led the search for and salvage of the USS *Scorpion* sub, lost at sea, and his expertise in sub design and structural analysis made him one of the program's most valuable consultants, even if his steadfast adherence to Navy habits—such as storing his pants under his mattress each night to keep them pressed—was a constant irritant to Brent Savage. The other captain was Fred Terrell, a Naval Academy grad who served on battleships and then later commanded a diesel submarine division. He would serve as the director of operations. Terrell hated the beard that the CIA insisted he grow as part of his disguise, and would surreptitiously shave away a little more each day, much to the amusement of Canby, who was the ship's unofficial barber. With days to kill, Canby and Jackson helped Terrell design the sailboat he planned to build after getting back, sketching it on brown paper that they unspooled on the deck.

41

West Coast Sea Trials

JANUARY 1974

By January, the schedule was in disarray and Parangosky was trying not to panic, an act of self-control that was increasingly difficult, as new problems arose almost daily. By this point, there was only so much time left for mistakes. Careful study of the weather and sea conditions in the area around the wreck site made it clear that the only period in which a recovery might be possible was from early July through mid-September. And the ship would need a minimum of fourteen and more likely as many as twenty-one days at the site to have a legitimate chance of success. That meant the *Explorer* needed to leave Long Beach by the end of June, or the entire mission would have to be delayed until the following summer. As far as Parangosky was concerned, the idea of maintaining the cover for another twelve months, while keeping all the contractors and key personnel on the books, was absurd. It was now or never.

On January 10, while union protesters agitated outside the gates, the *Explorer* departed Pier E for the West Coast sea trials, in which several of the systems would be tested for the first time. Two picketboats bobbed in the water just outside the pier, but neither interfered with the enormous ship as it headed for the test site, 160 miles west-southwest of the harbor, where the ocean depth was 12,500 feet.

The trials would focus on the pipe-handling (PHS) and heavy-lift systems (HLS)—which together were the linchpin of the entire recovery—as well as the readiness of the operators who would handle Clementine. Provided the trials went well, the *Explorer* would retract the pipe string, close the moon-pool gates, and head out on or about February 1 for Isthmus Cove, off Catalina Island, where the *HMB-1* would be waiting to submerge and transfer Clementine onto the *Explorer*—completing the final step for mission readiness.

Complications began almost immediately. Just outside the harbor, the *Explorer* stopped to run some quick tests of the PHS. The mining crew loaded a sixty-foot section of pipe and ran it through the automated system a few times to test its reliability. It didn't go smoothly. The system worked, but it was buggy, and considering that the recovery itself required that thirteen thousand feet of pipe be moved, assembled, lowered, and then raised again with millions of pounds on the other end, the PHS would need urgent tweaking, and it obviously wasn't going to be certified on this round of sea trials.

Were time not an issue, the *Explorer* would have turned back to harbor for repairs to the PHS, but to do so would likely mean missing the summer weather window, so the PHS team was asked to begin repairs at sea while the ship headed for deep water to continue its tests.

Then the real trouble began. The *Explorer* reached the deep-water test site on January 19, but rough seas and high winds foiled the crew's ability to do what they really needed to do: flood the moon pool, open the sea gates, and close them.

On the morning of January 22, the seas calmed enough for Curtis Crooke to arrive by helicopter and observe the test of the sea gates along with two very important guests: John Parangosky and Undersecretary of the Navy Dr. David Potter, who had also succeeded Bob Frosch as the second director of NURO. Several of the Agency's engineers, including Director of Recovery Dave Sharp, were also on board to observe the *Glomar Explorer*'s subsystems, which they'd been discussing and designing for three years, in operation at last.

For many of the men on board who weren't accustomed to being on the ocean but who would serve on the mission crew, these trials were also a chance to get some sea legs. John Parsons was one of them. Sherman Wetmore was another. Like most of the engineers at the program office,

Wetmore had been frantically busy during the design phase, but things had slowed down once the final ship preparations began in Long Beach.

Wetmore and all the others who had no actual job on the ship during the trials gathered around the railing above the moon pool to watch a test of those enormous gates—each one measuring one hundred feet by seventy-five feet. From his vantage, it was fifty feet to the floor, far enough that the immense scale of those gates, which slid open on rails, was difficult to grasp.

Outside, the winds had picked up and violent seas were tossing the ship around again. Had the whole schedule not been so far behind, the *Explorer's* crew would have postponed the tests for calmer weather, but Parangosky's urgency had infected everyone, and Crooke, as test supervisor, decided to go ahead anyway.

First, valves were opened by hand and millions of gallons of ocean water poured into the room through twenty-four-inch sea chests. An hour later, the pool was half-filled with dark green seawater, and the opening of the moon-pool gates could begin. The ship, meanwhile, had begun to buck, and that bucking grew worse as the rocking created an enormous wave that surged back and forth inside the two-hundred-foot pool in resonance with the swell outside. Each time the swell shifted and changed direction, the wave crashed into the ends of the 183-foot-long docking legs, causing an explosion of ocean spray that reached up over the railing, splashing down onto the observers and the deck under their feet. Underneath the ship, the sea gates slammed into the bottom of the hull. The sound was deafening, and the feeling for anyone standing on board was that this wasn't good, or right.

Wetmore knew that Graham's architecture was solid and would hold up. He'd actually anticipated this kind of stress on the ship. It was why the program office had flown the hydrodynamicist Jacques Hadler back and forth in the design stage—specifically to study the forces of that water on the wing walls. Still, standing there as a wave crashed back and forth, torquing the ship—so that the front half seemed to move one way, while the back moved in the opposite direction—was a frightening sensation. Potter and Parangosky both looked terrified, while Crooke, who appreciated the gravity of what was happening, attempted to ameliorate the situation by remaining stoic, as if this were all normal.

As the test continued, Wetmore himself began to worry. He didn't understand why it was taking the operators so long to close the gate doors, and the answer was soon apparent: They couldn't. The banging of the gates against the hull had damaged the drive in the aft operating machinery, causing a malfunction. Control of the rear door was lost; it would slide closed, but then water pressure would stop it before the two doors actually joined and were sealed by double rubber gaskets. Instead the aft gate kept opening and closing on its own, like a huge and very powerful steel mouth.

To calm the wave inside the pool, the captain turned the ship astern, and that maneuver worked, causing a change in the gate's momentum. The enormous gate, essentially a small barge, slid forward, then stopped, hung up on a gear tooth, just short of the forward gate. This left a three- or four-foot opening through which water emptied and surged up.

A team of safety divers was on board and standing by in case of emergency. If they could get down into the water by the gate opening, they could hook steamboat ratchets to both sides and force the gap closed manually.

None of the divers were enthusiastic about the idea. The violence of the waves and the unpredictability of the gate opening made it a perilous job. But two divers volunteered. One was Tony Acero, famous among the crew for his comfort with chaos and for the tattoo on his butt; there was a single *M* on each cheek, each one part of the setup for an elaborate joke that made no sense until he did a nude handstand, at which point the punch line was revealed.

Acero dove into the water carrying the ratchets, and the second diver followed.

From above, it was difficult to see exactly what the two were doing, and the crew stood there, transfixed. The difference in pressure between the inside of the pool and the water in the ocean below created enormous suction, and as soon as Acero approached the opening, he was sucked out through the gates. Up in the control room, engineers listening to the diver's net communication channel heard and would never forget the guttural howl that Acero, maybe the toughest man on the boat, let out when he was pulled under.

For a few seconds, the crew froze. A diving supervisor on the deck screamed at the other SEAL, who clung to a section of the intact gate. Then,

THE TAKING OF K-129

as quickly as he vanished, Acero reappeared. As the ship dropped and the water surged up through the opening, he popped out, thrust back through the hole and into the moon pool.

The other SEAL grabbed Acero and, with the ratchets in place, the crew pulled the aft gate forward until the gap was closed.

The gate failure wasn't just a setback to the schedule; it was a very real sign of the mission's risks—of taking an experimental ship loaded with untested systems and attempting the most daring act of military espionage ever undertaken, in the middle of the Pacific, in full view of the enemy. The CIA's naval architect who'd been Graham's chief counterpart on the S&T team, and who knew Soviet submarines as well as anyone, was so shaken by the experience that he removed himself from the mission roster.

Back at NURO, the organization's deputy and CIA liaison, Zeke Zellmer, recognized that this was a make-or-break moment for Azorian, a program he fought for and had shepherded for three years. He caught the next plane to LAX, where a helicopter was waiting on the runway to deliver him straight to the *Explorer,* where he met his boss, as well as Duane Sewell, second in command at Lawrence Livermore Lab, one of the country's most critical and secret centers for nuclear weapons research. Sewell was there to assess the situation for the Lauderdale Panel, a small, influential group of private sector scientists that had become the de facto advisory board for all major scientific and engineering decisions related to Azorian. Sewell was a meticulous man, revered for his judgment, who installed safety practices at Livermore, where extremely dangerous testing was common, around a motto: You can do anything safely, no matter how hazardous it might appear, as long as you pay attention and get the engineering right.

The presence of the two highest-ranking men at the organization that funded Azorian, as well as a key presidential scientific adviser, was a clear signal to Crooke and everyone else that this was the single most tenuous moment since the program's inception. Zellmer and Potter needed to know what would require repair, how the team was going to repair it, how much those repairs would cost, and where the funds would come from.

The failure of the gates proved to Zellmer and Potter what they already suspected—that the rush to get to sea in the summer of 1974 meant that some of the ship's key systems would not be as refined as they should be. This increased the risk of failure, but probably not enough to justify a full year's delay. That was the argument Parangosky made very persuasively when Zellmer voiced his concerns.

Crooke personally led an inspection of the moon-pool floor and was surprised and also impressed when both Potter and Sewell—august PhDs and giants of American science—crawled down into the gate opening behind him to assess the damage to the steel plating caused by the gear teeth. They had punched massive holes right through the plates.

When the ship got back to shore, Crooke felt compelled to blame someone, so he fired the ship's construction supervisor and ordered a hasty review of the incident. As the naval architect on board, Steve Kemp was left to explain the failure. At three to four feet, the sea state had been technically within the limits set by Graham, but those limits were based on calculations and with no real-world evidence to consider. The fact was, no one had ever built sliding nine-foot-thick doors—each one essentially a barge—on the bottom of a ship, and it was extremely difficult to predict how the wave action at that depth would affect them.

The water had been much more violent than he and Graham, who had tried to be conservative, had anticipated, so Kemp consulted with Charlie Canby and decided to rewrite the operating manual for the gates during the most critical period of operation. The period of time when the doors were in motion, no more than a couple of hours, was the primary point of vulnerability; therefore, they should be opened only in calm seas. Once the doors were open and secured to the ship's bottom, the sea state didn't matter anymore.

42

A Crack in the Facade

JANUARY 1974

As the *Explorer* labored back to port for urgent repairs, with only a short time to return to sea and mate with Clementine, a different crisis began to bubble up back in Washington. Seymour Hersh, the dogged, irascible *New York Times* reporter who'd won a Pulitzer for his exposé on the My Lai Massacre in Vietnam, got a tip from a source late in 1973 that the CIA was in the process of attempting to recover a sunken Soviet sub and that the mission was code-named Jennifer.

Hersh worked every possible intelligence source for confirmation but came up empty again and again until he happened to bump into a recently retired CIA officer he knew at a cocktail party in January. Why, Hersh asked the man, would the United States be trying to recover a submarine? The man acted as if that story was crazy. It couldn't possibly be true. But as soon as he left the party, he called newly installed CIA director William Colby to say that Hersh was, at a minimum, on the trail of Azorian.

Colby, in his early fifties, had been on the job just five months, but he recognized immediately that Hersh—a reporter known for being impervious to government power and influence—was on the verge of spoiling the Agency's biggest secret, an operation six years in the making. He decided there was only one way to deal with Hersh. He had to confront him and negotiate his way out of the trouble.

Colby was a veteran of the OSS's legendary Jedburghs, a group of spies recruited to parachute behind enemy lines in the early years of World War II and wreak havoc, organizing resistance and blowing up roads and bridges. The Jedburgh motto was "Surprise, kill, and vanish," and Colby was perfect in the role. A quiet, analytical man with a sharp chin and round, steel-rimmed glasses, his calm, reassuring presence made him particularly effective as a saboteur. He never panicked, and even though his arrival at *The New York Times* Washington bureau confirmed to Hersh that his story was valuable, Colby made no attempt to bully the reporter. For one thing, he couldn't legally compel Hersh to do anything. Instead, he offered a deal. He explained that the operation in question, the name of which he could not reveal, was of enormous importance to national security and that revealing it now would foil six years of work and a vast sum of taxpayer money. But he also knew that he needed to give Hersh an out. If he would just sit on the story until the Agency had finished the operation, Colby would be willing to give him a complete briefing of the program details.

Hersh, who didn't have enough to publish anyway, agreed. He also wanted Colby to answer some questions about the CIA's involvement with Watergate, the story he was really interested in pursuing at that time.

Colby had defused the situation, for the time being.

By mid-February, the *Explorer*'s gates were repaired, and the ship departed Pier E for a second set of sea trials. The ship moved first into shallow water off Los Angeles to deploy and retract forty doubles of pipe string, totaling twenty-four hundred feet. That went smoothly, with only minor control-panel issues, so the ship headed toward Catalina Island, where it would rendezvous with the *HMB-1* for a final mating with Clementine.

The capture vehicle was hiding in the belly of the world's largest submersible barge, which was already en route from Redwood City, towed behind a tug named *Wendy Foss*. The *HMB-1*'s stint in the Bay Area had been a matter of curiosity for locals, who were given no specifics about the nine-story-high vessel that had arrived under the Golden Gate Bridge from San Diego. THE SECRET REVEALED. WHAT WILL BARGE DO? announced an above-the-fold story in the *San Mateo Times* on the day of the *HMB-1*'s departure.

"We want to clear the air," Paul Reeve told reporters in a phone interview from Summa Corp.'s offices in Houston. The barge was part of an underwater mining operation and contained a "mining vehicle" that he was unwilling to discuss in detail because to do so would reveal proprietary technology that would damage Howard Hughes's competitive advantage. A UPI wire report said that the "football field–sized" barge had been outfitted "under top secret conditions behind a fenced compound watched over by guards" and was "apparently headed toward South America for an undersea mining venture." The AP story quoted Redwood City fire marshal George Asvos, who'd inspected the barge, reporting that the vehicle Reeve mentioned was a "submarine tractor that can be released to comb the sea bottom in search of mineral deposits."

The 350-mile trip to Catalina would have taken just under two days in calm seas, but again, the weather was uncooperative, and sixty-seven-knot winds driving thirty-foot waves bashed the tug and barge, creating conditions severe enough that the crew would have turned around and waited out the storm in port were time not so fleeting. Further delays were not an option.

On February 27—just a day behind schedule—the *Wendy Foss* pulled the *HMB-1* into Catalina Island's Isthmus Cove, in plain view of a beach packed with sunbathers and the dozens of sailboats anchored in the popular harbor. Local news reports had noted the arrival of the *Hughes Glomar Explorer* a day before, and swimmers gathered along the shore to snap photos of the enormous barge, which looked like a floating basketball arena, complete with domed roof.

The cove was an objectively terrible location for a sensitive operation, but the extremely public setting fit Walt Lloyd's cover story perfectly. Moving Clementine into the *Explorer* was an ungainly process—"like trying to mate a couple of elephants," as he described it—and required a flat sea bottom and very calm waters. And those were exactly the conditions in the 160-foot-deep Isthmus Cove, twenty-six miles from the California coast.

A small armada of escort vessels had arrived to participate in the operation, including three tugs, an anchor-pulling barge called the *Happy Hooker*, and several pleasure boats piloted by security staff whose job was to protect the perimeter, telling nosy boat owners to back off in the name of Howard Hughes's privacy.

The final mating was done after nightfall. Once the sun set, divers slipped into the water to activate the motors that opened the roof of the barge—which had been sunk and was sitting on the shallow floor of the cove—and were ready to fend off any foreign agents or curious tourists who might decide to scuba around these curious vessels. The *Explorer* itself was bathed in industrial spotlights, lighting up the cove and beach so much that an innkeeper would later complain to reporters that the popular local wild buffalo were scared away from the surrounding hills for weeks after.

Inside the *Explorer,* Charlie Canby opened the moon-pool gates and lowered the ship's massive docking legs through the hole and into the *HMB-1*'s innards, now exposed by the barge's retracted aluminum roof. Controllers maneuvered the legs so that their keyholes were aligned with docking pins on Clementine's strongback—actions requiring delicate control of enormous steel objects the size of dinosaurs. Once the two components were linked, the docking legs were slowly retracted, pulling Clementine up into the moon pool.

The only way anyone could have glimpsed the elaborate claw was from under the water, but even that possibility had been considered. In anticipation of such an event, Walt Lloyd asked Manfred Krutein and John Parsons to commission a scale model of a mining machine that looked similar to Clementine but which, upon closer inspection, would have had other adornments, such as giant tubes for sucking up manganese nodules. If blurry photos of Clementine were to surface, the model could serve as a useful distraction, a much shinier object for the media to focus on.

The process was meant to look defensive but not overly secretive. It had been described already in *Ocean Industry* magazine, using information "leaked" by Paul Reeve. "The mining vehicle is too large and heavy to be handled by the ship's gear in a conventional manner and must be installed from beneath the ship," the magazine reported.

As soon as Clementine was inside her mother ship, suspended over the floor by the docking legs, the sea gates were closed and the process of pumping out the seawater began. This was also Canby's job. The ship's naval architect opened the valves and fired up the fourteen-inch-diameter pump, which started up fine, ran for fifteen seconds, and then died.

The reason: Masses of fist-size squid, drawn into the pool by the interior floodlights, had jammed the pumps. The mating coincided exactly with an annual squid migration to the waters off Catalina.

Divers cleared the pumps, but the problem kept recurring and Canby was exasperated. Then a clever solution was posed. The ship raised anchor and moved to deeper waters, where the crew turned off the interior lights, opened the sea gates, and activated bright lights that had been hung over the sides of the ship. The lights would, in theory, attract the squid to the waters outside. And it worked, leaving only the large and smelly problem of shoveling thousands of pounds of dead squid from the well. The smell lingered for days after.

From Catalina, the *Explorer* headed back to sea while the *HMB-1* was pumped dry and towed back north to Redwood City to await the mother ship's return. The *Explorer* would next head farther out to sea, some sixty-five miles southwest of Catalina, ostensibly to test the roll-stabilization system. In reality, the location was selected because it put the ship just outside the boundary of America's territorial waters, which was how Walt Lloyd and Parangosky decided to work around a pesky problem that had arisen: On March 1, commercial vessels in California waters were to be subject to a special inventory tax. To avoid the scrutiny of that tax, which could force a revelation of the boat's true owner, they decided to skirt the problem entirely by being at sea.

The ship carried out the test, broadcasted an open message from international waters declaring the test complete, and then, just after midnight on March 2, headed back to Long Beach for thirty days of rigging and preparation.

For the next few weeks, the *Explorer*'s crew put the ship through repeated and rigorous examination just offshore of Long Beach. Every major system was tested and every part worked, sometimes, but almost never did everything work at once, and a small powerboat named the *Colleen* ferried crew and parts back and forth from the *Explorer* to Pier E, with key department heads flying almost daily to the program office by helicopter for debriefs with Washington.

The clock was ticking, morale was fraying, and many of Azorian's top engineers fretted openly about reliability, about system failures, and especially about rushing into a mission preloaded with complexity even in the best of circumstances.

Curtis Crooke wanted to do a basic test of Clementine in which they'd attempt to penetrate the seafloor with the tines of the claw, just to see how well the controls worked, and to look for any flaws or weaknesses in the tines. But every time he raised the matter with Parangosky, Crooke was told there was no time for another test. The idea bothered him, though, and he kept at it until, after three or four requests, Parangosky shut him down. "I don't have any more time to waste, Curtis," he said. "Mention this one more time and you're through."

At this point, the calendar was dictating most every decision. The final step before leaving for the mission was an integrated systems test that would require the crew to operate all of the various components required to complete the mission. Ideally, this would be done in the deep ocean, at a depth of twelve thousand feet, so that the rigging crew could deploy and retract a large amount of pipe, but there just wasn't time for that. Crooke, after serious discussions with the CIA engineering team, decided that they could accomplish a good enough integrated test in shallower waters. They chose a depth of twenty-four hundred feet, close to shore but adequate for operating all the systems. This wouldn't allow anything close to a full deployment of pipe, but the reality, everyone agreed, was that a deep test wouldn't tell them much anyway about the only thing that mattered—whether or not they could locate, grab, and lift a submarine three miles deep in the ocean.

The *Glomar Explorer* was one of the most specific tools ever built, designed for onetime use, and to carry out a series of iterative tests would be of only minimal value while unnecessarily stressing the various components. In truth, there was no way to truly test it all. So why even bother? Either it would all work, or it wouldn't.

43

Sub School

Beginning in April, every man on the crew was given a new order. Anyone going to sea who didn't have a job that required him to maintain a specific position for the entirety of his workday was assigned to a group. And on a date arranged by the security staff, each group would fly commercial up to San Francisco and follow instructions from there.

This was required of every man who might have flexibility on the ship, no matter his rank or job, and there was no hierarchy in the groups. Engineers were mixed in with grunts and government agents, just as they would be out at sea. For the roughnecks, it was some rare exposure to the spook world, and they relished it.

Upon arrival at SFO, each group was met by a security officer who took the men to pick up rental cars, then led them fifteen miles south to Redwood City, where they were checked into a Howard Johnson under fake names—Sherm Wetmore, for instance, became a Wetstein. The men got a rare night off, which included access to a suite stocked with Agency-supplied booze, a perk, it was made clear, provided for the specific purpose of keeping everyone (but especially the roughnecks) in the hotel and out of the local bars.

The next morning, Cotton Collier, with Howard Imamura as the security liaison, met the men in the hotel lobby and took the group in a caravan across the 101 freeway and into the barren marshlands along San Francisco Bay, where they proceeded along a series of unmarked dirt roads until they reached a green metal warehouse ringed by a security fence topped with barbed wire and bordered on one side by a dredged canal. Behind it, the enormous *HMB-1*, anchored in an inlet, dwarfed every other building on the Lockheed lot.

Once inside, the men were led into a large classroom, where a tall, thin man with wisps of graying hair who called himself Stan explained that they would be spending the next few days inside this metal-walled warehouse, preparing for the mission.

Stan was the school's nuclear materials expert, who would teach them all proper handling and decontamination procedures, but not before they learned first about the submarine itself. For that, Stan turned the room over to a man in his mid-thirties with a barrel chest, a bit of a belly, and a thick dark beard. He called himself Blackjack.

Blackjack—whose true name and work history were never revealed to the crew—was Azorian's submarine specialist, having served seventeen years in the Navy's Silent Service before the Agency recruited him to train the Azorian crew for the exploitation process. Rumor had it he'd come from the Navy's ultrasecret underwater espionage program, perhaps even from the legendary NR-1 nuclear spy sub. He was stern but friendly, and he sweated profusely, making frequent use of a rag in his back pocket to wipe away moisture from his forehead.

On the way into the building, Blackjack said, the men may have noticed a walled section to their right. That area was sealed off from the rest of the warehouse by army-green plastic that stretched from the top of the wall all the way to the corrugated metal ceiling, twenty-five feet above, and inside was a replica of the submarine wreck that they would all be dissecting over the course of the week. The point, he said, was to get familiar with what they would be seeing once the actual sub was raised, and to be prepared for anything. Everyone on the mission was cleared and should feel free to ask any questions that came up. If Blackjack could answer it, he would.

Instruction would be provided in the use of cutting tools, such as arc gougers and acetylene torches, as well as ultrasonic baths, which would be used on board to clean up and preserve, for instance, the sub's sensitive electronics, so that they could be reverse engineered later in some government laboratory.

In addition to studying the submarine's structure and working on the mock wreck itself, the crew would be given two hours per day of Russian-language instruction, lessons on the nuclear weapons the K-129 carried, and instruction on the risks and proper handling of radioactive materials. They were taught the risks of radiation exposure and drilled on the protocols of the Geneva Convention, which mandated the proper treatment of prisoners.

No one knew what condition the sub's warheads might be in, nor the types or levels of radiation that the wreck might give off, so the Agency's nuclear experts—from Livermore—were proceeding as if the entire wreck would be "hot." And that's the way the training was set up, with rope and red tape setting a cordon around the mock sub, a tangled mass of rusted steel twenty feet long and eight feet wide, complete with a damaged conning tower.

To maximize every minute, including the down period when the *Explorer* was sailing from the target site to whatever port was chosen for its return, workers from across the crew, no matter their job or rank, would be assigned to the exploitation team (on a voluntary basis only) and put to work searching the wreck immediately after Livermore's experts had scanned the sub and declared it safe enough for work.

Before any one of the men got close to the mock wreck, he had to suit up according to precise and methodical procedures designed by Livermore. First on was a base layer of normal working gear—underwear, pants, shirt, and boots, plus surgical gloves and rubber rain galoshes over the boots. From there, each man stepped into a cotton full-body suit similar to long johns, and then into the final, shiny outer layer, disposable and made of Tyvek, which felt and crinkled like paper. Work gloves went over the surgical gloves and assistants taped both wrists and ankles with duct tape to prevent air leaks where layers of clothing overlapped. Next, each man was given a hard hat and an oxygen mask hooked up to a tank on his back and controlled via a switch on his chest, and then, finally, a hood—with a built-in mic and earphones—went over all of that, and it, too, was duct-taped to make the entire inside of the suit airtight.

Once they were suited up, students were led into the mock contamination zone. And when finished, they exited through a cleanup zone, where trainers used handheld black lights to scan for signs of green powder that is invisible in natural light but which had been sprinkled throughout the tangled mess of metal to simulate the presence of radioactive particles, which are invisible to the naked eye.

The job, Blackjack explained, was fairly simple: Identify, record, cut, remove, save, and discard. Every shift would be staffed by a team of analysts from the Agency and Livermore, who could provide a second opinion on any object, but the general rule was going to be that if it looked even slightly interesting, it should be removed and handed over to a specialist.

Russian linguists would be aboard the *Explorer* to translate documents, assist in identification of signs, and communicate with the exploitation crew via two-way radios in the hoods, but the CIA wanted every man to receive cursory instruction in Russian in order, at least, to be able to identify warnings. Priority was given to a crash course in the Cyrillic alphabet, and especially in memorization of keywords such as "nuclear," "radioactive," "caution," and "danger."

Two Russian émigrés, both short and stout and clad in double-breasted, wide-lapel suits, pointy-toed shoes, and unfashionable eyeglasses, taught the sessions and were alternately entertained and frustrated by the process of teaching an unfamiliar language, with an entirely foreign alphabet, to men who didn't care much for English grammar and who in many cases hadn't finished high school. The Russians cringed, and often laughed, at the many ways in which their native language was butchered.

Stan and Blackjack alternated instruction on nuclear weapons, and submarine construction and mechanics, and then shadowed the men as they suited up and began to pick apart the mock wreck, which appeared to have been made of actual submarine parts. To enhance the realism, instructors stashed rotten meat inside to simulate the pungent, overpowering odor of rotting human flesh that would likely permeate the moon pool as soon as the submarine was exposed to surface air conditions after four years in the extreme cold and low oxygen of the deep ocean. Sherm Wetmore gagged and nearly puked the first time he entered the room.

The welding crew was taught to X-ray the hull before cutting any portion to avoid destroying valuable material on the inside—or worse, detonating explosives or damaging a nuclear warhead. Blackjack devoted entire sessions to teaching every possible component that could be valuable and worth saving, even when that wasn't obvious.

At day's end, it was time to decontaminate, a process even more laborious than suiting up. Clothing was removed one piece at a time, checked under the black light for particles, and then thrown into waste barrels. On the ship, checks would be done with dosimeters, and any man who tested positive would have to scrub himself in the shower, then be retested—repeating the process however many times it took to get clean.

Follow the procedures, the school's instructors said, and all would be fine. But make no mistake, either. "You're going to be working in an environment that is contaminated with multiple types of radiation, including plutonium," one of them said. "If, by any chance, you should suffer a puncture wound and what punctures you is contaminated with plutonium, you will die. You will be buried at sea and it will be recorded as an industrial accident."

44

Standing by for Green Light

On May 12, the *HGE* completed its final scheduled systems tests and headed back to port, where the crew would await next steps. Mission Director Dale Nielsen sent word to Washington that he and the *Explorer* crew were finally ready to go to sea and get the submarine.

"In spite of the fact that we have had to work through many problems, all systems have worked satisfactorily," Nielsen wrote in a report to Parangosky. "The crew has performed extremely well. I am convinced that they are qualified to begin the mission.... It is my recommendation that following the upcoming refit and crew rest period we begin the mission on or about 15 June."

Parangosky briefed Carl Duckett and presented the deputy director with a memo to deliver to Kissinger and the all-important 40 Committee, which would give its advice to the president. Those men would now have to decide if five years of work—and at least 250 million dollars in spending—would finally be put to the test out on the Pacific, or if the rising stakes of nuclear disarmament talks and the possibility of Soviet interference would cause the president and his team to cancel the entire operation, choosing caution over risk.

On May 28, Kissinger received the memo, a highly classified document titled "Project AZORIAN Mission Proposal." The memo summarized the situation at hand. "If approval to depart in mid-June is received, the ship would depart Long Beach, and at normal cruising speed arrive in the vicinity of the target in fourteen days, following which the recovery operation could commence. It is mandatory that recovery operation be initiated as early as possible in the 'annual weather window'—the period between 15 June and 13 August—when there is the highest probability for sea conditions in that area within which the recovery system can be successfully operated."

The recovery should take about three weeks, Parangosky suggested, but the unpredictability of weather and "other contingencies"—a catch-all euphemism for a host of unpleasant possibilities that could probably fill another entire memo—meant that the ship should plan for six weeks on station. The mission had to either go now, or wait a full year.

Of course, the CIA's urgency was in part self-inflicted. The failure of the moon-pool gates had caused an unplanned delay for repairs that forced the team to skip several important steps, including additional deep-water testing, as well as "simulated mining legs" that were supposed to be staged off the coast of Hawaii to, in Parangosky's words, "further condition the Soviets to the operation of the HUGHES GLOMAR EXPLORER." These fake mining stints were planned by Walt Lloyd to generate additional publicity and "provide the Soviets with further opportunities to observe the vessel," Parangosky admitted, but there was no assurance that this would actually have happened. "Deletion of these legs will not unravel the cover nor reduce the import of the considerable publicity in the media and trade journals developed over the past four years.

"It is reasonably certain that the Soviets are cognizant of the existance [*sic*] of the HUGHES GLOMAR EXPLORER and its purported deep ocean mining role by virtue of the extensive publicity, Soviet overhead reconnaissance, and the observational opportunities Soviet vessels have had at Long Beach." In other words, Parangosky was saying, there was no reason to worry.

Aware that some members of the committee were new and had not been privy to the operation throughout its life, Parangosky emphasized certain key points, in particular the risk of Soviet interference. The *HGE* had "reliable and secure communications" between the ship and the control center, and "in the remote possibility" that the Soviets interfered, plans were in place to shift command to the Navy's Pacific Fleet, at Pearl Harbor. If that situation were to escalate, he noted, dialogue with the Soviet Union at the highest levels could be enacted to "defuse the situation thus reducing the possibility of military confrontation at sea."

The mission team estimated that the *Explorer* would spend twenty-one to forty-two days doing the target recovery operation, before heading to Hawaii for subsequent analysis and recovery. By October 22, the ship should be safely back in Long Beach—hopefully with the greatest intelligence haul in history in its belly.

Three years after the keel had been laid in Chester, the cover story seemed to be intact. "The Summa Corporation Deep Ocean Mining Project (DOMP) is recognized and accepted by the media, both news and technical, for that which it purports to be," Azorian's director wrote. "The DOMP has been the subject of attention in a variety of technical and trade journals." The Agency had reams of evidence that the Summa project was accepted in the commercial mining world, and by the Soviets, who tended to observe and tap Western technical media for their own industrial and scientific needs.

All possibilities had been considered. Photographs clearly showed that the remains of at least one Soviet crewman were at the wreck site, so it was a virtual certainty that others would be found within the submarine itself. Walt Lloyd had been thinking about this for a while, studying both international law and Soviet military burial customs, and an interagency contingency review committee had approved his plans to handle and dispose of any remains in accordance with the 1949 Geneva Convention, and in a way that would not cause any issues with the Soviets should they someday find out.

Parangosky felt confident that the mission could be conducted in relative peace, since the recovery site was in international waters about twelve hundred nautical miles from the Soviet mainland, removed from commercial shipping lanes, and not in proximity to normal Soviet or American naval operating areas.

If the Soviets were to decide to surveil the *HGE*, the CIA thought, it would be because of curiosity about ocean mining from their scientific and economic communities, and not because of concern or caution from the military.

In summation, Parangosky said, the Agency was ready. "The mission team is technically trained and psychologically ready." The team was confident, the cover story was solid, and the window was about to open, but only briefly. To wait another year would put the whole thing in jeopardy, allowing more time for leaks. "I believe that we would have the maximum probability of success by initiating the mission as soon as the ship is ready; that is, on or about 15 June."

45

Twiddling Thumbs

Between the second sea tests and mission launch, NURO's leadership organized a final inquisition at CIA headquarters in Langley. Top officials from all of the important agencies—Navy, State, Justice—were asked to attend, and recognizing the gravity of the moment, Parangosky ordered every senior member of his team in so that they'd be prepared for any question that might be asked.

Norm Nelson and Dave Sharp led the technical portion of the meeting, defending against loud and aggressive criticism by the Navy brass, who cited equipment failures to suggest the systems were unready for live operation, and took real issue with the mission's contingency plans, which Parangosky knew to be flimsy since there was no real way to protect the ship and its crew should Soviets board the *Explorer.* Captain Walter N. "Buck" Dietzen, from the staff of the chief of naval operations, couldn't believe what he was reading. The plan, basically, was to try to maintain cover, pretending to be miners and refusing to allow any Soviets to board on the grounds that Howard Hughes wouldn't allow it. If that failed, the plan stated, the crew would blast the Soviet ship with fire hoses to fend off ladders and boarding parties, and if it all escalated to the point of armed invasion—well, the guys on deck would buy as much time as possible while the spooks dumped the classified documents overboard in the metal-wire baskets.

To a military lifer like Dietzen, this was outrageous, even shameful. The crew should stand and fight. One problem with that notion, he admitted when pressed, was that the nearest Navy ship or submarine would be at least four hundred miles away. So the *Explorer* crew would be alone. Any fight against a foreign vessel of war was unlikely to end well.

Still, the crew—or at least the onboard security—should have weapons, he barked. And Parangosky, aware that this was a particularly petty and terrible hill for his mission to die on, ceded the point. His security team would work out a plan for resisting Soviet aggression. Or at least that's what they told the Navy brass.

On June 3, 1974, Rob Roy Ratliff of the National Security Council staff delivered a memo to Kissinger in advance of what would be the final 40 Committee meeting before taking the matter to Nixon for a final decision. "Culminating six years of effort, the AZORIAN Project is ready to attempt to recover a Soviet ballistic missile submarine from 16,500 feet of water in the Pacific," the memo reported. "The recovery ship would depart the west coast 15 June and arrive at the target site 29 June. Recovery operations will take 21–42 days." This schedule was essentially inflexible, Ratliff wrote, because the "good weather window" was extremely narrow—a mere crack—and to miss that window would likely foil the entire operation, "since it is doubtful security could be maintained" until the window opened again in 1975.

Assigning probability to the chance of success felt like a pointless endeavor—there was so much unproven technology, so many variables. Nonetheless, Ratliff admitted that "estimates [of success] seldom go beyond 50%" and in the view of some were as low as 20 percent. He reminded the committee that at a prior review in late 1972, the group decided that "an estimate of 30–40% was considered sufficient to go ahead with the project" and that Parangosky's team was confident that, with integrated tests completed, the number was at least 40 percent.

The question, then, was: Is a 40 percent chance to recover "information which can be obtained from no other source, on subjects of great importance to the national defense," good enough?

The State Department continued to worry that the submarine, as a "man of war," was still the property of the USSR, even if the Soviets had no idea where it was. But intelligence is dirty business and rules are broken all the time. They're relevant only if you get caught. If that were to happen here, the Soviets might exploit it for propaganda and political purposes—or they might choose to sit quietly and say nothing out of embarrassment that they lost a nuclear ballistic missile submarine. What was more, Ratliff reported, "As Hal Sonnenfeldt pointed out in the 1972 review, détente is not going to terminate mutual intelligence operations which the target country will consider obnoxious and the collecting country vital." Given a similiar opportunity, the Soviets would probably do the same thing.

With the ship's departure imminent, and—at least for the moment—all of the engineering challenges solved, there was little to do but sit and wait. The only people who actually had work left to do were the security officers, and they were still scrambling to prepare for all eventualities. Paul Evans' staff worked up "the book," a three-ring binder filled with loose-leaf pages organized into sections with tabs color-coded to the progressive severity of threats that the *Explorer* could encounter at sea. Whoever was on communication back at the program office would have this book close at hand and would consult it upon receipt of certain urgent coded messages—messages that would be immediately relayed to the East Coast via the Donald Duck phone.

Security officers also visited the wives of all the key government employees who would go out on the mission—the CIA engineers, nuclear analysts, and Navy men. The security teams provided only very limited briefings as to what their husbands were doing. They wanted to make it clear, however, that the mission wasn't without risks, and also that secrecy was tantamount, so that attempts at communications should be limited to emergencies only. Each wife was given an officer as her point of contact.

Final preparations were increasingly nervy for everyone. As the CIA officers visited spouses, Cotton Collier told members of the roughneck crew that they'd each need to submit next-of-kin affidavits, to be filed away in case they were killed or taken prisoner.

In truth, no one directly associated with Azorian knew what would happen if the Soviets meddled. That extremely sensitive matter was above even Parangosky's pay grade. When he briefed Colby about the meeting with the

Navy in which Dietzen had scoffed at the CIA's plans to respond to provocations with water cannons and shrugged shoulders, Colby expressed some sympathy with the Navy's point. He asked how many Marines the ship could carry. None, Parangosky replied. There was no room for more personnel, and you can't very well hide Marines, or their arms, in a ship that was supposed to be commercial.

Colby accepted that explanation, but then thought more about it and called Parangosky back to say that he still thought the *Explorer* should carry a platoon of Marines. Azorian's chief explained—again, as calmly as possible—that this was a bad idea for the same reasons he'd stated before. It was a clear signal that the *Explorer* wasn't a mining ship. But he agreed at least to tell the ship's security team to reverse course and stow away some guns.

Not that this was simple, either. There was no time to use official channels to requisition guns from the Navy or the CIA, not without creating attention. If the ship's security crew was going to bring guns, they'd have to go rogue and buy them from stores. Brent Savage, being a former cop, offered to take care of it. He and two other officers went out and bought eight guns—a collection of shotguns and rifles selected because even the firearms required a cover story. If the *Explorer* was ever to be boarded and the security team overrun, they'd need a way to explain the fact that a commercial ship was carrying arms. The rifles, they were told to say, had been brought aboard to shoot flying fish and birds from the deck, for fun, while the shotguns were for skeet shooting. To bolster that explanation, Savage bought a launcher and a large supply of clay pigeons and stashed the whole arsenal in a crate under Dave Sharp's bunk.

Soviet submarine K-129, in an undated photograph.
COURTESY OF NIKOLAI CHERKASHIN

The crew of the K-129, in an undated photograph.
COURTESY OF NIKOLAI CHERKASHIN

The K-129's Ukrainian captain, Vladimir Kobzar, on the bridge of the sub in port.
COURTESY OF NIKOLAI CHERKASHIN

Alexander Zhuravin,
the K-129's second-in-command.

One of the few known
photographs of John
Parangosky, taken at a
base in Iran during his
time on the U-2 program.

R. F. BAUER, Chairman of the Board, was graduated (BSPE) from the University of Southern California in 1942 but previously had worked for a number of years as a drilling crew roughneck. Following his graduation, he joined Union Oil Company as a research engineer and served successively in technical, supervisory and administrative capacities. In 1953 he became manager of offshore operations for the CUSS Group, administering all phases of the work until formation of Global Marine in 1959.

A. J. FIELD, President, received his Master's Degree from Stanford University (BSCE, MSCE) following completion of undergraduate work at Cal Tech. During World War II he served as a supervisor in waterfront construction with the Seabees in the Pacific. In 1947 he joined Union Oil Company as a roustabout and subsequently was assigned to various supervisory and engineering positions in the Company. In 1953 he joined the offshore group where he assumed responsibilities for petroleum engineering programs and economics until formation of Global Marine in 1959.

R. C. CROOKE, Vice President — Engineering and Construction, graduated in 1949 from the University of California with a BS in Mechanical Engineering, specializing in fluid mechanics and hydrodynamics. He worked for the University for four years on special wave and ship motion projects, then joined a consulting firm, as oceanographer and development engineer, which was retained by the CUSS Group for developing offshore drilling techniques. He also has been consulted as an independent oceanographer. He was one of the founders of Global Marine in 1959.

The men who were running Global Marine at the time that Project Azorian
was born, from a company marketing brochure.

John Parangosky, in a photograph of unknown origin, supposedly taken the year the Azorian program began.
COURTESY OF CHRIS POCOCK

John Graham, the *Glomar Explorer*'s chief architect, meeting with his staff.
COURTESY OF JOHN AND JENNY PARSONS

Manfred Krutein, the program's "mining engineer" and a key figure in the cover story, on deck of the *Explorer,* off Hawaii, 1974.
COURTESY OF WEHRNER KRUTEIN

Some of the *Glomar Explorer* crew on the deck. Top row, left to right: Jim McNary, Charlie Johnson, Sherm Wetmore, Don Borchardt, John Parsons. Kneeling, left to right: Randy Michaelsen, Bob Cooper, John Hicks, John Owen.

The deep-ocean mining cover crew in a publicity photograph prior to the sailing of the *Sea Scope*. Clockwise from top left: Manfred Krutein, Paul Reeve, Lockheed's Connie Welling, George Sherry, and Dave Pasho.

Mission geologist Dave Pasho hoses down manganese nodules recovered on the faux mining voyage of the *Sea Scope*.

The *Hughes Glomar Explorer* hull is launched in November 1972.
COURTESY OF CHUCK CANNON

The patch affixed to the blue denim uniform worn by *Glomar Explorer* crewmen.
COURTESY OF DAVE PASHO

The *Hughes Mining Barge*, or *HMB-1*, anchored at Lockheed's base in Redwood City, south of San Francisco International Airport.
COPYRIGHT NORTON PEARL PHOTOGRAPHY/SAN MATEO HISTORICAL ASSOCIATION

An illustration and timeline of the pipe string, drawn by Sherman Wetmore while on station during the mission.

Chuck Cannon on the *HGE*, just after leaving the Strait of Magellan, en route to Long Beach.

The capture vehicle, inside the *HMB-1*, in 1975, after repairs and improvements in preparation for Project Matador.

Program dignitaries at the *HGE*'s launch, in Chester, Pennsylvania. Standing, left to right: Chuck Goedecke (Lockheed), Chester Davis (Summa), Jim LeSage (Summa), Nadine Henley (Summa), Bill Gay (Summa), Paul Reeve (Summa), Clinton Morse (Summa), and Curtis Crooke (Global Marine). Kneeling, left to right: Pat O'Connell (Honeywell) and Dick Abbey (Honeywell). COURTESY OF CURTIS CROOKE

The *Hughes Glomar Explorer*, off the coast of California.
COURTESY OF JOHN AND JENNY PARSONS

Curtis Crooke (bottom left) and executives from Honeywell, Lockheed, and Summa Corporation sign the transfer of ownership papers on the *Explorer*, off the coast of Catalina Island, June 1974.
COURTESY OF CURTIS CROOKE

The cover story was so well planned that it even had a cake to celebrate the "transfer of ownership" from Summa to Global Marine, off the coast of Catalina. COURTESY OF CURTIS CROOKE

An actual manganese nodule recovered with the K-129, photographed at the home of an Azorian veteran.
AUTHOR'S COLLECTION

A newspaper cartoon, drawn by Bill Garner, that appeared in *The Washington Star-News* on March 18, 1975, shortly after Jack Anderson blew the program's cover.
COURTESY OF ZEKE ZELLMER

John Wayne visited the *Explorer* in 1976 when the US government was trying to market it to new, potential customers. Bob Bauer, Global Marine president, is at center; Don White, CIA contractor turned Global Marine employee, is at far right.
COURTESY OF CURTIS CROOKE

46
Waiting, More Waiting

As final preparations were under way in Long Beach, CIA director William Colby began to lobby the national security establishment in Washington for a final, official green light. On May 23, he delivered a memo to Kissinger reasserting the target's "unique intelligence value." Colby did this not just as CIA director, but also as chairman of the US Intelligence Board, which had recently reviewed and updated the operation's projected intelligence bounty.

Colby summarized the board's identification of "five major categories of equipment which are believed to represent the more significant . . . intelligence targets," listed in presumable order of importance:

1. Cryptographic machines and materials

2. Nuclear warheads and related documents, which "would provide important new insight into Soviet nuclear technology, weapon design concepts, and related operational procedures"

3. The SS-N-5 missile, which "although not in itself the major SLBM threat, would provide important information on technologies relevant to the SS-N-6, and possibly to some aspects of the SS-N-8"

4. Navigation and fire control systems, especially "equipment and documentation in the missile fire control category," as well as "instruction books, internal circuit diagrams, spare parts, and

related documentation" that could "add significantly to our technical understanding of the GOLF-II strategic weapon system"

5. Sonar and other naval equipment, though in this case the board
   acknowledged that most sonar and antisubmarine warfare
   equipment would probably be obsolete based on the kinds actually in use by the Soviet Navy in 1974

Two weeks later, on the afternoon of June 5, the 40 Committee met in the
White House Situation Room to discuss Azorian. Parangosky, Duckett, and
Colby all quickly reviewed the state of the operation, telling the committee
that the *Explorer* was ready to go to sea in the small window of opportunity
that was about to open. Kissinger led the meeting, and his primary concern
was the potential for interference from Soviet ships in the target area. He
wanted assurance that he would be alerted immediately if a ship arrived on
the scene, and Duckett told the secretary of state that direct communication
was possible—through encrypted channels and even in the open, as certain
ship-to-shore messages would actually be embedded with code.

"What could go wrong?" Kissinger asked.

Colby and Deputy Defense Secretary William Clements answered this
one simultaneously: "Lots of things." Soviet ships could arrive and intervene. Best case, they would just harass the *Explorer,* causing delays and distractions. Worst case, they could send divers into the water after the
recovery had begun and would see the claw rising through the water with
the sub in its grasp. They could also decide to board the ship without provo-
cation. And then there were operational risks—most prominent among
them the possibility that the recovery itself would fail. It was, after all, one
of the most mechanically complex operations ever mounted by the United
States—and there was no real way to put the systems, working in unison, to
the test until it was time to do it for real.

Clements wanted Kissinger and the rest of the president's closest national
security advisers to consider the project carefully. If it worked, Azorian
would probably be a good thing for the United States. But a "flap," as he
called it, could be a disaster. And no matter how it turned out, Clements
said, there was no chance the United States could keep it all secret for long.

"Don't be so sure of that," Colby replied. The director was confident in his operational security, in the cover story, and in his ability to continue to obfuscate, if necessary. "There are 1,800 people who know about this project and we could tell 1,700 of them that it failed and nothing was accomplished," he said.

As the conversation continued, member support waxed and waned. The more they talked, the more Clements seemed to turn against the operation. He told the room that he had serious doubts about what the United States would gain from a six-year-old submarine and that Dr. Edward Teller, the theoretical physicist who led the creation of the hydrogen bomb and who had served as a key consultant to Azorian on the sub's nuclear weapons, had expressed serious doubts, too. "And he's been up to his eyeballs" in this project, Clements added.

Duckett dismissed the notion that Teller was involved "up to his eyeballs" and that the scientist was against the project. Teller was a consultant, and an important one, but he'd spent a relatively small amount of time actually working on Azorian. He also still supported the effort.

When Clement asked Assistant Secretary of Defense for Intelligence Albert Hall for his opinion on the value of what was sitting down there on the ocean floor, Hall seemed to be in favor of recovering it. He said that as much as Soviet weaponry might have changed since the K-129 sank, the Pentagon still had no idea how Soviet missile systems work, nor had they ever come into possession of an actual intact warhead. Reverse engineering the key components—guidance, telemetry, detonators—would be an enormous boon to US missile defense, and the country's nuclear scientists had a long list of questions that could likely be answered. In particular, the level of uranium enrichment the Soviets were achieving, the isotopic composition of plutonium in their weapons, and especially the control and security features on Soviet missiles—command and control of nuclear weaponry being a problem all designers struggled with.

The biggest skeptic in the room was Joseph Sisco, undersecretary of state for political affairs. Sisco's group would be the ones who had to deal with the fallout of any program exposure, and it would be coming at a particularly terrible time, with arms-reduction talks just beginning. Even if the operation worked, Sisco said, it was going to leak, and that would have real implications for any Cold War thaw.

"Keep in mind that we've been deep into this problem for four years without a leak," Duckett replied.

Kissinger considered that possibility. Did anyone really know how the Soviets would react to a leak? "Won't they say, 'Boys will be boys'?" Kissinger asked. "Or will they say, 'You dirty SOBs'?" His own opinion—informed by the Gary Powers U-2 episode—was that the Soviets wouldn't say much, if anything. They were more likely to view the operation as an intelligence coup that their own military allowed to happen by losing track of the submarine in the first place. Any blowback would be internal.

Opinion in the room seemed to be shifting. When Kissinger asked what the US public reaction to the program's exposure might be, Sisco thought it would be positive. The public was likely to be proud that its government could pull this off. On the other hand, if the project was canceled, and the news came out, the public would want to know why. Huge sums had been spent. What would the answer be?

"Morality," Kissinger answered, and then admitted that this was a problem in itself: The same public would want to know why the United States spent four years and a large amount of money on something it knew from the outset was immoral.

Ultimately, Kissinger said, only one person was in a position to weigh the foreign and domestic political implications, the same person who was going to be asked why the United States was in the covert operations business with Howard Hughes, and why he was willing to risk a direct confrontation with the Soviets over a mission that was morally questionable: the president. And although the committee was ready to recommend going forward with Azorian, Kissinger needed Colby to prepare a memo for Nixon.

As the meeting was breaking up, Kissinger grabbed the CIA director to give him one more order: The ship was to hold off on any recovery effort until after July 3, when the president returned from Moscow.

The late 1960s was a period of runaway acceleration for ballistic missile stockpiles. Realizing they were outgunned, the Soviets began a massive buildup of ICBMs that motivated and alarmed the US leadership. In 1967, Lyndon Johnson told the public that the Soviets had also begun constructing an antiballistic missile (ABM) system around Moscow, which only increased concern at the Pentagon, where military planners understood that a substantial nuclear stockpile plus adequate antimissile defenses by either nation would give that side a decided advantage and that having an advantage was a dangerous position to be in. Peace hinged on détente. Continuing such rapid escalation, Defense Secretary Robert McNamara warned, was "an insane road to follow."

So Johnson proposed the two nations begin Strategic Arms Limitation Talks (SALT), and in 1967 he and his Soviet counterpart, Premier Aleksey Kosygin, met at Glassboro State College in New Jersey, though official negotiations didn't begin until Johnson was out of office. At the prodding of his successor, Richard Nixon, SALT began on November 17, 1969, in Helsinki, Finland, and continued for more than two years, as negotiators from the United States and the Soviet Union haggled over the number of ICBMs, the extent and status of ABM systems, and submarine-launched ballistic missiles (SLBMs).

Finally, on May 26, 1972, Nixon and Soviet general secretary Leonid Brezhnev met in Moscow to sign an interim agreement that, for the first time ever, froze the total number of ballistic missiles at current levels and permitted each side to build only two ABM installations—one around the national capital and another at a single ICBM launch location.

Which wasn't the end, of course. Nixon and Kissinger made détente their Cold War strategy and immediately sought to pursue additional limits on arms, focusing especially on a large ICBM loophole. The SALT I agreement limited only the number of ICBMs, but both countries had developed a missile that could carry multiple independently targeted reentry vehicles (MIRVs)—a single missile that, once in orbit, can deploy multiple nuclear warheads, each steered to a different target site. (The Soviets had developed versions that could carry anywhere from ten to thirty-eight MIRVs on a single missile.) You can imagine why this would be problematic, and the haggling picked up anew on a subsequent round of negotiations, known as SALT II.

This is the background in which Nixon and Kissinger pursued and approved the Azorian mission, which—pending presidential sign-off—would finally depart for the target site while Nixon was in Moscow negotiating arms reduction.

47

Trouble on Romaine Street

JUNE 1974

hortly after midnight on Wednesday, June 5, Michael Davis was wrapping up his regular inspection of the perimeter of 7020 Romaine Street. The block-long two-story Summa Corp. office had once been a key outpost of the Hughes empire, but by 1974 it was little more than a storage facility for records and memorabilia. Davis was a father of six with thinning hair, caterpillar eyebrows, and a salt-and-pepper goatee that made him look significantly older than his thirty-nine years. He worked days selling Corvairs and Camaros at Crossroads Chevrolet in North Hollywood and nights working security for Summa, a quiet, easy job that offered ample opportunity to take naps and chip away at his sleep debt.

There were items of value inside Romaine Street, but its reputation as an impenetrable fortress filled with secret files—"the Bastille," as Summa's executive VP Nadine Henley once called it—was a vast inflation, especially by mid-1974. It was, as the Hughes PR rep Arelo Sederberg later wrote, "a neglected, lonely place—like a worn-out ship hulk moored at an abandoned pier."

Davis was the only guard on duty. He carried no weapon and the electronic burglar alarm system wasn't even working that night, when he unlocked a set of glass doors from the street and was immediately shoved inside and onto the lobby floor by two men whose faces he never saw.

"Be quiet and don't look around," one of them snapped as the other tied a blindfold around Davis' face, duct-taped his mouth and hands, and yanked him back to his feet. The men shoved the guard forward, through a second set of doors to the building's interior. Davis had walked those halls hundreds of times, often in the dark, so even though he could see nothing through the blindfold, he knew exactly where he was when the men stopped—inside the ground-floor office of Kay Glenn, a key aide to Hughes's most trusted lieutenant, Bill Gay, and an administrator of Hughes Aircraft.

The men hadn't asked Davis to direct them to any particular place, and yet they clearly knew how to find Glenn's office, where they ordered Davis to sit. He could tell by the clanking of tools on metal that they were working on a filing cabinet—one, it turns out, that contained a small safe—but he also heard a different, duller clanking sound, as well as the sounds of two more men, whose voices got louder as they approached and stopped across the hall, where the entrance to a large walk-in Mosler vault was located.

There was a hiss, then a pop, as the second pair of intruders began to cut away at the lock of the vault door using an acetylene torch.

Once the two men who'd grabbed Davis were finished in Glenn's office, they led him upstairs, to payroll, then into the office of Lee Murrain, another Summa executive. From there, the burglars went to Henley's office and finally into a large second-floor conference room where stacks of sensitive Hughes files were being sorted and compiled in preparation for the 17-million-dollar slander lawsuit filed against Hughes by his former confidant Robert Maheu. Davis heard the men sifting through papers and conferring on their relative importance.

"These look good!" one exclaimed.

"Let's take those," the other replied.

The burglars seemed to be in no hurry, and over the course of four hours of casual plundering they made stops in nearly every important room of the building before finally taking Davis to the basement, into a large room that served as a warehouse for excess supplies and furniture. Rolls of carpet lay on the floor and Davis tripped several times before he was finally shoved onto a couch. The thieves taped his legs and told him to "stay put." By this time, his blindfold was only half-on, but it was too dark to see much of anything and one of the burglars pulled it down around his neck, seemingly as a courtesy, as they rushed out.

Davis lay there for at least a half hour, until he was certain he could no longer hear footsteps, and then began to kick and struggle with his restraints. The tape on his ankles slipped a little, then a little more, until he had enough space between his legs to stand and hop-slide across the floor, falling several times onto carpet rolls and then flopping back to his feet. He managed to hobble to Kay Glenn's office, knock a phone off the hook, and dial Harry Watson, the company's operator on duty that night. It took two calls, using only muffled sounds he could make through his gag, but Davis managed to relay enough information that Watson called for help.

As Davis sat in Glenn's chair to await the police's arrival, he noticed two pieces of loose paper on the floor—papers that were clearly dropped by the burglars in their haste to loot the room.

The LAPD detectives assigned to the case were perplexed from the onset, and things got weirder two weeks later, on June 17, when a man identifying himself as Chester Brooks called Romaine Street looking for Nadine Henley or Kay Glenn. When the man who answered the phone told the caller that neither of the women was in the building, he replied with a set of bizarre instructions straight out of a spy movie. Either Henley or Glenn should proceed to a park across from Hughes's quasi-secret office on Ventura Boulevard in Encino and look for a white envelope on top of a trash can. Once the envelope had been found, they were to place an ad in the *LA Times* classified with the message "Apex okay" and a phone number, written backward.

An LAPD bomb technician retrieved the envelope and found a typewritten memo to Hughes from one of his underlings about the potential purchase of a Las Vegas hotel company. The memo, which was proven to have come from a typewriter at Romaine Street, showed that whoever Chester Brooks was, he had access to stolen documents.

FBI agents assigned to the case found many things to be fishy. They theorized internally that it could have been an inside job to cover up for Hughes's connections to Watergate, or alleged SEC violations in the mogul's recent purchase of Air West. Stranger still, Davis, the guard, refused to take a polygraph exam and was fired by Summa.

A few weeks later, an unnamed Summa executive notified the FBI that the company had neglected to mention one important thing—that "among the documents stolen was one that related to national security and the CIA."

Steve Clark, acting security chief at the program office, was at his LA apartment the next morning when Bill Gay called to ask if he could come to Summa's offices in Studio City immediately to discuss "something of critical interest." There, Clark was met by Gay and Nadine Henley, who told him about the break-in and explained that this important "something" was a single handwritten memo from Raymond Holliday to Hughes describing the basics of the CIA/Summa ocean-mining operation. She wasn't certain that the document had been among those stolen, but she hadn't seen it in some time, and she knew it had been kept in one of the burglarized safes in the past. She was worried enough that she wanted the CIA to be aware.

Clark briefed Parangosky, who briefed Colby, who made the difficult decision to approach and clear LAPD detectives who were already working on the break-in in conjunction with the FBI.

Two men claiming to be FBI agents flew out from headquarters in Washington to meet with the LAPD. They told detectives working the case that "a national security document" was among the papers stolen and that if it turned up, "they would recognize it and were to forget they'd ever seen it." These agents, who might not even have worked for the FBI—speculation later was that they might have been CIA officers posing as federal agents—stayed in Los Angeles and floated the rumor that there was a 1-million-dollar reward for the return of Hughes's stolen documents.

When two suspects emerged, by stepping forward to offer the documents for sale, the CIA's involvement intensified. It took a direct role in the investigation, an action in violation of its charter, which forbade the Agency from spying on US soil. Unknown officers from within the Agency began working directly with the FBI to set up an elaborate ruse. They would use an LAPD informant to introduce the alleged thieves to a fake attorney (an undercover FBI agent) who claimed to represent an interested buyer. The attorney would examine the documents and would be authorized to "negotiate the buy of individual pieces" if he felt his client would find them useful. The FBI authorized the release of one hundred thousand dollars in "show money" that the agent could use to make a buy if necessary, to bait the thieves and negotiate the return of the most important documents— including the Azorian memo.

The plot unraveled when one of the thieves, a struggling actor and screenwriter, was interviewed by cops and made a series of demands, including total immunity in writing. When the CIA learned that he had an extensive criminal record, the Agency changed its stance and quietly backed away from the case. It also urged that the FBI do the same, explaining that further attention would be harmful to national security.

And that, it seemed, was the end of it.

48

Let's Go Fishing!

Shortly after midnight on June 20, the *Hughes Glomar Explorer* backed away from Pier E and headed to sea under cover of darkness, not because of secrecy but because of the need for a high tide to make sure the giant ship, fully loaded with gear for its mission, wouldn't get hung up in the shallow channels off Long Beach. After more than five years of preparation, and numerous near cancellations, the crew now had only three thousand miles and a week or two of waiting before attempting the most daring intelligence mission in history.

Before the *Explorer* could depart for the target site, though, there was one last task to complete. As soon as the ship had cleared US waters, twelve nautical miles from port, it stopped and waited for the arrival of a large chartered helicopter, which left the program office shortly after dawn and landed on the *Explorer*'s helipad thirty minutes later, disgorging a gaggle of VIPs representing all of the major contractors. The largest group, by far, was from Hughes's Summa Corp. Out popped Bill Gay, Chester Davis, Jim LeSage, and Paul Reeve, as well as Nadine Henley. Chuck Goedecke represented Lockheed, Pat O'Connell and Dick Abbey came for Honeywell, and Curtis Crooke and Dave Toy were there on behalf of Global Marine. Finally, there was the day's host: Walt Lloyd, director of Azorian's Commercial Operations Division, and the event was both an important moment for the cover and a clever fix for a pesky problem that developed while the ship was docked in Long Beach.

For months, Los Angeles County tax assessor Philip Watson had been badgering Global Marine and Summa about the status of the *Hughes Glomar Explorer*. Back on February 24, he'd sent a letter to Summa Corporation's ocean-mining division requesting that the company complete and return a statement about the *Explorer*'s ownership. More than a month later, on March 29, V. C. Olson, VP and controller of Summa, wrote back, stating that the "subject vessel is registered in the state of Delaware, and is not based in California."

Watson wasn't buying it. He had papers that contradicted Olson's reply. Every vessel that arrives in a port has to be registered, and when the *Explorer* pulled into the Port of Long Beach, on October 2, the captain filed documents with the US Coast Guard stating that Summa had sole ownership of the vessel, on a contract to conduct research—documents that Watson had obtained. In his view, this giant ship, owned by one of the country's wealthiest men, was dodging taxes, and it was his responsibility to collect them. He threatened legal action and kept after the matter until Global Marine's project attorney, Dave Toy, finally sought backup. It became Lloyd's responsibility to get Watson off their back.

Lloyd recruited the support of the CIA's general counsel, Larry Houston, and arranged a meeting with Watson in the office of the deputy district attorney for Los Angeles a few days before the *Explorer*'s departure. The plan was to present a formidable show of government force, to show the county tax assessor who he was really dealing with, and to convince him to desist. But when Lloyd, Houston, Toy, and—because nobody went anywhere without a security officer—Paul Evans arrived at the DA's office downtown, Watson wasn't even there; he'd sent his attorney instead. This infuriated Lloyd, who dressed the attorney down, demanding that he pass a message to the tax assessor: The ship was engaged in "government activity" and Watson didn't have any claim.

The lawyer's reaction took them all aback. He asked, rather sheepishly, if they might at least offer some small sum—maybe three thousand dollars— so that Watson could feel as if he'd won something.

This only inflamed the situation. "We represent the federal government and the taxpayers of the United States and the expenditure of their money, and you're asking us to give you something just because you want to feel good!" Lloyd snarled.

What bothered Lloyd more than the meddling of an ambitious local official was the notion that his program was dodging tax regulations. This was a man who took the law, and accountability, very seriously. And it wasn't the first time he'd had to handle a tax problem. Back when Clementine was still under construction, Lockheed notified Parangosky that its local tax collector, in San Mateo County, was agitating about sales tax, too. So Mr. P called Lloyd. "We're having tax problems, Walt," he said. "Figure out what we do."

Lloyd gathered attorneys from all of the major contractors, and after several hours of debate they'd yet to agree on a solution, when one of them mentioned that his company wasn't required to pay taxes on an item shipped out of state. Lloyd perked up. "That's the answer," he said.

It was why, on the day the *Explorer* left Long Beach, the ship paused to receive a helicopter full of dignitaries—to put on a public show for the nation's tax collectors, as well as a photographer who took official photos of the transfer of ownership documents from Global Marine to Hughes Tool.

Had this transfer occurred within US territorial waters, the Agency would have been on the hook for 7 percent sales tax, which is no small number on a ship worth a reported 150 million dollars. Instead, it paid none, and it did so legally—a fact verified by the state tax authority's general counsel, who'd agreed to the plan in advance, when Lloyd and Toy went to see him.

Once the dignitaries had lifted off for their return to the mainland, the crew could finally, after nine months in Long Beach, put this ship and its systems to the test that many in Washington were still convinced would fail. The sky over the Pacific was "leaden," according to one of the CIA officers, but "the crew had spirits that were as bright as polished silver."

The ship's skipper, a former tuna boat captain named Tom Gresham, set a course west-northwest, pointed directly to the target site. With an average speed of eight knots, the trip was expected to take roughly thirteen days, meaning that they should arrive on July 4, a date that stood out to some of the CIA men as an auspicious one—a sign that after so many stumbles and bumbles the actual mission might have good luck. Not that "thoughts of jinxes" were on the minds of the crew, one officer later wrote in his journal. "We could do anything. Let Headquarters give us a last-minute change of targets—with this crew and this beautiful ship, no task was too difficult. Mission impossible? Nonsense! 'Impossible' was not in our vocabulary. Moments like this must contain the true meaning of team spirit, that extra ingredient that hardware will never possess. To experience it once is enough for a career."

On the second day at sea, Mission Director Dale Nielsen called a meeting for all of the CIA officers in the boardroom. The subject: What to do if any Soviet vessels interfered with or even boarded the *Explorer*. According to Nielsen, the options were limited. The first and primary goal for anyone was to stop any Soviets from getting on board. The captain would take whatever evasive action he could take. Fire hoses could be used to fend off men who might try to climb up the side, SEALs could be sent into the sea to meddle with boats or divers, and the security staff had already told any crew who might be nearby to move crates and boxes onto the helicopter pad to prevent any unwelcome choppers from touching down.

If all else failed, and a boarding party managed to get onto the ship, the security staff was to avoid the mistake made by the crew of the USS *Pueblo*. They were to destroy all the classified material immediately. A system was designed to make this emergency process as simple as possible—all classified documents were stored in a single location, in the control center van, in drawers made of steel mesh (except for the few that were hidden in Charlie Canby's fake pipe, which was a secret to most of the crew). If and when the order was given, those drawers would be pulled and dropped into a chute that went straight to the ocean, and once they were in the water, they'd be lost forever, headed three miles down to the bottom.

There was also a plan for the worst-case scenario—if the ship were to be taken by force, like the USS *Pueblo*, and was unable to communicate. Prior to leaving Long Beach, the security staff bought twelve three-gallon buckets of fluorescent green paint and handed them out to certain key crew members, who were instructed to keep them under their bunks. If the ship were to be seized, anyone who was able to get a paint can out of his stateroom should run to the highest point available to him—the helipad, for instance, or the roof of the bridge—and paint a symbol that would then be seen by the next surveillance plane or satellite to fly overhead.

Every day at five P.M., there was a staff meeting, and the holders of the green paint cans were to attend. Honeywell's Hank Van Calcar, the simulator architect, was one of those selected to stash a can, and during the initial days of the mission, he was looking for ways to mess with one particular security staffer, a former Navy officer who took everything way too seriously. At the end of a meeting, the room was opened to questions, and Van Calcar raised his hand. "Does anyone have any more of that green paint?" he said. "That damn bedroom of mine is so dull that I painted the walls to make it more homey and now I'm out."

Everyone in the room laughed, except for the Navy officer.

Even Jack Poirier was amused. The ship's security chief was beloved by the crew, and by the CIA staff who depended on him to protect the mission. He was an "absolutely wonderful guy," said one, who suggested he should be "consecrated" for his work. But with time to kill in the mission's early days, he, too, wasn't above being pranked.

About a week into the trip, some of the crew huddled up and asked a boyish Honeywell computer engineer whom few people knew very well if he'd be willing to participate in a prank. They shaved his beard, cut his hair, put him in a suit and tie, and handed him a suitcase, with instructions to report to the mess hall at lunch and seek out Poirier as if he had just arrived. The young man put on his most naive face and approached Poirier, asking if he was the purser. Poirier stared at the unfamiliar face, appearing suddenly after days at sea, and said yes.

"I'm here for my berthing assignment," the man said. "I just came aboard!"

And if anyone in the room had been able to hold his laughter, Poirier might actually have bought it for a few minutes.

The crew manifest had been set for weeks by the time the *Explorer* sailed, but there were a few last-minute additions. One of the most notable was John Parsons. John Graham's son-in-law was never supposed to go to sea, but he had proven to be such an adept engineer, useful to most any job that required extra hands, that Curtis Crooke recommended to Sherm Wetmore that he go out as a floater on the Global Marine engineering staff. Parsons could keep an eye on the air lines and hydraulic pumps, as well as numerous other pieces of systems that were too small to have been of concern unless the ship was at sea, and the *Explorer* needed someone there to fix them. And Parsons knew every valve on the ship.

Personally, he was conflicted about the mission. The prospect of contributing to an operation unlike anything that had ever been attempted was obviously exciting, but he'd be leaving behind a pregnant wife and a terminally ill mentor and boss who was also his father-in-law.

Shortly before the mission was to set out, Graham asked if he could come over to Parsons' house to have dinner with the family. His doctor, Graham said, had told him that there was nothing more they could do for him. The cancer had reached his brain and he was unlikely to live more than a few months. If he was lucky, he'd be alive to see the *Explorer* complete the mission, but he also might die while it was at sea, and he'd accepted this.

John Parsons and Jenny, however, weren't really ready for that news. They knew Graham was losing his fight with cancer, but they'd stayed hopeful and thought that maybe his intense pride in the *Explorer* could carry him a little longer—at least until the mission's end.

Instead, Parsons left Long Beach knowing that, in all likelihood, he would never see John Graham again, and he wouldn't be there to comfort Jenny if her father died during the mission. This bothered Jenny, with good reason, and she let that be known. But what bothered her more was the possibility, however remote, that this ridiculous ocean-mining trip could drag on long enough that her husband would also miss the birth of his second child. And in that case, she told John, he could just not come home at all, since she'd have made it fine on her own.

Others on the ship felt Graham's absence, too. The man had deeply influenced everyone who worked with him, and his absence caused a small but inescapable dark cloud to hover over the *Explorer* as it sailed out to make history, or at least try. "He was a great man to us," the electrical engineer John Owen explained. "We all appreciated what John led us through. To know that he was vulnerable, as we all are, was just another part of what we had to deal with."

49
Hurry up and Wait

Every man on the *Explorer* had a job to do, and with so many of the systems still works in progress, and only a very small window for the recovery, the crew had virtually no downtime. But when they could steal even a few hours, life was comfortable. A crew of fifteen cooks worked in the mess hall, keeping it provisioned twenty-four hours a day. At any moment, a crew member could stop into the mess and get a good, hot meal—rib eye steaks, lamp chops, burgers, seafood, as well as an array of salads, desserts, and freshly baked bread and pastries. For men who had only a few minutes, lounges around the ship were stocked with fresh fruit, nuts, candy, coffee, tea, and soft drinks. There was even a soft-serve ice cream machine. Two native New Yorkers had arranged for the cooks to buy and hide a large supply of bagels, lox, and cream cheese that they managed to conceal in the depths of the walk-in freezer—for a few days, until someone found the stash and word got out. In no time, it was all gone. The only luxury missing from the *Explorer* was alcohol, which was officially banned from the mission but could be found tucked away in trunks under certain bunks.

The feeling on the boat was egalitarian. Roughnecks ate with deck mates, Navy captains sat with mechanical engineers, and although it was obvious to the regular crewmen who the spies were, there was nothing intimidating about them. The only men on the entire mission who kept themselves separate were the mysterious mutes from the communications van, a quiet bunch of NSA guys who always sat together, at a table in the mess hall's far corner, so that the entire room was in front of them and no one could approach without being seen in advance.

Men worked twelve-hour shifts with no off days, but there were activities for anyone who didn't sleep the entirety of the time he was off. The *Explorer* had a game room, a fitness center, and a TV/movie lounge that had multiple showings a day of current-run movies from a library of nearly seventy titles that included a few pornos, one of which was *Deep Throat,* and even some subtitled foreign films, which the roughnecks hated and jeered. Workers jogged, sunbathed, and even played Frisbee on the helipad, which everyone called "the beach," and built model airplanes purchased from the ship's store, which they'd finish and then launch from atop the derrick, watching the miniature planes soar into the currents high above the deck, then drift away and crash into the surf.

For John Parsons, there was always something to fix or a meeting to attend. He often worked thirty hours straight, stopping to sleep a little only when his body finally developed immunity to the coffee he was guzzling. Parsons liked to walk around and visit the various sections, staffed by a crew that was wildly eccentric in makeup. It was, he thought, a seafaring version of the odd couple, only instead of two mismatched personalities, there were nearly two hundred. Roughnecks hammered on pipes with sledgehammers while Ivy League intel analysts worked on reports and, in the windowless control-room vans at the ship's very back, console operators recruited from the Nevada nuclear test site stared at screens installed to feed in video images with the sole purpose of making these men feel connected to the actual action happening elsewhere on the ship.

To these controllers, ship operations appeared to be easy. They pushed buttons and things happened. It seemed automatic, and they were oblivious to the reality that the *Glomar Explorer,* the world's most technologically advanced ship, was actually a greasy, human-powered machine held together by men who squirted lubricating oil on bearings and used brute force on systems just to keep them running.

One of the daily responsibilities of the security team was to be sure that the bulk of the classified paper generated was destroyed in the ship's shredders. The most sensitive documents went through a specialized shredder that worked so well that the resulting paper scraps were essentially a fine powder of secrets that was dumped overboard after dark. But there was so much paper being generated on a daily basis that the shredders kept jamming, and the security guys realized it was sometimes easier to just rip the paper into tiny pieces by hand and then dispose of it the old-fashioned way—by going to the top deck and making it rain. This process worked well enough, with one exception, when an overtired team working the late shift made the mistake of throwing the paper into the wind instead of with it, resulting in a blizzard of classified confetti that blanketed the deck, and causing the poor security guys to scramble and clear the evidence before Jack Poirier awoke and lost his mind.

Contact with the mainland was limited. To help the crew feel connected to their lives back home, operators in the communications van got regular radio reports and published a daily news sheet, complete with sports scores, that was posted around the ship. This was how the crew learned that White Sox pitcher Steve Busby set an American League record by registering thirty-three consecutive outs, that the government of Ethiopia was overthrown in a military coup, and that a thief in Port Chester, New York, set fire to a bowling alley to cover up a robbery, and the ensuing blaze consumed an adjoining nightclub, killing twenty-four people.

Men were free to move around the ship as they wished, so long as they didn't get in the way of the roughnecks, didn't bother the captain and crew on the bridge, and stayed out of the CIA's communications van, which monitored satellite intelligence, weather reports, and downlinks from the NSA "ears in the sky," which were constantly listening to Soviet ship signals. The communications van was a COMSEC-cleared facility, laden with high-security cryptogear that was used as infrequently as possible, to prevent the risk of Soviets somehow hearing the suspicious chatter of encrypted signals from an alleged commercial mining ship.

When possible, the NSA techs used open commercial code with innocent text embedded inside. Members of the crew, especially those with wives and children, could send very occasional messages back home, and sometimes one of the techs would ask to use that message to relay some code, promising that the recipient would get nearly the same message the crewman had originally intended and would have no idea that it had been modified to hide information. The only way whoever was listening on the other end knew if it was coded or not was by the way the message was labeled. Certain keywords on the header signaled that there was a code inside.

When an encrypted message was necessary, special measures were taken. Back in Philadelphia, the NSA had helped install and disguise a powerful log-periodic antenna on the ship's aft bridge to transmit and receive continuous-wave communications, which sent a signal over obscure frequencies and used gaps in the signals, comparable to the beeps in Morse code, to hide messages that only the person on the other end, who had a key to interpret those gaps, could understand. Encrypted messages had to be extremely brief, so that they were transmitted only for a very short time, and always on some distant, unused area of the spectrum that was never used again.

On July 4, thirteen days after leaving Long Beach, Captain Gresham slowed the engines to just a few knots as the *Explorer* approached the target site, which lay almost exactly at 40 degrees latitude, 180 degrees longitude. The position of the wrecked submarine was, in fact, so close to the International Date Line that there was some discussion on board about which date to use in the ship's log. Since the voyage originated east of the line, it was decided to use that date no matter where the ship was sitting.

The *Explorer* was outfitted with an early satellite navigation system, housed in an enormous box that filled up most of a container, but it was still very primitive and could take a reading only a few times a day, when the satellites passed over. The captain knew the location of the wreck on his maps, and once the ship was positioned over the coordinates he'd been given, he sent a signal to interrogate a transponder that had been left at the wreck site by the *Glomar II*. That transponder had been dormant for more than two years, but it woke up immediately upon being pinged and sent back a reply, which meant that the four onboard hydrophones, one in each corner of the moon pool, could begin communicating with it, too, providing the ship's station-keeping system with the information it needed to center itself.

The sky was lightly overcast, and rain clouds stood off on the horizon, as—at 1:01 P.M.—the first acoustic transponder was lifted by a crane and tossed overboard to begin the process of laying out the long baseline system, a network of sensors that would allow the ship to keep itself on station automatically for the duration of the time it was at the target site. Each transponder was a four-by-four-foot steel box filled with an array of twelve-volt DieHard batteries surrounded with kerosene to keep the box from compressing under pressure. They were designed to sink to the bottom at a specific point, the position of which was checked against a fix from overhead satellite navigation and plotted on a chart. For the rest of the afternoon, the ship inched carefully around the area as five more transponders were dropped into the water in a circular pattern around the target location, fifteen hundred feet from the center point.

The transponders could be pinged every two seconds, but they were so far under the surface that it took each signal three seconds to get down to the bottom and then another three seconds to come back up, so really the ship got a fix on its position every six seconds, often enough for its station-keeping system to keep the *Explorer* virtually still over the target.

For the next day, the heavy-lift crew worked in thick fog to get that system up and running, while the deck cranes lifted a set of beacons off the deck by a crane and dropped them, as delicately as possible, into the sea. These would form a grid around the target that Lockheed controllers would use to position and direct Clementine from three miles above.

Ideally, the sea would have minimal swell during the recovery operation, so the onboard meteorologist suggested that no one rush during preparations, since calmer weather was a few days away. It wasn't until July 8, day four on target, when orders came to start flooding the moon pool until the level of the water inside was equal to the level outside the ship's walls, at which point the heavy steel moon-pool gates would become neutrally buoyant and could be moved easily into the open position. Once the gates opened, the massive docking legs began to lower Clementine from her perch over the moon pool down into the water.

A day later, they paused at one hundred feet to prepare for the undocking—the point at which Clementine's three-legged bridle would be attached to the pipe so that the legs could be released. After that,

Clementine would be hanging from the pipe alone, and the long process of lowering her to the ocean floor could begin.

Some of the most stressful, mentally taxing work on the ship was in the control room. Because there had been no way to test the capture vehicle in advance, there was tremendous pressure on Clementine's operators. Hank Van Calcar had helped solve this problem with his amazing simulator, and during the many days when the ship was heading out to station and getting ready for recovery, the simulator ran nearly all day and night.

Van Calcar was a controls-theory specialist. He had asked the Agency to make a scale model of the wreck using the *Glomar II*'s images, and the resulting model was beautiful—two feet eighteen inches in length, and made of gold. The Honeywell software behind Clementine's controls was shockingly accurate. If an operator wanted to move the CV forward, backward, or to either side, he simply put in a command to, say, move forward six inches, and the thrusters would fire, moving it exactly six inches. And Van Calcar's simulator mimicked that perfectly—so much so, he noted proudly, "that you couldn't tell the difference between the simulator and the actual mission." Which didn't mean it was actually easy to use. The movements required were so precise, and the margin for error so slim, that operators were constantly on edge.

They alternated stints on the simulator and found that the experience was frying their nerves, which meant that it was working. By the time a session had finished, the operator was often drenched in sweat, and after a few rounds, Chuck Guzzetta, the Lockheed engineer in charge of the controls, came over to Van Calcar and said, glumly, "I don't like your trainer."

The simulator, like all of the major systems, ran on the most sophisticated computers available at that time. For the capture vehicle, that meant two redundant Honeywell 316s, each worth twenty-five thousand dollars and carrying sixteen kilobytes of hardwired memory in four thousand eight-bit boards.

Just observing practice was harrowing, and to decompress, Van Calcar liked to go out on deck. He'd never really spent much time at sea, certainly not on a ship as huge as the *Explorer,* and every day he saw something that impressed or terrified him. Once, after dark, he was out in a thick fog when a big storm rolled through. He was standing on the edge of the boat looking one hundred feet down when a gigantic wave went under one side of the ship and came up the other side, right below him. It was so huge that it reached nearly to his eyeballs, and he jumped back in reflex, then watched it disappear off through the fog.

The ship itself was an awesome thing, and it took him some time to get comfortable with the idea that it wasn't going to fall apart out there. When he stood at the back corner of the ship and looked straight out along its edge, he could actually watch the wing walls torque and twist in heavy seas. This was part of the design, he knew, but to watch metal bend was disconcerting. His favorite thing, though, was to climb all the way up to the crown block on top of the derrick and stand there, looking down at Clementine hanging inside the moon pool. The ship could be rolling and pitching, but if he turned his gaze and fixed it on the horizon, the feeling was of absolute stillness. The gimbaled platform and derrick, riding on those enormous bearings, didn't move an inch.

50

Trouble on the Horizon

ife on the trip out was rarely dull. The *Explorer,* according to Electric John Owen, was a "maze of machinery and control systems that needed constant maintenance and observation," and it seemed, according to one Navy officer, like there was a "thrilling experience" every day. The hydraulic system sprang regular leaks, the heavy-lift pumps jammed, the heave-compensation cylinders got dangerously out of sync, and a double section of the pipe string broke loose and was left dangling from the derrick, swinging erratically over the moon pool like a twenty-ton pendulum that could easily crush a man or men. Because the pipe's motion varied according to the ship's rocking motion, it did sometimes slow down, and a crew of roughnecks who'd grabbed steel cables positioned themselves to loop the cables around the loose pipes when they were at just the right place and speed. One of them, an amateur bullfighter, whooped and hollered as they pursued the rogue pipe, yelling that this reminded him of tussling with a bucking bull.

July 9, the twentieth day at sea, brought a host of issues—camera mounts on the docking legs had rusted and had to be replaced by divers; one of Clementine's lights kept failing, unpredictably, which indicated a wiring issue; and a pressure transducer, installed to track the load on each of Clementine's beams, failed. The next day, July 10, the forward well gate came loose and then one of the Lockheed engineers had a mild heart attack, causing the crew to scramble for a replacement who could take over his duties. The men on the ship, Sherm Wetmore liked to say, became comfortable with their failures. They weren't confident that things would always work, but they were very confident that whatever broke could be fixed.

Two days later, on July 12, the weather went south, again. The ship's on-board meteorologist, a retired Naval officer, spotted a prolonged disturbance heading their way in the data from the Fleet Numerical Weather Center back in Monterey. He predicted seventy-two hours of difficult conditions, including heavy rain, dense fog, and sea swells up to twelve feet. None of this was beyond the limits for undocking and lowering Clementine, but the high end of that prediction would create serious roll and make the whole process more difficult than it already was. Charlie Canby didn't like it.

For the next twenty-four hours, the crew ran further tests and prepared for undocking while the sea outside pounded the ship. The constant heaving created giant waves inside the moon pool, waves that slammed into the well walls and the docking legs, causing spray that reached the catwalks above. It was, as a mate wrote in the ship's log, "a maelstrom in the docking well"—easily the worst conditions inside the ship's most vulnerable section since the moon-pool gates failed back in California.

Late in the afternoon of July 13, the seas began to settle, and a distress call arrived over the radio on VHF channel 16. The M/V *Bel Hudson,* a British cargo ship bound for Seattle, was seeking immediate assistance because of a sick crewman. The ship's mess officer, who had a recent history of cardiac disease, was reporting severe chest pain and "felt that he had had another attack," according to his mates. The *Bel Hudson*'s medic wanted to know if the *Explorer*—the only ship within hundreds of miles—had a doctor on board.

The *Bel Hudson* didn't. She had only a medic, who had stabilized the crewman according to orders given by a doctor over the radio. He had given the man a dose of the coronary vasodilator Peritrate to help ease constriction, as well as an ounce of whiskey for good measure, but the man's condition wasn't improving. It actually seemed to be worsening. The man was reporting "severe constrictive pains" in his chest and could barely move.

A ship at sea is bound by maritime law to help another in distress, so Captain Gresham felt compelled to assist, and Nielsen agreed. Jack Poirier, though, was worried. This wasn't a total surprise. One of many contingencies that Paul Evans had gone over with the team before it left Long Beach was that a foreign vessel could exploit maritime courtesy and pretend to have a passenger emergency to get some agents inside the *Explorer*. But it was most important to maintain the cover, and a mining ship would not deny assistance to a sick sailor. Poirier and his staff understood this. They ordered a sweep of the ship to clear any sensitive materials that might be in plain view, closed access to the ship's more secure compartments, and asked the crew to go about business as normal.

Early the next morning, Poirier and Nielsen convened an urgent meeting with the ship's doctor, James Borden, to discuss how they might handle their reaction. A short visit wasn't a big concern; it wasn't that difficult to get a man onto the ship and into the hospital without his getting anywhere near the moon pool, nor would it seem suspicious to avoid that area. But what if the man's condition slipped to a point where he had to stay under medical supervision? A permanent stowaway was definitely not something the security team could or would risk.

As a first step, the *Glomar Explorer* offered to send over a medical team. So the *Bel Hudson*—which had stopped about one-third of a nautical mile off the port side of the *Explorer*—dropped a lifeboat into the water and picked up Borden, a medical technician, and Poirier, who was introduced as an "administrative officer."

By the time the men had reached the British ship, the patient had deteriorated into a state of "semi-delirium." Borden checked his vitals, took his blood pressure, and determined that the seaman wasn't in cardiac failure. He was clearly in distress, however, and Borden couldn't say for sure what was wrong with him. He decided that to be safe the man needed to be transferred back to the *Glomar Explorer* for further testing, including a chest X-ray, and observation.

This was easier said than done. The patient was in no shape to move very far, and the weather had worsened, kicking up into a squall. It took the group of them to load the man into the lifeboat, and as the deck crew lowered it into the water, the *Bel Hudson* rolled and bucked.

It was even worse on the other end. Borden and his men had climbed down a rope ladder to reach the skiff, but the patient was far too weak to ascend a rope ladder. The only way to get him up to the *Glomar*'s deck, seventy-five feet above, was to strap him into a stretcher and use a deck crane, typically used for loading cargo and heavy equipment, to lift it. Massive loads are what the crane's operator was accustomed to feeling on the other end, and a man on a stretcher felt practically weightless in comparison, so it would have been difficult enough for the operator to make a gentle lift under ideal circumstances. But with the seas churning, the stretcher bounced several times off the ship's side as it ascended and finally reached the deck, where the crane operator deposited the litter with a thud. If the man hadn't been feeling terrible before, he was then.

Borden wheeled the patient to the hospital on a gurney, with the *Bel Hudson*'s second mate following behind with Poirier. He was given a chest X-ray, and as soon as Borden slipped the print onto the wall-mounted illuminator, he recognized the problem: This wasn't a cardiac condition at all; the man had three broken ribs.

"How did you get broken ribs?" he asked.

The man stared back, perplexed. He had no idea. He had just woken up in horrible pain, and considering his history, the medic assumed it was a heart attack.

Poirier looked at the second mate. Did he have any idea what happened?

Well, the mate replied, there was something. He, the captain, and the mess officer had been drinking heavily in the wee hours with "some girls" when the other two men got into an argument. Recognizing trouble, he rushed the girls out of the room, he said, and didn't see what happened next. He found the mess officer "out cold" on the deck in the morning, and when the man woke up, he immediately clutched his chest and groaned with pain. Most likely, either the captain broke the man's ribs in the fight, or he stumbled out of the room and fell, breaking them that way.

Broken ribs hurt—a lot—but the man's health was clearly not perilous, so Poirier wanted him off the *Glomar* and back on the *Bel Hudson* as quickly as possible.

Dr. Borden wrapped the patient's chest in tape, doubling up around the sixth rib, where the worst break was, gave him Xylocaine and codeine for the pain, then sent him back to the top deck, where the man saw the stretcher being prepped to lower him back to the lifeboat and experienced a sudden renewal of vigor. He felt fine, he said, to climb down himself. By five fifteen P.M., the lifeboat was back, with a box of Scotch whiskey on board as thanks, and the *Bel Hudson* sailed off toward Seattle, with a batch of the *Explorer*'s mail in the hold. That night, every man on the crew got a single finger of whiskey as he arrived for dinner, poured by Poirier.

And then it was back to work. Preparations for the salvage could begin again.

51
Here Comes Trouble

lementine's trip to the bottom and back should have taken two days. It took two weeks. The problems were frequent and many, and the engineers assigned to the pipe-handling and heavy-lift systems ran from one fix to another, as the mission command group watched the days tick away while worrying about the constant threat of Soviet ships on the horizon.

Weather, though, was the biggest issue. Sea swells reached thirteen feet, which was more than the ship's systems were designed to handle, so for days on end, the mission froze, with Clementine dangling one hundred feet under the ship at the end of the pipe string, where it, too, was battered. Every day, the divers would be sent into the water to fix something—a light, a camera, a weld—and the work was so frequent that three of the four underwater welding torches broke.

On July 15, day twenty-six, the weather calmed, but only temporarily, as Tropical Storm Harriet spun up a few hundred miles away. The crew used this break to pull Clementine back into the well, so that they could more easily do repairs to both the claw and the docking legs.

The ship's log was filled with a litany of malfunctions, cracks, leaks, and "abnormal operational inconsistencies," not to mention fog, mist, rain, and wind. Nonetheless, by the morning of July 18, day twenty-nine of the mission, the crew had welded, patched, and jerry-rigged the various faulty parts to a point at which the mission director felt confident enough to proceed. Better yet, the weather was improving. After days of heavy seas, driven by distant storms, the ocean calmed and on the eighteenth the onboard fore-caster predicted calm seas and the imminent arrival of a high-pressure system that would keep conditions mild for at least a few days. "We should expect some stable good weather!" Sherm Wetmore scrawled in the heavy-lift log. The plan was to be ready to begin flooding the well at midnight that night.

There was just one small hitch: At 9:06 A.M., the *Explorer*'s radar picked up an "unidentified vessel continuously maintaining station" one and a half to two and a half miles out. There was no way to make a visual identification through the fog, but the ship appeared to be circling, and it made no attempt at contact. This was unnerving activity, not at all normal for a ship.

Nielsen told the crew to maintain radio silence while continuing with preparations for the undocking, later that afternoon. Around three thirty, the fog lifted, and there the ship was—not even a half mile off the *Explorer*'s starboard side. The vessel was white with no obvious markings or flags, but it had a spiky Mohawk of antennas that looked to naval analysts like the kind used for missile tracking. There was also a helicopter on a pad near its stern. Nielsen reported the sighting back to the mainland over the secure channel and was told that this was probably the *Chazhma,* a 459-foot-long Soviet "missile range instrumentation ship."

The *Chazhma* had been observed by the Pacific Command departing its home port, Petropavlovsk, on June 15, to support a Soviet *Soyuz* space launch and had just begun her return to Russia when, it seemed, she was diverted to check on the *Explorer.*

The arrival of a Soviet ship, even one without armaments, was ominous, and the helicopter in particular worried Jack Poirier, who asked his men to move more canvas-covered crates to the helipad, in case the ship decided to send over a recon mission. This was wise. At 3:42 P.M., twelve minutes after the fog lifted, the helicopter took off, turned, and flew directly toward the *Explorer.* As it approached and buzzed the deck the first time, the ship's provenance was confirmed by a large red star on the chopper's tail. The helicopter swung around and came back, then circled the *Explorer* for at least ten minutes, as a man sitting inside the open passenger-side door snapped photographs with a binocular camera. From the deck of the

Explorer, security officers dressed as crew fired back, taking numerous photos of the photographer.

At first, the crewmen who'd run to the deck to see the ship and helicopter were passive, even startled, but the more passes the chopper made, the more emboldened they grew. They shouted, jeered, flipped the bird, and even mooned the helicopter. Some of the roughnecks were especially angry and were loudly discussing how easy it would be to throw a steel wire over the chopper's rotors to bring it down when a security officer ordered them to shut up.

Then, having apparently exhausted the film, the pilot turned back toward the *Chazhma.* The act wasn't overtly provocative, but it was concerning to both Poirier and Nielsen, as well as Parangosky and everyone else back in Virginia. Nielsen told Poirier to stay vigilant and to have the officer in charge prepare to dump the classified documents if the *Chazhma* were to put skiffs in the water to attempt a boarding.

At four thirty P.M., less than an hour after the chopper flight, the *Chazhma* made its first attempt at contact, activating a blinking light that no one could decipher through the patchy fog. When that signal went unanswered, the *Chazhma* moved five hundred yards off the *Explorer's* stern and signaled that it would attempt to communicate using flags, the universal basic code of seamen. The *Explorer* signaled back that it understood, and stayed put while the *Chazhma* moved again, this time crossing the bow and announcing, in Russian, over the radio, that it was going to launch the helicopter. Once again, the chopper lifted off and circled, as a man with a large camera photographed the ship from all angles a second time. This time, the helicopter flew around and above the *Explorer* for thirty minutes, and Nielsen ordered his men to stay quiet and to keep their pants on, since even a joke had the potential of escalating a tenuous situation.

After several hours of failed communications, the *Chazhma* managed to locate a channel that reached the *Explorer* and the two ships began an awkward interaction in Russian. The Soviet ship announced itself as the "*UGMT*" and said that it was ready to receive the *HGE's* message.

"We have no message," Nielsen told his radio operator to reply. "Understand you have a message for us."

This was met with silence and then a message: "Stand by five minutes," followed by, "We were on our way home and heard your fog horn. What are you doing here?"

Nielsen, Poirier, and the rest of the mission control team all had the same thought at once: There was no way the *Chazhma* had come here because it heard a fog horn. The ship had been well out of range. Rather, it seemed to have set a very specific course to intercept the *Explorer,* here.

Nielsen decided to play it out. "We are conducting ocean-mining tests," he told the Soviets, who then asked what kind of vessel this was. "A deep-ocean mining vessel," he said, and, when the Soviets asked what kind of equipment was aboard, replied that it was "experimental deep-ocean-mining equipment."

"How long do you expect to be here?"

"We expect to finish testing in two to three weeks."

On the deck, nerves settled. Nothing about the conversation seemed unusual. The Soviets appeared to be accepting the story. A short while later, they called over one last time. "I wish you the best," the *Chazhma* said, and then, at nine P.M., turned and sailed toward the Russian coast.

As deputy chief of naval intelligence for underwater espionage at fleet headquarters in Petropavlovsk, Rear Admiral Anatoliy Shtyrov's job was to track and study the behavior of US vessels, military or commercial, and he tended to view any unusual activity as suspicious. Shtyrov had first noticed the *Glomar II* in the area of 40 degrees latitude, 180 degrees longitude in 1970—an area the Soviets referred to as Location K—and had made note of this to his superiors, only to be told not to worry. But he would later claim that American ships in the area could be involved in something that was occasionally whispered about in naval intelligence circles—a secret salvage of the K-129, which the Soviets called PL-574.

When another large "special" ship appeared at Location K in 1974, Shtyrov surveyed the Soviet naval options in the region and noticed that the telemetry vessel *Chazhma* was en route to Kamchatka from the South Pacific, after assisting in a space launch. He convinced the Pacific Fleet chief of staff to wire orders to the *Chazhma*'s commanding officer, a close friend of the K-129's former CO, Vladimir Kobzar: "Proceed to location and follow the US vessel *Explorer* to determine its activities." Shtyrov sent a second encrypted message to Captain Krasnov saying that he suspected the *Explorer* could be a military or espionage mission posing as a commercial vessel, but after extensive close-up observation for ten days, Krasnov sent word back that he believed the *Explorer* to be what she claimed to be: a drill-ship. Shtyrov radioed the ship, using a secure link, and pumped the captain for information. "He confirmed that all signs were that the Americans were looking for oil. A week later he implored: stores on his vessel were giving out!" With only enough fuel remaining to get home, the captain then turned and headed back to the Motherland.

52

Action All Over

The locus of operations during the recovery phase would be the control center, a series of connected vans located in the aft deckhouse. Anyone who worked on the various systems relating to the capture vehicle, as well as the mission director and his chiefs, would need to live in the control center for the duration of the recovery.

Once Dale Nielsen gave the order to begin the recovery mission, Captain Gresham would no longer be in charge; the men in this van assumed full control of the ship. If a catastrophe were to occur during the operation, it was likely to be noticed in the control van first. At that point, there might not be time for the bridge to react.

There were six operators in total, assigned to every specific function—video, control console, acoustic systems, and the capture vehicle operations—and these were the same men who'd designed them and knew them best.

Accurate signals from the bottom were critical, and as the guy who designed the telemetry cables at Hiller Helicopter and helped wire the whole system up, Ray Feldman spent his every waking hour in the control room, too, crawling around on the floor behind the consoles patching wires. On a ship with redundant systems in nearly every area, Feldman somehow had no backup himself. He was the only person who could maintain the link, so even though he had no direct role in the recovery operation, he was aware of every highlight and hiccup.

The control room wasn't the only key location on the ship during the recovery. Down in a small, claustrophobic box built into the ship's port wing wall, right at the waterline, was the heavy-lift control console. The story passed around by some of the contractors was that Graham put the controls at the ship's most vulnerable point because he didn't trust the pipe string, and if anything was going to sink his ship, it would be the steel umbilical. Graham wanted the guys controlling that string to feel the pressure, literally, by putting them into a part of the ship where the steel plates were under so much stress that they literally hummed. In reality, he'd put it there because it was the closest place to the gimbaled platform, creating the shortest run for all the cables from the console to the platform. Regardless, it was a hairy spot and the four operators—who worked rotating, twelve-hour, two-man shifts—felt the ocean's power, and the ship's relative fragility, on a second-by-second basis.

And then there was the pipe handling. Of all the things that gave the ship's engineers fits, none was more consistently frustrating. The process of moving one sixty-foot double section of pipe every 3.3 minutes from the storage hold to the rig floor one hundred feet over the deck was one of the most intricate and complicated on the ship, involving six different machines, all of which could—and at some point did—have problems.

53

Meanwhile, Back at LAX

While the ship was on station, the skeleton staff back in LA held a roundtable meeting at the program office to discuss what to do with items recovered from the sub that would be kept and brought back to the mainland for further study. In meetings of this kind, anyone was welcome to contribute, and the security staff would, as part of the process, poke and prod any valid idea for potential flaws. The general sentiment was that the items would be crated and off-loaded in Hawaii, then flown back to an undisclosed location in a chartered DC-10.

Brent Savage didn't like that idea. It was too easy to foil. If the Soviets had any suspicions at all about the *Explorer,* they could track the ship back to Hawaii, follow those loads, and then raise an alarm. The easiest way to do that, Savage said, would be to sprinkle some kind of radioactive particles around the crates or the plane and then call in a nuclear scare, which would start a huge commotion that would make secretly transferring the materials impossible. "Boy, would that raise hell," he said.

The safer idea, Savage suggested, was to box up everything from the sub worth keeping on the ship and take it back to Long Beach that way.

This discussion got CIA electrical specialist Don White thinking. Like any opportunistic contractor, White was already planning what he might do next, when the program was closed, and one afternoon he called his old friend and associate Wayne Pendleton into his office to discuss an idea he had. As far as the program staff knew, there was still no plan for where to take the materials recovered from the sub that required further analysis. I have the perfect solution, White told Pendleton. We used to work there: Area 51.

It was remote, secret, and extremely dry, an important feature when you're working on decaying materials that had spent a long time in water. Pendleton agreed that it was a good idea and went off to work on a pitch that White could deliver to Crooke. He was working on that when Steve Schoenbaum, another of the security guys, stopped by and asked what he was up to.

As soon as Schoenbaum heard the explanation, he stopped Pendleton. "No, you're not going to work on that," he said. "Come with me." He led Pendleton to White's office and asked if he had actually authorized this work, as described. "Is this really what he's doing?"

"Yep," White replied. "That's what he's doing."

"Well, he isn't going to be doing it anymore," Schoenbaum said. "We've got that covered. We don't want anybody else involved. So, forget it. Don't even think about it."

"Shit," White told Pendleton, once Schoenbaum was gone. "We lost a job there."

As an alternative, they were asked to help with other things. And Pendleton got a tedious assignment that felt a little like a punishment. Brent Savage came to his desk with reels of video footage taken mostly at the pier in Long Beach, but also some from Chester and Redwood City. They needed someone to go through every frame in more than forty thousand feet of film and "cut out anybody who couldn't be seen"—anyone who might be sight sensitive—using a hand slicer. "You know all these guys, so you're the natural person to do this," Savage said, and patted him on the back. It took Pendleton weeks to finish the job.

Dave Pasho, who'd been hired specifically to provide science in support of the cover story, had literally nothing of immediate relevance to the mission to do. He had taken the opportunity to work on actual mining concepts, in the hopes that Global Marine might decide to pursue this business for real later, when the security guys assigned him a job, too. Being young and single with no family to go home to, Pasho volunteered to be the night-duty officer, responsible for all communications from the ship after normal working hours. Pasho would sleep through lunch, then come into the office around six P.M., as everyone was leaving for the day, to sit by the radio and await telex messages that arrived via the communications officer inside the small, secure "box" that held the sensitive communications gear.

Once the mission was under way, the secret Harvey door was left open after dark so that Pasho had access to the box. Security officers briefed him on how to interpret messages passed from the communications officer and showed him what they called "the book," the three-ring binder filled with bad scenarios that might occur on the *Explorer,* as well as precise instructions on how to react.

"The book" was like an instruction manual for crises of varying severity, from some kind of industrial accident to a military encounter that could spark the third world war. Pasho was to sit and wait and hope that nothing of concern happened. If it did, though, he'd have to react quickly. If a message came through the radio officer that said, "Soviet ship moving to harassment pose. Divers going into water," Pasho would flip to the section of "the book" devoted to this scenario and react accordingly. In most cases, he was to call for immediate help from security. If the situation was truly dire—for instance, if a message said, "We are being boarded"—he would have no time to recruit help. In that case, he was to pick up the Donald Duck phone in the CIA's communication box and get word to the highest levels of government. "At that point," Pasho later observed, "I'm on the phone with Henry Kissinger."

Pasho and the engineers were also supposed to be available to listen for and help solve any technical problems that might arise. Log reports from the ship arrived often, with every new development. They were printed out on computer pages and tacked up in a long hallway so that anyone who came in, or was curious, could view the operational details in sequence—or go straight to a particular moment.

The office also kept tabs on John Graham's health. The *Explorer's* chief architect had officially left the program, but he remained a kind of guardian angel, as well as a giant brain on reserve should some engineering crisis arise during the recovery. His condition, however, kept deteriorating.

On July 19, Nell Graham drove her husband to Hoag Memorial Hospital in Los Angeles and had him admitted, but not without unusual security precautions. Doctors were searched and then observed anytime they came to treat Graham, and under no circumstances was his room to be unobserved. The Agency's paranoid fear was that Graham would be put under anesthesia or would become delirious—in either case, making him a risk for accidentally exposing program secrets. A security man, ostensibly working for Howard Hughes, was stationed outside the room at all times and would come in whenever a nurse, doctor, or visitor entered, unless that visitor was Nell, who made it clear that the mysterious guards were unwelcome in her presence.

Those who were closest to Graham, including his top architects, filed in over the final week of his life. He was barely alert the last time Chuck Cannon went to see him, but even near death, with his wife and loyal secretary, Laura, both at his bedside, Graham was thinking about the *Explorer*. "You gotta go make sure that those damn Enterprise diesels on the ship are doing alright," he told Cannon. The ship didn't actually have Enterprise diesels. It had Nordberg engines. Graham was delirious, but only in the specifics. What he was worrying about there, in his dying days, was the ship.

54

The Breaking Point

More than a month after leaving Long Beach, Clementine was back in the water, with her bridle on, attached to the pipe string. The crew was ready to begin the undocking at last. Just after midnight on July 21, the procedure began. The weather was calm and the sea as flat as it had been in days, but a pesky four-foot swell was rocking the ship from side to side. The *Explorer*'s ocean scientists, who were monitoring the wave-rider buoys, conferred with mission control and determined when the swells were farthest apart, so that the undocking could begin.

Conditions weren't ideal, but with a month gone and more severe weather on the way, this was as good as it was going to get. It was clear to everyone on board by this point that there was never going to be a perfect moment.

The first two sections of pipe to go down weren't attached correctly and had to be raised back above the waterline so that the fittings could be checked. That was an easy fix, and the process was just beginning again when a new signal appeared on the radar.

The blip showed up at around seven A.M., several miles out. Time was too valuable now to stop operations when they were going well, even with a suspicious ship approaching, so Nielsen ordered the pipe handlers to continue.

The process of retrieving, moving, and attaching pipe was a sight to behold, a complicated ballet of automated equipment working in coordination with skillful humans. Each sixty-foot double was pulled out of storage by a crane and put on conveyors that carried it to the top of the derrick, where another crane grabbed it and dangled it over the top of the attached pipe sections. There, a giant wrench applied two and a half turns to reach maximum torque. Down below, in the water, divers worked in shifts inside a cage, tying the two electromechanical cables to the pipe by hand, after several efforts to automate the process failed in Long Beach.

At virtually any moment, some piece of equipment was under repair, and nearly every engineer on the ship was working twenty-four-hour shifts by this point just to keep the schedule from falling further behind. Meanwhile, an inspection team led by Harry Jackson roamed the ship in search of larger structural issues—the kinds of things that could wreck the mission, or even worse, sink the ship—and when Jackson spotted something, resident architect Charlie Canby and the captain would be informed.

On the positive side, the mystery ship got within two miles but changed direction and grew more distant, then dropped off radar altogether. It seemed to be gone, until a man on lookout called out at eleven fifteen P.M. that he spotted the lights of a vessel—no more than two miles away.

Still, operations continued. Clementine, by now, was more than three thousand feet down, so there was little risk of a visiting ship seeing anything suspicious. Even if a ship were to send divers into the water, all they'd see was a heavy pipe string vanishing into the abyss—looking exactly like the tether of a mining vehicle on its way down to scoop up manganese nodules.

Which was good, because the approaching ship was no longer being coy. At midmorning, it set a course directly for the target site and just before eleven A.M. got within a few hundred feet of the *Explorer*'s starboard side, at which point it pivoted and began to circle.

This was a tiny ship relative to the *Explorer*—a 155-foot tug identified by the eyes and ears in the sky as the SB-10, an allegedly civilian salvage vessel of a type widely used by the Soviets as undercover intelligence ships. Often, these tugs accompanied submarines on patrol and carried divers.

Communication between the *Explorer* and the mainland was limited, and there was no way to safely connect the ship to Naval Intelligence in the Pacific, meaning that, save for the occasional encrypted cable from headquarters, the *Explorer*'s command was in the dark about the history and movement of Soviet vessels. What they didn't know was that the Navy was paying close attention. Bobby Ray Inman, a rear admiral and a rising star in naval intelligence, had been dispatched to Hawaii to oversee a small surveillance group that watched for any sign that the ship's true purpose had been detected. Inman had analysts inspecting radar and satellite feeds, linked in to the NSA's communications intercepts, but mostly what they did was observe the open movement of merchant marine vessels that could be Soviet Navy ships in disguise.

They'd seen the SB-10 coming and were fairly certain its arrival was just coincidence. Which didn't make the situation any less tense in Langley, in Hawaii, and especially on board the *Explorer*.

The SB-10 was close, so close that anyone on the *Explorer* could see an unknown number of crew in "fatigue-type outfits," as well as shorts and, in some cases, swimsuits. There was at least one woman on the tug, too—the first female anyone had seen in a month, woo-hoo—and several sailors emerged from the tug and took photos, making no effort to hide what they were doing.

Having observed the *Explorer* from all sides, the SB-10 backed off and sailed three miles out, where it took a position off the ship's stern, which seemed perplexing until someone noticed the current. It flowed that way, so that when anything was thrown overboard from the *Explorer*, it naturally carried in that direction. The Soviets were stealing the trash.

Ships outside of coastal boundaries disposed of their garbage by throwing it into the sea in plastic bags that eventually ripped, filled with water, and sank. The CIA was aware of this in advance, and nothing classified or even remotely sensitive went overboard. Those documents were shredded. So mostly what the Soviets were finding was useless junk. The trash had no intelligence value. But it was useful as a prank. The next day the trash went out with every item, including a few well-thumbed *Playboys* as a special gift, covered in a thick slime of Aqua Lube, a green grease used for lubricating pipe joints that is designed for use in deep-ocean environments. It is detergent- and solvent-resistant and is famous for its ability to ruin clothes and stay on skin for days, even after vigorous washing.

To make sure the Soviets didn't miss a single bag of slimy mail, the crew began to pump acetylene gas into the bags. This made them extra-buoyant, so much so that they'd skip across the waves when thrown overboard, often causing the SB-10 to change course and chase them.

Still, the mere presence of this second Soviet ship further stressed nerves that were already fraying, even if much of the crew was too frantic to actually worry much. Within hours of the SB-10's close pass, the heave-compensator cylinders sprang a serious leak that caused the immediate suspension of activity, as Western Gear's crew ran to suss out and solve the problem. This was potentially quite serious. The heave compensators were critical to keeping the platform isolated from the ship's up-and-down motion, allowing Clementine to stay in position relative to the sea bottom rather than following the motion of the ship in the swells. If the platform were to lose its stability, the pipe could bend, and that was something it wasn't designed to do. Too much tension, and it would snap—causing some portion to spring back up toward the surface violently, perhaps with enough force to sink the ship.

At the advice of Captain Gresham, Dale Nielsen ordered all nonessential personnel to evacuate the moon-pool and well-wall sections until the leak could be fixed, which it was in remarkably short order.

By Thursday morning, more than ten thousand feet of pipe had been laid, meaning that two-thirds of the trip was finished. The Soviet tug, however, was increasingly an issue. The SB-10 had assumed an erratic schedule of basic harassment, sailing in close to the *Explorer* and then veering away, or pulling within one hundred feet and holding course, so close that any sudden movements by either ship could cause a collision. However, the crewmen who weren't on duty grew less worried and more entertained by the tug, which looked tiny in comparison to their floating behemoth.

Poirier and his security team were less amused. The tug was too small to pose much of a takeover risk, but the SB-10's captain was being unnecessarily risky with the tug's maneuvers—behavior that seemed to grow bolder by the day. Fog made the tug's erratic actions even more troubling. John Owen was in and out of the radio room helping the NSA techs with electronic problems, and he happened to be there when a fogbank circling the

Explorer caused the tug to vanish completely from view. The radar operator could see it, though, and announced with some concern in his voice that the boat had turned again and was approaching the *Explorer* at high speed, as if to ram the side. Everyone stopped to stare at the console as the tug raced forward and then, just as it broke through the fog ring, slowed and cut its engines.

What most of the *Explorer* crew didn't know was that satellites were intercepting every message the tug sent and bouncing those messages directly to Washington, where NSA analysts listened and then passed word to the CIA that there was nothing serious to worry about. At least for now, the Soviets didn't seem to doubt that the *Explorer* was an ocean miner. In fact, the satellites had known this from the outset, when the SB-10 arrived and radioed home that it had encountered a strange ship. What is it doing? the captain asked. The answer, straight from fleet headquarters, was that this was an ocean miner, and we've been aware of it for years.

And yet, the SB-10 was a constant pest. It would appear, come close, then sail off and hang out a few miles away, before returning to a closer position. "The SB-10 made several dangerous passes," the ship's log noted on July 30. "Some dangerously close, apparently in disregard of common sense and good judgment!"

There seemed to be no schedule or rationale to the tug's actions, and often the approaches came after dark, in which case the captain would order the ship's high-intensity spotlight to illuminate the Soviet ship as long as it was operating in close quarters. The tug was annoying more than troubling, and as yet another tropical storm, Kim, churned up the ocean, some of the *Explorer*'s crew actually started to feel sorry for those Soviet sailors, sardined into a stuffy diesel tug bobbing around in giant swells.

Around the ship, a popular topic of conversation became what would happen if the Soviets stepped up their tactics. What if they boarded with weapons? No one really had a good answer. Very few people knew of the guns that the security staff had stashed under Dave Sharp's bunk. They had been told not to worry, but that didn't stop a series of rumors from spreading around, including one that the Navy had a submarine shadowing a safe distance away, and another that the ship had been wired with explosives that could, in a true emergency—if the Soviets were to board while the submarine was in the moon pool—be triggered, sinking the ship and crew.

Not even the mission command knew the true answer. They were aware that a special Naval Intelligence detachment under the command of Bobby Inman was in Hawaii monitoring ship traffic and could, in theory, order fighters to head for the target zone. Back at NURO, the leadership had discussed this eventuality many times. And even Dave Potter and Zeke Zellmer weren't sure what the worst-case-scenario plan should be. The US reaction would ultimately depend on circumstances. The first step would be to advise a Soviet vessel to stand down and not board. If that was ignored, the ship would issue an open distress signal to Naval Command that the mining ship *Hughes Glomar Explorer* was being boarded by men with guns from a vessel claiming to be a Soviet ship.

The trouble with sending a submarine, if one was in fact nearby, was that it would escalate the situation in a dangerous, even perilous, way. As NURO's founding staff director Bob Frosch later explained, "Once that submarine surfaces, that's when the guessing starts. Because they don't know what we're prepared to do, and we don't know what they're prepared to do."

55
Touchdown!

As Clementine approached the bottom, the control center was abuzz. The mission director and his key engineering leads had gathered there to watch the display from the capture vehicle's forward and side-scanning sonars, which probed in the darkness below for signs of the target. The display was simple—a series of yellow dots marching across the screen, over and over. "Then, on one pass, an irregular hemispheric hump displaced the flat line on the screen," one of those officers later observed. "It was the submarine hulk for sure. Word spread rapidly throughout the ship. We were on target."

From there, Clementine got close enough to the target for her CCTV cameras to begin sending back pictures—surprisingly clear images of what could only be a wrecked submarine appeared in the lens, which had cross-hairs in the middle.

After more than four years of preparation, and twenty-six days of struggles and stresses at the target site, the claw was in position over the submarine it had been designed to grab. The sub appeared to be lying exactly as the site survey from the *Glomar II* had predicted. But Hank Van Calcar wanted to test that accuracy. He directed the captain to move the ship to one end of the target and then to move in very small increments of just a few feet at a time, so that he could map the target with the high-resolution sonar. The measurements matched up precisely.

Everyone in the room closed in around the screen as an operator moved the joystick to position the crosshairs over various parts of the sub. He panned over the sail and along the top of the sub's deck to a mark that they'd all seen in the photos and planned to use as a point of reference for aligning the CV. But as he closed in on it, there was something else there, something in a familiar shape. It was a ball-peen hammer. No one in the room could recall a hammer from any of the photos. Erwin Runge, one of the original CIA task force engineers, ran out to get "the book," which contained all the images from *Halibut* and *Glomar II.* The hammer wasn't in any of them. Turns out it had been dropped by a diver working in the well and had fallen 16,500 feet down through the sea, landing right on top of the target.

Once word got around that the submarine was in the CV's camera sights, seemingly everyone on the *Explorer* was agitating to come to the control van for a look. Nielsen agreed to let anyone who was interested file through, in small groups. After that, the control room would be off-limits. Clementine may have reached her position over the top of the sub, but the work left to do was some of the most precise and difficult of the entire mission. The concentration and tension required by the controllers would be too great to risk any distractions, yet Nielsen was also bothered by the idea that he had to deny these men, who had all contributed so much to get to this point, the chance to watch the thing they'd all been working toward for so long. So he asked that TV monitors showing the same feed from the control room be placed in a few locations throughout the ship. "And these were intently watched by sailors, cooks, divers, drill crew—all hands—during the crucial moments of the recovery," a CIA summary later reported.

With Clementine parked over the wreck, operators panned and tilted her tripod-mounted cameras to film the sub, looking for anything unusual that they might want to be aware of—changes in the sub's orientation, previously unnoticed hull damage, or potentially hazardous seafloor features that could snag the claw. The site was coursing with sea life. Strange, almost extraterrestrial-seeming crabs plodded around on the seabed, and huge, bizarre, blind fish swam into and out of the camera's view. The sub itself looked exactly as it had in the thousands of pictures taken with Joe Houston's "catfish solution" cameras on the *Glomar II.*

With more than sixteen thousand feet of pipe deployed, plus Clementine on the end, the heavy-lift system had an astounding 12 million pounds hanging from the derrick. This was more than twice the weight that had been carried during the sea trials, and the stress on the ship was obvious. It creaked and groaned, and the strain on the well walls was so intense that crewmen witnessed them bending in and out—a terrifying sight that Charlie Canby assured everyone was normal; all steel structures are designed to give under stress.

The Soviet tug had chosen this inopportune moment to get even more reckless. It again passed within feet of the *Explorer* and began circling the ship, and this time several sailors were spotted taking height and distance measurements of the *Explorer*'s superstructure using a sextant and an alidade. The *Explorer* was as vulnerable at this point as it would be. The ship needed to maintain its station now or risk stressing the pipe, as the controllers positioned Clementine perfectly over the wreck to make the grab.

Clementine's operators had been practicing for the past month on Hank Van Calcar's simulator when they sat down to begin the procedure. For the first time, they began to fire the capture vehicle's eight hydraulic thrusters, which allowed them to position it with accuracy of less than a foot. Clementine had been outfitted with profiling sonars as a backup, with the expectation that the thrusters would stir up great clouds of silt, which would blind the cameras and render them useless. But oddly, the thrusters created only bubbles. The bottom was much firmer than anyone had expected.

Around nine A.M., as the SB-10 made one of its closest and most harrowing passes yet, coming within fifty yards of the *Explorer*'s bow, Clementine's controllers lowered the aft breakout legs to the seafloor and then tipped the capture vehicle's bridle so that the front legs touched down at the other end of the wreck. With the huge legs on firm ground, controllers were free to lower Clementine onto the target, using the towing eye on the K-129's bow and a crack at the aft end as reference points for an alignment they'd practiced over and over on the simulator.

They opened the claw as much as possible, spreading the finger-like davits wide, and then lowered the unit until it, too, contacted the floor, unloading 1 million pounds of weight from the string. The controllers had expected the floor to be soft and silty, so that the davits would actually sink into the mud under the sub, but this ground was firm, almost rocklike. It resisted, and an additional 2 million pounds were off-loaded from the heavy-lift system in an attempt to drive the tines into the ground under the sub.

One of the control engineers argued that the best way to ensure a full grab was to clamp the sub tightly, but Van Calcar, Dave Sharp, and the rest of the controllers disagreed. They were afraid of damaging the sub's pressure hull and instead directed the controller to slide around and under the sub lightly, which jolted it and caused the wreck to slip and tip over a bit farther.

Off-loading weight from the heavy-lift system had only minimal effect, but there was little more that could be done. The controllers had to hope that the tines had penetrated enough so that when the lift began, they would curl around and under the hull. Once they'd gone as deep as they were going to go, operators lifted upward until the tines were physically touching the sub.

They were ready to attempt the breakout. Pulling the submarine off the floor, out of the bed, would be done in two ways. The bulk of the force would come from the breakout legs, which had pistons that would push out into the seafloor when a flow of seawater was sent down the pipe hydraulically. This extended the length of each leg and would, in theory, break the sub out of whatever it was resting in. At the same time, the heavy-lift system would begin to pull up until the sub was hanging on the pipe, but with the vehicle's bridle still attached to the legs. It wasn't a violent process. The lift out was slow, to minimize stress on the system. The analogy that John Owen, who'd studied geology, used was of a stick stuck in the mud. You don't grab it in the middle and pull straight up, because that's the point of maximum load. Rather, you grab an end and peel.

And it all worked—the pistons pushed and the pipe pulled and the claw grabbed the sub and lifted it out of the soil. Around the ship, on the rig floor, inside the heavy-lift control room, and even in the crew quarters, men felt and heard the strain on the system, and as the enormous metal wreck popped out of the seabed, cheers rang out in the control van. All that remained now was to pull 16,500 feet of pipe attached to millions of pounds of submarine back to the surface without any major malfunctions. But just as the operators were about to initiate the lift, Western Gear's engineers noticed yet another breakdown in the heave-compensation system, a broken pump that was going to take at least a few hours to fix. This meant that the claw would have to hang there, with the immense weight of the sub on its most fragile components, the davits, for however long it took to fix the pump.

While engineers scrambled to fix the heave compensators, the captain kept the ship as still as possible while maintaining a close watch on the SB-10, which was still acting erratically, for no ostensible reason. Gresham tried flags, lights, and a radio call to tell the ship to back off, informing the Soviets that the *Explorer* was "maneuvering with difficulty," a message that was either not heard or flatly ignored.

During the lull, roughnecks fussed with the pipe system, removing some doubles and reconnecting the seawater hydraulic line, allowing controllers to push a little harder on the pistons. This provided some additional lift, easing the strain on the davits, but it also caused a shift in the position of the target itself. A wave of energy shot up the pipe into the ship, violently enough that many on board felt it. All eyes turned to the camera operators, who scanned the target and noticed that the sail portion of the submarine had dropped and turned, as if the davits holding it had let the load slip slightly. What that meant, however, wouldn't be known until the lift commenced.

Twenty hours after the first attempted breakout, the procedure was repeated, and this time controllers pumped seawater down the pipe and into each of the breakout legs, to activate the release function. Four pins, one in each leg, popped out, disconnecting the legs from the CV, leaving Clementine alone, with the sub inside her claw, at the end of the pipe string. The legs would be left behind on the floor, their usefulness exhausted, and the lift could finally begin.

When the *Explorer* arrived at the target site on July 4, the mission director's expectation was that the operation would be completed in six or seven days. Now, thirty days after arrival, they were only beginning the lift, a process that was going to take at least another two days. The heavy-lift system could move only so fast and was operating at its outer limits, with 14 million pounds of metal hanging under the ship. Fortunately, the sea was mostly cooperative, and every chunk of ground covered on the way up was a relief on the system, as each of the 274 doubles that came off the string removed fifteen tons of stress. During that first day, three thousand feet of pipe was recovered.

Nielsen felt comfortable enough in the lift progress to leave the control van and begin preparations for the ship's next move, out of the target area and into a friendly harbor. The *Explorer* went to sea with two possible destinations—Midway Island and Lahaina, Hawaii. The latter was a civilian port, and not a concern. But Midway was a Navy base, and to use it would require a cover story. Nielsen sent a message out over open channels that the ship's "nodule collector vehicle" had suffered damage after colliding with a silt-covered basalt outcrop and that he was requesting permission from the US Navy to proceed to Midway for repairs.

The plan from there was to have this fake mining-machine injury diagnosed as inoperable in Midway, at which point the ship would be sent back to the US mainland, where the necessary parts were located. In reality, CIA officers would remove the most sensitive documents recovered from the ship in Midway—ideally, missiles and code books—and secret them out under cover of darkness. Then the ship could continue the less urgent exploitation at sea, while en route to the United States for those fake repairs.

56

Tysons, We Have a Problem

AUGUST 4, 1974

For those men on the heavy-lift and pipe-handling crews, the slow process of raising Clementine and her target back to the surface was anything but boring. Every moment was tense as the system strained under the load, requiring constant attention and repairs. And then there was life inside the heavy-lift control room, where Fred Newton worked.

Newton was a nuclear physicist with a specialty in Soviet weapons and top-level clearance, which was why he was first recruited into Azorian, but he was also an electrical engineer, and during the construction phase, Newton contributed to the *Explorer*'s design.

On the ship, he was one of four men assigned to the heavy-lift controls. This was a critical job, considering the unprecedented loads that were being handled, and the four individuals worked in two-man, twelve-hour shifts inside a small, windowless room inside the portside wing wall, at the waterline. Newton had tremendous admiration for John Graham even though they'd barely interacted. In fact, he joked, Graham probably despised electrical engineers and nuclear physicists because he saw their sensors as fussy ornaments on his mechanical hardware.

When the heavy-lift system was in operation, it was in the hands of just two controllers, and no one else was allowed to be in that section of the ship. Each tandem included one engineer from Global Marine and one from

302

Western Gear, since the two companies shared responsibility for the heavy-lift and heave-compensation systems.

Newton had been in charge of installing the system's strain gauges, which measured the stresses being imparted during the lift and were monitored from the heavy-lift room, and Graham had helped him position them. As an intuitive engineer, Graham could just eyeball it all and know where the stresses would be highest, as well as what might cause them. If he could have been there, as the claw and sub rose through the water, approaching a mile above the floor, he would have hated the sight. Newton and his shift-mate, Tom Fry, were at a near panic for hours on end, screaming into the sound-powered headsets whenever a decision was required. The system was run by racks filled with eleven hundred CMOS logic cards and thirty-six switches on a board. Depending on the situation, Newton—or his Global counterpart, John Owen—needed to hit a certain one at a certain time, and the way it felt—for pretty much every minute he was in that chair—was that picking the wrong switch could sink the ship.

What made the system stressful, Owen thought, was the automation. The operator of an automated system is the emergency switch. He must sit there, vigilant, waiting for a problem and ready to jump in and take over. That's tedious when automation works well, but on the heavy-lift and heave-compensation systems, tested to their full capacities for the first time during the actual lift of the sub, it was nerve-fraying work in an environment that didn't exactly set a man at ease in the first place.

As the sub rose, one-inch-diameter steel bolts began to strain and hiss and eventually pop loose, firing across the deck like bullets. This wasn't necessarily a problem; in fact, it was expected. As the load settled, the pressure equalized and certain points released stress by finding weak spots. But those steel bullets could also kill a man. Owen cracked later that when he was up on the rig floor working on a heave-compensator control issue, the constant whiz and ping of the rivets reminded him of the sound effects from an old Hopalong Cassidy Western, when cowboy bullets were regularly ricocheting off boulders.

The first rivets startled Newton, but he quickly got used to them, distracted by scarier signs of straining, such as in corners and at the intersections of beams, where he hadn't put any strain gauges. What he realized, when the world's burliest lift system was finally in operation, was that there weren't enough strain gauges in the world to properly monitor the stresses being put on the pipe, tower, and ship. He was, he realized, an overly confident man in his twenties, alone on the frontier of something that had never been done before—something he might well not survive. Up in the pump room, probably the single most dangerous place on the ship, no one had ever seen pressures like the ones being experienced during the lift, as pump units handling three thousand pounds per square inch sprang leaks, causing streams of seawater to jet out with such force that they could cut off a man's hand.

For others on the ship, however, the lift period was painfully slow, almost boring. John Parsons had been awake for more than a day by the time the lift was actually under way, and knowing that the process of raising the sub would take much longer than a night's sleep, he went off to bed early in the morning of August 4, figuring he could get plenty of sleep and still be up in time to watch hours of pipe slowly ascending through the depths.

He was in his bunk, sleeping, when a crewman burst into his room shortly after nine A.M. "Something's wrong," the man said. "We've lost a lot of weight."

Parsons threw on his coveralls and ran to mission control, where all of the key spies and engineers were staring nervously at a screen that showed no obvious problems. There were Clementine and the sub, moving very slowly up toward the surface. But that couldn't be right.

That's what Sherm Wetmore thought, too. He'd been eating breakfast in the mess when he felt the ship shudder. It was like a little earthquake, and he recognized it immediately as an anomaly—either something had just run into the ship, or there was a problem with the pipe. Wetmore called the heavy-lift control cabin, where the operator on duty told him that they seemed to have lost some load. Whatever happened was sudden and violent, he said, because the heave compensator had stroked out, causing the pistons to shoot upward like a gigantic slingshot. Wetmore ran to the rig floor and saw crewmen rushing to bleed air out of the compensator so that it could equalize to whatever the new weight was on the pipe. They cranked open two large dump valves, one on each cylinder, and compressed air came screaming out, louder, Wetmore thought, than any jet engine he'd ever heard.

By the time Wetmore got to the heavy-lift control room, it was clear to his operators that a significant amount of load had been lost, but when he called up to the control van, he got a very odd reply. The Lockheed controller who answered said that he was staring at a picture of Clementine and everything appeared to be fine.

Hank Van Calcar, Ray Feldman, and the team in that control van were surprised by the frantic tone in Wetmore's voice. They had felt no visceral change or shift. And the picture they were seeing looked fine.

The spies, being bureaucrats, called a meeting, while the various technical teams scrambled to identify the problem. It didn't take long. The CCTV wasn't actually showing a live feed. To save bandwidth, the camera system had been designed so that the image updated only when there was a change in the picture, and Clementine's cameras didn't detect any change, so the feed had been showing an image of the claw from many hours before.

Once that signal was reset, the problem was apparent, in black and white: Several of Clementine's tines had broken during the ascent, and a chunk of the submarine, at least half and maybe more, had fallen back into the sea.

All around the room, men sank into their chairs. The feeling in every one of them was of total disbelief. With more than a third of the pipe reeled back in, the control-center crew had felt that success was imminent. The touchdown, grab, and lift had all presented opportunities for error—no one would have been surprised to see a major malfunction there—but once the lift had begun, everyone relaxed. They had shut down most of the consoles and were just waiting.

But now, suddenly, it felt like a failure. Some large portion of the submarine was gone, back to the ocean floor, where it would probably break into still smaller pieces.

The failure wasn't total, however. Something was still in the claw. And whatever remained in Clementine's grasp could still hold secrets.

Everything stopped while Nielsen and the command team met to consider how to proceed. Down in heavy lift, things were incredibly tense. Holding the pipe steady with the full load at the end strained the entire system, and Fred Newton was watching strain gauges nearly pop while hearing nothing from the control van except to hold his position and wait for orders. Periodically, he'd yell into his headset, asking for some direction, but for several hours, he heard nothing. It was not a good feeling.

Once reality set in, Nielsen directed the communications officer to send a secure message to Langley with the news that there had been a partial failure, and the lift would continue until whatever was left had been secured inside the ship.

Back east, Parangosky digested the news and called Carl Duckett, asking the deputy director to come to the program office as soon as possible. Duckett had been following the *Explorer*'s progress intently from Langley, making regular trips to the director's office to update Colby on how many feet the claw had risen since their last meeting. Like all of the operation heads, Duckett felt as if the hardest work had been done, and he took the news hardest of all. (Years later, Colby's former assistant still vividly recalled "the disappointment and devastation.") The program had come so far, having endured constant pressure from the Navy, and having solved a relentless barrage of technical challenges, and now—when every single insanely complicated piece of equipment had actually worked, and picked up this submarine—it was literally falling apart at the last possible minute, with success so close. It was too much for Duckett to accept and process, especially early in the morning.

He fired back a reply that stunned mission control. He wanted Nielsen to send Clementine back to the bottom to pick up the lost portion. Nielsen couldn't believe what he was reading. He handed the cable to Dave Sharp. "I guess you'd better answer this one," he said.

Sharp was the Agency's head engineer in charge of the actual capture and raising. His opinion on this mattered more than that of a nuclear physicist and, according to his own retelling of events in his memoir, he prepared a carefully worded cable laying out the situation for Duckett: The claw had been severely damaged, with at least a few tines broken; there were no longer any breakout legs on Clementine to land on the floor and position the claw; and there was no way to know where and in what state the lost portion would be in. Basically, Sharp told the directorate's most powerful man, there was no way to go back.

Sharp's response was sensible and correct. They could not try again. Clementine was broken. And yet, it wasn't well received. Within minutes, a cable came that was signed by Carl Duckett himself. "Return to ocean bottom and recover remainder of target," it said. "This is not a request. This is an order."

Sharp knew Duckett to be a smart, reasonable man. It was always possible to convince him, provided you made a logical case, and he was preparing to try again when another cable came in. "Proceed with plan to continue ascent," it said. "Disregard previous order."

Common sense, in the form of Mr. P, had prevailed. Sharp would later learn just how furious Duckett had been. For a period of hours that day, he'd been insisting not only that the *Explorer* make another attempt, but that Parangosky give him an open line—an unsecured radio channel—to the ship, so that he could make this point clear, with his voice. Parangosky convinced his boss that this would be a terrible idea and then very patiently asked if Duckett would allow the lone Azorian engineer who'd been left behind in Washington to explain why another trip to the bottom wouldn't work. Duckett was convinced. "But he hated it," Dave Sharp wrote in his book. "We had come so close to recovering the entire target. He was devastated."

As soon as Curtis Crooke walked in the door to the program office, around eight A.M. Pacific Standard Time, he knew something was wrong. The recovery attempt had continued through the night before, while he was asleep, and he half expected to arrive at the office to find a celebration under way. But the cases of champagne the admin staff had bought in preparation were unopened, stacked against the wall where they'd been put a few days before.

The night shift had experienced the emotional roller coaster in real time. There was an overly large staff in the office that night, to monitor the final stages of recovery, and they all erupted when the first secure telex arrived, saying, "Congratulations, break out the champagne!" Hours later, that enthusiasm was dashed by a follow-up: "Disregard the previous communication."

The security staff briefed Crooke with the little detail they had. Communication to and from the shop was extremely limited under the best of times, but the crew on the *Explorer* also didn't have much information to share at this point. The claw had suffered a partial failure during the lift, about nine thousand feet up from the ocean floor, and some of the target had been lost. No one knew yet how much, or what that was.

As the lift continued on the *Explorer,* and Clementine rose closer and closer to the ship's bottom, Nielsen followed a predetermined order and sent an open message, via station KPH in San Francisco, informing the ship's base that the nodule collector vehicle was more badly damaged than previously thought. This time, the reply came from Paul Reeve, Summa Ocean Mining Division general manager, and was addressed to "the Senior Summa representative" on the ship. This representative was to continue to assess damage and, as soon as he was certain of the specifics, begin twice-daily reports on the progress.

What this exchange did was set a precedent, and a framework, for an open conversation of the recovery process, once the sub was on board and could be studied. Because each of these innocuous twice-daily reports would be embedded with code that contained details of the sub's condition, as well as what if any important pieces of Soviet hardware had been recovered.

Outside, the SB-10 was back at it and seemed more persistent than ever, as if its crew somehow sensed that the big drillship was wrapping up its mission. It made a pass within seventy-five yards, and then another within fifty yards, and failed to heed all signals from the *Explorer* warning the tug that the drillship was having difficulties and was unable to move.

Worry spread through the security staff that the tug might be preparing something more bold. Jack Poirier, his security staff, and the onboard Navy analysts all conferred with Langley and came to the conclusion that, while the SB-10 probably did have divers on its crew, they weren't likely to make an attempt to get under the *Explorer.* Those divers were there to assist in submarine contingency and limited salvage operations. They were probably certified to perform hull inspections, but only in controlled conditions and at depths of up to thirty feet. Going into the open ocean and swimming under an unfamiliar ship the size of the *Explorer* in the middle of a drilling operation was unpredictable and dangerous. They'd also be easily spotted, allowing the *Explorer*'s captain and crew to react with evasive actions.

By Tuesday, August 6, the mood on the ship had settled into a kind of calm. The shock of the failure passed, and the pipe-handling crew was now working with renewed vigor, removing doubles at a faster and faster rate. Clementine was within one thousand feet of the ship and rising quickly.

Inside the moon pool, crewmen were preparing for its arrival. The docking legs had been lowered to their maximum depth and workers who weren't busy with a particular task were just watching the water, where they noticed some objects pop up out of the sea and bob around in the flooded pool. At first, it was unclear what these things were, and then someone identified the very clear outline of a fuel canister, followed by some clothing. These were objects from the sub itself, which had been shaken free by the more turbulent, wave-influenced depth where the wreck was now ascending, and they'd simply floated out of the sub and up into the well.

This created a new worry for Poirier: What if other detritus was floating up outside the ship? The SB-10 crew had been grabbing anything, no matter how small or filthy, that came off the *Explorer*, and if they were to fish out a Soviet naval uniform or a submarine fuel can with Cyrillic letters on it, the situation could get nasty fast.

Fortunately, that didn't happen. In fact, with the stolen Soviet submarine just an hour or two from reaching the surface, the SB-10 surprised everyone again. At 9:35 P.M., as the last light of the summer sun was disappearing over the horizon, the tug moved within seventy-five yards of the *Explorer*'s starboard beam, close enough that Captain Gresham signaled the tug to stay clear. This time, the SB-10 listened. The tug moved around to the stern, as its entire crew crowded onto the deck, turned their backs to the *Explorer*, and dropped their pants, exposing a row of extremely pale Russian butts. The men on the *Explorer*'s deck howled with laughter, and a few of them, including Hank Van Calcar, returned the favor, which caused more clapping and laughing and waving. "Mooning the Russians," he would later say, "was one of the highlights of my career."

The tug blasted its horn three times, turned toward Russia, and sailed away. Within an hour, it had vanished from radar and was cruising at full speed toward home, having spent thirteen days and sixteen hours observing a pretend mining ship that was really stealing a Soviet submarine.

In fact, the SB-10 had been sent purposefully to surveil the *Explorer,* but despite having what the fleet intelligence chief called "sharp-eyed lads" on board, the tug was also overly cramped and provisioned with only rudimentary spy gear—namely, binoculars and notebooks. After ten days, the ship was hot, smelly, and running out of food and freshwater. The crew had observed nothing suspicious and were suffering from poor morale.

Back at fleet command, Admiral Shtyrov was unconvinced, but he was also out of options. When his fleet commander told him to give it up, Shtyrov made one last desperate plea. He wrote a report to the Navy Main Staff and then awaited a reply. Two days later, it came. "I direct your attention to more qualitative performance of scheduled tasks," it said, and Shtyrov, he later wrote, got the message, through the bureaucratic doublespeak: "Don't come around with your nonsense."

There were no more ships to send after that; the only thing fleet command could offer Shtyrov was the occasional reconnaissance overflight by a pair of Tu-95RC jets, but each of the three times those flights went out they were foiled by overcast conditions and could confirm only the presence of a large ship in that location.

Desperate for any intelligence, Shtyrov even asked the chief of the Soviet Union's Far Eastern shipping division if container ships working the Yokohama–Los Angeles route could navigate past Location K. They agreed, but with no time or budget to stop or linger, they could do no more than the planes—only confirm that a large ship was there.

At 9:20 P.M. on August 6, the *Explorer*'s docking legs grabbed Clementine, relieving pressure at last from the pipe string and ensuring that whatever was in the capture vehicle's grasp would actually make it into the moon pool. "Miner on legs," Silent Jim McNary wrote in the heavy-lift log. Clementine was safe at last.

57

Assessing the Catch

When the pipe string cracked the five-hundred-foot mark, men began to gather around the rim of the moon pool, watching the murky black water for any sign of Clementine. And once the tug was gone, the *Explorer*'s crew could bring the target into the moon pool and pump it dry without fear of being caught in the act by divers.

Every man on board who didn't have other immediate responsibilities wanted to be there to get the first sight of the target. And those who'd gathered cried out when an intact jerry can of torpedo fuel from the K-129 popped up from under the water and onto the surface of the well, as one of the men observed, having "traveled over 3 miles to the bottom and back and been subjected to pressures of over 7000 pounds per square inch without spilling a drop."

When Clementine approached the ship's bottom, divers slipped into the water to assist in the final steps, and then returned with confirmation of the bad news everyone suspected anyway. At least half of the submarine had fallen away.

At last, fifty-one days after the *Hughes Glomar Explorer* left Long Beach, the claw was lifted carefully through the gates, with just ten feet of clearance on each side, and into the pool, where the docking leg operators continued to lift until it was dangling over the surface of the water. Jim McNary was the lone engineer on the scene, amidst a crowd of roughnecks. He was stunned at how little of the sub remained—just a small, dirty metal tube wobbling around in the precarious grasp of the claw. It looked to him like that last section could slip free, too, and he called Sherm Wetmore to suggest they hurry up and close the sea gates to secure the whole package inside the ship.

Once the gates were closed and the water pumped out, the scale of the failure was there for everyone to observe: Two-thirds of the submarine had been lost—everything from the conning tower back, which included both the missile tubes and the code room.

The mood around the pool and in the control room was funereal. The intelligence officers were especially stunned by Clementine's failure, since all of the major targets of the operation—the ballistic missiles and code machinery, in particular—appeared to be gone. Elsewhere, reactions were more mixed. To the roughnecks and pipe handlers, not to mention the *Glomar* engineers who'd worked on all the systems other than the capture vehicle, it was hard not to see what they'd accomplished as at least a partial success. They'd done their part. They'd delivered a very heavy pipe to a precise point on the seafloor and then pulled it back up with a huge weight at the end, fighting and solving problems along the way. As the oil industry saying goes, sometimes you drill a hole and there's no oil there.

The mission director ordered everyone who wasn't essential to leave the moon pool until further notice as he and his team viewed the scene from a balcony-like portion of the ladder that led down to the floor. Radiation monitors reported readings five times background even at that distance, indicating, as one officer noted, "that we were in for a nasty time."

First onto the floor were the radiation specialists from Livermore, who suited up and surveyed the wreck, sampling locations with Geiger counters and reporting back to mission command with good news: There was plutonium, but it wasn't floating around in the air, so the inhalation risk was minimal. Plutonium is denser than lead, which means that particles would stay where they lay unless disturbed. Getting particles on the skin isn't even a risk, since they wash off easily in water. The only time anyone would need to wear a breathing apparatus was when using cutting torches, because that would vaporize the plutonium and create a temporary airborne risk.

The fact that the sub was hot was something the crew needed to know.

The CIA's sub specialist, Blackjack, called a meeting in the mess hall to share that news and to say that anyone uncomfortable with the idea of working on the exploitation of the wreck could opt out at any time. No one would be forced to participate. But the process would be onerous, meaning that they needed bodies, as many as he could recruit. Those who were willing to help were appreciated, he said, and should feel confident that the ship's antiradiation procedures were sufficient. Livermore officials had designed the protocol with exposure in mind.

With the sub hanging up over the pool, in the grasp of Clementine and the docking legs, sand and water and organic material of unknown origin dripped from the wreck down to the floor. The first step, then, was to sift the gunk, and a team armed with shovels and saltwater hoses plodded into the pool, scooped up shovels full of material, and placed them in stainless-steel baskets with wire mesh on the bottom. They'd dump a pile in, then spray it to clear away the smallest particles, leaving only pieces too big to fall through the mesh, as if sifting for gold. Pieces of the sub were pulled out and handed to analysts, who'd carry them away for study, while human parts—jawbones, finger bones, bone fragments—were placed into bags and given to medics, who carried them off to the ship's refrigerated morgue.

Once the floor was cleared, it was the cutting crew's turn. And they were already in a staging van on the lower level where special antiradiation suits had been set out. Among them was big Billy Collier, whom most guys on the crew called Bimbo. He had been hired for his expertise with a torch, to be one of the first men to go to work once the sub was inside the moon pool—cutting at the sub's hard steel exterior to expose the parts inside that CIA analysts really wanted to see. Into the maw they went, careful not to bump into the sub's many sharp edges, where the violence of the implosion had twisted and torn and sheared two-inch-thick metal plates as if they were plastic. The implosion also caused compaction, when the forces of the sea became so great that all the open spaces that weren't filled with water compressed suddenly, like a toy placed into a garbage compactor. Nothing was easily accessed. Every inch had to be pulled apart.

The work was immediate and intense, because the men were fighting time and temperature. Crews worked in teams of six on two-hour shifts. For six years, the steel hunk had been sitting in thirty-two-degree water, where it would in theory have been preserved in good shape for centuries. But as soon as the sub was inside the *Explorer*'s belly, out of the cold water and exposed to warmer air, decay set in. Within hours, the hull began to oxidize, and a rancid stench permeated the air around the wreck, getting worse every minute. That was the smell of decomposing human flesh.

This, too, had been expected, and to combat the decay, more than one hundred industrial air conditioners were moved into the moon pool and cranked to maximum power.

The smell, one roughneck would later recall, "was terrible. Damp, rotten." Others were less bothered. Hank Van Calcar, for instance. He'd been assigned to work on the missiles, had they been recovered, because he'd helped design control systems for US ICBMs, but he was useful here, too. He'd grown up on a dairy farm, "in blood and guts from the day I was born," he said, and the smell, while pungent, "wasn't near as bad as a barn full of cow shit."

CIA handlers had specifically forbidden workers from taking any materials from the sub, but those orders were promptly forgotten, as cutters and grunts stripped the bodies and the wreckage of souvenirs—tucking rings, coins, and bracelets into the pockets of their suits. Buttons were a favorite souvenir, as they were easily popped off jackets and hidden away.

At the end of a shift, the men stripped down and the suits were thrown away in special trash receptacles. They were told to take hot showers, and if anyone tested positive on the dosimeter after his shower, he was sent back for another hot shower and told to scrub himself repeatedly until it felt like he'd lost a few layers of skin.

As the days went on, any man who wasn't worried about exposure was welcome to join in the exploitation, and many did. All twelve Lockheed men volunteered, including Ray Feldman, who served as the unofficial photographer, using a CIA-issued thirty-five-millimeter to document every piece pulled out of the wreck. John Parsons put on a bunny suit, too, and went in early, searching through the sub's former storage and bringing out cans of Soviet rations, including beans and cabbage, which he passed over to analysts for study. He also found a leg and, after moving some metal, the body attached to it, and as instructed he backed out and let the divers, who'd been assigned to handle human remains, come in and carefully move what was left of a Soviet submariner into the morgue.

Parsons was told to pull out anything that might be useful—he found pipes, valves, handles, and tattered clothing and carried them out to the Agency's consultants, who logged the items and put most aside for further study. The major targets of the mission might have been lost, but every piece could reveal some detail of value—what factories made the valves, the precise thickness of the inner hull, and the quality of the welds. The men were told to be fastidious and to overlook nothing, and after a complete shift it wasn't unusual for any one of them to look up and realize he'd spent the whole time on an area not much larger than a phone booth.

What struck Parsons most was how much it still looked like a submarine, despite an explosion, fire, and six years on the ocean floor. From the nose to the point at which the sub broke, where the metal had been violently torn, it was still very recognizable.

The room was cool but humid, and masks fogged up. It was also awkward to walk and work inside the suit, and even men who didn't get claustrophobia found themselves dying to get out of the masks and back into fresh air afterward.

It didn't take long for the Navy and CIA submarine experts to begin to glean valuable information. The Soviet submarine program was thought at that time to be more advanced than the US program, but what they saw of the K-129 was shocking. The steel hull plates were inconsistent, with varying thicknesses and irregular welds. They found two-by-four boards reinforcing some sections of the hull and hundreds of lead weights that they determined had been brought on board to adjust the submarine's trim manually as needed.

Some of the men who'd volunteered for duty completed a single shift and then decided that the work wasn't for them. This resulted in a new call for volunteers, and one of the CIA electrical engineers up in the control van decided to give it a shot. Prior to the mission's departure from port, he had volunteered to be the photographer of the warhead disassembly, if they were able to retrieve the Soviet SS-N-5s. That was to be done at sea, and while it was a job that terrified plenty of crewmen, the way this engineer looked at it, if the warhead were to detonate during disassembly, it didn't matter where you were on the boat. Everyone would die instantly, so he might as well see something interesting in the moments before being vaporized.

Fumbling around the sub, in comparison, sounded like much less stressful work. He went to the dress-out van, got a quick instructional in procedures, and then was led onto the floor. He was tentative at first, fumbling in the heavy gloves and sweating profusely in the stifling humidity of the suit, but got used to it and began to feel more confident on the floor.

He stepped through an opening in the hull and was surprised at how much space there was to maneuver even inside a submarine that had been crushed by the deep ocean. He was the first into an officer's berthing compartment, where he got on his knees and swept under a bunk with his arm until he felt some resistance—an object. With a little push, it came loose and he pulled it out, recoiling in shock at the sight of an entire human head, still largely intact. It had flesh and hair and a nose, but no eyes or ears, both of which had likely been eaten away by the large blind crabs that were crawling throughout the wreck.

On a later shift, the man stumbled upon the exploitation crew's most important discovery yet—a two-inch-thick journal, remarkably intact, in a berth where its owner, a young officer, had apparently been curled up asleep at the time of the accident. His body was still in the bunk, in good enough condition that he could be positively identified, and the book, filled with handwritten eight-by-ten-inch pages, was, remarkably, in extraordinary shape. The engineer handed it over to the CIA's paper-preservation crew and later discovered that it contained detailed notes written by the officer, who was apparently studying the never-before-known nuclear weapons capabilities of his refitted Golf-class attack submarine. The find, according to word that spread quietly around the ship, was important enough that it would be flown directly back to Washington upon the ship's return to Hawaii.

58

Down Goes Nixon

AUGUST 1974

wo major events occurred on the morning of August 9. The first was that the *Hughes Glomar Explorer* completed the recovery phase of Project Azorian. The second was that President Richard Nixon resigned and left the White House in shame, swearing even to his closest aides that he was not a crook.

Once the emergency work was completed on shoring up the sub and its armaments, Nielsen decided that it was best for the *Explorer* to leave the target site and resume the exploitation in safer waters, where the surprise arrival of a Soviet missile-tracking vessel would be a lot less likely. He told his communications officer to radio word via station KPH that the *Explorer* wished to head out. The message was overt, so anyone listening would have heard that Howard Hughes's mining ship was notifying "Summa headquarters" that it had finished "Event 36-A," a code that anyone in the program would recognize as the operation's recovery phase. In addition, the message stated, analysis of damage to the "nodule collector vehicle" would continue.

Back in Washington, Carl Duckett and John Parangosky discussed what to do next. The fact that the Soviet ships had left without causing any trouble was a relief, but other ships were within a day's sail, and there was no way to know if the Soviet Navy might get curious again. On the other hand, there was still valuable equipment in the water; in particular, the ship's wave-rider buoys, each worth twenty-five thousand dollars, had yet to be recovered, and to rush away without picking them up seemed riskier than actually sticking around to do what a commercial ship would do. So Parangosky ordered that the ship recover the buoys before leaving the site.

Nielsen continued to radio back, via open channels, the ship's progress. On August 10, he reported that engineers were still assessing damage to the collector to determine if it could be repaired at sea and that the ship would head, for now, toward a prearranged location near Midway Island where it could sit for repairs if necessary. The next day, however, he had bad news: Repairs to the collector would take at least thirty days.

This made Parangosky's decision easier. He had the B crew on standby, ready to meet the ship and begin the exploitation with just a few days' notice, so he told Nielsen to change course and return to American waters. The *Explorer* should set a course for "Site 130-1," code for Lahaina Roads, off the coast of Maui. There, Nielsen knew, the B crew—specially trained to recover, process, and package the sub's intelligence—would take over a more thorough process of exploitation. For cover purposes, this crew was described as an engineering team and would be led aboard by Summa's Paul Reeve, who was already en route to Lahaina.

One day after Gerald Ford was sworn in, telling America that "our long national nightmare is over," the new president met with his National Security Council in the White House Cabinet Room to get up to date on the most pressing crises on his agenda. One of those was the *Glomar Explorer,* which everyone in the room knew to be in possession of at least some portion of a stolen Soviet submarine and which, for much of the recovery process, was openly harassed by two different Soviet naval ships.

"Bill," the president said, addressing his CIA director. "What is the latest on our ship project in the Pacific?"

"Well, sir, as you know, the tines were damaged when we picked up the sub," Colby said, resulting in the loss of a significant portion of the K-129. "However, we have the rest of it inside the recovery ship and the ship has now steamed away from the area."

Colby also had good news. The Soviet tug that had caused so much worry had left the area and the *Explorer*'s security team was confident that the ship had no idea what the *Glomar*'s true purpose had been. It had been in the area on a standard precautionary mission, to be available to provide service for the new Yankee-class subs making their first crossings of the Pacific, and had merely hung around to bother the *Explorer* as a small act of Cold War posturing.

This eliminated, at least temporarily, Ford's most immediate worry. When he'd told his national security team to continue the mission during his first hours in office, he'd done so knowing that there was a Soviet ship in the area and that if that ship were to interfere, or even board the *Glomar Explorer,* the crew would be helpless. To maintain the ship's scientific cover meant that no US Navy vessels could be anywhere near the site, so there was the potential—however small—for a repeat of the USS *Pueblo* fiasco. And that troubled the president.

The director then moved on to the real question. What did the *Glomar* recover?

"It is very hard to tell what they have, but they have detected some radio-activity," Colby continued. "It will probably be as long as thirty days before they really know. We think that at least one of the missiles was loose and it may have fallen free, but it will be some time before we know just what the situation is. It is too bad that, with the whole mission having gone so very well, we lost the section that we did."

A few days out of Lahaina, a cable arrived in the *Glomar Explorer*'s communications center and the staff sent immediately for the ship's top officers and for John Parsons. John Graham, the message reported, had passed away at Hoag Hospital, back home.

News of Graham's death spread around the ship rapidly. Not every crew member on board had worked with Graham, or even met him, but they all knew that none of them would be there, at sea on a spy vessel with a stolen Soviet submarine in its belly, without him.

Parsons was gutted. Even worse, the cable had arrived as code, over the secure channel, meaning that he couldn't even send a message back to his wife acknowledging the news and expressing sympathy. This had been a mistake. Whoever sent the news did it over the secure channel unnecessarily, without considering the consequences, and it created a situation where Parsons couldn't reply until the news was rebroadcasted over open channels—which finally happened two days later.

As the ship approached Lahaina, the cover continued to hold. A new round of stories appeared upon the *Explorer*'s return to Hawaiian waters, which coincided with the departure of a Japanese mining research vessel, the *Hakurei Maru,* from Yokohama. This, reporters thought, signaled an escalation in the race for underwater riches—"the billion-dollar treasure hunt for manganese," the UPI called it—that was only just beginning. Down in Caracas, Venezuela, delegates at the Law of the Sea Conference were still debating the matter of ocean-mining rights, and an oceanography task force ordered by Hawaii governor John Burns had just taken samples from a three-thousand-foot undersea plateau between two Hawaiian Islands and declared that a mining ship could recover 1 million tons of nodules worth 785 million dollars in a single year.

As promised, the *Explorer* was met in port by Paul Reeve, followed by a parade of mostly unfamiliar faces who came aboard behind him and proceeded to fan out over the ship, inspecting every corner. This was the so-called Tiger Team, a group of nonaffiliated engineers, mostly from Sun Wong's Mechanics Research Inc., asked to figure out what went wrong, so that similar problems could be prevented if and when the ship went back out to complete the task.

Like many of the key engineers on board, Dave Sharp had mixed emotions. He was disappointed at the partial failure. But the more time he had to consider it all, the prouder he was of what had been accomplished, too. The fact that they'd retrieved even a part of a submarine from 16,500 feet was one of if not the greatest marine-engineering feat ever completed. Which was only a partial salve for the pain of knowing how close they'd come to getting it all.

One face Sharp was thrilled to see on the *Explorer* was that of Curtis Crooke, who'd been itching to get to the ship after spending almost two months in the program office feeling helpless and like he should have been out there at sea. The two men talked for a few minutes and then Crooke handed Sharp a package that was addressed to him under his code name, David Schoals. Inside was a plastic bag filled with bone fragments and ash and labeled, on a tag, "John R Graham."

When Graham was dying, he asked that his family have him cremated and his ashes sent to the *Explorer,* where he wanted them scattered. That way, at least in death he'd be able to spend some time on the ship that was the culmination of his career. Crooke had arranged to meet up with Nell before leaving for Hawaii and carried the architect's ashes out in a box on his lap. "I'm not sure if that was actually legal," he later said. "I'm sure I didn't care."

Sharp wrote in his book that he was able to spend some time with Graham before the ship sailed for the mission. Graham was weak as they walked around the ship at Pier E, stopping often to catch his breath. Sharp says that he told Graham his ship was "an amazing engineering achievement" and that he should be proud. "Thank you," Graham replied. "I am proud of it."

A few days after the return to Lahaina, just after seven P.M. on Monday, August 19, Sharp gathered on the *Explorer*'s fantail with Crooke, the ship's new captain, Elmer Thompson, and a small group of program engineers. They each said some words, bowed their heads, and tossed John Graham's ashes into the wind as the sun set over the Pacific, turning the sky a fiery red.

Crooke stayed in Lahaina another week to debrief his engineers, then returned to the program office to begin planning for repairs. When the next edition of the company's newsletter, *Global Marine News,* was printed, it included a touching memorial from the company's president, A. J. Field, who credited Graham with helping to make Global into the industry leader it had become. "John's finest achievement to me is the *Hughes Glomar Explorer* design and project management," Field wrote. "He literally created a wonder of the world both in the object itself and the short time it took to accomplish it. . . . We are grateful for having known him."

59
Crew Change

Up and down the coast, members of the B crew were on standby, just waiting for a call. John Rutten was asleep next to his wife, Laura, when their bedside phone rang at five thirty A.M. on Monday, August 5. It was Dr. Don Flickinger, Rutten's supervisor, calling from the program office. "The crew has the TO in the moon pool," said Flickinger, a Stanford-educated World War II flight surgeon who had been in charge of "human factors" for America's nascent space program, helping select the first seven astronauts in US history. "Someone you know will meet you at the United counter at LAX at 1310 on the 15th."

Rutten hung up the phone. "They got it!" he yelled. "I can't believe it!"

Rutten would be taking over from James Borden as the ship's doctor. An internist who ran a large medical clinic in Santa Barbara, Rutten had been recruited some years back to work on secret deep-submergence diving projects for the Navy, including the famous underwater habitat, SeaLab. In that role, he met Flickinger, who came calling again when Parangosky asked him to join Azorian to find divers and doctors for the mission.

Ten days after that call, Rutten met Flickinger and Mike Redmond, a physician who'd flown in from Hawaii to brief his replacements, as well as Jack Thiel, a new medical tech who would be joining Rutten on the B crew, at LAX. Flickinger took the men out for Wagyu steaks, then dropped them both at a safe house in Marina del Rey to get one more night's sleep on land before departing for Hawaii to board the ship. The next morning, Flickinger delivered them to the program office, where a man in a dark suit introduced by Curtis Crooke as "JP" briefed the men who would comprise the *Glomar Explorer*'s B crew on what had just happened at sea and what they could expect when they joined the exploitation process in Hawaii.

Before leaving this office, Parangosky said, the men would need to hand over any cameras to the security staff. The keeping of diaries and journals was also not permitted. He said that the flight to Hawaii would leave shortly after the meeting and that the group should gather their bags and go to the building's Walnut Street entrance, where a bus would pick them up and take them to the Continental Airlines terminal for boarding of a charter jet to Honolulu.

After takeoff, passengers were served filet mignon, and they arrived in Honolulu at 7:05 P.M., just as a bloodred sunset seeped across the sky. The men were transferred to a smaller plane across the runway and by 7:45 were back in the air, en route to Maui, where finally they boarded buses to La-haina. Rutten watched out the window as farmers set fire to the sugarcane fields, preparing for harvest, and the resulting smoke filled the air with the scent of caramel.

It was dark when the buses arrived at the port. A path lined with tiki torches led to a glass-bottomed boat called the *Coral Sea* that would shuttle the B crew from shore to the *Explorer*. The men were excited, but also exhausted from flying and eating and drinking, and said little as they dropped their canvas bags and walked to the boat, which puttered out across the harbor and stopped alongside the enormous *Explorer*. The ship's deck crane lowered a hanging basket, known as a Billy Pugh, down onto the *Coral Sea*, and groups of four or five tossed their bags onto it and then climbed aboard, at which point the crane yanked them straight upward and onto the deck, which felt to those who'd never experienced it like a thrill-park ride in the dark.

"One hundred fifty fresh-faced new crewmen and personnel boarded the Coral Sea and, without so much as an 'aloha,' climbed aboard the Glomar Explorer," a reporter wrote in *The Maui News* on August 24, which happened to be Rutten's twenty-fourth wedding anniversary. "They looked like a band of CIA agents heading for exile." That wasn't a lucky guess, or even a cagey assertion. It was the writer's attempt at a joke about a ship that was the hottest gossip item on the island, owned by an eccentric germophobe and chasing riches in realms that were barely explored. Stories from the papers were clipped and delivered both to the boat, where the crew laughed over the outrageous details, and in Washington, where Walt Lloyd and John Parangosky found a little humorous relief in the continued success of the mission's outlandish cover.

"Behaving not at all like the mystery ship she is, the Howard Hughes Glomar Explorer steamed in broad daylight into the quiet waters off Lahaina yesterday and dropped anchor," wrote *The Honolulu Advertiser*. "The Glomar Explorer thus becomes the first commercial contestant in the billion-dollar race for manganese nodules to make it to Hawaii, the nearest land mass to undersea treasure." That same story stated that the "Glomar Explorer is the first ship believed to possess the ability to harvest the nodules from the sea floor on a commercial basis."

The ship's arrival in Lahaina coincided exactly with the Circum-Pacific Energy and Mineral Resources Conference in Waikiki, which brought in more than a thousand people from sixty countries, and speculation was rampant around the Hawaii statehouse that some *Glomar* crew members had surreptitiously attended, to keep watch on the discussion.

Not only that, but the United Nations Law of the Sea Conference in Caracas ended during the stopover, following ten weeks of contentious negotiation sparked, in part, by Howard Hughes's effort to mine the ocean floor for precious metals that belonged to no nation. As the *Explorer* "rocked to the gentle swells off Lahaina yesterday," a reporter noted, "hundreds of delegates at the United Nations seabed conference in Caracas were arguing what to do about the mining potential of Summa Corp and others."

The reporter noted the vacuum of information from the ship's crew and representatives, saying that "those connected with the ship are as tight-mouthed as James Bond pursuing Goldfinger." A related story on the same front page reported that the state's acting governor, George Ariyoshi, planned to initiate an investigation "concerning the ownership of mineral rights in off-shore Hawaiian waters" and that the state attorney general had asked local authorities to keep a close watch on the ship.

A day later, the *Explorer* moved eight miles down the coast, anchoring off the less conspicuous Olowalu Point, one of the most popular snorkeling and diving areas on Maui, and the local papers were on it again. *Advertiser* science writer Bruce Benson noted that it was still "easy to recognize the ship's personnel in town—they were the ones who walked around with their mouths shut." Personnel wouldn't even tell anyone how long they planned to be in the area, nor where they'd go when the ship left. They mostly just wore sunglasses and looked conspicuous. These stories weren't plants, but the cover was so well constructed that they might as well have been.

John Rutten awoke early on August 17, his first morning aboard the *Explorer,* on the top bunk in the small stateroom that he shared with Carl Atkinson, the ship's chief steward. Their room was nice enough but had one major drawback; it was directly adjacent to the ship's movie room, so depending on the film playing—and the volume at which it was played—sleep was often interrupted by shouts, gunshots, or, on occasion, the lusty groans of Linda Lovelace.

The exploitation was still a twenty-four-hour operation, and the B crew picked up right where the A crew left off. This time, men worked rotating shifts of up to eight hours, and the hospital crew mimicked that schedule, too. Over twenty-four hours, each medical crewman worked eight hours, had eight hours of off time, and was "available" for eight hours—which meant the person would need to be in the hospital if required, but more often could use that time as additional rest. Rutten, as the ship's medical director, was also on call for emergencies twenty-four hours a day.

After his first breakfast, Rutten went to the moon pool to get a look at "the catch." He stood at the railing, fifty feet above the mangled sub, which looked to him remarkably similar to the fake version the CIA had built in Redwood City for the training program.

Enormous exhaust vacuums gulped air from the room through eight-inch ducts and vented it out the rear of the ship, so that the pool's exhaust was always downwind. The focus of the exploitation that day was on the Soviet crew's bunk rooms.

A few crew members in white Tyvek suits and breathing rigs were picking in the metal, and the only other person up on the gangway was a friendly, outgoing older man who told Rutten that he'd been working with submarines a long time, going back to World War II, when he'd run maintenance at a German U-boat base. His name, he said, was Manfred.

The scenery at this location, around Olowalu Point, was unreal: Rippled green hillsides rose four thousand feet above the beach on the ship's starboard side, while the vast pineapple plantations of Lanai, the smallest of the publicly accessible Hawaiian Islands, were clearly visible off port, as was the ten-thousand-foot summit of Haleakala peak, the massive volcano that dominates Maui's topography.

This spot was away from the city and just north of Kahoolawe, an uninhabited island used as a bombing range by Navy pilots stationed at Pearl Harbor. It was selected in advance for this reason, because no large vessels could get close, which was important because the *Explorer*'s crew would have to start disposing of debris, especially the tons of excess mud from the ocean bottom that had come up with the sub.

The next morning, Rutten woke at five A.M. and began a tradition that would continue for as long as he was aboard. He put on his bathing suit and running shoes and ascended to the helicopter pad, where he ran laps for forty-five minutes, until the fast-rising sun made outdoor exercise unbearable.

The next morning, Rutten ate breakfast in the mess hall, then headed for van 14, where he would practice a full dress out for the first time. He removed his clothes and stored them away in a locker, then put on shorts, a T-shirt, and socks, followed by a yellow one-piece jumpsuit with a drawstring around the neck, plastic booties, and rubber boots that were taped to his legs with yellow duct tape. A tech taped plastic gloves to the doctor's wrists and handed him thick leather work gloves, which he pulled over the plastic ones. At the end, he was given a hard hat and a respirator. "I felt like an astronaut heading for an Apollo spaceship at that point," Rutten would later write in the journal he wasn't really supposed to be keeping.

He left the dressing van and climbed down a long ladder to the floor of the moon pool, three stories below. This was Rutten's first time on the floor, and the wreck was far larger than he expected it to be. Huge sections of the sub had already been cut apart and picked through. Chunks of black metal lay in piles, and there was mud, rust, and organic waste floating in seawater that puddled around the wreck.

The K-129 fore section had begun to dissolve, so there was increased urgency to get it stripped. That was one reason Rutten had been asked to get familiar with the process, because even a slight change in expediency would increase the risk of injuries, from falls or cuts or whatever, and if there were to be an emergency, he'd need to get dressed and into the well as quickly as possible. He'd already prepared a full medical kit to stash in one of the dressing van lockers.

Many things in and on the sub came up in the capture vehicle, including crabs, shells, and, by total chance, some manganese nodules. These nodules, being loaded with metals, had tested hot, and were handled carefully. Irradiated objects had to be removed, bagged, and disposed of using strict procedures. Tests had also begun to pick up rising radiation counts around the capture vehicle, which hung over the moon pool, and the nuclear guys attributed that to metal vaporization from the cutting torches. At no point, now, could anyone be around the equipment without a full antiradiation suit and respirator.

Rutten was shown around the wreck, and then it was time to climb back out. Atop the deck, a fully suited radiation technician scanned him with a dosimeter, which detected a hot spot on his right boot. The boot was removed and taken away, where it would be cleaned with ultrasound purifier and then put into a bag for disposal, overboard, like all the other waste.

Several of the program officers who'd been unable to go to sea were put on the B crew as a token of appreciation, so that they could see and plunder the fruit of their labors. Dave Pasho also joined the crew in Lahaina, and because he was an amateur photographer, he had been trained in Redwood City to take photographs in a high-radiation environment. Once aboard the ship, he suited up and headed for the moon-pool floor to photograph anything of interest that came out of the wreck. He was welcome to participate in exploitation, too, and the first thing he noticed, when he stepped into the mangled former crew quarters, were the crude and uncomfortable-looking horsehide mattresses that the Soviet submariners had slept on.

A series of tables had been set up next to the wreck so that items retrieved from inside could be set down and analyzed. The job, Pasho later explained, "was basically to squeeze the mud and find anything from rings to knuckle bones, to whatever." Anything structural with printing, especially date or location, got the spooks excited. Analysts could use this information to figure out where the Soviets were manufacturing parts and how often certain components were replaced. It might even inform future target lists for American ICBMs.

One item that Pasho found would forever haunt him. It was an undeveloped roll of film he handed over to the photo analysts, who took it to the darkroom lab for processing. The film was badly damaged, pockmarked from the salt and water, but some images were still clearly visible and there was a series there that squashed Pasho's enthusiasm for the job: photographs of a Russian sailor, at the dock, with his family, just before shipping out.

Visitors were common while the ship was so close to shore, though it was never clear to most of the crew, Rutten included, who exactly these visitors were. Typically, they were introduced in some vague terms as being out "from Washington" or "Nevada," and on Saturday the twenty-fourth, a group came through the hospital with a surprise guest leading the tour—JP. Rutten didn't know JP's full name, only that he was the senior-most Agency man on the operation, and that one never knew when he might appear, nor what the purpose of his visit was.

Two days later, JP was back, this time to let Rutten know that Doug Cummings—his most trusted deputy—was in the sick bay. Azorian's boss was clearly concerned about the man's health, and during the course of their conversation, Rutten gleaned a rare personal fact about the mission's most mysterious man—this day, August 26, was his birthday.

Cummings had a history of recent medical issues, including a pulmonary embolism six years prior. He was taking medication to control arrhythmia and was showing mild atrial fibrillation. Though it wasn't normal practice, Rutten opted to spend the night in the sick bay because this wasn't a normal patient.

JP had other concerns, too. Two Soviet "barographs," or surveillance ships, were reported to be nearby, which caused a slight change in plans. The *Explorer* was scheduled to move farther offshore to a spot known as Area 3 to dispose of the larger hull sections that had been cut away in the process of exposing the sub's interior, with the exception of any areas that showed "penetration"—breaches from the explosion or the collision with the seafloor. The Navy had asked the CIA to save these parts for further study.

Because of the Soviets, this would all be done after dark, and while the ship was waiting to move, practically the whole crew showed up for lunch to celebrate JP's birthday. For one meal, an exception to the alcohol ban was made, and the mess hall staff filled small plastic cups with champagne so that everyone could toast the boss before he returned to the mainland.

Cummings' illness necessitated a crew change, and several new, grim-faced Agency officers arrived from Washington to take over operations and security for the next and last stage, which would ultimately end back in Long Beach.

The ship motored south, and then, at 4:20 A.M. on Friday the thirtieth, its motors slowed and then stopped as the ship anchored one hundred miles south of Hawaii, where a large crew assembled and began to dump the broken carcass through the open gate of the moon pool—pausing briefly around eleven A.M. so roughnecks could pull a cover over the large opening overhead in preparation for the daily pass of a Soviet spy satellite.

Two days later, Rutten volunteered for lookout shift as the ship moved slowly in a grid pattern to ensure that none of the material dumped overboard had floated back to the surface. Working lookout enabled him to spend the morning on the helipad, his favorite place on the ship.

Later, when he went below, Rutten saw the submarine's brass diving bell in the mess hall, where someone had placed it overnight as a totem of the mission's success. The bell looked filthy, like it had just spent six years in some ocean muck, but it had been cleaned with the ultrasound purifier, so that patina was now permanent. The bell had numerous dings, a large dent near the top, and the clapper was missing, but the fact that it had survived at all seemed remarkable to Rutten and the others who stopped to admire it.

Apparently, the crew had finished with the disposal because the ship turned east and headed for Maui at ten knots, its maximum speed. By September 3, the *Explorer* reentered Hawaiian waters and dropped anchor just off Maui. A boat skittered out with mail and some new crew, including a number of faces Rutten recognized as having been on the A crew. Having refreshed with several weeks of R and R, they were back for the duration of the sail to port in Long Beach, which was to begin the following day, after one very important final task—which would be carried out that night after dark.

60
Burial at Sea

Shortly after seven o'clock on a calm, cool night, nine miles off the coast of the Big Island, the *Explorer*'s tinny PA system crackled to life, and Mission Director Dale Nielsen began to speak. Seventy-five of the ship's crewmen had assembled on the top deck and stood in silence, facing a makeshift six-person honor guard—each member dressed in a spotless white suit and matching white hard hat borrowed from the exploitation team.

The honor guard stood in front of a large eight-by-eight-by-fourteen-foot box painted in rose red, which held the remains of six Soviet submariners, each one laid out on a shelf and shrouded by a Soviet naval ensign. The bodies had been carried on litters covered in the flag of the USSR—crimson, with the yellow sickle and star—one at a time, and because there was only a single Soviet flag on board, the pallbearers reused it each time a litter had been placed inside the vault.

These six bodies were recovered intact, but Nielsen wanted to make every effort to respect the lives of the others lost, too. Any human organic matter—body parts that were recognizable or not—had been carefully stored in the ship's morgue. These remains were also placed inside the box, in bags.

Two rehearsals were held earlier that afternoon to "ensure that the actual ceremony would proceed smoothly and with appropriate dignity," an official report of the proceedings stated. The necessity of staging a proper funeral had been considered far in advance and ordered at Parangosky's direction. Officers consulted the Agency's Soviet desk, which arranged for a contact at Naval Intelligence to enlist the help of Nicholas Shadrin, the code name for Soviet Navy captain Nikolay Fedorovich Artamonov, who defected to the United States via Sweden in 1959. Shadrin had served on submarines and had attended funerals at sea: He was flown to Hawaii with his Naval Intelligence handler to help Nielsen and the crew prepare for a proper burial at sea.

"The ceremony will now begin," Nielsen said, as a dirgelike version of "The Star-Spangled Banner" played, followed by the Soviet anthem.

"This service is being conducted to honor Viktor Lokhof, Vladimir Kostyushko, Valentin Nosachev, and three other unidentified Soviet submariners who perished in March of 1968 in North Pacific Ocean when their ship suffered a casualty of unknown origin," Nielsen said. "In a very real way this ceremony has resulted from the continuing tensions between our two nations. . . . Their casualty happened at a time when they were engaged in activities they deemed to be in service of their national protection. Their bodies have come into our possession some six years later through activities on behalf of our country which we feel fit the same criteria. The fact that our nations have had disagreements does not lessen in any way our respect for them and the service they have rendered. And so, as we return their mortal remains to the deep, we do so in a way that we hope would have had meaning to them, enclosed with a representative portion of the ship on which they served, and perished. As long as men and nations are suspicious of each other, instruments of war will be constructed, and brave men will die as these men have died, in the service of their country. Today we honor these six men, their shipmates, and all men who give their lives in patriotic service."

On the deck, the entire crew stood stoic, silent, as both the US and USSR flags fluttered.

Nielsen continued. "May the day quickly come when men will beat their swords into plowshares and spears into pruning hooks, and nations shall not rise up against nations. Neither shall there be war anymore."

A second voice took over the microphone and spoke, in a slightly less somber voice: "We know neither the exact burial ceremony of the Soviet Navy, nor the specific desires of what form a service these men might have desired. Accordingly, we have constructed a ceremony that we believe to be the closest approaching of an actual Soviet ceremony. Our intent is to preserve the meaning and symbolism of such a solemn occasion. In addition, the US Navy service for men at sea will follow."

There was a brief prayer, read from a copy of *Prayers at Sea,* by US Naval Institute chaplain Joseph F. Parker, and then the service continued, with each portion read in English first, followed by Russian.

"The officers and men of this ill-fated USSR submarine, pendant number 722, whom we honor here today have reached their journey's end. To you we entrust them that they find peace and contentment in their repose.

"We therefore commit these crew members of this ship to a proper resting place to join the Valhalla of sea heroes who have gone before them."

"At this time, please close the doors to the vault," Nielsen said as the *Explorer*'s deck crane pulled upward on one rose-red door, and then another. "Commence the hoist."

A member of the honor guard stepped in to bolt the vault door shut, and the crane hoisted the box up and over the side, depositing it as gently as a crane can, into the water, as the committal and benediction were read, and the "US Navy Hymn" played solemnly.

The *Explorer* was running south, slowly, and the sky off the starboard side changed from orange to red as the sun sank farther below the horizon.

At precisely 7:21 P.M., "during the final light of evening twilight," the vault broke the surface, filled with water, and sank under the ocean, as white foam crested and bubbled where it had just been. "Everyone on board," John Rutten later recalled, "was deep in thought and somber as the vault was let go into the open ocean."

"This concludes the ceremony," Nielsen said.

61

Good-bye, Azorian; Hello, Matador

The funeral at sea was the last major task for the *Explorer*'s crew. The exploitation work was completed, with the most valuable assets already packed up and flown back to wherever the Navy and CIA specialists would begin to mine the intelligence, most likely at Area 51, where the dry desert air was ideal for preservation of items recovered from the sea.

Picketing by the marine workers' union had resumed on the docks in Long Beach, forcing the captain to slow the *Explorer*'s approach to the mainland about halfway between Hawaii and California, to delay the scheduled arrival time of early morning on Thursday, September 19. Instead, the ship would enter port after midnight on a Saturday so that the Agency's team on the dock could unload the vans from the ship under the cover of darkness, on a weekend, and get them onto flatbeds and out of town before the protests regained strength with the daylight.

As Friday wound down, the *Explorer* approached its home harbor at last, more than ninety days since leaving port to begin the mission. For the final few hours it had been navigating on radar alone, as a thick fog blanketed the coast, making visual navigation extremely difficult.

Just after midnight, a pilot boat emerged from the fog and led the mining vessel through the narrow channel into Long Beach port, where a pair of tugs grabbed the ship and turned it around, so that it could be tied up on the starboard side, the bow facing out toward the ocean.

As the deckhands began the process of securing the enormous vessel to the pier, a dockside crew fired up a crane and began unloading vans, so that by the time the gangway had been dropped, the first set of trucks was already headed for the Nevada desert. These trucks had no special markings to indicate their origins. Only someone who'd worked in the black world would know that NoSoCalCo—the company name printed on the side— stood for North South California Company, the in-house transportation service for Lockheed's Skunk Works.

Parangosky was waiting at Pier E to greet the returning B crew, as was Doug Cummings, whose condition had stabilized. John Rutten was thrilled to see his patient there on the dock, looking happy if not as hearty as he'd once been. The ship's physician was told that he'd need to report to the program office on Monday for a debrief; then he, like the rest of the crew, would be free to take some well-earned vacation. He and his wife, Laura, already had a plan—to borrow their son's pickup with camper top and sleep their way up the coast, toward Santa Barbara, under the stars.

There'd been plenty of time to dissect and discuss the mission's shortcomings, and most everyone on the crew agreed that everything that didn't work on the mission could be fixed. The claw could be remade, better and stronger, and so could other elements of the ship that had been built or assembled hastily in the rush to get to sea in July.

By the time the *Explorer*'s personnel left Pier E, the general consensus was that those crewmen who wanted to go back and finish the job would be given their chance. And that process began a few weeks later, when the ship pulled back out of the harbor and sailed to Catalina, where the capture vehicle was demated, returned to the *HMB-1*, and carried north to Redwood City, where it would be rebuilt with some design changes, including a different, stronger steel for the tines.

Once he returned to Washington, Parangosky moved quickly to get a follow-up mission under way. Project Azorian might have come to a close, but Project Matador was only beginning. Those who'd been instrumental in bringing Azorian to fruition—in particular, NURO director Dave Potter— were mostly in support of a follow-up mission to recover the rest of the submarine, but critics of the operation were emboldened by the original recovery's failures.

The two factions argued through the late fall and over the holidays into early 1975, when Kissinger presented a memo to the president summing up the situation: "With justifiable pride, the intelligence community climaxed a six-year effort last year by lifting from the ocean floor in the Pacific a Soviet submarine which sank there in 1968," Kissinger wrote. This "unique accomplishment" was marred, he admitted, when a portion of the submarine broke away during capture, but the United States Intelligence Board (USIB) believed that the value of the intelligence assets still inside the sub, in combination with the "sizable investment ($250 million to date)," warranted a review, which had just been completed.

That review had been positive, Kissinger reported. "The USIB has reaffirmed its view" that the equipment aboard the submarine is of "unique intelligence potential," and its estimate of the overall gain from a successful recovery has not "measurably" changed. "Cover and security for this operation have been remarkably maintained, but there are obvious risks in extending the operation for several more months." The Soviets, as everyone knew, had been suspicious of the *Glomar* during the primary mission, and it seemed extraordinarily unlikely that they wouldn't at least return with more curiosity the second time the giant ship appeared in the same area of the Pacific. But nothing in the news reports so far had revealed any tangible information; the denials were plausible, and—Kissinger noted to Ford—preparations for a return had already begun. "The equipment that broke during the lifting of the heavy target is being redesigned. An estimated $25,576,000 has been committed, and $36,424,000 more will be required to complete a second operation." Lastly, and importantly, that money had already been allocated. No new funds would be required, which is the kind of fact that makes decisions a whole lot easier for politicians.

Which didn't mean that approval was a slam dunk. When the 40 Committee met to discuss Azorian, Kissinger told Ford, the loudest objections came from the undersecretary of state for political affairs, a man who would be directly in the line of fire for Soviet backlash, should there be any. The undersecretary argued that the risks of going back outweighed the value of the leftover intelligence on the seafloor, "and that a return to the exact spot of ocean will feed Soviet suspicion; and that new uncertainties in US–Soviet relations add to the substantial political risks should there be a Soviet reaction."

This was a reasonable objection, but it failed. All of the other members of the 40 Committee were in agreement that a second recovery attempt was worth it and should be approved. "The deep ocean mining cover story has been accepted widely and the Soviets did not show any undue suspicion during the first operation," Kissinger reported; "therefore it is reasonable to expect that they will accept a return to the site as what it will appear to be—a second deep ocean mining trial." In summation, Kissinger wrote, there was a consensus: "That the potential intelligence return from a successful second mission would be significant enough to accept the cost, cover/security and other risks."

Until someone told him otherwise, Parangosky was moving forward, and so was the organization that had been built up around him. NURO arranged for the USS *Seawolf* to depart her West Coast base and head to the target site. *Seawolf* was the latest special projects submarine to emerge and conduct covert activities in support of the CIA and NSA, in the tradition of the *Halibut*, and the sub slipped quietly out into the Pacific and took a new round of high-resolution photographs of the target—photographs that assured analysts that what had fallen back to the sea remained intact enough to justify another mission.

The program office had gone quiet for the interval after the mission, while the ship was off Hawaii, but it never closed, and as a plan to go back for the rest of the submarine was just being formulated back in Washington, Curtis Crooke reassembled his engineers to begin studying the necessary fixes.

The biggest problem, obviously, was the claw. The tines had broken, and that, a postmortem evaluation concluded, was due to a series of factors—the most important being a poor choice of steel. This, really, was a problem that could be traced all the way back to the *Glomar II*. That ship's inability to get a proper soil sample meant that no one knew what the seafloor was like, and engineers had therefore chosen the hardest possible steel. But extremely hard steel isn't infallible. It's stiff, but it won't bend. Subject it to too much stress and it'll crack, like glass. The tines had held up during the initial contact with the bottom, through the process of unloading more weight to force them into the soil, and even for the pickup and lift. But once the submarine was inside the grabber, it moved around, causing the weight to shift from one davit to another, which created a shock wave that snapped the fingers of two-inch-steel plate.

There was some bickering back and forth between the engineers of Lockheed and Global Marine after the mission's completion; in private, Parangosky felt that Crooke and the systems integration team should have picked up the problem in advance, but as a good manager he recognized that nothing positive could come of criticizing his key engineers in retrospect. We should have recognized it and we didn't, he told the team. Accept that and move on.

This time, the tines would be made of low-carbon HY-100 steel and handled by Global Marine, which subcontracted the job to their old friends at Sun Ship in Chester, where an enormous heat-treating oven built for the original ship construction came in handy once again.

Forging the new davits wasn't a complicated job for Sun Ship; getting them out to Redwood City for assembly on the rebuilt capture vehicle, however, was. The enormous steel fingers were too big to hide inside truck trailers and had to be strapped onto flatbeds that exceeded the typical size allowed on American interstates. The rigs would be officially oversize, requiring special clearance to pass through certain more persnickety states. The Agency hired one of its more clever trucking contractors, Leonard Brothers, from Miami. Leonard did various special transport jobs for the government and was known for having excellent relationships with the highway inspectors of most US states. Leonard Brothers agents kept detailed records of which inspectors were most difficult, and which were more lenient, and what shifts everyone worked. Schedules were then optimized to run the loads across problematic states when the friendliest inspectors were on duty. If necessary, they'd slip a case of Jack Daniel's off the truck when passing through as a thank-you.

As engineers at the program office awaited the next stage, morale was high. From the moment they all reassembled, Hank Van Calcar later said, the conversation was all about how to fix the problems and go back: "It wasn't, 'It's over with.' It was, 'Okay, on to the next phase.'"

62

The Beginning of the End

Sometime in the late fall, while the *Explorer* was back in port in Long Beach, and work had already begun inside the *HMB-1* at Redwood City to repair Clementine for a second trip to the bottom, a package was slipped under the door of the Soviet embassy in Washington. Inside was a note. It read: "Certain authorities of the United States are taking measures to raise the Soviet submarine sunk in the Pacific Ocean" and was signed by "Well-wisher."

Tips and leads poured into the embassy on a regular basis, and most were misinformed, useless, or completely without merit, but those with some credence were passed up the ladder to Ambassador Anatoly Dobrynin, who in this case took the note seriously enough to raise the matter with his superiors back in Moscow. Their response was nonplussed, even dismissive. Rumors of American meddling with the missing sub weren't a new thing, and now, as before, the naval command considered the prospect ridiculous. As far as the admirals were concerned, it was simply impossible for anyone to salvage a submarine from three miles under the sea—and this was hardly a stubborn position; most engineers on earth at the time would concur.

Whether and how the Soviets reacted internally is something we still don't know, and layers of obfuscation and misinformation have been settling on this story like silt ever since. But rumors, apparently, also began to scatter around Washington.

In December 1974, according to a former head of Naval Intelligence who told the author Norman Polmar, a Soviet officer approached a US Navy captain at an annual party for foreign naval attachés and said that the Russians were aware of the CIA's attempt and that it would be unwise for another mission to be launched. "If you go back," he allegedly said, "it would mean war."

Then, on Friday, February 7, the late edition of the *Los Angeles Times* landed on doorsteps around that city with a thump that echoed back to Langley and beyond. Above the fold on page A1 was a near-half-page headline that no one had seen coming: US REPORTED AFTER RUSS SUB. The story, by staff writers William Farr and Jerry Cohen, was accompanied by two large photos—one of a Soviet sub that wasn't anything like the K-129, and one of the *Glomar Explorer* docked in Long Beach—and sketched out the basics of the CIA–Hughes arrangement, "according to reports circulating among local law enforcement officials."

The story was riddled with mistakes and incorrect speculation, starting with the target of the operation. The *Times* story guessed that the mission, if indeed it was real, "is likely to have involved one of two Soviet undersea vessels"—both of them nuclear-powered subs lost after 1970 in the Atlantic Ocean.

News of the leak reached Washington late in the afternoon, and Director Colby happened to be going to the White House already, for a meeting with Ford and several key advisers, including Kissinger, Defense Secretary James Schlesinger, Chairman of the Joint Chiefs of Staff David Jones, and the president's main assistant, Donald "Rummie" Rumsfeld, in the Cabinet Room. January 1975 was a turbulent month for the intelligence community, with Sy Hersh's revelations of the CIA's so-called family jewels—a series of disturbing and in some cases illegal acts perpetrated by the Agency in recent years. Among the shocking admissions made by Colby in an open session of Congress was that the CIA had spied on US antiwar activists, opened Jane Fonda's mail from Russia, and made several unsuccessful attempts to assassinate foreign leaders.

That was not Ford's agenda on the day in early January when the *LA Times* story hit, however; he had called the meeting of his advisers to discuss leaks from the National Security Council.

"I hate to raise this, but the *Los Angeles Times* just asked whether we had raised a piece of a Soviet submarine," Colby told the president, adding that he'd already instructed Frank Murphy, on his security staff, to "try to kill it" and that "it doesn't seem to be a Washington leak."

And in fact it wasn't. The *Times* story really began with the June 1974 break-in at the Summa office on Romaine Street, and that was obvious from the text. "Confidential files on the operation" were "believed to have been among" those stolen in the robbery, the *LA Times* story reported, and the thieves had singled them out in the hopes that the US government would pay the 1-million-dollar ransom for their safe return.

Colby explained that when word reached the CIA that the files had allegedly vanished—files that really consisted of a single handwritten document that may or may not even have existed—he ordered his West Coast security staff to brief the FBI agents working the case, to alert them to the sensitivity of this document, and to ask them to make sure that the LAPD understood that if this document were to surface, it must be kept secret at all costs.

Well, the FBI did brief the LAPD detectives, who listened and then did the complete opposite of what they were asked; they let the murky story behind the document slip out, and Farr got a tip about it from a contact at the district attorney's office while reporting another story. With little more to go on than that rumor, Farr and Cohen spent several months on the investigation and managed, by February, to piece together a story with a basic premise juicy enough to occupy nearly the entire front page—even though beyond the CIA–Hughes connection, there was virtually no actual detail on the mission or its target.

By the time the story reached Colby, it was too late to do anything. He raced back to Langley after the White House meeting and called the West Coast program office on the Donald Duck phone. The security officer on duty ran to answer the squawk.

Colby ordered two security men to go straight to the *LA Times* office and tell the paper's editor, Bill Thomas, "anything he needs to know about the program to stop publication." The director said that he would call Thomas himself to alert him that they were on the way but that he wouldn't be able to make a case himself because the *Times* didn't have a secure line.

The security officers arrived at the paper's downtown headquarters and found that Thomas had already spoken to Colby. He knew that the CIA wanted him to kill the story and that the men had come to provide the reasons for this unusual request. Thomas, in his third year leading the powerful daily, was friendly and receptive, and when the two men told him that the operation was very much still in play, he agreed that this was a time when national security trumped news. But it was also too late—the late edition, with the story splashed across the front, had already been printed.

What Thomas could do was downplay the story in the next day's early edition and then drop the paper's coverage. And that's what he did. The next morning, a smaller version of the story appeared deep inside the front section, on page A18. There was no further coverage.

Late on Friday, Colby heard from *The New York Times*. That paper was also preparing a story, based mostly on the *LA Times*' reporting, and because it wasn't scheduled to run until Saturday, Colby still had time to act. He traveled to New York and met with the paper's publisher, Arthur Sulzberger. The situation there was a repeat of that in Los Angeles: Sulzberger told Colby that it was too late to fully kill the *Times* story but that it could be buried. It ran on page 30.

The director wasn't yet panicked. He strongly believed that if he could stifle the story fast, after just these two small leaks, the Soviets might miss it. So once he had successfully squashed the story at two of the country's largest dailies, he sat back and waited for the blowback.

Almost immediately, the phone began to ring at several outposts of the Hughes empire. Paul Reeve, in Houston, was besieged with inquiries, and he had no idea what to say. He consulted with the Agency and also called Hughes's personal PR rep, Arelo Sederberg. Sederberg was dumbstruck by the story. He'd been out dutifully trumpeting the *Explorer* and his boss's experimental mining effort for more than two years, one of the few Hughes business ventures he was allowed (and even encouraged) to promote in the media. He was one of the only top Hughes deputies who hadn't been told the truth, which made him a valuable part of the cover. "I was on a

last-to-know status for the project," he later wrote, "since in innocent ignorance, I could boost it as a commercial venture."

He hadn't heard a word about the submarine salvage until William Farr
called him the night before the story published and asked, obliquely, what
he knew about the *Glomar Explorer*. A true PR man, Sederberg replied with
a florid sales pitch of the ship's remarkable innovation and the new industry
it would help create. "Okay," Farr replied. "Get what you have on it to me."

When Sederberg saw Farr's story, he didn't know what to think, and
when Reeve called him for advice, it seemed like Summa's mining operations guy was also confused. When Sederberg asked what he was telling
reporters, Reeve replied, "I wish they'd go sit on a tack." Reeve was playing
dumb, and the two decided that the best way to respond was to discredit the
story based on one of its central—and clearly incorrect—facts, that the *Explorer* had participated in a submarine salvage operation in the Atlantic
Ocean. Maybe there had been a secret salvage, he would say, but it wasn't
our ship. We've never left the Pacific Ocean.

Reporters liked Reeve. That was a big reason Walt Lloyd made him the
single point of contact for the media. "He was accessible, friendly, and quot-
able," according to Sederberg. And reporters in this case seemed to believe
him, or at least were confused enough by what he was saying—that the ship
never went east—that the *Times* story seemed murky and possibly just
wrong. Even Sederberg was convinced, and he and Reeve doubled down on
the mining story. "We insisted that the Explorer was a commercial mining
venture," he later wrote. "No dark lanterns or eye-shaded CIA operatives
lurked around it." This tack, he says, "added to the confusion, which perhaps
was what the CIA wanted. When lies and deception no longer work, confusion might."

Many of those inside the program who saw the paper were certain that
this was the end of Azorian, but Colby wasn't so sure. His hope was buoyed
by a similar incident from the past: During World War II, a front-page story
in the *Chicago Tribune* revealed that the United States had broken Japan's
top secret Navy code, and the story caused President Roosevelt to go

bananas. But the Japanese either didn't see the story or didn't believe it, because they never stopped using the code, and the United States continued to intercept and crack messages until the war's end.

Colby felt there was a chance for a similar result here—that either the Soviets wouldn't see it or they'd discount the report as ridiculous, which wasn't just wishful thinking since the *Los Angeles Times* story hadn't even named the right ocean. "There was a real chance that the stories would be dismissed as just another of the hysterical tales about the CIA then crowding the press," Colby later wrote in his memoir. "And if the Glomar was careful to follow the manganese-nodule-collection scenario it could even escape another close inspection next summer."

What worried Colby more were the other investigative reporters who would notice this tantalizing story appear and then vanish literally overnight. In particular, he was concerned about Seymour Hersh, who had promised him nearly a year before to sit on his investigation only as long as no one else was reporting on it. Now Colby could no longer make that case.

For the next few weeks, during the most tumultuous period of his directorship—as the Rockefeller Commission and Church Committee began to ramp up on Capitol Hill, probing alleged nefarious and possibly illegal activities by the CIA—Colby said, he "raced around from newsrooms to editorial offices to television stations, trying desperately to plug any leaks on the story and feeling as if I were rapidly running out of fingers and toes with which to do the job."

Everywhere he went, the director ran into reporters and editors whose skepticism of the US government, and especially the CIA, was at an all-time high. The ripples of Watergate were still sweeping through Washington, and Colby's own revelations about the "family jewels" had made distrust of the CIA even worse. He made a bold decision to try to counter those feelings. The director knew that legal action to stifle further stories about Azorian would be unpopular and was likely to fail. It might actually piss off and embolden reporters like Hersh. The only way to stop the stories, he decided, was to treat the editors as equals—as Americans who could be trusted with sensitive material.

Colby was parsimonious with specifics, but he shared classified details with editors at twelve different publications, including the *LA Times, The New York*

Times, and *The Washington Post.* As he later explained in his memoir, "I took the gamble of responding to their questions to the minimum degree necessary to show my good faith, and only then, when I was sure they comprehended the seriousness of it, did I request that they hold back stories on the Glomar. In practically every instance, my urgings paid off and the press held back."

The director's frantic road show resulted in agreements from the *LA Times, The New York Times, The Washington Post, Newsweek, Time,* and *Parade.* In each case, Colby successfully argued that printing stories about Azorian—a name he never revealed—would cause the entire operation to fall apart, putting valuable intelligence critical to the US national interest at risk. *The Washington Post's* Katharine Graham told Colby that "it is not anything we want to get into" and that "we have no problem not doing it," but admitted that other *Post* reporters could be working in secret and that it was possible, even likely, that she wouldn't yet know about their projects.

One of Colby's most challenging encounters was with *Parade* writer Lloyd Shearer, who called the director shortly after the *LA Times* story to inquire about something called Project Jennifer.

At the mention of that name, Colby bristled. "We can't discuss this on the telephone," he said. "I'll have someone out to see you in a few hours."

Shearer slowly came around. "You are onto something very, very delicate," Colby told him on a subsequent call, after the writer had been briefed. "This one I really would like you to sit on." When Shearer warned the director that "entire news bureaus" were aware of the story, he replied that a cooperative media would later be rewarded in other ways. "And that is, I suspect, the best story—maybe in a year or so—the performance of the press," he said. "It will make a hell of a story, and I would be the first to give it." Later, Shearer told a lower-ranking Agency representative who'd called to follow up, "If he contains it, all you guys should be given a Medal of Honor."

Every time an editor or reporter agreed to sit on the story, Colby added his or her name to a list that he carried in his wallet—a list of people who would be called and told to go ahead with their stories the minute the cover was blown.

On February 19, an official Agency memo summed up his success: "To date, all of those in the mass media who have been briefed and whose cooperation was solicited have honored their commitments."

63
More Legal Troubles

A County tax assessor Philip Watson looked up from his desk in the Hall of Administration in downtown Los Angeles to see an FBI agent he knew walking into his office along with four men in suits, three of whom he'd never seen before.

"These men are representatives of the Central Intelligence Agency," the agent said quietly, then left the office, shutting the door on his way out.

Watson was preparing his case against Howard Hughes's Summa Corporation, which he was still sure had been ignoring a large tax bill it rightly owed on the massive mining ship that had been docked at Long Beach on and off for more than a year.

The four men introduced themselves as David Toy, Steven Schoenbaum, Clinton Morse, and George Kucera. Two were locals—including Toy, a lawyer whom Watson had previously met—one was from Houston, and the fourth said he'd come from Washington, but he offered no business card or other identification.

The man from Houston was Clinton Morse, a partner in a law firm who had come to represent Summa. Dave Toy was there to represent Global Marine, and Schoenbaum and Kucera were both with the Agency.

"We're here today to talk about the *Hughes Glomar Explorer*," Schoenbaum said, assuming the role of spokesperson. "To acquaint you with certain facts concerning its ownership."

He snapped open a briefcase and withdrew a short stack of paper.

"Before we go any further, you need to sign this," Schoenbaum said. He placed a piece of paper with an embossed seal that Watson couldn't immediately identify on the table. On the top were the words SPECIAL PROJECT SECRECY AGREEMENT. It went on in very clear language to lay out the terms that the person signing this paper was agreeing to. He was being cleared to receive information that was beyond top secret, and if he signed it and later disclosed that information, he was subject to prosecution under the espionage law (title 18, sections 793 and 794).

Watson scanned the paragraphs, one of which said: "I have also been informed that extraordinary security measures and controls have been established to protect Project information and that access to such information is restricted to those who 'must know' based upon their present position." He told the men that he was confused. He understood the *Glomar Explorer* to be a mining vessel owned by Summa worth 40 million dollars, and based on this, the company owed his county taxes—lots of taxes.

"The *Glomar Explorer* is and always has been the property of the United States government," Schoenbaum replied. "It is not owned by Summa Corporation, nor has it ever been operated by Summa Corporation, despite the fact that official documents—documents you've seen—state precisely that." Summa, Schoenbaum explained, was acting as an agent for the government, on a classified project. "It's our desire to cooperate in any way we can to protect the secret project and at the same time prevent embarrassment for your office or the city of Los Angeles."

Watson nodded. "Okay."

Schoenbaum handed the tax assessor a photograph of the *HMB-1* and told him it was a "submarine tractor," used in conjunction with the *Glomar Explorer*. It was a submersible barge, containing "electronic gear and other equipment which is used on the ocean floor." He said that the barge could also be used as "a storage bin for materials that have been picked up from the ocean floor."

"This barge is owned by the Lockheed Corporation," Schoenbaum said. "And your equivalent in San Mateo County, where the barge is based, has assessed a tax of 1 percent of its full cash value as an oceanographic research vessel pursuant to Section 227 of the California Revenue and Taxation Code."

Watson nodded, a little puzzled. He didn't quite know what the man was getting at.

The men would prefer Watson not tax the *Explorer* at all, but if he insisted, he should follow the lead of San Mateo.

"Assess taxes at 1 percent of the full cash value," Schoenbaum said, as he reached into a briefcase and pulled out a small, clear container about the size of a box of checks and handed it to Watson. Inside, a lump of black rock had been mounted.

"That's a manganese nodule," Schoenbaum said. "The *Glomar Explorer* sucked that up from the floor of the ocean, 17,000 feet down. There aren't many of these. And there never will be, at least from the Explorer. We went out with another ship and collected just enough to convince people that this is something Howard Hughes was really serious about."

He produced a flyer from Sun Shipbuilding welcoming the recipient to a "Family Day, featuring the launching of the Hughes Glomar Explorer, constructed for Global Marine." The flyer gave the ship's remarkable specifications and listed a few notes, the first of which was this: "The HUGHES GLOMAR EXPLORER is a deep ocean mining vessel built for Hughes. When delivered, Global Marine will operate the 51,000-ton ship."

"Actually," Schoenbaum said, "the *Glomar* is worth about $300 million and we"— meaning the CIA—"had it built for laying sensors on the ocean floor." These sensors, he explained, were designed to detect the test launch of Polaris-type missiles, fired from submarines, as well as other ship movements and activities.

Watson was surprised by this. He didn't actually need to know the true purpose of the ship's secret work in order to waive the taxes; he needed only to know that it belonged to the US government.

Most important, the man said, Watson couldn't mention this actual value to anyone. The boat's true cost was such an unusual—even outrageous—figure that public disclosure would certainly arouse suspicion. "Somebody is going to ask, 'Who the hell owns a $300 million boat?!'"

The man from Washington had been sitting quietly, but he spoke now. "Mr. Watson, we need your help here," George Kucera said. As Azorian's contracting officer, he had executed the original arrangements between the Agency, Global Marine, and Hughes. "We need you to trust us that this is not Howard Hughes's ship. It belongs to the United States government. Summa Corp does and should not owe any taxes to Los Angeles County." As a result, no one was going to pay the 25 percent tax that a typical commercial ship owner would owe. If necessary, the government would pay the same 1 percent rate paid to San Mateo County, based on a rate granted to privately owned oceanographic vessels conducting scientific research.

"But if it's a government-owned ship, you don't need to pay any taxes," Watson replied.

Kucera smiled. "I know. But it's not a government-owned ship." He held the silence after that statement a few seconds to let Watson absorb the subtext. "It's a mining research vessel and its owners should pay their fair tax."

Watson got the message. The Agency was asking him to play along with a story, the story he'd already fallen for when he went after Howard Hughes for unpaid taxes. He laughed. "I have to say this is the first time in my career as a tax assessor that anyone offered to pay me taxes they don't owe." Watson said that he was willing to accept the men's explanation, but he wanted a letter from the Agency—or from some federal agency—stating that the ship in his port belonged to the United States and not to Howard Hughes.

"I'm afraid that's impossible," Schoenbaum said. "There's too much at stake here to give you a piece of paper stating that."

On April 25, Toy and Morse returned to Watson's office with a letter dated April 23 and signed by V. C. Olson, Summa's controller. The letter stated that the vessel was registered in Delaware and was only temporarily in California. It contained no mention of government involvement.

When Watson pressed the matter, asking for a letter that stated the true arrangement, Toy and Morse demurred, because Watson had also invited an attorney from the office of the Los Angeles County counsel—an attorney who was not cleared for program knowledge. The rules were very clear. It could not be discussed in this attorney's company. Watson sensed the trepidation and afterward pulled Toy aside to ask for a copy of the classified government contract covering the *Glomar Explorer* project. Toy replied that it was very unlikely Watson could be given his own copy, but that "under appropriate circumstances," a copy of the contract might be shown to him. Toy said he'd speak with his government contacts, and later that day, he did.

On July 2, another group arrived to see Watson, and hopefully shut him up. This time, it was heavy hitters: John Warner, chief counsel of the CIA; John Howard, acting LA County district attorney; and Stephen Trott, his deputy DA. Watson told the group, again, that he was unconvinced of their story. In fact, he said, he had discovered a Coast Guard document dated October 2, 1973, stating that the *HGE* was registered by Summa Corporation upon entering Long Beach port.

As a result, he had assessed "for ad valorem property tax purposes" two bills to Summa Corporation of Las Vegas, the ship's owner—4,395,152.43 dollars for 1974 and 3,119,865 dollars for 1975. He also threatened to assess late fees if the bill wasn't paid on time.

Toy had warned Walt Lloyd that sending Warner would likely backfire. Watson was a grandstander with political ambitions and he'd see an opportunity to embarrass the federal government as a way to get himself some attention. And Toy was right. By the time Warner was back at his hotel, Watson had called a press conference to declare his intent to assess taxes on the *Hughes Glomar Explorer* to Howard Hughes's Summa Corporation.

He wasn't going away quietly.

64

What Are We Doing Again?

Despite everything that had happened—press leaks, Soviet complaints, rising resentment in Congress—the pursuit of K-129 somehow continued and had strong support from the people who mattered most, especially Henry Kissinger and the powerful 40 Committee.

On February 5, Kissinger presented a memo to the president summing up the recommendations of the US Intelligence Board, which had met several times over the fall and winter to consider whether or not to go forward with the follow-up to Azorian, in a mission that had been code-named Matador.

The USIB had reaffirmed its view that the equipment on the sub was still important and worth pursuing, and cover and security were somehow still intact. Kissinger said that nearly everyone on the 40 Committee agreed that the mission was worth keeping alive.

His recommendation: that Ford approve preparations for a second mission, code-named Matador.

The support for Matador was hardly effusive. The State Department, especially, was uncomfortable. Some portion of the argument to move forward with a new operation was that the 250 million dollars already spent constituted a sunk cost and that it would take only another 25 million dollars for the follow-up. When someone asked if the 250 million dollars was actually lost, or if the ship could be used for something else, Director Colby said that it could be repurposed into an actual ocean miner, and that he hoped the government could later sell it for 40 to 50 million dollars.

Colby's standing at this point was clearly in jeopardy. The morning after the 40 Committee meeting, Kissinger told the president that he lacked confidence in the director, who he felt was far too forthcoming with Congress, in part to cover his own ass. "Colby is a disaster and really should be replaced," Kissinger said. "There are so many people who have to be briefed on covert operations, it is bound to leak. There is no one with guts left."

65

Stranger Than Fiction

LOS ANGELES, APRIL 3, 1975

A Times reporter Bill Farr tried for more than a year to get an interview with Mike Davis, the security guard ambushed during the Romaine Street break-in, the strange event that tipped the first domino that led to exposure of the largest covert operation in CIA history. On April 3, 1975, Davis agreed to sit for an interview. And one of the first things Davis told Farr dropped the reporter's jaw. Davis said that while he was waiting for police to arrive, he'd picked up two papers the thieves had dropped and stuffed them in his pocket. "It was just an absent-minded type thing," he said.

Once police arrived and began questioning him, Davis completely forgot about the papers—until they fell out of his pockets while he was changing at home later that night. One of the papers, he told Farr, was a Bank of America certificate of deposit for one hundred thousand dollars made payable to Kay Glenn. The other was a typewritten memo from Raymond Holliday to Howard Hughes "saying that the CIA wanted to build a ship or something to bring up a Russian sub," Davis said. "I don't remember all the details but I recall that it said President Nixon knew about it and that the IRS would look the other way on how the money was being put in."

Davis hid both papers inside a dresser drawer and then, months later, when the Soviet sub scandal appeared in the news, he tore the memo into pieces and flushed it down the toilet. "Then I took Glenn's $100,000 note and put it in a friend's safe. . . . My god, if only I would have remembered those documents I stuffed in my pockets," he told Farr. "It would have saved me and a whole lot of other people an awful lot of trouble."

He said he thought that the memo was "of no personal value to anyone" and that "the person who wrote it knew its content," while the certificate of deposit seemed more likely to be "of some value to Glenn." He planned, in fact, to return it to Glenn once things calmed down and thought "I wouldn't get in trouble over it." But that never happened. When Davis refused to take a polygraph test following the break-in, he was fired. He subsequently also lost his job at the car lot, and by the time he met Farr, he was unemployed. He'd even sold his house and moved into a smaller, cheaper rental.

"Had I had any idea that the memo involved something of that magnitude, my whole course of action would have been different," Davis told Farr. "I grant now that I made a mistake but as tough as it is for me now, I want to clear everything up."

66

The SEC Butts In

ax problems weren't Walt Lloyd's only bureaucratic nightmare. There was also a possible patent lawsuit from Project Moho progenitor Willard Bascom and something he'd already tried to anticipate and fend off—interference from the Securities and Exchange Commission. Global Marine was publicly traded, but a single family owned a significant portion of the company's stock in a family trust. And unfortunately, back in the program's early days, just as Azorian was coming together, the family decided to break up that trust and hand each member a portion of the shares, so that he or she would be free to trade them on the stock market, like any other investor.

This wasn't in itself an unusual thing. It happens. But it triggers an SEC law requiring that when a large enough amount of stock is disbursed, the holders must explain their actions, in great detail, to the SEC, to prove that there's nothing improper going on. That filing is called a 10-K, and the results are made public to anyone who wants to view them. They list every client, every customer, and every business problem—basically, every way in which a company generates revenue. And it happens immediately, before the trust can be split. That meant that Global Marine's financials would be published for the world, revealing, at a minimum, that Howard Hughes had quietly hired them to mine the ocean—a story that wasn't going to be public until all of the program's security, including a robust cover umbrella, had been put in place. That was still months away.

When this news reached Curtis Crooke, he panicked. He called in his

355

lawyer, Dave Toy, who went to see Walt Lloyd, whose job it was to snuff out fires that could engulf the project.

"We've got a problem," Toy said. He'd flown directly to Virginia that morning and met Lloyd at his office, where they schemed furiously until well after midnight. Lloyd's concerns were many. He knew that, above all, they couldn't flat-out lie to the SEC, because if it were ever to become public that Hughes was only pretending to hire Global Marine, it could destroy the reputation of two major corporations. And to say that Hughes was acting on behalf of an undisclosed principal, without providing more information, would be highly misleading to investors, who might see this huge mining contract as a reason to invest when, in truth, it was all a lie. The solution, they decided, was to tell one small lie while being overly truthful about everything else. They'd admit that Hughes Tool was representing an undisclosed principal, without disclosing who that was, and then make it very clear that the whole venture was highly speculative and risky. The plan was to make the situation look so unpalatable that no investment adviser in his right mind would recommend Global Marine based on this single deal.

"This mining business could blow up tomorrow," they would say. "It's very uncertain. This secret customer is willing to invest his money, but there is no guarantee it's going to be more than one shot. You aren't going to make any money down the road. It's very doubtful."

In this way, Lloyd and Toy could explain the influx of income that Global Marine was making on the mining project in the near term while painting the worst possible picture of the nascent industry's longer-term prospects.

And that all worked out fine, until one attentive clerk at a Wall Street investment firm happened to see the *LA Times* story and recalled Global Marine's 10-K claiming that Howard Hughes's Summa Corp. was responsible for a very large piece of new business that inflated the company's earnings in 1971 and 1972. She pulled the 10-K, confirmed her suspicions, and then reported the discrepancy to the SEC's Division of Corporate Finance, pointing out that Global Marine had, in fact, made a false representation.

The SEC's enforcement division, in turn, charged Global Marine with filing false information, a type of fraud, and requested that Global Marine's leadership come to Washington to answer the charges. This was a serious matter. Were the charges proven, it would lead to criminal proceedings, potentially causing significant harm to the company and its shareholders.

All of the stockholders stood to lose out in that scenario, and it would have been the CIA's fault. Again, Curtis Crooke sent Dave Toy to see Walt Lloyd, who recognized the severity of the problem and reported it to the Agency's general counsel, John Warner.

Warner was not pleased. He told Lloyd to "find out how deep of water we're in here" and to report to his office in thirty minutes. Lloyd recruited a trusted colleague and asked him to pull anything he could find about securities exchange law that might be pertinent to the case.

The colleague returned with a stack of SEC regulation books, written mostly during and in response to the Great Depression, and Lloyd flipped through the index until he saw a reference to "security" and turned to that page. He smacked the desk. "Hot damn!" There was his answer, in very clear terms: "Nothing in the filings with the Security Exchange Committee including the 10-K shall include information of a classified nature." The text was plain and unambiguous.

"Holy Christ," Lloyd yelped. "This is the Golden Grail."

Warner told Lloyd that he wasn't sure that this would work but that it was good enough ammunition for him to take over to the SEC and make a very blunt case. "Tell them that we think they're pissing on one of our contractors," he said. "And show them this."

Lloyd did exactly that and ended up in a meeting with not only the head of the corporate finance group, who'd filed the complaint, but also Stanley Sporkin, the SEC's cantankerous enforcement division head—his nickname was the Enforcer—and three of his attorneys. One of them was particularly obnoxious and made a point to interrupt Lloyd and issue insulting orders like, "Stand up." (Sporkin, by the way, would go on to become the CIA's general counsel after leaving the SEC.)

For an hour, the SEC attorneys grilled Lloyd as he repeatedly insisted that the false information was necessary to protect a highly classified program. Hughes Tool Company was never an investor in Global Marine.

At one point, the obnoxious lawyer, who looked as if he was at best only a few years out of law school, threatened to sue Global Marine and the CIA.

Lloyd was prepared for that one. Prior to visiting the SEC, he and Warner had gone to the Justice Department, where the Attorney General's special counsel, Antonin Scalia—the future Supreme Court justice—heard the case and told them that, in his opinion, the Agency was on "solid ground." Prior to leaving, Lloyd asked Scalia a question: If this case were to go to court, who would the Justice Department represent, the CIA or the SEC?

"We represent you," he said. "But try not to tell them that."

As soon as the lawyer mentioned the threat of a suit, Lloyd put up his hand. "Now stop this," he said. "But let me ask you: Who is your attorney?"

"The Attorney General," the lawyer snapped.

"I'm sorry," Lloyd replied. "But I've already spoken to the Attorney General and he represents the Agency. You'll have to find someone else."

The SEC relented. If the CIA could produce a document from Hughes verifying all of this, they could probably work it all out. Lloyd called Chester Davis, who happened to be on his way to Washington and offered to come in to personally vouch for the arrangement.

The next day, he and Lloyd met briefly with Sporkin, who left the two to work out the particulars with his deputy, the annoying attorney whom Lloyd referred to in private as "Young Turk." The man was rude to Davis, too, insisting that his word was not good enough and that the SEC would need documents from Hughes himself.

Davis, who'd been listening calmly to that point, cut him off. "Young man, you don't seem to understand your own law," he said. "You shouldn't talk that way to a privately owned company. You don't have any jurisdiction over us. Mr. Hughes and I, we'll do anything we damn well please." He slammed his briefcase closed. "I think this conversation is done."

The Young Turk fought on. He was temporarily embarrassed but undeterred. Lloyd, like most CIA security officers, didn't carry official credentials. And because of this, the attorney said, the SEC had no proof that he was actually who he claimed to be.

What, Lloyd asked, if he could get a document from the CIA director describing the arrangement?

That would probably suffice, the man answered.

Lloyd said that he could produce such a document but it was going to be highly classified and the CIA security staff would want to know where it would be kept. "Can I see your safe?" he asked.

The man stammered. He didn't have one.

Lloyd stepped out to borrow a phone and called Paul Evans. It was around two o'clock on a Friday afternoon. "Paul, can you do something for me? I want you to find a four-drawer safe that we can use to give to the SEC. And I want you to bring it through the goddamn front door."

This was an unusual request, Evans said, but he could do it. When?

"About 4:30 when everybody is leaving."

Evans laughed. A four-drawer safe is a massive thing, weighing more than a thousand pounds. Evans' staff found one at the headquarters, dropped it onto some piano dollies, and rolled it out to a station wagon, which he drove across the Arlington Memorial Bridge into DC with the rear end riding so low it rubbed against the tires.

At precisely 4:30 on Friday afternoon, he rolled the safe through the front door of the SEC just as people were leaving for the weekend, and he asked where to find the enforcement department.

Lloyd was sitting with the attorney on the fourth floor when he heard the elevator ding and saw Evans, a huge grin on his face, walking behind four of his men, who were pushing the safe in their direction. "Bring it here," he said, and waved Evans and the safe into the man's office, which was small enough that the only wedge of free space aside from his desk, chairs, and file cabinet was in front of his lone window, so that's where Evans parked the safe.

"Hi, Paul," Lloyd said. He asked Evans to demonstrate the procedure for opening the dial, which like all Agency safes was protected with a glass cover that prevented users from leaving fingerprints, to make cracking it more difficult. Evans opened the door and pulled out a sheet of paper embossed with the CIA's logo.

"I want you to read this," Lloyd said. The document explained the Azorian arrangement in a single paragraph—that Global Marine was working with Hughes Tool, but Hughes Tool was in fact an agent of the Central Intelligence Agency. Once he'd finished, the Young Turk was asked to sign a receipt verifying he'd received it, and then Lloyd locked it back in the safe.

"You are now responsible for this document," he said. "You just signed for it. We are taking the receipt to headquarters. If anybody asks where that document is, you are the guy that's got it."

That Sunday, Easter, the SEC staged a secret meeting at four P.M. to hear the case.

Lloyd brought George Kucera, Azorian's contracting officer, in case there was a question about the contract's validity. The two presented their case and were dismissed to wait in the lobby while the commission considered the matter.

Six hours later, at ten o'clock on Easter night, Harvey Pitt, the SEC's general counsel, wandered out into the dark lobby. "You win, Walt."

When Lloyd related the good news to Warner, the CIA's counsel told him that Colby was so thankful that he wanted to invite the SEC's top commissioners to Langley to thank them personally. A few days later, Lloyd met the group's car in the garage under CIA headquarters and walked them up to the director's suite and into a conference room where Warner and Parangosky were already waiting. Both men expressed their appreciation that the SEC recognized the Agency's responsibility in this sensitive matter and how important it was to the national security; then Colby entered and said that he, too, appreciated how the SEC had handled the matter.

At the meeting's completion, Lloyd walked the men back out, and when they were inside the elevator with the doors shut, the SEC's head of corporate finance, the man who'd started the whole affair, exhaled and patted Lloyd on the back.

"Walt, you don't know how glad we were to see you."

"What are you talking about?"

"We were never real sure you were real." Throughout the process, he said, several people at the SEC insisted that he was a con man representing Global Marine.

The story doesn't quite end there. There's a coda.

Three years later, Lloyd retired from the Agency and was doing some investigative work for the Gaming Control Board for the state of Nevada. When corporations apply for gaming licenses, they are investigated, and part of that involves going to the SEC to look through records for complaints and violations. Lloyd accompanied a team of agents to Washington to work on one particular case, and while they went off to chase down some files, he excused himself to visit some old friends on the fourth floor.

The Young Turk spotted him immediately. "Walt!" he said. "I need your help."

He led Lloyd down the hall and into his office, where the safe still sat—occupying nearly a quarter of the space and blocking most of the view. "I want to get rid of that goddamn safe."

Lloyd was dying inside, but he played it straight. "That's government property," he replied. "I am out of the government. I have no control over it anymore."

Exasperated, the Young Turk explained the position that this safe had put him in. He had signed a pledge assuming responsibility for it, and he couldn't move until the safe was out of his custody. But only the CIA could move it, and no one ever returned his calls about the matter.

"I wish I could help but I can't," Lloyd said, and headed back toward the elevator, leaving the Young Turk and his giant safe, which stored just a single document, in place. It may still be there.

67

Damn You, Jack Anderson

Bill Colby's effort to convince America's investigative reporters to sit on the sub story was one of his most impressive accomplishments as director of the CIA. But there was one stubborn reporter who just wouldn't listen. His name was Jack Anderson.

Anderson, fifty-three, was at the height of his popularity as one of the nation's most famous and feared voices, a tenacious reporter acclaimed for breaking news, often in defiance of his government's wishes. His syndicated column appeared in more than nine hundred newspapers and his weekly radio show was among the most listened-to broadcasts in the country. A devout Mormon, Anderson saw muckraking—and speaking truth to power—as actual God's work. He won a Pulitzer in 1972 for a series of columns that revealed a shift in US policy away from India toward Pakistan and feuded for decades with J. Edgar Hoover, who hated Anderson so much that he had him investigated and harassed and later described him as "lower than the regurgitated filth of vultures"—this is fairly tame in comparison to revelations in 1972 that a few key Nixon aides openly plotted Anderson's murder by poison in retaliation for his dogged reporting.

Anderson wasn't always right, and he could be dogmatic and self-righteous, but the sum of his work was impressive. Upon his retirement, in 2004, the director of George Washington University's journalism school, which collected Anderson's work into an archive, described him as "part circus huckster, part guerrilla fighter, part righteous rogue."

And at nine P.M. on Tuesday, March 18, 1975, Anderson sat in front of a microphone and broadcasted his story about the most audacious covert operation in CIA history over his Mutual Radio Network show. He then rebroadcasted it immediately afterward, at nine thirty, for those who might have missed the first show. Anderson told the millions of Americans who listened to his show every week that CIA director Bill Colby had attempted to talk him out of the broadcast but that he considered the rationale for that request illegitimate because the *Glomar Explorer* operation had become a white elephant. "Navy experts have told us that the sunken sub contains no real secrets, and that the project, therefore, is a waste of the taxpayers' money," he said.

Colby lobbied Anderson right up until the end; the two were on the phone five minutes before the columnist went on-air and, as Colby later described it, "blew the *Glomar* on national TV." (It was actually radio.) Colby's appeals had worked on the no-less-dogged Sy Hersh, but Anderson in 1975, a Pulitzer Prize winner who honestly believed the First Amendment to be divinely inspired, was basically unflappable.

Anderson balked at the notion that he was compromising national security. Parts of the story had been exposed, he argued, and the mission had already gone out to sea, made an attempt, and failed. "I don't think the government has a right to cover up a boondoggle," he said later, by way of explaining his decision. "This was simply a cover-up of a failure—$350 million literally went down into the ocean."

Once Anderson broke the embargo, there was no longer reason to stop anyone else, and Colby understood that. He had made a promise to the other reporters who agreed to hold the story, so as soon as it was clear Anderson wasn't going to heed his request, Colby pulled the list out of his wallet and called those journalists to break the news. He said he wouldn't blame any of them for following Anderson's lead. So, as Colby himself later described it, "on March 19, newspapers and television programs bannered these programs from coast to coast."

Seymour Hersh had his story ready to go. On March 9, Hersh's story, which had far more detail than Anderson's, arrived under a five-column, three-line headline: C.I.A. SALVAGE SHIP BROUGHT UP PART OF SOVIET SUB LOST IN 1968, FAILED TO RAISE ATOM MISSILES. Hersh's story was long, detailed, and mostly accurate, though it had several key mistakes, including a report that the Agency recovered the bodies of seventy Soviet sailors. It also revealed that Hersh had been aware of the operation, in some part, since 1973, when he got a tip and then agreed, at Colby's request, to sit on the story in the interest of national security.

The Washington Post and *LA Times* versions of the *Glomar* story were also given huge chunks of real estate, revealing that in each case, while the editors had agreed to hold stories, they had not actually called off their reporters. This time, there would be no denying that this was the work of rogue, mistaken journalists. Project Azorian was now a national news story.

On the morning of March 19, as those stories splashed across America's newspapers and TV screens, Colby attended a meeting called by the president at the White House to discuss what would happen now. He went knowing that Matador was finished. "There was not a chance that we could send the Glomar out again on an intelligence project without risking the lives of our crew and inciting a major international incident," he later wrote. Colby brought along a copy of Nikita Khrushchev's memoirs to help inform the discussion he knew would follow—about how America should react, publicly, to the revelation of this outlandish operation to steal a sovereign nation's submarine. Khrushchev's book was relevant because the former Soviet premier wrote about the international incident over the shooting down of the U-2. In it, he explained that he'd been aware of a US spy plane overflying his country for some time and had been planning to blast America's "weather plane off course," referring to the official cover story.

The plane's existence wasn't what upset him to the point that he canceled the Paris summit, raising tensions between the two nuclear powers to a dangerous level. What upset him was Eisenhower's public mea culpa, when the president admitted on national television that he had approved the flights. This embarrassed the Soviets, and the way Khrushchev saw it, Eisenhower was the one responsible for his American pilot being held captive.

The lesson Colby learned from this was that while you might sometimes get caught spying on your adversary in unexpected and potentially very upsetting ways, it was worse to then add embarrassment by rubbing your opponent's face in it publicly. Discovering that the United States had found a sub that its own Navy couldn't locate would be humiliating to the Soviet armed forces, and to hear that the Americans then freely plundered it in open view of Russian ships would be an even more massive blow to confidence in the Soviet intelligence community. The only way to make that worse was to broadcast this fact. As long as the matter remained private, the Soviets could hide it from their own citizenry, and even most of the government, none of whom had access to American media.

So, as soon as Colby told the reporters it was okay to run their stories, he went silent on the topic. Literally from that day forward, the CIA director not only wouldn't deny stories about Azorian; he wouldn't even address them. And in that meeting at the White House, he recommended that Ford do the same.

The president concurred. As they discussed Azorian in the Cabinet Room, Ford listened to some of his closest advisers on the matter of the leaks.

"This episode has been a major American accomplishment," Defense Secretary James Schlesinger said. "The operation is a marvel—technically, and with maintaining secrecy."

"I agree," Ford replied. "Now where do we go?"

Schlesinger recommended a simple admission of only "the barest facts." Because Colby had already confirmed the story, privately, to numerous journalists, the options were limited. "There is no plausible denial story, so 'no comment' will be taken as a confirmation. If we move now we can take the high ground—if not we will be pilloried."

The president's counsel asked who would make such a statement and Schlesinger volunteered to do it—"unless the President wants to." He felt that going public was almost required because of the Navy involvement, "so that it doesn't look like they are part of a covert operation."

Ford looked at Colby. "Bill, what do you think?"

One asset of the Agency's director was that he never reacted to anything, making him notoriously hard to read. He responded quietly, patting the memoir that sat in front of him. "I go back to the U-2. I think we should not put the Soviet Union under such pressure to respond."

Once the story was public, the Soviets reconsidered their opinion on the matter. On March 29, Ambassador Dobrynin passed a note to Kissinger that said: "Moscow was concerned about press reports of work underway off Hawaii to raise a Soviet submarine armed with missiles that had sunk in 1968." In particular, he said, the Soviets were alarmed about the rumor that bodies had been recovered, and then returned to the sea. Dobrynin warned that the Soviet leadership "could not be indifferent" on the matter, if it was true, because this was a clear violation of maritime law—"a sunken warship remains the property of the nation whose flag it flew." He demanded that Kissinger address the matter. "My information is without doubt no news to you," Dobrynin wrote.

Kissinger had been waiting for a Soviet outcry, almost from the day the operation began. But faced with that resistance, he struggled to reply. "This whole problem has already caused extensive debate inside the government," he told the ambassador, admitting that he couldn't really say anything else until he had more information himself.

Soviet media later reported that the Ministry of Foreign Affairs openly accused the United States of violating international law, by clandestinely salvaging a submarine, but the US State Department replied that the Soviets had no such claim because they'd never announced the sub's loss, thus making the wreck, according to the norms of international maritime law, free game.

Backed into a legal corner, the Soviets subsequently gave up that argument, but they did not cede the actual arena. Instead, they assigned a rotating cast of combat ships to maintain a constant patrol over the target area, to project a formidable message—that any future attempts by Americans to salvage the sub would risk conflict.

Publicly, the Soviets did nothing, and the official channels were—with those few exceptions—also quiet. It was only in private, in a few quiet conversations, that the subject ever came up.

On March 27, the CIA presented a summary of the Soviet reaction to Ford in his President's Daily Brief. The matter was in the middle of the day's foreign policy crisis agenda, below the imminent fall of Da Nang to the North Vietnamese, and the continued gains of Khmer forces in Cambodia.

The Soviet media had still not mentioned the story, the report said, "even though it has been broadcast in Russian to the USSR on the Voice of America, and the BBC."

The CIA's read on the matter was that they had no clear read—"we can discern no pattern that would provide a clue as to the ultimate Soviet reaction."

Most notably, aside from the back channel to Kissinger, the Soviets had made no effort to open a dialogue at official "working levels" in the State Department. The Soviet leadership was showing no unusual behavior and all scheduled meetings over strategic arms limitation remained on track. "The episode does not appear to have affected bilateral relations," the report stated, in text that had been underlined for emphasis.

Two weeks later, the Soviets were still silent on the matter. The April 8 President's Daily Brief was the second—and final—time the CIA summarized the situation for Ford. "It is becoming clearer that they want to avoid the subject if possible," the report stated. It offered two incidents as evidence. A delegate at the 1975 Law of the Sea Conference told his US counterpart that the Soviets planned to say nothing and were pleased to know that the Americans had also chosen silence. And at a reception in Moscow, the Soviet premier greeted the US ambassador with "ostentatious cordiality" in earshot of many high-ranking US, Russian, and Eastern European officials, making a point to loudly declare that he was pleased to see the United States and USSR working toward détente despite the efforts of "those" who might try to divide the two nations.

Behind the scenes, Kissinger and the 40 Committee were already considering all of the potential outcomes. After his first message from Dobrynin, Kissinger prepared a memo for the president. "We could offer a quasi-confirmation and supply the names of the three bodies that were identified. This, however, would be extremely risky; any official, written confirmation by me would challenge the Soviets. Even if they did not react at present, they would have it in reserve and could spring it at any time. Moreover, there is no explanation that would assuage them. In particular, we cannot argue the legality or legitimacy of the operation without starting a polemic, and the Soviets cannot possibly concede its legality as their note indicates."

Clearly, that wasn't the answer. What Kissinger recommended instead was the same thing Colby had recommended—a continuation of Ford's standing order to say nothing further. Like the director, the secretary was a student of history, and he, too, considered Eisenhower's public reply to the U-2 failure to have been a huge mistake, escalating tensions when a more tactful approach could have allowed the Soviets to save some face.

In this case, Kissinger said, he was going to arrange a meeting with Dobrynin in which he would deliver a simple message. That message consisted of one paragraph, printed on special paper that could not be copied. It read: "The United States has issued no official comment on the matters related to the vessel Glomar Explorer. It is the policy of this government not to confirm, deny, or otherwise comment on alleged intelligence activities. This is a practice followed by all governments, including the USSR. Regardless of press speculation, there will be no official position on this matter."

Espionage at its highest levels is a game, and like any game, it has rules that all players agree to follow. These rules are sometimes broken, but even sworn enemies who have entire arsenals prepared for the specific purpose of annihilating one another try their best to abide by them. The specifics of spying are secret and closely guarded, but the fact that spying is being done is very much in the open. Everyone does it. And no one talks about it.

68
Tumbling Down

Summa's Paul Reeve was at a deep-ocean-mining conference when the earthquake of articles following Anderson's news report hit America's newspapers, and the shock waves reached him during a lunch break. Summa's mining-project chief, who'd been playacting a fake job for four years, didn't need anyone to tell him that this was the official end of the cover story, and knowing the storm he'd be facing if he returned to the conference, Reeve simply packed up and called it a day. There was no reason to continue the charade.

Naval architect Steve Kemp had left Pier E to join a new drilling ship, the *Glomar Coral Sea*, in Orange, Texas, after finishing work as John Graham's on-site gopher, and then was recruited away by Chevron several months later. He never heard another word about the *Explorer* until he arrived back in California in March of 1975 after a month at sea on an oil tanker. The ship anchored at Chevron's refinery in El Segundo and Kemp caught a launch into shore, which dropped him in Redondo Beach, where one of the first things he saw was a newspaper machine on the pier filled with extra editions of the *LA Times*. Across the top was a giant headline about the CIA's secret operation to steal a Soviet sub. In a fraction of a second, all of the little questions and peculiar memories Kemp had filed away from his time on the "mining project" came forward again and made perfect sense.

Hank Van Calcar received a call in the middle of the night from one of Azorian's security officers, who wanted him to know that the story was going to come out that day and would probably be everywhere. That evening,

Hank turned on the evening news and called his wife, Carolyn, into the den. "Come take a look at this," he said, as his wife sat down and watched, dumb-founded, as a newscaster told a story that she almost couldn't believe. The mining program she thought her husband had been working on for three years had been a lie.

"That is what you've been doing all this time?" she said, her voice shak-ing. "What else haven't you been telling me?"

Carolyn was distraught that her husband had hid something this big from her for years. She left the room and Hank gave her space, but eventu-ally she came back in and sat down again.

"You know, I was thinking about if I had had the opportunity to do what you're doing—would I have done the same?" she said. "I would have."

That was the end of it.

Captain Harry Jackson was back home in Groton, Connecticut, having breakfast with his wife, when a news segment came over the radio, explain-ing what had occurred on Jack Anderson's radio program.

Once the report finished, his wife looked over and locked eyes with her husband.

"Did you hear what I just heard?" she asked.

"Yep," he replied.

"Were you there?"

Jackson sipped from his mug of coffee.

"I don't know," he said.

69

The End Is the End, Isn't It?

The consensus in the intelligence community was that Matador was finished, and Parangosky knew it, too, but he'd yet to be given any official order, so out at the West Coast program office, three thousand miles away from the various rooms in which powerful men were pondering the operation's future, all of the Azorian engineers pushed on, having shifted fully into Matador mode.

It was a very different environment this time. Many of the engineers had been with the program throughout the design and buildup, adhering to strict protocols in place to maintain absolute secrecy, so it was hard to believe now that things could actually continue. For years, Mr. P's refrain had been that if any one person breathed a single word, publicly, the mission would be canceled. Then a story appeared in a major American newspaper and nothing happened. Later, it was on the radio, and then everywhere. And yet, as of mid-April, Matador wasn't dead.

Within a day of Jack Anderson's radio broadcast, Pier E became a hive of activity that was, for the first time since the union strike, barely controlled chaos. The *HGE* was now a fortress besieged, as local, regional, and national newspeople poured into Long Beach. Helicopters carrying network TV crews hovered over the ship. Reporters frequented the local bars and deployed many of the dirtier tricks of their trade to identify knowledgeable sources and persuade them to talk. Waterfront hangers-on were plied with drinks, and prostitutes were enlisted in attempts to buy crew manifests. Crew members were pestered, badgered, and propositioned.

The security team gave repeated crew briefings on the dangers of any kind of conversation with people from the news media; their admonition was: "Don't answer any question, no matter how trivial, about the *Glomar Explorer* or its purpose." And the crew and other workers responded by holding the line, even when the press contacted their families at home or came at them directly with offers of substantial sums of money.

Security was further heightened due to a series of bombing threats in the LA area, and especially after a Catalina tour boat was destroyed by a radical group at a pier in the nearby Los Angeles harbor. Howard Hughes and his reported relationship with the CIA made the *HGE* a natural target for radicals, and security mounted a deck watch to warn of any suspicious approaches to the ship from the harbor channel. Antiswimmer nets were made and kept on the main deck to be thrown into the water at the first sight of any swimmers approaching the hull. Packages, sacks, and bags were opened, inspected, and stamped by security.

There were more alarming signs, too. Russian ships began to arrive more frequently, docking at a pier directly across the channel, where suspiciously little activity seemed to take place around them. Because Matador was still an active program, anyone who'd been selected for the crew had no choice but to prepare as if the operation was happening, which meant assuring wives and loved ones that this wouldn't be a suicide mission—an argument complicated by reports that the Russians were planning naval exercises in the North Pacific, in the same area as the target site.

John Parsons was one of those men. His marriage had barely survived the first trip, and now, with an infant son at home, he was going to be asked to head back out, under much more perilous circumstances. He, like everyone in the program, was aware of the story of the USS *Pueblo,* the captured Navy ship that was never rescued. That crew went to sea believing that a plan was in place to intervene if it were ever seized. "We were told the same thing, that there's a plan, but that you aren't cleared to know what the plan is," Parsons later recalled. "I figured it out. There was no plan."

On April 16, at precisely midnight, the *Explorer* was tugged out to Long Beach's outer harbor to prepare for a new round of sea testing on the improved pipe system. As soon as the sun rose, news choppers resumed their hovering and harassed the ship until it sailed toward the Channel Islands and out of range. Those crew members who weren't preparing for the process of mating with Clementine watched their own ship sail out of the harbor on the evening news that night, in the mess, and when the *Explorer* reached the coast of Catalina Island again, on April 20, a fleet of private yachts and sailboats swarmed the famous ship to photograph its every movement.

Global Marine's VP for corporate planning, Corbett U. Allen, Jr., had told reporters in advance that the *Explorer* was going to sea "to test modifications" but refused to elaborate on what those modifications were, nor would he comment on any news reports about the submarine or CIA. "This ship is a prototype piece of equipment," he said. "The whole project is a sensitive project and there are a lot of things we can't say about it."

Despite some complications, the tests were seen as a success and the ship returned to Pier E on Sunday, April 27, the same day *Parade* magazine ran a feature titled THE RACE FOR RICHES ON THE OCEAN FLOOR. The story reported that "more than half a dozen companies" had been in competition to be the first to successfully mine manganese nodules from the ocean and said that, in light of revelations about the true purpose of the *Glomar Explorer,* a company called Deepsea Ventures was in the lead, having already used a vacuum-suction-type device to remove nodules from a depth of three thousand feet.

Three days later, on April 30, the *HMB-1* left Redwood City with the revamped Clementine in its belly and motored south toward Catalina. The plan, if Matador wasn't canceled, was to remate with the *Explorer* around May 5, spend a few weeks in port, then return to sea on May 29 for a final round of integrated sea tests before setting out for the target site, this time via Midway, because Hawaii had politely requested that the ship not use Lahaina as a base.

That was one of many signs that this trip would be different. Another, more ominous one, was a report that five Soviet missile-tracking ships had gathered four hundred miles off the coast of Midway—an act that could have been a coincidence, or a clear signal that the Soviets wouldn't be sitting back this time if the *Hughes Glomar Explorer* decided to go back out after the sub.

Other adventures during the sea tests included a brief encounter with the US Navy, which asked the ship to deviate course to accommodate a live-fire air-to-sea missile test, only to be told, by Captain Gresham—back at the helm—that the commander might want to check those priorities with Washington; and an influx of sharks that arrived in the moon pool during pipe-string tests, a problem that enterprising crew members took advantage of, baiting hooks with chunks of meat and sportfishing right there inside the massive vessel. Sharks weren't the only animal interlopers. Seabirds had gotten inside and went fishing, too, by diving into the water and catching an array of smaller fish that couldn't escape far without swimming into the well walls.

On May 5, the *Explorer* left Long Beach again and returned to the same cove off Catalina Island, to repeat the docking procedure that had first been done eleven months prior. The *HMB-1* was submerged, again. The *HGE* was positioned over the top of it, again. And the new, improved, even stronger version of Clementine was pulled up through the roof of the barge and into the ship's moon pool by the docking legs, again. Then the ship returned to port until May 31, when the ship and crew went back to sea to test all of the systems in preparation for a return to the target site, as soon as possible. By June 11, all of the required tests had been completed and the mission command felt ready to proceed.

70

That's All She Wrote

JUNE 1975

Matador had been doomed for months, but the final decision didn't come down until June 16, when Kissinger delivered his official recommendation to the president, in the form of a memorandum—more than a month after Clementine had returned to the *Explorer*'s belly.

The secretary of state began by repeating what he'd said in his last memo, just before the leaks broke in February—that "the intelligence exploitation of the part that was recovered was of such significance, and the prospects of what we might obtain if we were to recover more of the submarine were so promising," that the 40 Committee had wanted to go back to complete the job. "You approved these preparations on 6 February," Kissinger wrote, the day before the *LA Times* broke the story of the CIA's submarine mission.

"Preparations for a possible second mission continued because we wanted to avoid any official confirmation of the press revelations by abruptly terminating the operation," he wrote, and also because no one knew if or how the Soviets would react. Maybe, by some miracle, they'd miss the news, or ignore it. Since that time, Soviet officials had made their displeasure known, using back channels to keep the matter discreet. "It is now clear that the Soviets have no intention of allowing us to conduct a second mission without interference," he said. Most obviously, a "Soviet ocean-going tug has been on station at the target site since 28 March, and there is every indication that the Soviets intend to maintain a watch there."

As a result, Kissinger reported, the 40 Committee met on June 15—the previous day—to make a recommendation. "It was the reluctant, but unanimous, conclusion of the Committee that the risk of a Soviet reaction was too great to warrant a second recovery attempt. Postponement was considered, but any change in the Soviet position was deemed unlikely. Therefore, it was agreed that the Committee recommend that Project MATADOR be terminated." Kissinger noted that the process of disengaging from "this complicated program" would take some time, and that "additional publicity can be expected." A plan to dispose of "the assets" was already being explored and the president would be given options. He finished: "I recommend that you approve the termination of Project MATADOR."

The Matador crew had been ready to go for weeks, and for the first half of June, the men were mostly sitting idle at the program office, waiting for the phone to ring. And a week before the estimated departure date, in mid-June, it did.

Any call that came in over the bubble phone was significant, and this one certainly was. Dave Sharp knew Parangosky would be on the other end and that he'd have important news, which could be good or bad, and was probably bad. Parangosky told his most senior engineer, a man who'd been with the program from its very inception, that "the highest authority" was killing the program, effective immediately. There would be no return to the target site.

Parangosky was in no mood to talk at length, and the bubble phone's garbled line made conversation frustrating anyway, but Sharp was able to pick up the basics of what had led to this decision. The United States and Soviet Union had been negotiating by back channel and had agreed to a deal in which the United States would not publicly acknowledge or discuss in any way the 1974 recovery operation, and the Soviets, in return, would not publicly protest the events. For all intents and purposes, both sides would pretend as if the boldest and most outlandish intelligence operation in history had never happened. No one would ever speak of it again.

Sharp recalls that he pushed for only one detail: Was there a single argument or event that tipped the Ford administration toward canceling

Matador? "The Russians," Parangosky told him. "They told us that if we try it, they'll stop it."

Many Azorian veterans would never forget where they were when they got the news of the program's end. Dr. John Rutten had been home from the sea tests for just one day when he got the call from his superior, Dr. Flickinger. It was six thirty A.M. on Friday the thirteenth, of all days.

Rutten's work on the *Explorer* wasn't fully complete, however. On August 19, he drove back to Long Beach, stopping at the airport to drop his youngest son, who wasn't quite eighteen, off for a flight to North Dakota, and then went on to Pier E, where he was to board the ship and supervise the hospital during the *Glomar Explorer*'s final act—demating the CV into the *HMB-1* one last time.

At this point, not even that act, which no longer required secrecy, could be easily finished. Philip Watson was still pestering Parangosky, who'd told Walt Lloyd to find a way to solve the matter. LA's tax assessor managed to win a court order requiring the ship to stay in port until it paid a 7.5-million-dollar tax bill or produced proof that it was not owned by the Summa Corporation. Watson hadn't just delayed the ship's departure. He actually shut down the pier, ordering police to lock the gates and hang signs from the fences announcing NOTICE OF COUNTY TAX COLLECTOR'S SALE. If the Summa Corporation did not settle its tax bill, the signs stated, LA County would hold a public auction for the ship's sale on August 27.

Watson was grandstanding. He was also irritated because he felt that the government was giving him the runaround. He had already been told, in secret, that the ship belonged to the CIA—a process that required he be "read into" the program in order to hear the truth, and then "read out" so that he could never repeat that truth to anyone, or risk prosecution. What seemed to frustrate Watson was that every time he saw a news report, the US government denied owning the ship and repeated the lie that it was Summa's ship. That was the official story, even if most people now knew it was a total lie.

Eventually, Walt Lloyd got Watson off of Summa's back, and on August 20, the *Explorer* left port for its final mission as a CIA vessel. The destination, it announced, would be Catalina Island, but the specific purpose of the planned "sea tests" trip was not revealed. The CIA at this point was playing political games, trying to say nothing publicly as a favor to the Soviets, so when a foggy night turned into a clear day and the gigantic ship wasn't actually off Catalina, or anywhere on the horizon, the local media freaked out, again.

Yet the explanation was simple: a Soviet ship called the AGI *Sarachev* had been spotted and was on a rendezvous course to encounter the *Explorer* en route to Catalina around eleven thirty A.M. the following day. To avoid any interactions with the Soviet ship, the *Explorer* was told to take a more erratic course. The captain set his radar at forty-eight miles to keep an eye out for any suspicious traffic and then began to sail the *Explorer* in squares, proceeding straight ahead until any ship was seen to be tracking the vessel, at which point he'd turn ninety degrees and sail at the vessel, in the hopes that it would change course. And sure enough, the Soviet ship did just that. After a full day of zigs and zags, the *Explorer* changed course again and headed for Catalina, with its arrival planned for August 23.

GLOMAR VANISHES ON CATALINA TRIP, the *Long Beach Independent Press-Telegram* announced that morning. The famous spy ship, the paper reported, "vanished Friday" while on what should have been a simple twenty-six-mile journey south. "Its whereabouts were unknown to all maritime agencies, including the company that designed and says it directs the ship"—that company being Global Marine, which was under orders to say exactly that.

Two days later, the *Explorer* arrived at Isthmus Cove and, according to the paper, "unceremoniously anchored" in full view of the public, with no explanation for its recent whereabouts, or why it had taken three days to cover twenty-six miles of placid ocean. "I kept hearing on the radio about six o'clock this morning, 'Where is the *Glomar Explorer*?'" a Catalina resident told reporters. "Then I went down the hill to work, at about 7:45, and there sat the ship."

On the morning of August 24, the *Explorer*'s crew began preparations for transfer in thick fog, as an ever-growing fleet of rowboats, skiffs, fishing boats, and yachts bobbed off of either side, overloaded with passengers whose curiosity was piqued by the press reports. The crew began to flood the moon pool that night and then, hours later, lowered Clementine out through the sea gates and into the water, where the *HMB-1* waited on the ocean floor, 160 feet below.

Once the claw was gone, the last of the Agency engineers, led by Redjack Stephenson, caught the final helicopter back to shore.

Because of the mystery of the voyage to Catalina, even the *Explorer*'s seemingly simple final act attracted controversy. This time, it was a local treasure hunter named Chuck Kenworthy, whose company, Quest Enterprises, had acquired exclusive rights to explore for sunken riches in the area around Catalina. Kenworthy was suspicious of the *Explorer* and its location and decided that whatever the ship claimed to be doing was another lie; consequently, he announced to the local media in October, the *Glomar Explorer* had secretly raided the Spanish galleon *San Pedro,* which hit rocks and sank in 1598, and had stolen gold that was rightfully his.

"We believe the *Glomar* gobbled up a $30 million treasure, half of it belonging to the state of California, and half of it belonging to me," he told reporters, noting that he'd already spent sixty-five thousand dollars over ten dives in a search to find the treasure. His next dive, he said, had been planned in precisely the spot where the *Glomar* anchored, and because the Summa Corporation and the US government refused comment of any kind, he was now uncertain of what to do. "Now we don't know if we're throwing good money after bad if they've already recovered it," he said.

Mysterious in life, the *Explorer*'s legend only grew after the program's death—and the less the CIA said about it, the more people began to wonder if they'd actually been told the true story after all. For years after, a debate raged over whether the "leak" had actually been a leak. Maybe, some conspiracy theorists suggested, the mission wasn't a failure. Maybe the *Explorer* got the whole sub and created the leaked story so that the Soviets would never know the truth. It's not like they could swim down to 16,500 feet and check.

Years later, former CIA director Colby mused on this in his autobiography. "There were those who were convinced that the project was completely successful and that then, in order to keep this a secret, I deliberately went around to all those newsmen to plant on them a false story that it wasn't, fully aware that if I told enough people the story was bound to leak eventually. And there are others who are sure that I put the story out solely for public-relations reasons. According to this view, I reckoned that it would do the Agency's image a world of good at a time when the headlines were scourging it for assassination attempts and illegal domestic activities to get the press to report on a project of such daring and brilliance as the Glomar certainly was. I must say that this is all nonsense. The Glomar project stopped because it was exposed."

As predicted, the Soviets stayed quiet on the matter. At least publicly. In private, however, there was some blowback. The chief of staff of the Soviet Navy was called to appear in front of the Communist Party Central Committee at the Kremlin and given a stern dressing-down that he accepted stoically—and then passed on down the chain. He called the commander of the Pacific Fleet as soon as he was back in his office and screamed, "You really fucked up that one!" at a guy who wasn't even in the position when the *Explorer* was out at the target site. Rear Admiral Anatoliy Shtyrov happened to be in the office when the call came, and as soon as he hung up, the commander turned and screamed at him, "You really fucked up!"

Shtyrov, however, was prepared. He told his boss that Soviet naval intelligence had done everything it could do to stop the Americans from meddling with the wreck, but his warnings were repeatedly ignored by the high command. The leadership refused to help him, he said, and he had an entire file to back up what he was saying. The commander subsequently lashed out at Naval Command in Moscow, and both sides pointed fingers while doing almost nothing of consequence except firing Shtyrov, the one man who actually tried to do something.

71

All Good Things Come to an End

Six months after Matador's cancellation, in January 1976, Don Flick-inger called John Rutten to tell him that the *Hughes Glomar Explorer* would be sent to Suisun Bay, the inland graveyard where the US Navy keeps its so-called reserve fleet of mothballed ships, in March. He said that Azorian's program office had been permanently closed on January 8. Harvey, if it had even been left intact, would now and forever be just a staircase connecting two bureaucratically bland office blocks.

Rutten asked if he could make one last visit to the *Explorer,* and on February 4 he drove to Long Beach, where some old friends on the crew updated him on the various sad developments. Clementine, they said, had been cut into pieces and sold to a salvage company for 144,000 dollars. It "felt like I was visiting someone's tomb," Rutten wrote later in his diary.

No one intended to scrap the *Explorer.* The US government and Global Marine wanted to see the incredible vessel—loaded with state-of-the-art technology—find a new use. From March to June 1976, the General Services Administration published ads inviting companies to submit proposals to lease the ship; one bidder was the Lockheed Missiles and Space Company, which submitted a 3-million-dollar two-year lease proposal contingent on the company's ability to secure financing. Their plan was to use the ship to retrieve Soviet warheads. Unfortunately, they couldn't get a bank to lend the money.

More than anyone, Curtis Crooke wanted John Graham's incredible ship to find a new purpose. He called on John Wayne, who'd fallen in love with the *Explorer* while motoring around it on his yacht, to write a letter to President Ford and plead for its survival. Jim McNary and Abe Person were asked to write a paper describing the ship's remarkable gimbaled and heave-compensation platform systems. "It is now within the realm of possibility to do work in the deep ocean which was not even envisioned only a few years ago," they wrote. "Hopefully, the technology developed on the Glomar Explorer will be used for the benefit of all mankind."

In the spring of 1976, Global Marine released a short film it commissioned about the *Explorer* and its remarkable features. It was twenty-three minutes long and featured the actor Richard Anderson, best known for his role as Oscar from *The Six Million Dollar Man* TV show, as the tour guide and narrator. "I'm now aboard what is probably the most technologically advanced seagoing vessel in the world today: the *Glomar Explorer*," Anderson said while standing on the ship's deck. "Exactly what this ship does, and what it has been designed for, has been an area of controversy and speculation. And yet, the potential uses of this ship can be instrumental in our survival. . . . The capabilities of the *Glomar Explorer* are giant steps in technology," he continued. "There has never been a ship built like this one. The technology Global Marine offers us today can lead to resources never before available. Our future may depend on it."

Crooke had arranged for Global Marine to have right of first refusal on the *Explorer* for ten years after the mission, and he was actually willing to buy the ship outright, only to be told that the US government couldn't sell it because an environmental inspection showed that it was highly polluted with PCBs from the hydraulic systems.

The *Explorer* left a legacy, too. It introduced a host of new systems and also helped prove that a variety of technologies actually worked in deep water. It showed that a ship could handle tremendously heavy loads and that dynamic positioning really did work.

Those who knew a little or a lot about the *Glomar Explorer* and its covert activity were ordered to be silent. In March of 1976, Howard Hughes himself died, on a plane en route from Acapulco to Houston, taking with him the truth about how much he ever actually knew about the operation that will forever be part of his legacy. The Hughes businesses, of course, carried on, and Arelo Sederberg continued to help promote them.

On December 12, Sederberg got one of the funniest letters of his career from the First United Methodist Church of Inglewood, California. "Dear Sir," it began. "Our church group wants to establish a fact and we ask your help to determine if indeed the Glomar Explorer did entertain the crew with 'Deep Throat,' a pornographic X-Rated motion picture as reported in Time Magazine December 6, 1976. We are aware Time Magazine is not always accurate, if indeed they are able to read into any 'story' the sex deviate angle. Probably, they feel they are in competition with the numerous sex-pervert magazines which flood the market and degenerate the mind of the public. However, the Glomar was a federally funded operation and we want to know the TRUTH, the facts before initiating further complaints. We thank you for your cooperation." The letter was signed by the "Methodist Men of the United Methodist Church" and noted that a copy had been cc'd to "President-elect Jimmy Carter."

A few days later, Sederberg mailed a reply, noting that he could not comment on "matters relative to the Glomar Explorer, nor do I wish to address myself to accuracies or inaccuracies in Time. However, I will point out that in its December 20 issue, Time did question the validity of its source, a Mr. Rodriguez." Sederberg was still enjoying the memory of this exchange in 2013, when he wrote a memoir of his years working for Hughes. "In effect it was a no comment," he wrote. "We stonewalled even the elect of God."

A little over a year after canceling Matador, in August 1976, President Ford was given a memo from his assistant for national security affairs, Brent Scowcroft, titled "Disposal of the GLOMAR EXPLORER." The federal government had been trying since then to find a new home for the ship, he said, and had been turned down by the Department of Defense and "other Government agencies," many of which "expressed an interest, but lacked an approved program and financial resources to acquire and operate the ship." Congress, however, demanded that funding to the CIA to maintain the vessel be terminated by the end of fiscal year 1976.

When no government agency could take the ship, it was offered for lease, but again, "there were no satisfactory bids." (One, from a Nebraska college student, offered two dollars.) Two things seemed to stifle interest: the taint of its former life as a CIA vessel and what that might mean to operations abroad, and the tremendous cost of operating the vessel, estimated to be between 13 and 22 million dollars a year.

Selling the ship at a tremendous loss was rejected by the GSA, as was selling it for scrap. In the end, Scowcroft reported, "the Administrator of GSA joined others in recommending that it be retained as a national asset. Mothballing the ship in the reserve fleet was cited as the most feasible and economical option for retention." The CIA and Navy would share the 10-million-dollar cost. The CIA would also create a fund to pay for up to ten years of mothballing expenses.

On October 4, 1976, Ford wrote back to John Wayne, to reassure the star that the ship's fate was not sealed, despite rumors to the contrary. "Dear Duke," he began. "I have your telegram on the Glomar 'Explorer,' and I would like to assure you that there are no plans afoot to scrap the vessel. As you know, we were, regretfully, unable to find an immediate use for the 'Explorer.'" Ford went on to say that he remained hopeful that someone would want the ship and that until a new job was found for the *Explorer,* it would be placed "in reserve" at the Suisan Bay anchorage, east of San Francisco. To get the ship under the Bay Bridge, he explained, would require cutting off the derrick, "but that is the only use of the cutting torch planned."

In September 1976, the GSA turned the *Explorer* over to the US Navy for mothballing, and in 1977, it went to Suisun Bay. A December 6, 1976, *LA Times* story called the mission a success but had little new information to offer. George H. W. Bush was by then director of the CIA. Unlike Colby, the paper said, "he absolutely refused to discuss the event."

After a short period in mothballs at Suisun Bay, the ship was leased to Lockheed's Ocean Systems Division, which started an experimental deep-ocean-mining operation—this time for real. Lockheed had built a prototype miner in 1977 that proved its ability to harvest manganese nodules from the seafloor, and in 1979, the company put the *Explorer* back into use with a one-tenth-scale, one-hundred-ton "mining machine" that was, finally, just that. The ship successfully mined nodules from a depth of sixteen thousand feet in tests off Hawaii using a remote-controlled "miner" that crawled along the seabed. Like Clementine, the mining machine had lights, sonar, and CCTV cameras used by operators working in the same control room where others had hovered the CV over K-129.

Lockheed's own Jim Wenzel led the spin-off ocean-mining company, backed in part by Amoco Minerals and Royal Dutch Shell. They named it Ocean Minerals Company, and Conrad "Connie" Welling, VP of the new venture, wrote a series of articles arguing for the necessity of ocean mining and explaining why the time was, after all the false starts, right to go mining under the sea. The experimental system cost 100 million dollars, according to Welling. A commercial-scale version, he estimated, would require an investment of about 1 billion dollars. It never materialized.

In 1997, after a second stint in mothballs at Suisun Bay, the *Glomar Explorer* was leased back from the US government by GlobalSantaFe, as Global Marine had been renamed after a merger, on a thirty-year lease for 1 million dollars a year. Global refitted the ship to be a deep-ocean exploration vehicle and renamed her the *GSF Explorer.* The conversion was done at Cascade General shipyard in Portland, Oregon, and was the largest and most complicated job the yard had ever done. The architect in charge of overseeing the conversion said that, even nearly a quarter century later, the ship was like nothing he'd ever seen. In one room in the ship's forward section, he found a blackboard "with a sketch of the grappling hook with the sub in it" still there, in chalk. A specialized electronics integration company was called in to inspect and overhaul the ship's intricate systems, and the sophistication shocked the company's engineers. "The *Glomar Explorer* was decades ahead of its time and the pioneer of all modern drillships," the company's CEO said. "It broke all the records for working at unimaginable depths and should be remembered as a technological phenomenon."

In 1998, the *GSF Explorer* drilled its first well, for Chevron, in the Gulf of Mexico at a depth of seventy-eight hundred feet—a world record. In 2010, Transocean, the international conglomerate that swallowed GlobalSantaFe, bought the *Explorer* outright from the US government for 15 million dollars and made it the world's largest offshore oil-drilling vessel.

Other key components of Azorian lived on, too. The technology that made Hank Van Calcar's CV simulator possible was used in the late seventies to build a simulator to train operators to emplace a 750-million-dollar oil platform in several hundred feet of water off Louisiana. "In this way," a CIA engineering assessment reported, "the training procedures and hardware developed for Azorian have played a role in helping to develop the oil resources of the United States. . . . So the labor of love created by a group of Agency managers and engineers has borne a continuing reward."

After Matador's end, the *HMB-1* was towed to San Francisco's Todd Shipyards and stayed there until 1982, when Lockheed bought the barge back and, in conjunction with the Defense Advanced Research Projects Agency (DARPA), put it back into use as a concealed construction facility anchored at Redwood City, this time to build a top secret stealth ship code-named *Sea Shadow.* This was to be the seagoing version of Kelly Johnson's Blackbird, and it was just as odd-looking, with twin hulls and a jet-black paint job. *Sea Shadow* was tested first off Catalina in 1985, after dark, and then hidden back away inside the barge during daylight.

The *Sea Shadow* program continued, off and on, until 2006, when it was finally canceled and the prototype towed, inside the barge, to Suisun Bay and placed in the Navy reserve fleet.

In 2012, the *HMB-1* and *Sea Shadow* were purchased by Bay Ship & Yacht in Alameda and, when no museum could be found that was willing to pay for and store the stealth ship, it was disassembled at the Navy's direction and handed over for scrap. The *HMB-1,* however, became an important part of the yard and is today still being used, every day, as a floating dry dock.

As of this book's publication, the *HMB-1* is one of only two pieces of the incredible Azorian hardware still in use. The other is one of the two enormous floating moon-pool gates, which was sold to Diversified Marine in Portland, Oregon, to be used as the pontoon for a small floating dry dock in the shipyard.

What about the ship itself? In September 2015, Transocean announced that, because of plummeting oil prices, it would be selling the *GSF Explorer* to an unknown buyer for scrap. After forty years of operation, John Graham's masterpiece would be cut to pieces in a Malaysian port.

The week the news came out I happened to be talking to Jon Matthews, the former head engineer at Sun Ship who considered the *Explorer* to be one of his proudest accomplishments. And hearing that it would soon be scrapped tore him up. He suggested that for this book I find a good picture of the ship in its glory and run that next to a picture of a razor blade. "A before-and-after shot," he said. "Because that's what the steel will be when the ship's cut up."

The trend in underwater innovation in recent times has been small, light, and fast, Matthews told me. The *Explorer* was basically a sledgehammer. "It was just massive and designed to kind of overwhelm the natural depth of the water and all the pressures that were there." So much innovation and engineering at epic scale went into the ship, he said. "It'll probably never be repeated." And while the Space Station is a more sophisticated and complex feat of engineering, it was built with the use of computers, he said. The *Explorer* and its subsystems were designed on slide rules and John Graham's napkins. "I don't think we have the ability today to develop from scratch another ship like it," Matthews told me. Also, unlike the Space Station, it was not built for multiple missions. "It had one job," he said. "And it had to work or it would become an anchor."

AFTERWORD
The *Glomar* Response

hen the CIA's Office of Public Affairs launched its Twitter account on June 6, 2014, there was much internal debate over what the first tweet in the history of America's notoriously tight-lipped intelligence agency should be. The decision, it is said, went all the way up to Director John Brennan. Ultimately, @CIA went with this: "We can neither confirm nor deny that this is our first tweet."

It was a cheeky thing to say, playing on the now-so-common-that-it's-a-cliché denial/nondenial that all intelligence agencies and other governmental entities use, but there's an interesting history to this phrase and it relates directly back to Project Azorian.

After the mass of press leaks that led to the operation's disclosure, President Ford took the advice of Kissinger and Colby and said nothing officially about the operation to steal K-129. That silence continued after Ford and became official government policy—no one would say anything, at all, about the greatest covert operation in American history.

But that actually wasn't good enough. The story was out there in the media, and the CIA director had, at one time, confirmed it, at least privately. And in 1976, a *Rolling Stone* reporter named Harriet Ann Phillippi filed a Freedom of Information Act request for documents relating to the *Glomar Explorer,* especially Colby's efforts to stifle press coverage.

The Freedom of Information Act requires that a federal agency release documents unless there is a good reason that this is not possible—for instance, for national security, in which case it must say that a request is being denied for this reason. But that wouldn't work here. To deny the release of documents on national security grounds would be admitting that such documents really existed. And when the problem of the requests landed on the desk of John Warner, CIA counsel, he called on Walt Lloyd, once again, to help him solve it.

After Matador was canceled, Warner asked Lloyd to be assigned to his office, to be helpful in situations just like this one. Thanks to what Lloyd calls "the tremendous load of legal issues generated by the boat project," he had made himself an expert and Warner wanted him on his staff. The first big job Warner handed Lloyd was the FOIA problem. Requests had been pouring in and were piling up on the desks of the young attorneys who worked for Warner. "With all of your experience in this goddamn program," said Warner, who never loved Azorian, "you go down there and figure out how we should be answering the public."

It was a unique legal challenge. On one hand, the Freedom of Information Act provided, by law, that there would be more public transparency. When someone asks a federal agency a question about what it's been doing, it has to answer, by law. On the flip side, the director of Central Intelligence is responsible for protecting intelligence sources and methods. Both are federal laws.

Lloyd walked out and went to see the overwhelmed attorneys, buried in papers and under duress because they didn't know what to tell their boss about how to answer.

Okay, Lloyd said. "We can't confirm this allegation of this use of the ship to go and do all these things"—which was at that time still top secret, at the order of the president and the director. Basically, then, they couldn't confirm it without revealing an intelligence method. They also couldn't deny it, by law, without lying. "So we can neither confirm nor can we deny," Lloyd said.

He thought about what he'd just said. It made perfect sense. Lloyd wrote the phrase down and walked back into John Warner's office.

"This is the answer as far as I can see," he said.

Warner looked at the paper. It was clear. It was simple. It was legal. He tweaked a few words but said he was pleased. "That's the answer," he said. "I like it."

Phillippi and her attorney didn't, however. They appealed the CIA's non-denial and the case was heard by the US Court of Appeals. The judge listened to the arguments, considered the CIA's peculiar statement, and answered: It was a valid response.

Thus was born the *Glomar* response.

And that's the history of the most famous and frustrating cliché in PR.

EPILOGUE
The Last Days of Mr. P

The end of the program also meant the end of John Parangosky's incredible CIA career. When Matador was canceled, he retired at age fifty-four, having served the Agency almost from its inception through four of the boldest and most successful covert intelligence operations in history. In retirement, Mr. P settled into a quiet life nearly as mysterious as the one he inhabited at the Agency. He kept listening to opera, kept playing his violin, and kept eating out at his favorite restaurants, especially La Salle du Bois at Eighteenth and M in Washington, DC. There was one big change, however. Some years later—around 1980 is the best guess—the bachelor hero of the DDS&T got married, to a woman named Renee Davis.

Like Parangosky, Davis was fond of eating out at the same time every night, by herself, often at La Salle du Bois. The two saw each other, time after time, dining alone, and then one night decided to join forces and eat together. In short order, they were married.

Not long after, Walt Lloyd ran into the couple in a restaurant near Langley. "She had changed him," he recalls. "He was happy as hell." He'd even given up the slicked hair. It was, Lloyd recalls, "fluffed up." The marriage, alas, didn't last. The couple divorced a year later, but in that short time Parangosky had grown close to Renee's daughter, and they stayed close after.

Parangosky did take some occasional consulting work. Curtis Crooke hired him in the 1980s to go to Japan and look into a group of men who had asked Global Marine to help find the *Awa Maru,* the Japanese freighter sunk by an American submarine after World War II and rumored to have been carrying a fortune in gold. "The thought was, if you can steal a submarine, you can steal a freighter of gold," Crooke told me. That job never actually materialized, and the last Crooke heard, Parangosky had fallen on ice and was in a Virginia nursing home. He was no longer able to drive. Crooke bought him a CD player and several discs of Jussi Björling, the Swedish opera tenor Parangosky loved, and mailed it all to his stepdaughter. He never heard back.

Walt Lloyd kept in more regular touch. He and Parangosky would talk periodically on the phone, and when he heard about the fall, Lloyd called his old friend to find out what happened. It had been icy, Parangosky told him, and he'd fallen backward, hitting his head on the steps. He was knocked unconscious, and that's how a neighbor found him, out cold in the snow. Parangosky was admitted to a hospital and improved, but never fully. He had considerable trouble walking after the accident and his health deteriorated.

During a trip back east, Lloyd, along with his wife, Monte, went to visit his old friend. He rented a car and drove out to the Heritage Hall Nursing and Rehabilitation Center in Leesburg, Virginia. Parangosky was asleep when he got there. A nurse said, "I'm not sure he'll wake," and Lloyd replied that he didn't want to disrupt his sleep. He walked over and was leaning in, studying his former boss's face to get a sense of how his old friend was doing, when Parangosky snapped awake and looked at him, as surprised as anyone would be to wake from a nap and see an old friend staring intently from a few inches above one's face. Parangosky was immediately very alert, and his face, as always, swelled with character. Lloyd introduced him to Monte, and Parangosky seemed genuinely touched that Lloyd had thought to bring her. For several hours, the three of them just sat and talked. Lloyd felt both pleased and sad when he left.

Few people knew that a year after his retirement, in 1976, Parangosky was given the National Security Medal, an award created by President Harry Truman to honor Americans who had made an "outstanding contribution to the National Intelligence Effort," consisting of "either meritorious service performed in a position of high responsibility or an act of valor requiring personal courage of a high degree." Parangosky was just the nineteenth person to receive the medal since its creation in 1953.

This wasn't his only medal, either. On the occasion of the CIA's fiftieth anniversary, in 1997, Parangosky was given one of the Agency's highest honors, too. He was named one of the fifty "Trailblazers" who had shaped the CIA in its first half century. The award cited his work on the U-2, the A-12, and Corona, but did not mention the *Glomar Explorer*. "A pioneer in marshaling the technical capabilities of industry for the Intelligence Community, Mr. Parangosky is recognized for his management of the joint contractor team that produced the world's fastest and highest flying stealth reconnaissance aircraft," the accompanying citation stated. "His contributions paved the way for creating the Directorate of Science and Technology." Three years later, the National Reconnaissance Office gave Parangosky a similar honor, naming him one of the forty "Pioneers" in National Reconnaissance on the occasion of the NRO's fortieth anniversary. Mr. P. accepted the awards quietly and, one presumes, proudly, but never spoke of them with anyone. He brought his stepdaughter Theresa Vaughan to both ceremonies. And on September 9, 2004, he died of pneumonia at Loudon Hospital in Loudon, Virginia. He was 84.

The Long View

We thought, with luck, that we could keep the Glomar Explorer
project secret for a year. We kept it secret for over five years.

—Paul Reeve

*This is one of the darkest, most tragic, and most mysterious
tragedies of our Navy in all of its history.*

—Soviet naval historian and submariner
Nikolai Cherkashin

n October 1992, Robert Gates passed through the Kremlin gates in the
US ambassador's limousine, under police escort, on his way to meet Russian president Boris Yeltsin. Gates was the first CIA director ever to visit
Moscow, after forty-five tense years of crisis after crisis, some of which
nearly led the world's two superpowers to go to war. "As a gesture of intent,
a symbol of a new era, I arrived with the Soviet naval flag that had shrouded
the coffins of the half dozen Soviet sailors whose remains the *Glomar Explorer* had recovered when it raised part of a Soviet ballistic missile submarine from deep in the Pacific Ocean in the mid-1970s," he wrote in his
memoir *From the Shadows*. "I also was taking to Yeltsin a videotape of their
burial at sea, complete with prayers for the dead and the Soviet national
anthem—a dignified and respectful service even at the height of the Cold
War." Gates also handed over a few items that had been kept from the
K-129—most notably, the diving bell, with its dented top—and gave Yeltsin
the precise coordinates of the burial site, ninety miles southwest of Hawaii's
Big Island, so that any family members of the lost crewmen who wanted to
visit the site would now be able to do so.

This Moscow trip was indicative of the rapid thaw in relations between the two countries that followed the fall of the Soviet Union in 1991. It also caused the Russian government to publicly admit the loss of the K-129 for the first time, twenty-four years after it vanished under circumstances that remain, to this day, mysterious. That admission vindicated the tireless work of numerous family members of the lost submariners, in particular Irina Zhuravina, widow of the submarine's thirty-four-year-old executive officer, Alexander Zhuravin.

The loss of the ninety-eight men on the K-129 wasn't the only tragedy of the sub's sinking. The Soviet Union was disrespectful to the families in the aftermath, telling them only that the submarine had been lost and that its sailors were all presumed dead. Because the Soviet Navy couldn't locate the wreck and had no bodies to prove the men's deaths, the Soviet leadership refused to issue pension benefits to the widows and parents. "We were told nothing for months, and then warned, 'Do not place your personal interest above the interest of the state,'" Zhuravina told the author Ken Sewell more than thirty years later. One admiral advised her "to forget about it and not stir up the past."

On March 7, 1998, on the thirtieth anniversary of the disaster, the Russian government posthumously awarded Medals of Courage to all of the K-129's crew members. It was, according to Zhuravina, an empty gesture. She told a Russian TV show that the mother of twenty-year-old Yurii Dubov was ruined by the sub's loss. "For thirty years his mother lived with the hope that he was alive," Zhuravina said. "She couldn't believe that her son was dead. She lived, and waited, and hoped." Officers from each submariner's native region delivered those medals to the families, and it wasn't until Dubov's mother got hers that she finally accepted his death. And the next day, March 8, she died. "Just like her son," Zhuravina said. "Her heart gave out."

Zhuravina bought a stone etched with a photo of her husband in his Navy uniform and put it up over an empty grave in a Moscow cemetery, right next to the plot where their son, Mikhail, a nuclear plant engineer, was buried earlier in 1992, after dying of cancer. "I'll never be a seaman," he told his mother when he was a boy. And finally, after thirty years of fighting with the Soviet Navy, Irina was given a spot on a tanker ship headed for the

Pacific, to visit the wreck site. She brought Igor Orekhov, who was eight when his father, chief engineer Nikolai Orekhov, was lost at sea. The trip was long and rough—the tanker sailed through a typhoon en route—but when it reached the coordinates, 40 degrees latitude, 180 degrees longitude, it paused so that the two could drop flowers into the water, 16,500 above whatever remains of their loved ones were still down there.

◆

On July 20, 2006, dozens of surviving Azorian contractors gathered at the headquarters of GlobalSantaFe—the conglomerate that ultimately swallowed Global Marine—for a ceremony. The American Society of Mechanical Engineers was honoring Global Marine and the other contractors who contributed to the project by naming the *Hughes Glomar Explorer* a mechanical engineering "landmark"—just the 239th object ever to receive this revered distinction. "In the short years of its design and construction the modern limits of 'state of the art' were extended from the impossible to the possible," the ASME citation said.

Curtis Crooke accepted the award and told a few stories about the operation, saying that he was unable to even use the project's real name, because as of 2006, the word "Azorian" itself was still classified.

Praise for the engineering on Azorian has been near universal. William A. Nierenberg, a former director of Scripps Institution of Oceanography and a young science section leader on the Manhattan Project, has compared "the achievement of constructing the Glomar Explorer" with that project. Admiral J. Edward Snyder, former oceanographer of the Navy, told *Science* that the system "is probably the greatest technical achievement in ocean engineering in my lifetime."

The true story of how Azorian leaked to the media is one of the most enduring mysteries. Whether or not there ever was really a Hughes memo at Romaine Street is debated, as is the entire story of the break-in—numerous people have asserted over the years that it may have been a CIA inside job, as part of a cover-up of the Agency's ties to Hughes.

What I heard, again and again, from retired Agency personnel was that they are certain that—somehow, in some way—the leaks can be traced back to someone (or a few people) at the Navy. The feeling among CIA veterans is that certain factions of the Navy, particularly within its science and engineering group, never liked the program. They resented that a huge and complicated underwater operation would go to the CIA and that it was going to be paid for out of the Navy's own black budget. And once the mission failed to get the entire sub, these figures, whoever they were, weren't going to sit back and watch the CIA spend more money to go back and try again. So they found a way to kill the program using the media.

One veteran of several DDS&T black programs told me that he has no proof that this is the case, but his gut instinct tells him it's true. He says that the Navy watched the CIA take over spy planes and develop the first satellites and it took a vicious fight for the Air Force to regain control of space operations. "They said, 'Those sons of bitches are building a Navy.' That's motive."

An equally enduring mystery is how much Howard Hughes actually knew about Azorian, if he knew anything at all. There's little doubt that Hughes was falling apart by 1971, popping opioids like Tic Tacs and mostly slumped in a recliner watching movies, but a few credible sources have told me they're sure he was at least periodically paying attention.

His PR man, Arelo Sederberg, was certain. "There is no doubt that Hughes knew about it, if no doubt was possible with anything concerning him, and in his drug-fogged state he probably felt smugly content to do a favor for the powerful CIA, with no quid pro quo expected," Sederberg wrote. "The CIA said he knew, as did Raymond Holliday, the Hughes executive who had initially been approached by the CIA. [Bill] Gay and [Chester] Davis also knew."

I was unable to find a single person who met Hughes, but a retired intelligence officer who knew Parangosky well swore to me that Hughes did meet Azorian's maestro once. As the story goes, Hughes had a favorite plane, a Lockheed Constellation that he kept at Burbank airport and liked to visit when he was in Los Angeles, usually just to sit in the cockpit and hold the controls. At some point, the CIA decided that it needed a plane to use for trips back and forth to Area 51. The Agency inquired, through

Hughes's go-betweens, if they could use the Constellation. After many false alarms, the Agency was notified of a meeting—Parangosky was to be at the entrance to the LA city dump at midnight on a particular night. Shortly after he arrived, a limousine pulled up and stopped. A door opened, and out stepped Hughes himself. He said few if any words, handed Parangosky the keys, and got back into the car, which drove away.

The thing that people will probably debate forever about Azorian is whether or not the largest covert operation in CIA history should be considered a triumph. The fact that the Agency built and protected a cover story for five years is undeniable; by that measure alone, the project was a success. And the program engineers, led by John Graham, did design and build the most complicated ship in history, a vessel that everyone considers a marvel. That ship was able to do something that seemed nearly impossible—to reach down to the floor of the ocean and pick up a single object from 16,500 feet without anyone noticing. The depth alone is unbelievable.

Just ask Admiral Dygalo, the Soviet officer in command of the K-129's sub fleet at that time. "The fact that the US managed to build a ship of 60,000-tons displacement, to install equipment to sustain such a load, to make provision of how to accommodate the submarine under the ship and finally to lift it up—it seemed to us something unreal, fantastic," he told a Russian news program. "I can compare it with a mission to the moon in regard to technology and invested money. And another point—the ship was built in two years and the disinformation was organized outstandingly."

So while it's true that the CIA lost two-thirds of the K-129, including the ballistic missiles and code books, it also fooled an entire nation of spies who were staring straight at them. And it did recover a nuclear-tipped torpedo, a number of logbooks and documents, and pieces of the submarine's hull and controls. And that's just what we know. The CIA has never released a detailed accounting of items recovered and probably never will. Every year, the number of people who know what was boxed up and carted away from Pier E gets smaller. But several Agency officers coyly told me that the mission was more successful than any of us know.

One of them said that even the loss of the missiles wasn't as crushing as it seems. The warheads and their packaging had been in the water for six years, degrading, and probably had suffered damage in the original accident that caused the wreck. Radioactive isotopes from the weapons were found in the recovered portion of the wreck, and the types of isotopes and their relative distribution, he said, told Livermore's scientists—who themselves designed nuclear packages for missiles launched out of US submarines—"a lot" about Soviet warheads. With that information alone, they'd get a pretty good idea of how the explosive package was designed.

In the early 1990s, *New York Times* science writer William J. Broad went to see former defense secretary David Packard at his Bay Area estate while reporting for his book *The Universe Below*. There's a chapter in there about Azorian, and Broad asked Packard about the operation. Packard confirmed reports that a majority of the wreck did in fact drop back into the deep as the ship's claw broke. But he added that it was still a worthwhile venture, implying that much of the value was retrieved. "The Cold War probably would have turned out as it did without that endeavor," Packard told Broad. "But you never know."

Inside the current CIA, the memory is increasingly positive. After burying the story for decades, the Agency today seems very proud of what it pulled off with Azorian. Artifacts of Azorian are now prominently displayed in the CIA's private museum, which sums up the operation, and its engineering, in no subtle terms. "Imagine standing atop the Empire State Building with an 8-foot-wide grappling hook on a 1-inch-diameter steel rope. Your task is to lower the hook to the street below, snag a compact car full of gold, and lift the car back to the top of the building. On top of that, the job has to be done without anyone noticing. That, essentially, describes what the CIA did in Project AZORIAN, a highly secret six-year effort to retrieve a sunken Soviet submarine from the Pacific Ocean floor during the Cold War."

Feelings are mixed among surviving participants of the mission. Jim McNary, John Graham's head mechanical engineer, told me that "being able to see my projects being built, installed, and operating was a very fulfilling experience," but that he can't shake the feeling that, ultimately, the project failed. He was the only engineer in the moon pool when it was first pumped dry, so he was among the first people on the ship who could see what was left inside Clementine's broken jaws. "All I saw was a large cylinder covered in mud. I was very disappointed."

Ray Feldman, the Lockheed electrical engineer who designed the telemetry cables, has a rosier view. He thought the mission had about a fifty-fifty chance of recovering the sub when they went out. "The risks were tremendous that something would go wrong, and a lot of things did go wrong," he said. But that doesn't diminish what was done, for him. "The fact that we could go all the way down and all the way up with a piece was a significant achievement."

Walt Lloyd feels that way, too. Especially when you consider the bigger picture, with the cover story—a story so believable that it actually kick-started an industry. In retrospect, he says, it's even more impressive, because in 1985, the United States learned that a Navy communications specialist named John Anthony Walker had been selling US cryptocodes to the Soviets since 1968, the year K-129 sank. "Azorian was being run right at the time all that information was being revealed, right under the nose of the Soviets, and they didn't know about it," Lloyd said. Throughout the years that the program was going on, Walker and his coconspirators decoded more than 1 million secret Navy messages. "And they didn't get the Glomar communications."

Lloyd was given an Intelligence Medal of Merit for his work on Azorian. People often ask him why the United States never broadcasted exactly what was captured from the sub. "They say, 'You didn't get anything good! What a failure!'" He smirked. "The Soviets didn't know what we got. That's just as valuable."

Quantifying success can be difficult with programs as complicated as Azorian or the U-2. The spy plane was lauded for its secrecy, but the Soviets knew it was flying. They almost shot one down the first month of operation and worked furiously to improve their antiaircraft defenses afterward, pouring vast sums into the effort. That had a real effect on the Soviet economy. "We ran their enterprise into the ground," Lloyd says. "Defense operations caused by [the U-2] caused major economic impact on the Soviet Union. Secondary and tertiary consequences are an untold story."

Melvin Laird, Nixon's secretary of defense, told the journalist Christopher Drew that he didn't back the Azorian plan because he necessarily thought the cost justified the potential value of the intelligence. "I felt that the technology was important because we might be able to use it with one of our submarines if we got in a problem," he said. "I was always worried about crews getting trapped. . . . This idea that it was just done for that one submarine is a mistake."

Toward the end of my reporting, I visited a retired CIA officer who worked under a covert identity on the project. Even forty years later, he was uncomfortable with my using his real name. But he was quite proud of what they'd done. "Look, those guys did an engineering job that is world-class and unbelievable," he said. "I didn't appreciate at the time how spectacular it was, and that the fact that it was executed under such secrecy is amazing. I don't think you could do anything close to it today." As for the success: "If nothing else, the whole thing was worth it—whatever it cost," he said, "for the sheer fact of the embarrassment it caused the Soviet Union."

Acknowledgments

Really, this book exists because of David Grann. Back in early 2014, I had a proposal and was all fired up to write about an incredible story of murder and conspiracy in the American West that had somehow never received the book treatment it deserved. The day after we sent the proposal out, my agent, Daniel Greenberg, called me with gut-wrenching news: David Grann was writing this same book—and he'd been working on it, quietly, for two years. Obviously, we scrapped the proposal. Not only is a two-year head start by another journalist impossible to overcome, but in this case that journalist happens to be one of the most talented narrative nonfiction writers on earth (who, in the end, wrote an incredible book on that story, *Killers of the Flower Moon*). So after allowing me a few days to wallow in self-pity, Daniel asked me what else I had.

You're looking at it.

Needless to say, this book would not have been possible without the help of many people. Dave Sharp, Norman Polmar, and Michael White all contributed greatly to the recent Azorian literature and legacy, and their works helped get me started while filling in some critical blanks. Gene Poteat, a DDS&T ELINT superstar, welcomed me into his Alexandria home and later convinced Walt Lloyd and Zeke Zellmer that I could be trusted. Andrew Dunn, my brother's best friend and a guy so close to our family that my nephews call him uncle, encouraged me to pursue this idea and then opened the door to the crew at the CIA's Office of Public Affairs. I made three trips to see them in a windowless conference room at Langley and was always treated well. Ryan Trapani became my most frequent point of contact, and while he was often too busy dealing with the indefatiguable Jason Leopold to reply to my e-mails very promptly, he did let me use his employee discount at the gift shop and an Agency-approved recording device for an interview I did there. (Visitors must leave all electronics outside the Langley gate. The only things you can bring in are a notebook and a pen.) Trapani and his colleagues were also supportive of the project from the outset and helped where they could, which included assuring a few retired officers that I was trustworthy. David Robarge, the agency's lead historian, also did what he could.

By far the most important contributors to this book were the veterans of Project Azorian who are still around and willing to talk about it. Curtis Crooke and Walt Lloyd stand

405

out, of course, both because they were part of the operation's leadership and because they're wonderful humans. I visited Curtis and his wife, Jean, at their house above Carmel three times and was always made to feel very welcome. Jean even cut the crusts off my sandwiches, and when I brought a nice bottle of wine as a gift she insisted that we drink it, right there. So we did. I only got to Arizona to see Walt and Monte Lloyd once, but I stayed three days, and Monte sent me off to the airport at the end with a packed lunch. In Jacksonville, Zeke Zellmer and his wife bought me lunch and then let me borrow piles of irreplaceable clippings to take to Staples for photocopies. Zeke also made me a color photocopy of a painting of the *Glomar Explorer* by his former wife that hangs over my desk. I'm looking at it right now.

I wish the budget had allowed me to fly around visiting all the men who devoted years of their lives to the K-129 recovery effort, but alas, it did not. Most of my conversations with Azorian veterans were on the phone and often stretched over many hours. Those who took my calls and answered my many questions, even the dumb ones, are, in no particular order: Sherm Wetmore, Jim McNary, Chuck Cannon, Charlie Canby, Steve Kemp, John Owen, John Parsons, Vance Bolding, Dave Pasho, Hank Van Calcar, Joe Houston, John Hollett, Fred Newton, Wayne Pendleton, Tom Bringloe, Larry Small, Bill Swahl, Bill Tancredi, Jon Matthews, and a few retired intelligence officers who still aren't comfortable talking on the record even though these events took place forty-some years ago. (Old habits are hard to break.) I'm going to pull the project's attorney Dave Toy out of this list for a special and sad reason: He passed away a few months after we spoke.

Occasionally, though, I was in the neighborhood and caught someone in person. Ray Feldman was the first to show me a manganese nodule, still in the little box that Walt Lloyd had made, during a visit to Palo Alto. Bob Frosch and I had sandwiches in the café at his retirement home in Amherst, Massachusetts. I had no idea the beautiful Webb Institute existed until I caught a train out to Long Island's North Shore to spend the morning with Jacques Hadler, who is well into his nineties but still teaching future naval architects, and commuting back and forth from Long Island to the Washington, DC, suburbs on I-95 every week during the academic year. Jenny (Graham) Parsons was a joy, and eager to help me get to know her amazing father better. I never made it to Santa Barbara, but she and her husband, John, a *Glomar* veteran, happened to be in New York, so we had lunch—in New Jersey.

Vern Krutein, Manfred's son, digitized a video of his father giving a talk and sent me some pictures, one of which appears in the book. TD Barnes, who runs Roadrunners Internationale, a group of Area 51 veterans, helped me fill in a little of Mr. P's mysterious life and graciously invited me to join the club's annual gathering, which I wish I'd been able to attend. John Lahm, a retired electrician, successfully lobbied his local politicians to get a plaque installed on the Philly waterfront remembering the *Glomar Explorer*, not far from where the ship was built, and helped connect me with some former Sun Ship workers.

Others who contributed expertise and wisdom include Admiral (Ret.) Bobby Ray Inman, Admiral (Ret.) Paul W. Dillingham, Jr., Admiral (Ret.) Mal Mackinnon, John Halkyard, Charles Morgan, Miriam John, and Rich Wagner. Steve Bailey, a Lockheed engineer who worked on the *Glomar Explorer* during her stint as a *real* deep-ocean-mining ship, in the late 1970s, and later on the stealth vessel *Sea Shadow*, endured an interview and then, when I visited the Bay Area, took me to visit the *HMB-1*, now a floating dry dock at Bay Ship & Yacht, in Alameda, California.

Menschy writers include Chris Drew of *The New York Times*, naval historian W. Craig Reed, and Jim Steele, who gladly gave me access to the treasure trove of Howard Hughes material in the archive he and Don Bartlett donated to American University. Susan McElrath, who oversees that archive, helped show me around and had piles of copies of Hughes clips and memos made and mailed to me. Serge Levchin in New York and Dmitry Kvasnikov in Moscow helped find and translate Russian stories, books, and films. Dmitry also tracked down some photos, answered many annoying questions, and is just a generally kind and cheerful person whom I now consider a friend.

There would be no book at all if not for two very important people: Daniel Greenberg, my agent, for selling it, and Jessica Renheim, my editor, for buying it. They are, individually and collectively, the best. Approximately 100 percent of people who heard about the idea while I was working on it said, "That should be a movie!" so hopefully by the time you read this that's a real possibility. If so, it means that Michelle Kroes at CAA and Rick Jacobs at Circle of Confusion are working their magic.

Gillian Fassel, every writer's frenemy, turned her red pen upon the manuscript and absolutely made it better while only slightly bruising my ego. Keith Schlegel, a retired English professor and family friend, corrected my comma abuses. Chuck Cannon, Dave Pasho, Steve Kemp, and Joe Houston all read drafts and helped me avoid embarrassing engineering and science mistakes. Probably I still screwed a few things up. That's what the paperback is for!

I couldn't do this job without my incredible wife, Gillian Telling, allowing me to take off and stalk retired spies. She is an excellent writer herself, as well as an excellent magazine editor (her full-time job), and—most of all—excellent mother to our two boys, Charlie and Nicky.

Finally, I want to say a few things about my dad, David Dean. I dedicated this book to him for a couple of reasons. He's a retired history professor and an author himself, so he's a big part of the reason I'm out here doing this. He always encouraged reading and education and pushed me to do things like internships even when I didn't want to. He's a kind, generous, and only occasionally foul-mouthed man who did a lot of the child-rearing in an era when that wasn't very common for men. He's also the only parent I have left. My mom, also a former professor and writer, died rather suddenly while I was working on my first book. A few months ago, we found out my dad—who's run seventy marathons, biked across America three times, and hasn't smoked a cigarette in his life—had lung cancer. It was shocking and scary and seemed for a little while like I might be out of parents by the time my second book was published. But a surgeon at the Mayo Clinic removed a lemon-size tumor in February and found that the cancer hadn't spread. My dad will have four chemo treatments over a few months and then, with some luck, he'll be back to normal, running, biking, drinking beer, and complaining about Indiana University basketball. I fully expect him to be around for the next few books.

A Note About Sources

This book is a work of nonfiction. I have made every effort to verify all statements of fact, and direct quotes come either from existing documentation—official government records, court transcripts, and previously published books and articles—or from interviews with surviving participants, who recalled specific conversations to me. I have attempted to locate a second source for all facts that came to me from interviews, but that wasn't always possible, and this being a book about intelligence—a business that employs and relies upon some of the world's best liars—it's always possible that someone's memory is a little off, or that a person has intentionally misled me. I don't think that's the case, but I feel it's worth mentioning anyway.

No book of narrative nonfiction is possible without those works that came before it, and I am indebted to several in particular. The two most important are *Project Azorian* by Norman Polmar and Michael White, and *The CIA's Greatest Covert Operation* by David Sharp. Polmar is a naval historian, and his collaboration with White—a filmmaker who made an hour-long documentary in conjunction with the book—goes deep into the military and engineering specifics of this story, on both the Russian and American sides. Michael White's accompanying film, also titled *Project Azorian,* is excellent, too, and includes beautiful computer-generated images of the various complex systems that made up the submarine recovery system on the *Glomar Explorer.* If you can't quite picture Clementine and the heavy-lift system, watch White's film. Actually, even if you can picture it, you should watch the film.

Dave Sharp was a key member of Azorian's original CIA engineering team, and the head of recovery on the mission. His book is tremendous. It's part memoir, part history, and is chockablock with anecdotes and insider recollections about life inside John Parangosky's think tank. Sharp fought the CIA's notorious Publications Review Board for years for the right to publish. That permission was finally granted in 2011, a year after the National Security Archive got the CIA to release its heavily redacted internal history of the Azorian mission planning, engineering, and security apparatus.

No single document was more important to me than this official Agency history, which originally appeared in the CIA's classified journal, *Studies in Intelligence.* It was written by an unnamed Agency historian, based on interviews with Azorian officers (including, presumably, Mr. P) and the reams of official program material that are still locked away in a northern Virginia warehouse that I tried repeatedly, in vain, to get access to. I got as far as a meeting with a bureaucrat assigned to the office that weighs what remains classified versus what can be safely disseminated to journalists and FOIA cranks. Mostly he stared at me blankly and offered little hope when I pleaded for help. "Do you have any idea how much material there is for this one operation?" he asked. "Boxes." He meant this as a dismissal, but it only egged me on. I'm still after those boxes.

Two other, much earlier *Glomar Explorer* books I found helpful were *A Matter of Risk* by Wayne "Cotton" Collier, and Clyde Burleson's *The Jennifer Project*. These two were published long before any of the operation's details were officially acknowledged, which explains why Burleson's book used the wrong name for its title. Until very recently, Jennifer is what pretty much everyone called Project Azorian. Collier was hired by Global Marine to recruit the *Explorer*'s civilian crew, and I have no idea how he managed to write his somewhat myopic but very detailed account without going to jail. Roger Dunham's *Spy Sub* was also invaluable. It is, ostensibly, a work of fiction about a secret special projects sub called the *Viperfish*. In reality, it's a thinly veiled memoir of his time on the USS *Halibut*, focusing on the hunt for the K-129 wreck, and is a novel only because NCIS agents convinced Dunham that publishing a nonfiction account of this still-classified episode might land him in very hot water.

The heart and soul of this book, of course, are the humans who brought this incredible mission to life, and a surprising number of them were still alive to share their stories. They provided the best and most detail, by far, nearly all of it attributed and on the record—with only a few exceptions from retired spies. I'd be remiss if I didn't single out the contributions of two deceased Azorian veterans who kept diaries that are invaluable artifacts, for me and for history. Manfred Krutein's appears, in parts, in his fascinating, colorful immigrant memoir *Amerika? America!*, while John Rutten's was found by his son, Rand, in a storage unit after his father's death. Rand polished up the diary, submitted it to the CIA's PRB, and then self-published the parts the agency didn't redact as a book he titled *DOMP*.

You'll notice this edition lacks notes. That's because I'm trying something new. To avoid turning this book into, as my editor says, "a doorstopper," I'm including just a selected bibliography and this note. Complete notes, with links to online sources wherever possible, are online on a website I set up for the book. This allows me to go into much more detail and to update the notes and longer bibliography as mistakes or omissions surface. I will also include story updates, some interview excerpts, and photos. If I get ambitious, there'll be a blog. Check it out: www.thetakingofk129.com.

If you have a question about the source of a fact, or want to share additional stories for future editions, by all means drop me a line. I'm easy to find on all your major social media platforms (when in doubt, try @joshdean66), or you can e-mail me directly to a special account I set up for the express purpose of luring people out of the shadows, at thetakingofk129@gmail.com. You can also find me on Signal and WhatsApp, if end-to-end encryption puts you more at ease.

Selected Bibliography

Books

Amel'ko, Admiral Nikolai. *In the Interest of the Fleet and State.* Moscow: Nauka, 2003.

Bartlett, Donald L., and James B. Steele. *Howard Hughes: His Life and Madness.* New York: W. W. Norton, 1979.

Bauer, Robert F., with F. Jay Schempf. *Roughneckin'.* Charleston, SC: BookSurge, 2009.

Benford, Harry. *Naval Architecture for Non-Naval Architects.* Jersey City, NJ: Society of Naval Architects and Marine Engineers, 2006.

Broad, William J. *The Universe Below.* New York: Touchstone, 1997.

Bucher, Lloyd M., USN, with Mark Rascovich. *Bucher: My Story.* New York: Doubleday, 1970.

Burleson, Clyde W. *The Jennifer Project.* Englewood Cliffs, NJ: Prentice-Hall, 1977.

Burns, Thomas S. *The Secret War for the Ocean Depths.* New York: Rawson Associates Publishers, Inc., 1978.

Colby, William. *Honorable Men.* New York: Simon and Schuster, 1978.

———. *30 Ans de C.I.A.* Paris: Presse de la Renaissance, 1978.

Craven, John P. *The Silent War.* New York: Simon & Schuster, 2001.

Dobrynin, Anatoly. *In Confidence.* New York: Times Books, 1995.

Drosnin, Michael. *Citizen Hughes.* New York: Broadway Books, 1985. Digital edition.

Dunham, Roger C. *Spy Sub.* Annapolis, MD: Naval Institute Press, 1996.

Dygalo, Viktor. *A Rear Admiral's Notes.* Moscow: Kuchkovo Pole, 2009.

Feldstein, Mark. *Poisoning the Press: Richard Nixon, Jack Anderson, and the Rise of Washington's Scandal Culture.* New York: Farrar, Straus & Giroux, 2010.

Ford, Gerald R. *A Time to Heal.* New York: Harper & Row, 1979.

Ford, Harold R. *William E. Colby as Director of Central Intelligence, 1973–1976.* Washington, DC: Center for the Study of Intelligence, Central Intelligence Agency, 1993; declassified 2011.

Gates, Robert M. *From the Shadows.* New York: Simon & Schuster, 2006.

Hack, Richard. *Hughes: The Private Diaries, Memos and Letters.* Beverly Hills, CA: Phoenix Books, 2007.

Helvarg, David. *Blue Frontier.* San Francisco: Sierra Club Books, 2001.

Hersh, Seymour M. *The Price of Power: Kissinger in the White House.* New York: Summit Books, 1983.

Huchthausen, Peter A., and Alexandre Sheldon-Duplaix. *Hide and Seek.* New York: John Wiley & Sons, 2009.

Hutchinson, Robert. *Jane's Submarines: War Beneath the Waves from 1776 to the Present Day.* New York: HarperCollins, 2001.

Johnson, Clarence L. "Kelly," with Maggie Smith. *Kelly: More than My Share of It All.* Washington, DC: Smithsonian Press, 1985.

Krutein, Eva, and Manfred Krutein. *Amerika? America!.* Albuquerque, NM: Amador Press, 1997.

Mero, John L. *The Mineral Resource of the Sea.* Elsevier Oceanography Series 1. New York: Elsevier, 1965.

Podvig, Pavel. *Russian Strategic Nuclear Forces.* Cambridge, MA: MIT Press, 2001.

Polmar, Norman, and Michael White. *Project Azorian.* Annapolis, MD: Naval Institute Press, 2010.

Reed, W. Craig. *Red November.* New York: William Morrow, 2010.

Rich, Ben R., and Leo Janos. *Skunk Works.* New York: Little, Brown and Company, 1994.

Richelson, Jeffrey T. *The US Intelligence Community.* Boulder, CO: Westview Press, 2012.

———. *The Wizards of Langley.* Boulder, CO: Westview Press, 2002.

Riebling, Mark. *Wedge.* New York: Knopf, 1994.

Romney, Carl. *Recollections.* Bloomington, IN: Author House, 2012. Digital edition.

Ruffner, Kevin C., and the CIA History Staff. *CORONA: America's First Satellite Program.* Cold War Records Series 4. Washington, DC: Center for the Study of Intelligence, Central Intelligence Agency, 1995.

Rule, Bruce. *Why the USS Scorpion (SSN-589) Was Lost: Death of a Submarine in the North Atlantic.* Ann Arbor, MI: Nimble Books, 2011.

Rutten, R. John, M.D. *Deep Ocean Mining Project.* Bloomington, IN: iUniverse, Inc., 2012.

Sederberg, Arelo C. *Hughesworld: The Strange Life and Death of an American Legend.* Bloomington, IN: iUniverse, 2013.

Sewell, Kenneth, with Clint Richardson. *Red Star Rogue.* New York: Simon & Schuster, 2005.

Sharp, David H. *The CIA's Greatest Covert Operation.* Lawrence, KS: University of Kansas Press, 2012.

Sontag, Sherry, and Christopher Drew. *Blind Man's Bluff: The Untold Story of American Submarine Espionage.* New York: Public Affairs, 1998.

Spassky, I.D., ed. *Istoriya Otechestvennogo Sudostroeniya* [History of indigenous shipbuilding]. Vol. 5, *1946–1991.* St. Petersburg: Sudostroenie, 1996.

Varner, Roy, and Wayne Collier. *A Matter of Risk.* New York: Random House, 1977.

Werth, Barry. *31 Days.* New York: Anchor Books, 2006.

Woods, Randall B. *Shadow Warrior.* New York: Basic Books, 2013.

Articles

Aarons, Leroy F. "Glomar Sets Test Cruise." *Washington Post,* April 10, 1975.

Alexin, V. "Better Late Than Never." *Independent Military Review,* September 17, 1999. http://nvo.ng.ru/notes/1999-09-17/k-129.html. Article on the ceremony to honor the K-129 crew.

Baldwin, Jack O. "Secret Hughes Barge on Way to Catalina." *Independent* (Long Beach, CA), January 9, 1974.

"Behind the Great Submarine Snatch." *Newsweek,* December 6, 1976.

Belair, Felix, Jr. "S.E.C. Staff Finds Data About Glomar Misleading." *New York Times,* April 1, 1975.

Benson, Bruce. "Hughes Mineral Ship's at Lahaina." *Honolulu Star-Advertiser,* August 17, 1974.

Boyarsky, Bill. "Why Editors Withheld Details on Sub." *Los Angeles Times,* March 20, 1975.

Broad, William. "Navy Has Long Had Secret Subs for Deep-Sea Spying, Experts Say." *New York Times,* February 7, 1994.

——. "Russia Says U.S. Got Sub's Atom Arms." *New York Times,* June 20, 1993.

Chriss, Nicholas C., and Jerry Cohen. "'Good Old Boys' Raised Russian Sub." *Washington Post,* April 8, 1975.

——. "Sub Recovery: Anatomy of a Secret Mission." *Los Angeles Times,* April 7, 1975.

"C.I.A. Asked Tax Assessor's Aid on Ship." *New York Times,* April 4, 1974.

"CIA's Mission Impossible." *Newsweek,* March 31, 1975.

"CIA Plan Disclosed in Glomar Incident." *New York Times,* October 26, 1977.

"CIA Rebuffs Request in Trial for Data on a Hughes Burglary." *New York Times,* January 6, 1976.

Claiborne, William, and George Lardner, Jr. "Colby Called Glomar Case 'Weirdest Conspiracy.'" *Washington Post,* November 5, 1977.

Clarity, James F. "Soviet Is Silent on Sub Salvaging." *New York Times,* March 20, 1975.

Cohen, Fritzi. "The Unanswered Questions of the Glomar Explorer." *Covert Action,* no. 9 (June 1980).

Cohen, Jerry, and George Reasons. "CIA Recovers Part of Russian Sub." *Los Angeles Times,* March 19, 1975.

Crewdson, John M. "'CIA Men' Sought Tax Break on Glomar." *Washington Star,* June 8, 1975.

Eccles, Henry E., Rear Admiral, US Navy (Ret.). "The Russian Maritime Threat." *Naval War College Review* (June 1969).

"Engineering for Azorian." *Studies in Intelligence* 23, no. 2 (Summer 1979).

Farr, William. "Mystery of Hughes' Secret Memo Solved." *Los Angeles Times,* April 4, 1975.

Fazio, Marlene. "Mining Ship Is Launched." *Delaware County Daily Times,* November 6, 1972.

Foley, Charles. "Hughes Mining Ocean Floor, Report Claims." *London Observer,* November 5, 1973.

——. "Hughes Taking Plunge to Reap Ocean's Riches." *London Observer,* October 31, 1972.

Fountain, Henry. "Dr. Donald D. Flickinger, 89, a Pioneer in Space Medicine." *New York Times,* March 9, 1997.

"The Great Submarine Snatch." *Time,* March 31, 1975.

Hersh, Seymour. "C.I.A. Salvage Ship Brought Up Part of Soviet Sub Lost in 1968, Failed to Raise Atom Missiles." *New York Times,* March 19, 1975.

——. "Human Error Is Cited in '74 Glomar Failure." *New York Times,* December 9, 1976.

——. "Participant Tells of C.I.A. Ruse to Hide Glomar Project." *New York Times,* December 10, 1976.

Horrock, Nicholas M. "CIA Ends Plan to Raise Soviet Sub." *New York Times,* January 14, 1976.

——. "CIA Reported Pressing S.E.C. to Curb Global Marine Inquiry." April 27, 1975.

Howard, John, Lt. "Fixed Sonar Systems: The History and Future of the Underwater Silent Sentinel." *Submarine Review* (April 2011).

"Hughes Glomar Explorer Begins Sea Tests of Mining Systems." *Ocean Industry,* March 1974.

"Hughes Mystery Barge Slips Down the Coast." *Santa Cruz Sentinel* (Santa Cruz, CA), January 8, 1974.

"In Memoriam: John Parangosky, National Reconnaissance Pioneer." *National Reconnaissance,* date unknown.

"John Parangosky." Nevada Aerospace Hall of Fame. http://www.nvahof.org/hof/hof-2014/john-parangosky/.

Lardner, George, Jr. "CIA Covert Action Defended." *Washington Post,* April 8, 1975.

———. "Hughes Ship Tax Doubled by California." *Washington Post,* June 4, 1975.

———. "SEC Reaches a Truce on CIA Projects." *Washington Post,* April 9, 1975.

Lardner, George, Jr., and William Claiborne. "CIA's Glomar 'Game Plan.'" *Washington Post,* October 23, 1977.

Latham, Aaron. "How Glomar Really Surfaced." *New York,* April 7, 1975.

Lewis, John, Colonel, US Army. "The Deep Sea Resources." *Naval War College Review* (June 1969).

Lynch, Mark H. "FOIA and the CIA." Center for National Security Studies. *First Principles* 9 (September–October 1983).

Martin, Douglas. "Jack Anderson, Investigative Journalist Who Angered the Powerful, Dies at 83." *New York Times,* December 18, 2005.

"Mining Sailors Heading for Ocean Depths." *High Gear,* no. 1 (1978).

Mozgovoy, A. "The Silent Death of the K-129." *Top Secret,* no. 5 (May 1, 1999). http://www.sovsekretno.ru/articles/id/341/.

Mueller, William Behr. "Howard Hughes, CIA, and the Incredible Glomar Explorer." *Sea Classics,* September 1978.

Nelson, Jack. "Administration Won't Talk About Sub Raised by CIA." *Los Angeles Times,* March 20, 1975.

Nocera, Joseph. "Le Couvert Blown: William Colby en Francais." *Washington Monthly,* November 1980.

"Now Howard Hughes Mines the Ocean Floor." *Business Week,* June 16, 1973.

O'Leary, Jeremiah. "The CIA Pulls a Salvage Job on a Soviet Sub." *Washington Star,* March 19, 1975.

———. "Silence Reigns on Soviet Sub as U.S. Awaits Détente Impact." *Washington Star,* March 20, 1975.

O'Toole, Thomas. "CIA Raised Warheads, Sources Say." *Washington Post,* March 21, 1975.

———. "Glomar Hunt Revealed Soviet Submarine Code." *Washington Post,* December 17, 1976.

Parker, Ann. "Knowing the Enemy, Anticipating the Threat." *Science & Technology Review* (July–August 2002).

Peer, Elizabeth, with Ann Ray Martin. "Salvaging the Sub Story." *Newsweek,* March 31, 1975.

Phelan, James. "An Easy Burglary Led to the Disclosure of Hughes-C.I.A. Plan to Salvage Soviet Sub." *New York Times,* March 27, 1975.

Phillippi, Harriett. "The Story Behind the Story: Cracking Colby's Glomar Files." *Washington Post,* November 20, 1977.

Polmar, Norman. "How Many Spy Subs?" *U.S. Navy Proceedings,* December 1996.

"Project Azorian: The Story of the Hughes Glomar Explorer." *Studies in Intelligence* (Fall 1985).

Quale, Alan. "The Secret Revealed: What Will Barge Do?" *Times* (San Mateo, CA), January 8, 1974.

Roberts, Jeffrey. "What Happened to Glomar Explorer." *Ocean Engineering,* December 1976.

Rule, Bruce. "Acoustic Detections of the Loss of the GOLF II Class Soviet SSB K-129." Integrated Undersea Surveillance System Caesar Alumni Association (IUSSCAA) Message Board, June 30, 2013. http://pub10.bravenet.com/forum/static/show.php?usernum=774301397&frmid=32&msgid=1338762&cmd=show.

Sampson, Richard A. "The Hughes Glomar Explorer Project." *Journal of the OpSec Professional Society* 2 (1995). www.opsecsociety.org/039.html.

Sansweet, Stephen J. "Vessel Used in Bid to Lift Russian Sub Wasn't on Tax Rolls." *Wall Street Journal,* April 4, 1975.

Schudel, Matt. "Robert Maheu, 90; Tycoon's Aide, CIA Spy." *Washington Post,* August 6, 2008.

"Security: Hidden Shield for Project Azorian." *Studies in Intelligence* 22, no. 3 (Fall 1978).

Seib, Charles B. "The Confusing Coverage of the Submarine Story." *Washington Post,* March 27, 1975.

Shearer, Lloyd. "Parade and Project Jennifer." *Parade,* May 11, 1975.

Shtyrov, Anatoliy. "Tragediya PL K-129. Za kulisami operatsii Jennifer" [The tragedy of submarine K-129. Behind the scenes of Operation Jennifer]. Flot.com. Online article /blog post in response to a 2008 NTV film about the loss of the K-129. http://flot.com/history/si58.htm.

"SOSUS: The 'Secret Weapon' of Undersea Surveillance." *Undersea Warfare* 7, no. 2 (Winter 2005).

Steinbeck, John. "High Drama of Bold Thrust Through Ocean Floor." *Life,* April 14, 1961.

Stilwell, Paul. "The Recollections of Captain Harry A. Jackson, US Navy (Retired)." Naval Institute, 2002. Oral history.

"The Submarine from 'Grave Bay.'" *Izvestiya,* July 4, 1992.

Thomason, Robert. "CIA Cover Story Gives Birth to Deep Ocean Mining." DC Bureau, March 10, 2014. http://www.dcbureau.org/201403109664/natural-resources-news-service/cia-cover-story-gives-birth-deep-ocean-mining.html.

"Trying to 'Swipe' a Russian Sub Is Just Part of the CIA Saga." *US News & World Report,* March 31, 1975.

Turner, Wallace. "Publishers Offered Hughes Documents." *New York Times,* April 21, 1977.

United Press International. "Navy Fund Reported Diverted to Glomar." *New York Times,* February 26, 1976.

Wade, Nicholas. "Deep-Sea Salvage: Did CIA Use Mohole Techniques to Raise Sub?" *Science,* May 1975.

———. "Glomar Explorer: CIA's Salvage Ship a Giant Leap in Ocean Engineering." *Science,* June 1976.

Webster, Bayard. "Sea-Mine Rivals Did Not Suspect Sub." *New York Times,* March 22, 1975.

Weir, Gary E. "The American Sound Surveillance System: Using the Ocean to Hunt Soviet Submarines, 1950–1961." *International Journal of Naval History* (August 2006).

Welzenbach, Donald E. "Science and Technology: Origins of a Directorate." *Studies in Intelligence* 30, no. 2 (1986).

Zeman, Ray. "CIA Got Tax Secrecy for Hughes Ship." *Washington Post,* April 3, 1975.

Films

Azorian: The Raising of the K-129. Directed by Michael White. Studio not specified. 2011.

Propavshaya submarina. Tragediya K-129 [Vanished submarine. The tragedy of the K-129].
    Directed by Aleksei Bystritsky. VGTRK, 2012. Translated from Russian by Sergey
    Levchin. https://www.youtube.com/watch?v=H_XifByb9rg.

Index

About the Author

Josh Dean has written for dozens of national magazines including *Rolling Stone*, *Men's Health*, *GQ* and *Cosmopolitan*, and is a former editor at various magazines, including *Men's Journal*, where he was deputy editor. He is also one of the founding editors of *PLAY*, the *New York Times* sports magazine.